Minor Universality
Universalité mineure

Beyond Universalism
Partager l'universel

Studies on the Contemporary
Études sur le contemporain

Edited by / Édité par
Markus Messling

Editorial Board
Souleymane Bachir Diagne (Columbia University, NY)
Tammy Lai-Ming Ho (Hong Kong Baptist University)
Christopher M. Hutton (University of Hong Kong)
Ananya Jahanara Kabir (King's College London)
Mohamed Kerrou (Beït el-Hikma, Carthage)
Soumaya Mestiri (Université de Tunis)
Olivier Remaud (EHESS Paris)
Sergio Ugalde Quintana (El Colegio de México)

Volume 2

Minor Universality
Universalité mineure

Rethinking Humanity After Western Universalism
Penser l'humanité après l'universalisme occidental

Edited by
Markus Messling & Jonas Tinius

DE GRUYTER

This project has received funding from the European Research Council (ERC) under the European Union's Horizon 2020 Research and Innovation programme – Grant Agreement Number 819931

European Research Council
Established by the European Commission

ISBN 978-3-11-221475-6
e-ISBN (PDF) 978-3-11-079849-4
e-ISBN (EPUB) 978-3-11-079864-7
ISSN 2700-1156
DOI https://doi.org/10.1515/9783110798494

This work is licensed under the Creative Commons Attribution-NonCommercial-NoDerivatives 4.0 International License. For details go to https://creativecommons.org/licenses/by-nc-nd/4.0/.

Creative Commons license terms for re-use do not apply to any content (such as graphs, figures, photos, excerpts, etc.) not original to the Open Access publication and further permission may be required from the rights holder. The obligation to research and clear permission lies solely with the party re-using the material.

Library of Congress Control Number: 2023933217

Bibliographic information published by the Deutsche Nationalbibliothek
The Deutsche Nationalbibliothek lists this publication in the Deutsche Nationalbibliografie; detailed bibliographic data are available on the internet at http://dnb.dnb.de.

© 2025 the author(s), editing © 2025 Markus Messling and Jonas Tinius, published by Walter de Gruyter GmbH, Berlin/Boston
This volume is text- and page-identical with the hardback published in 2023.
This book is published open access at www.degruyter.com.

Cover image: based on an original idea by Hannes Brischke
Typesetting: Integra Software Services Pvt. Ltd.
Printing and binding: CPI books GmbH, Leck

www.degruyter.com

Acknowledgements

This book bears the imprint of many voices, experiences, and translations. It is an outcome of years of reflection with and international cooperation of the group *Minor Universality. Narrative World Productions After Western Universalism* based in Saarbrücken since 2019. The group itself has its own *préhistoire*: Important for its inception were activities with the Working Group *Experiences of the Global*, which Markus Messling co-founded at the Marc Bloch Centre, the Franco-German institute for research in the Social Sciences and Humanities at Humboldt-Universität zu Berlin.[1] Without Franck Hofmann, companion in long sessions at the State Library of Berlin, these reflections would in the end not have turned into an application for a Consolidator Grant funded by the European Research Council (ERC).

Many other encounters – and, incidentally, those that didn't take place due to the Covid-19 pandemic – shaped the content of this book. Among these, we wish to mention the thematic conversations we had throughout the years with Arjun Appadurai, Leyla Dakhli, Souleymane Bachir Diagne, Giovanni Levi, Gisèle Sapiro, Adania Shibli, Maria Stavrinaki, and David Scott which we also recorded for our video series *Universalisme & ....*[2] We want to thank our project partners and dear colleagues Leyla Dakhli and Mohamed Kerrou, with whom we organised the international colloquium *Universalismes, hégémonies et identités* in collaboration with the Académie tunisienne des sciences, des lettres et des arts (Beït al-Hikma) in Tunis in March 2022. We also thank our colleague Aïcha Filali, director of the Centre des arts vivants de Radès, for hosting and co-organising with us the international symposium *Universalisme et incertitude* during the same research trip in March 2022 to Tunisia. The question of how to bring into accordance the conflict between different universalisms (Islamic, French-Republican) and the struggles for dignity and participation of a wider social strata, did not just mark our conversations during this time. In June 2022, we had the fortune to discuss the work of Gilles Deleuze and Félix Guattari, especially the notion of the "minor", during a long session with Cord Riechelmann, which left an important mark on this book. We give thanks to our partners and colleagues at the Haus der Kulturen der Welt (HKW), especially Bernd Scherer and Olga von Schubert, with whom we realised our research artist-in-residence programme and exhibition *The Pregnant Oyster – Doubts on Universalism* (June/July 2022). The project found its form across several iterations, and we are grateful to those that hosted us in Athens as part of the *New Alphabet School*, in

---

[1] This is in thankful memory of the discussions with Petra Beck, Leyla Dakhli, Emmanuel Droit, Franck Hofmann, Teresa Koloma Beck, and Serge Reubi, and all those who participated in the many meetings.

[2] https://www.youtube.com/@ercminoruniversality4876/videos.

workshops in Berlin at the HKW, and to Bonaventure Soh Bejeng Ndikung and Elena Agudio for welcoming us at SAVVY Contemporary. Without the intellectual curiosity of the invited artists and curators Lynhan Balatbat-Helbock, Filipa César, Sagal Farah, Kelly Krugman, Emeka Ogboh, Adania Shibli, Camille de Toledo, as well as Bitsy Knox, Sana na N'Hada, and Shaly López, this project would not have been possible. We are most grateful to Sergio Ugalde Quintana, who kindly hosted and co-organised with us and Mario Laarmann the international conference *Universality after Universalism? Questions of Philology, Translation, and Intellectual Biographies* at the Colegio de México during our research trip to Mexico City, Puebla, and Teotihuacán in October 2022. The research trip to Mexico, and in particular the intense reflections on the universal claim of the Baroque as a way of understanding world and a cultural form relevant for the Mexican present, was of enormous importance for our research group's concern with central questions revolving around imperialism, "le roman national", Christianity and indigenous subversions. During the winter semester 2022–23, finally, we had the chance to discuss fundamental aspects of the problem of universalism in the seminar *Universalism: History, Theory, and Epistemology* with Olivier Remaud, Omri Boehm, Soumaya Mestiri, Julia Christ, and Souleymane Bachir Diagne.

 The initial project team (Elsie Cohen, Azyza Deiab, Franck Hofmann, Clément Ndé Fongang, Hélène Thiérard) as well as the extended team around Markus' chair for Romance Literatures and Comparative Literary and Cultural Studies (Nicole Fischer, Fatma Hotait, Mario Laarmann, Laurens Schlicht, Aurore Vanessah Reck, Sebastian Rost, Maria-Anna Schiffers, and Carla Seemann) took the project impulse to their respective fields, debated its implications, and let the project transform. Together, we discussed history politics and the function of narration for and in world-making in our ongoing research colloquium with Ananya Jahanara Kabir, Ibou Coulibaly Diop, René Aguigah, Camille de Toledo, Laurent Demanze, and Alexandre Gefen. In September 2020, the ERC-team organised the international symposium *Histoire / histoires: Le concret et l'universel dans les Sciences humaines et sociales* at Villa Vigoni, the Italo-German Center for European Dialogue, a place to which we returned in September 2021 in a short window in-between pandemic restriction for the realisation of the international summer school *Restitution, Reparations,* Reparation – *Towards a New Global Society?* This large event, which afforded exchange with many colleagues and PhD students from different parts of the world, was programmed by Mario Laarmann, Clément Ndé Fongang, Carla Seemann, and Laura Vordermayer, and realised in cooperation with the *Cluster for European Research* as well as the International Research Training Group *European Dream Cultures* directed by our colleague Christiane Solte-

Gresser (both part of Saarland University).³ We are very thankful to the director of the Villa Vigoni, Christiane Liermann-Traniello, who opened the doors of this marvellous place when the pandemic seemed to make any international meeting impossible and to Albrecht Buschmann, who spontaneously joined our sessions on the Lago di Como.

Translation is central to this book in many respects. As a subject, but also as a transformative process. We thank John Angell, Anna Galt, Michael Thomas Taylor, and Liz Carey Libbrecht for their translations, Elsie Cohen who assisted with scientific editing and language revision in several chapters, and of course Hélène Thièrard who has worked with us on this book project from the outset and provided crucial help in editing and formatting all the chapters in French. For editorial work with the index and the formatting of chapters, we are grateful to Ann-Christin Gelszat, Kaja Lilith Hauser, Freddy Ndi, and Tetyana Vorobyova.

Without the funding from a European Research Council Consolidator Grant, neither the project nor this book and the series in which it appears would have been possible. We thank Anne Nielsen, scientific officer at the ERC, as well as Adela Ruiz-Caabeiro, for their steady support. At Saarland University, we owe thanks to Claudia Theis and Nina Christmann for steering financial and administrative matters. Christine Guirriec undergirds the *Minor Universality* project with her support in all matters.

At de Gruyter, we thank Ulrike Krauss for her work in establishing the book series *Beyond Universalism. Studies on the Contemporary – Partager l'universel. Études sur le contemporain* of which this volume – and now quite a few more – form part, and Gabrielle Cornefert for her editorial support during all stages of this book's production.

Last but not least, we are beyond grateful to the contributors to this volume for bearing the weight of an all-around increased pressure on intellectual life and production during the Covid-19 pandemic and for engaging with and co-creating the reflections that led to this book.

Markus Messling & Jonas Tinius
Saarbrücken / Venice, 20 January 2023

---

3 See now the open-access volume *Reparation, Restitution, and the Politics of Memory. Perspectives from Literary, Historical, and Cultural Studies / Réparation, restitution et les politiques de la mémoire. Perspectives littéraires, historiques et culturelles*. Mario Laarmann, Clément Ndé Fongang, Carla Seemann, and Laura Vordermayer. Eds. Berlin, Boston: De Gruyter, 2023 ("Beyond Universalism / Partager l'universel", vol. 3).

Contents
Table des matières

Acknowledgements —— V

Markus Messling & Jonas Tinius
On Minor Universality —— 1

Part I: **Universality After Universalism**
Première partie : **L'universel après l'universalisme**

Souleymane Bachir Diagne
What Might a Truly Universal Universalism Be? Thinking the Universal With Étienne Balibar —— 35

Anil Bhatti
The Universal and the Particular: The Place of Similarity in Cultural Theory —— 43

Gisèle Sapiro
Le décentrement épistémologique conduit-il au relativisme ? —— 57

Part II: **Narrative (and) World Production**
Deuxième partie : **La fabrique narrative du monde**

Christopher M. Hutton
From Acoustic Space to the Global Village: Linearity and the Western Intellectual Imagination —— 75

Isaac Bazié
Porteurs d'universalité et fictions de l'Afrique-monde —— 91

Maria-Anna Schiffers
More-Than-Human Relations, or: Rethinking Narration and Relations With Bears —— 105

Mario Laarmann
Hybrid Aesthetics and Social Reality: Reading Caribbean Literature in the Postcolonial Present —— 119

Rukmini Bhaya Nair
Precolonial Universality and Postcolonial Diversity: The Example of the Indian Subcontinent —— 137

Part III: **Language, the Self, and Society**
Troisième partie : **Le langage, le sujet et la société**

Leyla Dakhli
Par-delà la pureté de la langue : révolutions et jeux de langues dans le monde arabe contemporain —— 157

Hélène Thiérard
Multilingual Literatures and the Production of Universality Through Translation: Cassin, Diagne, Tawada —— 173

Elsie Cohen
Exil et universalité —— 191

Ananya Jahanara Kabir
Creolising Universality —— 215

Part IV: **Restitutions and Reparations**
Quatrième partie : **Restitutions et réparations**

Bénédicte Savoy
Statues Also Trample —— 233

Albert Gouaffo
Décentrer la question des restitutions : l'exemple des biens culturels issus de contextes coloniaux en Afrique face aux micro-histoires régionales —— 251

Khadija von Zinnenburg Carroll
Repatriation From the Universal Museum: *Iyagbon's Mirror* **as a Performance of Minor-Universals** —— 265

Part V: **Human Rights and Universal Rights**
Cinquième partie : **Droits humains et droits universels**

Jean-Luc Chappey et Laurens Schlicht
Utopies égalitaires. De l'égalité aux techniques d'égalités : retour sur le « sauvage de l'Aveyron », 1799–1830 —— 285

Sergio Ugalde Quintana
La violence et la construction du « commun » : la littérature internationaliste écrite au Mexique dans les années 1940 —— 305

Stefan Helgesson
Universality From Within: The Challenge of Black Consciousness in 1970s South Africa —— 323

Nicole Fischer et Fatma Hotait
Penser l'universel à travers le féminisme islamique —— 335

Olivier Remaud
Raconter le vivant —— 353

Contributors —— 369

Index —— 373

Markus Messling & Jonas Tinius
On Minor Universality

Abstract: Our contribution seeks to render intelligible minor forms of a world-consciousness generated through social and cultural practices. Departing from Zineb Sedira's installation "Dreams Have No Titles" for the French Pavilion of the 2022 Venice Biennale and concluding with our project's research exhibition "The Pregnant Oyster: Doubts on Universalism" at Berlin's Haus der Kulturen der Welt, we discuss how narrative forms (beyond the book) produce experiences of a shared world. Shifting from an understanding of universality as effect of the universal in particular worlds, we return to the epistemological proposal of the *microstoria* (Ginzburg, Levi, Revel) to inverse this relation. In doing so, we suggest the concept of a minor universality, by which we describe the genesis of a universal consciousness from concrete contexts. Our notion mobilises Deleuze and Guattari's concept of the minor through their engagement with Franz Kafka. We draw on it to address the Algerian anti-colonial struggle and the practice of sonic radio resistance described in Frantz Fanon's "This is the Voice of Free Algeria". Not captured through the binary of power/resistance, minority/majority, ours/yours, the minor produces instead a potentiality for change, for the not-yet, which foreshadows and intuits a new humanity.

Keywords: universalism, decolonisation, Mediterranean internationalism, Venice Bienniale, exhibition-making, narrative, *microstoria*, truth-procedure, Alain Badiou, Gilles Deleuze, Frantz Fanon, Giovanni Levi, Zineb Zedira

> Minor literature is completely different; its cramped space forces each individual intrigue to connect immediately to politics. The individual concern thus becomes all the more necessary, indispensable, magnified, because a whole other story is vibrating within it. (Deleuze and Guattari 1986 [1975], 17)

Note: Research that led to the publication of this book chapter was supported by the project "Minor Universality. Narrative World Productions After Western Universalism", which received funding from the European Research Council (ERC) under the European Union's Horizon 2020 research and innovation programme (Grant no. 819931).

Translated by Michael Thomas Taylor

Open Access. © 2023 the author(s), published by De Gruyter. This work is licensed under the Creative Commons Attribution-NonCommercial-NoDerivatives 4.0 International License.
https://doi.org/10.1515/9783110798494-001

1 The dream of humanity?

"The Milk of Dreams" is the motto chosen by the Venice Biennale 2022 for its exploration of how human existence is being transformed. Its title borrowed from Leonora Carrington's eponymous book, the international exhibition aims to showcase artistic interrogations of what it means to live together on one planet. Keenly aware of a viral world crisis, confronted by the disenchantment that now attends technological progress, and powerlessness in the face of a pandemic of our own making, the Biennale is asking art to respond to the most existential form of the anthropological question: What does it mean to be human, in the shadow of humanity's destruction and exploitation of the nonhuman world? Or more radically: "What would life look like without us?" (Alemani 2022, 47).

The question touches upon a universal awareness of our humanity, of the shared experience of living on one planet – our only planet – in the face of its possible destruction. This is an awareness that the multifaceted Biennale seeks to capture and articulate – in the universalist tradition of world exhibitions – as the state of human history. Such a perspective has long claimed to be the pinnacle of the global cultural field: a view of the whole, both encapsulated and broken down within national pavilions that appear to resist any further abstraction – did universalist modernism not ultimately result from a universalisation of nations? This is a perspective that has repeatedly claimed to allow us to see and hear the Other, to see and hear those who have been silenced and rendered unseen, and which thus repeatedly comes up against the dilemma formulated by Horkheimer and Adorno – that the capitalist cultural industry has long since understood how to co-opt forms of resistance.[1] Can something "minor" be expressed in such a world exhibition, through such a view of the world?[2] Can this context give rise to

---

[1] See the seminal chapter on the "culture industry" in Horkheimer and Adorno's *Dialectic of Enlightenment* (2002 [1944]: 94–137); also Adorno (2009 [1957]). Boltanski and Chiapello describe how "the new spirit of capitalism", as they title their book (2005 [1999]), "incorporated much of the *artistic critique* that flourished at the end of the 1960s" (Boltanski and Chiapello 2005 [1999]: 419), along with its desire for liberation, autonomy, and authenticity. This leads them to speak of "the inherent ambiguity of critique: even in the case of the most radical movements, it shares 'something' with what it seeks to criticize" (Boltanski and Chiapello 2005 [1999]: 40). What they see emerging is what they term the "spirit of capitalism": "precisely the set of beliefs associated with the capitalist order that helps to justify this order and, by legitimising them, to sustain the forms of action and predispositions compatible with it" (Boltanski and Chiapello 2005 [1999]: 10).

[2] The title of our introduction departs from an understanding of the minor, which builds on the writing of Gilles Deleuze and Félix Guattari. For them, it is literature – and specifically, the writings of Franz Kafka – that serves as a starting point for their theory of the "minor", as a form of community mediated in language. In this introduction, we aim to mobilise this term deliberately

Figure 1: Installation View, *Les rêves n'ont pas de titre / Dreams have no titles*, Zineb Sedira, French Pavilion, Venice Biennale 2022. Credit: Markus Messling.

something that disturbs our shared sense of history and, precisely in this way, thinks the world as a space of shared experience?

In the French pavilion of the Biennale, one finds a rectangular display case resembling a large aquarium (Figure 1).[3] It contains a miniature of a living room made of cardboard, fully furnished with a fireplace, armchairs, a sofa table, houseplants, and bookshelves. The floor is covered with oriental carpets, where a female figure stands, recognisable upon closer inspection as a photograph of the artist Zineb Sedira. Slightly receding into the background, she occupies the vanishing point of the scene even as she gazes right back at us. The entire *tableau vivant* is in the style of

---

for modes of narration beyond the book, beyond literature, indeed beyond the canon of written texts that ultimately constitute what we are calling "minor universality": shared experiences and consciousness of the "world" and its horizons that emerge from concrete narrative practices. Or to quote Deleuze and Guattari: such narration is the "whole other story [. . .] vibrating within it" (Deleuze and Guattari 1986 [1975]: 17).

3 We are very grateful to Zineb Sedira for permitting us to print our photos of her work in this context.

late-sixties and early-seventies decor, with overly bright, pop art posters on the walls, red seat cushions, records, small objects, and other ornaments. At first glance, all of it has the look of a charming dollhouse, a piece of self-reassuring kitsch from an idealised age. Does this installation present us with the *intérieur* of a society that has been seized, time and time again, by the desire to exhibit its culture? Does it mean to embody the "nation universaliste"? Stepping into the main room of the pavilion, one has precisely this impression, because the overall scenario immediately evokes a feel-good cliché: an old-time bar (it's hard not to think of the "fabulous" world of

Figure 2: Installation View, *Les rêves n'ont pas de titre / Dreams have no titles*, Zineb Sedira, French Pavilion, Venice Biennale 2022. Credit: Markus Messling.

Amélie Poulain), with film reels and movie scenes, advertising posters from the post-war *Orangina* age. "Dreams Have No Titles" is the shimmering slogan from an old movie theatre billboard from which Sedira's installation takes its name.[4]

The oversized spotlight directed at the display case, though, creates distance; it marks the scene as staged and casts all of it in a different light (Figure 2). Only then does one notice the cameras all around, the monitors and spotlights, the fact that the entire installation is designed as a film set. If we arrived as passive onlookers, we now become active observers challenged to look more closely. In a play of multiple *mises en abyme*, Sedira guides us to an utterly different story.

We are the ones now inside the display case. One of the pavilion's side rooms is furnished just like the dollhouse, as if this little scene offered a set of building blocks for real life (Figure 3). In the same spot where the cardboard figure of the artist stood just a moment ago, we now find ourselves in the middle of a living room. This is a play with scales. The aquarium-like microcosm that seemed to represent Zineb Sedi-

Figure 3: Installation View, *Les rêves n'ont pas de titre / Dreams have no titles*, Zineb Sedira, French Pavilion, Venice Biennale 2022. Credit: Markus Messling.

---

4 *Le fabuleux destin d'Amélie Poulain*, film directed by Jean-Pierre Jeunet, Paris 2001.

ra's individual story becomes that of our own, or at least we are suddenly implicated in this world. And now, as we inspect its features, we begin to see so many details that provoke so many questions. There are photos of Algerian landscapes hanging on the walls, alongside family photos and a potpourri of film posters, many of them of Arabic origin, such as the poster for *Le doute mortel* (*The Murderer's Suspicion*, 1953) by the Egyptian director Ezz el-Din Zulfikar, whose work deeply influenced Arabic cinema. Wooden elephants serve as book stands, mixed in with African masks. There are records by the Algerian singer Zoubida and by the American Bob Destiny, the actor and musician who taught at the Théâtre National Algérien in the late 1960s and early 1970s. And of course there is the library, with editions of *Présence africaine* and the work of Frantz Fanon alongside Sartre and Lacan, with Detalmo Pirzio-Biroli's *Révolution culturelle africaine*, James R. Hooker's *Black Revolutionary*, and Guy Hennebelle's *Chroniques de la naissance du cinéma algérien* (Figure 4).

Figure 4: Installation View, *Les rêves n'ont pas de titre / Dreams have no titles*, Zineb Sedira, French Pavilion, Venice Biennale 2022. Credit: Markus Messling.

The ensemble of references points to the revolutions, upheavals, and reorganisation of societies in the processes of decolonisation – and to the period of political freedom following Algerian independence that promised such great hope, especially for many African societies. At the same time, it illustrates the change in the concept of culture itself that was brought about primarily by music and film.[5] This altered concept is characterised by an ambivalent relationship to the new possibilities of film – because of course we have also been left with a cinema of "la douce France", a tradition that produced imagery for the new, bourgeois world of the "Trente Glorieuses", the 30 golden years (1945–1975); and at times this cinema reduced the colonial question to mere kitsch. The many film reels piled up to fill the main room invoke cinema itself as a myth of French post-war

Figure 5: Cinema Installation View, *Les rêves n'ont pas de titre / Dreams have no titles,* Zineb Sedira, French Pavilion, Venice Biennale 2022. Credit: Jonas Tinius.

---

5 "What we call pop – pop music, pop philosophy, pop writing – Worterflucht [sic]. To make use of the polylingualism of one's own language, to make a minor or intensive use of it, to oppose the oppressed quality of this language to its oppressive quality, to find points of nonculture or under-development, linguistic Third World zones by which a language can escape, an animal enters into things, an assemblage comes into play" (Deleuze and Guattari 1985, 26f.). See also the influential work of Hall and Whannel (2018 [1965]).

modernism.⁶ Yet the very structure of myth implies that we are meant to see, like Oedipus who has lost his sight, only after the tragedy. It is only in remembering that we understand.

A minor detail opens the path for what has been repressed to penetrate into the living room like a spectre. In the space at the rear, behind the scene, is where the dead lie – where we find an empty coffin staring back at us (Figure 5), "filled" with associations evoked in references taken from Visconti's film adaptation (1967) of *L'Étranger* by Albert Camus (1942) – a novel that tells the story of the senseless murder of an unnamed Arab person by the callous French Algerian Meursault. Motifs of alienation from the world, and of the weight of guilt, steal back into the mind. Hence, the question remains: Whose dead do we mourn? Who lies in the coffin? The beholder is invited to the wake. Two chairs stand by the casket: one seat for France and one for Algeria? For the Algeria that France was so keen to assimilate that it carved the country up into French departments, and which became the place where France finally destroyed its own universalistic ideals with brutal violence.

Rather than simply reviving the myth of French cinema, then, Zineb Sedira reinterprets it in a new form by telling us the story of an intellectual opening and a cinematic avant-garde located between Algeria, the Maghreb more widely, France, and Italy. This story encompasses Pontecorvo's *Bataille d'Alger* (1966), Visconti's *Lo straniero* (1967), and Lorenzini's *Les mains libres* (1964), along with so many Algerian films that have largely been forgotten and to which Zineb Sedira also gives a material presence via the stack of film reels in the adjoining rooms. Yet what she emphasises is not the historical lines running between enemies and blocs: instead, she leaves us standing within a symbolic remake of an age of internationalism, in which hope was born for a humanity that might finally be worthy of this name.

Orhan Pamuk, in assembling his Istanbul *Museum of Innocence* (2012), programmatically rejected the institution's grand representational gestures. His installation focuses instead on the similarity of emotions and experiences that, when integrated into a narrative, make it possible to experience a wholeness shared by all. In it, experiences of objects and emotions make intensities of shared life present and point toward the common grounds of human gestures:

> What we feel when we open the curtains to let the sunlight in, when we wait for an elevator that refuses to arrive, when we enter a room for the first time, when we brush our teeth, when we hear the sound of thunder, when we smile at someone we hate, when we fall asleep in the shade of a tree – our sensations are both similar to and different from those of

---

6 With essays on the Romans in film, Greta Garbo, and Charlie Chaplin in his influential *Mythologies* (2009 [1957]), Roland Barthes ultimately elevated cinema itself from a producer of myths to the very myth of post-war society.

other people. The similarities allow us to imagine the whole of mankind through literature [. . .] (Pamuk 2010, 49).

Stylistically, too, Zineb Sedira's work evokes Pamuk's museum. She stages a scene that invites its visitors to explore performatively the possibilities of what it opens up: the power that art and other productions of culture possess – and for Sedira, this especially means film – to make connections between individual lives and a universal question, and thus to make possible an experience of universality from within a historically situated position. This kind of consciousness emerges from concrete contexts, in processes of remembering and translating – processes of repairing or even of making reparations. They aim thus toward a universal ideal of humanity – toward hope, solidarity, and shared human community. And it is this consciousness that we call "minor universality".

2 Micro-cracks and macro-cuts

A brief excursus into the German translation of Gilles Deleuze and Félix Guattari can help us to articulare more precisely what we mean, since the notion of minor that they develop in their reading of Kafka, and which we cited in our epigraph above, is stubbornly translated in German as "klein" – meaning "little" or "small". "Für eine kleine Literatur" – "Toward a small literature" – is the book's subtitle in German. But this isn't quite what "minor" means.[7] Of course, "minor" as used by Deleuze and Guattari also refers to a small, even micro frame of reference; it pertains to concrete situatedness, to the embodiment and enactment of a certain kind of speech that estranges the standard use of speech, escapes it. Still, "minor" for them primarily denotes literature which has not yet been adopted into the canon, has not yet entered into the main currents of social and cultural discourse, but which rather "speaks" from another place and thus takes shape in a different use

---

7 On this point, see the commentary by the German translator Burkhart Kroeber (Deleuze and Guattari 2019 [1975]: 24). "In French, this is not *petite littérature*, but a more capacious phrase: *littérature mineure* (as opposed to the grand, recognised, well-established *littérature majeure*). To indicate this richness of meaning, as a makeshift solution Kafka's characterisation of 'klein' will be furnished with a gloss of 'minder' [lesser/minor] or placed in quotation marks." – On the back cover of a 1980 collection of Gilles Deleuze's essays published in German by Merve Verlag under the title *Kleine Schriften* [Small writings], the following list appears vertically: "little, mini, lesser, low, minor, measly, minoritarian, inferior, underage, immature, idiotically, secondary, subordinate, mine worker, pioneer, minelayer, *frz. mineur*" (in the original: „klein, mini, minder, gering, niedrig, Moll, mickrig, minoritär, minderwertig, minderjährig, unmündig, schwachsinnig, zweitrangig, Untergebener, Bergarbeiter, Pionier, Mienenleger, *frz. mineur*.") We thank Cord Riechelmann for the hint.

of language and form. It denotes a literature which has not yet been polished by the weight of custom, or which even stands in its way as a counter-discourse; which is perhaps nothing more than a murmuring or rushing sound that is gradually perceived like a sub-tone, or like noise. This is a sound, though, that can also infiltrate a more dominant frequency to appear not as foreign, as coming from outside, but as itself bound to the dominant tone, that even expresses itself in this dominant language or form. When Deleuze and Guattari attribute to a minor use of language a "high coefficient of deterritorialization" (Deleuze and Guattari (1986 [1975], 16), this does not exhaust itself in the mobility, migration, or displacement of the writer or speaker; the use of language itself can change within a given language or aesthetic form, create variation, introduce deviation, depart from received grammar. Such variations of language – "linguistic *action*" (Bogue 2005, 132) – are forms of grappling with conventions, labels, and, ultimately therefore engagements with power relations. Interestingly, they act not in an entirely different language, but parasitically. Major and minor do not denote two different languages, but "two usages or functions of language" (Deleuze and Guattari (1987 [1980], 104). "In this sense, the minor both compels obedience and opens passages" (Parr 2005, 164).

This is how, for instance, Kafka inscribes his own way of articulating into German, which may seem unremarkable at first but in fact entails taking a position vis-a-vis an authority – as a sign of a "minor becoming" (Deleuze and Parnet 2007 [1977], 124–125). It was Deleuze and Guattari (1986 [1975]) who showed that Kafka's language, his writing, is a "becoming" which no longer signifies primarily through meaningful references but through effects of alienation, that tends more toward making it possible to experience the intensity of a position than references to the world that can be completely deciphered. In this case of Kafka's relationship to authority, they argue, the complexity of this relating lies in the fact that Kafka does not – indeed could not – rise up in an oedipal fashion against his father, but rather that he counterposes his own weakness to that of his father precisely because he has understood that the father is already in a position of symbolic disempowerment: as a Jew who moved from the Czech countryside to the German-dominated city of Prague, Kafka's father finds himself permanently displaced (one aspect of what Deleuze and Guattari call "deterritorialization"). What Kafka seeks, as they argue against a classical psychoanalytic interpretation, is not to assert himself against the father's generation but to find a "way out". This "line of escape" finds a subversive form in Kafka's language, which is a "machine" of metamorphosis, an undermining of sense, a whistling and a coughing and a whining (Deleuze and Guattari 1986 [1975], 7, 21).[8]

---

8 In this respect, one must ask whether Deleuze and Guattari are implicated in the critique that is the foundation for Gayatri Chakravorty Spivak's analysis of whether the subaltern can speak,

That a rushing sound of this kind, a tinnitus in the ears of society, can develop to become a powerful, penetrating tone – one that speaks with truth, as though the reality of world had only just been grasped – is what Kafka's literature revealed in dispatching its disruptive commentary into the faltering modernity of the Habsburg Empire and of (Imperial) Germany. For Deleuze and Guattari, Kafka's literature stands precisely for a kind of "minor" that does *not* exist independently of or outside the dominant forms of expression, but nests within them and creates, from and within them, another form of consciousness. The "minor" is accordingly not to be misunderstood as an alternative in a binary of either/or, minority/majority; rather, it is to be grasped as a form of co-dependent opposition, a footnote, a variation that does not exist without a given unmarked standard. It is not to be essentially reduced to statistics or to identities either. It is possible to belong to a majority in a given context and yet not be the supposed norm:

> Minority and majority are not only quantitatively opposed. Majority implies an ideal constant, a standard measure against which it is marked and evaluated. Let's assume this constant or measure was *human-white-western-male-adult-reasonable-heterosexual-city-dweller-speaker of a standard language* (as Ulysses in Joyce or Ezra Pound). Obviously, the "human" is in the majority, even if he is less numerous than the mosquitos, children, women, blacks, peasants, homosexuals etc . . . The majority presupposes a juridical relation and a relation of governance, and not the other way around (Deleuze 1980, 27).

The minor describes a form of relating, a capacity for change, for escape, for the *not-yet*, for potentiality. In this sense, it is a political, collective, and perhaps utopian use of language, since it conjures up a "people to come" (Deleuze 1997 [1993], 90). Hence it can be most readily thought in relation to what is normative or axiomatic, to the standard that enforces homogeneity. "Micro-cracks are also collective, no less than macro-cuts are personal" (Deleuze and Guattari 1986 [1975], 127).

In "This is the Voice of Algeria" (1965 [1959]), Frantz Fanon describes such collective "micro-cracks" as appropriating the normative language and media of French colonial power in order to find a disruptive Algerian frequency of liberation –

---

in which she accuses Deleuze and Foucault's thinking of indirectly reintroducing the European concept of the subject that they themselves criticise (Spivak 1988, 271–272). For Deleuze and Guattari, "marginalization", processes of "becoming small", or the production of unknown intensity are namely the prerequisite for any literature that effects a change by making it possible to feel something that cannot yet be said otherwise (Deleuze and Guattari 1986 [1975]: 18, 27). They therefore draw a line from Kafka to Artaud and Céline, and to Proust and Joyce. Moreover, one might even suggest that the very idea of "speaking" is undermined by their suggestion that the becoming-animal in Kafka's writing is no longer about anthropocentric forms of expressions, but takes on other forms of articulation. On the problem of the relations between critiques of representation, singularity, and universality in literature, see Messling (2021).

and of a solidarity that unfolds precisely within these dominant forms. The Algerian resistance, Fanon notes, exploited the French medium of radio, which was "essentially the instrument of colonial society and its values" (Fanon 1965 [1959], 69). In the years leading up the Algerian War of Independence (1954–1962), radio sets were not adopted by the Algerian society, since they threatened traditional types of sociability. Moreover, as Fanon points out: "For a European to own a radio is of course to participate in the eternal round of Western petty-bourgeois ownership" (Fanon 1965 [1959], 71). For the French occupies, "the radio reminds the settler of the reality of colonial power and, by its very existence, dispenses safety, serenity" (Fanon 1965 [1959], 71). The radio, in other words, was a system of colonial information and civilising standard, presumed to maintain a regime of power and keep the colonial situation safe and sane. "Algerian society, the dominated society, never participates in this world of signs", Fanon (1965 [1959], 73) notes. Just before the Algerian War, this radically changed. On 1 November 1954, when Algeria joined the anti-colonialist Maghreb Front, radio sets were acquired. "The Algerian who read in the occupier's face the increasing bankruptcy of colonialism felt the compelling and vital need to be informed" (Fanon 1965 [1959], 75). It was at this moment that the Algerians organised themselves in the medium of the French occupation. This created fear, disruption. "The European, after 1954, knew that something was being hidden from him" (Fanon 1965 [1959], 78). Inarticulate bursts of madness undermined their safety further; "Individuals in a fit of aberration would lose control of themselves. They would be seen dashing down a street [. . .], shouting, 'Long live independent Algeria! We've won!' (Fanon 1965 [1959], 78). These moments of interruption led to an anxiety, because the French didn't know anymore how these news spread, whether they were true, or not. By the end of 1956, Algerians bought radio receivers, and time tracts, broadcasting schedules, and wavelengths were distributed "announcing the existence of a Voice of Free Algeria" (Fanon 1965 [1959], 82). The medium of occupation became a medium of opposition, its function deterritorialised, its acts political, and its horizon the creation of a community to-come: "Since 1956, the purchase of a radio in Algeria has meant, not the adoption of a modern technique for getting news, but the obtaining of access to the only means of entering into communication with the Revolution, of living with it" (Fanon 1965 [1959], 82).

The French realised this, prohibited radio – even battery – sales. They shifted to engage in "sound-wave warfare" (Fanon 1965 [1959], 5), as they detected wave lengths of resistance, jammed the programmes, and rendered the *Voice of Fighting Algeria* temporarily inaudible. The medium of power became itself a battleground through the introduction of a minor function. The resistance distributed new wavelengths, Algerians tuning in for periods of two to three hours. Over the course of one broadcast, frequencies shifted several times. The French operator might have caught a glimpse of the *Voice of Fighting Algeria*. The bits of news that got through were distributed by word-of-mouth, retold and distributed. "Imperfectly heard, obscured by an incessant jamming, forced to change wave lengths two or three times in the course of a broadcast, the *Voice of Fighting Algeria* could hardly ever be heard from beginning to end. It was a choppy, broken voice" (Fanon 1965 [1959], 86).

La Voix de l'Algérie libre et combattante ("Sawt El Djazair el hourra el moukafiha") thus itself became a medium of battle, within the language of power. Liberation, as Fanon has shown in his phenomenological analysis, not only means inscription into the dominant medium, but always, too, an emphasis on what is one's own, on the negation of the opponent and the discourse of struggle:

> The natives' challenge to the colonial world is not a rational confrontation of points of view. It is not a treatise on the universal, but the untidy affirmation of an original idea propounded as an absolute. The colonial world is a Manichean world (Fanon 1963 [1961], 41).

The radio of the Liberation Front speaks in its own language – both symbolically and more concretely in Arabic and not (only) in French. The radio is thus transformed from a weapon of repression to the disruptive noise of self-assertion, yet of the demographic majority battling colonial hegemony with view to a political community that was in the process of becoming. "Under these conditions, claiming to have heard the *Voice of Algeria* was [. . .] above all the occasion to proclaim one's clandestine participation in the essence of the Revolution" (Fanon 1963 [1961], 87). Sedira's installation in the French pavilion aptly echoes this repression, as a protagonist reads passages from Fanon's *A Dying Colonialism* 1965 [1959] – yet another *mise en abyme* that allows us look behind the scenes built by violence (Figure 6).

Fanon thereby gained an unadorned view of a painful dilemma: "Illuminated by violence, the consciousness of the people rebels against any pacification" (Fanon 1963 [1961], 94). Yet any repair of the self, any self-reparations, are only a first step toward a new social order. "It is true to say that independence has brought moral compensation [in French: *réparation morale*] to colonised peoples, and has established their dignity. But they have not yet had time to elaborate a society, or to build up and affirm values" (Fanon 1963 [1961], 81). In this context, then, processes of resistance related to liberation, in which the fronts are clear even as they intersect and are deterritorialised, are particularly interesting, because this is where solidarities become visible that lie beyond the self. In his essay "This is the Voice of Algeria", Fanon, too, is interested in the subtle appropriations that allow a minor position to insert itself into a dominant discourse by co-opting language: during the Algerian War, he argues, buying leftist, anti-colonial French dailies served to sow further insecurity, adding to the choppy voice of *Fighting Algeria*. Hence French society itself became an accomplice to Algerian independence:

Figure 6: Coffin Installation View, *Les rêves n'ont pas de titre / Dreams have no titles,* Zineb Sedira, French Pavilion, Venice Biennale 2022. Credit: Jonas Tinius.

> For the Algerian to ask for *L'Express*, *L'Humanité*, or *Le Monde* was tantamount to publicly confessing – as likely as not to a police informer – his allegiance to the Revolution; it was in any case an unguarded indication that he had reservations as to the official, or "colonialist" news; it meant manifesting his willingness to make himself conspicuous; for the kiosk dealer it was the unqualified affirmation by that Algerian of solidarity with the Revolution. The purchase of such a newspaper was thus considered to be a nationalist act. Hence it quickly became a dangerous act. Every time the Algerian asked for one of these newspapers, the kiosk dealer, who represented the occupier, would regard it as an expression of nationalism, equivalent to an act of war. Because they were now really committed to activities vital to the Revolution, or out of understandable prudence, if one bears in mind the wave of xenophobia created by the French settlers in 1955, Algerian adults soon formed the habit of getting young Algerians to buy these newspapers. It took only a few weeks for this new "trick" to be discovered. After a certain period, the newsdealers refused to sell *L'Express*, *L'Humanité*, and *Libération* to minors. Adults were then reduced to coming out into the open or else to falling back on *L'Écho d'Alger*. It was at this point that the political directorate of the Revolution gave orders to boycott the Algerian local press (Fanon 2002 [1961], 81).

With Fanon, we find the threads stretching out across the Mediterranean that also made possible the cinema of the 1960s and 1970s – the art in which Zineb

Sedira finds hope for a new internationalism and a world bound together in solidarity, a world that joins both Mediterranean coasts into one horizon.[9]

In this sense, the term "minor universality" may at first seem like an internal contradiction: minor and yet universal. But it is precisely the initial bewilderment provoked by these seemingly paradoxical processes and connections that motivates this book – because horizons of universality that make connections, that remain open to experience or take shape in imagination, arise not (only) through standardising and totalising processes. History has certainly known a consciousness of world "from above", created through missionary work and power. Western universalism has set the mould here,[10] while also demonstrating its own implosion. Universality, we know, cannot be based on exclusion, but must always also think the minor, lest it lose integrity and collapse. This is exactly why the Marseillaise was sung by the slaves who had been freed in the Haitian Revolution: it is the liberation of those who have been oppressed in the name of freedom that promises the liberation of humanity.[11] We can think "a universal figure of minoritarian consciousness as becoming", and in doing so, we need to turn to fields and "forces of becoming that are other than those of juridical relation or a relation of governance" (Deleuze 1980, 29).[12] In this respect, the attitude that conceives of the demand for freedom from a minor position is not only a reaction, an anti-thesis, to Western universalism; it aims at something more fundamental, at something that invents its own resources in articulating the idea of humanity and freedom.

Julia Christ has attempted to categorise the historical forms in which critiques of universalism have been articulated as attempts to address the concept's political and social "blind spots". She defines a first category as a "reconfiguration of the universal we try to achieve, through the particularities that the universal reintegrates"; this universalism aims to integrate what has not yet been considered into the existing concept of the universal. A second category, by contrast, refuses to include the particular and instead demands an "alternative universal", a kind of counter-universal that begins with what universalism declares to be particular.

---

9 Deleuze and Guattari speak tellingly of Kafka's "own third world" or his "own desert" – a process of marginalization even within "great (or established) literature" – as the only place where narrative has the power to enunciate collectives (Deleuze and Guattari 1986 [1975]: 18).
10 See also Wallerstein (2006, 1–29) and, on the violence inherent in a functionalist European rationalism, of course, still Horkheimer and Adorno (2002 [1944]).
11 On this historical tension, see Buck-Morss (2009) and also Hofmann and Messling (2021).
12 Lila Abu-Lughod's ethnography *Veiled Sentiments. Honor and Poetry in a Bedouin Society* (1986) offers a rich account of poetic forms of expression that articulate otherwise hidden and sanctioned narratives in a context of patriarchal authority; ones which show how a minor consciousness, a minor community to-come can be formed and enacted within fields otherwise marked by hegemony.

And finally, she defines a third category which does not think unity from above, but is "structurally generated – and thus horizontally constructed – by certain distinctive oppositions relevant to the thought" (Christ 2021, 13–25). Creating relevance out of such fundamental contradictions is the task taken up by critical universalism. And it is Christ's third category of critique that we have also taken up as our task, as a project that emphasises both a future creation of the universal, of the normative, out of concrete tensions, and the production and experience of the relevance this claims. The "minor" is thus no site or identity that can be fixed, but a relationship to the dominant standard that governs adaptation, just as thinking, producing, and demanding universality from within the minor is no relativistic gesture that would exhaust itself in reclaiming, pluralising, or provincialising Western, Northern modernity.[13] Nor is it a process of re-juxtaposition, of re-canonisation following de-canonisation, or of simple re-territorialisation. Minor universality instead describes narratives that arise from a position embedded within a concrete situation, from unexpected social intensities, variations of standard expression, or from a particularised enunciation, to develop a power for our ability to conceive of "world" and of humanity, – and for our desires and obligations to do so (Messling 2019; 2023). Against the experience of violence that threatens and divides society, it is precisely from similar concrete minor practices and fields, which witnessed and incorporated the forces of destruction, that we derive our urgency and hope for a new universalism. Analytically speaking, this is the experience, which contemporary cultural practices seek to produce, since this is the way, it seems to us, that Zineb Sedira conceives her time of hope.

3 Universality after universalism

Hope is a driving force in the emergence of European universalism. In his book on *Saint Paul: The Foundation of Universalism* (2003 [1977]), Alain Badiou invokes Paul's doctrine of faith precisely to emphasise the groundlessness of the universal. Reformulating what at first seems to be a paradox – namely, a groundlessness in the face of a belief – Badiou argues that for Paul, the pre-Christian religious law shapes the universal as a specific way of life whose observance aims at salvation *after* life. But faith in love, Badiou continues, as expressed in Christ's

---

[13] Anthropologist James Laidlaw discusses cultural relativism as "an incoherent solution to a non-existent problem" (2014, 24), suggesting that "either the claim that all truths are relative applies to itself, in which case it is only relatively true, or it doesn't, in which case there is at least one non-relative truth" (2014, 26).

resurrection, is what gives birth to the hope of overcoming death *in* life (Badiou 2003 [1977], 81–92). Badiou elaborates that for Paul, what is significant is thus not any interpretation of death and resurrection, a way of explaining what the event *means*, but rather a "truth procedure" (Badiou 2003 [1977], 84), it is about faith in the event itself – "love is precisely fidelity to the Christ-event" (Badiou 2003 [1977], 90). Faith in this event nevertheless needs to be publicly confessed, because the subjective experience of the truth is the same as the truth itself: "Truth is either militant or it is not" (Badiou 2003 [1977], 88).

What Alain Badiou proposes with his interpretation of Paul is thus not an understanding of truth that we could describe through interpretation, but a theory of epistemic form: it is only in the event that truth shows itself, and it is only faith in truth as an event that endows truth with power. For Badiou, however, this truth also reflects something universal: the fact that it equally encompasses all human beings (Badiou 2003 [1977], 76). What is decisive here is the direction of the movement: this is a universalism that comes from above. It is only because the event – the overcoming of death – transcends any form of particularity that it can be universal. What matters for Badiou here is the difference between the particularity that emerges from cultural and religious forms of life, and a singularity. No universal can arise from particularity, he argues, because particularity must determine the one truth according to its own contents and rules (in the same way that a religion determines its own conception of God). Singularity for Badiou is by contrast the transformation of the individual that comes from believing in the event, for it is precisely in believing that an individual becomes part of the universal and experiences their determination as part of the human community (Badiou 2003 [1977], 96–97).

The strength of this "Pauline universalism" therefore lies in the fact that it can cut through particular communities and reconnect human beings to truth that transcends particular limits. In a way, this also provides an explanation for the historical success of early Christianity throughout the Mediterranean. In 1977, in his first chapter on "Paul, Our Contemporary", Badiou emphasised the power of this idea to shape community as an answer to the identity politics of Jean-Marie Le Pen's radical right-wing party:

> Although himself a Roman citizen, and proud of it, Paul will never allow any legal categories to identify the Christian subject. Slaves, women, people of every profession and nationality will therefore be admitted without restriction or privilege. As for ideological generality, it is obviously represented by the philosophical and moral discourse of the Greeks. Paul will establish a resolute distance to this discourse, which is for him the counterpoise to a conservative vision of Jewish law. Ultimately, it is a case of mobilizing a universal singularity both against the prevailing abstractions (legal then, economic now), and against communitarian or particularist claims (Badiou 2003 [1977], 13–14).

Badiou's book suggests a formation of the universal that in some ways repeats within the great upheavals of modernity. One might say: 1789 is above all the event of postulating human rights, and its legitimacy stems from a faith that this truth will prevail. "Universalism" would thus be a Western experience of truth, closely tied to monotheism – to the idea of the One God – that has nevertheless been universalisable since Paul. And yet what is also clear is that the significance of any transcendent truth is bound up with the specific ways in which it can be realised in different forms of life, in laws and social practices. The early Christian idea of living in faith and love so that this truth prevail is, after all, a specific experience shaped by a belief that the Last Judgment is nigh, which may appear to be insufficient in the context of enduring social structures where action requires long-term, institutional justification. In societies without any expectation of divine justice, what is needed are processes for identifying the universal, for articulating it as law and social practice, and this leads to particularisations. But this generates precisely those attributions that might link human rights to specific prerogatives, rights, or privileges, and that tie their unrestricted validity to economic, social, and political conditions. No sooner did the French Revolution claim to fulfil a mission in the name of humanity by spreading human rights than its revolutionary wars became wars of conquest that yoked this mission to a program of domination. Now, as Immanuel Wallerstein (2006) has shown, the universal was to be founded from within the cultural particularity of its origins, giving rise to the ideology of universalism, as an "ism", that justifies domination.

Faced with the fact that life thus always embeds the universal within a social context that particularises it, microhistory, as a method, has elevated the relationship between the concrete, specific case and the general, singling it out as a problem in its own right. And in doing so, it has also given the question of truth a new, scholarly cast, by asking about the method of its production (Messling 2020). Two fundamental aspects are relevant here.

On the one hand, this approach reverses the truth procedure by addressing the general from a concrete context. The general, which historiography poses as a question about an epistemic order of the world, is thereby compelled to acquire new plausibility at the micro-level. We find this exemplified in how generalised assumptions about early modern peoples' view of the world are challenged in the case of the miller Menocchio in Carlo Ginzburg's *The Cheese and the Worms* (2013 [1976]). The miller Menocchio was not the least bit convinced of the divine order preached by the church, to which he opposed his own, entirely "realistic" idea of life. His fate opens a rift in our homogeneous conception of the estate-based early modern social order, and our understanding of how "simple" people in the late Middle Ages understood their world. Menocchio's particular, concrete understanding of world stands here before us as an obstacle, as a methodological challenge, for even if the question posed to contexts like his can be generalised, his individual case cannot. For Carlo Ginzburg, this necessitated comparison with the work of anthropologists and their rejection of ethnocentrism, which led him to "the minute analysis of a circumscribed documentation, tied to a person who was otherwise unknown" (Ginzburg 1993, 22). Aptly describing this approach, Ginzburg notes that by "reducing the scale of observation, that which for another scholar could have been a simple footnote in a hypothetical monograph on the Protestant Reformation in Friuli was turned into a book" (Ginzburg 1993, 22).[14]

On the other hand, however, this reversal of perspective does not obscure the fact that the universal horizon is postulated here as a series of questions: it is the horizon that makes it possible to play with these different scales; it allows the particular to appear in the light of perspective (Revel 1996). If the universal in Badiou's work finds its true power precisely in this sense, that is to say, as the event whose identity cannot be determined, then this also applies structurally to an approach such as microhistory, which begins by considering the particular. For while the concrete becomes all the more visible in the question of the general, the universal also becomes visible within the particular, and this happens by virtue of the fact that a question is posed to the particular from within a universally valid framework. The very act of addressing a human horizon thus holds an epistemological power. When experienced individually, as happens in moments of solidarity or liberation from the confines of restricted worlds, this act can indeed retain the character of an event.[15]

---

[14] At the conference "Universalismes, hégémonies et identités", which we organised in March 2022 as part of the ERC project "Minor Universality", in cooperation with Leyla Dakhli and Mohamed Kerrou at the Académie tunisienne des sciences, des lettres et des arts (Beït al-Hikma) in Carthage, Giovanni Levi therefore insisted that the hermeneutic cultural and social sciences are not "sciences" in a strict sense, meaning they cannot generalise what is particular or specific. Rather, they offer plausible reasons for a general understanding. See https://www.beitalhikma.tn/fr/colloque-universalismes-hegemonies-et-identites-17-18-mars-2022/ (last accessed 23 October 2022). See also Levi (2018).

[15] Little could demonstrate this more clearly than the narrative through which Levi grounds an interview with the ERC team (ERC Minor University 2020). In a short village in the Piedmontese alps, to which the Levi family fled to escape deportation from the Nazis, and where Giovanni's father joins forces with Leone Ginzburg, the father of Carlo Ginzburg, and the partisans, the young Giovanni digs out a medal from the cracks of a villa road through which Napoléon Bonaparte sent his loyal freedom fighters his "dernière pensée" from Saint Helena. In this story, which Giovanni Levi recounted to Markus Messling and Franck Hofmann in Venice in March 2023, rests, in nuce, the narrative of a humane resistance against the violence of National-Socialism, of a personal engagement, and thus the inner tension of *microstoria* (on this, see the forthcoming publication of our interview in volume 5 of the series *Beyond Universalism. Studies on the Contemporary*).

For a question of the universal that is thus transformed – in a secular age – into an epistemological problem, the narrative processes that are employed to interlink and weigh these various levels plays a central role. Ginzburg writes of *The Cheese and the Worms* that it "does not restrict itself to the reconstruction of an individual event; it narrates it" (Ginzburg 1993, 23). Out of the concrete contexts in which we seek the universal, this event becomes visible through procedures concerned with shaping perspective, establishing narrative stance, or extending the narrative. Tzvetan Todorov, for instance, noted of Roland Barthes's late autobiographical trilogy *Roland Barthes, par Roland Barthes* (1975), *Fragments d'un discours amoureux* (1977), and *La chambre claire* (1980) that Barthes' aim was not to develop a subjective perspective from any first-person form:

> It was necessary, in order not to impose his truth upon others, to limit the field of application of his statements to the minimum: to himself. Thereby he did not necessarily opt for the subjective to the detriment of the objective; I am tempted to say: quite the contrary; for the "objective" is frequently no more than a personal fantasy, whereas to speak of oneself consists precisely in making oneself an object. Nor did he opt for the singular to the detriment of the universal: here again, the collective for which one commonly authorizes oneself to speak is often no more than a fiction; and Barthes' final trilogy is certainly the most universal of all his writings (Todorov 1981, 453).

That is to say: for Todorov, the individuality that is most firmly situated in a place, and that is most specific, also appears most powerfully as universal. This is, on the one hand, because rather than simulate any kind of universality that would ultimately do nothing more than incorporate or annex the particular, it stands – in its idiosyncratic character – as the truest (most universal) representation of the particular. And on the other hand, it points in its very particularity most forcefully to the tension it must overcome in moving toward generality. It thus points to the universal, while simultaneously displacing this target.

For this reason, it makes sense not to think of universality as a scaled category or as an analytical level of aggregation, but rather to consider it from the perspective of concrete, embodied human experiences, within the spectrum of relations to the world. By "experience" we understand a process of directed formation of meaning (in a critical recourse to Husserl 1991). Considered phenomenologically, experience of a universal horizon is consequently a precondition for specific forms of appropriating reality, each time specifically incorporated in one's habitus and translated into language. If the experience itself is "invisible", it emerges, in language, as awareness, as practice.

Disengaging with 'classical', particularly Hegelian, aesthetics, the analysis of culture often distances itself from the claim that analysing narratives also means analysing a form of consciousness.[16] This skepticism is justified insofar as it rejects problematic presuppositions of the philosophy of spirit (*Geistphilosophie*). Our reflections on minor universality, however, assume that narratives express consciousness. This is not a "pure" consciousness in an idealistic sense, but one that is always already embodied in the processes of linguistically formulating concrete, material, social, political, and emotional factors. Consciousness is thus based here on a concept of narration which integrates the body that we are (*Leib*, not *Körper*).

Four aspects are decisive in these acts of "translation": 1) embodied experience as linked to social practices; 2) language as a medium for producing "world"; 3) narration; and 4) the transposition of narrative structures to material forms of producing "world", including such diverse forms as (oral and written) texts, cultural forums, and architecture.

First, in our apprehension of the world, biographical and cultural elements are always embodied. Hence experiences are always already related to the world and historically profound. When they are translated into language, a specific attitude toward reality and a specific production of the world emerges out of this embodiment. On the one hand, this is created in narration and can be described in aesthetic terms (Rancière 2000). And on the other hand, experiences in and of the social context through which a subject lives unfold narrative dimensions beyond the written text and induce practices which structure social life (Bourdieu 1984 [1979]). Perception, practice, and experience are situated in "the socially informed body" (Csordas 1990, 7; see also Mauss 2013 [1934]). As Tomas Csordas puts it, with reference to Bourdieu's notion of practice: "if we begin with the lived world of perceptual phenomena, our bodies are not objects to us. Quite the contrary, they are an integral part of the perceiving subject" (Csordas 1990, 36). To understand how world is produced through the embodied and the situated, is to return a crucial capacity to experience.

Second, language is the medium of producing the world in which experiences attain awareness. We must consider that the natural languages (in the sense of French *langue*, not *langage*) necessarily produce "world" by expressing the world in a certain way, and not in another. We no longer understand this world-making in the deep hermeneutic sense as developed from Romantic thought (Trabant 1990), but in the sense that languages "colour" a perspective on the world, that is, they enable us to grasp the world in a historically and structurally specific way (Deutscher 2011; Trabant 2014). Languages thus possess a historical, semantic,

---

[16] Today, for example, it is hard to think of Goethe's *Faust* as a representative of "the German spirit", a generaliseable German consciousness of being in history. Both the late Adorno and the movement of deconstruction have permanently shaken the notion of a suspension of subjectivity in generalised conceptual discourse and of the identity of thought and world.

poetic surplus and never completely fuse together. Understanding that languages, individually and collectively, cannot be translated without loss or surplus into other languages, opens a relation to a cognitive position implying a universal understanding beyond the monolingual experience. This position does not exist *a priori*; it is only gained and incarnated within this constellation: it constitutes an understanding that both languages do not fully grasp a concept but exceed it in semantic determination; that both address a "third", virtual concept, which refers to the universal core of understanding. The idea of "non-translatability" (Cassin 2014) therefore does not entail imprisonment in relativistic understandings of culture and human articulation. To the contrary, it means that we take a position "beyond", where the process of translation has already taken place. Against this backdrop the capacity to translate proves to be the art of dealing with difficulties, allowing for the invention of a new "monde commun" (Cassin 2016, 9). And multilingualism proves to play a central role in the complexity of the world and for the question of what constitutes a shared horizon (Diagne 2014, 2022).

And yet, instrumental translation in a wider sense may also be a hindrance to a joint universal concern. In *Prisoners of Freedom* (2006), his study of foreign aid and human rights activism in Malawi and Zambia, Harri Englund has shown how translation of ostensibly universal notions, such as human rights, came to be defined in particular ways, steered by the rhetoric and interests of foreign donors and creditors. Through his fieldwork with foreign NGOs and local legal volunteers, Englund reveals how "human rights discourse – even as it asserts that all individuals are equals – can be deprived of its democratising potential and made to serve particular interests in society" (Englund 2006, 49). As he observes: "translation as a cultural and political process" can hamper the "situational characteristic" of human rights mobilisation, "obscured by human rights activists' commitment to abstraction and universalism" (Englund 2006, 49).

Third, if Tim Parks's answer to the polemic question of whether we really need stories is negative, he admits that there is nothing which shapes subjectivity more than narrations since the concept of *self* on which it is based is both unavoidable and essentially in need of explanation. Any explaining terminology, he argues, in itself already contains narratives (Parks 2015, 3–8). This declaration is true for subjects as much as for cultural collectives, organisations, or institutions (Mattingly 2013; Tinius 2018). Narrations are historically formed and subject to a multifarious dynamics. This becomes obvious even in the meta-narration of Western universalism itself. Narrations are not "simple" verbal processes. They are rather constitutive of identity and can materialise socially as reality (Koschorke 2018, 24). In narrations, forms of producing the world become manifest.

Lastly, this becomes particularly evident in the constitutive elements of museums – architecture, curating, and collections – and more so in such museums that lay claim to represent "world" and encompass difference; hence in these fields of knowledge production and those cultural practices from which we departed in this introduction and to which we now wish to return. The creation of museums with such scope have been caught up since the nineteenth century in processes of managing, assembling, and creating differences of every imaginable kind and therefore in creating a kind of similarity, or the sense of a universal claim (Bennett 1995, Macdonald 2016). This is not just the case for ethnographic and anthropological museums; even if these have co-constituted the *méta-récit of* (imperial) modernity more than any other (Amselle 2016, Penny 2002). The post-literary narrative dimension of museums extends both outwards (from their collections to their exhibitions and architectures) and inwards (from universal ambition to situated provenance investigations), depending on their interpretation, use, and construction (Macleod, Hanks, and Hale 2012, Martinez-Turek and Sommer-Sieghart 2009, Tinius and Zinnenburg Carroll 2020). The work taking place within them – collections management, provenance research, and the practice of curating – form part of their three-dimensional poetic and political narratives (Lidchi 1997, Macdonald 2022, Oswald and Tinius 2022, Savoy 2022). The curatorial work of assembling universal museum collections is a constant practice of witnessing the constructions and destructions of worlds. Their architectural narratives, too, are no less caught up in the friction between the global or universal horizons they create, and the particular places in whose narratives universal museums are entangled, which may variously take on or be refused by their concrete contexts (Raad 2014, Tinius 2020, Tschumi and Cheng 2003, Yarrow 2019). The "constructed narratives" (Adjaye 2016) of their architecture pertain not just to the buildings; they are also entangled with the interests, interpretations, and refusals that visitors bring. As material creations within the symbolic construction of cultures and societies, (universal museum) architecture is an expression of epochal consciousness and, as a practice, also an instrument of its fashioning (see Hofmann 2017). Taken together, narratives in museums – and the forms of "world" that they engender – allow for a host of questions to be opened about their possibilities in thinking shared and divided humanity.

4 In our present: A search

"Minor universality" is (also) a research project. It was conceived and launched in Berlin to then find a home in Saarbrücken.[17] This shift is emblematic of the underlying concept that defines its structure – of a universality that is no longer understood to mean the universalisation of the centre. The centre of our project is now the peripheral area between Germany and France – a region that considers itself to be the "heart of Europe", even though its infrastructure and social status belong more to Europe's margins. Yet the project was also funded by the European Research Council, that is to say, from the political centre of the European Union in Brussels. Hence it was all the more important that the project develop multi-polar ways of thinking its paths and aims – that right from the start it fashions its epistemological framework in concert with partners in Mexico, Tunis, Hong Kong – and beyond. When the project first got going, it seemed important to us to emphasise human horizons and to rethink universality in a moment that increasingly sees identity as something inherent to the self and closed off, as something that limits and isolates the (collective) self. Today, this concern seems more urgent than ever.

This would mean that the problem of constructing "world" in the aftermath of Western universalism is also an attempt to find a common scholarly narrative. The idea was to structure our methods and insights from the very beginning together with horizons of knowledge and experience that lay beyond our own. But our attempt to realise a multi-polar research project based on a common narrative that we developed in coming together and exchanging our experiences and ideas – that is to say, a narrative that would be concrete, embodied, and shared – repeatedly failed in an almost symbolic way. The list of our unsuccessful attempts to bring people together is long, as is that of the reasons why: borders closed by the pandemic; delays of a work visa; overworked immigration authorities; *Fiktionsbescheinigungen*, as they are called in German (literally: "certificates of fiction") – an immigration status that confers an unsatisfactory kind of residency, allowing an international researcher, for instance, to remain in the country while prohibiting international travel; delays in visas being issued and related travel restrictions to international conferences for non-European participants; cancellation of project meetings, conferences, and get-togethers; interruptions of field research; and not least personal troubles and health problems, long Covid, and pandemic-related deaths.

The further the project progressed, the clearer it became that these problems were not acute individual cases, isolated failures, or simply bad luck, but that they

---

17 See https://www.uni-saarland.de/forschen/minor-universality.html (last accessed 22 December 2022).

corresponded to the systematically produced asymmetries of our world. In 2020, Achille Mbembe posed the question of a "universal right to breathe" ("le droit universel à la respiration"), which evidently resonates with the racist violence against George Floyd ("I cannot breathe"):

> If, indeed, Covid-19 is the spectacular expression of the planetary impasse in which humanity finds itself today, then it is a matter of no less than reconstructing a habitable Earth to give all of us the breath of life. We must reclaim the lungs of our world with a view to forging new ground. Humankind and biosphere are one. Alone, humanity has no future. Are we capable of rediscovering that each of us belongs to the same species, that we have an indivisible bond with all life? Perhaps that is the question – the very last – before we draw our last dying breath (Mbembe 2021).

As the world's nations compare the statistics that track their rising and falling cases of Covid, engendering a competition among countries of the Global North, the same international solidarity that rushes forth united against Russia's war of aggression in Ukraine seems to vanish when it comes to open patents and ties to the Global South. Globalisation and a universalist consciousness of "world" are not one and the same. Neither capitalism nor a functionalist concept of freedom, the identitarian reinterpretation of particularity and situatedness, or the nationally shaped global-Western world order have produced a convincing new awareness of humanity in the void left by modernity's great universalisms (secular monotheism, liberalism, Marxism). Instead, the Western world – finding itself unable to breathe (Mbembe 2021), while once again locked in confrontation with post-Soviet imperial power, united along the borders of communist ecumenism – is now searching for a unifying narrative that cannot be found. The West is no longer – *can* no longer be thought and enacted as – monolithically synonymous with universalistic ideals of freedom, equality, and fraternity as human solidarity. But not only in the West, critical reflection on a post-universalist self-understanding has aimed to fill this vacuum with an identitarian relativism, conversely giving rise to new forms of identitarian self-assurances characterised by nativism, identity politics rooted in anti-modernist essentialisms, neo-fascism, and racist ideology. Faced with this relativism, universalist arguments are the strongest we have. David Scott put it aptly when he described this tension as inherently instable and uncertain:

> It is a moment when hitherto established and authoritative conceptual paradigms and political projects (those defined in relation to Marxism and cultural nationalism, for instance, or various admixtures of nationalism and socialism, and so on) seem no longer adequate to the tasks of the present, and when, at the same time, new paradigms and projects have yet to assert themselves fully in the place of the old. These essays inhabit, in other words, a sort of Gramscian interregnum, a transitional moment that I shall characterize as "after postcoloniality" (Scott 1999, 10).

As part of our *Minor Universality* initiative, we are exploring various practices and media that claim to seek and collectively fashion narratives from locations beyond these responses to critiques of universalism, beyond relativism and identitarian particularism. We aim to understand how a new consciousness of universality is now tentatively *being produced* in contemporary social practices and cultural expressions such as oral transmissions and narrations of the self, literatures and archives, films and festivals, or curatorial spaces and museums. Such narration tries to think what we share by attending to small things, minor things – to produce "world" from experiences that always remain concrete. Constantly moving between the scales of the individual and the whole, each individual project has grappled with the problems that face multi-polar attempts to conceive of "world" from a minor position, and with the urgency of this political endeavour. This is apparent even with the publishing of this volume itself. The fact that it can appear open access, funded by the European Union, allows its ideas to be disseminated free of cost, worldwide. And yet this opportunity also means a problem is emerging: funding an open-access book, which is increasingly becoming the standard of scholarship and thus constitutive for the dominant, officially defined discourse of "excellence", remains a privilege available to but a few, often Western, research projects.

What these difficulties indicate is that we may not want any longer to derive a commonly conceived universality from any philosophical *a priori*, but from concrete projects and situations. One such concrete practice that was fundamental to our project is that of artistic production and curatorial work in, at, and beyond the museum. From the beginning, the project has sought to incorporate artistic research and practice as a form of narration into our collaborative work, as an epistemological and aesthetic displacement of specific scientific modes and forms of thought. This was why we developed an artist residency as part of the project, selecting seven artists with various aesthetic approaches in the fall of 2020 to join our dialogue in two residencies each in June and September 2021 at the House of World Cultures (HKW) in Berlin. In June 2021 we travelled with all the artists to Athens, and in March 2022 to Tunis, where we held research colloquia and seminars with the Académie de Carthage ("Beït al-Hikma") and the Centre des arts vivants de Radès. These residencies were accompanied by an attempt to think about and experience the decentring of epistemological production in our research project from the point of view – and in the language and form of – artistic practice. These artists' work foregrounded concrete, embodied, acoustic, and shaped aspects of narration and its forms.[18]

---

[18] We were delighted that these artists accepted our invitation to cooperate: the writers Camille de Toledo and Adania Shibli, the multimedia artist Emeka Ogboh, the filmmaker Filipa César, and

Figure 7: Congress Hall Berlin, 18 May 1980, Credit: Herbert Orth. Public Domain.

The positions developed by our artistic residencies derived from situated forms of doubt and from engaging with dominant forms of discourse through the minor; they share an urgency to work with the birth of a world within the ruins of the former West. And in speaking of ruins, we do not use the term metaphorically or playfully (see Figure 7). The artists were invited to respond, react, or altogether develop their own minor practices in response to the exhibition space, chosen to be the central auditorium of the former Congress Hall, now Haus der Kulturen der Welt (HKW) in Berlin. This space is laden with historical and contemporary significance pertinent to our project, since it was gifted to West Berlin by the United States as a token of the country's commitment to liberty, liberalism, modernism, and the "free world". However, when the free-floating modernist roof of the Congress Hall collapsed in 1980, a Western symbol of US universalism crumbled with it, offering us an apt starting point for our exhibition.

Taking inspiration from the ambivalent nickname – the "pregnant oyster" – that Berliners gave the building, on account of its form, where the HKW has found a home since 1989, our project asks how horizons of a shared world are born out of

---

the curators of radio SAVVYZAAR, Lynhan Balatbat-Helbock and Kelly Krugman, as well as the curator of the archive SAVVY.doc, Sagal Farah, from the Berlin art space SAVVY Contemporary. For more information, see http://www.hkw.de/minoruniversality (last accessed 23 October 2022).

a concrete and situated narrative. The oyster as a queering animal that changes its gender at will, occasionally producing precious surprises, ones which are fragile and valuable, is a metaphor for this meandering search. The exhibition *The Pregnant Oyster – Doubts on Universalism* (June–July 2022) was thus deliberately staged both in Berlin and beyond at the HKW, arguably a site that represents Western universalism and its questioning. We hoped to harness our learning process in order to confront the ways in which notions of the multipolar and the minor are being increasingly tied to geographic locations, with a design that resisted being trapped in identitarian closures or any insistence on what is properly one's own. As Okwui Enwezor conceives of it, geographical distance is no longer a marker of alterity; we live in an age of "intense proximity" (2012), he writes, in which near presence can just as intensely allow us to bring together other productions of "world". At the same time, the loss of seemingly easy global access that is increasingly being imposed by the climate-driven urgency to change our travel habits is another deep and painful loss of opportunity for dialogue and cosmopolitan exchange, which raises new questions.

The exhibition *The Pregnant Oyster – Doubts on Universalism* brings us back to the "game of scales" that unfolded in the French pavilion in Zineb Sedira's work – to the minor details in the major narratives that opened this introduction. In an unfathomable diversity of ways and places, the minor forms they represent have always already begun to produce horizons of a shared world – to realise hope and humanity – from the situated, embodied experiences that we all possess. This volume assembles some of their idiosyncrasies, investigations, and reflections for our present.

References

Abu-Lughod, Lila. *Veiled Sentiments. Honor and Poetry in a Bedouin Society*. Chicago: University of Chicago Press, 1986.
Adjaye, David. *Constructed Narrations*. Ed. P. Allison. Zurich: Lars Müller Publishers, 2016.
Adorno, Theodor W. "Kultur and Culture." Transl. Mark Kalbus. *Social Text* 27.2 (99) (1 June 2009): 145–158.
Alemani, Cecilia. "The Milk of Dreams". *The Milk of Dreams: Biennale Arte 2022: Short Guide*. Venice: La Biennale di Venezia, 2022. 44–47.
Amselle, Jean-Loup. *Le Musée exposé*. Paris: lignes, 2016.
Badiou, Alain. *Saint Paul. The Foundation of Universalism*. Transl. Ray Brassier. Stanford: Stanford University Press, 2003 [1977].
Barthes, Roland. *Mythologies*. Introduction by Neil Badmington. Transl. Annette Lavers. London: Vintage, 2009 [1957].
Bennett, Tony. *Birth of the Museum: History, Theory, Politics*. London, New York: Routledge, 1995.

Bogue, Ronald. "The Minor". *Gilles Deleuze. Key Concepts*. Ed. Charles J. Stivale. London, New York: Routledge, 2005. 131–141.

Boltanski, Luc, and Eve Chiapello. *The New Spirit of Capitalism*. London: Verso, 2005 [1999].

Bourdieu, Pierre. *Distinction. A Social Critique of the Judgement of Taste*. Transl. Richard Nice. Cambridge/MA: Harvard University Press, 1984 [1979].

Buck-Morss, Susan. *Hegel, Haiti, and Universal History*. Pittsburgh: University of Pittsburgh Press, 2009.

Cassin, Barbara. "Introduction". *Dictionary of Untranslatables: A Philosophical Lexicon*. Ed. Barbara Cassin. Princeton: Princeton University Press, 2014. XVII–XX.

———. Ed. *Après Babel, traduire*. Catalogue of the exhibition at the Musée des civilisations de l'Europe et de la Méditerranée (MuCEM). Marseille, Arles: Actes Sud / Mucem, 2016.

Christ, Julia. *L'oubli de l'universel: Hegel critique du libéralisme*. Paris: Presses universitaires de France, 2021.

Csordas, Tomas J. "Embodiment as a Paradigm for Anthropology." *Ethos* 18.1 (1990): 5–47.

Deleuze, Gilles. *Kleine Schriften*. Transl. K.D. Schacht. Berlin: Merve Verlag, 1980.

———. *Essays Critical and Clinical*. Transl. D. W. Smith & M. A. Greco. Minneapolis, London: University of Minnesota Press, 1997 [1993].

Deleuze, Gilles, and Félix Guattari. *Kafka. Toward a Minor Literature*. Transl. Dana Polan. Minneapolis, London: University of Minnesota Press, 1986 [1975].

———. *A Thousand Plateaus. Capitalism and Schizophrenia II*. Transl. Brian Massumi. Minneapolis, London: University of Minnesota Press, 1987 [1980].

———. *Kafka. Für eine kleine Literatur*. Transl. Burkhart Kroeber. Berlin: Suhrkamp, 2019 [1975].

Deleuze, Gilles, and Claire Parnet. *Dialogues II*. Revised edition. Transl. Hugh Tomlinson and Barbara Habberjam. New York: Columbia University Press, 2007 [1977].

Deutscher, Guy. *Through the Language Glass. Why the World Looks Different in Other Languages*. London: Arrow Books, 2011.

Diagne, Souleymane Bachir. "L'universel latéral comme traduction". *Les pluriels de Barbara Cassin ou le partage des équivoques*. Eds. Philippe Büttgen, Michèle Gendreau-Massaloux and Xavier North. Lormont: Le Bord de l'eau, 2014. 243–256.

———. *De langue à langue : l'hospitalité de la traduction*. Paris: Albin Michel, 2022.

Di Cesare, Donatella. *Heidegger, die Juden, die Shoah*. Frankfurt am Main: Klostermann, 2016.

Englund, Harri. *Prisoners of Freedom: Human Rights and the African Poor*. Berkeley: University of California Press, 2006.

Enwezor, Okwui. "Intense proximité: de la disparition des distances." *Intense proximité. Une anthologie du proche et du lointain. La Triennale 2012*. Eds. Okwui Enwezor, Mélanie Bouteloup, Abdellah Karroum, Émilie Renard, and Claire Staebler. Paris: Éditions Artlys, 2012. 18–36.

ERC Minor Universality. "Universalisme & histoires concrètes. Entretien avec Giovanni Levi." Universalisme & ... Youtube. https://www.youtube.com/watch?v=xZyqYDA3KhA&t=9s, last accessed, 16 April 2023.

Fanon, Frantz. *The Wretched of the Earth*. Preface by Jean-Paul Sartre. Transl. Constance Farrington. New York: Grove Press, 1962 [1961].

———. "This is the Voice of Algeria." *A Dying Colonialism*. Transl. Haakon Chevalier. New York: Monthly Review Press, 1965 [1959]. 69–97.

Ginzburg, Carlo. "Microhistory: Two or Three Things That I Know about It." *Critical Inquiry* 20.1 (1993): 10–35.

———. *The Cheese and the Worms. The Cosmos of a Sixteenth-Century Miller*. Transl. John and Anne C. Tedeschi. Baltimore: Johns Hopkins University Press, 2013 [1976].

Hall, Stuart, and Paddy Whannel. Eds. *The Popular Arts. Selected Writings*. Durham, London: Duke University Press, 2018 [1965].

Hofmann, Franck. "De/Konstruktionen des Südens – Die Méditerranée im planetaren Horizont der documenta 14." *kritische Berichte* 4 (2017): 10–17.

Hofmann, Franck, and Markus Messling. "On the ends of universalism." *The Epoch of Universalism / L'époque de l'universalisme (1769–1989)*. Eds. Franck Hofmann and Markus Messling. Berlin, Boston: De Gruyter, 2021. 1–39.

Horkheimer, Max, and Theodor W. Adorno. *Dialectic of Enlightenment: Philosophical Fragments*. Transl. Edmund Jephcott. Stanford: Stanford University Press, 2002 [1944].

Husserl, Edmund. *Ding und Raum*. Ed. K.-H. Hahnengreß and S. Rapic. Hamburg: Meiner, 1991.

Koschorke, Albrecht. *Fact and Fiction. Elements of a General Theory of Narrative*. Transl. Joel Golb. Berlin, Boston: De Gruyter, 2018.

Laidlaw, James. *The Subject of Virtue. An Anthropology of Ethics and Freedom*. Cambridge: Cambridge University Press, 2014.

Levi, Giovanni. "La storia: Scienza delle domande generali e delle risposte locali." *Psiche* 2 (2018): 361–377.

Lidchi, Henrietta. "The Poetics and Politics of Exhibiting Other Cultures". *Representation. Cultural Representation and Signifying Practices*. Ed. Stuart Hall. Milton Keynes: SAGE, 1997. 151–222.

Macdonald, Sharon. "New Constellations of Difference in Europe's 21st-Century Museumscape." *Museum Anthropology* 39.1 (2016): 4–19.

Macleod, Suzanne, Laura H. Hanks, and Jonathan Hale. Eds. *Museum Making. Narratives, Architectures, Exhibitions*. London, New York: Routledge, 2012.

———. Ed. *Doing Diversity in Museums and Heritage. A Berlin Ethnography*. Bielefeld: transcript, 2023.

Martinez-Turek, Charlotte, and Monika Sommer-Sieghart. Eds. *Storyline. Narrationen im Museum*. Wien: Turia + Kant, 2009.

Mattingly, Cheryl. "Moral Selves and Moral Scenes: Narrative Experiments in Everyday Life." *Ethnos: Journal of Anthropology* 78.3 (2013): 301–327.

Mauss, Marcel. "Notion de technique du corps." *Sociologie et Anthropologie*. Paris: Presses universitaires de France, 2013 [1934]. 363–372.

Mbembe, Achille. "The Universal Right to Breathe". Transl. Carolyn Shread. *Critical Inquiry* 47.2 (2021) https://doi.org/10.1086/711437 (last accessed 24 April 2023).

Messling, Markus. *Universalität nach dem Universalismus. Über frankophone Literaturen der Gegenwart*. Berlin: Matthes & Seitz, 2019.

———. "La difficile fabrique d'une revue « globale »." *Annales. Histoire, Sciences Sociales* 75.3–4 (2020): 667–679. https://www.doi.org/10.1017/ahss.2021.7.

———. "Mit Barthes: Subjektivität und Universalität." *Bilder in Bewegung. Transdisziplinäre Ansichten des Bildlichen zwischen Kunst und Wissenschaft*. Eds. Patricia Gwozdz, Tobias Kraft, Markus Lenz. Berlin, Boston: De Gruyter, 2021. 35–48.

———. *L'universel après l'universalisme. Des littératures francophones du contemporain*. Préface de Souleymane Bachir Diagne. Transl. Olivier Mannoni. Paris: Presses universitaires de France, 2023.

Oswald, Margareta von, and Jonas Tinius. "Introduction: Across Anthropology." *Across Anthropology: Troubling Colonial Legacies, Museums, and the Curatorial*. Eds. Jonas Tinius and Margareta von Oswald. Leuven: Leuven University Press, 2020. 17–42.

Pamuk, Orhan. *The Naïve and the Sentimental Novelist. The Charles Eliot Norton Lectures 2009*. Cambridge/MA, London: Harvard University Press, 2010.

———. *The Innocence of Objects: The Museum of Innocence, Istanbul*. New York: Ambrams, 2012.

Parks, Tim. *Where I'm Reading From. The Changing World of Books*. New York: The New York Review of Books Publishers, 2015.
Parr, Adrian. Ed. *The Deleuze Dictionary*. Edinburgh: Edinburgh University Press, 2005.
Penny, H. Glenn. *Objects of Ethnography: Ethnology and Ethnographic Museums in Imperial Germany*. Durham/NC: University of North Carolina Press, 2002.
Raad, Walid. *Walkthrough*. London: Black Dog Publishing, 2014.
Rancière, Jacques. *Le partage du sensible : esthétique et politique*. Paris: la fabrique, 2000.
Revel, Jacques. Ed. *Jeux d'échelles. La micro-analyse à l'expérience*. Paris: Gallimard / Le Seuil, 1996.
Savoy, Bénédicte. *Africa's Struggle for Its Art: History of a Postcolonial Defeat*. Princeton: Princeton University Press, 2022.
Scott, David. *Refashioning Futures. Criticism After Postcoloniality*. Princeton: Princeton University Press, 1999.
Spivak, Gayatri Chakravorty. "Can the Subaltern Speak?" *Marxism and the Interpretation of Culture*. Ed. Cary Nelson and Lawrence Grossberg. Basingstoke: Macmillan, 1988 [1985]. 271–313.
Tinius, Jonas. "Porous Membranes: Alterity, Hospitality, and Difference in a Berlin District Gallery." *Across Anthropology: Troubling Colonial Legacies, Museums, and the Curatorial*. Eds. Jonas Tinius and Margareta von Oswald. Leuven: Leuven University Press, 2020. 255–276.
———. "Capacity for Character. Fiction, Ethics, and the Anthropology of Conduct". *Social Anthropology / Anthropologie Sociale* 26.3 (2018): 345–360.
Tinius, Jonas, and Khadija von Zinnenburg Carroll. "Phantom Palaces: Prussian Centralities and Humboldtian Horizontalities." *Re-Centring the City. Global Mutations of Socialist Modernity*. Eds. Jonathan Bach and Michal Murawski. London: UCL Press, 2020. 90–103.
Todorov, Tzvetan. "The Last Barthes". Transl. Richard Howard. *Critical Inquiry* 7.3 (Spring 1981): 449–454.
Trabant, Jürgen. *Traditionen Humboldts*. Frankfurt am Main: Suhrkamp, 1990.
———. *Globalesisch oder was? Ein Plädoyer für Europas Sprachen*. Munich: Beck, 2014.
Tschumi, Bernard, and Irene Cheng. Eds. *The State of Architecture at the Beginning of the 21st Century*. New York: The Monacelli Press / Columbia Books of Architecture, 2003.
Wallerstein, Immanuel. *European Universalism: The Rhetoric of Power*. New York: New Press, 2006.
Yarrow, Thomas. *Architects: Portraits of a Practice*. Ithaca/NY, London: Cornell University Press, 2019.

Part I: **Universality After Universalism**

Première partie : **L'universel après l'universalisme**

Souleymane Bachir Diagne

What Might a Truly Universal Universalism Be? Thinking the Universal With Étienne Balibar

Abstract: Working through the work of Aimé Césaire, Étienne Balibar, and Léopold Sédar Senghor, this chapter addresses ways to think the universal beyond exclusion and domination, and thus to conceive of a "truly universal" universalism. Drawing on Balibar, this text discusses the tensions between the constitution of citizenship and the struggle for its universal extension in a decolonial movement of emancipation. If the postcolonial universe can only arise from the horizontality of the relationships between cultures and languages, then the universal can be said to be generalised translation. The point is then not to renounce the universal in order to embrace the multicultural, but to realise and accept that anthropological differences are not obstacles but a point of departure for a "subject-becoming of the citizen" (Balibar); a process under way and to be accompanied, politically.

Keywords: Étienne Balibar, Aimé Césaire, Léopold Sédar Senghor, Négritude, translation, lateral universal, hegemony, citizenship, equaliberty

In a major essay in English entitled "Sub specie universitatis" (2006, 3–16), Étienne Balibar reflected on the future of philosophy from the perspective of its relationship to the question of what is meant by "speaking the universal". As he explained, speaking the universal entails three completely different strategies: the theory of double truth exemplified by Spinoza and Wittgenstein, the construction of the universal as "hegemony" analysed by Hegel and Marx in terms of collective consciousnesses or ideologies, and the programme of generalised translation that he describes as emerging from the critique of traditional "paradoxes of the untranslatable" by contemporary sociolinguists and pragmatic philosophers.

My remarks here focus on the second and third of these strategies. Speaking the universal as hegemony? To configure the question, I will recall here the famous

Note: This text is a translation of Souleymane Bachir Diagne, "Penser l'universel avec Étienne Balibar". *Raison publique* 19.2 (2014): 15–21. The editors would like to thank *Raison publique* and the author for the courtesy.

Translated by John Angell

Open Access. © 2023 the author(s), published by De Gruyter. This work is licensed under the Creative Commons Attribution-NonCommercial-NoDerivatives 4.0 International License.
https://doi.org/10.1515/9783110798494-002

letter Aimé Césaire (2016 [1956]) sent to Maurice Thorez in 1956 to inform him that he was resigning from the French Communist Party (PCF):

> [. . .] there will never be an African variant [of communism], or a Malagasy one or a Caribbean one, because French communism finds it more convenient to impose theirs upon us [. . .] there will never be an African, Malagasy, or Caribbean communism because the French Communist Party conceives of its duties toward colonized peoples in terms of a position of authority to fill, and even the anticolonialism of French communists still bears the marks of the colonialism it is fighting (Césaire 2010, 150).

And Césaire goes a step further:

> There are two ways to lose oneself: walled segregation in the particular or dilution in the universal. My conception of the universal is that of a universal enriched by all that is particular, a universal enriched by every particular: the deepening and coexistence of all particulars (Césaire 2010, 150).

That the universal is hegemony and that one senses and rejects it when one speaks of a place other than the one where it is expressed *sub specie universitatis*, that is, the experience underlying the reasons expressed by Aimé Césaire to justify his resignation from the PCF. In the discourse arguing that the universal is a matter of hegemony, it is, so to speak, natural that it be taken as something to inscribe (subscribe, i.e., to *write under*) under a hegemony or other colonial reality, which is never anything other than a deeply secondary contradiction: The universal is played elsewhere, in its own places, which cannot be the colony. This is why Engels could calmly write that when the revolution was victorious in Europe (the theatre of universal history), colonised countries would have to be "temporarily entrusted to the proletariat [of former colonial nations], who would lead them as rapidly as possible to independence" (Alleg 2010).[1] Clearly, Césaire's criticisms of the PCF were not accidental, but stemmed from an entirely natural position that was directly aligned with Engels' proposals.

Lenin's declaration can always be cited as a counterpoint when he says, "the socialist revolution will not be only nor principally a struggle of the revolutionary proletariat of each country against its bourgeoisie. No, it will be the struggle against international imperialism by all the colonies and every dependent country" (Alleg 2010). It remains true that emancipation will come from the universal class. Once it is understood that the universal has a place, colonial paternalism

---

[1] Extract from Engels' letter to Kautsky dated September 1882. The letter is cited by Henri Alleg in his interview with Francis Arzalier and Jean Louis Glory in the Chapter "Socialisme et domination coloniale au XXe siècle", published in Arzalier (2010, 251–267).

can easily be translated into a (big brother) fraternalism of the central communist parties, which is no better.

Even the Sartrean message in *Orphée noir* continues to extend self-assured universalism, which assumes the character of Hegel-Marxian dialectics that reduce the Négritude's protests to nothing more than a single moment in a process whose driving force – whose veritable agent – is the proletariat of European countries.

Césaire calls for a "universal that will be rich in every particular", that opposes a tranquil universalism with its imperturbable good conscience, what Immanuel Wallerstein also called a "truly universal universalism" (Wallerstein 2006, 2). It is noteworthy in this regard that in Wallerstein's book – a critique of European universalism – the only hint of what this "truly universal universalism" might actually resemble is an expression oft-cited by Négritude authors, particularly Senghor: "the rendezvous of giving and receiving" (Wallerstein 2006, 79). Indeed, Wallerstein's book concludes that our epoch "signals the end of [this] immense era" that could be called "the age of European universalism", adding that available alternatives include "the blossoming of a multiplicity of universalisms that form a network of universal universalisms". He concludes that this would introduce the world of Senghor's "rendezvous of giving and receiving" (Wallerstein 2006, 79).

Arguably, these different expressions – "universal rich in every particular that coexists," "universalisms forming a network", "rendezvous of giving and receiving"– remain poetic in their ecumenical dimension, not to say naïve, because they bear no trace of conflict, except for the obvious denunciation of a universalism of exclusion. The Balibarian conception of the universal could be said to advance the cause of this quest for a "truly universal" universalism:
1) by in turn insisting on the necessity, emphasised by the thinkers of decolonisation, of questioning the *Eurocentric universal* precisely in order to consider the totally emancipatory – the *insurrectional* (an often-used word in Balibar's writing) – and thereby decolonising, but without the inevitable equivocation;
2) by specifically insisting on the dimension of the inherent conflict of universalism as a "demand that those who have been kept outside the 'common good' or the 'general will' be counted", as Balibar wrote in his remarks on Jacques Rancière's assertions concerning the "share of the shareless" (Balibar 2010, 6).

Regarding this first point, it is important to cite the following lines from the chapter "the antinomia of citizenship" in their entirety:

> We cannot delude ourselves [. . .] that *organised* class struggles will naturally be immunised against the internal authoritarianism that results from their transformation into a 'counter-

state', and 'hence in counter-power and counter-violence', nor that they represent a principle of unlimited or unconditional universality. The fact that the majority of the European worker's movement and its class organizations remained blind to the problems of colonial and domestic oppression and of domination over cultural minorities (when it was not explicitly racist, nationalist, and sexist), despite considerable effort and acute internal conflicts that formed something akin to an 'insurrection within the insurrection', *owes nothing to chance*.[2] It must be explained not only by one material condition or another, through such and such corruption or degeneration, but also by the fact that resistance and protest against determined forms of domination or oppression always rely on the emergence and construction of *counter-communities* that have their own principles of exclusion and hierarchy. This entire, often dramatic, story calls our attention to the finite character of 'insurrectional moments', in other words, to the fact that there is no such thing as 'absolutely universal' emancipatory universalities, escaping the limitations of their objects. The contradictions of the politics of emancipation are thus transposed onto and reflected in the most democratic *constitutions of citizenship*,[3] thereby contributing, passively at least, [. . .] to the possibility of their de-democratization (Balibar 2010, 25–26).

This crucial passage leads us to the dimension of conflict, which is none other than political, and which could find offense in the ecumenism of the expressions that I evoked earlier. Indeed, it is simultaneously a matter of the "constitution of citizenship" and the "construction of the universal" (Balibar 2010, 271), this construction then being able to be understood as the struggle for a universal extension of the constitution of citizenship, which itself is continuous. Citizenship, "the proposition of equaliberty", is clearly the affirmation of the fact that freedom equals equality, and that to combat absolutism is to combat privilege. What we are also told is that this same equality is constructed in the movement and in the conflict between limitation or, on the contrary, universal extension. Thus – and this is the full intention of "the proposition of equaliberty" – should the principles of the Revolution of 1789, based on "intensive" universality, be, or able to be, limited – and the politics of emancipation that produced them will thereby find themselves de-democratised (such as when slaves were excluded from the rights that these principles conferred) or, on the contrary, will manifest their "indefinite opening" to the claims of "wage-earners, or dependents [. . .], women, slaves, the colonized . . .?" (Balibar 2010, 71)

The universal that concerns us here is a universality whose utterance is negative, thus marking its "absolute indeterminacy", which as Balibar tells us, comprises "all the force of the utterance, but also the practical weakness of enunciation" (Balibar 2010, 72).

---

[2] Here, I emphasise and call attention to the manner in which this statement echoes Césaire.
[3] Author's emphasis.

The political thus once again imposes itself when we are facing struggle, the construction of "power relations" on which depends, as a practical matter, the fulfilment of the open promise of equaliberty and co-citizenship that is borne by intensive universalism that refutes difference and this hierarchy whose stigmata Césaire identified in the very movements that presented itself as emancipation. We are thus able to see why Balibar, while acknowledging what he says as paradoxical, speaks of a "supplement of universality" that corresponds to "the incorporation of differences and singularities in the very construction of the universal" (Balibar 2010, 163).

I would now like to broach the question of the universal as translation, a notion about which I reflect explaining what Balibar wrote on the subject, particularly in the lines that he devotes to the subject in "Sub specie universitatis".

Allow me first to evoke briefly what I am attempting to accomplish by addressing this notion. I came across a concept in Merleau-Ponty which, despite its difficulties, I felt was important to underline how much light it sheds on an important philosophical task for our time: this concept is the "lateral universal". Merleau-Ponty essentially explains that our period, which is a period of decolonisation, signals the end of a top-down universal (*universel de surplomb*): the postcolonial universe can only arise from the horizontality of the relationships between cultures and languages. This is what the work of Barbara Cassin also helps to complete, particularly in her *Dictionnaire des intraduisibles* (2004): the lateral universal is related to translation – and to the untranslatable (cf. Merleau-Ponty 2010).

The universal can thus be said to be generalised translation. We could therefore extend to the entire planet what Umberto Eco said about Europe when he declared that the language of Europe is translation. So be it. But does this mean that it suffices to simply adopt the model of generalised translation to achieve the ideal of a lateral universal? Balibar calls attention here to three crucial points that, once again, forbid naivete and simple ecumenical enthusiasm.

First, the model functions only if one does not begin by taking as a given that cultures and languages are merely hermetically sealed insularities. To fully understand this, let us consider how Levinas describes our decolonised world, which he calls "disoccidentalised" (*désoccidentalisé*) and therefore "disoriented" (*désorienté*).

If the model is one of a saraband of innumerable cultures, "each justifying itself solely in its own context", there is simply no reason to speak of translation (Levinas 1972, 55–56). In reality, though, no culture is closed inward – a point that the thinkers of Négritude also made, even though they are often called essentialists (this is also often our interpretation of them, itself essentialist and involving petrifying a *movement* in a few well-known formulae that unfolded, with its contradictions, recantations, and rectifications, over a period of decades).

Second, one must know how to take the singularity of individuals into account and to understand that translation is not only interculturality, but also intracultural. Translation shows the dividing lines that cross communities and that should therefore not be essentialised. On this question, Balibar gives the example of suburban youth and their language. It is naturally common for us to say that we "do not always speak the same language" as young people, but in this specific case, do we even *share* the same language? In any case, the model of the passage from one cultural group to another via translation will assuredly complicate itself to integrate the process of individuation, the way in which the individual "constructs" him or herself as a capacity for moving through the universe (multiverse) that is traversed by "the contradictory tendencies toward standardisation, but also the claim of differences, identification with traditions, and resistance to normalisation" (Balibar 2006, 15).

Third (and for Balibar, this was the second point), it is important to recall that when one adopts generalised translation as the model, it always takes place against a background of *misunderstanding* (Zygmunt Bauman) or *dispute* (French *différend*, Lyotard). It is worth noting, too, that Merleau-Ponty made the same argument using different words:

> The equipment of our social being can be dismantled and reconstructed by the voyage, as we are able to learn to speak other languages. This provides a second way to the universal: no longer the overarching universal of a strictly objective method, but a sort of lateral universal which we acquire through ethnological experience and its incessant testing of the self through the other person and the other person through the self. It is question of constructing a general system of reference in which the point of view of the native, the point of view of the civilized man, and the mistaken views each has of the other can all find a place–that is of constituting a more comprehensive experience which becomes in principle accessible to men of a different time and country (Merleau-Ponty 1964, 119–120).The system of general reference, then, generalised translation, is not about a problem-free co-presence of different languages and the perspectives they enclose, but rather a co-presence of "errors", of *misunderstanding* and of *unresolved dispute*.

Must I conclude? Yes, I must, in terms of stopping here, but not of pulling this all together into tidy, closed formulae. It is not a question, Étienne Balibar reminds us, of renouncing the universal in order to embrace the multicultural, but of being aware of "the process" in which anthropological differences, far from being "obstacles to the universalisation of the citizens' rights and to the citizen-becoming of the subject", represent, on the contrary, the point of departure for "a subject-becoming of the citizen" (in the active sense, as he points out); this process is indeed "already under way" (Balibar 2010, 163). It is a question of how we accompany it with our reflection. Politically.

References

Alleg, Henri. "Socialisme et domination coloniale au XXe siècle". *Expériences socialistes en Afrique. 19601990*. Ed. Francis Arzalier. Paris: Le Temps des Cerises, 2010. 251–267.

Balibar, Étienne. "Sub specie universitatis." *Topoi* 25 (2006): 3–16.

———. *La proposition de l'égaliberté. Essais politiques 1989–2009*. Paris: Presses universitaires de France, 2010.

Cassin, Barbara. Ed. *Vocabulaire européen des philosophies: Dictionnaire des intraduisibles*. Paris: Seuil / Le Robert, 2004.

———. Ed. *Dictionary of Untranslatables: A Philosophical Lexicon*. Translation Eds. Emily Apter, Jacques Lezra, and Michael Wood. Princeton, Oxford: Princeton University Press, 2014.

Césaire, Aimé. "Lettre à Maurice Thorez (24 octobre 1956)". *Écrits politiques* (1935–1956). Ed. Édouard de Lépine, préface Marc Césaire. Paris: Jean-Michel Place, 2016. 387–394.

———. "Letter to Maurice Thorez". Transl. Chike Jeffers. *Social Text* 103 (2010): 145–152.

Levinas, Emmanuel. *Humanisme de l'autre homme*. Saint-Clément-de-Rivière: Fata Morgana, 1972.

Merleau-Ponty, Maurice. *Signs*. Transl. Richard McCleary. Evanston: Northwestern University Press, 1964.

———. "De Mauss à Claude Lévi-Strauss". *Œuvres*. Ed. Claude Lefort. Paris: Gallimard, 2010. 1409–1421.

Wallerstein, Immanuel. *European Universalism. The Rhetoric of Power*. New York: The New Press, 2006.

Anil Bhatti
The Universal and the Particular: The Place of Similarity in Cultural Theory

Abstract: The context for the brief reflections in this paper is the increasing entanglement of the world under conditions of colonialism characterised by the creation of borders, demarcations, border crossings, social and cultural transformations and transgressions as part of the process of globalisation, 'mondialisation', or 'planetarisation'. Goethe's interest in *Weltliteratur* is based on an increasing awareness of this historical situation characteristic of complex societies. Goethe's work, especially the *Divan* and his stray remarks on *Weltliteratur* also lay the foundations for the comparative cultural analyses of complex societies. This analysis has until now been largely characterised by a culturalisation of difference. This is the point of departure for the alternative viewpoint of similarity, which also emerges from Goethe's poetic praxis. The point of view of similarity permits us to develop a critical approach which thematises entanglements and historical overlapping in order to grasp cultural, social diversity, and the comparison of cultures not so much under dichotomous categories, but rather under overarching moments of simultaneity and 'correspondance' as features of complexity. The perspective of thinking in terms of similarity functions now increasingly as a counter moment to the dominant cultural practices of thinking in difference.

Keywords: cultural complexity, difference, Johann Wolfgang Goethe, Evald Ilyenkov, Bernhard Bolzano

Identity, exclusionary nationalism, and religious difference are at the forefront of our discussions, which is precisely why it is apposite to talk about the place of similarity in culture theory. I am interested in the question of the universal and the particular in a specific historical context within the German tradition during nineteenth-century Europe when this ancient philosophical problem became relevant and topical. The philosopher Georg Lukács wrote about the singular importance of the dialectical understanding of the Nineteenth century in his *Lob des*

Note: This chapter is a revised and annotated version of a speech with the original title "Beyond Difference and Identity: Goethe and The Place of Similarity in Culture Theory", delivered during the Annual Conference of the Goethe Society of India, 11–14 November 2019 at the Jawaharlal Nehru University in New Delhi. I thank Jyoti Sabharwal for transcribing the original speech and the editors of the present volume for revising it for publication.

∂ Open Access. © 2023 the author(s), published by De Gruyter. [CC BY-NC-ND] This work is licensed under the Creative Commons Attribution-NonCommercial-NoDerivatives 4.0 International License.
https://doi.org/10.1515/9783110798494-003

neunzehnten Jahrhunderts (Lukács 1971, 659–664). During the nineteenth century, as a result of the congealment and consolidation of colonialism, crucial changes took place in the world, which made it possible to see that the world was interconnected, but at the same time to see that this interconnection was itself a problem. This conundrum is the starting point for my interest in thinkers and scholars in the German tradition, foremost Goethe and Hegel, but also those around him, mainly the two Humboldt brothers.

Roughly from the early part of the nineteenth century onwards, ascendant colonialism brings the world together in the form of trade linkages, exploitation, and reconfigurations of established countries so that many borders, as they existed until then, became vulnerable. Borders were questioned and new countries came into existence in place of old countries. The end of WWI gave rise to the Wilson plan on whose basis empires, like the Habsburg Empire broke down and nation states were established. The reasons for empires breaking down is crucial, because all classical empires, such as the Habsburg Empire, were characterised by what has been called an indifference to difference, or to be more specific, to cultural difference as it is often affirmed in theories of multiculturalism (Bhatti 2016, 171–180; Csáky 2019; Judson 2016).

I specifically use this term indifference in a technical sense and would not want it to be confused with Derridean *différance* (1973 [1967]). I refer specifically to the indifference to the question of the nation. Empires functioned as supranational entities characterised by a great deal of multi-lingual or plurilingual competence. They were systems of exploitation. But they had something that the nation-state did not have: the positive connotation of plurality, pluriculturalism (as distinct from multiculturism which often leads to parallel societies), and plurilingualism, a term I prefer to multilingualism. They were non-identitarian at the level of the state. All empires were by definition plurilingual; they had a positive connotation of mobility among classes (in India this also meant castes and classes). The positive connotation here is the ability to see territory not as an ontologised phenomenon but as a fluctuating system of rule. As a result of colonialism, these traditional empires broke up and became oriented more and more towards something called a border-oriented economy and a border-oriented society. From this emerged the proto nation-state.

This proto nation-state is characterised by borders, and borders are meant to demarcate. From empires, which were by definition based on overcoming borders, the colonial enterprise created nation-states, which were invested in borders and boundaries.

Later in the post-colonial phase, borders and boundaries have been relocated, new definitions have come up, new states have sprung up. But empire, indifferent initially to the question of nation, now invested its entire political, moral, and intellectual economy in upholding the necessity of having an entity called the nation based on a border. This border then, in the classical sense which we inherited from the German tradition, is the Herderian notion of the unity of territory, religion, history, memory, and language (Herder 1989).

This kind of nation-state became the model against which other empires began to founder. The Habsburg Empire was one of the main victims of this assertion of the need for a nation. Some of the great philosophers and thinkers in the Habsburg Empire (Robert Musil, Joseph Roth, Hermann Broch and many other writers like Bronisław Malinowski and Ludwig Wittgenstein) were all aware of these dynamics.[1] They developed philosophies and thought processes which are against the formation of a nation. The philosopher Bernhard Bolzano (see Künne 2019), for instance, mediated between the Bohemian and the German population and their cultural traditions in Bohemia in the Austro-Hungarian Empire. He did so in a spirit of accommodation, and with a positive connotation of the many languages present. For him they were part of a formation in which the epistemological principle of similarity and of becoming similar (*Ähnlichkeit / Verähnlichung*) was characteristic of diversity in pluricultural social formations (Bhatti and Kimmich 2018).

Nations invest in borders. Colonialism overcomes this kind of bordering to create a supranational enterprise of exploitation, suppression, and power, which, at the same time, gives to these borders an almost theological significance. Borders may start off as something arbitrary, but they do not remain so. They are not arbitrary in the sense of linguistic theory, which posits that signs are arbitrary as de Saussure (1972 [1916]) affirmed. Borders are invested with meaning; they have something sacrosanct about them. It is this almost theological notion of the nation which becomes the cornerstone of the formation of nations in the nineteenth century and leads to the creation of empires, like the British, which are built around nations. If these nations' borders are transgressed, it is according to a finely calibrated system of power.

The colonial enterprise consists of ontologising the border and creating the notion of transgression, where it actually does not exist. This is a fiction, which is essential to the maintenance of an empire *as* an empire. We can here consider a number of instances in literature, which show how important it was to think and talk about the border. In Joseph Conrad's fiction, for instance, in particular *Heart of Darkness* (2018 [1899]), he constantly problematises the border and transgressing the border. The problem is also at the heart of E.M. Forster's novel *A Passage*

---

[1] Grillparzer's famous lines on how nationalism degenerates to bestiality could be recalled here (Grillparzer 1960, 500).

to India (1985 [1924]) and it is central to Saadat Hasan Manto's work, for instance, in the short story *Toba Tek Singh* (present in *Kingdom's End and Other Stories*, translated from the Urdu by Khalid Hasan, see Manto 1989).

What happens in this period during which reflections on the border and the nation are taking place in context of the globalisation of empire is that you can negotiate between nations, but you cannot transgress them. That is how racism comes into being as a system of demarcation, of finding ways in which to characterise on what basis racism can exist. Skin colour is one such system of demarcation as is so clearly shown in Herman Melville's work, in particular in the story *Benito Cereno* (2019) and in discussions of the question of the colour line in the theoretical work of W.E.B. Du Bois, such as *The Souls of Black Folk* (2015).

In a system wherein borders are given privilege and literature emerges as a reflection on the border, we notice a remarkable phenomenon in German and World Literature. In Goethe's *West-östlicher Divan* (1994) the predominant theme that emerges is the transgression of the border. This is a notable cultural, historical achievement – a point which cannot be emphasised often enough. At a time when borders were being cemented by colonialism, Goethe problematised transgressing borders, un-cementing them, and making them fluid. In other words, when the borders were hard, he was talking about the fluidity of borders and this fluidity is here expressed in a language of poetry.

Goethe thinks of the possibility that he, as a poet in nineteenth-century Weimar – a very small German town at that time –, could travel in his imagination to the great empire of Iran, Isfahan, and meet his colleague Hafiz in the thirteenth and fourteenth centuries so that there would be a conversation of poets across the centuries – nineteenth-century Germany and the thirteenth- and fourteenth-century Iran without borders.

Instead of focusing upon this moment of transgressing borders in the *Divan*, what cultural theory and literary theory has done is to reinforce the nationalised version of literature as dialogue. In this version, we find a nation called Germany, a national writer called Goethe, talking to a nation called Iran, to a national writer called Hafiz and the two have a dialogue across the centuries. With this dialogue, the question only is: "Is the dialogue *auf Augenhöhe*?" Is it a dialogue of equals, a peer-to-peer dialogue – or would it be a dialogue in the patronising sense of "I bring the cultural theory, you bring the texts"? This is what Goethe is supposed to do with Hafiz. This is substantiated in the monument to Hafiz and Goethe in Weimar, where you have the image – Goethe, the monumental figure, on one side of the monument – and Hafiz as another monumental figure on the other side of the piece. Both look at each other at the same level. This is based on the hermeneutic principle of dialogue. I suggest a different way of looking at this, namely as a non-hermeneutical way of affirming transformation, metamorphoses – and a bit of science fiction.

In this way of looking at things, Goethe's *Divan* talks in a different way. It talks of the possibility of Goethe becoming Hafiz, of Hafiz visiting him across the centuries and Hafiz becoming partly Goethe. Thus, it is not a dialogue in the older sense of the term, but more of what can be captured by a hologram, rather than by a static image of one talking to the other. It is one merging into the other as a possibility, and the other merging into one as a possibility, as a historical possibility of a universal moment in history, which does not exist *now*, in the immediate present of Goethe's writing, because colonialism is there, is dominant, and deforms every possibility of contact and communication. Rather, because they become a moment in which this contact can be overcome, it may be possible in some other universe that Goethe wanders through Isfahan and Hafiz wanders through Weimar with Goethe and these two merge together in a moment of history which has overcome colonialism.

In fact, it is science fiction *avant la lettre* – at a stage where science fiction did not exist in this form. Their contact evokes a possibility and, of course, we have more dignified names than science fiction for this. It is the possibility of injecting utopia, the one important way of thinking in the nineteenth century in a nineteenth-century system of literature and correspondences, which was being undercut by the colonial enterprise that would like its poets to remain in certain clearly defined bounded centres of influence and thinking. From this, we receive an entire aesthetics which emerges from the traditional interpretation of the *Divan*.

Literatures that emerge in one country take an interest in another country. They encourage multilingualism of learning another language and encourage translations from other languages, but you do not have a continuum of languages in which you can move around and deal with them. Much in the way of an earlier context in India, one moved between languages without necessarily dealing with codified grammars.

The introduction of grammar into the continuum of language is the way in which borders are created and interest spheres are demarcated. Therefore, what the dialogical notion of the *Divan* implies is this: We have a poet called Goethe, who uses this wonderful piece of poetry called the *Divan*, and he is inspired by Hafiz. Hafiz, in turn, is read because of translations, and the whole matrix of aesthetic terminology emerges to explain this enterprise of Goethe. It is then part of a system of influences, system of reception, system of articulations, which are ultimately based on the fact that all this knowledge is only available to Goethe because colonialism brought texts back from India and the Orient to the West, and therefore, scholars could translate (see Hammer-Purgstall 1812). Therefore, Goethe was able to read it and he could talk about it. But the essential significance was that Goethe wrote about this when he himself travelled, albeit not between countries, in a coach going back and forth between Weimar and Jena, Jena and Weimar. This poetry emerges out of travel, out of movement. It was mobile. This angle on and through mobility is crucial to understand why the *Divan* has such paradigmatic significance. It is for the first time that we note movement as part of poetic enterprise in a world which privileges the static principle of sedentarism.

Goethe did this with his experiment about Hafiz. The *Divan* has a second part called *Noten und Abhandlungen zum West-östlichen Divan* (see Goethe 1960), in which Goethe falls into the role of an Orientalist, who tries to define and classify the external world and to put things into order to create literary history out of the relationship between European poetry and Iranian or Persian poetry. He develops a theory of translation to accommodate all this. But that is the less interesting part of the *Divan*. The more interesting part comprises poetry and prose in which Hafiz and Goethe are in a very peculiar relationship to each other, literally merging into each other in the form of poetry.

This creates, as it were, an aesthetic of *similarity* in their poetic enterprise. This is different from the dialogical hermeneutical principle. We should note that his writing constitutes a fiction and markedly an experiment. It is, moreover, a fictional similarity because Hafiz never wrote of this. Goethe did, on behalf of Hafiz, as a projection of his own interest in transgressing from the boundaries of Weimar and opening the cultural possibility of becoming another. This becoming another is the way in which you overcome borders which have been created. We can consider the overcoming of these borders a possibility of writing in a new aesthetic mode. This new aesthetic mode was very important for Goethe, and he stuck to it for a long time, but it not necessarily ossified. The *Divan* was an experiment, and in some ways, like the *Farbenlehre* (Goethe 2016), an oddity on his part.

The *Divan* was discovered in the twentieth century through a variety of literary scholars, who, as a result of the rise of fascism and migration, were looking into the world as it was, and discovered that here was something unique in the German tradition. But it was only so if one recognised this form of uniqueness as transgression. If one only understood it in a conventional sense, that is, as a relationship between literatures, nations, national literatures, and dialogues, one would miss the point entirely.

Goethe's interest in the *Divan* is an experiment and experiments are meant to be given up. Goethe, at some stage after the *Divan* had been completed, mentioned that he looked back at the *Divan* like a "Schlangenhaut" (*snakeskin*), which he shed. Goethe's personal secretary, the poet Johann Peter Eckermann, recalls a conversation with Goethe, dated to a Sunday evening, 12 January 1827, after a "musical party at Goethe's" (Eckermann and Soret 1850 [1836], 317):

After the party had left, I remained some moments alone with Goethe. "I have," said he, "this evening made the remark that these songs in the 'Divan' have no further connection with me. Both the oriental and impassioned elements have ceased to live in me. I have left them behind, like a cast-off snakeskin on my path (Eckermann and Soret 1850 [1836], 318).[2]

Herein, we read also another message from the *Divan* – namely, that it is not an ontological or essential piece of literature. It is an experimental possibility of dealing with the question of being something else, other than being what you are. Goethe's opening to the world beyond Weimar could be schematised as an ambivalent relation to India, the Orient as metamorphoses, and the world of China as a part of the aesthetic of similarity.

This is what we could call the literature of migration (see Muschg 1986 on Goethe as a migrant). This principle of migration emerged in Germany, which at that moment did not have a publicly acknowledged colony, but supported the colonies being established by the British and the French. At the time, large number of experts from Germany and the Habsburg Monarchy, Austrians and Hungarians, worked in the interest of the British and the French empires as experts. Thus, a portion of the British Empire is also part of German and Habsburgian heritage.

This migration meant that not only an aesthetics existed, but a certain attitude to literature, too. This was an attitude shared among other great writers, especially by Alexander von Humboldt. He saw that in this entire period, the German literary, aesthetics, and philosophical field established the conditions for the ability to see similarity where until now only differences had been seen.

I shall provide a short example. As already noted, colonialism creates borders and difference, leaving us with the question: How do you deal with such demarcations of difference? The British Empire dealt with it by creating boundaries – for example the difference between the cantonment and the market. They did not do so as in South Africa, but firmly enough to make it impossible for somebody from the market to be in the cantonment, and for somebody from the market to become part of the club to which only the cantonment people could belong. These were invisible boundaries, which were very important, and the empire functioned on the basis of these boundaries. Violation of these boundaries meant transgression, and anybody who violated these was punished. This is part of the theme of E.M. Forster's *A Passage to India* (1985 [1924]); his violation of the border, which takes place either consciously, unconsciously, or sub-consciously, remains present.

---

2 "Ich habe [. . .] diesen Abend die Bemerkung gemacht, daß diese Lieder des Divans gar kein Verhältnis mehr zu mir haben. Sowohl was darin orientalisch als was darin leidenschaftlich ist, hat aufgehört in mir fortzuleben; es ist wie eine abgestreifte Schlangenhaut am Wege liegen geblieben" (Eckermann 1836; Goethe 1999, 628–629).

It was a very important theme of Joseph Conrad's Novel *Heart of Darkness* (2018 [1899]), too. We can recall the moment on the river as the protagonist sees black masses and does not know what he witnesses. The ability to see these masses as other human beings would have cost so much epistemological violence to himself that he preferred to remain with the other epistemological violence of *not* accepting them as human beings and supporting a system of oppression, the critique of which is a part of the secret of *Heart of Darkness*.

In his voyages to Latin America and especially in his trenchant critique of colonial economies in Cuba (1992), Alexander von Humboldt recognised something that was not noticed at his time, because it was largely censored. It took a long time for these revolutionary passages in Alexander von Humboldt to become accessible. As a result of his travels, he was attuned to the possibility that much of what he saw as a research traveller was also there in other forms elsewhere. In other words, what he saw could be rescued as memory of other places which were also part of memory. What he saw may have been very different from what he witnessed elsewhere in Germany, but he had an ability to link up memories and therefore to establish similarities, rather than to see the obvious differences. If one remains with the obvious differences, one misses again the entire point, which is that by recognising similarity, we break up ontological systems of differences and an epistemological way of looking at these differences, and deriving conclusions from them. The whole science of historical classification in the nineteenth century is based on this wish to see difference instead of similarity. If similarity had been given the same emphasis, it would have led to a completely different science of classification – of diversity, science, philology, and linguistics (cf. Messling 2016).

The rise of a migratory consciousness in the nineteenth century is marked in Alexander von Humboldt, because he looks upon the world as a *Zusammenhang*. The term *Zusammenhang* is difficult to translate. If we translate it as totality, it is philosophically wrong, because totality is a philosophical term mainly popularised by Lukács. However, *Zusammenhang* is more and at the same time less than totality. It is the *way* in which everything holds together. And in this way, it is a fundamentally Goethean term.

This idea of *Zusammenhang* is at the basis of what Goethe and Alexander von Humboldt, but also the early August Wilhelm and Friedrich von Schlegel, see in the general principle of diversity – be it of languages, cultures, or traditions. *Zusammenhang* captures the sense of plenitude and abundance. It connects plenitude and abundance to variety and diversity. This kind of diversity can either be ontologised and made into hard borders, or it can be softened and made into a system of similarities.

At some stages, similarity vanishes, and at other stages it may become very important. The key to understanding *Zusammenhang* is the kind of memory that one is summoning up from one's own work, one's own writings, one's own reading, and one's own interactions. We mobilise such sorts of memories in order to create organising principles and order. Understanding how this process works is a search for what constitutes a *Zusammenhang*, what makes it work, how it is connected. "Was die Welt zusammenhält" (what holds the world together?) was Faust's question (Goethe 1808).

In a conversation on 31 January 1827, his private secretary Eckermann asked Goethe what he had been doing (see Eckermann and Soret 1850 [1836]; Eckermann 1836). Goethe responded that he had been doing nothing special, but that he had been reading a Chinese novel recently. "Chinese novel" – exclaimed Eckermann horrified, for he was a petty bourgeois and the thought that the master Goethe might have been reading a Chinese novel was for him a transgression. Chinese novels might have appeared strange for a bourgeois during nineteenth-century Weimar. But Goethe, in his typical way of saying important things in a sleight of hand manner, calmed down Eckermann by saying that the Chinese novel he had been reading actually was not really very different. In fact, it was more or less the same as what he was accustomed to, he explained. Now, this, for Eckermann, was another disturbing statement. The Chinese, Goethe continued, are not very different, they do more or less what he does. Some of it even reminded him of his own poem *Hermann and Dorothea* (1796/1797):

> Dined with Goethe. "Within the last few days, since I saw you," said he, "I have read many and various things; especially a Chinese novel, which occupies me still, and seems to me very remarkable." "Chinese novel!" said I; "that must look strange enough. "Not so much as you might think," said Goethe; "the Chinamen think, act, and feel almost exactly like us; and we soon find that we are perfectly like them, excepting that all they do is more clear, more pure, and decorous, than with us. "With them all is orderly, citizen-like, without great passion or poetic fight; and there is a strong resemblance to my 'Hermann and Dorothea,' as well as to the English novels of Richardson (Eckermann and Soret 1850 [1836], 348–349).[3]

---

3 "Bei Goethe zu Tisch. »In diesen Tagen, seit ich Sie nicht gesehen,« sagte er, »habe ich vieles und mancherlei gelesen, besonders auch einen chinesischen Roman, der mich noch beschäftiget und der mir im hohen Grade merkwürdig erscheint.« – »Chinesischen Roman?« sagte ich. »Der muß wohl sehr fremdartig aussehen.« – »Nicht so sehr, als man glauben sollte« , sagte Goethe. »Die Menschen denken, handeln und empfinden fast ebenso wie wir, und man fühlt sich sehr bald als ihresgleichen, – nur daß bei ihnen alles klarer, reinlicher und sittlicher zugeht. Es ist bei ihnen alles verständig, bürgerlich, ohne große Leidenschaft und poetischen Schwung und hat dadurch viele Ähnlichkeit mit meinem ›Hermann und Dorothea‹, sowie mit den englischen Romanen des Richardson" (Eckermann 1836).

In a way, Goethe's remark to Eckermann is a shocking statement, which strikes at the very foundation of all colonial ideology, since it is ultimately based on radical difference. And Goethe's statement in response is also tremendous, since he puts it forward so casually. His way of underplaying the drive towards seeing that *it is* Chinese and that *therefore* it is different, is captured in Goethe's comment that the work he is reading does more or less what he also does. The fuzziness of this *more or less* is crucial. The things we treat as unimportant parts of our vocabulary, the fuzzy more-or-less terms are loaded theoretically. Instead of saying either/or, he says *sowohl als auch* (this as well as that).

The universals that Goethe tries to look for are not abstract universals. On the contrary, it is through the concreteness of our examples that we rise in a dialectical manner to an enriched level of the abstract. In the same way, we could see the dialectical need to go from the concrete, that is, the real world to the abstract, so that we can come back to an enriched concrete. The nineteenth-century was adept in this dialectical movement from that which one might call the obvious, abstract real, through the motion of dialectics to concrete, to abstract, and thereby to go on the reverse moment to enrich the concreteness with a new meaning. Goethe embodied this, but of course, it was sanctified in Hegel's *Phenomenology* (1988). In this way, the concrete migration, the concrete *Hermann und Dorothea*, the concrete question of the *Divan*, the concrete translations from Hafiz, are the concrete reality of Goethe's world.

The transformation of this reality into poetry is the movement from the concrete to the abstract through a dialectical process of enrichment, which brings them back to the concrete as an enriched raw, meaningful concrete. This happens in a casual way, and this casualness is essential to the process. It is needed, first, to get the movement correctly. This is very important for looking at the particular and the universal. The movement, which takes this concreteness through a process of this ascendance, of *Aufsteigen* in the Hegelian sense, is captured by the philosopher E.V. Ilyenkov (2008). We can summarise this process through classification, but another way of understanding it is to take this complexity seriously, and to see the availability of things and their situation as part of what *Zusammenhang* is and how this *Zusammenhang* can become enriched through a dialectical motion.

Goethe was working on a contradictory process during the nineteenth century. This process was marked by colonialism. Colonialism divides. It would not survive if it could not divide. Any attempt to overcome the division are subversive. This subversion must be brought down by systems of oppression and terror.

The theoretical opposition to this division is the noticing of similarities where actually the colonial emphasises differences. We can evoke writings of British colonial officers, who were disturbed in a manner similar to Conrad's protagonists.

These officers were disturbed by the possibility that the people they were governing could be so similar to themselves. We know of officers, who, in their diaries, do not manage to justify to themselves the system of oppression that they established in India, because the people were so similar. Their system works by internalising the artificial notion of difference in order to keep the system of oppression alive. But this is undercut by the remarkable theoretical possibility of similarity that I discussed in this essay for nineteenth-century Germany and central Europe. The writings of Alexander von Humboldt, Wilhelm von Humboldt, early Friedrich and August Wilhelm Schlegel, culminating in Hegel, Marx, and Engels, and certainly including Goethe, lead to a way of looking at the world as a world of possible similarities.

The similarities I refer to are not *actual*, but possible similarities. The possibility, the recognition of the possibility of similarity, is a valuable part of the epistemology we inherited from this era. Marx and Engels recognised this in the first chapter of the *Communist Manifesto* (2012 [1848]), in which they show how for the sphere of intellectual production the intellectual creations of individual nations become common property. "National one-sidedness and narrow-mindedness become more and more impossible, and from the numerous national and local literatures, there arises a world literature" (Marx and Engels 2012 [1848], 77).

It is my aim to point out that it is possible for World Literature to become an empty slogan. World Literature does not exist; it will emerge. The emergence of World Literature, after all exploitation is over, is the key point which Marx and Engels, following Goethe were underlining. There are, thus, two paths, which we could take. We can talk of World Literature in the form of the great books of the world and state merely that their existence constitutes World Literature. We can also remark that these are stepping stones for the possibility of World Literature to emerge out of the world; a world that has pacified itself through the resolution of various contradictions that exist. We can therefore say that there is no World Literature as such *now*, but that it will *come*. For it to come, the Indians already had the vision of a *Viśvasāhitya*, a World Literature, which Tagore discussed in 1907 (see Chaudhuri 2021). This could come only after India got rid of the external subjugation through colonialism and the internal subjugation through the caste system as a universal system of exploitation. This *Viśvasāhitya* would come after colonialism, just as it was for Iqbal when he wrote the answer to Goethe's *West-östlicher Divan*, and called it *Payam-e-mashriq*, or *A Message of the East* in 1923 (see Iqbal 1977). In the foreword to *A Message of the East*, Iqbal reflects on the many writers and many thinkers who have talked about the relationship between the East and the West. But he remarks that it will only be possible to do so in a free manner after colonialism has been overcome. World Literature is a moment in Goethe, Iqbal, and Tagore in which anti-colonial writers meet.

Many others after them in many other countries took up the notion of World Literature as a possibility of non-colonial, non-divisive writing, which would emerge in the future. This is a form of enlightenment, but not in the text-book sense of *Aufklärung*, because it should not be misunderstood as a moment of diffusion. It is, rather, a co-emergent way of emancipation, which emerges in a world deeply shaken by the colonial enterprise and the revolts against it. How much of this possibility realised itself as success was not my question in this contribution, but rather the question as to whether it can partially be understood as the beginning of an answer. It is not the answer itself, but the fact that it can be seen as such is an answer. The overall matrix of universalism and particularity, difference and similarity, and the possibility of a World Literature, are part of the extraordinary nineteenth-century encounters I described. This matrix was obvious, but not immediately noticed.

References

Bhatti, Anil. "Plurikulturalität." *Habsburg neu denken: Vielfalt und Ambivalenz in Zentraleuropa. 30 kulturwissenschaftliche Stichworte*. Ed. Johannes Feichtinger and Heidemarie Uhl. Wien: Böhlau Verlag, 2016. 171–180.

Bhatti, Anil and Dorothee Kimmich. *Similarity. A paradigm for culture theory*. New Delhi: Tulika Books, 2018.

Chaudhuri, Rosinka. "Viśvasāhitya: Rabindranath Tagore's Idea of World Literature." *The Cambridge History of World Literature*. Ed. Debjani Ganguly. Cambridge: Cambridge University Press, 2021. 261–278.

Conrad, Joseph. *Heart of Darkness*. Ed. Knowles, Owen, and Allan Simmons. Cambridge: Cambridge University Press, 2018 [1899].

Csáky, Moritz. *Das Gedächtnis Zentraleuropas. Kulturelle und literarische Projektionen auf eine Region*. Wien: Böhlau Verlag, 2019.

Derrida, Jacques. *Speech and Phenomena. And Other Essays on Husserl's Theory of Signs*. Evanston: Northwestern University Press, 1973 [1967].

Du Bois, W.E.B. *The Souls of Black Folk*. New Haven, London: Yale University Press, 2015.

Eckermann, Johann Peter. *Gespräche mit Goethe in den letzten Jahren seines Lebens*. Leipzig: Brockhaus, 1836. Projekt Gutenberg: https://www.projekt-gutenberg.org/eckerman/gesprche/gsp1075.html (last accessed, 25 July 2022).

Eckermann, Johann Peter and M. Soret. *Conversations of Goethe*. Vols. 1–2. Transl. John Oxenford. London: Smith, Elder & Co., 1850 [1836].

Forster, Edward Morgan. *A Passage to India*. Ed. Oliver Stallybrass. Harmondsworth: Penguin Books, 1985 [1924].

Goethe, Johann Wolfgang. *Faust. Eine Tragödie*. Tübingen: Cotta, 1808.

———. *Noten und Abhandlungen zum West-östlichen Divan*. Ed. Wolfgang Lentz. Hamburg: Augustin, 1960.

———. *West-östlicher Divan. Sämtliche Werke, Briefe, Tagebücher und Gespräche*. 40 vol. Section 2, vol. 3, part I–II. Ed. Hendrik Birus. Frankfurt am Main: Deutscher Klassiker Verlag, 1994.

———. *West-östlicher Divan. Studienausgabe*. Ed. Michael Knaupp. Stuttgart: Reclam, 1999.

———. *Zur Farbenlehre*. Ed. Karl-Maria Guth. Berlin: Contumax-Hofenberg, 2016.

Grillparzer, Franz. *Sämtliche Werke. Ausgewählte Briefe, Gespräche, Berichte*. München: Hanser Verlag, 1960.

Hammer-Purgstall, Joseph Freiherr von. *Der Diwan von Mohammed Schemsed-din Hafis. Aus dem Persischen zum ersten Mal ganz übersetzt*. Tübingen, Stuttgart: Cotta, 1812.

Hegel, Georg Wilhelm Friedrich. *Phänomenologie des Geistes*. Ed. Hans-Friedrich Wessels and Heinrich Clairmont. Hamburg: Felix Meiner Verlag, 1988.

Herder, Johann Gottfried. *Ideen zur Philosophie der Geschichte der Menschheit. Werke in zehn Bänden. Vol. 6*. Frankfurt am Main: Deutscher Klassiker Verlag, 1989.

Humboldt, Alexander von. *Cuba-Werk. Studienausgabe*. 7 vol. Vol. 6. Ed. Hanno Beck. Darmstadt: Wissenschaftliche Buchgesellschaft, 1992.

Judson, Pieter M. *The Habsburg Empire. A New History*. Cambridge/MA: Harvard University Press, 2016.

Ilyenkov, Evald. *Dialectics of the Abstract and the Concrete in Marx's Capital*. Transl. Sergei Syrovatkin. Delhi: Aakar Books, 2008.

Iqbal, Mohammed. *A Message from the East*. Lahore: Iqbal Academy Pakistan, 1977.

Künne, Wolfgang. *Bernard Bolzanos Erbauungsreden (und ihre Edition)*. Baden-Baden: Academia, 2019.

Lukács, Georg. "Lob des neunzehnten Jahrhunderts." *GLW*. Vol. 4. Berlin, Neuwied: Luchterhand, 1971. 659–664.

Manto, Saadat Hasan. *Kingdom's End and Other Stories*. Transl. Khalid Hasan. New Delhi: Penguin Books, 1989.

Marx, Karl, and Friedrich Engels. *The Communist Manifesto*. Ed. Jeffrey C. Isaac. New Haven: Yale University Press, 2012 [1848].

Melville, Herman. *Benito Cereno*. Ed. Brian Yothers. Peterborough / Ontario: Broadview Press, 2019.

Messling, Markus. *Gebeugter Geist. Rassismus und Erkenntnis in der modernen europäischen Philologie*. Göttingen: Wallstein, 2016.

Muschg, Adolf. *Goethe als Emigrant. Auf der Suche nach dem Grünen bei einem alten Dichter*. Frankfurt am Main: Suhrkamp, 1986.

Saussure, Ferdinand de. *Cours de linguistique générale*. Paris: Payot, 1972 [1916].

Gisèle Sapiro
Le décentrement épistémologique conduit-il au relativisme ?

Abstract: Universalist claims are based on the denial or at least the bracketing of the fact that science is a social product, that it is inscribed in specific cultures. But does cultural relativism automatically lead to epistemological relativism? Against a widespread tendency to infer the latter from the former, this chapter proposes a negative answer to the question. This implies a critique of the traditional conceptions of the history of science as linear and Western. A decentred and transcultural history of science reveals the numerous contacts and circulations of scientific concepts, theories, and methods between cultures, including those called "non-Western". Moreover, the holistic idea of incommensurability between epistemes or paradigms does not mean they are impervious to each other, since any circulation between paradigms implies operations of borrowing, displacement, and reinterpretation. The plurality of paradigms or competing theories neither calls into question the existence of a reality that is external to them, nor the validity of some of them (more than others).

Keywords: cultural relativism, epistemology, holism, Occidentalism, progress, universalism, untranslatability

1 Introduction

Le concept d'universalisme est une construction sociale qui a servi à justifier l'impérialisme occidental et l'imposition d'une hégémonie culturelle dans le monde à partir du XVIIIe siècle. On peut ainsi parler, avec Pierre Bourdieu, d'un « impérialisme de l'universel », qu'il attribue en particulier à la France depuis la Révolution française (Bourdieu 1992). La notion de mission civilisatrice qui accompagna les conquêtes coloniales leur servait de justification lettrée et de sociodicée. Cet universel prenait des formes spécifiques selon les domaines : philosophie, science, littérature, arts plastiques. Des canons étaient constitués pour chacun de ces domaines et une histoire universelle qui a marginalisé voire effacé les apports non-occidentaux, lesquels furent pourtant consistants, que l'on pense aux mathématiques ou à la médecine égyptienne, à la médecine et à la philosophie indienne, à la philosophie arabe d'Andalousie ou au Haiku japonais.

Si les canons sont en cours de révision, la question se pose différemment sur le plan épistémologique. Y a-t-il une seule épistémologie (au sens de philosophie de la connaissance scientifique), dont la validité serait universelle, ou devons-nous parler d'épistémologies au pluriel ? Autrement dit, l'épistémologie dépend-elle de la diversité des cultures ? Si tel est le cas, cela doit-il nous conduire au relativisme épistémologique ? Et quelle serait la signification d'un tel relativisme épistémologique ? Telles sont les questions qui seront examinées ici, à partir d'une réflexion en cours[1]. Sans prétendre la résoudre, je suggérerai des pistes pour poser le problème de façon plus adéquate.

Le relativisme culturel appliqué à la connaissance scientifique risque de nous conduire à un relativisme épistémologique extrême, tel que développé par Feyerabend (1975), qui nie toute différence entre les propositions scientifiques, les mythes, et les énoncés religieux ; ou, plus extrême encore, à l'idée de Nelson Goodman (2007) selon laquelle nos catégories créent ou construisent la réalité, et que ces catégories qui constituent une pluralité de mondes sont façonnées par leurs conditions sociales et culturelles de production, et par des intérêts circonstanciels, liés au contexte.

D'autre part, la prétention universaliste est fondée sur le déni ou au moins la mise entre parenthèses du fait que la science est un produit social, qu'elle s'inscrit dans des cultures spécifiques, ou dans ce que Foucault (1966) a appelé, dans *Les Mots et les Choses*, une épistémè, qui varie dans le temps et dans l'espace[2].

Ma réflexion se fonde sur trois observations. Premièrement, les concepts et théories ont une origine sociale, et sont plus ou moins encastrés dans leur culture d'origine, mais ils peuvent parfois résulter de rencontres transculturelles. Par exemple, l'anthropologie structurale est née de la rencontre entre deux chercheurs exilés à New York, le français Claude Lévi-Strauss et le russe Roman Jakobson, pendant la Deuxième Guerre mondiale (Jeanpierre 2004 ; Loyer 2015).

Deuxièmement, les concepts ne sont pas de purs produits du savoir, leur production est plus ou moins encastrée dans des croyances et dans des intérêts sociaux, qu'illustre de façon paradigmatique la fausse science : par exemple, le pseudo-concept de « race » dans son acception biologique était le produit de préjugés racis-

---

[1] Des étapes de cette réflexion ont été présentées lors d'un colloque à l'Université de Dakar les 4–6 janvier 2018, à l'occasion du séminaire « Experimental Critical Theory seminar » à UCLA le 27 février 2020 et dans l'entretien sur « Universalisme & savoir(s) » avec le groupe Minor Universality de Sarrebruck le 4 février 2021 (https://www.youtube.com/watch?v=AF-hEDCOGmI). Que les participantes à ces événements soient remerciées pour leurs questions et commentaires qui ont enrichi la réflexion.

[2] Notons que le sens de la notion d'épistémè a évolué entre *Les Mots et les Choses* et *L'Archéologie du savoir*, Foucault ayant restreint progressivement son usage aux sciences ou aux champs des savoirs scientifiques (Foucault 1968, 250).

tes et d'intérêts coloniaux (voir notamment Reynaud-Paligot 2006) ; ou, autre exemple plus récent, celui de « underclass » (Wacquant 2022).

Troisièmement, les concepts sont liés à d'autres concepts, ils ne peuvent être isolés de la théorie dans laquelle ils sont inscrits, ni même d'un paradigme, comme William Orman Quine (1951) et Thomas Kuhn (1962) l'ont avancé. C'est ce qu'on appelle la position holiste. Or, à l'instar de Quine, Kuhn considère que les paradigmes sont incommensurables.

Ces trois observations devraient logiquement nous conduire au relativisme épistémologique : si les concepts dépendent des théories et des paradigmes, et si ceux-ci sont encastrés dans des cultures, alors les théories provenant de différentes cultures sont incommensurables. Cependant, l'exemple de la rencontre entre Lévi-Strauss et Jakobson nous indique une autre option. Tout en souscrivant au relativisme culturel (on peut se référer aux arguments de Geertz [2010] contre l'anti-relativisme culturel), j'avancerai que le décentrement épistémologique ne conduit pas nécessairement au relativisme épistémologique.

Avant de revenir à la question de l'incommensurabilité, il nous faut faire un détour par les biais de l'histoire traditionnelle des sciences, à savoir la notion de progrès et le caractère occidentalo-centré de cette histoire, lequel repose sur l'occultation de maints contacts interculturels. Elle doit donc elle-même être décentrée afin que l'on puisse examiner à nouveaux frais le problème des rapports entre relativisme culturel et relativisme épistémologique. Il sera également nécessaire de rappeler les limites épistémologiques de la pensée scientifique.

2 La notion de progrès

La variation des connaissances dans le temps est regardée dans le monde occidental, depuis le XVIIIe siècle, comme un « progrès ». Le concept de « progrès » est au cœur de l'idéologie scientifique qui considère l'histoire des sciences comme un développement téléologique et linéaire vers la vérité. Or ce récit linéaire a été remis en cause aussi bien par Lévi-Strauss que par Popper, Quine et Kuhn.

Selon Popper (1962), comme on sait, il est impossible de confirmer une théorie, on ne peut que l'invalider. La réfutation est l'opération qui permet de résoudre le problème de l'induction et de réconcilier le domaine du probable avec la logique. Il en découle que la science n'évolue pas par accumulation mais par conjectures et réfutations. On peut néanmoins considérer que, bien que non linéaire, ce schéma d'évolution par ruptures demeure compatible avec la notion de progrès scientifique, dans laquelle Popper croyait.

Dans son fameux article « Two dogmas of empiricism », Quine (1951) a toutefois contesté l'idée réductionniste selon laquelle un énoncé singulier peut être vérifié empiriquement. Quine souligne en effet l'interdépendance des énoncés scientifiques. Sa conception holiste de la science remet en cause la théorie vérificationniste des positivistes logiques. En effet, il y a plus d'une façon de résoudre les contradictions entre énoncés théoriques et énoncés empiriques, et elles ne conduisent pas nécessairement au rejet des théories. Il en déduit, à l'instar de Pierre Duhem (2016 [1906]) avant lui, qu'il y a une sous-détermination des énoncés théoriques par les énoncés empiriques.

Quine tire de cette démonstration deux conclusions. La première est que la science ne diffère pas par essence de la religion ou d'autres systèmes idéalistes, mais seulement du point de vue de son efficacité. La seconde est pragmatique : la fonction de la science étant de prédire les expériences futures en fonction de celles du passé, le choix entre explications ne repose que sur le degré avec lequel elles « facilitent nos interactions avec nos expériences sensorielles » (Quine 1980, 120). Toutefois, ainsi qu'il l'explique dans un article postérieur, étant donné qu'il est possible de décrire les mêmes données empiriques à partir de plus d'une théorie plausible, les théories peuvent être à la fois incompatibles et équivalentes (Quine 1970).

Avec la notion de « paradigmes », Kuhn (1962) combine les conceptions holistes et discontinuistes de la science. L'incommensurabilité des paradigmes fait que l'évolution de la science n'est pas linéaire mais s'opère par révolutions. Comme les révolutions politiques ou les conversions religieuses, le passage d'un paradigme scientifique à un autre implique un changement de vision du monde.

Dans *Les Mots et les choses*, Foucault (1966) esquisse quant à lui une histoire non linéaire, ou plutôt une archéologie, des sciences humaines à l'aide de la notion d'épistémè, qui est plus large que celle de paradigme, en ce qu'elle inclut toutes les formes et types de savoir. L'épistémè est un mode de connaissance qui implique un rapport particulier entre langage et choses, signifiant et signifié. Foucault évoque trois phases de cette archéologie (qui reste chronologique) et en voit poindre une quatrième. Avant l'ère classique prévaut la ressemblance, la similitude, l'analogie, des correspondances, le langage signifiant. L'ère classique (XVIIe–XVIIIe siècles) leur substitue la question des identités et des différences (le discernement) par comparaison de la mesure et de l'ordre (les taxinomies), séparant les mots et les choses pour imposer aux choses une logique (le cartésianisme, la logique de Port-Royal, le recensement). On sépare histoire et science : d'un côté, l'érudition, la lecture des auteurs, le jeu de leur opinion, de l'autre, la science (le langage doit traduire la vérité, il est neutre, transparent). L'ère moderne (début XIXe–XXe) est marquée par le retrait du discours de représentation (grammaire générale, analyse des richesses, histoire naturelle) et par l'apparition de l'homme dans l'épistémè : l'homme qui parle (philologie), vit (biologie) et travaille (économie politique). Foucault pensait qu'on entrait dans une ère post-moderne caractérisée par la disparition de l'homme et le retour au langage comme signifiant non transparent. Il se trompait : après le moment structuraliste et post-structuraliste, on a assisté au retour du sujet et à un recentrage de l'intérêt scientifique sur l'être humain. Mais c'est une autre histoire.

Critiquant la notion de « progrès » dans *Race et histoire*, paru en 1952, Lévi-Strauss signalait que « le développement des connaissances préhistoriques et archéologiques tend à *étaler dans l'espace* des formes de civilisation que nous étions portés à imaginer comme *échelonnées dans le temps* » (1987, 38). Il en déduit que le « progrès (si ce terme convient encore pour désigner une réalité très différente de celle à laquelle on l'avait d'abord appliqué) n'est ni nécessaire, ni continu ; il procède par sauts, par bonds, ou, comme diraient les biologistes, par mutations » (*ibid.*). Ainsi, pour Lévi-Strauss, c'est « seulement de temps à autre que l'histoire est cumulative [...] » (*ibid.*, 39). Ce qui nous conduit à interroger la vision du monde à partir de laquelle a été élaborée cette notion de progrès.

3 Un récit occidental

Tous ces récits de l'histoire de sciences, qu'ils soient linéaires ou non, sont centrés sur le monde occidental, comme si l'Occident détenait le monopole du savoir scientifique dans le monde, comme s'il n'y avait pas de savoirs valables dans d'autres cultures. Ce récit occidental est remis en cause non seulement par des anthropologues comme Lévi-Strauss, mais aussi par l'histoire de sciences. Il suffit d'évoquer l'histoire des mathématiques, notamment en Egypte (Mankiewicz 2004 [2001]), la philosophie et la médecine indienne ou chinoise (sur la première, voir Raj 2007), ou les philosophies arabes ou africaines, pour ébranler toute tentative de monopolisation de la science par l'Occident.

Comme l'a montré Kapil Raj (sous presse), ce récit est, à l'origine, moins le produit d'un ethnocentrisme aveugle que d'une entreprise volontaire et consciente, qui situe « La » révolution scientifique dans l'Europe du XVIIe siècle, en instrumentalisant la thèse d'Alexandre Koyré dans ses travaux sur Copernic et Galilée, dans un contexte de construction de l'hégémonie américaine et de décolonisation. Alors que Kuhn, s'inspirant de Koyré, parle de « révolutions scientifiques » au pluriel, cette thèse de « LA révolution scientifique » s'est imposée comme doxa savante d'une histoire officielle de la science à partir de cette époque.

Si l'on admet la notion de « révolutions scientifiques » au pluriel, il faut toutefois se demander comment elles ont circulé d'un endroit à l'autre. L'histoire des sciences apporte maintes preuves de l'existence de contacts interculturels non seulement en Europe mais aussi avec des cultures non-européennes (on évoquera, par exemple, l'intérêt de Leibniz ou de François Quesnay pour la philosophie indienne au XVIIIe siècle). Après Kapil Raj (2007), James Poskett (2022) s'est récemment attelé à une histoire des sciences décentrée, qui révèle les nombreux contacts et circulations occultés entre savants « occidentaux » et « non occidentaux » à l'ère moderne, pour restituer « ce que la science moderne doit aux sociétés non européennes », comme le précise le sous-titre de son ouvrage. On peut d'ailleurs s'interroger sur la pertinence de cette distinction entre « occidental » et « non-occidental » avant sa construction en contexte colonial, comme l'a montré Edward Saïd (1978) dans son livre sur l'orientalisme.

Une deuxième question se pose : celle de l'exclusion de ces traditions « non occidentales » et de ces interférences du récit canonique de l'histoire de savoirs. La science « occidentale » s'est construite en occultant les savoirs qui se sont développés ailleurs, en les niant ou en se les appropriant, et cette histoire commence à peine à s'écrire. Peter Park (2014) l'a entrepris pour la philosophie. Dans son livre *Africa, Asia, and the History of Philosophy : Racism in the Formation of the Philosophical Canon*, il montre que jusqu'au moment de leur exclusion dans la seconde moitié du XVIIIe siècle, certaines traditions dites orientales bénéficiaient d'une place pionnière dans l'histoire de la philosophie. Il en donne plusieurs exemples (au chapitre 4, n. 5) : *De orthographia* de Giovanni Tortelli commence par Zoroastra ; *Bibliotheca philosophorum classicorum authorum chronologica* (1592) de Johann Jacob Fries débute avec la confusion des langues suite à la destruction de la tour de Babel ; *History of Philosophy* (1655–1662), de Thomas Stanley, commence avec Thalès, dont il rappelle qu'il est d'origine phénicienne et qu'il a voyagé en Asie et a étudié en Egypte ; le livre traite à la fin des philosophies orientales, Chaldéennes, Perse et Sabéenne, leur reconnaissant la primeur. Ces systèmes étaient en effet bien connus au XVIIIe siècle, en Allemagne comme en France : par exemple, Schlegel a inclus la philosophie indienne dans son histoire de la philosophie, la reconnaissant comme une « vraie philosophie à la fois dans sa forme et dans sa méthode » ; il liste quatre écoles : Vedanta, Sankhya, Nyagya, Mimansa (cité dans Park 2014, chap. 3, n. 86 ; je traduis).

Schlegel réagissait à l'exclusion de la pensée orientale de la nouvelle histoire de la philosophie qui se développait en Allemagne dans les années 1780. Ces nouveaux historiens de la philosophie étaient les disciples de Kant qui ont constitué une histoire de la philosophie distincte de l'histoire tout court, définie comme l'histoire du progrès de la pensée.

Cet acte qui opère une révolution symbolique, en rompant avec le genre établi des vies et doctrines de philosophes, et en séparant en même temps la philosophie de l'histoire des sciences et des histoires de la littérature, peut être considéré comme un des actes fondateurs de l'autonomisation du champ philosophique (au sens de Bourdieu 1988), qui établit dès lors ses règles, son histoire propre, ses références légitimes. Le paradoxe est que cette autonomisation passe dans ce cas par l'exclusion des autres traditions de pensée (ainsi que par l'exclusion des femmes soit dit en passant). Il n'empêche que les penseurs allemands, français ou anglais du XVIIIe siècle avaient d'ores et déjà absorbé des pans entiers de savoirs non-occidentaux.

La reconnaissance du non-monopole de la science par l'Occident signifie que des systèmes de connaissance peuvent coexister parallèlement, voire simultanément, qu'il y ait interférences ou non, ce qui remet en cause l'approche chronologique qui prévaut en histoire de sciences et conduit à la question de l'incidence du relativisme culturel sur le relativisme épistémologique. En effet, s'il existe parallèlement des épistémai incommensurables, s'inscrivant dans des traditions et histoires différentes, comment arbitrer entre elles ? Et cela signifie-t-il que notre savoir est toujours relatif ? Avant de revenir à cette question, je voudrais aborder le problème des limites épistémologiques de la pensée scientifique et du caractère situé des savoirs.

4 Les limites de la pensée scientifique

Selon Gaston Bachelard (1993 [1938]), le savoir n'est pas cumulatif. Il est conquis contre les savoirs antérieurs et surtout contre le sens commun. Parmi les obstacles épistémologiques les plus coriaces, il y a les préjugés, que Durkheim (1986 [1895]) appelait les « prénotions », en s'appuyant sur Francis Bacon, lequel mettait en garde contre les « idoles », ces notions vulgaires qui se placent entre notre esprit et la réalité, tel un voile.

Les théories racistes sont un exemple extrême d'une pseudo-science qui vient conforter les stéréotypes. Il en va de même de la physiognomonie de Lavater (Dumont 1984). La fausse science est là pour nous rappeler que les entreprises scientifiques remplissent des fonctions et objectifs autres que la connaissance pure. Dans son livre sur la notion de totémisme, Lévi-Strauss (1962) analyse une erreur scientifique paradigmatique. Tentant de comprendre d'où vient l'erreur commise par nombre d'anthropologues (notamment Frazer) à ce propos, il montre qu'elle réside dans la confusion entre deux phénomènes : d'un côté, le totémisme comme système de dénominations collectives (les noms d'animaux donnés aux clans) ; de l'autre, le culte des animaux ou les croyances dans l'esprit gardien, qui sont des phénomènes d'ordre religieux. De fait, le recours aux noms d'animaux pour désigner les clans n'a rien de religieux. Lévi-Strauss montre qu'il s'agit d'un système de classification d'ordre logique : le monde des animaux propose un système de représentations qui permet de les distinguer par des rapports métaphoriques. Et Lévi-Strauss d'expliquer que cette confusion relève d'un ensemble de préjugés d'idées reçues, d'erreurs méthodologiques et de généralisations hâtives en termes utilitaristes ou psychologisants. Or ces erreurs, poursuit-il, ne sont pas le fruit du hasard. Elles sont fondées sur des intérêts sociaux. La confusion provient de la croyance en une différence d'essence entre les conduites du « primitif » et celles de l'homme blanc occidental, différence qui repose sur l'opposition entre nature et culture. La proximité à la nature différencierait l'homme « primitif » de l'homme occidental « civilisé », dont la conduite aurait un fondement culturel. La notion de « mentalité pré-logique » forgée par Lévy-Bruhl condense cet ensemble de préjugés sous une forme savante. Elle empêche de voir la pensée logique qui sous-tend le système de dénominations collectives.

Lévi-Strauss rapproche cette attitude de la conception de l'hystérie selon Charcot, conception qui rendait les malades (en l'occurrence les femmes) radicalement différents des gens « normaux ». Cette notion fut critiquée par Freud qui montra qu'il n'y avait pas une différence d'essence entre les malades et ceux qui ne l'étaient pas, car ce qu'on appelait hystérie était juste l'accentuation ou l'involution de certains traits partagés par tout le monde.

Ainsi, la nécessité – d'ordre plus social que scientifique – d'établir une frontière entre gens « normaux » et « anormaux » ou entre « civilisés » et « primitifs » nous rend aveugles à l'examen de phénomènes comparables dans nos sociétés : on préfère, dit Lévi-Strauss, ne pas voir que « le malade est notre frère »[3] ; et l'anthropologue de poursuivre qu'il était « plus confortable de voir dans le malade mental un être d'une espèce rare et singulière, le produit objectif de fatalités externes ou internes, telles que l'hérédité, l'alcoolisme ou la débilité » (Lévi-Strauss 1962, 6).

Cet exemple rappelle combien notre savoir est dépendant de la culture dans laquelle il s'inscrit et de nos préjugés. Autre exemple : la théorie des climats de Montesquieu, qui étudie son influence sur les hommes et la société. Comme l'a montré Bourdieu (1980), l'argument de Montesquieu repose sur une série d'oppositions construites sur le binôme masculin/féminin : dur/mou, froid/chaud, actif/passif, conduisant à une opposition entre le sang-froid des peuples du Nord, pleinement maîtres de

---

[3] Citation qui semble faire écho à une phrase des « adieux » du vieillard dans le *Supplément au voyage de Bougainville* (1773) de Diderot : « Celui dont tu veux t'emparer comme de la brute, le Tahitien est ton frère ; vous êtes deux enfants de la nature. »

leurs facultés, et pouvant donc être autonomes dans leurs opinions politiques, et le sang chaud des peuples du sud, qui seraient passifs et sujets à des gouvernements despotiques. Ces biais questionnent la limite entre vraie et fausse science, et l'hétéronomie des savoirs par rapport à la vision du monde d'une société.

5 Comment dépasser le relativisme épistémologique ?

Faut-il en conclure au relativisme épistémologique, qui conduirait à contester le statut particulier de la science par rapport à la vérité ? Ou cet obstacle peut-il être surmonté ? Qu'est-ce qui permet de différencier la vraie science de la fausse ? Le triomphe d'une théorie sur une autre n'est-il que le résultat d'un rapport de force socio-politique et/ou économique, comme le laissent penser certains historiens et sociologues des sciences ? Et s'il est impossible de nier que la science soit aux prises avec ces forces sociales, quelle peut être sa validité ?

Dans le dernier ouvrage qu'il a publié avant sa mort, *Science de la science et réflexivité*, Bourdieu (2001) proposait une solution sociologique à la question du relativisme. Selon Bourdieu, qui est proche en cela du sociologue américain Robert Merton, la validité de la science réside dans la capacité des savants à s'émanciper des intérêts sociaux extra-scientifiques. Cette capacité est l'expression de l'autonomisation d'un champ scientifique imposant ses propres lois, ses intérêts spécifiques, son *illusio*, à savoir la croyance dans la science, que partagent les scientifiques. L'autonomisation du champ scientifique crée les conditions d'un intérêt au désintéressement. Il faut rappeler que le concept de désintéressement était synonyme, en allemand, de celui d'objectivité au XVIIe siècle, à propos précisément des sciences (Dear 1992).

La loi du champ scientifique impose des règles spécifiques aux luttes pour la reconnaissance et l'imposition de théories, qui sont l'argumentation, l'usage de concepts communs, la cohérence, la vérification empirique, l'administration de la preuve selon des protocoles d'expérience explicites et admis par la communauté scientifique, etc. L'autonomie n'est jamais complète, mais le non-respect des règles du jeu entraîne des sanctions, voire l'exclusion et la perte de capital symbolique.

Si le développement de la science dépend en bonne partie du degré d'autonomie des sciences dans un lieu et une période donnés, et n'est donc pas linéaire[4], il n'y a

---

[4] Il y a des périodes de perte d'autonomie, comme en témoigne l'instrumentalisation de la science sous le nazisme ; voir Ash (2021).

pas de raison de penser que de telles conditions n'ont existé que dans ce qu'on appelle l'Occident, même si l'émergence de champs scientifiques est largement un phénomène moderne, qui s'inscrit dans le processus de sécularisation. En outre, le degré d'autonomie varie d'une science à l'autre et selon les configurations socio-politiques. Par exemple, la sociologie a été constituée comme une science à l'époque du colonialisme conquérant, qui a vu fleurir les théories raciales, lesquelles servaient de justifications lettrées des agissements coloniaux (Reynaud-Paligot 2006). Mais l'école durkheimienne affirme son autonomie à l'égard des intérêts coloniaux, reconnaissant pleinement l'existence d'autres sociétés et d'autres cultures contre les théories évolutionnistes qui voyaient dans les peuples dits « primitifs » des résidus d'étapes passées du processus de civilisation. Durkheim a d'ailleurs été violemment attaqué pour avoir traité les religions non-monothéistes comme des religions à part entière (Sapiro 2004a). De même, l'anthropologie structurale de Lévi-Strauss a offert un paradigme qui permettait de sortir l'ethnologie française des prénotions coloniales dont elle était saturée.

Bourdieu donne un exemple de ces prénotions en évoquant ses recherches en Algérie. Il avait lu les orientalistes qui disaient « les primitifs n'ont pas d'avenir ». Or Bourdieu, qui recourait à des méthodes d'observation ethnographique, observait les paysans kabyles faire des provisions pour l'hiver : ils se projetaient donc bien dans un à-venir. Il s'agissait toutefois d'un temps cyclique, différent de la conception linéaire du temps de la modernité capitaliste, où l'on fait des projets pour le futur (épargne, scolarisation des enfants, etc.). Pour comprendre ce rapport au temps, Bourdieu a recouru à la philosophie de Husserl, qui distingue « la protension comme visée pratique d'un à-venir inscrit dans le présent, donc appréhendé comme déjà là et doté de la modalité doxique du présent, et le projet comme position d'une future constitué comme tel, c'est-à-dire comme pouvant advenir ou ne pas advenir » (Bourdieu 1987, 22). Cette conception du temps est en rupture avec la conception spontanéiste et discontinuiste de la théorie de l'action que Sartre reprend à la tradition rationaliste cartésienne, celle de la libre projection du sujet dans le futur, que Bourdieu va critiquer d'un point de vue sociologique (Sapiro 2004b).

Enfin, si l'on s'accorde pour dire que la science n'est pas homogène et unifiée, et qu'il y a parfois des théories concurrentes, voire incommensurables, dans un même domaine, dont certaines continuent à être valides à une certaine échelle à l'instar de la physique de Newton, sans l'être à un autre niveau, comme l'a montré la théorie de la relativité d'Einstein, alors on peut admettre qu'il y a des domaines du savoir hors du monde occidental. Qui plus est, les contacts interculturels du passé témoignent de l'enrichissement que peuvent apporter les épistémologies dites du sud. On sait au moins depuis Kuhn, et aussi depuis l'étude sociologique de Ben-David et Collins (1966) sur le cas de la psychologie, que les systèmes de connaissance, les paradigmes, les théories scientifiques se renouvellent par emprunts et importation d'éléments, concepts, méthodes, d'autres sciences, voire d'autres domaines (par exemple les arts) ; ou encore par des synthèses raisonnées entre théories (Bourdieu a, par exemple, opéré une telle synthèse des théories de Durkheim, Marx et Weber, en proposant un dépassement). Ces confrontations stimulent l'imagination scientifique, et soulèvent des problèmes qui demandent à être résolus – c'est par cela que la science progresse (Zald 1995).

Se pose néanmoins la question de l'incommensurabilité. Comment peut-on emprunter des concepts s'ils dépendent d'un autre système ? Faut-il tomber dans l'éclectisme que revendiquaient les philosophe populaires allemands du XVIIIe siècle ? Pas nécessairement. On peut en effet suggérer une autre voie.

Dans un article sur les rapports entre la philosophie et l'histoire, le philosophe Pascal Engel (1995) évoque la controverse entre Claude Panaccio et Alain de Libera à propos de l'usage que fait Panaccio des concepts d'Occam en les extrayant de leur contexte, usage que de Libera conteste au nom du holisme et du relativisme historique. Prenant partie pour le premier, Engel distingue entre deux acceptions du holisme : l'une supposant des « liens d'interdépendance entre les thèses d'un philosophe dans divers domaines et entre son œuvre et celle de ses contemporains » ; l'autre impliquant que la « réalité » dont parle un philosophe est toujours interne au « monde » qu'il élabore et à celui qu'élaboreraient ses contemporains. Si le premier sens lui paraît une évidence, le second est selon lui inacceptable.

Or l'idée d'incommensurabilité, de même que la notion d'intraduisibilité qui lui est souvent associée, ne dit rien sur l'existence ou non d'une réalité extérieure, elle parle juste des différentes manières d'appréhender une telle réalité, à l'instar de l'étoile du soir et de l'étoile du matin de Frege. Davidson (1973) a de longue date pointé les incohérences du présupposé d'intraduisibilité du relativisme conceptuel. Par ailleurs, le saut ontologique opéré par Goodman à partir de la pluralité des perceptions du monde vers la pluralité des mondes n'a rien de nécessaire. Mais la position de relativisme historique radical qu'adopte de Libera ne paraît pas acceptable pour d'autres raisons : tout notre savoir est fait d'emprunts et d'importations de système en système, et même si les termes prennent un sens nouveau dans le nouveau système sémantique dans lequel ils s'inscrivent, cela n'invalide pas le système en soi.

Par ailleurs, l'approche historique discontinuiste ne permet pas d'expliquer la transmission qui s'opère malgré tout (même si de façon variable) d'une période à l'autre (transmission d'un corpus de connaissance, de modes de raisonnement, etc.), et qui rend la communication possible, fût-ce au prix de malentendus. Comme l'expliquait Bertrand Russell, la communication suppose nécessairement une discontinuité entre le contexte où le concept a été élaboré et celui où il est réemployé, et où il produit de nouvelles associations. Au sein d'un même paradigme, on peut du reste aussi constater des variations dans l'interprétation et l'usage des concepts.

De même, si l'on peut s'accorder sur l'incommensurabilité entre systèmes occidentaux et non-occidentaux, il faut tenir compte des circulations de ces savoirs dans les deux directions. Par exemple, tandis que les missionnaires identifiaient les doctrines chinoises traditionnelles comme de la « philosophie », cette notion fut introduite en Chine via le Japon au XIXe siècle et a produit une intense activité, y compris la relecture de la pensée traditionnelle chinoise par ce nouveau prisme : Hu Shi a ainsi tenté de trouver une pensée philosophique pragmatique dans la Chine ancienne, tout au long de son livre de 1922 *The Development of the Logical Method in Ancient China*, qui a exhumé des penseurs auparavant marginalisés par le courant confucéen dominant (Defoort 2005 ; Feng 1983, 73).

Si l'incommensurabilité et l'intraduisibilité étaient complètes, comment pourrait-on expliquer les phénomènes d'apprentissage, d'appropriation et d'hybridation ? Holisme ne signifie pas étanchéité, cela signifie juste que les éléments prennent sens dans un système, il faut donc comparer les systèmes et trouver des homologues structuraux ou fonctionnels. Si la notion d'intraduisible (Cassin 2004) vient rappeler les limites des équivalences structurales dans les systèmes de communication (Apter 2006), elle ne rend pas compte des opérations de traduction qui s'effectuent malgré cela. Certes, celles-ci ne sont pas exemptes de malentendus (Bourdieu 2002). Et certes, l'apprentissage d'un autre système de pensée est coûteux, coût qui est un des freins les plus puissants aux révolutions scientifiques, comme l'a souligné Kuhn. L'être a intérêt à persévérer dans son être selon Spinoza. C'est pourquoi la confrontation aux épistémologies dites du sud doit reposer sur un acte volontariste. Et il nous incite à suivre l'invite de Hilary Putnam (2002) à dépasser l'opposition entre historicisme et positivisme.

6 Conclusion

En conclusion, le relativisme culturel ne mène pas nécessairement au relativisme épistémologique. Une histoire décentrée et transnationale des sciences porte actuellement au jour les contacts et circulations entre les cultures, notamment dans le domaine scientifique, qui n'étaient pas des univers étanches. Elle révèle aussi le processus historique d'occultation de ces échanges et de construction d'une histoire « occidentale » épurée de ses apports « non occidentaux », notions qui sont elles-mêmes le fruit de constructions ayant eu pour effet (recherché) d'accentuer les différences culturelles et de dénier les circulations. Ces échanges témoignent du fait qu'incommensurabilité ne signifie pas étanchéité et que si les emprunts, importations, appropriations, modifient, transforment les concepts, théories et méthodes (ce qui est vrai aussi quand on s'approprie les auteurs canoniques), les systèmes de pensées, ou paradigmes, ou programmes de recherche suivant le concept du philosophe Imre Lakatos, se nourrissent les uns des autres même lorsqu'ils sont incompatibles, voire incommensurables. Il en résulte que la progression des savoirs n'est pas et ne peut être linéaire. Mais la pluralité de paradigmes ou de théories concurrentes ne remet en cause ni l'existence d'une réalité qui leur est extérieure, ni la validité de certaines d'entre elles (plus que d'autres), que cette validité ait une portée universelle ou située dans l'espace-temps, d'ordre causal, probabiliste ou structural, atemporel, tendanciel ou conjoncturel[5].

Références bibliographiques

Apter, Emily. *The Translation Zone. A New Comparative Literature*. Princeton: Princeton University Press, 2006.
Ash, Mitchell. « The Suppression and Misuses of Academic Freedom During the Nazi Regime. » *TRAFO – Blog for Transregional Research*, 03.03.2021. https://trafo.hypotheses.org/26855.
Bachelard, Gaston. *La Formation de l'esprit scientifique*. Paris : Vrin, 1993 [1938].
Ben-David, Joseph, et Randall Collins. « Social factors in the origins of a new science : the case of psychology. » *American Sociological Review* 31.4 (1966) : 451–465.
Boghossian, Paul. *La Peur du savoir. Sur le relativisme & le constructivisme de la connaissance*. Trad. Ophelia Deroy. Marseille : Agone, 2006.
Bourdieu, Pierre. « Le Nord et le Midi : Contribution à une analyse de l'effet Montesquieu ». *Actes de la recherche en sciences sociales* 35 (1980) : 21–25.
———. *Choses dites*. Paris : Minuit, 1987.
———. *L'Ontologie politique de Martin Heidegger*. Paris : Minuit, 1988.
———. « Deux impérialismes de l'universel ». *L'Amérique des Français*. Ed. Christine Fauré et Tom Bishop. Paris : F. Bourin, 1992. 149–156.
———. *Science de la science et réflexivité*. Paris : Raisons d'agir, 2001.
———. « Les conditions sociales de la circulation internationale des idées ». *Actes de la recherche en sciences sociales* 145 (2002) : 3–8.
Cassin, Barbara. Ed. *Vocabulaire européen des philosophes. Dictionnaire des intraduisibles*. Paris : Seuil / Le Robert, 2004.
Davidson, Donald. « On the Very Idea of a Conceptual Scheme. » *Proceedings and Addresses of the American Philosophical Association* 47 (1973–1974) : 5–20.

---

5 A rebours de la thèse de « l'égale validité » avancée par nombre de constructivistes (voir la critique de cette thèse par Boghossian 2006, 155–156), je pense comme nombre d'épistémologues que ce n'est pas parce qu'il y a différentes manières de construire et de représenter le monde qu'elle se valent toutes.

Dear, Peter. « From Truth to Distinterestedness in the Seventeenth Century. » *Social Studies of Science* 22 (1992) : 619–631.

Defoort, Carine. « Existe-t-il une philosophie chinoise ? Typologie des arguments d'un débat largement implicite ». *Extrême-Orient, Extrême-Occident* 27 (2005) : 67–89.

Duhem, Pierre. *La Théorie physique : son objet, sa structure*. Lyon : Presses de l'ENS, 2016 [1906].

Dumont, Martine. « Le succès mondain d'une fausse science ». *Actes de la recherche en sciences sociales* 54 (1984) : 2–30.

Durkheim, Émile. *Les Règles de la méthode sociologique*. Paris : Presses universitaires de France, 1986 [1895].

Engel, Pascal. « La philosophie peut-elle échapper à l'histoire ? » *Passés recomposés. Champs et chantiers de l'histoire*. Ed. Jean Boutier et Dominique Julia. Paris : Autrement, 1995. 96–111.

Feng, Youlan. *A History of Chinese Philosophy*. Princeton : Princeton University Press, 1983.

Feyerabend, Paul. *Against Method : Outline of an Anarchistic Theory of Knowledge*. London : New Left Books, 1975.

Foucault, Michel. *Les Mots et les choses*. Paris : Gallimard, 1966.

———. *L'Archéologie du savoir*. Paris : Gallimard, 1968.

Geertz, Clifford. « Anti Anti-Relativism. » *Relativism. A Contemporary Anthology*. Ed. Michael Krausz. New York : Columbia University Press, 2010. 371–392.

Goodman, Nelson. *Manières de faire des mondes*. Trad. M.-D. Popelard. Paris : Gallimard, 2007.

Jeanpierre, Laurent. « Une opposition structurante pour l'anthropologie structurale : Lévi-Strauss contre Gurvitch, la guerre de deux exilés français aux États-Unis ». *Revue d'Histoire des Sciences Humaines* 11.2 (2004) : 13–44.

Kuhn, Thomas. *The Structure of Scientific Revolutions*. Chicago: The University of Chicago Press, 1962.

Lévi-Strauss, Claude. *Race et histoire*. Paris : Gallimard « Folio Essais », 1987.

———. *Le Totémisme aujourd'hui*. Paris : Presses universitaires de France, 1962.

Livingstone, David. *Putting Science in Its Place : Geographies of Scientific Knowledge*. Chicago : University of Chicago Press, 2003.

Lloyd, G.E.R. *Disciplines in the Making*. Oxford : Oxford University Press, 2009.

Loyer, Emmanuelle. *Lévi-Strauss*. Paris : Flammarion, 2015.

Mankiewicz, Richard. *The Story of Mathematics*. Princeton : Princeton University Press, 2004 [2001].

Park, Peter K. J. *Africa, Asia, and the History of Philosophy : Racism in the Formation of the Philosophical Canon, 1780–1830*. Albany : State University of New York Press, 2014.

Popper, Karl. *Conjectures and Refutations : The Growth of Scientific Knowledge*. New York : Basic Books, 1962.

Poskett, James. *Copernic et Newton n'étaient pas seuls. Ce que la science moderne doit aux sociétés non européennes*. Trad. Charles Frankel. Paris : Seuil, 2022.

Putnam, Hilary. « On historicism. » *Realism and Reason. Philosophical Papers*, t. 3. Cambridge : Cambridge University Press, 2002. 287–308.

Quine, William Orman. « Two dogmas of empiricism. » *The Philosophical Review* 60 (1951) : 20–43.

———. « On the Reason for Indeterminacy of Translation. » *Journal of Philosophy* 67.6 (1970) : 178–183.

———. « Les deux dogmes de l'empirisme ». *De Vienne à Cambridge*. Trad. Pierre Jacob. Ed. Pierre Jacob. Paris : Gallimard, 1980, 93–120.

Raj, Kapil. *Relocating Modern Science : Circulation and the Construction of Knowledge in South Asia and Europe, 1650–1900*. Basingstoke, New York : Palgrave Macmillan, 2007.

———. « History of science and intellectual history ». *The Routledge Handbook to the History and Sociology of ideas*. Ed. Sefanos Geroulanos et Gisèle Sapiro. London : Routledge, sous presse.

Reynaud-Paligot, Carole. *La République raciale (1860–1930). Paradigme social et idéologie républicaine, 1860–1930*. Paris : Presses universitaires de France, 2006.
Saïd, Edward. *Orientalism*. London : Routledge & Kegan Paul, 1978.
Sapiro, Gisèle. « Défense et illustration de 'l'honnête homme'. Les hommes de lettres contre la sociologie ». *Actes de la recherche en sciences sociales* 153.3 (2004a) : 11–27.
———. « Une liberté contrainte. La formation de la théorie de l'*habitus* », suivi d'un entretien avec Pierre Bourdieu. *Pierre Bourdieu, sociologue*. Ed. Louis Pinto, Gisèle Sapiro et Patrick Champagne. Paris : Fayard, 2004b, 49–91.
Wacquant, Loïc. *The Invention of the 'Underclass' : A Study in the Politics of Knowledge*. Cambridge : Polity Press, 2022.
Withers, Charles W. *Placing the Enlightenment : Thinking Geographically about the Age of Reason*. Chicago : University of Chicago Press, 2007.
Zald, Meyer. « Progress and Cumulation in the Human Sciences after the Fall. » *Sociological Forum* 10.3 (1995) : 455–479.

Part II: **Narrative (and) World Production**

Deuxième partie : **La fabrique narrative du monde**

Christopher M. Hutton
From Acoustic Space to the Global Village: Linearity and the Western Intellectual Imagination

Abstract: Linearity is a key organising concept in modern Western thought. It is central to Saussure's *Cours de linguistique générale* (1972 [1916]), and to intellectual debates concerning the relation of writing to speech. In the background to the *Cours*, an ongoing revolt against linear notions of time and space was taking place. This foregrounding of the non-linear was characteristic of modernist art and literature, as well as science, in particular mathematics and physics. The critique of linearity defined French poststructuralism of the 1960s and 1970s, and has been integral to feminist, anti-modern, anti-universalist, as well as postcolonial, interventions. Marshall McLuhan identified in writing, and in particular printing, a powerfully deterministic reductionism; more radical critics saw the introduction/imposition of writing and printing as destructive of many non-western cultural ecologies. It is proposed that non-linearity be seen as a minor universal, and linearity as a form of order created out of it.

Keywords: linearity, writing versus speech, modernism, poststructuralism, postcolonialism, Marshall McLuhan

1 Introduction

This chapter reviews the concept of linearity as set out in Saussure's *Cours de linguistique générale* (1972 [1916]). The discussion then surveys the pervasive intellectual attacks on linearity which became fashionable towards the end of the nineteenth century, and which, in the twentieth century, characterised the *avant garde*, much of artistic and literary modernism, post-WWII counter-culture, and postmodernism. Linearity refers to *sequence* in space or time. An utterance can be thought of as a sequence of spoken words, just as in writing there is a sequential order that leads from the beginning of a sentence (paragraph, page, or book) to the end. Linear reasoning follows a line from premise to conclusion (for example, the syllogism). Effect

Note: My thanks go to Adam Jaworski, David Karlander, Don Kulick, Markus Messling, and Adrian Pablé for helpful discussion and suggestions.

follows cause. The passage of time is a line or arrow leading from the past through the present into the future. For its critics, linearity is associated with the oppressive features of Enlightenment modernity, as symbolised by the universalist ideal of the straight line. Linearity stands for the colonisation of human consciousness and the lifeworld by regimented temporal and spatial organisation, and the destruction of non-linear human social orders and ecological systems.

2 Linearity in Saussure

The *Cours* made the linear character of the signifier the second fundamental principle of the study of language, the first being the arbitrary nature of the sign. Linearity followed directly from the oral character of spoken language (1972 [1916], 103): "Le signifiant, étant de nature auditive, se déroule dans le temps seul et a les caractères qu'il emprunte au temps: a) il représente une étendue, et b) cette étendue est mesurable dans une seule dimension: c'est une ligne." In contrast to visual signs, e.g., nautical signaling systems, where more than one dimension might be exploited at the same time, speech was purely linear (1972 [1916], 145), "leurs éléments se présentent l'un après l'autre; ils forment une chaîne. Ce caractère apparaît dès qu'on les représente par l'écriture et qu'on substitut la ligne spatiale des signes graphiques à la succession dans le temps." Speech was continuous and undifferentiated (1972 [1916], 145): "Considérée en elle-même, elle n'est qu'une ligne, un ruban continu, ou l'oreille ne perçoit aucune division suffisante et précise; pour cela il faut faire appel aux significations". In listening to an unfamiliar language, there was no way of dividing the "ruban amorphe" of sound into discrete units.

Yet, for Saussure, the primacy of speech notwithstanding, writing was key to knowing and grasping language (1972 [1916], 44): "Ainsi, bien que l'écriture soit en elle-même étrangère au système interne, il est impossible de faire abstraction d'un procédé par lequel la langue est sans cesse figure; il est nécessaire d'en connaître l'utilité, les défauts et les dangers". This was the case, even though studying writing in order to understand language was akin to scrutinising the photograph rather than the actual face of the person one wanted to know (1972 [1916], 45). While writing offered a potential trap, it was also indispensable (1972 [1916], 55): "Quand on supprime l'écriture par la pensée, celui qu'on prive de cette image sensible risqué de ne plus apercevoir qu'une masse informe dont il ne sait que faire. C'est comme si l'on retirait à l'apprenti nageur sa ceinture de liège". Given this, the link between word and written image was much more easily grasped than the link between word and sound. The visual was more powerful (1972 [1916], 46):

"l'écriture voile la vue de la langue: elle n'est pas un vêtement, mais un travestissement" (1972 [1916], 51–52). But this link to sound was "le lien naturel, le seul véritable, celui du son" (1972 [1916], 46). Chinese writing was ideographic, and therefore did not mislead in the same way as alphabetic script (1972 [1916], 48).

While arbitrariness is the property of relationships established by the system (*langue*), temporal sequence is a property of speech (*parole*). There is no succession or sequence in *langue*: "denn in der *langue* gibt es keine Sukzessivität, sondern nur Simultaneität (was eine hierarchische Ordnung nicht ausschließt" (Wunderli 1972, 228 fn).[1] The Saussurean sign is somehow required to be both atemporal and temporal (Hutton 1990). *Langue* is a closed or, rather, semi-closed system, in that it reorganises in a non-teleological process under stimulation from *parole*. Self-organising systems cannot be linear, by definition. Unlike land, where value reflects potential income, and therefore its value has some kind of natural basis, linguistic values cannot be traced through time and are not anchored in the world of things (Saussure 1972 [1916], 116–117). This model places all languages (*langues*) on the same level as autonomous, autopoietic structures.

The *Cours* gives priority to the temporal (sound sequence) over the spatial (visual arrangement). Vandendorpe echoes this priority:

> La linéarité se dit d'une série d'éléments qui se suivent dans un ordre intangible ou préétabli. Parfaitement exemplifiée par la succession des heures et des jours, elle relève essentiellement de l'ordre et du temps, mais s'applique aussi à un espace réduit aux points d'une droite (1999, 41).

Chandler counters (2007, 110): "Reversing Saussure's priorities, we will begin with spatial rather than temporal relations." Attacks on the concept of linearity frequently reflect distrust of the manner in which writing, in particular alphabetic writing, represents, or distorts, speech. One response to the *Cours* therefore is to argue that it fell victim to the very pathology which it warned against, namely the tyranny of the alphabet (Harris 1987, 69–78). If this is correct, it would imply that the universalism of the Saussurean model is illusory, given that the representation of speech offered there is mediated through the affordances of alphabetic writing.

A further way in which linearity is attributed to the *Cours* is in relation to the "circuit de la parole" (1972 [1916], 26–27). For many commentators, this represents a one-dimensional, highly reductionist, model of communication, with the linguistic system as "the conduit through which 'meanings' are transmitted from 'speaker' to 'hearer'" (Blommaert 2014, 2). This model is perceived as linear because it suggests

---

[1] "In *langue* there is no succession, but only simultaneity (which does not preclude a hierarchical ordering)."

direct transmission. Harris (1987, 163–174) characterises this as a "telementational" theory of communication. In media studies this is sometimes referred to as a "transportation model" (see E. McLuhan 2008).

3 The late-nineteenth century intellectual context

Saussure's foregrounding of linearity stands in dramatic contrast to the late nineteenth century attack on linear modes of representation in artistic and literary modernism. Developments in non-Euclidian geometry and physics had raised complex questions about straight lines in space and time (Henderson 2013, 101–103). These debates were part of the intellectual public sphere, with mathematicians like Henri Poincaré having an impact in the visual arts: "Poincaré offered a conception of space as a joint experience of visual and tactile space, which intrigued pictorial artists, and even writers" (Botz-Bornstein 2021, 135). Poincaré's *Méthode nouvelles de la mécanique celeste* (1892) was an important landmark in the development of chaos theory, which in popularised form was to have extensive ramifications in the humanities and social sciences (see for example Manzoor 2003; Yesilorman 2017). The popular science notion of a fourth dimension was a hot topic in theosophy, Occultism, *avant garde* art, and modernist literature, and was debated in periodicals such as *Revue philosophique* and the *Revue de Métaphysique et de Morale* (Henderson 2013). Esprit Jouffret's *Traité élémentaire de géométrie à quatre dimensions* (1903) had an impact on Cubist practice (Henderson 2013, 22, 126). Atonality in musical composition reflected a desire to break with linearity: "the quintessential expression of linearity is the tonal system" (Kramer 1981). Literary modes such as stream of consciousness, as exemplified in Édouard Dujardin's *Les lauriers sont coupés* (2001 [1888]), sought to capture the associative nature of thinking, as did the psychologist William James in his famous image of the "river" or "stream" of thought: "Consciousness [. . .] does not appear to itself chopped in bits" (1890, 239). More radically, the symbolist movement rejected both linear forms and unitary consciousness. Stéphane Mallarmé's *Le Livre,* while not published until 1957 (Scherer 1957), reflects an intellectual scene which sees the break with linearity and the unitary self as the key to renewing and revitalising literary form (Benoit 1993). Experiment with typographical arrangement blurred the boundary between the linguistic and the pictorial, notably in Guillaume Apollinaire's *Calligrammes* (1918) (Shingler 2011). Given this search for renewal and vital forms, there are extensive links between the *avant garde* and fascism (Adamson 2001), as in Filippo Tommaso Marinetti's anti-linear *Distruzione della sintassi: immaginazione senza fili; parole in libertà* (1998 [1913]).[2]

The modernist break with linearity and a unified point of view is exemplified in Virginia Woolf's story *Kew Garden*, first published 1919 (Woolf 1921). The celebration of the non-linear, associative consciousness is fundamental to James Joyce's *Ulysses* (1922). In *Finnegan's Wake* (1939), the rejection of linearity is pushed close to the point of simultaneity as nonsense, with dense punning, word-association, and etymological games. At the macro-level, *Finnegan's Wake* foregrounds cycles of history over linear time and plot, drawing, it has been argued, on Giambattista Vico's *Principj di Scienza Nuova* (New Science), first published in 1725 (Verene 1987). This turn to ideas of contingency and flux constituted for Wyndham Lewis a "mystical time-cult" (1927, I, 3). Lewis associated this cult in particular with Henri Bergson's "Time-view, the flux" (1927, I, 3). Einsteinian relativity and quantum mechanics had been popularised, and these theories were now treated as being of general philosophical and political significance (Lewis 1927, I, 12–14). This elevation of "intuitive, instinctual world of interpenetration and constant flux" led to forms of relativism and the shattering of "the order and stability associated with space by seeing everything as time and motion" (Campbell 1983, 362, 351).

One way to frustrate linearity in artistic production was to inject chance and spontaneity into the creative process, thereby breaking the causal linear link between the artistic intention and the product. Tristan Tzara's "Pour faire un poème dadaïste" (1920 [1916]) describes a cut-up procedure (*découpé*) for rearranging the words of a text at random. The artist Joseph Cornell cut up, rearranged, and reduced George Melford's feature film, *East of Borneo* (1931), adding new scenes, projecting it at a slower speed and through blue glass. In creating the experimental film *Rose Hobart* (1936), Cornell "eliminated any obligation to the linear time and causality, the straight story, of Melford's film" (Hammond 2000, 18). According to Charles Sirató's *Manifeste Dimensioniste* (1936), literature was now obliged to escape the constraints of the line: "sotrir [sic] de la ligne et à passer dans le plan". Gertrude Stein's *Ida* (1941) sought to undermine linear ways of reading and thinking: "Without temporality, Ida's oppositional discourse becomes "spatial" and therefore frustrates the readerly desire for linearity, order, and sense" (Murphy 2001, 5).

---

2 'Destruction of syntax–imagination without strings –words in-freedom'.

4 Post-war intellectuals and linearity

The critique of Saussurean linearity defined the French intellectual scene of the 1960s and 1970s, identifying its uncanny non-linear opposite in Saussure's obsession with anagrams (Lacan 1957, 1966; Starobinski 1964; Testenoire 2012). As Joseph (2012, 488) puts it, there seemed to be two Saussures, one "who insisted by day on the linearity of linguistic signs" and another who "by night sat in his study obsessed with signs broken up and arranged in non-linear order." In poststructuralism, the text became a dynamic object without a unitary, agentive author (Barthes 1968), set in an intertextual field of relations with other texts. One key influence was Mikhail Bakhtin, whose work was first promoted in France by Julia Kristeva (Kristeva 1967, 1969). A text was "un appareil translinguistique qui redistribue l'ordre de la langue, en mettant en relation une parole communicative visant l'information directe, avec différents types d'énoncés antérieurs ou synchroniques" (Kristeva 1968, 103). In Kristeva's *La Révolution du langage poétique*, a study of Mallarmé, the *chora* can be equated with non-linearity, in that it describes "une articulation toute provisoire, essentiellement mobile, constituée de mouvements et de leurs stases éphémères" (Kristeva 1974, 23). In revolutionary poetic language there is a struggle between deep rhythm and linearity:

> Toute la rythmique dont nous avons parlé plus haut est un combat contre la linéarité syntaxique à travers, avec et dans sa nécessité inévitable. La mélodie, les intonations, les scansions de phrases obtenues par des inversions, visent à découper cette linéarité, à la varier à l'intérieur de ses propres limites (Kristeva 1974, 270).

Feminist theorists of the period shared a common rejection of linear modes (Irigaray 1977). Derrida's *De la grammatologie* included a sustained engagement with Saussurean linearity, drawing on the work of André Leroi-Gourhan (see Mainberger 2019, 400). Linearity is characterised by the unsustainable repression of an underlying pluri-dimensionality:

> La ligne ne représente qu'un modèle particulier, quel que soit son privilège. Ce modèle est devenu modèle et il reste, en tant que modèle, inaccessible. Si l'on tient pour acquis que la linéarité du langage ne va pas sans ce concept vulgaire et mondain de la temporalité (homogène, dominée par la forme du maintenant et l'idéal du mouvement continu, droit ou circulaire) dont Heidegger montre qu'il détermine de l'intérieur toute l'ontologie, d'Aristote à Hegel, la méditation de l'écriture et la déconstruction de l'histoire de la philosophie deviennent inséparables (Derrida 1967, 128).

For Baudrillard, linearity was at odds with the complex simultaneities and affective density of the human mind, and offered an impoverished view of time, space, and in particular history:

> Dans l'espace euclidien de l'histoire, le chemin le plus rapide d'un point à un autre est la ligne droite, celle du Progrès et de la Démocratie. Mais ceci ne vaut que pour l'espace linéaire des Lumières. Dans le nôtre, l'espace non euclidien de la fin du siècle, une courbure maléfique détourne invinciblement toutes les trajectoires. Liée sans doute à la sphéricité du temps (visible à l'horizon de la fin du siècle comme celle de la terre à l'horizon de fin de journée) ou à la subtile distorsion du champ de gravité (Baudrillard 1992, 25–26).

Textual difficulty or obscurity was celebrated as a stimulus to non-linear reading and re-reading practices. Discussing Rimbaud's prose poem "Promontoire", Michael Riffaterre (1982, 632) concluded: "L'obscurité n'est donc pas simplement une difficulté, voire une impasse. C'est un passage initiatique, c'est le moyen d'un exercice verbal qui consiste pour le lecteur à se soumettre à une autre discipline que celle de la linéarité. L'obscurité est donc de nature figurale. L'obscurité est un trope". A work such as *Mille plateaux* (Deleuze and Guattari 1980) – to put it at its simplest – seeks to perform an even more radical step away from Saussurean linearity, most obviously with concepts such as *agencement* and *rhizome*. Much the same could be said of the entire post-modern pantheon (Landow 1994, 25).

One can trace these ideas down through the twentieth century and beyond, across a wide range of contexts and genres. William Burroughs reanimated the *avant garde* technique of cut-up in producing novels such as *The Soft Machine* (1961). Cran (2013, 308) argues that these texts are a form of collage, and that the reader should "disregard expectations of verbal linearity and plot and view the page as a sequence of images." As Timothy Leary put it: "Books are too static, outdated, linear" (cited in Perry 1991). Experimentation with LSD was intended to expand consciousness beyond the confines of linearity. This dovetailed with the new electronic age:

> The generation gap is a species mutation. Electronics and psychedelics have shattered the sequence of orderly linear identification, the automatic imitation that provides racial and social continuity. The kids today just won't grow up to be like their parents. They are pulsating television grids. They move consciousness around by switching channel knobs. Tune in. Tune out. Flick on. Correct image focus. Adjust brightness (Leary 1968, 162).

Linear time was associated with western modernity and a destructive teleology that sought dominance over the natural world (Meyer 1967). Ingold describes how the straight line has been misleadingly identified with artificiality, describing "a powerful impulse in modern thought to equate the march of progress, whether of culture or civilisation, with the increasing domination of an unruly – and therefore non-linear – nature" (2007, 155). The esoteric philosopher Raymond Abellio juxtaposed the impoverished linearity of language with the spherical nature of reality: "Parler de l'émergence de la conscience transcendantale et de la transformation de la linéarité en sphéricité est une seule et même chose" (Abellio 1965,

92; see Faivre 1996). In similar vein, Alan Watts, the populariser of Zen Buddhism, argued that "the linear one-at-a-time character of speech" was at odds with life itself "which does not proceed in this cumbersome, linear fashion" (2011 [1957], 8).

5 The Toronto School and linearity

One sustained challenge to linear modalities came from the Toronto School of communication studies. This diverse grouping of scholars included Harold Innes, Marshall McLuhan, George Grant, Edmund Carpenter, Dorothy Lee, Walter J. Ong, and Robert K. Logan. To this list one should add the historian of art and architecture Sigfried Giedion, and the British classicist Eric Havelock, who was professor at the University of Toronto from 1929 to 1947. One feature of this school was an emphasis on modalities of interconnection, technologies of communication, and pathways of economic and cultural exchange (Innis 1950). Havelock argued that the invention of alphabetic writing in ancient Greece was the key technological innovation that led to the rise of the West. Printing was a further, more abstract, stage in the development of linear modes of organisation. The affordances of alphabetic writing represented a profound leap forward in human development, enabling new forms of societal organisation, revolutionising cognition, extending individual and collective memory, and allowing sequential reasoning and abstract normative thinking as found in logic and law (Havelock 1982, 1986). Put simply, "the alphabet creates the environmental conditions under which abstract theoretical science flourishes" (Logan 1986, 54). However others noted a balance of loss and gains (Ong 2002 [1982]). There was anxiety about the effects of technological modernity, in particular the saturation of modern media (Grant 1969; Postman 1992). Technology and mechanisation were threatening to alienate humanity from the authentic grounds of its being (Giedion 1948). Taylorism and the Fordist production-line were symptoms of the linearity of industrial civilisation (Maier 1970). Some off-shoots of the Toronto school found in alphabetic writing the source of the destructive impact of Western modernity on non-Western cultures (Abram 1997). Shlain (1988) argued that the rise of patriarchy reflected the impact of alphabetic writing and literacy. It had led to the domination of the brain's left hemisphere, which was linear, abstract, masculine, over the holistic, iconic, feminine right.

Reflecting a common trope, the anthropologist-linguist Dorothy Lee saw the lineal versus non-lineal as the key to the Western/non-Western binary (1960, 140): "In our own culture, the line is so basic that we take it for granted, as given in reality. We see it in visible nature, between material points, and we see it between metaphorical points such as days or acts." The Trobriand islanders by contrast "do not describe their activity lineally; they do no dynamic relating of acts; they do not use even so innocuous a connective as *and*" (1960, 144). While their activities are patterned, "the Trobrianders do not act on an assumption of lineality at any level" (1960, 454). Benjamin Lee Whorf argued that the Hopi had no notion of linear time:

> I find it gratuitous to assume that a Hopi who knows only the Hopi language and the cultural ideas of his own society has the same notions, often supposed to be intuitions, of time and space as we have, and that are generally assumed to be universal. In particular he has no notion or intuition of time as a smooth flowing continuum in which everything in the universe proceeds at an equal rate, out of a future into a present and into a past (Whorf 1956, 57).

The Hopi understanding of time was closer to the reality of the universe in flux, that is, the picture presented by modern physics, than the static, abstract (Aristotelian) categories reflected in the structure of European languages (Rollins 1972).

At the centre of these debates was Marshall McLuhan. McLuhan is best known for the slogan "the medium is the message" (McLuhan 1964, 7) and the term *global village*. Fundamental to his understanding of media was the notion that technology including speech and writing, functions as an *extension* of the human nervous system (McLuhan 1964).[3] Speech was a technology or medium, just like writing, albeit the most fundamental one (Carpenter and McLuhan 1956, 46): "English is a mass medium. All languages are mass media. The new mass media – film, radio, television – are new languages, their grammars as yet unknown." Communication was not a matter of transporting ideas from sender to receiver, but rather of transformation (E. McLuhan 2008, 31–32). The natural/artificial distinction was of no relevance, given that speech represented the most fundamental extension of man. Speech was not linear, since it was a process of continuous reaction "even to our own act of speaking." By contrast writing "tends to be a kind of separate or specialist action within which there is little opportunity or call for reaction" (McLuhan 1964, 79). Speech then is a technology, which in extending the self also can be said to alienate that self. McLuhan referenced Henri Bergson, who believed "that language is a human technology that has impaired and diminished the values of the collective unconscious." It was the extension of speech "that enables the intellect to detach itself from the vastly wider reality" and in effect alienates by abstraction or reflexivity. For Bergson, as explained by McLuhan (1964, 79): "Language extends and amplifies man but it also divides his faculties. His collective consciousness or

---

[3] Similar ideas can be found in Kapp (1877), Merleau-Ponty's *Phénoménologie de la perception* (1945, 167), and Bateson (1960, 481). Contemporary notions of extended, embodied, distributed, and enacted mind reflect ecological, anti-linear models of human consciousness (see Noë 2009).

intuitive awareness is diminished by this technical extension of consciousness that is speech." With each successive technology of communication, this self-alienation increases.[4]

McLuhan offered an analogy between rows of letters and teeth (1964, 83): "Teeth are emphatically visual in their lineal order. Letters are not only like teeth visually, but their power to put teeth into the business of empire-building is manifest in our Western history." The phonetic alphabet set up an arbitrary set of pairings, in that it was the only one in which "semantically meaningless letters are used to correspond to semantically meaningless sounds". This represented a parallelism between the visual and the auditory which was "both crude and ruthless, culturally speaking". Hieroglyphs and the Chinese character were culturally richer, but they could not facilitate "the transfer from the magically discontinuous world of the tribal word into the cool and uniform visual medium" (McLuhan 1964, 83). This breach between visual and auditory experience gave "its user an eye for an ear" and freed "from the tribal trance or resonating word magic and the web of kinship" (McLuhan 1964, 84). The Chinese character was "an inclusive *gestalt*, not an analytic dissociation of senses and functions like phonetic writing" (McLuhan 1964, 84). Notions of cause and effect, and logical reasoning, were derived from the sequence represented by the alphabet, as was the assembly-line: "Only alphabetic cultures have ever mastered connective lineal sequences as pervasive forms of psychic and social organization" (McLuhan 1964, 85). The reduction of experience to "discrete units" enables forms of industrial and military control; it allows for acting without reacting, and underlies "the endless succession of blunders achieved by visual and civilized Americans when confronted with the tribal and civilized cultures of the East" (McLuhan 1964, 86). In terms of writing praxis, McLuhan's so-called *mosaic style*, which used short sections, discontinuity, and arbitrary sequencing, performed a form of non-linearity (McLuhan 1951). John Cage's *A Year from Monday* (1967, 3) also used the term "mosaic". *The Medium Is the Massage* (McLuhan and Fiore 1967) employed montage of text and image. The designer Quentin Fiore likewise collaborated on Buckminster Fuller's *I Seem to be a Verb* (1970). For McLuhan, "the personal and social consequences of any medium – that is, of any extension of ourselves – result from the new scale that is introduced into our affairs by each extension of ourselves or by any new technology" (1964, 7). Given that the direction of technological change cannot be changed (because we grasp it too late to act upon it), McLuhan's stance became one of ironic detachment: "I accept media as I accept cosmos" (cited in Stearn 1967, 272).

---

4 There are echoes here of Lucien Lévy-Bruhl's notion of *participation mystique* (1910).

McLuhan's notion of *acoustic* or *auditory space* offers an exact counterpoint to Saussurean arbitrariness and linearity. A purely acoustic space was "the space evoked by the spoken word in a pre-literate world" (McLuhan 1956, 16). Once writing was introduced, it alienated the word from its object, that is, it introduced the arbitrary nature of the sign: "The complex harmonic structure of the word can never be a sign or reference before writing. It evokes the thing itself in all its particularity. Only after this acoustic magic has been enclosed in the fixed written form can it become a sign" (McLuhan 1956, 16). Auditory space (an alternative label) is not enclosed in determinate lines, and has no middle, and no edge:

> Auditory space has no favoured focus. It's a sphere without fixed boundaries, space made by the thing itself, not space containing the thing. It is not pictorial space, boxed-in, but dynamic, always in flux, creating its own dimensions moment by moment. It has no fixed boundaries; it is indifferent to background (Carpenter 1973, 35).

The centre is everywhere, and the periphery is nowhere. There is an evident analogy here with notions of God in Christian mysticism (Findlay-White and Logan 2016). The electronic age, while increasingly joined in a global village of instant decentred communication and non-linear hypertext, was also analogous to a vast acoustic space. Yet this new electronic quasi-aurality/orality, as McLuhan foresaw, would not lead to a new mystical integration of self, world, and word (interview in Stearn 1970, 272–273): "The more you create village conditions, the more discontinuity and division and diversity" (on this point, see Flusser 1988 and Guldin 2008). The global village ensures that there will be "maximum disagreement on all points". It is characterised by "spite and envy" rather than "uniformity and tranquility". This village is not a harmonious place: "The tribal-global village is far more divisive – full of fighting – than any nationalism ever was. Village is fission, not fusion, in depth. [. . .] I don't *approve* of the global village; I say we live in it." In response to information overload, humanity "resorts to myth", as a conceptual short-cut: "Myth is inclusive, time-saving, and fast." McLuhan's dystopian global village puts a pessimistic gloss on the idea that the escape from linearity is the key to a more balanced and ecologically sustainable world order. Yet there remains a latent mysticism in McLuhan's thinking, represented by his affinity for Pierre Teilhard de Chardin's concept of *noosphere* (Krüger 2007).

6 Conclusion: The end of the line?

The physicist Steven Weinberg, discussing Sokal's (1996) hoax on postmodernism, noted that "for some postmodern intellectuals, 'linear' has come to mean unimaginative and old-fashioned, while 'nonlinear' is understood to be somehow perceptive and avant garde" (Weinberg 1996, 12). Richardson (2000, 685) questions the frequent assumption that the linear novel is "by its very nature conservative or reactionary", and that narrative techniques are "in themselves progressive or liberatory". For the anthropologist Tim Ingold this raises an obvious question (2007, 2): "Why does the very mention of the word 'line' or 'linearity', for many contemporary thinkers, conjure up an image of the alleged narrow-mindedness and sterility, as well as the single-track logic, of modern analytic thought?" There is in any case no clearly identifiable proponent of linearity. Saussure is the most obvious candidate. Yet the *Cours* arguably denies linearity at one level, the level of *langue*, whilst affirming its centrality at another, *parole*. Taken as a whole, there is neither structure nor linearity in language: "Le tout global du langage est inconnaissable, parce qu'il n'est pas homogène" (1972 [1916], 38). For all that, the political or ideological question raised by the *Cours* lies in its universalism and its adoption of epistemic reductionism expressed as methodological homogeneity (see Connell 2020, 40). Saussure did not invent this reductionist frame, which has deep roots in the Western tradition, but rather sought to theorise it. Dorothy Lee for example was not advocating epistemological relativism (1960, 136): "My own position is that there is an absolute reality, and that communication is possible." Given the latent universalism and methodological homogeneity of linguistic analysis, difference in worldview is recuperable at the level of linguistic analysis. This reductionism emerges most clearly if we look at the study of non-European languages in the colonial context. Colonial linguistics had a dramatic impact on pre-existing linguistic ecologies, leading to "the construction of languages within a universalizing/totalizing colonial framework" (Makoni 2013, 87).

In parallel to this, colonialism (and subsequently, globalisation) brought with it the imposition of an alien concept of time (Mbiti 1970, 21): "The linear concept of time in western thought, with an indefinite past, present and infinite future, is practically foreign to African thinking." For Edouard Glissant, this represented a violent breach: "Il n'y a pas de linéarité temporelle dans la mémoire historique du colonisé mais une espèce de chaos dans lequel il tombe et roule; 'nous dévalons les roches du temps'" (cited in Artières 2003, 5). In Glissant's aesthetic, "[t]he reassertion of space is also a resistance to linear time"; it involves "juxtaposition, non-linearity, polyphony" (Coates 2001, 12, 13). As explained by Messling (2017), Glissant in his *Philosophie de la Relation* (2009) rejects the totalisation of "continental thinking" in favour of "archipelagic thinking". This seeks "to cope with unpredictability, incompatibility, and non-simultaneity, without intentionally directing the world according to a model, and physically shaping it". In similar vein, Derek Walcott's *Omeros* (1990) appropriated and transformed the epic into a non-linear form.

At one level linearity reflects the ineluctability of closure and death. A linear consciousness is one that is moving towards extinction. Linearity is *Thanatos*, anti-linearity *Eros*; alternatively, it can stand for the Apollonian as opposed to the

Dionysian. The linear/non-linear is one of a set of powerful dichotomies that have shaped modern self-understandings, and within which forms of difference and resistance have been framed. Yet the rejection of linearity organises itself around, and understands itself in relation to, linearity. One approach to the linear/non-linear problematic would be to invert the universal/particular dichotomy. This would mean to begin with non-linearity as the universal, and linearity as the formal exception: "Linear text may be seen as a special case of the non-linear in which the convention is to read word-by-word from beginning to end" (Aarseth 1994, 51). Given this, linearity is best seen as a specific type of order ("figure") created out of, or imposed on, background non-order ("ground"). Non-linearity would be a minor universal, in that there are as many non-linearities as there are linearities.

References

Abellio, Raymond. *La structure absolue*. Gallimard: Paris, 1965.
Adamson, Walter. "Avant-garde modernism and Italian Fascism: cultural politics in the era of Mussolini." *Journal of Modern Italian Studies* 6 (2001): 230–248.
Aarseth, Espen. "Nonlinearity and literary theory." *Hyper/text/theory*. Ed. George Landow. Baltimore: Johns Hopkins University Press, 1994. 51–86.
Artières, Philippe. "Solitaire et solidaire. Entretien avec Edouard Glissant". *Terrain* 41 (2003): 9–14.
Abram, David. *The Spell of the Sensuous: Perception and Language in a More-Than-Human World*. New York: Vintage, 1997.
Apollinaire, Guillaume. *Calligrammes*. Paris: Mercure de France, 1918.
Barthes, Roland. "La mort de l'auteur". *Mantéia* 5 (1968), 12–17.
Bateson, Gregory. "Minimal Requirements for a Theory of Schizophrenia." *AMA Archives General Psychiatry* 2 (1960): 477–491.
Baudrillard, Jean. *L'illusion de la fin ou la grève des événements*. Paris: Galilée, 1992.
Benoit, Eric. "Non-linéarité et discontinuité dans l'élaboration du Livre de Mallarmé". *Modernités* 4 (1993): 81–98.
Blommaert, Jan. "Meaning as non-linear effect: the birth of cool." *Tilburg Papers in Cultural Studies*. Tilburg: Tilburg University, 2014.
Botz-Bornstein, Thorsten. *The Philosophy of Lines*. Cham: Palgrave, 2021
Buckminster Fuller, Richard. *I Seem to Be a Verb: Environment and Man's Future*. New York: Bantam, 1970.
Burroughs, William. *The Soft Machine*. Paris: Olympia Press, 1961.
Cage, John. *A Year from Monday. New Lectures and Writings*. Middletown/CT: Wesleyan University Press, 1967.
Campbell, SueEllen. "Equal opposites: Wyndham Lewis, Henri Bergson, and their philosophies of space and time." *Twentieth Century Literature* 29 (1983): 351–369.
Carpenter, Edmund. *Eskimo Realities*. New York: Holt, 1973.
Carpenter, Edmund and Marshall McLuhan. "The new languages." *Chicago Review* 10 (1956): 46–52.

Chandler, Daniel. *Semiotics: The Basics*. London: Routledge, 2007.
Coates, Nicholas. *Gardens in the Sands: The Notion of Space in Recent Critical Theory and Contemporary Writing from the French Antilles*. Doctoral dissertation, University College, London. 2001. https://discovery.ucl.ac.uk/id/eprint/10108445.
Connell, Raewyn. *Southern Theory: The Global Dynamics of Knowledge in Social Science*. London: Routledge, 2020.
Cran, Rona. "'Everything is permitted': William Burroughs' cut-up novels and European art." *Comparative American Studies: An International Journal* 11 (2013): 300–313.
Deleuze, Gilles and Félix Guattari. *Mille plateaux*. Paris: Minuit, 1980.
Derrida, Jacques. *De la grammatologie*. Paris: Minuit, 1967.
Dujardin, Édouard. *Les lauriers sont coupés*. Paris: Flammarion, 2001. First published in the *Revue Indépendante*, 1888.
Faivre, Antoine. *Accès de l'ésotérisme occidental*, volume 2. Paris: Gallimard, 1996.
Findlay-White, Emma and Robert Logan. "Acoustic space, Marshall McLuhan and links to medieval philosophers and beyond: center everywhere and margin nowhere." *Philosophies* 1 (2016): 162–169.
Flusser, Vilém. *Krise der Linearität*. Bern: Bentel, 1988.
Giedion, Sigfried. *Mechanization Takes Command*. New York: Oxford University Press, 1948.
Glissant, Édouard. *Philosophie de la Relation*. Paris: Gallimard, 2009.
Grant, George. *Technology and Empire: Perspectives on North America*. Toronto: Anansi, 1969.
Guldin, Rainer. "Die zweite Unschuld: Heilsgeschichtliche und eschatologische Perspektiven im Werk Vilém Flussers und Marshall McLuhans." *Flusser Studies* 6 (2008): 1–24.
Hammond, Paul. "Available light." *The Shadow and its Shadow: Surrealist Writings on the Cinema*. Ed. Paul Hammond. San Francisco: City Lights Books, 2000. 1–45.
Harris, Roy. *The Language Machine*. London: Duckworth, 1987.
Havelock, Eric. *The Literate Revolution in Greece and its Cultural Consequences*. Princeton: Princeton University Press, 1982.
———. "The alphabetic mind: a gift of Greece to the modern world." *Oral Tradition* 1 (1986): 134–150.
Henderson, Linda Dalrymple. *The Fourth Dimension and non-Euclidean Geometry in Modern Art*. Revised edition. Cambridge/MA: MIT Press, 2013.
Hutton, Christopher. "Meaning and the principle of linearity." *Language and Communication* 10 (1990): 169–183.
Innis, Harold. *Empire and Communications*. Oxford: Oxford University Press, 1950.
James, William. *The Principles of Psychology*. New York: Henry Holt, 1890.
Joseph, John. *Saussure*. Oxford: Oxford University Press, 2012.
Ingold, Tim. *Lines: A Brief History*. New York: Routledge, 2007.
Irigaray, Luce. *Ce sexe qui n'en est pas un*. Paris: Minuit, 1977.
Jouffret, Esprit. *Traité élémentaire de géométrie à quatre dimensions et introduction à la géométrie à n dimension*. Paris: Gauthier-Villars, 1903.
Joyce, James. *Ulysses*. Paris: Shakespeare & Co., 1922.
———. *Finnegan's Wake*. London: Faber and Faber, 1939.
Kapp, Ernst. *Grundlinien einer Philosophie der Technik*. Braunschweig: Westermann, 1877.
Kramer, Jonathan. "New temporalities in music." *Critical Inquiry* 7 (1981): 539–556.
Kristeva, Julia. "Bakhtine, le mot, le dialogue et le roman". *Critique* 23 (1967): 438–465.
———. "Le texte clos". *Langages* 3 (1968): 103–125.
———. *Séméiôtiké: recherches pour une sémanalyse*. Paris: Seuil, 1969.

———. *La Révolution du langage poétique. L'avant-garde à la fin du XIXᵉ siècle: Lautréamont et Mallarmé*. Paris: Seuil, 1974.
Krüger, Oliver. "Gaia, God, and the internet: the history of evolution and the utopia of community in media society." *Numen* 54 (2007): 138–173.
Lacan, Jacques. "L'instance de la lettre dans l'inconscient ou la raison depuis Freud". *La Psychanalyse* 3 (1957): 47–81.
———. *Écrits*. Paris: Seuil, 1966.
Landow, George. *Hyper/text/theory*. Baltimore: Johns Hopkins University Press, 1994.
Leary, Timothy. *The Politics of Ecstasy*. Berkeley/California: Ronin, 1968.
Lee, Dorothy. "Lineal and nonlineal codifications of reality." *Explorations in Communication*. Eds. Edmund Carpenter and Marshall McLuhan. Boston: Beacon Press, 1960. 137–141.
Lévy-Bruhl, Lucien. *Les fonctions mentales dans les sociétés inférieures*. Paris: Algan, 1910.
Lewis, Wyndham. *Time and Western Man*. London: Chatto & Windus, 1927.
Logan, Robert. *The Alphabet Effect*. New York: Morrow, 1986.
Maier, Charles. "Between Taylorism and technocracy: European ideologies and the vision of industrial productivity in the 1920s." *Journal of Contemporary History* 5 (1970): 27–61.
Mainberger, Sabine. "Graphism(s)." *The Bonn Handbook of Globality*, volume 1. Eds. Ludger Kühnhardt and Tilman Meyer. Cham: Springer, 2019. 397–408.
Makoni, Sinfree. "An integrationist perspective on colonial linguistics." *Language Sciences* 35 (2013): 87–96.
Manzoor, Shahida. *Chaos Theory and Robert Wilson: A Critical Analysis of Wilson's Visual Arts and Theatrical Performances*. Doctoral dissertation, Ohio University, 2003.
Marinetti, Filippo Tommaso. "Distruzione della sintassi. Immaginazione senza fili. Parole in libertà." *Filippo Tommaso Marinetti, Teoria e invenzione futurista*. Ed. Luciano De Maria. Milano: Mondadori, 1998 [1913]. 65–79.
Mbiti, John S. *African Religions and Philosophy*. New York: Anchor, 1970.
McLuhan, Eric. "Marshall McLuhan's theory of communication: the Yegg." *Global Media Journal* 1 (2008): 25–43.
McLuhan, Marshall. *The Mechanical Bride: Folklore of Industrial Man*. New York: Vanguard, 1951.
———. *Understanding Media: The Extensions of Man*. New York: McGraw-Hill, 1964.
———. *The Medium Is the Massage: An Inventory of Effects*. London: Penguin, 1967.
McLuhan, Marshall and Quentin Fiore. *The Medium is the Massage*. London: Penguin, 1967.
Merleau-Ponty, Maurice. *Phénoménologie de la perception*. Paris: Gallimard, 1945.
Messling, Markus. "Chaos world. Édouard Glissant and the question of universality." *Untie to Tie. On Colonial Legacies and Contemporary Societies*. Exhibition series at ifa Gallery Berlin, 2017; chapter 1: Global Relatedness. https://untietotie.org/en/media-link/chaos-world/ (last accessed, 1 December 2021).
Meyer, Leonard. *Music, the Arts and Ideas*. Chicago: Chicago University Press, 1967.
Murphy, Sean. "'Ida did not go directly anywhere': symbolic peregrinations, desire, and linearity in Gertrude Stein's *Ida*." *Literature and Psychology* 47 (2001): 1–11.
Noë, Alva. *Out of Our Heads*. New York: Hill and Wang, 2009.
Ong, Walter J. *Orality and Literacy: The Technologizing of the Word*. London: Routledge, 2002 [1982].
Perry, Tony. "Voice from the past claims to have a vision for the future." *Los Angeles Times* (October 18, 1991), available at: https://www.latimes.com/archives/la-xpm-1991-10-18-me-475-story.html.
Poincaré, Henri. *Méthodes nouvelles de la mécanique céleste*. Vol. 1. Paris: Grauthier-Viltars, 1892.
Postman, Neil. *Technopoly: The Surrender of Culture to Technology*. New York: Vintage, 1992.

Richardson, Brian. "Linearity and its discontents: rethinking narrative form and ideological valence." *College English* 62 (2000): 685–695.

Riffaterre, Michael. "Sur la sémiotique de l'obscurité en poésie: *Promontoire* de Rimbaud". *French Review* 55 (1982): 625–32.

Rollins, Peter. "The Whorf hypothesis as a critique of western Science and technology." *American Quarterly* 24 (1972): 563–583.

Saussure, Ferdinand de. *Cours de linguistique générale*. Paris: Payot, 1972 [1916].

Scherer, Jacques. *Le "Livre" de Mallarmé. Premières recherches sur les documents inédits*. Paris: Gallimard, 1957.

Shingler, Katherine. "Perceiving text and image in Apollinaire's *Calligrammes*." *Paragraph* (2011): 66–85.

Shlain, Leonard. *The Alphabet Versus the Goddess: The Conflict Between Word and Image*. New York: Vintage, 1988.

Sirató, Charles. "Manifeste Dimensioniste". *La Revue N + 1*. Paris: José Corti, 1936.

Sokal, Alan D. "Transgressing the boundaries – toward a transformative hermeneutics of quantum gravity." *Social Text* 46–47 (1996): 217–252.

Starobinski, J. "Les anagrammes de Ferdinand de Saussure". *Mercure de France* 1204 (1964): 243–262.

Stearn, Gerald. Ed. *McLuhan Hot & Cool*. New York: Signet, 1967.

Stein, Gertrude. *Ida: A Novel*. New York: Random House, 1941.

Testenoire, Pierre-Yves. "La linéarité saussurienne en rétrospection". *Beiträge zur Geschichte der Sprachwissenschaft* 22 (2012): 149–170.

Tzara, Tristan. "Pour faire un poème Dadaiste". *Littérature* 15 (1920 [1916]): 18.

Vandendorpe, Christian. *Du papyrus à l'hypertexte: Essai sur les mutations du texte et de la lecture*. Paris: La découverte, 1999.

Verene, Donald. Ed. *Vico and Joyce*. Albany: SUNY Press, 1987.

Walcott, Derek. *Omeros*. New York: Farrar, Straus & Giroux, 1990.

Watts, Alan. *The Way of Zen*. New York: Vintage, 2011 [1957].

Weinberg, Steven. "Sokal's Hoax." *The New York Review of Books* 43.13 (1996): 11–15.

Whorf, Benjamin Lee. "An American Indian model of the universe." *Language, Thought, and Reality: Selected Writings of Benjamin Lee Whorf*. Ed. J.B. Carroll. Cambridge/MA: MIT Press, 1956. 57–64.

Woolf, Virginia. *Monday or Tuesday*. New York: Harcourt, Brace, 1921.

Wunderli, Peter. "Zur Geltung des Linearitätsprinzips bei Saussure." *Vox Romanica* 31 (1972): 225–252.

Yesilorman, Mehtap. "Chaos theory and modern jurisprudence: an essay on deconstruction of parameters' order and linearity." *Hacettepe Hukuk Fakultesi Dergisi* 7 (2017): 7–32.

Isaac Bazié
Porteurs d'universalité et fictions de l'Afrique-monde

Abstract: The issue of Africa in the world raises diverse and contradictory positions on questions such as racial identification, conflicting memories, and policy-making (slavery, colonisation, globalisation), etc. In this context we witness the publication of literary works with a common denominator: to approach this Africa-World tandem in a critical way. Starting from the criticisms of Western universalism, I present my contribution about universality based on these literary works about Africa and the world. I analyse vulnerable subjects that I call "bearers of universality". These subjects allow us to hear alternative stories of a human community that must define itself on other bases than those erected by universalism.

Keywords: African memory, universality, migrant subjectivity, Black women, colonisation, Rodney Saint-Éloi, Tanella Boni

1 Introduction

Dans un long souffle poétique, une voix de femme, « fille du baobab brûlé », compte ses pas à travers l'histoire et les espaces dont son corps de négresse porte les mémoires accumulées :

> J'ai marché marché j'ai marché / comme une négresse en pays rouge / Ils n'ont pas regardé mes jambes / Le sable blanc a avalé ma soif / J'étais seule sur la route brune / Ils ont dit que j'ai un pacte avec l'exil / J'étais seule et moi-même et mes souliers / L'étoile de la chance disparaissait / Elle n'avait de royaume que le feu / Elle n'avait de géographie que le portage / Elle n'avait de nom que l'oubli de sa présence / Je n'avais de liberté que le cri de l'aigle / / Le chien jaune me montra la route / J'avais une chanson qui m'abandonna / Je n'ai rien qui vaille / Rien que ce morceau de ciel lézardé (Saint-Éloi 2015, 40).

Cette femme qui marche se présente, insistante, avec un énoncé itératif et auto-réflexif qui a donné son titre au recueil : *Je suis la fille du baobab brûlé*. Dans cette scansion de soi qui émaille le poème-trajectoire de Rodney Saint-Éloi se trouve le paradoxe d'un sujet marginal et en même temps universel : femme, négresse sur les chemins du monde (tropicalité afro-caribéenne, nordicité américaine), prise dans un mouvement réticulaire (solaire, lunaire, stellaire), dans un corps poreux au visible et à l'invisible, le tellurique et le céleste, tenant « dans une main le soleil et dans l'autre la terre » (Saint-Éloi 2015, 10). La fille du baobab brûlé est l'incarnation d'un sujet fortement singulier et pourtant intrinsèquement inscrit dans les fondements de l'humain en général, par sa conscience du vaste, très vaste monde, à tel point qu'elle se lise dans une dimension cosmique.

Le baobab, figure d'une Afrique pérenne et résiliente, sage et tenace face au vent de l'harmattan et aux pluies des hivernages jamais assez longs, a enfanté d'une voix de femme en lui léguant une identité marquée par sa propre brûlure. Contrairement à la stable présence de l'arbre millénaire, durablement enraciné là où il voit le jour, la fille est nomade, elle arpente les lieux du monde avec la marque du feu qui consume les identités, elle est un corps, stigmate, et une conscience singulière et humaine, à l'échelle du cosmos ; elle se sait à la jonction de ce particulier et du général : « Je suis l'humanité en détresse et le drapeau / en berne / Dans les yeux des chiens qui n'ont plus la force d'aboyer » (Saint-Éloi 2015, 44).

Ainsi, une conscience poétique se signale, insistante et se dévoile comme une porteuse d'universalité, une humanité qui semble avoir trouvé ses mots et ses images dans le mélange de la stabilité-mobilité d'un sujet minoré au fil du temps – la négresse.

Partant de la conception du lieu originel auquel renvoie le baobab dans les imaginaires, c'est-à-dire l'Afrique, je place le sujet lyrique de Saint-Éloi au début de cette contribution pour penser l'universalité à partir de l'Afrique comme lieu-monde. D'un point de vue théorique, je m'attarderai à appréhender ce qu'est le « lieu-monde » et ses caractéristiques, ses mises en fiction, d'une part. D'autre part, je donnerai l'exemple de sujets « mineurs » dont les expériences et les parcours ont façonné la conscience au point d'en faire les « porteurs » d'une humanité qui doit se redéfinir, à l'image de la fille du baobab brûlé. Ces porteurs d'universalité sont entre autres les migrants dont Patrick Chamoiseau dit qu'ils connaissent « une autre manière de vivre et d'habiter le monde » (Chamoiseau 2017, 117). Les fictions de l'Afrique-Monde que je vais analyser font une cartographie imaginaire d'une universalité dont les porteurs pratiquent les lieux-monde de manière particulière, signalant toujours l'ailleurs dans l'ici et l'imbrication irréversible des histoires. Ils sont des sujets porteurs d'imaginaires et de savoirs alternatifs à la mondialisation/occidentalisation courante et dominante. C'est en cela qu'ils incorporent au sens fort la « production d'une nouvelle universalité » (Messling 2023, 31).

2 L'Afrique, un lieu-monde : baobabs, lieux et sujets errants

La fille du baobab brûlé de Saint-Éloi n'est pas la seule à le tenir de l'arbre millénaire qui localise et enracine les sujets et les mémoires en Afrique, ou les y ramène, même quand ils se retrouvent très loin du continent. Elle a une figure gémellaire qui comme elle, entremêle les empreintes et les appartenances, sans renoncer au lieu qu'est l'Afrique : *Gorée, île baobab* ! (Boni 2004). À l'inverse cependant de la fille du baobab brûlée, qui est déjà sur les chemins du vaste monde, la femme-poète de Gorée est pèlerine de l'île prédiquée, comme la fille errante chez Saint-Éloi, du baobab. Cette dernière a « [. . .] remisé [sa] vie au fond d'une calebasse / [. . .] voyage au gré des ouragans / [sans] certitude géographique / [sans] consolation tellurique / [sans] race ni origine à revendiquer » (Saint-Éloi 2015, 26). Son alter ego chez Boni se rend sur une « île-mémoire » et le baobab avec lequel ce lieu de mémoire est déterminé, joue le même rôle chez l'une que chez l'autre : il convoque un imaginaire tropical, garant des mémoires millénaires, depuis l'Afrique vers le vaste monde, ou du vaste monde vers l'Afrique.

Aussi bien sous la plume de Rodney Saint-Éloi que sous celle de Tanella Boni, ce qui revient dans les déclamations, errances et déprises de ces femmes-poètes, c'est un dénominateur commun qui les renvoie à un arbre, le baobab, et à un lieu et un imaginaire, l'Afrique. Ce lieu devient donc un référent plastique dans la mesure où il est singulier certes, mais extensible aux limites du monde par l'expérience des femmes errantes ou pèlerines qui le portent et l'incarnent. L'Afrique est ce faisant un lieu-monde, pensé par Mbembe comme le point de déploiement de regards historiquement marqués et potentiellement novateurs sur le monde (cf. Mbembe 2013a).

Le monde comme concept a servi à élargir l'entendement dans l'expérience de l'espace en permettant de parler avec Marc Augé par exemple de « Monde-ville » et de « ville-monde » (Augé 1992 ; 2010). Mais c'est chez Patrick Chamoiseau que se retrouve l'usage du concept de lieu-monde tel qu'il peut être considéré comme complément à l'esquisse des contours de ce qu'est l'Afrique-monde, à la suite de Mbembe et Sarr. Chez l'auteur de *Frères migrants*, l'expérience de la traversée crée un univers propre à chaque individu par la fréquentation de lieux qu'il découvre dans la relation :

> Qu'elle soit consciente ou pas, la relation déterritorialise. Elle crée dans nos imaginaires individuels ou collectifs des « Lieux sensibles » qui se superposent aux lieux sensibles du monde. L'expérience du monde que vit chaque individu (son *ingenium*, ainsi que le disent les philosophes) s'accumule en lui, enrichit sa mémoire, lui concrétise un « Lieu-monde » qui n'appartient qu'à lui : un précipité de paysages, de musiques, de danses, d'œuvres,

d'images ou de rencontres . . . qui font matière sensible dans le concret et le virtuel (Chamoiseau 2017, 91–92).

Le lieu-monde de Chamoiseau est le fait d'une sédimentation faite de strates qui se superposent au fur et à mesure des lieux foulés dans la traversée et la relation : c'est un univers intérieur et singulièrement lié à l'expérience de sujets sensibles au contact du monde. L'Afrique comme lieu-monde comprend cette acception intrinsèque du lieu, mais lui associe un autre sens : il n'est pas seulement intérieur et phénoménologique *a priori*, mais physique et mémoriel, historiquement marqué par l'expérience des violences auxquelles renvoient les femmes-poètes de Saint-Éloi et de Boni : esclavage, colonisation, et toutes ces formes de violence énoncées par la parole poétique au féminin. L'Afrique comme lieu-monde est ce continent singulier qui a été le théâtre des violences historiques, là où le monde s'est invité et imposé, avant et pendant que l'Africain cherchait à se connecter à la vastitude. Comme je l'ai démontré ailleurs, elle est un lieu-monde parce qu'elle a en elle l'écho de la vastitude (Bazié 2020, 137) et parce que, comme l'eau qui ne se ramasse plus une fois versée, elle a accueilli les influences venues du monde dont elle ne peut plus se défaire, et qui font d'elle le réceptacle des hybridations forcées, mais aussi le laboratoire des innovations et des expériences imprévisibles.

Le lieu-monde dans ce cas est un lieu ouvert par définition, par la force de l'Histoire. Déjà avant le départ et l'expérience par l'errance chère à Chamoiseau et à Saint-Éloi, l'Afrique en tant que lieu-monde trouve sa généralisation à l'échelle globale par l'empreinte qu'elle porte de l'étranger notamment occidental, sur l'endogène africain, le sceau violent du global sur le local. Il est « monde » avant aussi le caractère cosmopolite que Felwine Sarr identifie dans les « villes-mondes » (si proche de ce qu'en dit Marc Augé[1]) :

> Les lieux cosmopolites, les villes-monde, donnent un aperçu de ce que peut être un monde non compartimenté, pleinement habité par la diversité de ses peuples et la pluralité de ses

---

[1] « L'urbanisation du monde s'inscrit dans cette évolution, ou plutôt elle en est l'expression la plus spectaculaire. Le fait que la vie politique et économique de la planète dépende de centres de décision situés dans les grandes métropoles mondiales, toutes interconnectées et constituant ensemble une sorte de « métacité virtuelle » (Paul Virilio), complète ce tableau. Le monde est comme une immense ville. C'est un monde-ville. Mais il est vrai aussi que chaque grande ville est un monde et même qu'elle est une récapitulation, un résumé du monde, avec sa diversité ethnique, culturelle, religieuse, sociale et économique. Ces frontières ou ces cloisonnements dont nous aurions peut-être parfois tendance à oublier l'existence, au spectacle fascinant de la globalisation, nous les retrouvons, évidents, impitoyablement discriminants, dans le tissu urbain étrangement bariolé et déchiré. C'est à propos de la ville que l'on parle de « quartiers difficiles », de « ghettos », de « pauvreté » et de « sous-développement ». Une grande métropole aujourd'hui accueille et cloisonne toutes les diversités et toutes les inégalités du monde » (Augé 2010, 173).

cultures. Dans ces espaces, on rencontre la multiplicité des individus, des visages de l'humanité, des langues, des saveurs, des manières d'occuper l'espace, des sensibilités et des temporalités. Ces endroits sont ceux de la plus grande créativité humaine (Sarr 2019, 39).

L'Afrique est un lieu cosmopolite, mais mieux encore, un lieu-monde parce qu'elle abrite en substance ce mélange, cette pluralité qui lui est propre, intrinsèque, du fait de sa propre diversité culturelle et linguistique, mais aussi et surtout du fait de ces « peuples et [de] la pluralité de ses cultures [. . .] la multiplicité des individus, des visages de l'humanité, des langues, des saveurs, des manières d'occuper l'espace, des sensibilités et des temporalités » (Sarr 2019, 39). À elle s'appliquent donc toutes les caractéristiques du « lieu cosmopolite » de Sarr, à la seule différence qu'elle n'est pas le fait d'un processus d'urbanisation, mais de cristallisation historique. On pourrait dire que l'Afrique-monde et un lieu cosmopolite qui s'est constitué verticalement, sur l'axe paradigmatique, par l'imposition et le temps, appelant à l'ouverture qui assume les violences historiques venues d'ailleurs ; alors que le lieu cosmopolite de Sarr, à la suite de la Ville-monde d'Augé, se constitue horizontalement, par l'agrégation bigarrée de sujets qui se retrouvent dans le même espace urbain sans partager les mêmes cultures, les mêmes langues et les mêmes arrière-plans. Le lieu-monde a la mémoire longue et sinueuse parce qu'il a été la scène de faits majeurs de l'histoire et le point de départ de sujets projetés durablement dans le vaste monde, mais aussi le lieu de résidence de sujets tout aussi durablement marqués par la présence irréductible du vaste monde dans le proche et l'endogène.

Une des caractéristiques majeures d'un tel lieu-monde est qu'il est marginal dans sa conception primaire, du point de vue de l'Histoire qui l'a choisi pour s'y déployer violemment. L'Afrique dans ce sens fut l'échelle dont l'acquisition confirmait l'universalisme du conquérant, qu'il soit esclavagiste ou colonisateur. Marge nécessaire à l'expression d'une dialectique du centre et de sa périphérie, elle s'est conçue d'un point de vue axiologique à l'extrême opposé des valeurs cardinales qui ont présidé à sa conquête. Paradoxalement, il se trouve par la suite que l'Afrique-monde est grande à l'échelle du monde par cette même présence historique et imposée de l'universel dans son particulier, et par la marginalisation-annexion qui a arrimé son sort à celui du monde, à tout le moins de l'Occident (cf. Mudimbe 1988 et Bazié 2020). On retiendra donc qu'en dépit, et grâce à cet universalisme marginalisant et aliénant, surgit une expérience humaine de la différence assimilée par des sujets minorés mais riches de l'étranger et du soi, de l'exogène et de l'endogène, porteurs d'une humanité acquise par la découverte violente et la lente et résiliente ingérence de la différence qui leur a été imposée : cette humanité-là est universalité. Elle est minorée *per se* du point de vue des idéologies dominantes et des histoires qui l'ont produite dans la violence ; elle est plus grande que l'échelle particularisante (universalisme) qui l'a produite, parce qu'en tant qu'expérience de la violence, elle est portée par des sujets qui désormais sont en connexion avec des sujets qui souffrent, en quelque lieu du monde que ce soit. C'est d'ailleurs pour cette raison que la femme-poète de l'île baobab ressent la douleur de Bagdad :

> Bagdad la résistante de tous les temps / ceux de Gorée ne savent plus pleurer / la mer des horreurs a séché leurs larmes / depuis les siècles des ancêtres / maintenant / ils gardent le silence des abysses / mais s'inclinent jusqu'à terre / devant ta douleur indicible / ceux de Gorée marchent avec toi / et l'île-mémoire honore tes pas / les mains levées vers le ciel / non pas en signe de soumission / mais pour clamer la victoire et la liberté des âmes / contre les chaînes des corps en souffrance (Boni 2004, 99–100).

C'est également avec cette capacité à faire cause humaine avec l'humain qui souffre à l'échelle du monde que la fille du baobab brûlé rêve d'une héritière dont la seule richesse sera les ossements des sans-espoirs :

> J'aurai une fille qui s'appellera Esperancia / Elle balaiera mes os en psalmodiant / Toute mère porte dans ses entrailles / Les convulsions du monde / Elle inventera un miroir aux abeilles / Nous sommes abandonnées / Nous sommes abandonnées / Abandonnées à la joie / Abandonnées à la furie (Saint-Éloi 2015, 65).

Les lieux-mondes comme l'Afrique sont donc le moule de sujets *réellement* marqués par la mondialisation, et par conséquent *potentiellement* à même de sentir le monde, et de faire preuve d'une montée en humanité. Porteurs de mémoires et d'universalité, ces sujets sont l'expression des défis d'un monde qui a pris la standardisation du particulier pour du général (occidentalisation serait ainsi égale à mondialisation) et l'imposition du soi pour le tout (universalisme serait égal à humanité et universalité).

Tanella Boni, Rodney Saint-Éloi, Felwine Sarr, Patrick Chamoiseau tels que convoqués dans cette réflexion, pensent le local et le global et pointent le sujet porteur d'expériences diverses tel qu'il s'incarne dans la figure du migrant, sur le chemin de l'exil et du pèlerinage. Ils sont les victimes de ce que regrette Sarr dans son *Essai de politique relationnelle* :

> Nous faisons encore les frais d'un sentiment d'appartenance étriqué et de processus d'identification aux autres êtres humains limités à ceux que l'on considère comme nos semblables. Une humanité ne se reconnaissant pas encore assez dans sa diversité, sa richesse, sa multiplicité, mais surtout dans son unité fondamentale (Sarr 2019, 33).

Je postule à partir de cette projection de Sarr que le sujet qui saurait vraiment « habiter le monde » est par excellence celui qui est issu d'un lieu-monde comme l'Afrique, et qui saurait traduire le potentiel héritage des dépôts multiples en une conscience qui lui permette de s'enrichir dans l'expérience de la diversité réelle du vaste monde. Le sujet porteur d'universalité, sujet afromondial de mon point de vue, saurait

> [. . .] pleinement habiter les histoires et les cultures de l'humanité : *endosser* [mon emphase] ses multiples visages, se sentir héritier des gisements de sens provenant de ses cultures plurielles. Ne plus être d'une culture particulière, mais *partir* [mon emphase] de celle-ci pour habiter les imaginaires multiples, riches et féconds des langues du monde, de ses mythes, des déclinaisons multiples des opérations de mise en sens que ces imaginaires permettent (Sarr 2019, 34).

« Endosser », « se sentir héritier », et surtout « partir » que je choisis d'entendre ici au sens propre et au sens figuré : tous ces verbes indiquent la mesure de l'effort et du dépassement auxquels il faut se soumettre pour arriver à cette pleine expérience d'une humanité pleinement vécue par une conscience individuelle, en relation avec la terre, et avec toutes les personnes qui l'habitent.

Puisque ceci est plus vite écrit que vécu, la question est donc de savoir ce qu'il en est concrètement et quelles sont les voies les plus à même d'y conduire. De mon point de vue, le sujet afromondial, comme tout sujet héritier de la colonisation occidentale des deux derniers siècles, aurait dans son bagage une compétence avec laquelle il pourrait embrayer : il a déjà en héritage une version de l'exogène et du lointain, non pas de manière superfétatoire, mais intrinsèque et constitutive de son identité. Il est donc réellement et symboliquement ici et déjà là-bas, et il a appris, bon gré mal gré à composer avec le proche et le lointain, l'endogène et l'exogène. L'ouverture chez lui est expérience du quotidien, c'est la fermeture qui est son défi, en sa qualité de sujet postcolonial systématiquement éduqué à être étranger à lui-même. Il est donc *potentiellement déjà* dans cet exercice difficile qui consiste à « habiter le monde », entendu comme capacité à faire harmonieusement cohabiter les mondes. Il ne faut cependant pas être naïf : il faut plus qu'un héritage hétérogène pour « habiter le monde » au sens de Sarr, ou se constituer en porteur d'universalité au sens fort du terme. L'héritage prédispose à apprivoiser le mélange, l'étranger, mais il ne protège pas des replis réactifs et du ressentiment victimaire. C'est la raison pour laquelle on n'insistera pas assez sur le caractère *potentiel* d'une telle aptitude à monter en humanité, à être un porteur actif d'universalité.

Nul besoin cependant d'aller jusque-là pour voir ce que signifie les figures afromondiales, surtout quand elles deviennent des sujets migrants mobilisés dans la consciente traversée des frontières géographiques et culturelles, à l'assaut d'un monde historiquement venu à eux, mais qui actuellement se ferme devant eux.

3 Fictions afromondiales, sujets migrants et universalité

3.1 Partir de l'Afrique-monde vers le monde

Une femme-poète, nostalgique d'un temps de paix et de solidarité entre les peuples soupire à l'oreille complice de son amie lointaine et constate : *Il n'y a pas de parole heureuse* (Boni 1997). À côté du réfugié, compagnon d'infortune elle témoigne :

> Nous avons apprivoisé / la marche qui nous accompagne / Sur les chemins de l'exil impromptu / Nous avons érigé le soleil et la lune / en guides éclairés / Parmi la faune et la flore / Où nous traînons nos blessures intarissables / Là-bas tombent les obus sur la ville des fauves / Et nous comptons nos pas de nulle part / D'ici vers un ailleurs sans lendemain (Boni 1997, 71).

Dans cet autre recueil, Tanella Boni dessine les contours de ces figures lancées sur les sentiers incertains de la migrance, du fait de la guerre et des précarités diverses qui grèvent la dignité humaine. Le refugié de Boni est l'une des facettes du migrant de Chamoiseau, parti depuis l'Afrique vers l'Europe, pris au piège d'une traversée qui le mène plus probablement vers la mort que vers l'Eldorado rêvé depuis les rives de la Méditerranée[2]. Ces sujets de la traversée sont devenus l'expression d'une humanité qui appelle à l'acceptation, porteurs d'une universalité minorée qui s'invite au centre et force l'arrêt utile à une réflexion sur la manière de faire monde et d'être en relation. Les fictions africaines des années 2000 creusent cette trajectoire de plus en plus, et suivent comme la femme-refugiée et poète de Boni, le parcours incertain de figures exilées, afromondiales en l'occurrence.

Ces fictions s'inscrivent pleinement dans le registre de l'imbrication caractéristique de l'Afrique-monde, chère à Mbembe[3] ; les auteurs de ces fictions mettent en

---

[2] « Le continent des Africains du fond de l'Atlantique – continent sans adresse, où les cales du bateau négrier ont pu broyer durant des siècles les fondements de l'Afrique, les fils aînés du genre humain – rejoint dans une exacte sidération son double en Méditerranée. Bleu glacial, oublié des cartes ! C'est comme un hoquet général, un spasme de nos histoires, sans doute un vomissement – de fait, un vrai recommencement, non du même, mais des forces réadmises de l'horreur » (Chamoiseau 2017, 23–24).

[3] « Au demeurant, notre manière d'être au monde, notre façon « d'être-monde », d'habiter le monde, tout cela s'est toujours effectué sous le signe sinon du métissage culturel, du moins de l'imbrication des mondes, dans une lente et parfois incohérente danse avec des signes qu'ils n'ont guère eu le loisir de choisir librement, mais qu'ils sont parvenus, tant bien que mal, à domestiquer et à mettre à leur service. La conscience de cette imbrication de l'ici et de l'ailleurs, la présence de l'ailleurs dans l'ici et vice versa, cette relativisation des racines et des appartenances primaires et cette manière d'embrasser, en toute connaissance de cause, l'étrange, l'étranger et

scène des sujets porteurs de cette mondialité-universalité avec l'Afrique comme fond et conscience. Ils l'inscrivent dans une dynamique mondiale, repensent le rapport des personnages au continent à travers leurs expériences de la migrance et de cet ailleurs constitué historiquement en l'autre de l'Afrique ; cela se fait cependant dans une perspective non plus d'altérification exclusive, mais inclusive, imbriquée. Ces écritures de l'Afrique et du reste du monde opèrent selon le principe de la polyvalence, au-delà donc des dichotomies ; elles tissent des liens contraignants entre l'Afrique et le monde, et trouvent leurs figures de prédilection dans les traits des sujets migrants qui font l'expérience du monde avec comme bagage imaginaire et culturel l'héritage de l'hétérogène afromondial. La migrance dans ce cas n'est pas seulement traversée des frontières géographiques, elle est pour le sujet afromondial passage de la sphère réduite de l'expérience du monde (le lieu d'origine africain) à son expérimentation dans le vaste monde : ce qui était de l'ordre du potentiel et du concentré se déploie dans cette détente du départ comme un ressort comprimé qui se détend pour être dans l'expansion ce qu'il était déjà dans la compression.

3.2 Fictions afromondiales comme poétiques d'une universalité en déploiement

Achille Mbembe postule dans *Critique de la raison nègre* la nécessité de tenir compte de ce que peut produire ce qu'il appelle le « génie hérétique au fondement de la rencontre entre l'Afrique et le monde. De ce génie hérétique découle [dit-il] la capacité des Africains d'habiter plusieurs mondes et de se situer des deux côtés de l'image simultanément » (Mbembe 2013a, 151). Les fictions afromondiales dont il est ici question s'écrivent dans la conscience aiguë de cette présence dans « plusieurs mondes » qu'on n'essaie plus de démêler, mais plutôt de faire converger et de rendre fréquentables. Les littératures africaines ont longuement thématisé et déploré l'invasion du continent, quand elles n'essayaient pas vainement de différencier le propre de l'étranger dans des gestes désespérément d'exclusion et de redécouverte d'un soi idéalisé. Partant de l'hypothèse de cette « falsification » historique de l'Afrique, Mbembe pose la question à laquelle les fictions afromondiales s'attaquent : « Si, comme on tend à le croire, l'Afrique a été falsifiée au contact de l'extérieur, comment rendre compte de la falsification à laquelle, dans leur

---

le lointain, cette capacité de reconnaître sa face dans le visage de l'étranger et de valoriser les traces du lointain dans le proche, de domestiquer l'in-familier, de travailler avec ce qui a tout l'air des contraires – c'est cette sensibilité culturelle, historique et esthétique qu'indique bien le terme « afropolitanisme » (Mbembe 2013b, 228–229).

effort pour ingérer le monde, les Nègres ont, en retour, soumis le monde ? » (Mbembe 2013a, 151–152). Cette ingestion du monde passe par une mise en scène de son caractère hétérogène d'une part ; et d'autre part, par la description complexe du parcours de sujets lancés à la conquête de la vastitude, dotés qu'ils sont des signes imposés et apprivoisés. Retenons deux exemples qui permettront d'en cerner les contours de manières plus clairs.

Le sujet en contexte de crase[4] : Dans ce cas de figure, l'imbrication qui nourrit les poétiques afromondiales est le fait durable et très manifeste d'une histoire dans laquelle l'exogène s'était violemment appliqué sur l'endogène, contraignant les sujets à être les porteurs obligés des violences, et à négocier difficilement le résultat culturel et identitaire de ce mélange issu de la crase. Il ne s'agit pas de sujets en migrance du point de vue géographique, mais plutôt de ces personnages à l'image de ceux de Kopano Matlwa dans son roman *Coconut* (2007) : ces *born free* en Afrique du Sud qui ont en héritage un état libéré de l'apartheid mais non de ses clivages aliénants, pris dans une traversée de frontières psychologiques et objectives, à l'intérieur du même pays. Ces sujets afromondiaux font l'expérience la plus visible de la crase quand ailleurs en Afrique, celle-ci se signale de manière plus insidieuse dans des attitudes qui peinent à se décoloniser. Si la crase est caractéristique de toute l'Afrique telle qu'elle est le produit des violences historiques et des influences extérieures, elle se manifeste dans sa forme la plus évidente là où les différences ont été durablement réifiées et ont produit des effets qui structurent dans le long terme les imaginaires et les comportements, comme en Afrique du Sud.

Le sujet migrant : Nous le retrouvons par exemple dans un roman tout aussi célèbre que *Coconut*, *Il nous faut de nouveaux noms* de Noviolet Bulawayo (2014). Dans ce roman de l'exotopie et de l'aliénation, le global prête ses mots au local pour nommer les lieux, et inversement : les noms des pays du monde, selon leur degré de richesses, sont utilisés par les enfants pour désigner les quartiers. Dans ce Zimbabwe de Bulawayo, « Paradise » est un bidonville que l'on rêve de quitter, pour se rendre de préférence à « Budapest » (un quartier riche) où une des petites filles se projette : « Un jour, j'habiterai ici, dans une maison exactement comme celle-là [. . .]. Elle montre la grande maison bleue avec le long escalier, tout entourée de fleurs. Une maison vraiment bien, mais pas plus que celle où on vient de trouver nos goyaves » (Bulawayo 2014, 19). Le sujet migrant ici est pétri des connais-

---

[4] À la différence de « l'osmose » (connotée comme processus sans violence) ou de la « greffe » (mise en relation d'entités qui n'y étaient pas destinées), Jacques Demorgon dit des « crases » qu'elles se produisent à partir de fortes contraintes extérieures et procèdent par tous processus lents et rusés ou brefs et violents pour faire « tenir » ensemble des données culturelles ordinairement peu associables ou en tout cas auparavant peu associées » (Demorgon 2000, 39).

sances d'un monde lointain tel qu'il lui a été vendu, stéréotypé et fallacieux, producteur de concepts aliénants avec lesquels le local est appréhendé : c'est le prélude au départ réel et à l'expérience des Budapest et des New York lointains, la traversée non plus imaginaire mais réelle des frontières, avec un ancrage au sol africain, porté par la mémoire et le corps migrant.

Il faut suivre Chamoiseau quand il élève le migrant – dans sa fragilité sur la Méditerranée – à la hauteur d'une incarnation de la mondialité (et non de la mondialisation) par son expérience particulière d'humain appartenant à une totalité dispersée dans le vaste monde, hétérogène mais en même temps unique. Il existerait par conséquent des sujets porteurs comme lui par excellence de cette humanité :

> Pensons à ces enfants qui ont vécu, qui vivent encore cela. /
> Ils ont connu la violence du monde qui vous refuse. /
>
> De leurs parents, ils ont connu la violence de l'énergie vitale qui se rebelle à l'extinction et qui vous branche au seul souci de vivre. Ils ont connu le « tout-donner » et « tout-tenter » d'un bond dans l'inconnu. De camp en camp, de murs en barbelés, ils ont connu l'ivresse et la mort, et l'asphyxie et l'oxygène, toutes les nuances des chaleurs et du froid. Ils ont vu pleurer ceux qui les secouraient, ont vu aussi des yeux de glace. *Ils ont de fait connu une autre manière d'habiter le monde*. Ce que nous avons à plaindre en eux, c'est notre propre misère avec laquelle nous avons tenté de nier leur existence, de tolérer leur mort. Ce que nous avons à envier chez eux, c'est désormais ce qu'ils lisent dans le monde, que le monde lit en eux, et donc : *ce que nous ne savons plus du monde et que le monde ne peut plus lire en nous* (Chamoiseau 2017, 117–118).

4 Conclusion

L'esclavage, les conquêtes et les colonisations européennes du monde ont constitué des manières d'investir la globalité, en lui imposant le particulier. Sur les routes du monde se sont retrouvés des sujets forts d'une idéologie universaliste, dont on n'a pas fini de mesurer l'impact jusqu'à présent ; au 21e siècle, d'autres sujets se retrouvent sur les routes du monde, habités non pas par des valeurs qui peuvent se prévaloir des armes du conquérant d'antan, mais riches d'une expérience et d'une capacité qui en fait des sujets du monde : c'est cette « *autre manière d'habiter le monde* » que leur identifie Patrick Chamoiseau, et pour laquelle plaident et Felwine Sarr, et les femmes-poètes de Saint-Éloi et de Boni. Le sujet afromondial, migrant de l'intérieur (Matlwa) ou de l'extérieur (Bulawayo) est porteur d'un récit alternatif, celui d'une universalité mineure qui s'incarne dans des quêtes individuelles. Pour entendre ce récit, il faudra savoir prêter l'oreille et apprendre un autre alphabet, faire preuve d'humilité[5], s'ouvrir à une géographie des narrations qui localisent des voix précaires, rendues vulnérables par le fait de l'Histoire et qui se déploient de leurs localisations particulières avec le potentiel d'humanité et d'universalité dont elles sont porteuses. Pour les entendre, il faut, comme le relève à juste titre Messling (2023)[6], se départir d'une conception réifiée de la réalité telle que l'a établie l'universalisme européen, pour prendre en compte des narrations décentrées, historiquement marginalisées et embrayant à partir de lieux désormais divers. La fille du baobab brûlé donne les conditions favorables à l'éclosion d'une telle énonciation à même de « générer l'universalité » :

> Acceptez-moi comme la braise / Acceptez-moi comme je suis / [. . .] Et je vous dirai les montagnes / Je vous dirai les prairies / Rien n'est plus beau que de marcher / Dans la confusion des soleils / Les fantômes au bras des silhouettes / Planter les vergers de menthe / Et la soif des matins vagabonds / La nuit demeure une étoile / Tant que les orages sont des cerfs-volants (Saint-Éloi 2015, 47–48).

Références bibliographiques

Augé, Marc. *Non-Lieux. Introduction à une anthropologie de la surmodernité*. Paris : Seuil, 1992.
———. « Retour sur les « non-lieux ». Les transformations du paysage urbain ». *Communications* 87/2 (2010) : 171–178. https://doi.org/10.3917/commu.087.0171.
Bazié, Isaac. « Violences de l'englobement et expériences du lieu originel dans le roman africain ». *Caietele Echinox* 38 (2020) : 297–308.
Boni, Tanella. *Il n'y a pas de parole heureuse*. Limoges : Le bruit des autres, 1997.
———. *Gorée, île baobab*. Limoges : Le bruit des autres, 2004.
Bulawayo, Noviolet. *Il nous faut de nouveaux noms*. Trad. Stéphanie Levet. Paris : Gallimard, 2014.
Chamoiseau, Patrick. *Frères migrants*. Paris : Seuil, 2017.
Demorgon, Jacques. *L'interculturation du monde*. Paris : Anthropos, 2000.
Ki-Zerbo, Joseph. *À quand l'Afrique ? Entretien avec René Holenstein*. Lausanne : Éditions d'en bas, 2013 [2003].
Mbembe, Achille. *Critique de la raison nègre*. Paris : La Découverte, 2013a.
———. *Sortir de la grande nuit. Essai sur l'Afrique décolonisée*. Paris : La Découverte, 2013b.

---

[5] Joseph Ki-Zerbo relève dans son analyse de l'attitude de l'Occident face à l'Afrique : « Il faut que le Nord ait suffisamment de bon sens et de modestie pour comprendre qu'il peut apprendre quelque chose des pays du Sud [. . .]. L'Afrique a apporté, depuis des siècles, beaucoup d'éléments que la civilisation occidentale a captés et intégrés [. . .]. Il y a un art de vivre africain, un art de la solidarité, un art de l'altérité, de l'ouverture aux autres que les Européens ne retrouvent plus chez eux » (Ki-Zerbo 2013, 181–182).
[6] « Ainsi s'installe donc une différence entre l'universalisme, qui s'était élevé au rang d'unique véritable régime de connaissance, et une attitude attachée au contexte concret et qui, seule tente de générer l'universalité » (Messling 2023, 42).

———. « Penser le monde à partir de l'Afrique ». *Écrire l'Afrique-Monde*. Ed. Achille Mbembe et Felwine Sarr. Dakar : Jimsaan, 2016. 379–392.
Matlwa, Kopano. *Coconut*. Trad. Georges Lory. Paris : Actes Sud, 2015 [2007].
Messling, Markus. *L'Universel après l'universalisme. Des littératures francophones du contemporain*. Préface de Souleymane Bachir Diagne. Trad. Olivier Mannoni. Paris : Presses universitaires de France, 2023.
Mudimbe, V.Y. *The Invention of Africa. Gnosis, Philosophy and the Order of Knowledge*. Bloomington : Indiana University Press, 1988.
Saint-Éloi, Rodney. *Je suis la fille du baobab brûlé*. Montréal : Mémoire d'encrier, 2015.
Sarr, Felwine. *Habiter le monde. Essai de politique relationnelle*. Montréal : Mémoire d'encrier, 2019.

Maria-Anna Schiffers
More-Than-Human Relations, or: Rethinking Narration and Relations With Bears

Abstract: The article focuses on more-than human relations and the role of narration. What are possible ways to improve the *quality* of relations that manage to keep up with the speed and problems brought about by the *quantity* of relations in a globalised world? By following the traces of a bear in Nastassja Martin's book *In the Eye of the Wild* (2021), I draw attention to a specific aspect of more-than-human relations. Martin's text creates a specific form of relationality and tells a story of how to narrate the relation between different worlds. It is precisely this kind of relationality we can think of as a common ground; a new, minor form of universality beyond Western Logocentrism, without denying differences or falling into a relativism that does not do justice to the material implications of the relation and the narration.

Keywords: relation, narration, more-than-human, minor, logocentrism (critique of), Nastassja Martin

In his essay "Habiter le monde", Felwine Sarr attests to a "profound crisis of relationality" (2017, 12).[1] The problem, he specifies, doesn't arise from the quantity of relations – after all, we certainly live in a highly connected, globalised world –, but in the *quality* of relations we inhabit. "After millions of years of hominisation and millennia of human civilisation, the quality of the relationships we produce between individuals, societies and with the living world that surrounds us remains mediocre" (Sarr 2017, 11). On the one hand, this is a diagnosis that echoes the analysis of major researchers in the past decades concerning the problems of modernity, globalisation and the anthropocene (see Braidotti 2013; Chakrabarty 2009; Haraway 2016a; Latour 2018). This kind of crisis is not just one on a material level, but also a crisis of ideals and the struggle for common ground without collapsing into relativism or the ideology of European Universalism (see Messling 2019).

---

[1] All translations by the author, unless otherwise noted.

Note: This article is part of the research project "Minor Universality. Narrative World Productions After Western Universalism", which received funding from the European Research Council (ERC) under the European Union's Horizon 2020 research and innovation programme (Grant agreement no. 819931).

On the other hand, Sarr introduces a new focus on the quality of relationality to a more general diagnosis of crisis by not only stressing the deep interconnectedness of our contemporary world. In a similar vein to Hofmann and Messling's reflections about the end(s) of European Universalism (2020), Sarr raises different problems and makes a profound crisis in the self-construction of the human being increasibly more visible.

What are possible ways to improve the *quality* of relations that manage to keep up with the speed and problems brought about by the *quantity* of relations in a globalised world? However, we are experiencing a world that we no longer know how to inhabit in peace and harmony with those with whom we share it. This crisis is rooted in the imaginary relationship that we establish with our fellow human beings, our environment and the living world in general.[2] Sarr hints in his diagnosis of crisis at the different entities involved (human and non-human) and the importance of the imaginary to improve the quality of relations in a globalised, highly connected world.

Addressing primarily human relations in his essay, I want to widen the view in focusing on more-than-human relations and the role of narration in facing this "profound crisis" (Sarr 2017, 12). Echoing Sarr's emphasis on relations, Donna Haraway states: "The relation is the smallest unit of analysis, and the relation is about significant otherness at every scale. That is the ethic, or perhaps better, mode of attention, with which we must approach the long cohabitings of people and dogs" (Haraway 2016a, 116) – or bears, the anthropologist Nastassja Martin might add, whose book *Croire aux fauves* (Martin 2019) will be the focus of this chapter.[3] We cannot exclude our relation to non-human worlds when thinking-about how to relate to the world and how to relate the world (see for example Latour 2018; Haraway 2016a; Henao and Toledo 2022). This is the case not only, because we, as species, live in a globalised and entangled world with its various connections to other species and non-human entities, who influence and shape the world we inhabit. We are also a species highly dependent on other species (Chakrabarty 2009, 219). We need to rethink our relation to the non-human worlds, because it matters how we put ourselves, as human-animals, in relation to what Haraway calls "significant otherness" (Haraway 2016a, 116).

What does it mean to relate to non-human animals? At first glance, we might think of relationships with pets, of the spiky attempts at communication with our

---

2 « Nous faisons cependant l'expérience d'un monde que nous ne savons plus habiter en paix et en harmonie avec ceux avec qui nous l'avons en partage. Cette crise se noue dans l'imaginaire de la relation que nous établissions avec nos semblables, notre environnement et le vivant en général » (Sarr 2017, 14).
3 The book was published in English in 2021 under the title *In the Eye of the Wild*.

dogs and cats, by whom we feel, at best, *seen* in Derrida's sense (2008).[4] At the same time, human-animal relations became more and more ambivalent during modernity. How we relate to the more-than-human has changed profoundly in the past decades (see Latour 2004; Toledo 2021). This change can be described as both, a symptom and as being part of a crisis (Hofmann and Messling 2021, v). In western thought, humans have defined themselves in distinction to the animal. As not only Derrida famously taught us in his way of deconstructing western logocentrism, in this kind of thought non-human animals become universal signs for the Other (Derrida 2011). The deconstruction of metaphysical categories of order, as evident in the antinomies of nature/culture, woman/man, subject/object, mind/body corresponding to the human/animal dualism, is currently polarising itself above all at the boundary between animals and humans, which was previously perceived as stable (Bodenburg 2012, 9). The countermovement to this development is the attempt to establish ever new criteria to secure this boundary between "us" and the "Other". Not only language and rationality become distinguishing features; intentionality and agency become new fields of negotiation (see Bühler-Dietrich 2015). "Man is the animal plus X", as the philosopher Markus Wild (2008, 26) critically summarises it, referring to western traditions of thought, deeply rooted in European Universalism. But securing borders has never improved the quality of relations. With Universalism as ideology coming to an end we need to think about a different common ground: a "minor universality" (Hofmann and Messling 2020; Messling and Tinius, this volume). Sarr develops such an idea in his analysis by placing relations at the very center of the world itself: "This world we have built and continue to create is the result of multiple relationships: inter-human, inter-state, with matter, with the living and the cosmos" (Sarr 2017, 20).[5] I would like to draw the attention to a specific aspect of more-than-human relations following the traces of a bear, asking: How can we narrate our relationship to non-human animals and how do we relate by narrating?

---

4 In his book *The Animal therefore I am (More to follow)*, Jacques Derrida famously coined the concept of "the animal gaze". He ponders a scene where the philosopher steps out of the bathroom naked, being looked at by his cat and feeling seen by the animal (2008 [2006]). Haraway gets back to this scene in *When Species Meet*. She praises Derrida for understanding "that actual animals look back at actual human beings" yet, crucially, the philosopher does not "seriously consider an alternative form of knowing something more about cats and *how to look back*, perhaps even scientifically, biologically, and *therefore* also philosophically and intimately." Although largely complimentary of his attempt to address the question of the animal, Haraway surmises that Derrida "failed a simple obligation of companionship" to the specific animal other (Haraway 2008, 19–20).
5 « Ce monde que nous avons construit et que nous continuons de créer est le résultat de multiples relations: interhumaines, interétatiques, ave la matière, avec le vivant et le cosmos » (Sarr 2017, 20).

1 *Croire aux fauves*. Rethinking relations with a bear

In her book *Croire aux fauves / In the Eye of the Wild,* French anthropologist Nastassja Martin relates the story of a near fatal encounter with a bear (*ursus arctus beringianus*) in the mountains of Kamchatka, Siberia.[6] The narrative opens *in medias res* by introducing the two main characters of the story. The bear precedes the human "I", even though the animal has long since left the scene: "The bear left some hours ago now, and I am waiting, waiting for the mist to lift" (Martin 2021, 1). Their encounter is anything but peaceful, and yet Martin creates a specific form of narration in order to explore her unique relationship to the bear that injured her so badly on a physical level as well as on an inner, psychological level. She relates narratively to the bear. At first, everything seems nebulous, "[a]s in the time of myths, obscurity reigns" (Martin 2021, 1). This mist that obscures everything, including the self-construction of the narrating "I" will only clear up much later. "I am this blurred figure," Martin goes on, "features subsumed beneath the open gulfs in my face, slicked over with internal tissue, fluid, and blood: it is a birth, for it is manifestly not a death" (Martin 2021, 1). This birth is an encounter at "this abyssal limit, these edges, this plural and repeatedly folded frontier", the *limitrophy* (Derrida 2008 [2006], 30) of different species, of western thought, knowledge and medicine and Soviet medicine, of knowledge of different indigenous groups in Alaska and Siberia.[7] In short, it is the implosion of the frontiers of worlds (Martin 2021, 101). At the same time, it is the birth of a relation with all its political and ethical implications:

> Recovering from this clash is not only an act of self-focused metamorphosis, it is a political act. My body has become a territory where Western surgeons parley with Siberian bears. Or rather, where they try to establish communication. [. . .] Our work, hers [i.e. the doctor's] and mine, and that of the indefinable thing the bear has left deep in my core, consists from now on of maintaining the lines of communication (Martin 2021, 54).

---

[6] The book was originally published in 2019 in French.
[7] Derrida develops the concept of limitrophy in *The Animal that Therefore I Am* (2008 [2006]) in the following sense: "*Limitrophy* is therefore my subject. Not just because it will concern what sprouts or grows at the limit, around the limit, by maintaining the limit, but also what feeds the limit, generates it, raises it, and complicates it. Everything I'll say will consist, certainly not in effacing the limit, but in multiplying its figures, in complicating, thickening, delinearizing, folding, and dividing the line precisely by making it increase and multiply . . . . [The limit] has an abyss: The discussion is worth undertaking once it is a matter of determining the number, form, sense, or structure, the foliated consistency, of this abyssal limit, these edges, this plural and repeatedly folded frontier" (Derrida 2008 [2006], 29–30.)

Martins text evokes a different crisis of relationality from Sarr's essay: In its mixture of different genres, the anthropologically-informed text narrates an autobiographical story. It raises the question of how to 'maintain the communiction' to this *significant otherness* that the bear has left in the "I" and how to narrate this difficult relation. However, Martin shares with Sarr a diagnosis of the crisis of relationality on a less general and more situated level:

> That my world had been drastically altered before my encounter is undeniable. An alteration of the relationship to the world – this is how academics define madness. How is it manifested? By a period of time, a moment, short or long, during which the borders between ourselves and the outside world dissolve, little by little, as if we were gradually disintegrating and sinking into the depths of oneiric time where nothing is settled, where the boundaries between living beings are still in flux and everything is still possible (Martin 2021, 87–88).

She tries to embrace this state conceived by western psychology as "madness" and searches a way to relate her story differently than in categories only informed by European modernity and its presumptions of madness, otherness *and* self-identity. Her story is not one of madness, but one of a relation to different worlds and the creation of a relational subject position.

At first sight Martin writes about a personal crisis following her severe injuries after her confrontation with the animal (Martin 2021, 36). On closer examination, however, other dimensions become more important in this text. The issue at stake is not only a personal crisis, but a struggle and discussion about how the anthropologist can place herself in relation to the world as a western educated and socialised person, without considering this to be the only layer of identity: "On that day, August 15, 2015, the event is not: a bear attacks a French anthropologist somewhere in the mountains of Kamchatka" (Martin 2021, 101), which would be the simple story in the newspapers and even in the talking off the staff at the airbase hospital in Russia.

> The event is: a bear and a woman meet and the frontiers between two worlds implode. Not just the physical boundaries between the human and the animal in whom the confrontation open fault lines in their bodies and their minds. This is also when mythical time meets reality; past time joins the present moment; dream meets flesh (Martin 2021, 101).

Martin reflects about painfully entangled stories of herself, the bear, myths of the Evens she lives with in Kamchatka, her studies about Animism *as* an anthropologist and western believes and medicine. In order to heal, "to scar" (Martin 2021, 52), she needs to relate to different ways of being and creates a situated and very concrete concept of relation to the world and a relational "I" that inhabits different worlds at the same time.

As a literary text, the book deals with the question of how the narrating, remembering and dreaming "I" can inhabit the world in the face of all its knowledge and undeniable relationalities. The text presents itself *par excellence* as a privileged source of knowledge of "Lebenswissen" as coined by Ottmar Ette, which is referring to a literature "that has gathered knowledge about life, about survival, and about living together, without either falling into discursive or disciplinary specializations or functioning as a regulatory mechanism for cultural knowledge" (Ette 2016, xxi). Martin's text creates a specific form of relationality and tells at the same time a story of how to narrate the relation between different worlds. It is precisely this kind of relationality that we can expect to be a common ground, a new, minor form of universality I want to focus on in the following. We put ourselves in relation to the world by telling stories, as the indigenous Daria in Martin's book, or Nastassja Martin herself. For Martin, the decision "to write it all" is an important part of her healing process: "At the heart of the Russian healthcare system am I. [. . .] I reflect that no one will believe me when I tell them about this when I get out, if I get out. I decide to write it all as soon as I can" (Martin 2021, 8).

Humans create themselves narratively and often do so – informed by presumptions of European Universalism – in distinction to animals. With Martin, things seem to be different as she focusses not on the distinction but on the relation: considering other ontologies (Descola 2013), other ways of relating to the more-than-human, the world seems to multiply. There are worlds opening up. Narrative texts considered "as sensual carriers of a discursive knowledge that is specialised in not being specialised" offer a possible way out of "simple dichotomies" (Ette 2017, 1). With their many different logics, they provide a possible counter-design to western logocentrism criticised by Derrida, with special regard to humans and non-human animals. In contrast to the disciplined knowledge of life science, the literatures of the world offer a multi-logical access to knowledge that transcends the different discourses and disciplines.

That is the force of the narration: In contrast to memorials and historical sites immobilised in stone, narrations can entangle histories. To connect, or even entangle the histories of suffering of modernity carries an ethic dimension, but, moreover, makes it necessary to reflect the own standpoint from where a narration shall be constructed (Hofmann and Messling 2020, 35). Hofmann and Messling highlight the importance of the situated standpoint. Édouard Glissant even coins the idea of a "poetics of relation" by presenting archipelagic thinking as an alternative to the globalisation-nationalism dichotomy (Glissant 1997). "Let us understand 'relation' in the sense of narration, the narration of the genealogical narrative, for example, but more generally as well, in the sense that Édouard Glissant imprints upon the expression when he speaks of Poetics of Relation just as one could speak of a politics of relation", states Derrida (1998, 19), emphasising the link between narration and relation. By referring to Glissant, he highlights the political implications of relations. Sarr stresses the importance of the imaginary and the poetics to create a different way to inhabit the world as well but with a slightly different focus on inhabiting the world:

> This world in which we live is a collective work that we create and produce. Through creativity, we make it expandable and immeasurable. Through poetry and the arts, we can inhabit the infinity of the world, as well as its subtlest and highest dimensions. It is possible to create within the ordinary order of time, a different way of inhabiting the common sensible world: a poetic way of being in the world (Sarr 2017, 38–39).

In consequence, "we need other kind of stories", as Haraway states in the film *Story telling for earthly surviving* (2016c). At the same time it is a question of form, not only a question of content, as Haraway (2016, 111) argues regarding human-animal relations:

> Living with animals, inhabiting their/our stories, trying to tell the truth about relationship, cohabiting an active history: that is the work of companion species, for whom "the relation" is the smallest possible unit of analysis.

Martin reminds us of "material-semiotic" (Haraway 2016, 13) consequences of narratives, myths and dreams, to really relate to the world. The attack of the bear doesn't only force the narrating "I" to relate to that specific animal differently and to tell her story, but it changes the human relationships as well, as Daria and Martin's mother meet for the first time:

> An odd new family comes together: my mother, my brother, and Daria and her children, the first occasion these people have ever been in the same space-time, all cast into this precarious, liminal zone. I have become an unlikely link, between these people as human beings and between them and the world of the bears up in the high tundra (Martin 2021, 20).

As Haraway points out, referring to the anthropologist Marilyn Strathern: "Strathern wrote about accepting the risk of relentless contingency; she thinks about anthropology as the knowledge practice that studies relations with relations, that puts relations at risk with other relations, from unexpected other worlds (Haraway 2016, 12). The relation is only possible in what Martin calls "this precarious, liminal zone" (Martin 2021, 20). Accepting the relation thus means to accept this risk of relentless contingency.

By relating to different worlds, Martin gets in touch with the world around her as well as within her, since she has to relate with the bear inside her.[8] But

---

[8] One can see some similarities to Glissant's conception of relation as present in *The Poetics of Relation* but Martin clearly adds a physical, embodied dimension to her concept as I will show.

Martin's way to get in touch with the world, to relate to the she-bear and the bears' world isn't very peaceful.⁹ Rethinking relations with 'her bear' means pain and struggle as well. To relate means also to weep the loss of a simple, unrelated subject position formed by western thought:

> I drop to the floor and let my tears wash everything else away. I weep like a little girl left alone, I weep for all that had to happen, I weep for my bear, for my old, lost face, for my previous life, which too is certainly lost, I weep for everything that will never be the same again (Martin 2021, 32).

And yet, there is still a narrating "I" even though it is clearly situated and embedded into relations, it is a related subject position. In Martins conception of how to build a relationship to the world dreams, and the Evens' knowledge about entangled worlds play an important role. In order to understand her relation to the bear, she needs "to go back to those who know bears and the questions they bring with them, who still speak with them in their dreams, who know that nothing happens by chance and that our life paths always cross for very particular reasons" (Martin 2021, 63). The task to understand what happens, is to understand the layers of the relationships as constitutive elements of the subject position:

> You must forgive the bear. I don't reply straightaway; I know I have no choice, and yet for once I want to disobey, to reject fate, our bonds, to reject everything we move towards that is inexorable, I want to shout that I wish I had killed him, to expel him from my system, that I am so angry he has disfigured me like this. But I don't, I say nothing. I breathe. Yes. I have forgiven the bear. [. . .] He didn't mean to kill you, he wanted to mark you. Now you are *medka* she who lives between the worlds (Martin 2021, 19).

Being *medka* means inhabiting what Derrida calles *limitrophy* and it forces her to relate to the world differently and to narrate the story differently.¹⁰ It means to understand the irresolvable and painful connection between the bear and the "I". Those unlikely relations are only possible in this "liminal zone" (Martin 2021, 20) at the frontier of worlds and they are narratively created.

Similar to Sarr's argumentation regarding his diagnosis of crisis, Martin's problem leading to "the crisis of her life" (Martin 2021, 36) isn't the *quantity of relations*. Indeed, she feels related to very different worlds and it seems to be easy for her to relate to those worlds. However, in order to heal, "to scar" (Martin 2021, 52), she needs to embody the relations, which have always been there and thus to improve the quality of relations. Martin starts to inhabit the world by

---

9 For the Evens, Martin is *mathuka*, which means "she-bear".
10 The Evens word *medka* is used to indicate people who are "marked by the bear," having survived their encounter with one. From that time on, people called *medka* are considered to be half human, half bear.

embodying the relation: "I need to scar. Closing means accepting that everything left inside is now a part of me, but from now on nothing more" (Martin 2021, 52).

Similar to Sarr, Haraway emphasises a deep connection between the imaginary and the world. She reminds us that there is a link between the imaginary, the narration, and the material world; a kind of process she grasps in the concept of *worlding*. "Ontologically heterogeneous partners become who and what they are in relational material-semiotic worlding. Natures, cultures, subjects, and objects do not preexist their intertwined worldings" (Haraway 2016, 13). Being is a relation of more than one entity or in Sarr's words: "To be is to be in relation. The relationality completes us and reveals us" (Sarr 2017, 21). It is also a question of form, of how to be in relation and how to narrate the relation. Or in Strathern's words: "It matters what ideas we use to think other ideas" (1992, 10). For Martin, the way of relating the story of herself, of being a relational being, a creature of metamorphosis, matters. At the same time, she reminds us of the fragility of this relational form of being:

> The relationships being spun within the little country my body has become are fragile, delicate. [. . .] I propose that surviving the confrontation with the bear, just as much as confronting *what's to come* in this world, means accepting recreation in the shape of structural transformation. The unity that so fascinates us is finally revealed for what it is: a delusion. The figure is reconstituted following its own unique pattern, but out of elements that are completely exogenous (Martin 2021, 54).

The subject position is never a simple one and this embodiment of relations isn't easy or peaceful. At the same time, the relations have always been there: Martin was "she-bear", *mathuka*, before her physical encounter with the bear. The relation pre-exists the encounter. Who follows whom must be constantly renegotiated.[11] The way we relate to one another and to other worlds never comes naturally in an essentialist way.

> What truly do I share with this wild creature, and since when? The truth as I see it is that I've never sought to bring peace to my life, far less to my encounters with others. On this point my therapist is correct: I am not at peace. I don't even know what the word means (Martin 2021, 59).

---

11 Derrida (2008) hints at this question of who follows whom, human-animal or nonhuman-animal with the title of his book and a lecture at Cerisy: *L'animal que donc je suis – à suivre*, with its ambivalent double-meaning in French of *being* and *following*.

This entanglement with the bear, troubles the anthropologist and the trouble is at the same time the one thing we should stick with, *Staying with the Trouble* as Haraway (2016b) puts it. It reveals the political and ethical claim Haraway shares with Martin.[12]

> Staying with the trouble does not require such a relationship to times called the future. In fact, staying with the trouble requires learning to be truly present, not as a vanishing pivot between awful or edenic pasts and apocalyptic or salvific futures, but as mortal critters entwined in myriad unfinished configurations of places, times, matters, meanings (Haraway 2016b, 1).

The subject position is thus an embedded and relational one, but at the same time situated with painful material and semiotic consequences. This kind of 'ontology of relation' found in Sarr's, Haraway's, and Martin's work, prevents from collapsing into essentialism, as being is always conceived as 'being in relation', as being-more-than one entity, as being "ontologically different partners" (Haraway 2016, 13) in relation.

2 More-than-human relations with a bear as minor universality

The question remains urgent: How to think those more-than-human relations and how can we, as human-animals, relate to more-than-human worlds beyond European Universalism? And how can we relate to stories such as the ones I analysed above?

Martin's story of an unlikely relationship with a bear, with the world of the Evens in Kamchatka. Her narrative of the world of the Gwichi'in in Alaska reminds us that to relate can be a painful process and healing means most of the times to scar. Martin embodies the blurred frontiers between human-animal and bear, and she narrates at "this abyssal limit, these edges, this plural and repeatedly folded frontier" (Derrida 2008 [2006], 30).

She does so in order to go on living, not necessarily to heal on a superficial level, but to be able to relate to the world and to herself again, Martin needs to relate to the world around her differently, to embody the relation. She does so by

---

[12] Derrida and Glissant combine an aesthetics with ethics as well, but not as explicit as Haraway and Martin do it. As I have shown, Glissant and Derrida do it on a rather theoretical level, but Martin and Haraway share a very practical, material, and semiotic way to develop an ethical way of writing and living.

relating her story, by remembering, writing it down, banning it on paper (Martin 2021, 36). She also tries to do this by going back again, by finding a way to connect to the bear in a way that combines western presumptions about the world, her anthropological knowledge, and different ontologies. Considering non-western ways to relate to the world means to consider other "ontologies" (Viveiros de Castro 2004) or at least other modes of identification (Descola 2013). But it doesn't mean to refer randomly to them in a quasi-esoteric shift, rightly criticised as cultural appropriation.

Martin's text teaches ways to relate to worlds which are perceived as radically different according to Western Universalism. Her narration is an example of how the different relations that span like a net can be told without repeating dualisms. But also, without denying differences or falling into a relativism that does not do justice to the material implications of the relation and the narration.

In order to repair the relation, to improve the quality of relation, the relation itself has to be at heart of the subject position – not the frontier.[13] Inhabiting the relation means to put the subject position at risk and situating it at the same time: "I am at the frontier of humanity, at what feels like the very edge of what a person can stand" (Martin 2021, 7). It means to scar, to make the borders of the worlds which implode visible and to embody the different relations. The relation isn't innocent; it is sometimes painful and always political. As I showed, it matters how we relate the world and how we relate to the word. Embracing a relational way of inhabiting the world implicates scars but to relate truly and honestly is also a "poetic way of inhabiting the world" (Sarr 2017, 39). This kind of worlding, this relational way of inhabiting the world can be conceived as a form of minor universality (see Messling 2019). The relation is placed at the very center of inhabiting worlds and forms a world, which appears as a common ground. In this conception with relations at the very heart of being, relations matter, they are significant, and we must take them seriously, because they shape our subject positions and our world. This means at the same time that we have to put ourselves at risk by relating, but to situate this relational subject position at the same time: we need to root ourselves in relation to different worlds (see Glissant 1997). Considering the way Martin creates and narrates her relational self, we can think of a minor universality without collapsing into pure relativism nor claiming truth in the tradition of Western Universalism. It seems possible to achieve a "new global awareness that can provide ethical and institutional frameworks of a world-society" (Messling and Tinius, this volume) that considers more-than-human entities. In this sense minor universality

---

13 Regarding the question of repair, see the first issue of *Rhinozeros. Europa im Übergang* (Basil et. al. 2021).

also means to tell different stories of relationality, to relate differently by narrating more-than-human relations differently.

References

Basil, Priya, Franck Hofmann, Teresa Koloma-Beck, Markus Messling. Eds. *Rhinozeros. Europa im Übergang*. Berlin: Matthes & Seitz, 2021.
Bodenburg, Julia. *Tier und Mensch. Zur Disposition des Humanen und Animalischen in Literatur, Philosophie und Kultur um 2000*. Freiburg, Berlin, Wien: Rombach Litterae, 2012.
Bühler-Dietrich, Annette: *Topos Tier: neue Gestaltungen des Tier-Mensch-Verhältnisses*. Bielefeld: transcript, 2015.
Braidotti, Rosi. "1 Posthuman relational subjectivity and the politics of affirmation." *Relational Architectural Ecologies: Architecture, Nature and Subjectivity*. Milton Park: Taylor & Francis, 2013. 21–40.
Chakrabarty, Dipesh. "The Climate of History: Four Theses." *Critical Inquiry* 35.2 (2009): 197–222.
Derrida, Jacques. *Monoliguism of the Other; or, The Prosthesis of Origin*. Stanford: Stanford University Press, 1998.
——. Derrida, Jacques. *The Animal that Therefore I Am*. Ed. Marie-Louise Mallet. Transl. David Wills. New York: Fordham University Press, 2008 [2006].
——. *The Beast and the Sovereign*. Volume I. Transl. Geoffrey Bennington. Chicago: University of Chicago Press, 2011.
Descola, Philippe. *Beyond Nature and Culture*. Chicago: University of Chicago Press, 2013.
Ette, Ottmar. *Writing-between-worlds: transarea studies and the literatures-without-a-fixed-abode*. Transl. by Vera M. Kutzinski. Berlin, Boston: De Gruyter, 2016.
——. *WeltFraktale. Wege durch die Literaturen der Welt*. Stuttgart: J.B. Metzler, 2017.
Glissant, Édouard. *Poetics of relation*. Transl. Betsy Wing. Ann Arbor: University of Michigan Press, 1997.
Haraway, Donna J. *Manifestly Haraway*. With Cary Wolfe. Minneapolis: University of Minnesota Press, 2016a.
——. *Staying with the Trouble: Making Kin in the Chthulucene*. Durham/NC: Duke, 2016b.
——. *Story Telling for Earthly Surviving*. Dir. Fabrizio Terranova. Icarus Films, 2016c.
Henao, Juan Carlos, and Camille de Toledo. *Les droits de la Nature: Vers un nouveau paradigme de protection du vivant*. Paris: Humensis, 2022.
Hofmann, Franck and Markus Messling. "On the ends of universalism." *The Epoch of Universalism 1769–1989 / L'époque de l'universalisme 1769–1989*. Eds. Franck Hofmann and Markus Messling. Berlin, Boston: De Gruyter, 2020. 1–39.
Latour, Bruno. *Politics of Nature: How to Bring the Sciences into Democracy*. Transl. Cathy Porter. Harvard: Harvard University Press, 2004.
——. *Down to Earth: Politics in the New Climatic Regime*. Transl. Cathy Porter. Cambridge: Polity Press, 2018.
Martin, Nastassja. *Croire aux fauves*. Paris: Collection Verticales, Gallimard, 2019.
——. *In the Eye of the Wild*. Transl. Sophie Lewis. New York: New York Review Books, 2021.
Messling, Markus. *Universalität nach dem Universalismus. Über frankophone Literaturen der Gegenwart*. Berlin: Matthes & Seitz, 2019.

Messling, Markus and Jonas Tinius. "On Minor Universality." *Minor Universality. Rethinking Humanity After Western Universalism*. Eds. Markus Messling and Jonas Tinius. Berlin, Boston: De Gruyter, 2023. 1–31.
Sarr, Felwine. *Habiter le monde. Essai de politique relationnelle*. Montréal: Mémoire d'encrier, 2017.
Strathern, Marilyn. *Reproducing the Future*. Manchester: Manchester University Press, 1992.
Toledo, Camille de. *Le fleuve qui voulait écrire: Les auditions du parlement de Loire*. Paris: Les liens qui libèrent, 2021.
Viveiros de Castro, Eduardo. "Exchanging Perspectives: The Transformation of Objects into Subjects in Amerindian Ontologies." *Common Knowledge* 10.3 (2004): 463–84.
Wild, Markus. *Tierphilosophie zur Einführung*. Hamburg: Junius, 2008.

Mario Laarmann
Hybrid Aesthetics and Social Reality: Reading Caribbean Literature in the Postcolonial Present

Abstract: With the work of authors such as Édouard Glissant, Patrick Chamoiseau, Edwidge Danticat, Earl Lovelace, Junot Díaz, Maryse Condé, Antonio Benítez-Rojo, or Dany Laferrière, Caribbean literature looks back on a prolific and influential tradition of 'hybrid' aesthetics and transcultural social realism. Simultaneously, contemporary literary and cultural scholarship is increasingly becoming aware of its post-postcolonial and post-postmodernist condition, deferring text-immanent arguments of deterritorialisation, agency, or representation for the sake of a more material criticism which questions the very premises of our modern social systems. The concept of a minor universality reflects this necessity. Against this backdrop, the present paper investigates the potential of critics such as Jacques Rancière, Stuart Hall, Pierre Bourdieu, and Shalini Puri to both (re)read the aforementioned tradition and also approach the present generation of Caribbean writers.

Keywords: Caribbean literature, postcolonial present, literary sociology, aesthetics, hybridity, cultural studies, conjunctural reading

> Rather than the anticolonial problem of overthrowing colonialism (or the West), or the decolonization of the West's representation of the non-West, what is important for this present is a critical interrogation of the practices, modalities, and projects through which modernity inserted itself into and altered the lives of the colonized. (David Scott 1999, 17)

> [W]e need to connect a poetics of hybridity to a politics of equality. (Shalini Puri 2004, 1)

1 Prelude

"These texts [. . .] speak to my childhood, to the magic, the free vision, the differing vision, to the factors that have structured my imagination, shaped my sensibility, and that would abound today in the schemes of my writing" – with these

---

Note: This article is part of the research project "Minor Universality. Narrative World Productions After Western Universalism", which received funding from the European Research Council (ERC) under the European Union's Horizon 2020 research and innovation programme (Grant agreement no. 819931).

∂ Open Access. © 2023 the author(s), published by De Gruyter. This work is licensed under the Creative Commons Attribution-NonCommercial-NoDerivatives 4.0 International License.
https://doi.org/10.1515/9783110798494-008

words, Patrick Chamoiseau (1996 [1990], 12) introduces his autobiographical trilogy *Une enfance créole*.[1] In the three volumes of the series, he remembers episodes from his childhood and invites his readers to share his innocent and magical worldview at the time. Simultaneously, however, these descriptions trace Chamoiseau's socialisation as a *créole* subject – that is, his inheritance of the culture and traditions of Martinique's transracial and transcultural society; a sensibility and cultural knowledge his fictional and non-fictional oeuvre aims to keep alive.[2]

As a consequence, *Une enfance créole* features an aesthetics similar to most of his fictional work; the "imagination" or "sensibility," whose development inspires the narrative of his childhood, clearly informs Chamoiseau's way of writing, of relating to the world. Much has been said and written about this aesthetics, but there seems to be a consensus that – inspired by *créole* deconstruction of racial categories and subversion of French language – it has a certain proximity to postmodernism (Ueckmann 2014, 14–16), or at least poststructuralist theory. One might argue that these markers – transracialism and transculturalism, cultural and linguistic subversion, deconstruction of the novel – have long been relevant in Caribbean literature beyond his work. Inspired by their societal reality, by poststructuralist criticism of Western cultural imperialism, postmodernist writing, magical realism, and other sources, writers such as Earl Lovelace, Edwidge Danticat, Junot Díaz, Antonio Benítez-Rojo, or Dany Laferrière all experiment with a *hybrid* aesthetics to a greater or lesser extent.

The strategic thrust of this paper is not a generic eulogy or criticism of such experimental Caribbean writing. Rather, I want to propose a theoretical framework that would permit to specifically locate individual literary projects in the light of questions that are pressing today: To what extent is Chamoiseau's *créole* aesthetics able to address the lived reality of different social groups in Martinique? Torn between French republican universality and poststructuralist deconstruction of identity per se, does his writing still find ways to think and express differently gendered, racialised, or class-experiences of *créolité*? To what extent do his deconstruction of language and literary genre and his focus on 'culture' permit a material – social, or sociological – criticism? What is his take on social and ecological implications of the *modern* mode of living which seems antagonistic to pre-colonial, but also *créole* cultural forms? These are some of the questions my reflections on literary theory will need to be capable to address. But what is this contemporary moment that makes these questions – developed here at the example of Patrick Chamoiseau – so pressing?

---

[1] Unless indicated otherwise, all translations into English are my own.
[2] For Chamoiseau's theoretical interventions on the subject, see for example his *Écrire en pays dominé* (1997) or the influential *Éloge de la Créolité* (1989).

2 Post-postcolonialism and Caribbean literature

In his 1999 *Refashioning Futures. Criticism after Postcoloniality*, anthropologist and *Small Axe* editor David Scott sketches the moment he calls the *postcolonial present*. As the title of his study already suggests, this contemporary moment in artistic and philosophical discourse goes beyond the criticism of what has come to be known as the postcolonial school. In the postcolonial present, Scott argues, additional and new questions are relevant that exceed the anti-essentialist impetus of postcolonial deconstruction and put the emphasis on concrete social issues – even questioning the very constitution of "the social" (Scott 1999, 16).

The postcolonial present, as Scott describes it, is marked by a new global condition, "defined by the collapse of the Bandung project and, with the dismantling of the Soviet Union, of the international communist movement as well, and the rise of a revived/revised liberalism" (Scott 1999, 14). The collapse of the Soviet Union and the advance of neoliberalism Scott evokes here are crucial markers, as they seem to corroborate the longstanding promises of a Western idea of modernity. With Francis Fukuyama, who calls out the "end of history" in his 1992 *The End of History and the Last Man*, one could be tempted to declare the Hegelian dialectic development towards greater liberty to have reached its final phase. At the turn of the millennium, "liberal democracy remains the only coherent political aspiration that spans different regions and cultures around the globe," Fukuyama (1992, xiii) writes, making a case for the (apparently indispensable) benefits of the 'free market' and its "limitless accumulation of wealth" (Fukuyama 1992, xiv). But while it is arguably true that 'the West' has triumphed over the socialist vision of modernity, the promise of a completed progression toward universal well-being has certainly not fulfilled itself after 1989. "On the whole, we are living better today", Felwine Sarr (2017, 9) put it in his *Habiter le monde*. But:

> The times we are living in, without yielding to alarmist disaster-mongering, are characterized by crises in various forms. Misery projects its multiple faces on them, namely economic and ecologic crises, the rise of violent nationalisms and religious extremism, terrorism, and the large-scale production of social inequalities and structural conditions of human indignity for a majority of individuals (Sarr 2017, 11).

The importance of 1989 for Scott's postcolonial present is therefore not the *celebration* of Western modernity, but much rather the realisation that this ideology can serve as a solution to neither ecologic nor social issues. As opposed to the postcolonial school, whose central impetus lay in the deconstruction of (neo)colonial discourse, Scott argues that fundamentally new questions need to be asked today – going to the core of the very premise of Western modernity. Similarly *radical* approaches – which go to the *roots* of the issue – have of course existed for a long time; one might think of Audrey Lorde's call to "dismantle the master's house" or Paulo Freire's *critical pedagogy*. But now that the principal and major alternative utopias have failed since 1989, the question of alternatives becomes ever more urgent.

If we turn to literature, the central focus of this paper, it is relevant to note that a similar argument has been advanced over the last years by a number of scholars working in literary and cultural studies, often criticising not postcolonial, but *poststructuralist* theory and *postmodernist* aesthetics. For the *post-post*-moment which they describe, the collapse of the Soviet Union in 1989 arguably plays the same pivotal role: An important strand of contemporary literature foregrounds social questions, constituting what Wolfgang Asholt (2013) has called a *new literary realism*, and the search for adequate tools to address and analyze this new realism – and also older literature, but from a contemporary vantage point – is common to both these arguments one might describe as *post-postcolonial* and *post-postmodernist*.[3]

The new literary realism, this "desire to write about the Subject, the Real, about historical or personal memory" (Viart and Vercier 2008 [2005], 16), is 'political,' for a start, due to its ability to capture a societal sensibility of the present. It often is a melancholic sensibility, Markus Messling (2019, 19–20) writes, arguing that contemporary French literature, for example, "has returned its attention to the question of 'reality' and has brought to the fore the intensities haunting Europe today: uncertainty, rage, a yearning for ideals, melancholia." It is an inquisitive literature, a tentative one, that replaces the old European or 'Western' habit of self-assured interpretation. Thereby, the post-post momentum does not simply draw on pre-deconstructivist notions of 'essence' and 'truth' when describing social realities, but clearly is mindful of the insights of deconstruction. It is to this effect that Scott (1999, 14) argues: "There is a real sense in which we now write *in the wake* of Edward Saïd". Wolfgang Asholt (2013, 28–29), in his article on contemporary francophone literature, observes that despite the renewed interest in social realism, "all these writers have given up [. . .] on generalizing projects that would explain the 'real world' in its totality, or at least some of its social or cultural milieus." They inherit "the debates of postmodernity and of poststructuralism, even though they would less and less claim this 'theoretical' heritage openly. Therefore, if there is today such a thing as a narrative 'realism,' it can only be a fragmented one" (Asholt 2013, 28–29).

---

[3] The terms *post-postcolonial* and *postcolonial present* (after Scott) are used interchangeably in this article. See also Graham Huggan's notion of *second wave postcolonialism* in his 2008 *Interdisciplinary Measures* and Lorna Burns' observations in her recent article "World Literature and the Problem of Postcolonialism" (Burns 2021).

It is in this sense that I understand the notion of *minor universality* to which this volume is dedicated: Poststructuralist and postcolonial discourse has dismantled the Western claim to universal values and knowledge as a potentially self-serving "rhetoric of power" (Wallerstein 2006; cf. Diagne 2018). Truth can no longer be found in universalist stances uttered from a presumably neutral position, but only in forms of situated, *minor* knowledge. Nevertheless, contemporary literature and thought go beyond the relativism and potential a-morality of continuous *deterritorialisation* and postmodernist aesthetics, reintroducing notions of justice and lived experience that hold for social groups or society at large. What is crucial is the return of normative claims that can no longer be discarded (see Messling 2019, 173, 19–20). These approaches suggest a universality again. They permit to locate individual positions – of writers or characters, when it comes to literature –, but always in reference to social justice in society as a whole; they don't give up the idea of global justice but look for it in forms of situated knowledge. The supposed universality of Western modernity has given way to a multitude of analyses of its pitfalls, a localised and *radical* questioning of *the social* and a decolonial quest for alternatives. It is a new *relation* to the world, Felwine Sarr (2017) contends, which both literary projects and their critics are looking for. As privileged sites for reflection and self-invention through narration and aesthetics, literature and art play a crucial role in the quest for these minor universalities and for the profound questioning of modernity it entails.

Against this backdrop, my question as a literary scholar in Caribbean studies is how to read Caribbean literature in the postcolonial present. What are literary and cultural approaches from and about the region that provide insights into the post-postcolonial moment? To what extent can the insights of post-postmodernism be relevant to Caribbean literature? I thereby start from the premise that a simple 'application' of (Western) post-postmodernist theories to Caribbean literary studies would be a perpetuation of western universalism; it would be a form of epistemic violence – the West producing again all knowledge, this time of its own deconstruction – and would risk missing some of the crucial elements of situated knowledge. At the same time, trying to neatly separate the West from the non-West would be artificial and equally misleading, as concepts are notoriously travelling and supposedly 'Western' knowledge has often long been appropriated by the Global South, as Dipesh Chakrabarty reminds us in *Provincializing Europe* (2000). The very concepts and traditions of poststructuralism and postcolonialism, for example, have mutually influenced each other and are entangled through the common tool of deconstruction.[4] In

---

4 While Gayatri Chakravorty Spivak, in her famous *Can the Subaltern Speak?* (1988 [1985]), discards Deleuze and Foucault on principle as idealists, Jacques Derrida, for example, in both

the following I therefore propose weaving together different positions that might foster a better understanding of the post-postcolonial problem space and of how to approach contemporary Caribbean literature – or rather, how to approach Caribbean literature per se, contemporary or not, from our present moment of relation to the world, bearing in mind the political and epistemological struggles they have been waging at given moments in time. Thereby, the notion of *transculturality* or *cultural hybridity* will repeatedly play a role. As a longstanding subject of discussion in the Caribbean, this notion has been widely used as a central aspect of postcolonial theory. While earlier criticism has already been pointing to some epistemological issues with the concept – such as its racialist baggage (Young 1995; Krämer 2015) – or has tried to develop new concepts capable of breaking with this baggage (see Derrida 1972 [1971], or Ette and Wirth 2014, 10), I will argue here that the postcolonial present demands an analysis of the role it has played in various social contexts.

3 Rancière's politics of literature and aesthetics

If we intend to trace the return to social questions in literature after a period of postmodernist writing (or evaluate earlier writing for its social criticism), and if it is true that contemporary literature often comes in the form of a new, fragmented realism, the question of *aesthetics* is crucial. How to determine whether the composite writing of Edwidge Danticat, Patrick Chamoiseau, or Junot Díaz, for example, originate in a postmodernist logic of *anything goes*, the aesthetics of "late capitalism" (Jameson 1991), or in a form of social realism? In what sense would their writing be more than the postmodern self-sufficient aesthetics and become *political*, this is, relevant beyond the framework of artistic propositions itself?

Jacques Rancière's *Politique de la littérature* (2010 [2007]) is a seminal study on the interplay of aesthetics, realism, and social structures, and it has proven useful for an analysis of new realist literature (Messling 2019). Therefore, one of the axes I explore is whether his engagement with nineteenth-century French bourgeois realism can be of use for the analysis of Caribbean literature in the postcolonial present, and how it connects to other scholarship in and on the region.

L'autre cap (1991) and *Le monolinguisme de l'autre* (1996), points towards the anti-colonial background to his notion of deconstruction. See also Kwame Anthony Appiah's "Is the Post- in Postmodernism the Post- in Postcolonial?" (1991).

Rancière bases his approach to literature on his broader argument concerning the politics of art. This argument starts with an extra-textual case for what he calls the "distribution of the perceptible" (*le partage du sensible*) – the discursive and material structure of society:

> This distribution and this redistribution of space and time, place and identity, speech and noise, the visible and the invisible, form what I call the distribution of the perceptible. Political activity reconfigures the distribution of the perceptible. It introduces new objects and subjects onto the common stage (Rancière 2010 [2007], 4).

Politics, for Rancière, is therefore not simply the implementation of political laws and decisions or the struggle for the power to decide on them, but the more general "configuration of a specific form of community" (2010 [2007], 3) which is lived on an experimental level as the distribution of the perceptible. Consequently, the politics of literature, or even of art more generally, is the way literature / art makes a particular distribution of the perceptible tangible through their aesthetics.

Beginning his analysis at the onset of the modern concept of literature, when around 1800 the term *literature* comes to denote the art of writing, replacing its prior significance as written scholarly knowledge, Rancière focusses on Flaubert and the bourgeois realism of the time, but his approach to aesthetic products is not confined to this time and genre. The same can be said for Pierre Bourdieu's *Les règles de l'art* (1992), which equally analyses Flaubert's literature in its capacity to shape the newly developing literary field, but also simply in its (realist) engagement with contemporaneous social structures. If apparently both Bourdieu and Rancière find that Flaubert's oeuvre "supplies all the tools necessary for its own [. . .] analysis" (Bourdieu 1995 [1992], 3), this can potentially be argued for most aesthetic projects engaged with extra-textual social reality, whether contemporary autosociobiographic writing, magical realism, or Afrofuturism. These approaches to understand aesthetics in relation to the extra-textual are useful for our interest in the determination of a new realism and the realist potential of literature influenced by deconstruction.

While realism obviously endeavours to portray reality, the politics of its literature does not pretend to simply reproduce this reality, however. Realism is not simply a fictionalised rendering of social structures, as Rancière makes clear from the beginning of his study. The politics of literature, he writes, does not concern "the way writers represent social structures, political movements or various identities in their books" (2010 [2007], 4). Instead of focusing on the presentation of these structures and movements – which constitute, after all, the distribution of the perceptible – Rancière focuses on the aesthetics of literature. But what is this *eigenvalue* literature can conserve when it comes to the critique of social reality?

This question is crucial since postmodernist and modernist art has often been reproached of a self-sufficient and ultimately elitist obsession with aesthetics. How can art claim to engage with social reality while being, by definition, removed from it through the process of fictionalisation? As Nick Nesbitt (2003, 207) has it, there is a guilt attached to any aesthetic representation of suffering, for "in speaking of suffering, in representing it aesthetically, the writer participates in a theft in which images are taken from the living and, perhaps worse still, from the dead, and merely represented". This is the reproach Chris Bongie (2008, 322–324), for example, brings to Édouard Glissant's emphasis on the poetic (*le poétique*). Nesbitt and Bongie stress the importance of self-conscious, at least partially metafictional writing in breaking this remove. But can there also be, thinking with Rancière, a valid politics within the aesthetic itself?

Markus Messling argues that literary *eigenvalue*, for Rancière, consists in the potential of language to develop a new understanding of, and a new approach to, society. Instead of showcasing a mirror-image of the world, nineteenth-century realism, in his understanding, wants to "generate an *intensity* impossible to resolve through existing notions of emotions, producing a sensation in the reader which has yet to be named" (Messling 2019, 39–40, emphasis added). An aesthetics, in this way, might well be able to search for and express new approaches to reality; intentionally or despite itself. This is what Messling calls *Welthaltigkeit*, "an intensity through which an author gets to the heart of a knowledge about their time" (2019, 39), and what Viart and Vercier call a *poétique de la langue*, "which, without wanting to imitate, voices the Real in its very intensity" (2008 [2005], 218).

I suggest that this approach to literature and aesthetics can be highly relevant in the light of our postcolonial present with its necessity not simply to criticise social injustices within the existing tools of the modern framework, but to go to the core of the social as such. This analysis is at the same time necessarily a decolonial one, but the emphasis has shifted with respect to the decolonisation of the 1960s or the school of postcolonial studies:

> This is what the postcolonial present demands. Rather than the anticolonial problem of overthrowing colonialism (or the West), or the decolonization of the West's representation of the non-West, what is important for this present is a critical interrogation of the practices, modalities, and projects through which modernity inserted itself into and altered the lives of the colonized (Scott 1999, 17).

We might want to ask: What is the relation to modernity – or *modern power*, as Scott calls the colonial "discourse of progress and improvement" (1999, 16) – that speaks out of a given novel? What problems and emotions does this modernity produce in the logic of the novel? Which alternatives are being explored, and to what results? This approach will permit not only for the reader to think and *live* differently in relation to the pitfalls of modernity and Western universalism, but also to come to a clearer evaluation of aesthetic projects inspired by cultural hybridity and deconstruction; it speaks to recent novels (Jamaica Kincaid's 2013 *See Now Then*, for example, in which a new language is being crafted to capture the despair and rage of an unhappily married West Indian woman) as much as to older ones (such as Andrew Salkey's 1960 *Escape to an Autumn Pavement* whose aesthetics transports the emotional tensions of West Indian gay men in 1950s London; cf. Ellis 2015a).

Reading Caribbean literature with a focus on aesthetics, and the intensities this aesthetics produces in its confrontation with the premises of modernity, draws a heightened attention to the time and space of utterance as well as the speaking subject, both on an intra- and an extra-textual level. If minor universality is always produced in concrete, subjective instances, what are these instances for the narrator and characters, but potentially also the author of a novel? Whose sensibility is being expressed, and by whom? What are their lived realities? These questions are crucial, because the politics of any given novel or artwork are highly personal in their reaction to social reality: Rancière traces the democratic aesthetics in Flaubert's post-revolutionary bourgeois realism, but all other sensibilities on the political and moral spectrum are possible; we might think, for example, of the horror in settler-colonial guilt of a Kenneth Cook or the lament of white male privileges of a Michel Houellebecq. Rancière himself avows that his politics of literature is a *metapolitics*, "leaving the great racket of the democratic stage to the orators in order to tunnel into the depths of society" (Rancière 2010 [2007], 21); it permits locating the politics of an aesthetics without inherent tools to judge its propositions. As an analytic instrument, it remains a-moral, the very term *intensity* carrying the epistemological baggage of poststructuralist a-morality. In order not simply to describe, but also to evaluate a specific politics of literature, it is therefore necessary to bring extra-textual knowledge to the reading of the text.

4 Stuart Hall's cultural studies approach

The generation of extra-textual knowledge, crucial for the evaluation of a text's aesthetic propositions, has often been achieved through a transdisciplinary dialogue between literary and social sciences in recent years. A forerunner of this dialogue between literary and social sciences is the field of cultural studies, both its continental and its British strand, that started in the 1950s and 1960s and regards literary texts as part of the larger context of cultural production. It will therefore not come as a surprise that David Scott cites Stuart Hall, the long-time director (1969–1979) and maybe most prominent voice of the Birmingham Centre for Contemporary Cultural Studies, as a major influence on his thinking. In a similar vein, Nadia Ellis, in a 2011 survey of Caribbean literary critique at the turn of the millennium, observes a "striking methodological shift towards the incorporation of cultural studies approaches into more traditional literary criticism" (Ellis 2011, 136–137), pointing to the disciplines heightened relevance in contemporary criticism. I therefore propose that cultural studies, and more specifically the work of Stuart Hall, is an important entry point into the study of Caribbean literature in the postcolonial present.

We have seen that Ashold observes a *fragmented* realism in contemporary literature, which does not claim one universal Truth while still crafting *minor* truths and knowledge through narration. The same can be said for literary theory and its connection to social sciences. The problem space of the *post-post* does not centre deconstruction as its main impulse anymore, but clearly inherits it as an epistemological necessity. Therefore, in theory as in literature, insights into social reality now need to be explorative.[5]

In an extensive interview with Scott for the first issue of *Small Axe* in 1996, Stuart Hall already displays a very similar understanding, embracing the heritage of deconstruction while simultaneously claiming the possibility to name *formations* and *articulations of power*. This is evident, for example, in the quote from the interview Scott choses as an epigraph for his introduction of *Refashioning Futures*, where Hall says: "I honour the moment that I am trying to surpass [. . .]. I'm not afraid of positionalities. I am afraid of taking positionalities too seriously" (Hall and Scott 2019 [1996], 258). Three central analytic tools that are helpful to Hall in this approach are the notions of strategy, contingency, and conjuncture, Scott proposes in his foreword to the interview:

> Hall is preeminently a strategic intellectual. Because he has given up the epistemological preoccupation with First Principles, with the search for a Final Philosophical Ground of True Knowledge, his approach to political questions depends crucially on such concepts as "contingency" and "conjuncture." That is to say, it depends on reading, at any given historical moment, the play of social forces and discursive hegemonies, and on identifying the

---

5 This is the approach of scholars such as Laurent Demanze (*Un nouvel âge de l'enquête*, 2019) who is interested in contemporary textual forms he calls *récits d'enquête*, narratives of investigation, that draw on journalism and empirical sciences, blending fiction and non-fiction – not in a positivist search for 'truth,' but for tangible social realities. Or of Ivan Jablonka (*L'histoire est une littérature contemporaine*, 2014), who argues that the nineteenth-century's division between 'literature' and the social sciences is not tenable anymore.

move that will produce a shift in the cognitive-political configuration (Scott in Hall and Scott 2019 [1996], 235).

Scott here reads Hall as a forerunner to the problem space of the postcolonial present whose cultural studies approach analyses a certain *conjuncture* – that is, the entanglement between discourse and social forces at a given moment – with the intention to advance the possibilities of thinking and acting upon it. Scott's observation thereby comes very close to Hall's formulations in his influential 1992 essay "What is this 'Black' in Black Popular Culture?":

> I begin with a question: what sort of moment is this in which to pose the question of black popular culture? These moments are always *conjunctural*. They have their historical specificity; and although they always exhibit similarities and continuities with the other moments in which we pose a question like this, they are never the same moment. And the combination of what is similar and what is different defines not only the specificity of the moment, but the specificity of the question, and therefore the *strategies* of cultural politics with which we attempt to intervene in popular culture, and the form and style of cultural theory and criticizing that has to go along with such an intermatch (Hall 1992, 21, emphases added).

Hall's essay, following this introduction, can be read as an endeavor to spell out the conjuncture, that is, the conjunctions or *entanglements* within the aesthetical / political / economic field in which black popular culture finds itself at the historical moment Hall alludes to and which he calls *the global postmodern*. His interest in popular culture connects to the general argument of cultural studies, moving away from elitist views on cultural expression in order to 'read' the semiotic propositions of a wide range of cultural products. By turning from his 'orthodox' Marxist training toward Althusser's notion of *ideology*, Hall refines the argument of base and superstructure, arguing for a more complex analysis of social and economic forces and cultural expression, including literature. Having witnessed the colonial structure of class differences during his childhood in Jamaica, Hall's turn away from high culture thereby goes along with a turn away from Western hegemony over the notion of *culture*. The growing importance of popular culture, connected to American cultural hegemony, in conjunction with the rising prominence of "decolonized sensibilities" (Hall 1992, 22), maps the field of black popular culture to which much of his work is dedicated. Significantly, the location of these decolonised sensibilities within the global postmodern, their politics and aesthetics, have little to do with a playful *anything goes*; Hall reads them as "modernism in the streets" (Hall 1992, 22). This approach, that is, to read aesthetic expression and sensibility (in the sense of both Hall and Rancière) *in conjunction* with the social, political, and discursive forces they are shaped by and they respond to, is what the postcolonial present demands.

5 Bourdieu and literary sociology

Before probing the notion of conjunctural reading some more in the last part of this essay, I return first to the usage of social sciences in literary studies, and more specifically to the relationship between author, society, and aesthetic propositions. I believe that we can gain important insights into the entanglements that Hall is interested in through the tools of literary sociology, a field which has gained in prominence in recent years. Both approaches – cultural studies as well as literary sociology, and connections to social sciences more broadly – can generate the extra-textual knowledge necessary for an aesthetical analysis of literature that would be *political* in Rancière's sense of the term.

Interestingly, perhaps the most influential study in literary sociology, Pierre Bourdieu's *Les règles de l'art* (1995 [1992]), equally bases its analysis on the literature of Flaubert – on his 1869 novel *L'éducation sentimentale* to be precise –, and like Rancière, it declares to find all the clues for its 'political' analysis in the novel itself. Bourdieu generates the necessary background knowledge to these clues through sociological insights, however; both with regards to society, and to the individual author. How Rancière as a philosopher generates this knowledge is less clear.

In the beginning of his study, Bourdieu challenges the longstanding argument of the independence of 'pure' art, asking: "Is it true that scientific analysis is doomed to destroy that which makes for the specificity of the literary work and of reading, beginning with aesthetic pleasure?" (Bourdieu 1995 [1992], xvi). While Rancière salvages literary *eigenvalue* through a focus on the aesthetic, Bourdieu simply proceeds to redefine aesthetic *pleasure*. Instead of purely intra-textual formal craftmanship, it is a deeper understanding of the social criticism inherent in a given novel – "that is to say, its informing formula, its generative principle, its *raison d'être*" (Bourdieu 1995 [1992], xix) – that makes reading enjoyable; the act of reintroducing into an "apparently self-contained literary space [. . .] the neglected 'margins' of the text, all that ordinary commentators leave aside" (Bourdieu 1995 [1992], xviii). While more formalist literary scholars have reclaimed a certain *incomprehensibility, ineffability,* or *transcendence* in their readings of Flaubert according to Bourdieu (1995 [1992], xvi),[6] he himself shows that one may "construct the social space of *Sentimental Education* by relying for landmarks on the clues that Flaubert

---

6 Glissant's notion of *opacité* might lend itself to similar readings and will require a more extensive analysis.

supplies in abundance and on the various 'networks' that social practices of cooptation such as receptions, soirees and friendly gatherings reveal" (1995 [1992], 5).

The shift that Bourdieu – but also Scott, Rancière, and Hall – effect in literary studies is a fundamental one. They break with the *dictum* of the *death of the author* and make the long-standing distinctions between author, narrator, and characters somewhat more complicated. This does not mean, evidently, that authors simply fictionalise their own lived experiences and that the logic of a novel needs to be linked back to its author's biography. Instead, an author obviously invents and thereby *chooses* the intensities unfolding in the fictional social space. But the latter can potentially find its counterpart in an actual social space, in the case of literary realisms habitually linked to the author's own experiences and sensibilities. In his discussion of *L'éducation sentimentale*, Bourdieu goes as far as to suggest that Flaubert sees in his main character, Frédéric, "an enterprise of *objectification of the self*, of autoanalysis, of socioanalysis," but that by the very act of "writing a story which could have been his, he shows that this story of a failure could not be the story of the person who wrote it" (1995 [1992], 25–26).

This becomes even more complicated in the various contemporary genres of *creative nonfiction, literary journalism*, and so on, and in what Annie Ernaux calls *autosociobiography*. In these genres, the author often does assume the position of both narrator and main character. While studies on autosociobiographical writing frequently focus on Ernaux, Didier Eribon, and Édouard Louis, whose interest in sociology is evident, rereading the autobiographies of various Caribbean authors in this light is also generative, as I have suggested in my Prelude with reference to Patrick Chamoiseau's autobiographical, and even, one might suggest, autosociobiographical, publications.

While Bourdieu's text-immanent analysis of Flaubert gives credit to the author to affect his own social analysis and criticism, others have conducted extra-textual sociological analyses on an author's social background or on the reception and circulation of their work (see e.g. Gesine Müller's *How is World Literature Made?* 2022). However, taking a sociological approach to Caribbean literature or using sociological insights for an aesthetic analysis does not claim the complete determination of writers by social structures. Just as the notion of *habitus* was conceived to prevent that an agent would "disappear" by reducing them "to the role of supporter or bearer (Träger) of the structure" (Bourdieu 1995 [1992], 179), literary sociology is mindful of the author's ability to make their own choices:

> [S]cientific analysis of the social conditions of the production and reception of a work of art [. . .] seems to abolish the singularity of the 'creator' in favour of the relations which made the work intelligible, only better to rediscover it at the end of the task of reconstructing the space in which the author finds himself encompassed and included as a point (Bourdieu 1995 [1992], xix).

This eventual *rediscovery* of the author's individual choices and positions with respect to social structures permits association to a specific socially locatable habitus or believe system by "either filiation or affiliation," as Rodolphe Solbiac (2020, 75) puts it in a recent socio-historical study on Martinique. An approach of literary sociology therefore requires both, an insight into the structures of a given society more generally and into the individual positions of an author, in order to make sense of a novel's aesthetic propositions.

6 Shalini Puri's conjunctural reading

I close with an intriguing example of a sociological study that I consider fundamental for an understanding of the Caribbean postcolonial present and contemporary literary sociology. Shalini Puri's *The Caribbean Postcolonial* (2004), which carries the subtitle *Social Equality, Post-Nationalism, and Cultural Hybridity*, goes to the core of the post-postcolonial problem space and can serve as a solid base for a reassessment of literary hybridity, both through its insights and its methodology.

The Caribbean Postcolonial is a social analysis of the various concepts of 'cultural hybridity,' such as *mestizaje*, *créolisation* and *Créolité*, *douglarisation*, *jibarismo*, and others, thereby approaching postcolonial notions with post-postcolonial criticism. "At the core of my work is the belief that we need to connect a poetics of hybridity to a politics of equality," Puri (2004, 1) writes, pointing to the connection between aesthetics, discourse, and politics her study effects.

Puri starts by acknowledging some of the epistemological criticism that has been brought forward against the notion of 'cultural hybridity,' such as the aforementioned conceptual legacy it carries of the Victorian extreme Right's discourse on race (Puri 2004, 4) or its reliance on concepts of *nationalism* as a "structuring absence" (Puri 2004, 27). However, her main criticism is another one, aiming at the sociopolitical mobilisations of the various notions of hybridity in given historical contexts. Significantly, the concept she employs for this post-postcolonial analysis is the same we have already encountered in Scott's reading of Stuart Hall: *conjunctural reading*, a notion she herself develops from a quote by Ella Shohat:

> A celebration of syncretism and hybridity per se, if not articulated in conjunction with questions of hegemony and neo-colonial power relations, runs the risk of appearing to sanctify the *fait accompli* of colonial violence. [. . .] As a descriptive catch-all term, hybridity per se fails to discriminate between the diverse modalities of hybridity, for example, forced assimilation, internalized self-rejection, political cooptation, social conformism, cultural mimicry, and creative transcendence (Shohat 1992, 109–10).

Similar to Hall, Puri uses the notions of *conjuncture* and *conjunction* to address aesthetic concepts "in relation to material and discursive issues at the time" (Puri 2004, 52). Conjunctural reading permits her to lay bare the origins of various notions of hybridity, the classist, racialised, and gendered interests that are connected to them and the political purposes they may serve. Another recent example of a similar undertaking is Deborah Thomas' *Modern Blackness*, also from 2004. Like Puri, Thomas elaborates the social and historical background to notions of cultural hybridity, but with a focus on the specific case of the Jamaican People's National Party's "mid-twentieth-century creole multiracial nationalism" (Thomas 2004, 48).

The insights and the methodology of both Puri's and Thomas' studies are instructive in the light of my discussion of the postcolonial present. Not only do they engage critically with postcolonial notions of cultural hybridity, they are also driven by a radical enquiry into the classist, racialised, and gendered foundations of *the social* in Caribbean societies. Connecting this form of *conjunctural reading* to a thorough investigation of the aesthetic politics displayed in a given novel could be a promising way of reading Caribbean literature in the wake of Scott's *Refashioning Futures*, and it might draw us closer to the *minor universalities* proposing responses to the crises of Western modernity, in the Caribbean and beyond.

7 Coda

An investigation of literary and cultural theory, this chapter has perhaps raised more questions than it provided answers. The issues proposed at the example of Patrick Chamoiseau in the beginning have not been resolved, but rather multiplied and complicated with reference to the postcolonial present. They have given way to a more general reflection on Caribbean literature within the current problem space, be it forms of 'hybrid' writing, contemporary new realism, or other literary projects we might want to reread from our contemporary vantage point. The Caribbean has itself brought forth an important corpus of literature and literary scholarship. Nevertheless, I hope that the connection of post-postcolonialism to post-postmodernism may elucidate some aspects of the study of literature from the region, and that it does not lead to a lack in specificity, but rather foster this specificity in the prerogative of conjunctural reading.

References

Appiah, Kwame Anthony. "Is the Post- in Postmodernism the Post- in Postcolonial?" *Critical Inquiry* 17.2 (1991): 336–357.

Asholt, Wolfgang. "Un renouveau du 'réalisme' dans la littérature contemporaine?" *Lendemains – Études comparées sur la France* 38.150–151 (2013): 22–35.

Bongie, Chris. *Friends and Enemies: The Scribal Politics of Post/Colonial Literature*. Liverpool: Liverpool University Press, 2008.

Bourdieu, Pierre. *The Rules of Art: Genesis and Structure of the Literary Field*. Stanford: Stanford University Press, 1995 [1992].

Burns, Lorna. "World Literature and the Problem of Postcolonialism: Aesthetics and Dissent." *The Work of World Literature*. Eds. Francesco Giusti and Benjamin L. Robinson. Berlin: ICI Berlin Press, 2021. 57–74.

Chakrabarty, Dipesh. *Provincializing Europe: Postcolonial Thought and Historical Difference*. Princeton: Princeton University Press, 2000.

Chamoiseau, Patrick. *Éloge de la Créolité*. Paris: Éditions Gallimard, 1989.

———. *Une enfance créole I: Antan d'enfance*. Paris: Éditions Gallimard, 1996 [1990].

———. *Écrire en pays dominé*. Paris: Éditions Gallimard, 1997.

Demanze, Laurent. *Un nouvel âge de l'enquête. Portraits de l'écrivain contemporain en enquêteur*. Paris: J. Corti, 2019.

Derrida, Jacques. "Signature événement contexte". *Marges de la philosophie*. Ed. Jacques Derrida. Paris: Éditions de Minuit, 1972 [1971]. 365–93.

———. *L'Autre cap*. Paris: Éditions de Minuit, 1991.

———. *Le monolinguisme de l'autre ou la prothèse d'origine*. Paris: Éditions Galilée, 1996.

Diagne, Souleymane Bachir. "De l'universel et de l'universalisme". *En quête d'Afrique(s): Universalisme et pensée décoloniale*. Ed. Souleymane Bachir Diagne et Jean-Loup Amselle. Paris: Albin Michel, 2018. 365–93.

Ellis, Nadia. "The Eclectic Generation: Caribbean Literary Criticism at the Turn of the Twenty-First Century." *The Routledge Companion to Anglophone Caribbean Literature*. Eds. Michael A. Bucknor and Alison Donnell. London: Routledge, 2011. 136–46.

———. "Between Windrush and Wolfenden: Between Windrush and Wolfenden: Class Crossings and Queer Desire in Andrew Salkey's Postwar London." *Beyond Windrush: Rethinking Postwar Anglophone Caribbean Literature*. Eds. J. D. Brown and Leah Rosenberg. Jackson: University Press of Mississippi, 2015. 60–75.

Ette, Ottmar, and Uwe Wirth. *Nach der Hybridität: Zukünfte der Kulturtheorie*. Berlin: edition tranvía – Verlag Walter Frey, 2014.

Fukuyama, Francis. *The End of History and the Last Man*. New York: The Free Press, 1992.

Hall, Stuart. "What Is This 'Black' in Black Popular Culture?" *Black Popular Culture: A Project by Michele Wallace*. Eds. Gina Dent and Michele Wallace. Seattle: Bay Press, 1992. 20–33.

Hall, Stuart and David Scott. "Politics, Contingency, Strategy: An Interview with David Scott." *Stuart Hall: Essential Essays, Volume 2, Identity and Diaspora*. Ed. David Morley. Durham/NC: Duke University Press, 2019 [1996]. 235–62.

Huggan, Graham. *Interdisciplinary Measures: Literature and the Future of Postcolonial Studies*. Liverpool: Liverpool University Press, 2008.

Jablonka, Ivan. *L'histoire est une littérature contemporaine. Manifeste pour les sciences sociales*. Paris: Seuil, 2014.

Jameson, Fredric. *Postmodernism, or the Cultural Logic of Late Capitalism*. Durham/NC: Duke University Press, 1991.
Krämer, Philipp. "Kreolistik Als Hybridologie, Kreolisierung Durch Physiognomie: Lucien Adam, René de Poyen-Bellisle und die Französischen Kreolsprachen." *Rassedenken in der Sprach- und Textreflexion: Kommentierte Grundlagentexte des Langen 19. Jahrhunderts*. Eds. Philipp Krämer, Markus Lenz, and Markus Messling. Paderborn: Wilhelm Fink, 2015. 465–81.
Messling, Markus. *Universalität nach dem Universalismus: Über frankophone Literaturen der Gegenwart*. Berlin: Matthes & Seitz, 2019.
Müller, Gesine. *How is World Literature Made? The Global Circulations of Latin American Literatures*. Berlin, Boston: De Gruyter, 2022.
Nesbitt, Nick. *Voicing Memory: History and Subjectivity in French Caribbean Literature*. Charlottesville: University of Virginia Press, 2003.
Puri, Shalini. *The Caribbean Postcolonial: Social Equality, Post-Nationalism, and Cultural Hybridity*. New York: Palgrave Macmillan, 2004.
Rancière, Jacques. *The Politics of Literature*. Cambridge: Polity Press, 2010 [2007].
Sarr, Felwine. *Habiter le monde: Essai de politique relationnelle*. Montréal, Québec: Mémoire d'encrier, 2017.
Scott, David. *Refashioning Futures: Criticism After Postcoloniality*. Princeton: Princeton University Press, 1999.
Shohat, Ella. "Notes on the 'Post-Colonial'." *Social Text* 31–32 (1992): 99–113.
Solbiac, Rodolphe. *La destruction des statues de Victor Schoelcher en Martinique: L'exigence de réparations et d'une nouvelle politique des savoirs*. Questions contemporaines. Paris: L'Harmattan, 2020.
Spivak, Gayatri Chakravorty. "Can the Subaltern Speak?" *Marxism and the Interpretation of Culture*. Ed. Cary Nelson and Lawrence Grossberg. Basingstoke: Macmillan, 1988 [1985]. 271–313.
Thomas, Deborah A. *Modern Blackness: Nationalism, Globalization, and the Politics of Culture in Jamaica*. Durham/NC: Duke University Press, 2004.
Ueckmann, Natascha. *Ästhetik des Chaos in der Karibik: 'Créolisation' und 'Neobarroco' in franko- und hispanophonen Literaturen*. Bielefeld: transcript, 2014.
Viart, Dominique and Bruno Vercier. *La littérature française au présent: Héritage, modernité, mutations*. Paris: Bordas, 2008 [2005].
Wallerstein, Immanuel. *European Universalism: The Rhetoric of Power*. New York: New Press, 2006.
Young, Robert. *Colonial Desire: Hybridity in Theory, Culture and Race*. London: Routledge, 1995.

Rukmini Bhaya Nair
Precolonial Universality and Postcolonial Diversity: The Example of the Indian Subcontinent

Abstract: This essay focuses on the semantic link between the notions of 'universality' and the 'university'. It does so by tracking changes in the specific roles played by universities on the Indian subcontinent, a region of the world with a legendary reputation for cultural diversity and difference. Plotting a narrative arc from the longue durée of the precolonial 'Axial Age', followed by the colonial Age of Empire, and now the postcolonial Age of the Anthropocene which has as its central motif the destruction of nature by humans, the essay explores the complex morphology of that dual and ambiguous construct 'human nature' as it is shaped by the technologies deployed and the epistemologies of 'indifference' developed in Indian universities at various historical junctures. Finally, mention is made of the constitution of a 'we' within the apparently benign halls of academe with a view to understanding the putative 'minor universalisms' of the future.

Keywords: colonialism, India, diversity, indifference, technology, universality, university

History, in its simplest rendition, is the narrative process by which geography is relentlessly converted into territory. When a landscape of undulating plains, a series of jagged hills, an isthmus here or a dim horizon there, come to be marked by lines and coded script on paper, we begin to see what was invisible before – the human face on nature's torso. And it is not always pretty.

This essay attempts to stretch the concept of 'minor universality' so that it spirals back to what has been called the Axial Age in human history (Jaspers 1953; Pinheiro et al. 2020) and then rebounds to the current Age of the Anthropocene (Williams et al. 2015). If a concept survives this 'stretch test', it is surely a worthy candidate for inclusion in the social science lexicons of the future; if not, it remains precariously subject to the 'space clearing' mechanisms of the modern marketplace (Appiah 1993). For reasons of parsimony and restricted word length, the putative workings of minor universalism will be explored here with respect to the case of the Indian subcontinent – the region that Alexander crossed into in 326 BCE after cutting the Gordian knot in Asia Minor at the apogee of the Axial

Age (roughly dated from the eighth to the third century BCE). This long durée of 'pre-colonialism', I want to suggest, contra historical convention, lasted through several rehearsals, rebounds and remembrances until the modern variants of colonialism were invented and put into practice across the globe from the late seventeenth to the twentieth centuries.[1] In this sense, the 'high colonialism' of the nineteenth century marked a narrative watershed between the precolonial and the postcolonial, this latter a troubled term that we may date for practical purposes to begin with the decolonisation of several countries across the globe in the mid-twentieth century (India, Indonesia, Ghana, Mozambique, Nigeria, and many others).[2]

Few concepts have been as protean in their manifestations as 'universalism'. Legend, however, tells us that while Proteus, the elusive, form-changing sea-god from whom the adjective 'protean' derives its name, would do all he could to hide 'the truth' from others, if one held on persistently enough, he would at last reveal the shape of things past, present and future. That is why he was also known as a prophetic god. One way to capture the complex morphologies of 'universalism' in a 'post-truth' era – to hold them as tight and constant as possible – is, I suggest, to 'imprison' them within a related concept. This is the strategy I adopt in this essay by considering the specific role that universities played on the Indian subcontinent during the precolonial Axial Age, the colonial Age of Empire and now the postcolonial Age of the Anthropocene.

---

[1] Like Jaspers' notion of an Axial Age in antiquity that so many professional historians dispute, the divisions of 'history' that I have postulated in this essay are undoubtedly questionable. It does seem contrarian to stretch the already shaky notion of 'axiality' right up to the edge of the eighteenth century. I do not dispute this but wish to suggest that my arguments about the 'axial' or the 'pivotal' are narrowly tied in this essay to the idea of 'memory storage' via devices external to the software of the brain (Donald 1991, 1997). In general, I would suggest that the decision to 'stretch' or to 'constrain' the role of historical agency depends on the specific arguments being presented. For example, Hofmann and Messling (2020) use a 'coincidence' of dates, namely, the year of Napoléon Bonaparte's birth (1769) and the year that the Berlin Wall fell (1989) to identify an 'epoch of universalism' that lasted 120 years. As they see it, "Napoleon's appearance on the scene of world history seems to embody European universalism" while "the fall of the Berlin Wall stands for an epistemic earthquake, which generated a world that can no longer be grasped through universal concepts" (Hofmann and Messling 2020). In short, their strategy is to approach "the idea of Europe and of its relation to the world itself" with "an ironic wink". I have myself used this technique while 'dating' the complex transitions between colonialism and postcolonialism and I gesture in this direction again in this essay. For a wonderful philosophical perspective on irony and the body politic, see Richard Rorty (1989).

[2] Stuart Hall's classic 1995 essay 'When was the Postcolonial?' deals with some sophistication on this matter of dating 'postcolonialism' (Nair 2002, 2011a).

The common etymological roots of the words 'universalism' and 'university' are obvious. For example, this is how a standard dictionary describes the modern 'western' university, the first recorded usage in English apparently being in 1300 with reference to St Edmund's Hall in 'Oxenford'. A university comprises:

> the whole body of teachers and scholars engaged, at a particular place, in giving and receiving instruction in the higher branches of learning; such persons associated together as a society or corporate body, with a definite organization and associated powers and privileges (esp. that of conferring degrees), and forming an institution for the promotion of education in the higher or more important branches of learning, also the colleges, buildings, etc. belonging to such a body (*The Oxford English Dictionary*, Volume II, 245).

Wholeness and the coming together of a like-minded community, an agentive 'we' so to speak, a society gathered together at a particular location with the common purpose of teaching and learning: what could constitute a more enticing preface to the story of western universalism? Yet even here there is telling mention of 'powers and privileges', of being a 'corporate body' and of territorial possession over both knowledge and 'buildings'. I want to maintain, further, that we could track this narrative of the university and its imbricated tale of universalism back to long-ago 'Axial' roots on the Indian subcontinent and elsewhere until we arrive at the apex of colonialism in India – and of course, elsewhere – in the nineteenth century. At this point, the narrative around 'universalism' changes dramatically and then changes direction sharply once again when we arrive at the postcolonial moment – a moment that we still seem not to have quite left behind. Thus is the Angel of History propelled forward buffeted by the gale-winds of the past and always facing backwards, as Walter Benjamin reminds us in his poignant analysis of Paul Klee's painting. In the next brief segments (or fragments), I piece together some of the shards of memory and event that the said Angel may have spotted in his hurtling journey towards the future.

Precolonial Investigations: The psychologist Karl Jaspers characterised what he termed "the Axial Age" as "an interregnum between two ages of great empire, a pause for liberty, a deep breath bringing the most lucid consciousness" (1953, 51). According to Jaspers, this period of psychic 'deep breathing', which began around the eight century BCE, saw the independent and coincidental rise of innovative and 'universal' systems of thought in several civilisational complexes across the Eurasian landmass. On the Indian subcontinent, various schools of philosophy (*darshana*) conduct vigorous debates on the nature of reality and human existence, taking their cue from post-Vedic Upanishadic thought; and the 'revolutionary' schools of Jainism and Buddhism took root, the latter being described by India's representative, Swami Vivekananda, at the Chicago World Congress of Religions in 1893 as "the fulfilment of Hinduism". In China, Confucius, Laozi and other thinkers debated the codes of conduct by which both rulers and the common people should live. In Persia (modern Iran), the monotheistic and arguably Manichean doctrines of Zoroastrianism were articulated and adopted as the state religion of Persia's rulers for over a millennium; and in Greece, a long line of 'Pre-Socratic' philosophers such as Thales, Anaximander, Pythagoras, Democritus, and Parmenides whose thoughts abutted and informed the writings of Plato and Aristotle, produced theories about the origins of the universe and much else.[3] Socrates, Plato, and Aristotle's own influential works came at the very end (or perhaps the glorious apex) of this Axial Age. We must also not forget the attested historical footnote which informs us that Philip of Macedon appointed Aristotle tutor to his young son Alexander. Alexander's respect for his teacher, who had scant respect for 'barbarians' and was supportive of his royal pupil's unbounded territorial ambitions, reportedly led him to carry Aristotle's works with him on his triumphant conquest of Persia – beyond which lay India where Alexander's exhausted troops at last mutinied and refused to cross the Ganges river, forcing him to turn back. Alexander died sick in Babylon at the age of 33 without ever making it home to Macedonia. But narrative memory is strangely enduring and to this day, there are towns, localities and even hotels across northern India and Pakistan proudly – or ironically – named after Alexander or 'Sikandar' in local parlance.[4]

Such a summary foreshortening of the Axial Age, its ending in a miasma of mutiny, sickness and myth, was probably not one with which Jaspers would have agreed; but there have been other, more substantive. criticisms of his celebration of this 'age' (MacCulloch 2006; Provan 2013), since its boundaries are so historically vague. Why, for instance, does Jaspers not include Christ and Muhammad in his inventory of thinkers by 'stretching' the axiality of his age just a few centuries? What was the connection between the pre-Axial world and the sudden appearance of a phalanx of 'Axial' thinkers? Jaspers' responses to such questions are, at best, sketchy, but perhaps we should view his account from a *narrative* rather than a strictly historical perspective. Jaspers speaks as a psychologist interested in the motives or 'goals' for the creation of history; one might say his concern is with the historiographical question of how history comes to be constituted or how it becomes persuasive to distant civilisational 'others' and not with the events of history *per se*. Jaspers's narrative presents Buddhism, Taoism, Zoroastrianism and the Greeks as players in the creation of thought-worlds committed to 'universal explanations' of human behaviour and aspiration; these systems of thought crossed civilisational boundaries and were 'religious' (see Geertz 2011) in the broadest possible sense.

---

3 The pre-Socratics are traditionally held to have had connections with India: see Drew (1998).
4 Not to be confused with Sikandar Shah II (1330–1395), ruler of the Bengal Sultanate.

Additionally, Merlin Donald's (1991, 1997) argument that 'external memory storage devices' such as handwriting – and later, the printing press and now e-storage on computers and cell phones – were, and are, critical in the history of human thinking seems compelling in this regard. Donald theorises human symbolic thought as possessing three aspects that were also stages in human cognitive evolution: the *mimetic*, involving imitation of gestures, actions and sounds; the *mythic*, involving narration; and the *'technologically supported'*. In this connection, it could be argued, as Pinheiro et al. (2020) have done, that the Axial Age was one in which the writing as a technology for the transmission of ideas truly came into its own (Herodotus and Thucydides, rival scribes, both wrote their histories during the Axial agA) and even though Socrates may have railed against writing in the *Phaedrus* as an invention that would destroy memory, induce forgetfulness, and rob oral communication of its stimulating vitality by reducing it to the dumb charade of a painted likeness, he was fighting a rear-guard battle (see Nair 2022c).[5] The technology of writing (on stone, clay, brass, vellum, parchment, and what have you) was to become the mainstay of permanent, often public, record-keeping for the next couple of millennia. It was to exert powerful narrative control over forms of 'knowledge transmission' until printing press technologies began to create new, private reading publics in, roughly, the eighteenth century. We will return to this point in the next section on the institutionalisation of colonial power; here, I shall only note that the dominance of (hand-)written texts as the main mode for the transmission of information from 800 BCE all the way to the eighteenth century constitutes one sort of argument in favour of 'stretching' the contours of the Axial Age as one in which the impulses of religious proselytisation and territorial expansionism were simultaneously – and ably – aided by hierarchical, even patriarchal, writing technologies that tended to sternly subjugate oral 'female' modes of community building (Nair 2009b, 2022c).

Writing was also among the main tools that sustained the first 'universities' that came up in the Axial Age (see also Nair 2017b). Returning briefly at this point to my contention concerning universities as a locus of the 'universal', I should note here that when Alexander began his Indian campaign right after his conquest of the Persian Achaemenid Empire which then extended all the way to the Indus valley, several records explicitly mention a particular city that he crossed. This was the city of Takshashila ('Taxila' in the Greek histories) – already a renowned urbanised centre for cross-cultural exchanges of knowledge since it was situated at the

---

5 While speech in its modern form has been part of the human communicative apparatus for at least 40 to 50,000 years, writing is a surprisingly late 11th hour invention, dating back, experts say, only 5000–7000 years or thereabouts (see Nair 2002c).

confluence of three major trade routes, and hospitably accommodated a broad range of Hindu, Buddhist, Persian and Indo-Greek perspectives on learning. While scholars have debated whether Takshashila counts as a university in the modern 'western' sense, it was certainly known as a center for medical training and instruction in arts ranging from archery to disputation/law. The archaeologist John Marshall who excavated Takshashila in the early twentieth century reported that ancient Buddhist texts refer to it as a "university center where students could get instruction in almost any subject" (Marshall 1960, 23). More recently, Cochrane excellently summarises several scholarly commentaries on ancient Asian sites of learning and, likewise, concludes that this "evidences a strong holistic content in its training curriculum. Taxila . . . emerges as the meeting ground of east and west" (Cochrane 2009, 32). Nor is this by any means esoteric information; school textbooks in India routinely include references to the ancient universities of Takshashila and Nalanda (see the AICTE online guide). I would therefore submit that an Axial University such as the one Alexander encountered in Takshashila begins to offer us a glimpse of what 'universalism' may have looked like under an early non-western banner.

Colonial Indifference: Two millennia after Takshashila, the British found their way to India, first as East India Company traders and then after 1857 as administrators for the Crown – and this time they brought with them their own ravishing version of an 'universalist' ideology. At the time, India still retained its reputation as a land of myth and mystery – as well as of considerable wealth (see Maddison 2007, who has estimated that India share of the world economy was 22.6% in 1700, almost equal to the whole of Europe's share of 23.3%). On the basis of copious written records, we can safely surmise, though, that when the British began to arrive in India small adventurous batches, they not only found widespread evidence of wealth; they also confronted an India so diverse and complicated with hundreds of different languages and bewildering ethnic differences that it was only in the beholding eye of a committed colonial mindset that it could ever be rendered as a single cultural region (Nair 2002, 2010, 2021a, and 2021c). The year 1857 was particularly critical in this respect as it was the year of the Sepoy Mutiny (now known as the First War of Indian Independence) which witnessed a united 'rebellion' of Hindus and Muslims forces against the British and so alarmed them that the Crown formally took over forthwith the following year from the East India Company. Strikingly ironic is the fact that 1857 was also the year in which three major universities were first instituted in Calcutta, Madras, and Bombay. The language of instruction at these universities was, needless to say: English.

English was of course hardly a surprising choice of language to educate the Indian populace on the protocols of modern western universalism. It was, rather, a foregone conclusion – for, as Thomas Babington Macaulay had already declared in his widely quoted Minute of 1835:

> The question now before us is simply whether . . . we shall countenance, at the public expense, medical doctrines which would disgrace an English farrier, astronomy which would move laughter in girls at an English boarding school, history abounding with kings thirty feet high and reigns thirty thousand years long, and geography made of seas of treacle and seas of butter (Macaulay 1965 [1835], 166).

The 'us' here is no inclusive 'we'; it is the British Parliament – and so we might be justified in wondering exactly whose 'public expense' Macaulay had in mind, given that a staggering £9.2 trillion (or about $44.6 trillion at today's rates) was siphoned out of India during the 200 or so years of Company and Crown rule over India (Patnaik and Patnaik 2016).

It hardly needs restating, moreover, that the colonial period was when certain institutional forms of governance were homogenised the world over, whether the colonisers were Spaniard, Dutch, Portuguese, French, or British. Throughout the eighteenth and nineteenth centuries, these gene carriers of the 'high culture' of modern Western democracies traveled outward in a frenzy of occupation, so that the being of 'high colonialism' is, in turn, inseparable from the 'official gaze' of administrative processes that the stamped upon an astonishing variety of societies one consolidated ideology of how to 'run a state'.

In short, while the 'universalism' of Takshashila in the Axial Age could perhaps lay claim to a certain cross-cultural inclusivism, the 'universalism' of the colonial university was markedly different. It was *linguistic* and *bureaucratic* and one of its main goals seems to have been to impose sameness via linguistic exclusion. By decreeing an 'apex predator' institutional format with English at the top of the food-chain as the main language of instruction, both administrative and educational, the colonial period in India – and perhaps elsewhere – effectively reconstituted Jaspers' metaphor.

At this point, the 'deep breathing' of the Axial Age metamorphosed, so to speak, into an age of language suffocation(s). My suggestion therefore is that colonialism was that 'watershed' era in which the technology of the printing press was forcefully used to produce textbooks, censuses, dictionaries, newspapers, and journals such as the august *Journal of the Asiatick Society* in which William Jones and others published their authoritative views on Sanskrit and the other languages of India. It is in this sense that Indians may have been said to have been 'subalternised', robbed of voice and cultural jurisdiction, becoming ever more expert as English language ventriloquists the higher they climbed up the colonial and postcolonial administrative ladders. In order to be comprehended and rewarded by their rulers, they had to constantly translate themselves into the singularity of English. Elsewhere, I have called this phenomenon the "institutionalization of indifference" (Nair 2002, 2018, 2022b).

Just as Edward Saïd's 'Orientalism' offered scholars in the 1980s a powerful matrix concept that enabled an understanding of how the Western 'Occident' created and reproduced itself through a continuous, mostly unilateral, process of inventing its Oriental 'Other', the idea of 'indifference' is another a matrix within which the workings of colonialism and postcolonialism may be analysed. Modern and postmodern theories of meaning in the west have relied, especially *après* Saussure and Derrida, on the key notion of 'difference' to describe relationships between signifiers – calling up a sort of joyous polyphonic buzz. The concept of indifference, however, unlocks the door into yet another significant chamber of semantics concerning negative emotion and affect. Unlike its opposite counterpart, 'indifference' as a colonial/postcolonial pathology is a subjective mental state rather than any objective property of objects. Derrida, we know, playfully refashioned Saussure's strict concept of difference as a standard marker of relations between signifiers (for example between the minimal pairs *pest/post*) with his famous postmodern pun – *differ/defer*. Difference, in this sort of analysis, as I see it, is an 'out-there' quality, which can be deictically indicated (for example via *dress codes/address terms* etc.). It is a visible, audible, tangible quantity, an external observable. In grammatical terms, it is a count-noun from which we may derive several parts of speech (for example *differentiate/differ/differences*). Indifference, on the contrary, is an 'in here', invisible, subjective mental state, signifying an interior condition rather than any objective property of objects. Linguistically, 'indifference' is a verbal monolith: non-count, antonymous, and tending towards the anonymous. But how does such a description apply to understanding 'minor universalism' – or Western Universalism in very small caps – in colonial/postcolonial contexts?

Well, here's a familiar example: 'western' visitors to India are instantly struck by its complicated legal and bureaucratic discourses of form-filling. But this addiction is not exactly *sui generis*; it is, in large part, the heritage of an empire that once had, as its colonial rulers repeatedly complained, to deal with the problem of overwhelming otherness. Variously valorised as 'objectivity', 'impartiality', and 'stoicism', indifference, I suggest, was in fact a very particular intellectual stance invented during the colonial period for the precise purposes of organising the complex and extremely heterogeneous domain of the colony. It was an institutionalised mode of response to pluralism, necessarily reductionist in its erasure of differences of style, opinion and culture.

By and large, in modern and postmodern Western academia, the inherent plurality of the semantics of difference has ensured that its political alliances have been with multiculturalism and its natural constituency the modish left liberal establishment. Indifference, on the contrary, in a postcolonial state, even in academia, is ultimately associated with the dimly ambiguous conservative corridors of power. Although much critical attention is devoted in 'objective' sociological descriptions of colonial/postcolonial societies to the high levels of corruption and violence said to characterise them, the underlying structure that accounts for these disparate ills could comprise the bureaucratic manufacture, on paper, of the unremarkable attitudinal substance I term 'indifference'. Gilles Deleuze writes enigmatically in *Difference and Repetition*:

> Indifference has two aspects: the undifferentiated abyss, the black nothingness, the indeterminate animal in which everything is – but also the white nothingness, the once more calm surface upon which float unconnected determinations like scattered members: a head without a neck, an arm without shoulders, eyes without brows (Deleuze 1994, 28).

In other words, the bureaucratic power of the printed word – "the black nothingness" plus "the white nothingness" – are all the "determinations" required for ideological state apparatuses (see also Althusser 2014) to instil obedience in colonial/postcolonial states. Such structures of knowledge are articulated in a top-down language (English, in the Indian case) that permits little intimacy, let alone sensuousness or playfulness (see Nair 2002, 2011a, 2011b, 2015). Postcolonialism, it should be borne in mind, differs from its grand predecessor, colonialism in one crucial respect. No temporal sequence of events identifies it – no Minute of 1835, no battle of Plassey, no war of 1857, no salt marches to Dandi, signpost its territory. Rather, the postcolonial is a region of shadows, indicative of a mentality, an inherited condition of the psyche. It is this potent paradigm of colonial indifference that is now built into the structure of reigning postcolonial institutions where the official language remains English (or whatever other language the former colonisers used) and 'good' university education is still in English (or whatever the former colonial language was). That is why Gandhi wrote with conviction in 1909:

> To give millions a knowledge of English is to enslave them. The foundation that Macaulay laid for education has enslaved us. I do not suggest that he had any such intention, but that this been the result. Is it not a sad commentary that we should have to speak of Home Rule in a foreign tongue? (Gandhi 1997 [1909], Chapter XVIII 'On Education')

Rabindranath Tagore, who whole-heartedly agreed with Gandhi on this issue, went further. He set up his own university 'Visva Bharati' (roughly 'The World in India' but this is a terrible translation!) in 1921 in rural Bengal at Shantiniketan long before India gained Independence in 1947. Tagore passionately believed that his interpretation of intellectual 'universalism' contrasted fundamentally with the colonial apparatus of modern 'western' education (see Nair 2017a, 2017b, 2018, 2021b, 2021c). His university offered instead a boldly cosmopolitan ideal of education, ecologically attuned to the natural environment, broadly interdisciplinary and creatively 'free'. Interestingly, Tagore also recognised the printing press was a great technological asset in the dissemination of knowledge and made an early decision to publish in the Indian languages as well in English by setting up his own University Press at Visva Bharati. This 'alternative university' and its press-imprint still thrive today and, once again, embody a locus of ideological conflict concerning interpretations of 'universalism' in non-western locations, since it is resistant to those other formats of indifference perpetuated in India's more conventional universities modelled on the colonial system – a system that still ensures that citizens of even the most emancipated and progressive postcolonial states (of which the Indian state may or may not be a member) can remain subject to an internalised orientalism that in effect denies the value of actually being surrounded by a vital buzz of multiple cultures and languages. It is this continuing battle from ancient Takshashila to Tagore in the colonial/postcolonial period over what constitutes the narrative of universalism today that is the theme of my next and final fragment.

Postcolonial Insurrections: Among the most radical decisions made by the newly independent Indian state post-1947 was the one to overhaul the homogenising language and cultural policies of the former colonial power. It did so by attempting to replace what we might call a 'mono-literacy' educational model with a 'multi-literacy' model. That is:

a. it created 'linguistic states' whereby many of the major languages of India (Gujarati, Kashmiri, Oriya, Telugu, Tamil etc.) would have their own federal dominions;
b. it decided on 'Hindi' as an official language;
c. it adopted a 'three-language formula' which meant that every child schooled in India had to learn three languages: his or her mother-tongue, Hindi the 'official' language of the state, and one 'international' language, which de facto overwhelmingly meant English;
d. and finally, it declared English as an 'interim' official or associate official language for an initial period of 15 years, until Hindi and the 'other languages' of India became sufficiently 'strong'.

These moves were made with the laudable goal of reversing the attitudinal indifference of nearly two centuries of colonial rule. By acknowledging the enormous cultural pluralism of India, its undeniable diversity, the Indian state believed that it was taking an emancipative stance, as Tagore had done, on shared 'universal' ideas of equality, freedom of speech, democracy and the whole nine yards of human well-being.⁶ But today, it is common knowledge that English is far from being 'given up' after 15 years. Ironically, it remains the primary language of elite aspiration in India (Nair 2008, 2012, 2019). Economic globalisation, the rise of the IT industry in India and the privileging of electronic media the world over, as well as the dominance of America as a super-power, have changed language contexts in such a way that Indian democracy must now respond to these forces in a manner that was unforeseen when India's language and educational frameworks was first laid out after decolonisation (Nair 2012). The postcolonial enactment of 'minor universalism' could aptly be described as a period of irregular and ragged but life-preserving breathing across the world.

Worth recalling here is the apparent point that the words 'diversity' and 'university' seem to stand in a complementary relationship to each other. If the former implies variety (Latin, *diversus*), the latter stands for a sort of gravitational force, a centrum, that pulls together these different modes of thought. But how is new life to be breathed into this creaky old slogan of 'unity in diversity' as we consider the metonymic zone of university education today in a technologically dominated world? In this brave new world, our cell phones have arguably become our most intimate knowledge companions. We suffer paroxysms of anxiety if we are separated from these extra limbs magically attached to us in the past few decades – and to which we have equally 'become attached' in Jaspers' psychological sense (see Nair 2022a, 2022b). In such an environment, the boundaries between fact and morphed fact, truth and opinion, hate and empathy, speech and writing, have been, like it or not, dramatically revised. Hence the question seems moot: how do we manage the 'cognitive dissonance', the potentially violent struggles for intellectual dominance that the current phase in the global evolution of our institutions of higher learning entail? How do we create a 'diversity friendly' social ecology in our universities in the midst of the sort of revolutionary and bewildering technological changes that we find ourselves in?

After all, diversity today signals the sorts of difference that the scholars who set up universities all the way from the Axial Age to the colonial period could not have dreamt of. To consider an obvious example, whereas in the past the control of 'higher learning' was obviously patriarchal and worked mainly by gender exclusion, today gender 'inclusion' is a buzzword. This is a 360-degree turnaround. It is a given in contemporary democracies that 'pluralism' is a desirable social good across categories such as gender, language, religion, disabilities, and economic and

---

6 This phrase in American English is of unknown origin but 'nine yards' is coincidentally evocative in the Indian context since it also refers to the gorgeous nine-yard full length 'sari' worn in Southern India.

social class (Nair 2003a, 2003b, 2009a, 2012, 2022a, 2022b). And it is easy enough to think of the merits of such universal inclusive practices. We can, for instance, immediately list the following advantages of increasing gender diversity in universities. Such diversity:

- *disrupts staid thinking:* The entry of hitherto 'excluded genders' into a place of 'higher education' encourages lateral thinking and disturbs conventional norms.
- *increases community bargaining skills:* Women and transgender individuals are culturally adept and this increases collective bargaining power in the university arena.
- *expands skill sets:* The more a university/institute aims to expand and grow, the more skill sets, including specialist language and cultural skills, are required in its domain.
- *encourages thinking on rights and social justice issues, even beyond gender:* Because of entrenched discrimination of various sorts, 'other genders' are more likely to bring wider concerns into universities.
- *brings economic benefits to the organisation entered after university:* A growing body of research indicates better economic performance in jobs is linked to higher levels of gender diversity.
- *increases social capital and creates vital role models:* Beyond regulatory compliance and reservations, there is a need to highlight gendered role models.

Ideal as this scenario may be, we know that in practice gender statistics can be damning, especially in countries like India which has slipped 10 places to 108 (out of 144 countries) over the past decade in the WEF's Gender Gap report. Women represent less than half (about 48.5%) of India's population. India's labor force reflects this skewed sex ratio and low visibility for women across the country's professional spectrum: only 27% of Indian women had a job in 2017, versus 35% in 1990, according to the World Bank. At 17% of GDP, the economic contribution of Indian women is less than half the global average. Women earn 57% of their male colleagues' earnings for the same work and India brings up the rear of the rankings at 139 out of 144 in economic participation and opportunity. This situation has worsened, as grimly expected, during the 2019–2022 Covid-19 pandemic. When we consider 'diversity' of any kind in a postcolonial universe, we have to place it against this sort of depressing backdrop.

Meanwhile, our best universities continue to churn out, within our current 'meat-grinder' model of higher education inherited from the monochromatic colonial model, 'certified' knowledge with little attention to any dire statistics. Institutions that trade in degrees and identity tags (historian, sociologist, literary critic, biologist, etc.), such universities can, in theory, accommodate the whole human community and all diversity. However, by the same token, they can also be coercive and reductive in a manner memorably described by Michel Foucault as 'discipline and punish'. Precisely because it aims to be wholly 'inclusive', the contemporary bureaucratised university ends up being 'exclusive' and persistently engaged in the meta-task of creating 'fair' and thus ever more bureaucratic, rules of exclusion. This is the curious paradox we must resolve if we are to realistically espouse diversity in university education. At least the following four initial moves seem necessary:

First, we cannot afford to ignore the stark facts of economic disparity like the ones detailed above. I would argue that the cognitive logic of our universities today follows on from the facts of economic and social deprivation; and that actual malnutrition is a good predictor of epistemic starvation in higher education. India is a country that suffers in equal measure from both epistemic hunger (see Dennett 1991; Nair 2002, 2019) and real hunger (the latest Hunger Index has seen India slip to 101 among 116 countries). This is that human face on nature's torso – grim.

Indeed, if we dare look these unpalatable facts in the face, there seems to be only one viable solution. It is to shift our focus from the stern, faux rigorous, rank-ordering modes of university assessment to more flexible experiential and embodied modes of empathy. We must, that is, accept that discussing and resolving pressing problems such as that of world hunger and malnutrition, particularly among children, is not embarrassingly low-status activity in university seminars (Nair 2021a). Rather, it is on par and goes hand in hand with discussing philosophical problems of 'well-being' (see, for example, Nussbaum 1999) and the ideals of a good life. If we are not to fall into the colonial error of snobbish indifference one more time, we must admit this primary postcolonial insight. In fact, to my mind, the great intellectual revolutions of the twenty-first century on the Indian subcontinent are likely to arise out of the struggles of various disadvantaged groups and communities such as women, Dalits and tribal communities to enter the literacy stakes and insert their own texts, and even more excitingly, their *theories* of text into international university canons. This would constitute a signal contribution to the annals of 'minor universalism'(Nair 2002, 2003a, 2003b, 2015; Nair and deSouza 2020).

Second, ancillary to the point above, we may wish to map a new set of codes to describe a psychological terrain to which we have long been indifferent and which has therefore been damagingly invisible. This is the common vocabulary that we as inhabitants in all regions of the world share *outside* of academia in every culture. A foundational effort in this direction was made in the aftermath of WW II by Raymond Williams in his iconic work *Keywords: A Vocabulary of Culture and Society* (1976). In India, we have recently tried to repeat Williams' monumental experiment at a time of great global ground-shifts and groundswells, this time with over 200 Indians from various disciplinary backgrounds writing on the words that matter to them in a post-technological universe that is nevertheless heir to an infinite store of past narratives, both mythical and historical. Our hope is that this locally anchored, yet 'universalist', venture will also offer a template for further research on minor universalisms (Nair and deSouza 2020).

Third, as a species, we are tool-using animals addicted to the ceaseless invention and consumption of technologies from simple handwriting to complex computers. But today we are at a crisis point in the Age of the Anthropocene where our technologies of communication appear to have colonised our minds to the extent that they ominously exceed our socio-cultural understanding of how best to use them. As Donald (1997) puts it:

> The externalization of memory was initially very gradual, with the invention of the first permanent external symbols. But then it accelerated, and the numbers of external pre-presentational devices now available has altered how humans use their biologically given cognitive resources, what they can know, where that knowledge is stored, and what kinds of codes are needed to decipher what is stored . . . . the human cognitive system is affected not only by its genetic inheritance, but also by its own peculiar cultural history (Donald 1997, 362–363).

Fourth and finally, in order to redesign our shared stores of internal and 'external' cultural memory, university professors should now perhaps seriously attempt to stretch the language of theory to include narrative – not just as 'data' but as a robust method for "conjecture and refutation" (Popper 1963). Narrative is an empathy generating mechanism. Just think of what happens to us physiologically when we listen to an engrossing, if 'false', story – our pulse rates go up, our eyes fixate, our palms sweat. In fact, we have many of the same reactions that we would have if we were in the real situations that these stories depict. This is why fictions (epics, myths, novels) manifest as discourse universals, found in every known human culture. They train our species in cultural survival. All cultures may not erect impressive 'theory-houses' such as modern western-style universities, but it is my contention that they all exchange stories as primary explanatory devices (Nair 2003a, 2011b, 2014, 2015).

Stories as a cross-cultural genre are in my view cognitively designed to probe into contexts, present conflicting hypothesis, examine causal evidence, and come to some resolution. In this sense, stories are a species of 'natural theory' and embody an instinctive research methodology. As I have argued elsewhere (Nair 2014, 2021b), the history of cultural evolution has worked by introducing us to 'primitive' but foundational versions of biological theory (how the leopard got its spots); political theory (Robin Hood was a revolutionary who challenged the oppressive class structures of a feudal society); moral theory (Cordelia's 'sin' was to plainly tell the 'truth' and Lear's to stubbornly refuse to hear it); aesthetic theory (the mirror on the wall in 'Snow White' proved itself a dispassionate judge of beauty); and so forth. These stories perform, in essence, a function not dissimilar to the cultural 'work' done by Darwinian theory for biology, Marxist theory for political science or Christianity for ethics or Platonic theory for aesthetics. Naturally, this process constitutes hard intellectual labour. At the same time, fictions sugar-coat this cognitive labour we undertake uncomplainingly each day by appealing to our emotions, thus giving readers and listeners the seductive affective practice so necessary to cultural survival (Nair 2003a, 2011a, 2011b, 2014, 2019, 2021c).

The sociolinguist William Labov (1972) further suggests that all narratives, fiction or factual, display in their 'full form' a six-part structure that he found among African American oral youth narratives in which the first person protagonists find themselves in 'danger of death' situations. These consist of the *Abstract* (pertaining to the theme of the story); the *Orientation* (describing scene, time, and other contextual details); the *Complicating Action* (focusing on narrative crisis); the *Evaluation* (bringing out emotional reactions in the characters as well as among listeners to the story); the *Resolution* (resolving the narrative crisis); and the *Coda* (returning to the narrative time to the present so that the audience is freed from the grip of the story). While these six features comprise the 'full form' of a story, the only 'essential' part of narrative, according to Labov, is the element of 'complicating action' or crisis. As he puts it, it is always relevant to say, 'I saw a man fall off a bridge today'.

Narrative, that is, is a discourse universal meant for the theorisation of crises, danger and distress – and the production of future hope. As an primary instrument of thought, it teaches us to breath in different rhythms for different cognitions: let's say, if we take recourse to a musical metaphor for a moment, from adagio to andante to allegro to vivace and presto. Jaspers writing in Germany under the shadow of Nazism knew this, as did Macaulay casting the looming shadow of empire over the Indian subcontinent. Today, we should take equally sharp note of these great, protean power of narrative in the crisis-ridden geological era of the Anthropocene (Nair 2009a, 2021b, 2022c; Nair and deSouza 2020). It is here that a footnote to Labov's original analysis appears essential. With our cell phones always at the ready, bombarded as we are with an excess of information, personal and public, it could be that we are becoming globally addicted to just one style of breathing and of narrative movement – that is, the fast-paced, hyperventilating presto (Nair 2019). The world is "too much with us, late and soon" as Wordsworth once phrased it. The result is that we are tossed from complicating action to complicating action, crisis to crisis, and have begun to ignore, at our peril, the other time-tested parts of the 'full-form' of narrative. Haunted as we are each day by thoughts of universal destruction by our own species agency, it could therefore be an urgent duty for university academics today to recover, reinstate, discuss and devote time and care to the study of those other five parts of narrative so neglected in the Age of Anthropocene. Perhaps we can then hope to find at last the hint of an ironic smile on that human face we have placed on nature's torso.

References

Althusser, Louis. *On the Reproduction of Capitalism: Ideology and Ideological State Apparatuses*. Transl. and ed. G.M. Goshgarian. London: Verso, 2014.
Appiah, Kwame Anthony. "The Postcolonial and The Postmodern." *My Father's House: Africa in the Philosophy of Culture*. Oxford: Oxford University Press, 1993. 137–157.
All India Council for Technical Education (AICTE). *Ancient Universities in India*. https://www.aicte-india.org/downloads/ancient.pdf (last accessed, 15 October 2021).
Cochrane, Steve. "Asian Centres of Learning and Witness before 1000 C.E.: Insights for Today." *Transformation* 26.1 (2009): 30–39.
Deleuze, Gilles. *Difference and Repetition*. Transl. Paul Patton. Columbia: Columbia University Press, 1994.
Dennett, Daniel. *Consciousness Explained*. London: Allen Lane, 1991.
Donald, Merlin. Origins of the Modern Mind: *Three stages in the evolution of culture and cognition*. Cambridge/MA: Harvard University Press, 1991.
———. "The mind considered from a historical perspective: human cognitive phylogenesis and the possibility of continuing cognitive evolution." *The Future of the Cognitive Revolution*. Eds. David Johnson and Christina Ermeling. Oxford: Oxford University Press, 1997. 478–492.
Drew, John. *India and the Romantic Imagination*. New Delhi: Oxford University Press, 1998.
Gandhi, M.K. *Gandhi 'Hind Swaraj' and Other Writings*. Ed. A.J. Parel. Cambridge: Cambridge University Press, 1997 [1909].
Geertz, A.W. and Jeppe Sinding Jensen. *Religious Narrative, Cognition and Culture: Image and Word in the Mind of Narrative*. London: Equinox Series in Religion, Cognition and Culture, 2011.
Hall, Stuart. "When was the Postcolonial? Thinking at the Limit." *The Post-Colonial Question*. Eds. Iain Chambers and Lidia Curtis. London: Routledge, 1995. 1–19.
Hofmann, Franck and Markus Messling. Eds. *The Epoch of Universalism 1769–1989 L'époque de l'universalisme 1769–1989*. Berlin, Boston: De Gruyter, 2020.
Jaspers, Karl. *The Origin and Goal of History*. Transl. Michael Bullock. London: Routledge & Keegan Paul, 1953.
Labov, William. "The transformation of experience in narrative syntax." *Language in the inner City*. Philadelphia: University of Pennsylvania Press, 1972. 354–397.
Macaulay, Thomas Babington. *Minute on Education*. Bureau of Education. Selections from Educational Records, Part I (1781–1839). Ed. H. Sharp. Calcutta: Government Printing, 1920. Reprint Delhi: National Archives of India, 1965 [1835].
MacCulloch, Diarmaid. "The Axis of Goodness." *The Guardian*, 18 March 2006. https://www.theguardian.com/books/2006/mar/18/highereducation.news (last accessed, 15 October 2021).
Maddison, Angus. *Contours Of The World Economy 1–2030 AD*. Oxford: Oxford University Press, 2007.
Marshall, John. *A Guide to Taxila*. Cambridge: Cambridge University Press, 1960.
Nair, Rukmini Bhaya. *Lying on the Postcolonial Couch: the Idea of Indifference*. Minneapolis: University of Minnesota Press and New Delhi: Oxford University Press, 2002.

———. *Narrative Gravity: Conversation, Cognition, Culture*. London: Routledge, 2003a.

———. "Sappho's Daughters: Postcoloniality and the Polysemous Semantics of Gender." *Journal of Literary Semantics* 32.2 (2003b): 113–35.

———. *Poetry in a Time of Terror: Essays in the Postcolonial Preternatural*. New Delhi, New York: Oxford University Press, 2009a.

———. "Language and Youth Culture." *Language in South Asia*. Eds. B.B. Kachru, Y. Kachru, and S.N. Sridhar. Cambridge: Cambridge University Press, 2008. 466–494.

———. "Learning to Write: Integrational Linguistics and the Indian Subcontinent." *Language Teaching: Integrational Linguistics Approaches*. Ed. Michael Toolan. London: Routledge, 2009b. 47–72.

———. "Yudhishthira's Lie: The Fiction of India." *Poétiques Comparatistes/Comparative Poetics* (2010): 227–242.

———. "The Nature of Narrative: Schemes, Genes, Memes, Dreams and Screams!" *Religious Narrative, Cognition and Culture: Image and Word in the Mind of Narrative*. Eds. Armin W. Geertz and Jeppe Sinding Jensen. London: Equinox Series in Religion, Cognition and Culture, 2011a. 117–146.

———. "Thinking out the Story Box: Creative Writing and Narrative Culture in South Asia." *TEXT* 10 (2011b): 1–22.

———. "Bringing English into the 21st Century: A Perspective from India." *The International Journal of Language, Translation and Intercultural Communication* 1.1 (2012): 103–122.

———. "Narrative as a Mode of Explanation: Evolution & Emergence." *Modes of Explanation: Affordances for Action and Prediction*. Eds. Michael Lissack and Abraham Garber. New York: Palgrave Macmillan, 2014. 140–154.

———. "Virtue, Virtuosity and the Virtual: Contemporary Experiments in the Genre of the Indian English Novel." *The History of the Indian Novel in English*. Ed. Ulka Anjaria. Cambridge: Cambridge University Press, 2015. 251–266

———. "Language, Nation. Freedom: Rabindranath Tagore and Ludwig Wittgenstein on the Epistemology of Education." *Tagore and Nationalism*. Eds. K. L. Tuteja and Kaustav Chakraborty. New Delhi: Springer Nature, 2017a. 219–244.

———. "Imaginaries of Ignorance: Five Ideas of the University in the 21st Century." *The Place of the Humanities in the Indian University*. Ed. Mrinal Miri. London: Routledge, 2017b. 140–175.

———. "Post-colonialism Outsourced." *Reframing Critical, Literary and Cultural Theories: Thought on the Edge*. Ed. Nicoletta Pireddu. New York: Palgrave Macmillan, 2018. 299–325.

———. "Epithymetics: The Psychology of Desire". *Annual Review of Indian Psychology*, Volume 1: *Cognitive and Affective Processes*. Ed. Misra, G. Oxford, New Delhi: Oxford University Press, 2019. 204–270.

———. "Caged Childhoods? Human Capabilities, Migrating cosmopolitanisms and Educational Experimentation." *Migrating Minds: Theories and Practices of Cultural Cosmopolitanism*. Eds. Didier Coste, Christina Kkona and Nicoletta Pireddu. New York: Routledge, 2021a. 247–260.

———. "'Do you believe in God, doctor?' The Atheism of Fiction & the Fiction of Atheism." *Sophia: International Journal of Philosophy and Traditions* 60 (2021b): 749–768.

———. "Language: Editor in Chief?" *Seminar* 743: Special Issue on 'Editing History' (2021c): 81–88.

———. "New Technology, Language and Gesture in Contemporary Indian Political Discourse." *Psychology of Democracy*. Ed. Ashley Weinberg. Cambridge: Cambridge University Press, 2022a. 195–228.

———. "Postcolonial Pragmatics." *Handbook of Pragmatics*. Eds. Jan-Ola Ostman and Jef Verschueren. Amsterdam, Philadelphia: John Benjamins, 2022b. 35–77.

———. "Arche-writing: narrative, emotion, embodiment and empathy." *Oxford Handbook of Human Symbolic Evolution*. Eds. A. Lock, C. Sinha and N. Gontier. Oxford: Oxford University Press, 2022c.

Nair, Rukmini Bhaya and Peter deSouza. Eds. *Keywords for India: A Conceptual Lexicon for the 21st Century*. London: Bloomsbury, 2020.

Nussbaum, Martha. *Women and Human Development: The Capabilities Approach*. Cambridge: Cambridge University Press, 1999.

Oxford English Dictionary. Volume II P-Z. Oxford: Oxford University Press, 1971.

Patnaik, Utsa and Prabhat Patnaik. *A Theory of Imperialism*. New York: Columbia University Press, 2016.

Pinheiro, Sylvia et al. "The History of Writing Reflects the Effects of Education on Discourse Structure: Implications for Literacy, Orality, Psychosis and the Axial Age." *Trends in Neuroscience and Education* 21 (2020): 100142. https://doi.org/10.1016/j.tine.2020.100142.

Popper, Karl. *Conjectures and Refutations: the Growth of Scientific Knowledge*. London: Routledge, 1963.

Provan, Ian. *Convenient Myths: The Axial Age, Dark Green Religion, and the World That Never Was*. Waco/TX: Baylor University Press, 2013.

Rorty, Richard. *Contingency, Irony, Solidarity*. Cambridge: Cambridge University Press, 1989.

Williams, Mark et al. "The Anthropocene Biosphere." *The Anthropocene Review* 2.3 (2015): 196–219.

Williams, Raymond. *Keywords: A Vocabulary of Culture and Society*. New York: Oxford University Press, 1976.

Part III: **Language, the Self, and Society**

Troisième partie : **Le langage, le sujet et la société**

Leyla Dakhli
Par-delà la pureté de la langue : révolutions et jeux de langues dans le monde arabe contemporain

Abstract: This chapter explores the place of languages in political and social struggles in the modern Arab world. Beyond the questions raised by the impact of colonial languages and their dominant positions, it explores the assignations to linguistic purity conveyed by a certain vision of the Arabic language and the once needed arabisation. In the Arab postcolonial space, the revolutionary gesture also takes on a linguistic dimension, challenging this mythical purity of identity and claiming a more organic and playful link with Arabic languages.

Keywords: language, history, Arab worlds, revolutions

L'histoire dont il s'agit ici suit le fil de mes recherches de manière un peu libre. Elle commence par moi. Si j'ai choisi d'écrire sur les langues, c'est parce que se niche au creux de ma vie personnelle et intellectuelle une déchirure, ou plutôt de multiples brisures de langues[1]. Je suis née en Tunisie, dans une famille où, enfant d'un couple mixte, c'est la mère française qui nous élevait la plupart du temps en solitaire. Ma langue est celle de ma mère d'abord, puis celle de la vie extérieure, ce créole arabe qu'est l'arabe tunisien, un joyeux mélange fabriqué au fil des occupations et des installations, dans lequel on trouve de l'italien, du français, du maltais, un peu de berbère et bien sûr de l'arabe. J'ai choisi, sans conscience, en inconscience, de travailler sur ce qu'on appelle – et que je continue à appeler pour pouvoir m'y confronter – le « monde arabe contemporain » de la Syrie au Liban, à la Palestine et aujourd'hui à la Tunisie[2], en historienne, sans savoir à quel point les trois termes qui constituent cette désignation académique deviendraient progressivement des problèmes, des mots que je porte avec précautions, et sans vouloir pour autant les remplacer tant je sais que c'est en leur sein que

---

[1] Cette expérience n'est évidemment pas isolée, elle fait écho à de nombreux témoignages et se met au cœur de travaux, y compris artistiques, sur la déchirure, la brisure, la réparation. Je pense ici en particulier à l'œuvre de Kader Attia.
[2] Ce travail prend la forme aujourd'hui de la coordination d'un projet de recherche financé par le European Research Council intitulé DREAM (DRafting and Enacting the revolution in the Arab Mediterranean).

réside une partie des questions que je me pose. Revenons tout d'abord sur la locution « monde arabe contemporain ».

D'abord, le terme « monde » au singulier, qui semble embrasser un ensemble cohérent et lui donner une unité alors que par bien des aspects ce monde arabe, dans ses différentes parties, fait – ou a fait, au cours de l'histoire – monde et unité avec d'autres lieux qui l'entourent : la *umma* qui rassemble les musulmans par exemple, la *koiné* du pourtour méditerranéen, ou bien encore des franges du Sahara. Par ailleurs, il semble tout aussi évident qu'il est possible de diviser ce monde en de multiples sous-régions, des sous-ensembles dont les derniers avatars sont les États nations issus des élaborations impériales et des segmentations coloniales et qui pourtant sont pour la plupart revendiquées comme des espaces de reconnaissance.

Ensuite, le mot « arabe ». Il va en être question dans ce texte, car d'évidence cette appartenance pose bien des problèmes et ouvre sur la question de l'identité ou de formes d'identifications concurrentes dans l'espace que l'on appelle « le monde arabe ». Car en son cœur se trouvent des minorités non-arabes revendiquées, des populations conquises et « devenues arabes », des formes d'être-arabe très différentes. L'usage de ce mot doit à mon sens se comprendre dans une histoire continue pour ne pas courir le risque de coller à une définition figée, le plus souvent idéologisée (Dakhli 2009a).

Enfin, j'ai qualifié ce monde arabe de « contemporain », avec la conscience de ce que ces scansions temporelles académiques impliquent comme réflexions possibles sur la contemporanéité elle-même (Ruffel 2016 ; Bardawil 2020). Elles embarquent les mondes que je souhaite ici saisir, ou plutôt avec lesquels je souhaite cheminer dans un régime de temporalité linéaire alors qu'il semblerait plus riche d'appréhender des régimes de temporalités différenciées, qui se rejoignent parfois, et qui, en voulant les englober, empêchent de voir les bifurcations qui nous sont propres, par-delà l'artificialité des frontières.

Ces précautions prises, il me semble important de continuer à comprendre ensemble cet espace qui, dans son artifice et par-delà les idéologies, travaille à construire des passages et des ponts, qui passent souvent par la langue. Il s'agira ici de saisir la question linguistique par les usages, et de s'attarder en particulier sur les processus d'arabisation en les situant dans les cadres successifs de l'aspiration à la renaissance arabe (*nahda*) (Dakhli 2021, 2014), de l'élan national postcolonial et des révoltes et révolutions récentes.

1 S'arabiser : une des figures de la *Nahda*

Il est devenu récurrent, dans les mondes postcoloniaux, de se poser la question de la langue que l'on possède, ou d'énoncer une situation où l'on n'en possède aucune en propre (Memmi 1957 ; Derrida 1996 ; Harchi 2016), dans des contextes où l'on naît dans des régions de polyglossie, où l'on apprend d'autres langues à l'école, et où parfois on émigre dans une autre langue encore. Le travail historien, qui met en présence de mots et de traces textuelles, permet de se confronter à cet exercice d'écart linguistique, de traduction prise dans le sens de relation (Glissant 2009), comme la décrit finement Souleymane Bachir Diagne pour la rapprocher de la notion d'hospitalité (Diagne 2022). Même lorsque l'on écrit dans la langue de ses archives – ce qui n'est pas mon cas – une partie de l'exercice consiste à saisir les usages passés de la langue et à se mettre en capacité de les traduire. Ce labeur implique de laisser couler la langue des autres en soi pour en saisir non pas seulement ce que l'on veut y lire[3], nous, mais ce que leurs auteurs et autrices cherchaient à y dire. C'est alors se mettre en présence de fantômes, dont parfois les traces sont infimes.

Travaillant sur une partie du monde arabe dans les temps de l'émancipation des tutelles impériales et coloniales, j'ai découvert dans mes archives, en écoutant les voix, une écriture de la dépossession et de la reprise en main. En réalité, je ne l'ai pas découverte : je l'ai reconnue. Et j'ai reconnu le pouvoir qui se conquiert par la conquête des mots, une autorité, celle que construisent les intellectuel·le·s. Se saisir de la langue arabe, en faire une langue moderne, quel beau projet pour ceux qui voulaient se défaire de l'emprise coloniale. En travaillant sur les académies arabes, en lisant les jeux de langue qu'ils opèrent pour se donner les moyens de désigner ce qu'ils appellent le monde moderne, on décèle l'élaboration d'une autorité par la langue, et une jubilation créatrice. On y voit aussi une ambition unificatrice qui s'engage dans deux voies complémentaires, toutes deux contenues dans le vocable d'arabisation et saisies par l'idée de rectification : la fabrication de mots nouveaux pour traduire le vocabulaire moderne le plus souvent entré dans des langues européennes et l'unification de langues nationales à travers la rectification des erreurs régionales, c'est-à-dire des dialectes en usage. L'Égypte réformatrice de Mohammad Ali (Fahmy 1998), la Tunisie de Khayreddine (Guellouz et al. 2010), l'Académie de Damas issue du Royaume arabe de Faysal (Dakhli 2009b, 227–234). Tous ces moments sont pour les penseurs, écrivains, administrateurs, journalistes, des temps de conquête de leur autorité (Hourani

---

[3] On rejoint ici les réflexions de Sheldon Pollock sur la philologie et sa place dans le monde contemporain dans *Philologie und Freiheit*, où il évoque notamment le devoir de vérité, de solidarité humaine et de réflexivité critique (« Verpflichtung zur Wahrhaftigkeit, zur menschlichen Solidarität und zur kritischen Selbstreflektion »), Pollock (2018, 19).

1962). Cette entreprise, initiée dans les premiers temps de la *nahda* et qui prend son élan véritable dans les États-nations en construction, semble être une quête sans fin, comme si les peuples arabes ne cessaient de s'arabiser[4]. D'où vient que cette entreprise soit sans fin ? D'où vient qu'elle ne cesse de se renouveler cette question ?

C'est qu'en réalité, la langue arabe a été saisie le plus souvent dans le cadre d'un projet nationaliste[5]. Le pouvoir intellectuel et culturel que les intellectuels du tournant du 20e siècle sur lesquels j'ai d'abord travaillé se construisait sur une réappropriation, inégalitaire et élitaire, mais ouverte. Dans le temps des émancipations on re-fabriquait l'arabe, mais aussi le Tamazight, l'arménien, le syriaque, l'hébreux, on se réappropriait ce que d'autres avaient cherché à codifier ou à enfermer, voire à effacer. Dans le cadre des luttes anticoloniales et dans la forge des États-nations, ces questions tendent à se durcir. Si l'on veut bien comprendre ce qui se joue derrière ces tensions de ce que l'on appelle alors la modernité, il faut interroger ensemble les puretés linguistiques qui semblent s'affronter. Comme le dit Jocelyne Dakhlia, à propos de la Tunisie :

> La colonisation, ainsi que la réaction nationale qu'elle induit chemin faisant, produisent concurremment un puissant processus de réduction identitaire et de purification des représentations de la langue et en certains cas de la langue elle-même. Dorénavant, et ce tableau est à peine caricatural, on est soit arabe, soit français, et la gamme des langues est censée se réduire à ce couple de l'arabe et du français (Dakhlia 2004, par. 20).

Ce chemin n'était pas tracé d'avance.

La piste de la colonisation et de ses suites, de la modernité qui clive, mérite d'être suivie ici, entre l'arabe et ses autres. Si l'arabe semble ne pas avoir de créole, ne pas en admettre, c'est probablement surtout par sa volonté d'être moderne, d'entrer en modernité, de quitter le lieu « hachuré » fait de violence et de souffrance dont parle Fanon[6]. Bien plus, on peut penser que la modernité a fait, de multiples manières, de ce lieu hachuré un lieu de douleur à force de vouloir le blanchir ou le noircir. Écrire cette histoire, c'est alors saisir les mécanismes d'entre-deux pour les insérer dans une histoire de la modernité qui la rende plus complexe et plus compréhensive. En effet, cette dualité liée à la modernité colo-

---

[4] Je ne fais pas ici référence à la querelle de l'arabisation telle qu'elle a pu s'exprimer, notamment en Algérie, autour de positionnements tranchés, voire de guerres de tranchées autour de « l'expression française » ou de la défense du bilinguisme. Parmi tant d'autres, cf. Djebar (2003).
[5] Pour une synthèse un peu ancienne des enjeux d'unification nationale à partir des cas de la Syrie et de l'Égypte, voir Eberhard Kienle (1996).
[6] Pour une réflexion sur les entremêlements linguistiques qui se poursuivent dans les interstices du pouvoir, Dakhlia (2000). Voir aussi le chapitre « La Femme de couleur et le Blanc » dans *Peaux noires, masques blancs* de Fanon (1952, 35–50).

niale et post-coloniale ne s'exprime pas que dans la langue, elle traverse les mondes, dans leur spatialité (la ville « arabe » /la ville moderne – donc coloniale) comme les manières de s'habiller (voiles, tarbouches, et autres couvre-chefs, habits dits européens . . .), les affects, les usages et même les manières de dire ou d'habiter le monde. Mais si la rhétorique de la modernisation, appliquée à l'économie ou à la société, a été beaucoup travaillée et critiquée, notamment par les théoriciens du postcolonial, la question de la langue me semble être restée bien souvent prise dans les pièges que sont la langue des locuteurs eux-mêmes ou les difficultés à formuler des énoncés.

Les États indépendants inventaient et cherchaient des façons de faire avec les langues, à plusieurs échelles. Aux archives du ministère de l'éducation nationale à Tunis, je suis tombée sur un mémoire de fin d'études de l'école d'instituteur qui date du milieu des années 1950[7]. C'est un lexique des mots empruntés des langues européennes dans la langue tunisienne (*darja*). Certains passages et certains mots ont une résonnance particulière et s'ancrent dans le dialecte, comme le « casse-croûte » des soldats et des écoliers, devenu une vraie spécialité tunisienne (sous la forme d'un sandwich au thon et aux légumes, arrosé d'huile et d'harissa). Il en est de même de l'usage du mot « cartouche » pour désigner le fusil à partir de la guerre de 1914–1918, aujourd'hui encore employé pour désigner les tirs et coups de feu.

Parfois, dans son modeste travail lexical, il reste des mystères dans les circulations linguistiques, comme le mot qui s'est imposé pour dire rue en tunisien, *kayyâs*, qui serait emprunté à un mot fort peu en usage en français (caillasse, pour un chemin fait d'éboulis). Par-delà le plaisir de la lecture de ce glossaire très resserré, quelques remarques sur « ce que fait le dialecte », la volonté de désigner de manière précise les réalités qui entourent les femmes et les hommes (mais ici, plutôt les hommes), les transformations des sons qui s'opèrent, les usages citadins et ruraux, le pragmatisme de la langue, annoncent autre chose. C'est aussi la manière dont apparaît la langue arabe, comme une langue qui est « trop loin » qui apparaît comme un indice, l'annonce d'un discours sur la langue qui s'est ancré dans les discours des « francophones » de manière pérenne.

La volonté que l'on y lit, de formaliser simplement, parfois de manière fantaisiste, la langue de la rue, n'est pas seulement le résidu d'un savoir colonial, qui on le sait, a été obsédé par l'observation et la codification des dialectes. Le mémoire, écrit à la main, classe les mots et en donne les usages. En cela, il cherche à dire le monde qui l'entoure et qui se transforme, un peu comme les académiciens en

---

7 Les mémoires de fin d'étude de l'École Normale ne sont pas classés dans le catalogue, je ne peux donc pas me référer à une cote d'archive.

leur temps. La trace de ce travail, effectué par un apprenti enseignant, signale bien que les voies sont encore ouvertes pour accueillir les multiples qui résident dans « la langue nationale », pour faire entrer des mondes dans le monde qui est en train de s'ouvrir.

2 L'école de la langue arabe commune

Pourtant, l'histoire de l'éducation comme celle de la constitution des cadres des États postcoloniaux arabes est prise d'une part dans des logiques d'arabisation qui tendent vers l'unification et d'autre part dans des logiques de « bilinguismes » portés par les exigences du « monde moderne ». Une partie de l'explication de cette relative impasse linguistique, de laquelle découlent de fortes tensions politiques sur la définition de l'identité nationale ou de l'authenticité tient à l'histoire de la postcolonie telle que décrite par Achille Mbembe (2000). Car si toutes les questions posées dans le cadre du mouvement de la *Nahda* sont saisies par les modernités postcoloniales, elles y perdent leur caractère ludique et créatif, et une partie de leurs potentialités dans l'entrée en nation, et plus encore dans l'entrée dans le « concert des nations », exigeant toujours plus d'ajustements et d'alignements entre une forme de pureté d'un idéal national (ou supra-national si l'on pense en terme de « monde arabe ») et les exigences de politiques prises dans les échanges inégaux qui fondent la mondialisation. Ainsi dans un premier temps faut-il admettre que, malgré les émancipations nationales, la langue arabe, bien que parlée par plusieurs millions de locuteurs, reste une langue marginale dans l'économie mondiale. Elle ne permet pas encore de naviguer dans les premiers mondes. À l'utopie d'une langue arabe médiane et unifiante, s'adjoint l'exigence d'un accès au reste du monde *en traduction* ou par des médiations, qui se trouvent être souvent la langue de l'ancien colonisateur.

Si l'on écrit cette histoire à grands traits, on peut la comprendre comme une série de restrictions se surimposant à l'ambition émancipatrice issue des décolonisations. Comme le signe de la fin d'une fiction et comme conséquence même de la difficulté à se dégager des dépendances, les politiques d'ajustements structurels, à partir de la fin des années 1970, valident le canal étroit dans lequel il va falloir désormais penser le « développement » des anciens pays colonisés. Dans le monde arabe, la question linguistique se trouve dès lors piégée par la libéralisation des systèmes scolaires qui installent et confortent des régimes linguistiques où le marché des langues a remplacé la question de la langue commune. On pourrait y voir une résolution par le marché des questions identitaires qui ont pu agiter les jeunes nations. En réalité, les questionnements identitaires ne cessent pas avec la mondialisation et ses exigences, elles sont au contraire renforcées et rigidifiées.

Dès lors, la langue arabe que nous apprenons tous·tes à l'école, c'est une langue qui ne doit pas avoir d'histoire. Son essence, sa fierté, est précisément de ne pas avoir d'histoire. Elle ne prend pas en charge les débats infinis des intellectuelles de la *Nahda*, qui jouaient avec la langue et ses bâtardises. Elle devient sacrée, coranique, on peut en décrire la grammaire et les richesses infinies, mais pas l'histoire. Comment embrasser simplement une telle langue ? Comment ne pas être intimidé par toute cette pureté, toute cette sacralité ? comment se projeter dans une littérature si vaste qu'elle dit tant de mondes lointains, qu'elle raconte un monde qu'on peine à s'imaginer ? les ruines du campement ? des centaines de mots pour dire les couleurs du désert, tant d'autres pour dire l'amour mais lequel est le nôtre, lequel est le vôtre ?

Il faut prendre la mesure de la croyance qui accompagne le règne de l'arabisation sous cette forme savante et unificatrice. Samir Amin l'énonce en ces termes au milieu des années 1970 :

> Le monde arabe se limite-t-il alors à un groupement de peuples parlant des langues parentes ? s'il en était ainsi, les langues arabes parlées évolueraient vers une différenciation croissante comme, à partir du noyau commun latin, les langues romanes ont évolué pour devenir le français, l'italien ou l'espagnol. Mais le mouvement de l'évolution des langues arabes va précisément dans le sens inverse : la langue littéraire tend à devenir la langue parlée de l'ensemble du monde arabe (Amin 1976, 13).

L'erreur que fait ici Amin, fidèle en cela à son éducation française (Trabant 2002), c'est de penser que la langue vient d'en haut. Les Arabes vivent avec et apprennent cet idiome surplombant, qui définit des espaces, des classes, des écarts entre ceux qui le maîtrisent et ceux pour qui il est, comme les langues étrangères, le signe d'une appartenance inaccessible. Coupée des usages communs, des dialectes qui la nourrissent, la langue peut s'égarer. Ces égarements provoquent aujourd'hui de l'ironie et de la distance, elles sont pourtant des intimidations. Un article d'abord publié en arabe dans *Mada Masr*, puis traduit dans *Orient XXI*, relève quelques-uns de ces épisodes :

> Mahmoud Abderrezak, un Égyptien fondateur de la page Facebook *Nahw wa sarf* (syntaxe et morphologie) dont l'objectif est de « diffuser la langue arabe de manière simple et fluide », évoque des tentatives passées de l'Académie d'imposer le mot *marna* à la place de *telfaz* pour désigner la télévision. Elle avait avancé comme argument le fait que ce mot était forgé à partir d'un verbe qui signifie « regarder longuement et en silence ». Abderrezak fait remarquer ironiquement qu'on « peut également regarder longuement un avion en silence, faut-il l'appeler *marna* au lieu de *tayyara* ? (Waël 2019)

Il y a de multiples occasions de se moquer, mais aussi de s'attendrir, à la lecture des débats d'académiciens cherchant des instruments pour nommer le monde qui les entoure, leur contemporanéité, ce qu'ils qualifient de modernité. Ce sont des histoires d'échecs devant l'usage, le plus souvent, de rattrapages de mots qui, à partir d'une langue européenne, se sont arabisés, sont passés directement dans les lignes des journaux, des commerçants, des artistes et qu'il faudrait repêcher pour les remplacer par d'autres, qui n'évoquent rien ou pas grand-chose.

Dans le moment moderne, voire modernisateur, du monde arabe, une certaine économie de la pureté s'est installée dans le discours politique et dans la morale publique alors que dans le même temps, l'économie s'est mise à valoriser les hybridations parce qu'elle pouvait les monnayer. C'est pour cette raison qu'une histoire sociale et transnationale du politique ne peut faire abstraction des transformations qui ont été opérées dans les systèmes marchands et dans les échanges de valeurs entre les années 1950 et aujourd'hui.

Pendant que perduraient les aspirations à construire des identités stables et sécurisantes, les migrations se sont intensifiées, la taylorisation des activités économiques à l'échelle mondiale s'est poursuivie, les échanges inégaux se sont installés dans de nouveaux habits décolonisés. L'habileté à traduire est devenue une valeur marchande à haute valeur, et le marché mondial de la traduction s'est construit à la défaveur des petites langues nationales, et même de certaines grandes langues transnationales comme l'arabe[8]. Réussir dans le monde de la modernité triomphante, c'était de plus en plus apprendre d'autres langues, parler d'autres langues que la sienne, non pas par le fait du colonisateur, mais bien par le fait du marché. Cette distorsion-là, loin de pousser à l'émergence d'un éloge de l'impureté, a au contraire renforcé les discours sur l'authenticité, la séparation entre nous et les autres, la survalorisation d'une essence à laquelle il ne faudrait pas renoncer. Le monde moderne veut protéger les espèces en les séparant et en les conservant dans des milieux étanches. Si l'on veut risquer une comparaison un peu osée, c'est ce qui s'est passé avec la langue arabe, standardisée et conditionnée à la suite des efforts de la *Nahda*, installée dans des refuges bien gardés. Son explosion et son développement ne se sont pourtant pas arrêtés, comme nous allons le voir, mais elle est restée comme en réserve, coupée de milieux qui auraient pu lui permettre un développement plus harmonieux.

Aujourd'hui, les élites du monde arabe parlent peut-être arabe, mais elles mettent leurs enfants dans des écoles francophones ou anglophones, où l'arabe est certainement la dernière roue du carrosse. Dans le même temps, on voit les dialectes

---

8 Sur le marché mondial de la traduction, Casanova (1999, 2015). Sur la langue arabe et ses traductions voir Leonhardt Santini (2006).

se développer, s'afficher sur les murs, se chanter et s'échanger dans les produits culturels, à la fois les plus massifs et les plus expérimentaux. Les « partisans » des dialectes ne sont pas sans arrière-pensée. Les débats sur la généralisation de la langue dialectale dans les écoles mettent au premier plan ceux-là qui veulent perpétuer des hiérarchies de langue. Car si le dialecte s'enseigne, c'est d'abord comme véhicule d'une culture au rabais, fermée sur elle-même, bien suffisante pour celles et ceux à qui on n'imagine pas d'autre horizon que celui de son étroit sol natal.

C'est aussi par le libéralisme économique, l'affichage publicitaire qu'est entrée dans nos vies une écriture de la langue parlée. Parce que si les politiques pouvaient continuer à nous bercer de leur langue de bois, les publicitaires eux devaient toucher au cœur et inventer des slogans dans la langue de tous les jours.

3 Révolutions

Déplaçons-nous à présent pour écouter les voix des révolté·e·s et écouter ce qu'elles ont à nous dire au moment où elles prennent la parole comme nous y a invité de Certeau (1994). Il est possible dès lors de percevoir un autre tissage linguistique, qui s'est opéré dans l'ombre de ce que j'ai appelé ici l'arabisation. C'est un tissage qui n'est pas un processus continu et uniforme, mais il appartient en propre à la langue arabe, ou plutôt aux langues arabes. Dans le temps long des parlers et des orfèvreries quotidiennes ou savantes de la langue, dans l'accueil de ses hybridations et de sa contemporanéité s'est inventée une nouvelle façon de se parler, entre les dialectes, les langues apprises, celles qui permettent de passer d'un lieu à l'autre.

D'évidence, les sons et les voix de 2011 ont été le surgissement d'une langue, et son affirmation. Alors que l'on tendait à nous présenter les mobilisations dans la région comme les cris inarticulés d'une rue arabe aux contours flous de laquelle répondait des paroles inaudibles, non politiques, perçues comme des vagues de révoltes irrationnelles, même les médias et les analystes d'ordinaire peu enclins à écouter se sont mis à percevoir ce que les peuples arabes avaient à dire. Ils ont articulé, par la révolte et le courage de la mise en jeu de leurs corps, un discours qui peut d'abord se savourer, se regarder, et permet à chacun et chacune de se recharger.

Cette langue s'est d'abord présentée comme un silence qui laisse circuler des gestes et des rituels. Lors des premières semaines des révolutions de 2011, l'un des symboles qui circulaient le plus souvent était une sorte de cercle de mains qui se tenaient par les poignets et formaient un cercle. Ce symbole, détournement politique d'un vocabulaire développé dans des cadres plus intimes, s'est ajouté à des symboles plus directement politiques, notamment les drapeaux nationaux. Cette manière de mêler les couleurs de la nation avec des empreintes corporelles définit une nouvelle grammaire, un peu kitsch et issue des réseaux sociaux. Mais elle définit aussi un usage renouvelé du réemploi, des collages et des montages devenus familiers aux usagers du numérique, pour dire des émotions collectives. Peu importe ici la langue, les Gif ou les montages vidéo se saisissent de la colère, des espoirs, des joies et des peines pour inventer de nouvelles langues. Ce bricolage contestataire fait place aux corps à la fois dans la violence qui les touche et celle qui en émane ; il fait place aussi à de l'amour, les cœurs sont souvent là pour le symboliser sous la forme d'amour de la patrie, d'amour du peuple, d'amour de ce qui se tisse dans la lutte face à la haine libérée du régime qui se dresse en face.

Il est fait de nombreux gestes, comme celui qui consiste à nettoyer, à faire place nette sur les lieux de la révolte. Ce geste est particulièrement fort, car il est aussi ambigu. S'agit-il d'un acte tactique, qui vient dire en miroir que le peuple est « propre » face à la saleté du pouvoir, ou un renversement de la saleté qui lui est accolée par les dominants ? Est-ce un acte écologiste ? On peut le lire dans tous les cas comme un discours sur le monde à construire, non pas forcément « propre » car ce serait aller vers des discours de la pureté qui sont bien loin de ce qui s'exprime dans le désordre des rues, mais où tout le monde et chacun·e prend en charge la question des déchets, prend sa part de nos restes, de ce que nous laissons derrière nous.

Au centre de cette prise de parole, on trouve des mots qui circulent entre les langues et inventent d'autres manières de se parler et de se dire. Certains sont repris, réappropriés et re-signifiés. J'emprunte ces notions à l'usage qui est fait notamment d'une terminologie raciste, homophobe ou sexiste au service de causes d'émancipation par le phénomène de réappropriation. Dans le cas présent, la réappropriation est une reconquête des espaces du politique par un nouvel usage. Il s'agit en particulier de mots transformés depuis des décennies en langue de bois, intégrés dans un discours figé du pouvoir. On reprend des mots, à commencer par celui de révolution, *thawra*[9]. Dans certains contextes en particulier, comme celui de pays dont l'indépendance s'était faite sous le signe de la révolte, ce registre avait été confisqué par la dictature : il en est ainsi de la révolution algérienne, ou de la révolution nassérienne en Égypte, ou encore de la révolution baathiste en Syrie, qui avaient usé jusqu'à la corde la possibilité même de faire usage de ces vocables.

Mais la « révolution » est un mot que l'on reprend également à ses terres du nord. La révolution appartient aux Lumières, qui l'ont en partie dégagée de ce

---

9 Il en est de même du mot « peuple », *shaab*, cf. « Lorsqu'un jour le peuple veut vivre » (Dakhli 2020, 103).

qu'elle contient de troubles, d'incertitudes et de désordre[10]. *Thawra* est un mot qui a une connotation désordonnée, il désigne le mouvement et l'agitation qui renverse. Il ne semble pas présentable en des temps où l'on pense le changement politique comme une transformation démocratique. L'usage de ce mot est enfin dénié par les analyses froides et normées qui savent ce qui peut être qualifié de révolution : un processus que l'on jauge à l'aune de son résultat, qui doit être une transformation profonde du régime. Alors, les soulèvements qui se nomment eux-mêmes révolutions ne sont pas jugés dignes d'user de ce terme s'ils ne sont pas en mesure d'aller au bout de la démarche révolutionnaire.

Quelles que soient ces objections, elles ne masquent pas le fait que les acteurs et actrices utilisent encore et encore ce mot de *thawra*, ou alors ce beau mot de *hirak* en Algérie et dans le Rif marocain[11]. Ces mots encapsulent une expérience, pas une théorie politique. Une expérience qui se nomme sans se vulnérabiliser, en l'occurrence parce qu'elle s'énonce en se faisant.

Par-delà ces réappropriations, on observe des inventions, des hybridations et des traductions, comme des échos plurilingues, entre les langues et les dialectes. *Ytnahaou ga !* ont répété les Algériens pendant tant de semaines, qu'ils partent tout simplement, *Dégage !* a-t-on entendu en Tunisie, *irhal* (va-t-en) en Egypte ou en Syrie, *kullun yani kullun* (tous, ça veut dire tous), au Liban encore. Tous sont de l'arabe, et se déclinent en traductions réciproques d'un même désir d'en finir avec un ordre honni. Mais ils font aussi écho au *Que se vayan todos* argentin de 2001, ainsi qu'à des slogans ou des groupes comme le « Y en a marre » sénégalais qui se dit en wolof *Le ëppe Tuuru* (trop c'est trop), qui fait lui-même écho à ce mouvement égyptien qui s'appelait aussi ça suffit, *kifaya!* plus de 10 ans avant la révolution de 2011.

Si j'évoque ces différentes occurrences, ce n'est pas simplement pour dire que les revendications sont les mêmes partout. Ce qui s'exprime ici est évidemment un ras-le-bol de la classe politique et du « système », qui s'énonce aussi autour du slogan phare des révolutions arabes « le peuple veut la chute du système » *al-shaab yurid isqat al-nidâm* (en arabe classique). Ce qu'on y entend aussi c'est le choix des mots qui remettent en jeu, redonnent en partage, le mot de peuple (*shaab*), sa volonté, et la caractérisation évidente pour tous de ce que c'est que le système.

---

10 Sur cette question de l'universalisme et de la révolution, voir l'entretien mené par l'équipe de recherche Minor Universality (2020).
11 Il est à noter que le mot *Hirak* (mouvement) n'est pas chargé du même sens et de la même symbolique au Maghreb occidental qu'au Moyen Orient. Ainsi a-t-on vu les manifestants libanais chanter « notre *thawra* n'est pas un *hirak* », non pas pour se distinguer des Algériens, mais pour dire quelque chose comme « notre révolution n'est pas seulement un mouvement social ». Dans le contexte algérien et rifain, le *Hirak* renvoie à l'idée de soulèvement.

Ces mots-là ne se sont pas forgés dans les académies de langue arabe. Leur forge se situe ailleurs, dans les luttes répétées, dans les échos de ces luttes, mais aussi dans des espaces d'apprentissage qui sont en marge du politique. Pour en saisir l'émergence et la circulation, il faut regarder ailleurs, écouter les chansons, les blagues, les films. Et aussi des lieux comme les stades où s'inventent des chants du monde. Ces surgissements racontent aussi des sociétés de relégation et de séparation. Ce qui se dit dans les stades, c'est ce qu'ont appris à mépriser, ou en tout cas à ignorer, les intellectuel·le·s et les élites des pays ou dont ils et elles se sont simplement séparé·e·s.

Cette langue forge un vocabulaire qui vient dire l'aspiration à la dignité (*karama*), dans sa pluralité : qu'elle se dise sous la forme de revendications syndicales, de mouvements populaires, ou de chants de supporters lancés à la foule comme des cris contre l'oppression ou l'humiliation. On a en tête la Casa de la Mouradia des supporters algérois reprise par la foule lors des premières journées de soulèvement en 2019. En écho, on peut aussi écouter le chant des supporters du Raja Casablanca, *F'Bladi Delmouni* (Ils m'ont opprimé dans mon pays). Créée en mars 2017 par le groupe musical des ultras du Raja, Gruppo Aquile (Groupe des Aigles), cette chanson raconte les souffrances d'une jeunesse. La chanson a dépassé les frontières du stade, et même celles du Maroc pour devenir un hymne puissant. Elle a notamment été entendue en Tunisie lors des manifestations populaires de juillet 2021 :

> Dans ce pays, on vit dans un nuage d'ombre
> Ils nous ont laissés comme des orphelins
> À attendre le jugement dernier [. . .]
> Vous avez volé les richesses de notre pays
> Les avez partagées avec des étrangers
> Vous avez détruit toute une génération . . .
> (Gruppo Aquile 2017)[12]

Le chant des supporters de l'Ittihad de Tanger est peut-être l'un des plus poignants. Voici ce qu'il dit, à l'unisson, appelant à l'exil pour fuir une terre de souffrance :

> C'est une terre de Hogra[13],
> Où nos larmes ont coulé
> La vie y est amère
> Ils n'ont pas menti ceux qui ont dit

---

12 On peut l'écouter par exemple sur YouTube : https://www.youtube.com/watch?v=kJvFAUZiK-Q.
13 La *hogra* désigne l'humiliation et le mépris.

Qu'ils nous ont tués avec des promesses
Nous n'en avons rien vu dans ce pays
Pour Mawazine Shakira a été payée des milliards
Nos demandes sont modestes
Vous nous avez tués avec des prix qui flambent
Par dieu, c'est une grande mafia
Tout le monde est devenu voleur
Dans les quartiers, les pauvres forment des files d'attente
Une bougie nous éclaire
Notre seule eau provient des robinets publics
Et ils se moquent de nous
Avec notre argent ils s'achètent des villas
Emmenez-nous sur un bateau
Sauvez-nous de cette terre ![14]

Ces paroles qui sont chantées à pleine voix dans les stades, circulent à plus basse intensité dans les conversations quotidiennes, elles sont une forme d'infra-politique[15], très directement énoncé mais porté dans des espaces particuliers, des espaces de tolérance relative et de confrontation réglée que sont les stades, elles sont aussi le terreau dans lequel se développent les langues de la révolte. Ce qui circule depuis longtemps à bas bruit se trouve hissé et porté très haut dans les moments, parfois éphémères, de communion dans la révolte. Ainsi les Algériens et les Algériennes ont-ils porté ces chants du stade dans la rue et, ce faisant, ils réparent littéralement, reconstruisent le lien entre les générations et entre les mondes séparés par le « système ».

Si l'on tend l'oreille, comme nous y invite par exemple le sociologue John Holloway, ces paroles et ces chants sont déjà audibles avant leur explosion dans l'espace public commun par un « ça suffit » ou par un « trop c'est trop » (Holloway 2010). Ils ne sont pas pour autant des signes annonciateurs, ils sont des potentialités qui ne se déploient pas nécessairement, qui peuvent se développer dans l'ombre longtemps et peuvent aussi prendre d'autres formes. Ces potentialités circulent par les productions artistiques, la scène musicale notamment. Le rap est aujourd'hui un des lieux de cette traduction-relation, un lieu de prise de parole où l'on prend des risques. Au Maroc, les rappeurs L'Zaar, Weld Legriya et L'Gnawi ont été condamnés pour leur morceau « 'ach al-cha'b » (que vive le peuple) en 2019[16]. On y retrouve des mots très proches des chansons des supporters :

---

14 « C'est un pays de hogra », YouTube, Middle East Eye. Cette vidéo a beaucoup circulé sur les réseaux sociaux en 2019 : https://www.youtube.com/watch?v=9KrmIB0a72E.
15 Cette notion est bien entendu empruntée à l'anthropologue James Scott (1990).
16 Sur cette affaire, voir l'article d'Omar Brousky (2020) paru dans le journal Orient XXI.

> Qui a broyé le pays et qui continue à chercher la richesse ? [. . .] Qui nous a mis dans ce pétrin ? Vous avez violé notre dignité [. . .]. Si on est 40 millions dans ce pays, 30 millions restent avec toi parce qu'ils y sont forcés [. . .]. Ma vie n'a pas de but [. . .]. Je suis celui qui t'a fait confiance et qui a été trahi [. . .]. Je suis le Rifain qui rêve d'un Rif meilleur . . . (L'Zaar 2019)[17]

Enfin, dans l'ordre des mots, les militants révolutionnaires contemporains ont leur mot à dire. Les décisions des Académies se font dans la lenteur du cycle de travail. Des années peuvent s'écouler avant que des solutions linguistiques pour dire le monde ne soient trouvées, bien après que les blogueurs et blogueuses ont de leur côté fait entrer par effraction des mots qui se répandent. L'article de *Mada Masr* précédemment cité évoque le cas du mot genre :

> L'Académie arabe du Caire a ainsi validé le mot *jounoussa*, en avril 2009, pour désigner les « traits distinctifs entre les sexes masculin et féminin » en arguant qu'il s'agit d'un nom d'action sur le schème de *fou'oula* semblable à *dhoukoura* (masculinité), *ounoutha* (féminité) et *bourouda* (frigidité). Cependant, relève Farah Berkaoui, rédactrice et coordinatrice du projet Wikigender, « le mot *jounoussa* ne s'est pas répandu contrairement à *gender* et genre social ». Selon elle, ce manque de succès du mot tient probablement à la ressemblance du mot *jounoussa* avec sexualité (*jinsâniyya*) et sexe (*jins*) (Waël 2019).

Les espaces pour dire les questions liées aux genres s'étaient depuis longtemps emparé de *gender*, et avaient cultivé d'autres manières de dire, y compris en retournant des stigmates.

Finalement, il y aurait bien sûr mille choses à entendre et à écouter, à décrypter et à traduire peut-être. Elles sont semées un peu partout sur le chemin des femmes et des hommes qui habitent le monde arabe contemporain. Elles n'ont pas surgi par miracle en 2011, elles avaient déjà tissé des toiles, fourni des refuges et des lieux pour se reposer alors même que les langues du pouvoir se développaient pour devenir, bien loin de leur élan émancipateur, des langues qui ferment, qui élèvent des murs, qui excluent, des langues qui humilient et relèguent.

Une image vient au moment de conclure, celle d'un manifestant dans les rues d'Alger en 2019. C'est un homme muet, et il harangue la foule. Les gens se rassemblent autour de lui et l'écoutent alors qu'il ne parle aucun langage articulé. Et pourtant, tout le monde le comprend. Sa position, le lieu où ils se trouve, le moment qu'il partage donnent les clés d'un discours à l'unisson. Que peut-on imaginer de plus « impur », que peut-on imaginer de plus digne d'être écouté ?

La position des locuteurs et locutrices de langues indigènes pourrait se situer bien loin d'une réflexion sur les universalités possibles. Leur position est au seuil de plusieurs « puretés » présentées, enseignées et brandies comme inatteignables et à atteindre. L'intelligence politique des révolutions arabes réside dans la fabrique

---

[17] On peut écouter la chanson ici : https://www.youtube.com/watch?v=hiW7ByHWJhg.

d'une langue concurrente, non unique, non unifiée, mais qui, contrairement aux langues savantes, est au plus proche des êtres vivants, de leurs émotions, de leurs désirs et de leurs aspirations les plus élevées et les plus abstraites. En son cœur, la notion de dignité, qui puise ici sa puissance politique.

La tâche du chercheur ou de la chercheuse, nous le savons, est d'écouter et de regarder. A cette place, voici donc ce que j'ai entendu, ce que j'ai vu et ce que j'ai lu : des sociétés sur le fil, qui dessinent par bribes le sens qu'elles donnent à leur « volonté de vivre », pour reprendre les mots du poète tunisien Abul Qassim al-Shabbi. Pour qui veut bien les entendre, ces voix des luttes, mais aussi de la vie quotidienne, nous embarquent dans un nouveau récit dont la première formulation est l'abandon même de la notion d'idéal abstrait à atteindre par une forme de pureté. La langue est le terrain par lequel il nous est peut-être permis de comprendre ce qu'on peut entendre par là, une forme de nouvel universel multilingue qui se bâtit sur les relations qu'il permet de nouer entre les êtres. Ces relations se passent parfois même de langue tant elles se comprennent, immédiatement, comme la langue de la dignité humaine.

Références bibliographiques

Amin, Samir. *La Nation arabe. Nationalisme et lutte de classes*. Paris : Minuit, 1976.
Bardawil, Fadi. *Revolution and Disenchantment. Arab Marxism and the Binds of Emancipation*. Durham/NC : Duke University Press, 2020.
Brousky, Omar. « Au Maroc, l'étouffement des dernières voix dissidentes ». *Orient XXI*, 29 janvier 2020. https://orientxxi.info/magazine/au-maroc-l-etouffement-des-dernieres-voix-dissidentes, 3566 (15.06.2022).
Casanova, Pascale. *La République mondiale des lettres*. Paris : Seuil, 1999.
——. *La Langue mondiale. Traduction et domination*. Paris : Seuil, 2015.
« C'est un pays de hogra ». Chant des supporters de l'Ittihad de Tanger, 2019. https://www.youtube.com/watch?v=9KrmIB0a72E (15.06.2022).
Dakhli, Leyla. « Arabisme, nationalisme arabe et identifications transnationales arabes au 20e siècle ». *Vingtième Siècle. Revue d'histoire* 103.3 (2009a) : 12–25.
——. *Une génération d'intellectuels arabes. Syrie et Liban (1908–1940)*. Paris : Karthala, 2009b.
——. « Nahda ». *Encyclopédie de l'humanisme méditerranéen*. Ed. Houari Touati. 2014. http://www.encyclopedie-humanisme.com/?Nahda (15.06.2022).
——. *L'Esprit de la révolte. Archives et actualité des révolutions arabes*. Paris : Seuil, 2020.
——. « Napoléon a-t-il réveillé le monde arabe ? » *The Epoch of Universalism 1769–1989*. Ed. Franck Hofmann et Markus Messling. Berlin, Boston : De Gruyter, 2021. 43–54.
Dakhlia, Jocelyne. « Mémoire des langues ». *La pensée de midi* 3.3 (2000) : 40–44.
——. « No man's langue : une rétraction coloniale ». *Trames de langues. Usages et métissages linguistiques dans l'histoire du Maghreb*. Ed. Jocelyne Dakhlia. Tunis : Tunis-IRMC, 2004. 259–271. http://books.openedition.org/irmc/1472 (15.06.2022).

de Certeau, Michel. *La Prise de Parole, et autres écrits politiques*. Paris : Seuil, 1994.

Derrida, Jacques. *Le Monolinguisme de l'autre*. Paris : Galilée, 1996.

Diagne, Souleymane Bachir. *De Langue à langue. L'hospitalité de la traduction*. Paris : Albin Michel, 2022.

Djebar, Assia. *La Disparition de la langue française*. Paris : Albin Michel, 2003.

Fahmy, Khalid. *All the Pasha's Men : Mehmed Ali, his Army and the Making of Modern Egypt*. Cambridge : Cambridge University Press, 1998.

Fanon, Frantz. *Peau noire, Masques blancs*. Paris : Seuil, 1952.

Glissant, Edouard. *Philosophie de la relation. Poésie en étendue*. Paris : Gallimard, 2009.

Gruppo Aquile – ظلموني في بلادي (Ultras Eagles). *F'Bladi Delmouni* (Ils m'ont opprimé dans mon pays), mars 2017. https://www.youtube.com/watch?v=kJvFAUZiK-Q (15.06.2022).

Guellouz, Azzedine, Abdelkader Masmoudi, Smida Mongi et Ahmed Saadaou. *Histoire générale de la Tunisie. T. III « Les temps modernes »*. Tunis : Sud Éditions, 2010.

Harchi, Kaoutar. *Je n'ai qu'une langue, ce n'est pas la mienne. Des écrivains à l'épreuve*. Paris : Pauvert, 2016.

Holloway, John. « À quelle distance est l'Amérique latine ? » *Variations. Revue Internationale de Théorie Critique* 13–14 (2010) : 12–18.

Hourani, Albert. *Arabic Thought in the Liberal Age, 1798–1939*. Oxford : Oxford University Press, 1962.

Kienle, Eberhard. « De la langue et en deçà : nationalismes arabes à géométrie variable ». *Égypte/Monde arabe* 26.2 (1996) : 153–170.

Leonhardt Santini, Maud. *Paris. Librairie arabe*. Marseille : Parenthèses, 2006.

L'Zaar, Weld Legriya et L'Gnawi. « 'ach al-cha'b (que vive le peuple) », 2019. https://www.youtube.com/watch?v=hiW7ByHWJhg (15.06.2022).

Mbembe, Achille. *De la postcolonie. Essai sur l'imagination politique dans l'Afrique contemporaine*. Paris : Karthala, 2000.

Memmi, Albert. *Portrait du colonisé*. Paris : Buchet-Chastel, 1957.

Minor Universality. « Universalisme & révolution. Entretien avec Leyla Dakhli ». *Les entretiens du groupe de recherche Minor Universality*, le 14 juillet 2020. https://www.youtube.com/watch?v=OCz3dq8TOAY (15.06.2022).

Pollock, Sheldon. *Philologie und Freiheit*. Trad. Reinhart Meyer-Kalkus. Berlin : Matthes & Seitz, 2018.

Ruffel, Lionel. *Brouhaha. Les mondes du contemporain*. Lagrasse : Verdier, 2016.

Scott, James. *Domination, and the Arts of Resistance. Hidden Transcripts*. New Haven : Yale University Press, 1990.

Smith, Julia A. *Mediterraneans. North Africa and Europe in an Age of Migration, c. 1800–1900*. Berkeley : University of California Press, 2011.

Trabant, Jürgen. *Der Gallische Herkules. Über Sprache und Politik in Deutschland und Frankreich*. Tübingen : A. Francke Verlag, 2002.

Waël, Ahmed. « L'Académie égyptienne au défi des mots ». Trad. Hamid Larbi. *Orient XXI*, octobre 2019. https://orientxxi.info/magazine/l-academie-egyptienne-au-defi-des-mots,3384 (15.06.2022).

Hélène Thiérard
Multilingual Literatures and the Production of Universality Through Translation: Cassin, Diagne, Tawada

Abstract: Does the failure of European universalism imply that we should get rid of the universal as a pernicious idea or does it, on the contrary, reveal the urgency of defining a truly universal concept of universality? In the current debate touching both societal and geopolitical issues, philosophers Barbara Cassin and Souleymane Bachir Diagne position themselves similarly, both tracing the epistemic dimension of the problem back to the beginning of the European history of ideas. Considering the abstract logos of philosophy as the bedrock of a "pathology of the universal" (Cassin) – in Diagne's words an "overarching", "imperial" universal – they put it to the empirical test of translation. My paper argues that the strategy of "untranslatables" that they explore is also at work in contemporary multilingual literature and examines the political potential of its poetic thinking. If writers are capable of letting the reader experience this "more complex" (Cassin) or "lateral" (Diagne) universality on the basis of translingual poetics, then they are privileged protagonists in the intellectual debate outlined above.

Keywords: universality, translation theory, translingual poetics, Barbara Cassin, Souleymane Bachir Diagne, Yoko Tawada

Note: This chapter is part of the research project "Minor Universality. Narrative World Productions After Western Universalism", which received funding from the European Research Council (ERC) under the European Union's Horizon 2020 research and innovation programme (Grant agreement no. 819931). An earlier version of this text has been published in German in the volume *Mehrsprachigkeit und das Politische* edited by Marko Pajević (see Thiérard 2020).

Translated by Anna Galt

1 Translation and multilingualism in the universality debate

The current debate in the humanities around the notion of universality is not just a theoretical one. As Immanuel Wallerstein puts it in his seminal book *European Universalism: The Rhetoric of Power* (2006, xv), establishing a (genuinely) "universal universalism" is a task we must tackle if we want to have a say in "how the future world-system into which we will be entering in the next twenty-five to fifty years will be structured". Starting from the critique of European universalism as articulated in postcolonial approaches as well as in theories of modernity and globalisation (Appadurai 1990; Chakrabarty 2000; Conrad and Randeria 2002), it is necessary to completely reconceive the category of the universal in order to not leave the field of thought and political action open to cultural relativism and ethnonationalism (Balibar 2016; Mbembe 2016; Messling 2019; Hofmann and Messling 2021) and their spreading of "murderous identities", as Amin Maalouf (1998) once called it. Within this debate, philosophers Barbara Cassin and Souleymane Bachir Diagne take a similar stance, both tracing the epistemic dimension of the problem back to the beginning of the European history of language thinking.[1] Considering the abstract *logos* of philosophy as the bedrock of a "pathology of the universal" (Cassin) – in Diagne's words an "overarching", "imperial" universal – they submit it to the empirical test of translation. Translation, they argue, in the back and forth between languages, makes possible the production of a more complex universality – as the title of Cassin's book *Éloge de la traduction: Compliquer l'universel* (2016) suggests – than the supposed universalism of the *logos* claimed from within a culturally dominating language. Following Merleau-Ponty, Diagne calls this universality conceived out of the diversity of languages "lateral", for it presupposes the negotiation of two particular points of view, in contrast to an "overarching universal" (*universel de surplomb*) imposed from above (Diagne 2014).

The problem that Cassin and Diagne articulate here on a theoretical level has become a more and more central focus in multilingual literatures – this seems to me to be the main reason for their political relevance today. If their translingual poetics are capable of letting the reader experience this new form of universality based on translation processes, then these writers are privileged protagonists in the intellectual debate outlined above. I argue that, like literary translators (Thiérard 2019), translingual writers produce a poetic thinking about language, and by doing so have

---

[1] The position of François Jullien (2008) should also be considered in this context, which unfortunately the limited space of this article does not allow.

a substantial influence on shaping the world of tomorrow. My contribution therefore intends to establish a dialogue between two disconnected fields of research: on the one hand Diagne's and Cassin's philosophy of translation, and on the other hand current research on literary multilingualism that focuses on overcoming the monolingual paradigm or the modern invention of monolingualism (Yildiz 2012; Gramling 2016; Dembeck and Mein 2014; Dembeck and Parr 2017). I will take the work of the writer Yoko Tawada as a paradigmatic example, whose poetics between languages displays certain similarities with Cassin's strategy of observing "untranslatables" as areas of tension that produce knowledge.

2 Thinking in tongues: Against the eurocentric universalism of the *logos*

The ethical and political implications of the European philosophy of language (*Sprachdenken*) have been highlighted in the last few decades by philosophers and critics such as Henri Meschonnic (1982),[2] Jürgen Trabant (1986; 1990), and Barbara Cassin (2016)[3] – all working in the linguistic anthropological tradition of Wilhelm von Humboldt.[4] In particular they reveal the disastrous consequences of the prevailing dualistic understanding of language for shaping our society and denounce this model dating back to Aristotle, which under the guise of the universality of language (*langage*), establishes the superiority of a certain language (*langue*) or language family. In *De interpretatione*, Aristotle posits universal abstract concepts, as if words were merely clothing, uninvolved in the process of knowledge. As Trabant points out, in this "probably most influential European text on language – after the Bible passages", "language is degraded to a tool for the communication of thoughts that have been formed without words" (Trabant 2003, 30, 34).[5] This supposed universality of the *logos* based on the radical division between *conceptus* and *vox*, between cognition and communication, is in fact conceived from a particular language and is therefore strongly ethnocentric: Thus

---

[2] Meschonnic's most important texts on Humboldt are reprinted in Meschonnic (2012, Chapters 28–30).
[3] See the chapter "Le dispositif Humboldt" in Cassin (2016, 177–226).
[4] On the founding of a linguistic anthropology in Trabant and Meschonnic, see Pajević (2012, 124–191).
[5] Unless otherwise specified, all the German and French quotes have been translated for the purpose of this article.

Greek declares itself to be the language of reason and being, excluding those who speak other languages ("barbarians") from participating in reason.[6] This "overarching universal" is "the position of those who declare their own particularity to be universal" (Diagne 2018, 68–69) and can only interpret alterity as inferiority. Depending on the age, the self-declared language of reason is Greek, French or English – the "barbarians" are then accordingly renamed "primitives". Diagne urges us not to confuse universalism with universality, pointing out that African languages are still commonly considered to be deficient compared to European languages: they lack writing, abstract concepts, the future tense, the verb "to be", etc. (Diagne 2018, 69–70). Must we remind ourselves that philologists in the eighteenth and nineteenth centuries provided arguments for a theory of European linguistic and cultural superiority, which largely justified the Europeans' colonial rule over the rest of the world and not least helped obtain public acceptance as a "mission civilisatrice" (Messling 2016)? To paraphrase Meschonnic, the Aristotelian conception of language that has so strongly influenced the history of linguistic thought in the occident is dangerous, because a theory of language always implies a theory of society (Meschonnic 2012 [2005]).

Against this dualistic tradition in language philosophy and its inherent "pathological universal", Cassin deploys Humboldt's conception of language as a dynamic synthesis of sound and idea, of communication and cognition, in which the material word participates in the concrete process of forming thoughts. In contrast to Aristotle, Humboldt considers the diversity of languages epistemically interesting, because he does not regard it as being a purely material: "Their diversity is not one of sounds and signs, but a diversity in the ways of viewing the world itself" (Humboldt 1903–1936, IV, 27). While language (*langage*) is "the formative organ of thoughts" for Humboldt (1903–1936, VII, 53), this world-constituting process necessarily takes place within a certain language (*langue*) and is therefore partly conditioned by a particular historical setting. Based on this understanding of individual languages as worldviews, Cassin wants to grasp epistemic universality in a "more complex" way, which first of all means moving away from the postulate of a given, abstract universality of human language – as in Aristotle, but also, for example, in Chomsky's idea of an innate universal grammar. In order not to reduce it to similarity with a dominant language, we should rather consider universality as a never-ending task, which, out of the concrete differences of individual languages, allows a common world to appear on the horizon.

In this sense, Cassin and Diagne understand translation as a philosophical method. The monumental reference work coordinated by Cassin, *Vocabulaire*

---

[6] Trabant raises the same objection against Chomsky's neo-Aristotelian position, which leads to indifference about the diversity and materiality of languages (Trabant 2003, 279–283).

européen des philosophies. Dictionnaire des intraduisibles (2004), took more than ten years and the work of almost 150 contributors to complete. It tackles four hundred lemmas that show noticeable resistance to translation and are therefore treated as important symptoms of the difference between (European) languages.[7] Philosophical texts in translation teem with such "untranslatables", whether they lead to neologisms or are simply adopted in the translation as loan words (Heidegger's *Dasein*, Hegel's *Aufhebung*). Other cases are less obvious:

> Does one understand the same thing by "mind" as by *Geist* or *esprit*, is *pravda* "justice" or "truth", and what happens when we render *mimesis* as "representation" rather than "imitation"? Each entry thus starts from a nexus of untranslatability and proceeds to a comparison of terminological networks, whose distortion creates the history and geography of languages and cultures (Cassin 2014, xvii).

This historical and comparative approach on the one hand makes the *Vocabulaire* an essential reference work for the humanities today, and on the other promotes an awareness of how we philosophise in tongues, i.e. how our thought categories are to a certain extent dependent on our language categories, as Nietzsche already identified.[8] Thus the epistemological gesture of the *Vocabulaire* is altogether a (linguistic) political one: the commitment to a (rich) many tongued, European tradition of philosophising vehemently opposes the increasing monolingualisation of the academic world in its use of English as a (European and global) *lingua franca* (Globish) (Cassin 2016, 55–60). Furthermore, Cassin also explicitly attacks a part of the analytical philosophy in the English-speaking tradition, which, she argues, demonstrates its own flaws with its monolingual attitude of dominance (Cassin 2016, 59–60).

It should be noted that with the plural noun "intraduisibles" (untranslatables), Cassin does not invoke untranslatability in the name of an absolute language relativism, which sacralises language difference as opacity – "the untranslatable is rather what one keeps on (not) translating" (Cassin 2014, xvii).[9] Following Humboldt, Cassin values the zones of incommensurability between the languages as an opportunity for the work of the mind [*Geist*], because "[t]he sum of what may be known, as the field to be cultivated by the human mind [*Geist*], lies between all languages" (Humboldt 1903–1936, IV, 27). If the conception of individual languages as worldviews means a limitation of perspective and therefore the knowable, then decentring can

---

7 Each lemma deals with a multilingual keyword group, meaning that in total there are about 4,000 philosophical keywords from fifteen European languages in the *Vocabulaire*.
8 Diagne (2014, 252) quotes the famous part from Nietzsche's *Jenseits von Gut und Böse* (para. 20) and refers to Crépon's reading of it (see Crépon 2000).
9 A form of the plural that leads to neologisms in translation, thus performatively realising the idea of "intraduisibles".

only have a productive effect. This decentring is the source of the productivity of untranslatables, which, employed as a method, may shed new light on old philosophical problems. Fundamentally it is about de-essentialising the language of European philosophies – from Aristotle to Heidegger – that is to refute the position of a "national essentialism" (Meschonnic 1990), which assigns certain languages (for instance Greek, German) an ontological status (Cassin 2016, 60–62). To philosophise in tongues therefore also means, based on the canonical philosophical texts' resistances to translation, revealing this form of the "overarching universal" as an historically particular construction. Although the *Vocabulaire* is not a postcolonial project per se, still we can identify a strong resonance with Achille Mbembe's criticism of European universalism in its inherent impetus (Syrotinski 2019). In this regard, Syrotinski draws attention to the English, as well as especially the Spanish and Portuguese editions of the *Vocabulaire*, which were published in the USA (2014), Mexico (2018), and Brazil (2018), and which shift the originally internal European dimension of the criticism[10] into a postcolonial context.[11] Among the members of Cassin's team working on the *Dictionary*, Diagne best articulates what is at stake in a postcolonial world in this conception of universality as a process of translation (Diagne 2013; see also Diagne's article in this volume).

Diagne takes a clear stance in favour of a decolonisation of knowledge/thinking, pleading for African languages to become (once again) languages of philosophical production.[12] However, he also points out a danger within postcolonial studies when the critique of European universalism leads to abandoning the idea of universality altogether.[13] In his essay "L'universel latéral comme traduction", he illustrates this danger by contrasting the approaches of two African philosophers, Alexis Kagamé und Kwasi Wiredu (Diagne 2014, 2022).[14] Since as early as 1955, Kagamé has been demonstrating the epistemological imperialism of the

---

10 In Cassin's approach, the dominant universalistic tradition of the European *logos* is criticised from the inside out, with recourse to post-structural and deconstructionist theories, especially Derrida, Lacan, and Deleuze (Cassin 2016, 64–67, 122–123).
11 On adapting the *Vocabulaire* in various editions through the process of translation (also into Romanian, Arabic, Ukrainian, Russian, Italian) see Cassin (2016, 70–76).
12 Diagne frequently refers to the writer Ngũgĩ wa Thiong'o and his influential book *Decolonizing the Mind* (1986).
13 On this tension within the postcolonial studies see the interview with Souleymane Bachir Diagne conducted by the ERC Minor Universality research team, "Universalisme et multilatéralisme" (ERC Minor Universality 2021).
14 For further reading see Diagne's chapter "De l'universel et de l'universalisme" (Diagne 2018, 69–72) in the volume he edited with the anthropologist Jean-Loup Amselle E*n quête d'Afrique(s). Universalisme et pensée décoloniale* (2018). In this book, the dialogue with Amselle about their diverging views on universality brings Diagne to expand on his argument from the 2014 essay.

European languages using the example of Aristotelian ontology, which with its eight or nine categories of being is clearly indebted to the grammatical categories of the Greek language, and whose translation into Indo-European languages is quite unproblematic. Had Aristotle thought in one of the Bantu languages, his ontology would very likely have had four categories of being instead. But is it therefore a justifiable position to set up a Bantu ontology against the Greek-European ontology, as Kagamé proposes, thereby replacing one national essentialism with the other? Distancing himself from this relativist position, Diagne favours that of Wiredu, much closer to his and Cassin's idea of translation as a method. Wiredu does question the logicians' concept of truth based on his difficulties translating it from English into the Akan language (Ghana). However, he does not oppose it with any particular Ghanaian concept of truth, but rather uses this zone of incommensurability between the languages critically in order to pose the philosophical problem in a new way – to find a lateral way in, which makes the concept less ethnocentric, that is, more universal.

3 The strategy of *intraduisibles* in multilingual literatures: Against the monolingual paradigm as overarching universal

The growing body of research on multilingualism in recent years has led to a questioning of the idea of monolingualism as a cultural norm and highlighted its historical indebtedness to the modern ideology of the nation (Dembeck and Mein 2012; Gramling 2016; Yildiz 2012). To address multilingualism in a more complex way, Gramling proposes to adopt M.A.K. Halliday's sociolinguistic distinction between "glossodiversity (diversity of linguistic codes) and semiodiversity (diversity of conveyed meanings)" (Gramling 2016, 31). I would like to argue here that this distinction from the field of applied linguistics ahistorically opposes the two main positions, unequally represented in the history of European linguistic thought, regarding language diversity: today's prevailing conception of glossodiversity on one hand, characteristic for a technocratic multilingualism as it appears for example institutionally in the European Union ("a diversity of codes in service of common meaning-making"), reflects the Aristotelian indifference towards the supposedly neutral materiality of languages; semiodiversity on the other hand again picks up Humboldt's theory of languages as worldviews. In this respect, it is not surprising when Gramling refers to Barbara Cassin and the *Dictionnaire des intraduisibles* and calls it "an extended experiment around semiodiversity in comparative intellectual history" (Gramling 2016, 32, fn. 29).[15]

In *Beyond the Mother Tongue: The Postmonolingual Condition* (2012), Yasemin Yildiz argues that multilingual, contemporary writers such as Emine Sevgi Özdamar, Yoko Tawada, and Feridun Zaimoğlu are subverting from the inside the "monolingual paradigm" that established dominance during the course of the formation of nations. This means that these literary works performatively demonstrate a kind of multilingualism that disrupt the very idea of glossodiversity. The sheer presence of several languages in one and the same literary text does not necessarily have this subversive force. In Tolstoy's *War and Peace*, for example, the integration of French mostly contributes to the social characterisation of the Russian officers belonging to the nobility. What makes multilingual literatures particularly explosive today is their ability to tightly interweave an epistemological and a cultural-political critique of language in their poetic thinking: this is how multilingual literatures make the affinity between the monolingual paradigm and what Cassin identifies as the pathological universality of the European logos tangible, and how they subvert both of them.[16] The disastrous social consequences of a conception of language that postulates a single epistemological model have already been outlined. What is at stake in the subversion of the monolingual paradigm is no less than the de-essentialisation of the relationship between language and nation. The sharp contrast between mother tongue and foreign language, in other words the idea that individuals are naturally in possession of only one language in which they can express themselves with authenticity and which shapes their subjectivity, is one of the cores of the monolingual paradigm. From an historical perspective, this is one of the most powerful inventions of modernity, since the idea of national ethnicity is constructed based on this community of feeling in the mother tongue. Viewed in its macrohistorical context, Herder's idea of the *Volk* (the people of a nation) originally had an emancipatory goal: it was intended to dismantle a political order based on aristocratic legitimacy in favour of a new political order which postulates the people as the new criterion of legitimacy (Thiesse 1999). As is well known, literature played a major role in this process by endowing the respective peoples with cultural capital (Casanova 2011), so that they could assert themselves against the aristocracy, which until then possessed all the legitimate symbolic power. What matters here is that literature attests to the existence of a certain people as a collective as far back into the past as possible, for what gives birth to a nation and keeps it alive

---

15 Gramling wonders in this footnote why Cassin does not use the term "semiodiversity" herself.
16 On the aspect of critique of language in multilingual literatures, see Heimböckel (2014).

is above all the belief in this "imagined community" (Anderson 1983). Although national identities in Europe have emerged as relational co-constructions – constructed out of frictions between neighbours for example – in which the forming of national literatures also plays a role,[17] the traces of their historical construction have later been erased in order to essentialise these identities.[18] Indeed, the excluding mechanism of national communities works better if one declares them to be a naturally given fact (Anderson 1983). Politically of course, the idea of the nation as a new form of collective identification serves not only to weld a people together, but also to set one people against another, for in cases of conflict it must feel natural to go to war in solidarity with one's fellow countrymen and women.

The conflation of linguistic, cultural, and national identity stems from the ideology of the mother tongue at the centre of the modern invention of monolingualism (Dembeck and Parr 2017, 27–33). Two closely related postulates support this ideology and contribute to shaping the modern understanding of linguistic diversity and translation (see Sakai 2009). The first one posits the idea of individual languages as homogenous, complete, and closed language systems – an idea towards which the national philologists in the nineteenth century worked conscientiously with their descriptive and normative linguistic tools. Grammars and dictionaries of the time systematically disregard phenomena like contact between languages, to provide clear, unambiguous contours. This idea of homogeneity also gains ground in national literatures over the course of the nineteenth century and slowly forces back the internal traditions of multilingual writing (Anokhina, Dembeck, and Weissmann 2019). The second postulate establishes the interchangeability of individual languages in the sense of an unproblematic, "systematic transposability" (Gramling 2014) of utterances from one language system to another. This notion of translation shows most clearly how deeply the monolingual paradigm is indebted to the Eurocentric universalism of the *logos*, for it presupposes a rational concept of language (*langage*) striving towards the ideal of mathematics (Dembeck and Mein 2012, 137–138). In this modern understanding of multilingualism as glossodiversity, languages (*langues*) may be involved in the cultural identity of individuals, but do not have an epistemological relevance.

The strategy of *intraduisibles*, whether adopted in philosophy such as in the work of Cassin, Diagne, and Wiredu, among others, or in multilingual literatures, not only undermines one of the key assumptions of the monolingual paradigm,

---

17 On national literature emerging in a national-transnational process in Germany and France, see Jurt (2009).
18 Casanova's distinction between *littératures majeures* or *pacifiées*, which understand themselves as universal, and *littératures mineures* or *combatives*, which still participate in the national struggle, is based on how any trace of the construction of the nation was erased (Casanova 2011).

but also works towards another, more complex or lateral way of producing universality. In contemporary translingual poetics, we often observe translation processes taking place within the text: as this writing between languages unveils zones of resistance to translation and shifting images, it reclaims the detours and derailments of meaning in translation to engage poetically in an intercultural critique of language. Whether in the form of poetry (Yoko Tawada's *Abenteuer der deutschen Grammatik*, 2010), autobiographical essays (José F.A. Oliver's *Mein andalusisches Schwarzwalddorf*, 2007; *Fremdenzimmer*, 2015) or language autobiographies (Eva Hoffman's *Lost in Translation*, 1989) and language-learning fictions (Xiaolu Guo's *A Concise Chinese-English Dictionary for Lovers*, 2008), of novels that reflect on language (Luigi Meneghello's *Libera nos a Malo*, 1969),[19] and fictions about translation (Annette Hug's *Wilhelm Tell in Manila*, 2016; Cécile Wajsbrot's *Nevermore*, 2021), these writers are exploring areas of incommensurability between languages as worldviews. In their poetic thinking about language, they do not just reflect the problematic, conflict-ridden change of perspective that takes place in the search for a lateral universality, but also make their readers experience it in their own bodies, in order to bring about a change in their consciousness.[20] In this regard, the poetic strategy of *intraduisibles* goes perhaps a step further than the philosophical one, when one considers the potential for social change.

4 Yoko Tawada's poetic strategy of *untranslatables*: Exploring a minor form of universality

The Japanese-German writer Yoko Tawada holds a PhD in literature and has a comprehensive education in the areas of philosophy and cultural studies, which also informs her multilingual writing practice. Drawing creatively on approaches to language, culture and translation theory from Walter Benjamin to Jacques Derrida via Roland Barthes and Claude Lévi-Strauss, Tawada has produced one of the most complex translingual poetics in contemporary German literature. One could almost claim that in her fictional short prose, literary essays, and poems, she is systematically pursuing the goal of turning the monolingual paradigm on its

---

19 The 2010 French translation by Christophe Mileschi makes Meneghello's novel contemporary literature again.
20 On this performative aesthetic in Tawada and Oliver, see Thiérard (2018).

head. She usually takes the concrete experience of everyday life as a starting point to make the zones of incommensurability between languages tangible, thus performing Humboldt's idea that "thought is embodied" (Trabant 2017, 23).[21] Tawada's poetic strategy of untranslatables appears most clearly in *Überseezungen* (2002), *Talisman* (1996), *Sprachpolizei und Spielpolyglotte* (2007), *Abenteuer der deutschen Grammatik* (2010), and *Akzentfrei* (2016). These works provide a good overview of the many textual techniques involved in her translational poetics and how they undermine the core assumptions of the monolingual paradigm.[22]

Tawada's short narratives, somewhat overloaded with language reflexivity, often counter the postulate of the mother tongue as a natural and most suitable medium of expression with its insidious violence, showing that in a mother tongue the conventional relationship between word and thing is essentialised without the speakers being aware of it. For example, the story "Eine leere Flasche" (An Empty Bottle) (Tawada 2002, 53–57) demonstrates the embodied violence of the personal pronoun "I" (*boku, ore, watashi, watakushi*) in her Japanese mother tongue. In this understanding of the mother tongue "the thoughts cling so tightly to the words" (Tawada 1996, 15) that Humboldt's worldview threatens to turn into a linguistic prison, as Mauthner suspected.[23] Tawada's first-person female narrator repeatedly liberates herself from her mother tongue by learning a foreign language, which works like a "staple remover": "It removes everything that staples and clings together" (Tawada 1996, 15). The estrangement of her own language consciousness is narratively staged as a liberation from a linguistic determinism, which restricts the ability to think and perceive due to habituation and automatisation. In Tawada's work, however, mother tongue and foreign language by no means remain in a static relationship, for this would mean opposing them to one another as an essentialising and an emancipatory principle. Quite the contrary, an essentialisation of linguistic conventions also takes place in the foreign language, when it no longer feels foreign. In *Überseezungen*, Tawada shows how the narrator's language consciousness, shaped by German as a second language, is in turn defamiliarised in contact with other foreign languages, such as English ("Porträt einer Zunge"), French ("Musik der Buchstaben"), and Afrikaans ("Bioskoop der Nacht"). This repetition of the process of defamiliarisation is necessary if one does not want to fall from one national language ontology into the next –

---

21 See Pajević (2020) for this focus.
22 Since this aspect is well documented in Tawada research, I will not undertake an in-depth textual analysis in the following and instead refer the reader to the relevant chapters in Gutjahr (2012); Ivanovic (2010); Banoun and Ivanovic (2015).
23 In his epoch-making work *Beiträge zu einer Kritik der Sprache* (Contributions to a Critique of Language), Fritz Mauthner (1923) calls attention to the limitations of language to gain knowledge of reality, insofar as it determines what people think instead of enabling them to think.

a risk already pointed out by Diagne in objection to Kagamé's philosophical agenda. For Tawada is not just concerned with the fact that individual languages shape cultural identity, but much rather that they are archives of a productive interpretation of the world and therefore also have a share in social and geopolitical power relations.

Tawada quite often deconstructs the postulated homogeneity and closed completeness of individual languages using text-internal translation as a means of demonstration. The translingual poem *Die Mischschrift des Mondes* (The Mixed Writing of the Moon) (Tawada 2010, 41), written halfway between German and Japanese, merges two systems of writing considered incompatible. The genesis of this poem involves a double process of translation: long after having published a German translation of one of her Japanese poems, Tawada transcribed the German text back into Japanese, while leaving some passages untranslated.[24] On the one hand, this mixed writing exemplifies the inherent heterogeneity of the Japanese writing system, in which word stems are written using Chinese ideograms, while Japanese characters phonetically notate the "hands and feet of the words". On the other hand, Tawada's multiscriptual *réécriture* of the poem combining Latin letters and Chinese ideograms shows, according to the author's note, "that one can also write German with this mixed method." The poem thereby urges German readers to deconstruct the supposed homogeneity of the German language as well.[25] Furthermore, many of Tawada's short stories draw attention to a second heterogeneity of the Japanese language which results from the double-pronged constitution of meaning – phonetic and visual – in languages with ideograms. This kind of semiodiversity internal to languages is particularly irritating for European speakers, since it conflicts with their common understanding orientated around alphabetic writing systems: script only records what is said, without participating in thinking. In "Die Botin" (The Messenger) (Tawada 2013 [2002], 44–50), the entire narrative relies on the technique of surface translation to stage this internal semiodiversity of Japanese: the German speech to be transmitted, transcribed into ideograms of roughly the same phonic value, is thus rendered unrecognisable, which turns out to be a powerful way of celebrating the signifying materiality of languages.[26] Here we can draw a further parallel with Cassin's fondness for homophony and homonymy relationships in the Greek language, which she uses to subvert Aristotle's dualistic theory of language (Cassin 2016, 87–145).

---

[24] On the relationship between the original poem, the German translation by Peter Pörtner and the *réécriture*, see Ette (2012, 318–323).
[25] Schmitz-Emans (2012) interprets Tawada's mixed-writing poetic practice in relation to the problem of the untranslatability of script.
[26] On the technique of surface translation, also known as homophonic translation, see Dembeck (2015).

In Tawada's poetic thinking about language, the cultural-political aspect is just as inseparable from the epistemological one as in Diagne's strategy of *intraduisibles*. Dieter Heimböckel (2015) reads Tawada's "fictional ethnography" as a form of writing back,[27] appropriating and rewriting European ethnographic discourse about Japan and the Orient, as it is known, for example, in Roland Barthes' *Empire des Signes*. Tawada's "intercultural language criticism" should therefore be read in relation to her literary and cultural study *Spielzeug und Sprachmagie in der europäischen Literatur: Eine ethnologische Poetologie* (2000). Her fictional ethnography does not fall back into the dichotomies of an orientalist discourse any more than she inverts this discourse into an occidentalism. Much rather she deconstructs cultural identities and proposes an aesthetic experience which makes the constitutive relationality of languages as discursive constructs (Sakai 2009) tangible for the reader.

Although Diagne's idea of a universality produced by translation can certainly not be reduced to the necessity of an intercultural dialogue in the postcolonial age (on this interpretation see Amselle 2018), nonetheless it is based on an "ethnological experience". Maurice Merleau-Ponty, whose work Diagne draws on, describes the process of moving from an overarching universal to a lateral universal, as follows:

> [. . .] the equipment of our social being can be dismantled and reconstructed by the voyage, as we are able to learn to speak other languages. This provides *a second way to the universal*: no longer the *overarching universal* of a strictly objective method, but a sort of *lateral universal* which we acquire through ethnological experience and its incessant testing of the self through the other person and the other person through the self (Merleau-Ponty 1964, 119–120).

The power of transforming subjectivity that Merleau-Ponty ascribes to learning other languages testifies to an embodied concept of language (*langage*). This idea of language as "the organ of thought", as Trabant reminds us, was historically coined by Humboldt: "As an organ, language is more closely interwoven into the corporeality of man, [. . .] situated on a deeper level of consciousness than it is when conceived as a tool" (Trabant 1986, 59).[28] This deep transformation of subjectivity in contact with other languages is central to Tawada's poetic thinking about language, as expressed through the metaphor of "the lens of flesh" (*Fleischbrille*) in her essay

---

27 Originally coined by Salman Rushdie, the term "writing back" became a central concept in postcolonial studies in the 1990s, describing a counterdiscursive strategy constitutive of postcolonial texts. Among other things, it undermines the supposed hegemony of knowledge of the (former) colonial power and its construction of the colonial "other" (see Ashcroft, Griffith, and Tiffin 1989).
28 On the conception of language as organ in Humboldt, see Trabant (1986, 51–61).

"Eigentlich darf man es niemandem sagen, aber Europa gibt es nicht" (I really should not be saying this, but Europe does not exist) (Tawada 2015 [1996]):

> In order to see Europe I need to use a Japanese lens. Since anything resembling a "Japanese point of view" did not and does not exist – and that is not an unfortunate fact as far as I am concerned – this lens must inevitably be fictitious and constantly needs to be manufactured anew. In this respect my Japanese point of view is not authentic, despite the fact that I was born and raised in Japan. Yet my Japanese lens is not an instrument that can be bought from a store. I cannot put it in or take it out at will. This lens grew out of my eyestrain and grew into my flesh, as my flesh grew into the lens (transl. Takabvirwa 2014, 56–57).

Although immediately suspended as fictitious, the metaphor of the "intercultural lens" is nonetheless reactivated by the physical dimension of pain. Tawada's translingual poetics forces the reader to engage, during the act of reading, in the "ethnological experience" between the languages as described by Merleau-Ponty. It also reminds us that the epistemological change of perspective proposed by Diagne and Cassin is a painful, never-ending process, not produced on an abstract level, but rather in one's own flesh.

References

Amselle, Jean-Loup. "L'universalisme en question". *En quête d'Afrique(s). Universalisme et pensée décoloniale*. Eds. Souleymane Bachir Diagne, and Jean-Loup Amselle. Paris: Albin Michel, 2018. 41–63.

Anderson, Benedict. *Imagined Communities. Reflections on the Origin and Spread of Nationalism*. London: Verso, 1983.

Anokhina, Olga, Till Dembeck, and Dirk Weissmann. *Mapping Multilingualism in 19th Century European Literatures. Le plurilinguisme dans les littératures européennes du XIXe siècle*. Zürich: LIT, 2019.

Appadurai, Arjun. *Modernity at Large. Cultural Dimensions of Globalization*. Minneapolis, London: University of Minnesota Press, 1990.

Ashcroft, Bill, Gareth Griffith, and Helen Tiffin. Eds. *The Empire Writes Back: Theory and Practice in Postcolonial Literature*. London, New York: Routledge, 1989.

Balibar, Etienne. *Des universels: Essais et conférences*. Paris: Galilée, 2016.

Banoun, Bernard, and Christine Ivanovic. Eds. *Eine Welt der Zeichen. Toko Tawadas Frankreich als Dritter Raum*. München: Iudicium, 2015.

Casanova, Pascale. "La guerre de l'ancienneté ou il n'y a pas d'identité nationale". *Des littératures combatives: L'internationale des nationalismes littéraires*. Ed. Pascale Casanova. Paris: Raisons d'agir, 2011. 11–31.

Cassin, Barbara. Ed. *Vocabulaire européen des philosophies: Dictionnaire des intraduisibles*. Paris: Seuil/Le Robert, 2004.

———. Ed. *Dictionary of Untranslatables: A Philosophical Lexicon*. Translation Eds. Emily Apter, Jacques Lezra, and Michael Wood. Princeton, Oxford: Princeton University Press, 2014.

———. *Éloge de la traduction. Compliquer l'universel*. Paris: Fayard, 2016.

Cassin, Barbara, and Danièle Wozny. *Les intraduisibles du patrimoine en Afrique subsaharienne*. Paris: Demopolis, 2014.
Chakrabarty, Dipesh. *Provincializing Europe: Postcolonial Thought and Historical Difference*. Princeton: Princeton University Press, 2000.
Conrad, Sebastian, and Shalini Randeria. Eds. *Jenseits des Eurozentrismus. Postkoloniale Perspektiven in den Geschichts- und Kulturwissenschaften*. Frankfurt am Main: Campus, 2002.
Crépon, Marc. "Nietzsche et la question de la langue maternelle". *Le malin génie des langues (Nietzsche, Heidegger, Rosenzweig)*. Paris: Vrin, 2000. 13–36.
Dembeck, Till. "The Poetics and Cultural Politics of Homophonic Translation." *Critical Multilingualism Studies* 3.1 (2015): 7–25.
Dembeck, Till, and Georg Mein. "Zum Jargon der Philologie. Postmonolingual schreiben?" *Zeitschrift für interkulturelle Germanistik* 3.2 (2012): 133–147.
———. Eds. *Philologie und Mehrsprachigkeit*. Heidelberg: Winter, 2014.
Dembeck, Till, and Rolf Parr. Eds. *Literatur und Mehrsprachigkeit. Ein Handbuch*. Tübingen: Narr Francke Attempto, 2017.
Diagne, Souleymane Bachir. "On the Postcolonial and the Universal?" *Rue Descartes* 78 (2013): 7–18.
———. "L'universel latéral comme traduction". *Les pluriels de Barbara Cassin ou Le partage des équivoques*. Eds. Philippe Büttgen, Michèle Gendreau-Massaloux, and Xavier North. Lormont: Le bord de l'eau, 2014. 243–255.
———. "De l'universel et de l'universalisme". *En quête d'Afrique(s). Universalisme et pensée décoloniale*. Eds. Souleymane Bachir Diagne, and Jean-Loup Amselle. Paris: Albin Michel, 2018. 65–85.
———. "Translation as Method." Transl. Philippe Major. *Comparative Philosophy and Method: Contemporary Practices and Future Possibilities*. Eds. Steven Burik, Robert Smid, and Ralph Weber. London: Bloomsbury, 2022. 89–96.
ERC Minor Universality. "Universalisme & multilatéralisme." Interview with Souleymane Bachir Diagne conducted by the ERC Minor Universality research team in 2021. https://www.youtube.com/watch?v=pgWoVx7igpk&ab_channel=ERCMinorUniversality (last accessed, 1 December 2022).
Ette, Ottmar. "Archipele der Literatur. Die neuzeitliche Tradition des Insulariums und das transarchipelische Schreiben Yoko Tawadas." *Yoko Tawada, Fremde Wasser. Vorlesungen und wissenschaftliche Beiträge*. Ed. Otrud Gutjahr. Tübingen: Konkursbuch, 2012. 296–332.
Gramling, David. "The Invention of Monolingualism from the Spirit of Systematic Transposability." *Philologie und Mehrsprachigkeit*. Eds. Till Dembeck, and Georg Mein. Heidelberg: Winter, 2014. 113–134.
———. *The Invention of monolingualism*. London: Bloomsbury, 2016.
Gutjahr, Ortrud. *Yoko Tawada. Fremde Wasser. Vorlesungen und wissenschaftliche Beiträge*. Tübingen: Konkursbuch, 2012.
Heimböckel, Dieter. "Einsprachigkeit – Sprachkritik – Mehrsprachigkeit." *Philologie und Mehrsprahigkeit*. Eds. Till Dembeck, and Georg Mein. Heidelberg: Winter, 2014. 135–156.
———. "wie Dreirad und Derrida. Yoko Tawadas Writing Back." *Eine Welt der Zeichen. Yoko Tawadas Frankreich als Dritter Raum*. Eds. Bernard Banoun, and Christine Ivanovic. München: Iudicium, 2015. 251–268.
Hofmann, Franck and Markus Messling. "On the ends of universalism". *The Epoch of Universalism 1769–1989 / L'époque de l'universalisme 1769–1989*. Eds. Franck Hofmann and Markus Messling. Berlin, Boston: De Gruyter, 2021. 1–40. https://doi.org/10.1515/9783110691504-001
Humboldt, Wilhelm von. *Gesammelte Schriften. 17 Bände*. Eds. Albert Leitzmann et al. Berlin: Behr, 1903–1936.

Ivanovic, Christine. *Yoko Tawada. Poetik der Transformation. Beiträge zum Gesamtwerk*. Tübingen: Stauffenburg, 2010.

Jullien, François. *De l'universel, de l'uniforme, du commun et du dialogue entre les cultures*. Paris: Fayard, 2008.

Jurt, Joseph. "Le champ littéraire entre le national et le transnational". *L'espace intellectuel en Europe: de la formation des États-nations à la mondialisation XIXe-XXIe siècle*. Ed. Gisèle Sapiro. Paris: La Découverte, 2009. 201–232.

Maalouf, Amin. *Les identités meurtrières*. Paris: Grasset, 1998.

Mauthner, Fritz. *Beiträge zu einer Kritik der Sprache. 3 Bände*. Leipzig: Meiner, 1923.

Merleau-Ponty, Maurice. *Signs*. Transl. Richard McCleary. Evanston: Northwestern University Press, 1964.

Meschonnic, Henri. *Critique du rythme: Anthropologie historique du langage*. Lagrasse: Verdier, 1982.

———. *Le langage Heidegger*. Paris: Presses universitaires de France, 1990.

———. *Langage, histoire, une même théorie*. Lagrasse: Verdier, 2012.

———. "Réalisme, nominalisme: la théorie du langage est une théorie de la société". *Langage, histoire, une même théorie*. Lagrasse: Verdier, 2012 [2005]. 717–726.

Mbembe, Achille. *Politiques de l'inimitié*. Paris: La découverte, 2016.

Messling, Markus. *Gebeugter Geist. Rassismus und Erkenntnis in der modernen europäischen Philologie*. Göttingen: Wallstein, 2016.

———. *Universalität nach dem Universalismus. Über frankophone Literaturen der Gegenwart*. Berlin: Matthes & Seitz, 2019.

Pajević, Marko. *Poetisches Denken und die Frage nach dem Menschen. Grundzüge einer poetologischen Anthropologie*. Freiburg i. Br.: Karl Alber, 2012.

———. "Sprachabenteuer: Yoko Tawadas exophone Erkundungen des Deutschen." *Mehrsprachigkeit und das Politische. Interferenzen in zeitgenössischer deutschsprachiger und baltischer Kultur*. Ed. Marko Pajević. Tübingen: Francke, 2020. 213–228.

Sakai, Naoki. "How do we count a language? Translation and discontinuity." *Translation Studies* 2.1 (2009): 71–88.

Schmitz-Emans, Monika. "Yoko Tawadas Imaginationen zwischen westlichen und östlichen Schriftkonzepten und -metaphern." *Yoko Tawada. Fremde Wasser. Vorlesungen und wissenschaftliche Beiträge*. Ed. Ortrud Gutjahr. Tübingen: Konkursbuch, 2012. 269–295.

Syrotinski, Michael. "Postcolonial untranslatability: Reading Achille Mbembe with Barbara Cassin." *Journal of Postcolonial Writing* 55.6 (2019): 850–862.

Takabvirwa, Oscar. *Stories in Transit. An Anthology of Texts by Exiles, Migrants and Émigrés, translated from the German with an introduction and conclusion*. Thesis submitted to the faculty of Wesleyan University, Middletown, Connecticut, 2014.

Tawada, Yoko. *Sprachpolizei und Spielpolyglotte*. Tübingen: Konkursbuch, 2007.

———. *Abenteuer der deutschen Grammatik*. Tübingen: Konkursbuch, 2010.

———. *Überseezungen*. Tübingen: Konkursbuch, 2013 [2002].

———. *Talisman*. Tübingen: Konkursbuch, 2015 [1996].

———. *Akzentfrei*. Tübingen: Konkursbuch, 2016.

Thiérard, Hélène. "Récits du moi entre les langues chez Yoko Tawada et José F.A. Oliver". *Cahiers d'Études Germaniques* 73 (2018): 121–138.

———. "Pensée du langage et pratique de la traduction chez Georges-Arthur Goldschmidt". *Traverser les limites. Georges-Arthur Goldschmidt: le corps, l'histoire, la langue*. Eds. Jürgen Ritte, Wolfgang Asholt, and Catherine Coquio. Paris: Hermann, 2019. 167–185.

———. "Mehrsprachige Literaturen gegen die 'Pathologie des Universellen'. Die politische Relevanz von poetischem Sprachdenken heute." Ed. Marko Pajević. *Mehrsprachigkeit und das Politische. Interferenzen in zeitgenössischer deutschsprachiger und baltischer Kultur*. Tübingen: Francke, 2020. 229–246.

Thiesse, Anne-Marie. *La création des identités nationales. Europe XVIIIe–XXe siècle*. Paris: Seuil, 1999.

Thiong'o, Ngũgĩ wa. *Decolonizing the Mind. The Politics of Language in African Literature*. London: Currey, 1986.

Trabant, Jürgen. *Apeliotes oder der Sinn der Sprache. Wilhelm von Humboldts Sprach-Bild*. München: Fink, 1986.

———. *Artikulationen. Historische Anthropologie der Sprache*. Frankfurt am Main: Suhrkamp, 1990.

———. *Mithridates im Paradies. Kleine Geschichte des Sprachdenkens*. München: C.H. Beck, 2003.

———. "Vanishing Worldviews." *Forum for Modern Language Studies* 53.1 (2017): 21–34.

Wallerstein, Immanuel. *European Universalism. The Rhetoric of Power*. New York: The New York Press, 2006.

Yildiz, Yasemin. *Beyond the Mother Tongue. The Postmonolingual Condition*. New York: Fordham University Press, 2012.

Elsie Cohen
Exil et universalité

Abstract: Based on the trajectories, productions, and narratives of contemporary intellectuals in exile in France and Germany, this contribution seeks to understand the relationship between exile and universality. Edward Saïd, in his memoirs, has portrayed exile as a situation of marginality and decentering, favorable to the production of universalist thought that is critical of the hegemonic universalism of the West. Based on this assumption, this essay seeks to construct a sociological approach to the position of the "exiled intellectual" and the different types of world narratives that arise from the radical experiences of loss intimately linked to exile and migration. It shows that the positions of exiled intellectuals in the fields of cultural production oscillate between the construction of an exiled identity endowed with an "epistemological privilege" (Traverso 2004), and the rejection of the status of foreignness as a cultural producer, as well as between universalism and particularism. It also examines, by way of a discussion of two contemporary authors whose trajectories have been affected by forced migration, the social and biographical determinants relevant to understanding the nuances of their stances taken towards the idea of universality and Western universalism.

Keywords: intellectual, exile, migration, narratives, intellectual field, universalism, universality

1 Introduction

« I have argued that exile can produce rancor and regret, as well as a sharpened vision. » écrivait Edward Saïd dans son introduction à ses *Reflections on exile* (2000, 54). À l'instar du penseur de l'*Orientalism* (1978)[1], l'exil est souvent dépeint par les intellectuels qui l'ont vécu, entre autres, comme la source d'une pensée universaliste. Cette pensée ne se réduirait pourtant pas à la reproduction d'un

---

[1] Sur cette lecture d'Edward Saïd, voir Bridet (2013, 499–508).

Note : Cet article s'inscrit dans le cadre du projet *Minor Universality. Narrative World Productions After Western Universalism*, financé par le Conseil Européen de la Recherche (ERC) (Programme cadre de recherche de l'UE « Horizon 2020 », convention n° 819931).

universalisme occidental – historiquement impérialiste et dominant[2] – mais se logerait dans la posture critique que confère la position marginale de l'exilé, suspendu entre deux mondes et décentré en tout lieu, « out of space » selon le titre éponyme des mémoires de Saïd (1999). La littérature historique sur les exils individuels ou collectifs d'intellectuels au XXe siècle montre que ces déplacements ont pu favoriser la rencontre de différentes épistémologies/méthodes et la remise en question de savoirs et de certitudes qui apparaissaient, à une époque et un lieu donnés, comme universels[3].

Aujourd'hui, de nombreux intellectuels et créateurs se déplacent dans le cadre de migrations forcées[4], qu'il faut distinguer des mobilités étudiantes et professionnelles d'une élite cosmopolite (Wagner 1998 ; 2020), bien que les intellectuels exilés appartiennent généralement aux classes sociales supérieures[5]. L'urgence et la violence des départs peuvent inciter certains à emprunter les mêmes chemins que les réfugiés les plus défavorisés, et transiter par des camps, avant de réussir à aboutir leur périple. Les origines nationales et les raisons de ces exils, solitaires ou collectifs, dépendent des cadres politiques et sociaux : ces départs sont liés à des contextes de guerre, aux manques de ressources dans un pays, à des catastrophes naturelles, ou encore provoqués par les persécutions directes dont ces citoyens font l'objet en raison de leurs activités professionnelles dans des pays où les libertés publiques et individuelles sont menacées par les régimes autoritaires et la montée des extrémismes (Scholars at Risk 2015–2021). Ce dernier cas peut toucher des communautés nationales

---

2 Sur les aspects de cet universalisme et ses conséquences voir Hofmann et Messling (2021).

3 Entre autres, l'exil des penseurs et artistes européens fuyant les régimes nazi et fasciste pendant la Seconde Guerre mondiale aux États-Unis (Ash et Söllner 1996 ; Azuelos 2008 ; Coser 1984 ; Fermi 1968 ; Fleck 2003 ; Hagemann et Milberg 2017 ; Jeanpierre 2004a, b ; Loewenberg 2006 ; Loyer 2007 ; Rösch 2014 ; Steinmetz 2010), ou en Angleterre (Crawford et al. 2017) ; celui des intellectuels d'Europe de l'Est fuyant les régimes communistes pendant la Guerre Froide (Popa 2000 ; Fleury et Jilek 2009), ou encore celui des intellectuels postcoloniaux aux États-Unis (Brisson 2018). Pour une revue de littérature non exhaustive, voir Cohen et Schultz (à paraître).

4 Le tournant des années 2000 a vu l'accroissement en Europe des flux d'arrivée de populations en danger fuyant les crises humanitaires et politiques – principalement du Moyen-Orient, de l'Afrique Sub-saharienne, d'Amérique latine, et désormais d'autres régions du monde (The UHCR Refugee Population Statistics Database, https://www.unhcr.org/refugee-statistics/ (consulté le 28 mars 2022).

5 Si les phénomènes migratoires contemporains montrent que les frontières ne sont pas si nettes entre « migrations économiques » et « migrations politiques », la notion d'exil se distingue par le caractère forcé du départ, que ce soit pour des raisons économiques, dû à des persécutions, ou une situation de danger subie en raison d'opinions politiques, religieuses, d'appartenance à une minorité, un manque de ressources dans un pays etc. De plus, la condition des exilés se dissocie souvent de celle d'autres types d'émigration : dans les formes de sociabilités développées, les modes d'intégration dans les pays d'accueil, etc. (Groppo 2003).

professionnelles qui s'opposent aux régimes en place. Exemples récents : celui des 200 journalistes iraniens contraints à l'exil après la réélection de Mahmoud Ahmadinejad à la présidence de la République Islamique d'Iran (Reporters sans Frontières 2012), celui d'intellectuels et d'activistes égyptiens fuyant les persécutions perpétrées par les nouveaux dirigeants égyptiens après le coup d'état militaire de 2013 (Dunne et Hamzawy 2019), ou encore le cas des centaines d'universitaires turcs qui ont été purgés des universités par le gouvernement d'Erdogan après avoir signé une pétition pour la paix en janvier 2016 dénonçant « le massacre délibéré et planifié » du peuple kurde (Academics for Peace 2016)[6].

Nous proposons ici d'étudier des trajectoires et expériences d'intellectuels contemporains en exil en Europe pour repenser la dyade exil/universalité dans une perspective empirique et sociologique[7]. Quels rapports les intellectuels exilés en Europe entretiennent-t-il aujourd'hui avec la modernité occidentale et ses savoirs ? Quels types d'universalités locales, « mineurs » et tangibles, sont produites aujourd'hui par des intellectuels et créateurs en exil, à travers leurs récits de vie et leurs discours – politiques, scientifiques, littéraires, leurs œuvres, et leurs modes d'intervention intellectuels et politiques ?

Le contexte hérité des années 1970–1980 où une pluralité de revendications culturalistes et politiques différentes a émergé pour faire contrepoids à la domination de la modernité libérale occidentale (Brisson 2018), persiste aujourd'hui, à une époque où les débats confrontent de manière dualiste, en France, les défenseurs des particularismes et identitarismes aux défenseurs de l'universalisme républicain. Catégorie marquée par le modèle de l'engagement (Matonti et Sapiro 2009), les intellectuels sont particulièrement à même de formuler, diffuser sur la scène publique, des pensées et des discours sur l'universalité telle qu'ils la conçoivent[8]. En sociologie, la construction de l'universel a été notamment pensée par

---

[6] Environ 700 universitaires sur près de 2000 signataires ont été poursuivis en procès pour « propagande en faveur d'une organisation terroriste ». 191 ont été condamnés à des peines d'emprisonnements selon un article du *Monde* (Jégo 2019). Sur le cas des universitaires turcs et les Académies de Solidarité voir aussi Mestci (2021).

[7] Les résultats sont basés sur une thèse menée dans le cadre du projet ERC « Minor Universality. Les productions narratives du monde après l'universalisme occidental » dirigé par Markus Messling. Les entretiens cités sont réalisés avec des intellectuels (principalement écrivains et chercheurs en SHS) dans deux pays, France et Allemagne, et complétés par des sources de seconde main : interviews dans la presse, tribunes, publications et travaux.

[8] On entend par « universalité » le caractère de ce qui est universel. Tandis que la notion ici d'universalisme est entendue comme idéologie qui découle de la définition de cet universel, ou encore comme « Toute doctrine qui considère la réalité comme un tout unique, ce qui revient à dire universel, dans lequel les individus ne peuvent être isolés, si ce n'est par abstraction » (Lalande 1993 [1902–1923], 924).

Pierre Bourdieu à partir de l'exemple historique des bureaucraties prussienne ou française qui illustrent, selon lui, l'intérêt que certains groupes sociaux ont eu « à inventer l'universel (le droit, l'idée de service public, l'idée d'intérêt général, etc.) » pour exercer leur domination au nom de l'universel (Poupeau 2020)[9]. Cette logique existe également dans les champs intellectuels et artistiques, « dans lesquels sont engagés des agents ayant en commun le privilège de lutter pour le monopole de l'universel et de contribuer ainsi à faire avancer, peu ou prou, des vérités et des valeurs qui sont tenues, à chaque moment, pour universelles, voire éternelles » (Bourdieu 1994, 224). L'universel peut constituer un appareil de domination – notamment idéologie d'Etat qui justifie la hiérarchisation des identités légitimes – mais également, être une arme de résistance et de revendication pour des minorités. Ramenés à différentes prises de positions normatives, morales et politiques, les discours sur l'universel portés par les intellectuels sont donc à comprendre à l'aune des enjeux de luttes sociales et de parcours biographiques situés dans des contextes sociohistoriques définis.

Expérience de socialisation hétérogène et de rupture avec la normativité, l'exil engage une pluralité de dispositions chez les exilés qui sont confrontés à une nouvelle vie, une nouvelle culture, ce qui nous conduit à interroger les effets de cette situation sur leurs perceptions du monde. Cependant, il faut préciser que la possibilité de créer de nouvelles visions du monde pour les intellectuels et artistes exilés, qui pourront être diffusées dans le temps et l'espace, est étroitement associée à la capacité de poursuivre son travail et de le rendre visible dans les champs des savoirs, notamment en sciences humaines et sociales, ou littéraires. Or, à l'échelle individuelle, la capacité de travail et de création en exil est inégale et nécessite de surmonter plusieurs contraintes et difficultés que nous aborderons par la suite. Edward Saïd dans ses *Réflexions sur l'exil*, comme Hannah Arendt (1943) dans son texte « We Refugees » combattaient ainsi les visions romantiques de l'exil et prévenaient des risques de minimiser le poids des contraintes sociales, de l'aliénation, la perte et la souffrance, qu'il représente souvent. Les parcours d'exil, et la chance de poursuite du travail intellectuel et d'accès à la reconnaissance, sont inégaux, et dépendent d'un certain nombre de facteurs à prendre en compte (pays d'origine, professions, pays d'immigration, raisons du déplacement, caractéristiques sociales – âge, genre, sexe –, ressources linguistiques, degré d'insertion dans des champs internationaux etc. (Sapiro 2022). De même, l'engagement politique, ou la pensée cri-

---

9 L'« ambition de l'universel » (Bourdieu 1992, 552) est intrinsèque à la fonction d'intellectuel : « en défendant leur activité, les intellectuels défendent une cause qui ne se réduit pas à celle de leurs intérêts particuliers. En se posant ainsi comme « fonctionnaires de l'humanité », pour reprendre l'expression de Husserl, les intellectuels ne doivent cependant pas cautionner l'imposition de modèles culturels dominants [. . .] » (Poupeau 2020, 870).

tique qui découlerait de la position de l'exilé, peuvent constituer une dimension de l'exil, mais ce n'est pas toujours le cas. Mettre en lumière les trajectoires des intellectuels exilés suppose d'interroger la complexité d'un parcours de vie soumis à la migration, et les continuités autant que les ruptures intellectuelles, identitaires, politiques induites par l'exil.

Dans une première partie, nous montrerons la position ambivalente des intellectuels exilés dans un espace de réception européen, qui doivent jongler entre plusieurs injonctions et aspirations contradictoires, et dont découle un conflit entre la figure universaliste de l'intellectuel et celle spécifique (Sapiro 2009b)[10]. Dans un second temps, nous examinerons à partir des pensées de deux auteurs, l'écrivain Omar Youssef Souleimane, et Mudar Al-Khufash créateur d'*Awhām* magazine, deux façons de concevoir l'universalité. Pour conclure, on s'interrogera sur les déterminants individuels et collectifs qui permettent de comprendre les effets de l'exil sur les représentations de soi et du monde et la nuance du continuum des prises de position par rapport à l'idée d'universalité.

2 La position d'intellectuel exilé, entre particulier et universel

Dans l'entretien qu'elle a accordé à l'équipe de recherche Minor Universality, Gisèle Sapiro a exprimé un paradoxe :

> l'Université elle-même, comme le dit son nom, « universitas », a une vocation universelle depuis ses origines, et elle est un lieu très important de circulation des personnes et des idées. Toutefois, la nationalisation de l'enseignement et la recherche et la compétition internationale ont cloisonné les champs académiques nationaux dans un espace mondial où les ressources et le prestige sont inégalement distribués : en témoignent les flux asymétriques entre les pays (Minor Universality 2021).

Cette remarque soulève la question de la convertibilité ou non du capital culturel dans le passage d'un champ académique ou artistique à l'autre, national ou transnational[11], des exilés, et les effets sur la réception de leurs travaux et l'accession à la reconnaissance. Ces inégalités s'expriment à travers la hiérarchie des langues

---

10 Il faut préciser que selon les cadres de référence et les traditions nationales, les figures de l'intellectuel, et les modes d'intervention peuvent être différenciés. Voir les travaux par exemple de Christophe Charle (1990, 1996) et Sapiro (2009a) pour l'Europe, ou pour une perspective croisée d'études de cas asiatiques, africains et occidentaux voir Kouvouama et al. (2007).
11 Sur cette notion voir Sapiro et al. (2018).

et les traductions (De Swann 1997, 1998a, b) qui jouent un rôle important dans l'insertion ou non des intellectuels étrangers[12]. Ces représentations sont particulièrement effectives dans la réalité, car la réputation d'un chercheur ou d'un écrivain, dépend en partie de la place symbolique des cultures nationales à l'échelle globale (Sapiro 2022). La possibilité de la venue en France, encore plus qu'en Allemagne aujourd'hui, est conditionnée par un capital social, et des réseaux antérieurs : professionnels et/ou politiques dans le cas des réfugiés politiques, notamment ceux dotés d'un « capital militant » (Matonti et Poupeau 2004) ou « capital révolutionnaire » (Baczko et al. 2016). Les intellectuels qui arrivent dans les pays d'Europe sont bien souvent celles et ceux qui ont le plus d'affinité sociale, intellectuelle, linguistique, avec les pays qui les accueillent[13]. Ce paradoxe s'inscrit dans l'expérience des intellectuels exilés et met à l'épreuve la vision universaliste de production de la science ou des arts. Au contraire, leurs trajectoires font apparaître un système inégalitaire et de rapports de force des champs intellectuels. Consacrés comme figures exemplaires des défenseurs des droits humains d'un côté, mais de l'autre, souvent positionnés en marge dans les champs intellectuels des pays d'accueil, assignés à leur particularisme et « spécialisés » sur leur pays/région d'origine, les intellectuels exilés sont en partie privés de ce « profit d'universalisation » conféré à la figure de l'intellectuel critique universaliste traditionnellement incarnée en France[14].

2.1 Entrer dans une catégorie

Tristan Leperlier (2016) montre que, dans le cas des écrivains algériens durant la décennie noire, l'offre d'écrivains nouveaux en exil répond à cette époque à une demande éditoriale française qui a une attente « ethnographique », souvent caractéristique des grands centres littéraires à l'égard des périphéries, et qui accorde une part importante à la notion d'authenticité des textes. Cette attente documentaire a causé aux écrivains algériens une grande difficulté à articuler leur ambition

---

[12] Voir notamment les phénomènes d'asymétrie dans les flux des traductions qui desservent les ouvrages – entre autres – en langue arabe (Glasson–Deschaumes Deschaumes 2011).
[13] Cette remarque s'applique à des degrés variables selon les pays d'accueil. La France présente un écart important dans ses statistiques d'octroi des demandes d'asile par rapport à l'Allemagne : la France a enregistré par exemple 2,2% des demandes d'asile des réfugiés syriens contre 55% en Allemagne (Héran 2022).
[14] Qui « s'engage à titre personnel pour des causes particulières au nom de valeurs universelles comme la liberté ou la justice, affirme son autonomie par rapport à la demande politique externe » (Sapiro 2009b, 15).

de témoigner et leur ambition littéraire, car « l'exigence de concrétude et d'exactitude » (Detue et Lacoste 2016) est souvent associée, dans les discours du champ, à un manque de littérarité, et donc d'universalité. Comme les écrivains algériens de la décennie noire, nos entretiens montrent que les écrivains contemporains en exil vivent cette ambivalence causée par cette double injonction/ambition : celle de témoigner des drames historiques de leur pays d'origine et de l'exil ou celle d'être en littérature. En d'autres termes, être considéré comme un écrivain « étranger », « exilé », ou un écrivain tout court[15]. Un poète d'origine syrienne et palestinienne qui réside à Berlin témoigne ainsi, à l'occasion d'un entretien :

> You lost your heritage, your privilege position, and you begin from zero. And you find yourself like . . . automatically, you are in a category. You are invited for evenings where they speak about exile or refugee rights. The struggle is here. A German poet could seat and speak about his poetry. And you, they ask you about exile or your trip.

La labellisation ou catégorisation des genres littéraires va de pair avec l'étiquetage d'un auteur selon son groupe social et ethnique. La formation historique de la littérature française s'est, en effet, appuyée sur un imaginaire de la « race », masqué par la rhétorique universalisante du projet littéraire républicain, et ayant eu pour conséquence la dévalorisation ou l'exclusion des belles-lettres de celles et ceux qui ne correspondaient pas au modèle de l'écrivain français – homme blanc (Burnautzki 2017 ; Harchi 2018). Kathryn Kleppinger (2016) montre dans son ouvrage *Branding the « Beur » Autor, Minority writing and the Media in France 1983–2013* sur l'apparition de la littérature dite « beure », la tension entre particularisme et universalisme qui est performée dans les médias. En interview, les auteurs issus de minorités ethniques, sociales, culturelles, sont renvoyés à leurs attributs sociaux particuliers (la vie de femme, la vie en banlieue, etc.) et on les incite à prendre position par rapport à leur vécu personnel. Pour les auteurs masculins d'origine locale, on s'intéressera, à l'inverse, à leur œuvre, la littérarité de leur textes (questions de formes ou d'esthétique) ou sur leur opinion ayant trait à des valeurs considérées comme universelles (la justice, la liberté, etc.).

Une différence existe entre les écrivains déjà expérimentés, d'âge avancé, et une génération de jeunes écrivains dont l'aspiration à la littérature est née parfois en l'exil. Bien que la profession soit peu réglementée, cette conversion affecte l'exercice de l'écriture, tant du point de vue de la production à travers le choix des thèmes traités et les genres adoptés par les auteurs (témoignages et autobiographies peuvent être favorisés plutôt que la fiction), que celui de la diffusion des textes à travers des choix éditoriaux.

---

15 Sur les contraintes que les écrivains peuvent affronter pour publier et traduire leurs textes en exil, voir aussi Popa (2010).

Il en va de même pour les professions les plus organisées, codifiées et professionnalisées telles que les chercheurs en sciences humaines et sociales qui sont également pris dans ces dilemmes. Les universitaires exilés, sont bien souvent convertis – par choix ou contrainte – à de nouvelles spécialités en lien avec leur capital linguistique, culturel et leur pays d'origine. Plusieurs orientent leurs objets d'étude pour refléter leur expérience (l'exil, la migration, ou des sujets liés aux luttes politiques menées dans le pays d'origine). Un certain nombre de programmes d'aide et de réseaux formés par des acteurs du monde académique et culturel en danger ont été mis en place en France et en Allemagne sur le modèle de structures qui existaient déjà dans d'autres démocraties[16]. On peut citer pour les scientifiques en danger, le programme Pause en France ou la Philipp Schwartz Initiative en Allemagne. D'autres dispositifs semblables, à la fois programmes d'urgence humanitaire et programmes de réinsertion professionnelle (résidences, bourses, offres de poste, mises à disposition de lieux d'exposition), existent pour les autres professions intellectuelles et artistiques[17]. On retrouve cependant le même biais décrit plus haut dans les cas des écrivains, et que les chercheurs en sciences humaines et sociales considèrent, pour la plupart, comme un stigmate qui entrave leur fonction. Comme témoigne une chercheuse turque exilée en Allemagne et qui a bénéficié d'une bourse de la Philipp Schwartz initiative :

> In many conferences or meetings, or workshops, I was asked to tell about my story. And that was quite annoying, I must admit. I understand that they like to authenticized this speech of mine and make the organization more shiny to the audience to show where I am speaking from. But it's not nice to be put in a category.

Le poids spécifique sur ces trajectoires intellectuelles des schèmes de perceptions véhiculés par les politiques publiques, les médias et les institutions d'accueil, tels que les programmes d'aide qui financent des bourses, est encore à définir.

Yana Meerzon montre, à propos du théâtre en exil, le jeu d'équilibriste de l'artiste ou de l'intellectuel exilé qui refuse, d'une part, l'assimilation complète dans la société d'accueil ; d'autre part, de n'être que « le chroniqueur de l'exil »

---

[16] Sur les politiques de secours et les dispositifs institutionnels sur le long terme et dans une perspective comparative voir Dakhli et al. (2021).

[17] Par exemple, à l'échelle internationale le réseau de villes-refuges International Cities of Refuges Network (Icorn) se destine à aider les écrivains et artistes persécutés ; et aux échelles nationales : en France, notamment à Paris, La Maison des Journalistes (Pasquet 2014) accueille depuis 2002 des journalistes exilés en résidence et l'Atelier des artistes en exil oeuvre pour offrir un espace de création aux artistes exilés depuis 2017. En Allemagne, nous pouvons citer le programme *Journalists in Exile* (organisé par *Neue Deutsche Medienmacher* et *Hostwriter*) ; le *Goethe-Institut Damascus In Exile* pour les artistes (Berlin) ou encore le projet *Weiter Schreiben* du collectif *Wir Machen Das*.

(Meerzon 2011). Cela peut mener à des « conflits de rôle » (Ben-David et Collins 1997) dont découle un sentiment d'illégitimité en tant qu'intellectuel pour parler d'un point de vue universel. Le sentiment d'illégitimité de cette chercheuse en sciences humaines et sociales, est révélateur de ce phénomène, qui a débuté en Syrie pendant la révolution et est réactualisé en France :

> Je ne me sentais pas toujours légitime, j'étais à fond avec la révolution, mais je ne me sentais pas tout à fait légitime parce que je ne représente pas ces gens, je ne représente pas le peuple, le petit peuple. Je suis classe moyenne supérieure, un petit peu bourgeoise [. . .]. Quand j'écrivais, c'était toujours avec un pseudonyme parce que je ne me sentais pas légitime. Quand je suis sortie du pays, je me suis sentie encore moins légitime, parce que je suis sortie, parce que je les ai lâchés, je ne peux pas parler au nom de ces gens. Et là, je parle de migration, je ne suis pas légitime. J'avais mon réseau à Paris. Je ne représente pas les immigrants, que je vois d'ailleurs dans les rues de Paris, parce que je fais une recherche là-bas [. . .] Et puis il y a des éléments identitaires plus anciens aussi parce que je ne suis pas du tout pratiquante, je suis athée, mais je suis d'une famille chrétienne orthodoxe en Syrie. Et tout le monde veut présenter la révolution comme une révolution des Sunnites, la majorité sunnite, ce qui n'est pas vrai. Les chrétiens sont considérés comme pro régime, du coup, je ne suis pas légitime[18].

Sollicitée régulièrement pour témoigner de l'exil dans des conférences, la chercheuse exprime son inconfort : « je suis lasse de ma nouvelle profession, celle de migrante », et craint de voir se réduire le champ de possibilités des chercheurs exilés. On peut faire l'hypothèse ici, qu'elle répugne à parler au nom du général, car elle est issue de minorités sociales et ethniques, en Syrie, son pays d'origine, et aussi en France. De plus, ses paroles reflètent cette culpabilité citoyenne et politique, à la fois assignée et intériorisée, des intellectuels syriens activistes qui sont pris entre plusieurs sentiments et identités contradictoires : d'un côté le statut de « victime », de l'autre celui de « coupable », l'exil étant vécu par les activistes syriens comme « un abandon de la cause de la révolution et des camarades restés sur place » (Fourn 2018).

2.2 Entre sentiments de déclassement et « privilège épistémologique »

Quels sont les effets de cette particularisation dans le champ intellectuel sur les carrières et les positions d'intellectuels et créateurs exilés ? La situation de forte incertitude qui caractérise l'exil, entraînant souvent une souffrance psychique dont les modalités ont été étudiées par certains travaux en sociologie des migrations (Sayad 1999 ; Wang 2017) – désubjectivisation (Wierviorka 2004 ; Boucher

---
18 Paroles précédemment citées dans Cohen (2019).

et al. 2017), abattement, sentiment « de n'être de nulle part », temporalité figée etc. – et les processus de déprofessionnalisation induits par la migration, sont en contradiction avec les dynamiques plus linéaires liées à la construction des identités sociales et professionnelles (Dubar 1992). La précarité, le statut d'étranger, qui résultent de l'immigration, marquent une rupture dans les trajectoires des intellectuels en exil notamment parce qu'ils engendrent un sentiment de déclassement social, sentiment particulièrement prégnant dans le cas des intellectuels qui appartiennent en majorité à une élite économique et sociale dans le pays de départ. Des chiffres récents montrent en effet que le phénomène de chômage et de déclassement social et professionnel en France touche une majorité des primo-arrivants et que ce risque est accru pour les femmes diplômées[19].

L'exil change la façon d'envisager sa place, en tant que professionnel ou intellectuel, dans la société. Les intellectuels qui sont arrivés à un âge plus avancé, laissant une carrière déjà construite derrière eux, ont du mal à se projeter dans une installation durable et à se représenter leur avenir dans la société d'accueil. Nombreux sont celles et ceux qui évoquent l'impression de devoir « repartir de zéro », c'est-à-dire passer à nouveau par certaines étapes pour entrer dans une carrière, construire une vie d'autonomie, matérielle et sociale. S'ajoute à cette précarité l'expérience ressentie de discrimination liée aux hiérarchies symboliques qui existent entre les différents pays et qui créent des limites à l'embauche, notamment par la non-reconnaissance des diplômes : « Quand vous êtes en Afrique ou au Burundi, vous savez que l'Europe, c'est un endroit d'apprentissage et c'est vrai. Sauf que dans ce pays, on dira que le niveau intellectuel en Afrique ou ailleurs, il est différent du niveau intellectuel ici. Déception. Ce mot, je le dirais mille fois. » (Une journaliste originaire du Burundi désormais en France).

Fréquents sont les phénomènes de reconversion et la poursuite d'activités intellectuelles non rémunérés, souvent associés à l'exercice d'un travail « alimentaire ». Certains universitaires qui bénéficient de contrats d'un an ou deux, financés par les dispositifs d'aide évoqués, ont pu se réinsérer dans leur profession, mais le privilège est relatif car de courte durée. Pour les écrivains, l'impact au niveau de la carrière n'est pas le même puisque la profession n'est pas salariée et organisée. L'exil impacte cependant les conditions psychiques et matérielles de création, comme l'explique la journaliste burundaise :

> La première chose, c'est la perte de la plume. Avec le stress, avec tout ce qui est procédures administratives et pour tout ce qui est stabilité, vous la perdez. Et je pense qu'à partir du moment où je me suis mise dans la logique de trouver de l'emploi pour résoudre la question de trouver du logement, j'ai réduit mes productions. Maintenant, si je vais écrire, c'est pour

---

[19] Selon le rapport de l'Insee (2018).

mon plaisir. Mais, tout doucement, la vie d'ici vous emporte ailleurs. Et ça, c'est ce qu'on appelle reconversion. Vous vous reconvertissez, sans le vouloir et sans le savoir[20].

Malgré les difficultés objectives que provoque l'exil, d'un point de vue interne et subjectif, il peut être vécu positivement comme une épreuve qui transforme sa façon d'être dans le monde et à laquelle est attribuée un pouvoir cognitif et moral. À partir du cas des intellectuels juifs allemands qui se sont retrouvés exilés aux États-Unis pendant la Seconde Guerre mondiale, Enzo Traverso (2004) définit le « privilège épistémologique de l'exil » comme une disposition intellectuelle découlant de la position sociale et culturelle d'*outsider*, qui permettrait aux migrants de voir ce que les autres ne peuvent pas voir et favoriserait ainsi les innovations intellectuelles. Nous pouvons étendre cette acceptation du terme à la création artistique de la même manière que Seidel qui voit l'exil comme « an enabling fiction [...] a fiction enabling me to address the larger strategies of narrative representation » (Seidel 1986, 142). S'appuyant sur une expérience sociale, ce privilège épistémologique est présent dans les récits des écrivains, mais aussi chez les chercheurs en sciences humaines et sociales puisqu'ils ont un objet commun, l'humain. L'écrivain Omar Youssef Souleimane, dans son texte *L'exil ne finira pas* (2019), considère ainsi l'exil comme une « grande école », au sein de laquelle :

> On peut apprendre beaucoup de choses. On peut vivre beaucoup d'expériences avec beaucoup de cultures, on peut regarder le monde d'une autre manière qui, à mon avis, est plus profonde. On peut sentir les autres, les gens, leurs souffrances, leurs douleurs. On peut savoir d'où ils souffrent. Et on peut croiser beaucoup d'exilés comme nous, spécialement si on vit dans une grande ville, parce que la solitude est riche aussi et je pense qu'on peut trouver, on peut voir les points positifs là-dedans, parce qu'à chaque fois qu'on est exilé on est tout seul, on cherche un chemin, ce chemin qui va nous sauver. (2019, 130)

A l'instar de l'enseignante-chercheuse que nous avons évoquée et qui déclare en entretien :

> Je suis très libre avec beaucoup d'amertume. Mais je suis très libre psychiquement, par rapport aux codes sociaux . . . Les capitaux symboliques dans une société, je suis complètement libre, je m'en fiche complètement parce que j'ai perdu beaucoup. Donc je sais de quoi il s'agit. Ça me donne beaucoup de force.

La position de l'exil, selon elle, comporte le danger d'une prise de position autoritaire, l'exilé pouvant tirer de son expérience de la brutalité du monde, le sentiment d'une supériorité morale et intellectuelle sur les autres :

> Parfois, quand on vient d'un contexte très traumatisé ou de guerre, on devient tortionnaire psychiquement, c'est-à-dire on essaie d'imposer ce concept de la vie et de l'expérience hu-

---

20 Paroles précédemment citées dans Cohen (2019).

maine sur les autres. Et les autres ne sont pas obligés d'être dans la terreur. Mais nous, puisqu'on a goûté à ça, on a l'impression qu'on est plus fort. Et ça c'est très pervers.

Cet extrait montre que souvent, l'exil génère des sentiments d'ambivalence dans le rapport au pays d'origine, entre culpabilité, envie de s'engager, mais aussi critique des bénéfices symboliques que cette politisation peut apporter.

Il faut cependant préciser que ce capital épistémologique de l'exil et le profit d'authenticité sociale ne sont pas des ressources convertibles par tous, en fonction notamment des disciplines : les sciences qui ne sont pas humaines et sociales, comme les sciences naturelles, ne peuvent bénéficier du savoir social que représente la position d'exil. D'autres critères entrent en jeu, tel que l'âge et la position sociale antérieure qui peuvent notamment amenuiser les stratégies d'ouverture à une nouvelle langue, ou à de nouveaux corpus de connaissance[21].

Nous avons vu que ceux qui travaillent, écrivent et publient pour un espace de réception européen sont tiraillés entre plusieurs injonctions ou aspirations contradictoires. Entre le refus du statut d'extranéité en tant que producteur culturel auquel ils sont assignés, et qui a un effet concret sur la poursuite de leur activité : non reconnaissance des diplômes, précarisation, reconversion... et la nécessité de témoigner, mais aussi de poursuivre leur activité et de voir leurs textes publiés. D'autre part, l'aspiration à toucher des thèmes globaux et universels et à voir leur travail légitimé pour sa valeur littéraire ou scientifique. Cette position affecte autant les productions que la posture intellectuelle puisque la revendication de l'identité d'exilé, pour un intellectuel, peut apparaitre comme un travail de présentation de soi qui est influencé par son degré d'engagement, la valeur du capital symbolique accordée à l'exil selon le pays d'origine et la cause défendue, mais aussi les opportunités professionnelles rencontrées dans l'exil.

3 Penser l'universalité en exil ?

Dans cette partie, nous présenterons deux positionnements différents vis-vis de l'idée d'universalité : d'un côté, la défense des valeurs de l'universalisme européen pour nourrir les luttes actuelles ; de l'autre, une critique forte de cet universalisme, identifié comme un système d'oppression.

---

[21] La comparaison faite par Laurent Jeanpierre (2004b) des trajectoires de Lévi-Strauss et de Gurvitch en exil pendant la Seconde Guerre mondiale, nous éclaire dans ce sens.

3.1 Omar Youssef Souleimane (Paris) : défense de la liberté

Né en Syrie en 1987, l'écrivain (poésie, roman) et journaliste Omar Youssef Souleimane passe une partie de son enfance en Arabie-Saoudite où il est éduqué au sein d'une famille salafiste. Il relate cette éducation dans son récit autobiographique *Le petit terroriste* (2018), écrit en français, dans lequel il défend la liberté de critiquer l'islam. Dans ce récit d'apprentissage, ou de désapprentissage, il décrit l'itinéraire d'un enfant « apprenti terroriste », qui s'éloigne de la religion au fur et à mesure que ses doutes, aspirations et désirs grandissent. Écrivain et journaliste en Syrie entre 2006 et 2010, il prend part aux manifestations contre le régime de Bachar Al Assad, puis est recherché par les services secrets syriens lorsque la guerre civile éclate. Il arrive en France en 2012, où il a obtenu l'asile. Son dernier roman d'inspiration autobiographique, *Une chambre en exil* (2022), met en scène l'épreuve d'un jeune Syrien réfugié qui doit reconstruire sa vie à Bobigny, en banlieue parisienne, entre nostalgie du pays quitté et déception de retrouver dans cette ville un islam radical qu'il pensait avoir fui. Intellectuel qui se définit comme « engagé », Omar Youssef Souleimane assure, tel qu'il le conçoit, la permanence de ses engagements par l'écriture : « J'ai tout de suite choisi d'apprendre le français et continuer ce que je faisais en Syrie avant la guerre, mais sur des sujets où je pourrais attaquer le régime. Parce que les régimes fascistes ont très peur des écrivains, surtout des poètes ». Ses deux derniers romans ont été écrits en français, « la langue de Paul Éluard », dans laquelle il dit se sentir libre.

Pour Souleimane, l'exil est « lié à la question de l'universalité », car l'exil change la représentation de soi et du monde :

> Vivre en exil ça veut dire qu'on a perdu son identité [. . .] Une nouvelle racine, un nouveau, pays, une nouvelle culture. Un refuge. Tout dépend d'où on est venu et de comment on vivait auparavant. Parce qu'en Syrie, on avait aucun droit, on avait aucune liberté d'expression, c'était la dictature. On était déjà nés comme exilés. L'exil n'est pas nouveau. Mais ce qui est nouveau, c'est de se retrouver tout seul dans une nouvelle culture, dans un nouveau monde, s'adapter dans ce monde et retrouver un nouveau chemin, qui est très loin de ses racines. [. . .] Je pense toujours que mon identité maintenant, c'est l'exil[22].

L'auteur trouve dans l'exil une nouvelle liberté, pour laquelle il s'est battu en Syrie et qu'il érige en valeur fondamentale de l'universalité : « *[Ce chemin] je ne l'identifie pas avec la tristesse pourtant, mais la liberté. Parce que, quand on est exilé, on a vraiment une liberté. On a le choix, on peut choisir par qui on est entouré : une certaine famille, un entourage, une communauté. Exilé, ça veut dire se libérer de tout.* »

---

22 Les extraits sont issus d'un entretien mené avec l'auteur le 21 novembre 2021 à Paris.

Le statut de l'exilé est, dans sa conception, transnational et « déracialisé ». Il donne en effet un sens à l'exil dans son texte *L'Exil ne finira pas* (2019), en y trouvant une certaine continuité biographique, et en revendiquant son appartenance à une communauté qui n'a « ni terre, ni pays » (Souleimane 2019, 130). Il fait ainsi de l'exil une condition universelle et permanente. Permanente, car « même en rentrant en Syrie, les exilés resteront toujours des exilés » (Souleimane 2019, 132) puisque le pays et les Syriens sont transformés par la guerre et les événements. Universelle, car l'exil n'a pas de frontières et devient, selon lui, la condition de tout homme ou femme vivant la solitude et le manque de reconnaissance, tels les « des écrivains qui ne peuvent pas publier leurs livres », y compris les nationaux dans leur propre pays. Dans son texte, la non-reconnaissance d'un écrivain, quel que soit l'endroit du monde où il habite, devient la métaphore de l'exil.

Une quête d'universalité doit être basée, selon lui, sur l'échange perpétuel et l'ouverture, l'exilé jouant un rôle d'intermédiaire, mais ne doit pas s'appliquer à celles et ceux qui ne respectent pas ses valeurs fondamentales :

> Honnêtement, je ne crois pas du tout à ce qu'on appelle ‹ citoyen du mond ›. Citoyen du monde, ça veut dire que les agresseurs, et les fascistes, et le régime de baasistes, pourraient aussi être citoyens du monde. Et moi aussi, je suis un citoyen du monde. Pour moi, c'est inacceptable. Mais je crois à l'idée de l'échange. Je pense que c'est le rôle principal pour ceux qui vivent dans une nouvelle culture, de créer un pont entre ce nouveau monde où ils vivent, où ils sont plongés, et d'où ils sont venus. Peu importe d'où. C'est ce dont on a besoin en ce moment dans un monde où il y a tellement de diversité, de séparation face à l'extrême droite, face au racisme, surtout dans un pays comme la France.

L'auteur prévient des effets pervers qui peuvent être impliqués dans le désir de fonder une société sur l'universalité, et considère qu'elle ne devrait pas être basée sur une religion ou idéologie politique. Dans ce sens, il aspire à un universalisme « extensif » en opposition à l'universalisme « intensif » des Lumières. Nous reprenons ici la distinction proposée par Etienne Balibar (2016) ou Walzer (1992)[23] : le premier serait l'apanage des *dominants*, appui d'un projet hégémonique et expansionniste. Tandis que le second est une réponse des *dominés*, porté par le mouvement post-colonial notamment, pour revendiquer une humanité multiple mais unie, où les groupes humains seraient reconnus dans leurs différences :

> Est-ce qu'il y a un mauvais côté de l'universalisme ou est-ce que c'est toujours positif ? À mon avis, il y a un mauvais côté. Exemple récent, c'est l'union soviétique. Parce qu'ils ont détruit des peuples, des cultures différentes. Le côté mauvais de l'universalisme, c'est quand il ne respecte pas la culture de l'autre. Quand il ne respecte pas l'existence et la différence de l'autre. L'islam malheureusement, souvent, pendant toute l'histoire, n'a pas respecté la

---

23 Walzer (1992) utilise les termes d'universalisme surplombant ou de réitération.

différence entre sa culture, ses principes, et la pratiques des autres. [. . .] la religion pourrait être changée d'une culture à une autre, mais elle a toujours des principes, surtout les religions monothéistes, comme l'islam, qui ont une prétention universelle. Donc la religion pourrait être universelle, mais c'est horrible. Comme n'importe quelle idéologie, comme les communistes d'ailleurs.

Cependant, Souleimane défend également dans ses travaux, une universalité qui reprend les termes de l'universalisme traditionnel hérité des Lumières : la laïcité, la liberté. Ses critiques portent à la fois sur l'islamisme politique, et sur une certaine gauche en France qui tomberait dans la défense de particularismes dangereux (Souleimane 2021). Les tribunes, qu'il écrit pour l'*Express* et *Le Point*, entraînent des réactions souvent violentes, de la part de celles et ceux qu'il identifie comme partisans de l'extrême droite ou de cette gauche « au casque colonial » :

> Qu'un migrant, comme ils disent, critique l'islam ou le Moyen-Orient, pour eux, c'est indésirable. Il faut que ce migrant reste malheureux, pauvre, victime, n'aime pas la France, râle tout le temps, comme ça, ils se représentent comme des protecteurs qui empêche que ce migrant passe à l'extrême droite. J'appelle ça du racisme, le casque colonial. C'est-à-dire, qu'ils deviennent nos défenseurs comme exilés et nous, on n'a pas le droit de s'exprimer.

Les paroles et les écrits d'Omar Youssef Souleimane mettent en lumière une façon de lier narration et représentation de soi et du monde avec l'expérience de l'exil. L'auteur trouve une certaine continuité biographique dans l'exil – il a été, est, et sera toujours, exilé – de même qu'il en fait une catégorie universelle à travers une définition matérielle et métaphorique de l'exil : les exilés sont celles et ceux qui ne sont pas reconnus dans le pays où ils vivent, qu'ils soient natifs ou immigrés. Son fort attachement aux valeurs de liberté et de laïcité peut être compris à l'aune de la vie et du combat qu'il a mené en Syrie, au cours d'une révolution durant laquelle les intellectuels se sont interrogés sur l'héritage de la Révolution française. En effet, les liens entre la Syrie et la France, hérité d'un passé colonial[24], et la coopération diplomatique, scientifique et culturelle historique, expliquent en partie les trajectoires géographiques des intellectuels syriens exilés. Comme témoigne Omar Youssef Souleimane :

> J'ai contacté l'ambassade française parce que, pour moi, c'était le pays de la littérature, de la poésie. J'avais lu Paul Éluard quand j'étais adolescent, j'étais fan de lui – c'est toujours le cas. C'était mon poète préféré. C'était l'exemple de la liberté. Deuxième raison : la réputa-

---

24 La Syrie a été administrée par la France, désignée comme puissance mandataire par l'ONU, à partir de 1920 jusqu'à l'indépendance en 1946 (Tannous 2017). Ce lien perdurera à travers une politique diplomatique au niveau économique et culturelle, qui connaîtra néanmoins certaines périodes de suspension au gré des crises politiques.

tion de la France au Moyen-Orient qui est connue comme un pays qui protège les réfugiés politiques, et surtout les journalistes[25].

Également, sa position d'écrivain désormais reconnu et médiatisé en France – comme l'indique le nombre d'ouvrages qu'il a publiés chez son éditeur Flammarion, ses prix, et ses nombreuses invitations à différents événements organisés dans des institutions réputées dans le champ littéraire, le rapproche de la figure consacrée et universaliste de l'écrivain engagé. Il est notamment décrit sur la quatrième de couverture de son ouvrage *Le Petit Terroriste* (2018), comme un « écrivain français » (nationalité qu'il a désormais obtenue), et prend la défense des droits et valeurs fondamentaux qu'il considère aujourd'hui comme menacés. Nous allons voir avec la partie qui suit que les discours sur l'universalité depuis la position de l'exil peuvent prendre une forme différente, et être appuyés par des pratiques intellectuelles collectives.

3.2 Mudar Al-Khufash et Awhām Magazine (Berlin) : une critique migrante, queer et décoloniale

Dans le domaine littéraire, le projet d'*Awhām magazine* s'inscrit dans une volonté de porter des voix exilées et transnationales, souvent invisibilisées[26]. Créé à Berlin en 2017 sous l'impulsion du créateur et « storyteller » – tel qu'il s'auto-définit – Mudar Al-Khufash, financé par des dons participatifs, ce magazine pluriel, d'art, de littérature, et d'essais, présenté comme queer, « anti-orientalist », décolonial, est composé essentiellement de rédacteurs exilés à Berlin. La motivation des auteurs engagés dans ce projet est celle de diffuser des récits qui manquent de visibilité dans l'espace public. Ils aspirent ainsi à des formes plus universalisées de partage des histoires et des savoirs, pour lutter contre une « histoire unique » (Ngozi Adichie 2009), comme le suggère le manifeste en introduction du second numéro : « We are given voices to tell narratives that otherwise threaten the ‹ true stor ›. To challenge it and to establish a real discourse, where all parties involved are given space to voice their critique to exceed. So lay back or take a seat, and immerse yourself in brimming pages with authentic reads[27]. »

Mudar Al-Khufash explique la genèse du magazine en ces termes :

---

[25] Propos recueillis lors de la présentation d'Omar Youssef Souleimane à la conférence de PSL « Exil et Culture », 1e décembre 2021 à l'Université Paris-Dauphine.
[26] Pour plus d'informations, voir le site web du magazine. http://Awhāmmagazine.com/about (consulté le 27 mars 2022).
[27] Extraits issus d'un entretien mené avec l'auteur le 30 juin 2021.

> I thought that there was no space for people like me to express themselves artistically. Whenever there was an opportunity in that way, it was edited to the point that it doesn't match what, actually, I set myself up to do. I wanted to create a platform where me, people like me, could express themselves artistically. In Germany, some aspects or some stories were not necessarily welcomed or some points of views were also not understood. Although, there is no space to be understood. [. . .] when I was visiting galleries or went to theatre, I only saw white people. Even in the middle of Neukölln where the population is in majority migrants. But if you go to the galleries, if you go to the bars there, you don't see Brown people participate, actually the locals.

Le projet porte une critique décoloniale, qui ancre l'expérience de l'exil dans la « racialisation » et les inégalités de légitimation culturelle vécues par les exilés. Il montre que l'exil peut également favoriser la création de nouvelles formes alternatives et collectives d'intervention, intellectuelles ou politiques, à l'instar du champ académique – phénomène parfois lié à la déprofessionnalisation induite par la non reconnaissance des diplômes et des équivalences de postes (Mestci 2021).

D'origine palestinienne, exilé d'abord en Jordanie jusqu'à ses 18 ans puis à Amsterdam, et Berlin depuis 2006, Mudar Al-Khufash est impliqué dans la défense de la cause palestinienne, une prise de position qui l'avait fait quitter l'Allemagne pour la Grèce au moment de notre rencontre et qui réactualise son expérience de l'exil :

> I am kind of used into basically not being in one place. At the moment, I am in Athens. Because of what happened, I feel like I exile myself now again because I couldn't be in Germany because of last cycle of Israel affecting Gaza and the Palestinians inside of Israel, and so on . . . A lot of the demonstrations that we were doing and how the state was extremely violent, and my German friends not reaching out because they are not sure what to say . . . . So, I needed to be out of Germany. I think, this experience, for me, because I moved a lot, it became a norm.

Dans ses propos, la question de la représentation des paroles des exilés, des personnes « Brown », rejoint celle de l'enjeu de l'universalisation des causes politiques :

> Germany is a main player on the global politic arena. So, if we manage to change a bit of narrative in Germany, if more Brown people have more space to talk or they are giving a stage to express themselves, politically be active, I think it would definitely help. I mean, I can look at the United States and see Ilhan Omar or Rashida Tlaib and it's already changing the narrative a lot. I would aspire for this kind of change in Germany because that would definitely have an impact globally.

A ces enjeux globaux, Mudar-Al-Khufash répond par une « utopie », celle d'un magazine qui offre la possibilité aux écrivains et artistes exilés de redéfinir leur identité en dehors de celles qui leur sont assignées, à travers les armes de la narration et de l'esthétique. Le magazine entretient des liens avec les champs politiques et universitaires : les auteurs puisent leurs références dans la littérature, des figures militantes, et des chercheurs en sciences humaines et sociales. Dans son essai « Queeronomics : Neoliberal Co-Optation of Queer Masculinities », Mudar-Al-Khufash (2021) s'appuie sur les travaux de la sociologue Eva Illouz sur les emodities, sur les théories décoloniales et celles de la biopolitique, pour proposer une réflexion sur les effets du néolibéralisme sur la formation des identités queers. Il conçoit l'identité comme fluide, plurielle, agentive, ce qui reflète sa conception de l'identité exilée. Ces identités sont menacées selon lui par les « sytèmes oppressifs » : le capitalisme qui modèle les identités à travers la consommation, et contribue à « dépolitiser les identités queers », mais aussi le grand récit de l'Universalité Blanche (« White Universality ») ou les épistémologies eurocentriques de la liberté personnelle et des identités queers (Khufash 2021, 12).

A la fin de son essai, Al-Khufash propose une résolution des problématiques qu'il présente à partir d'une fiction projective du monde qu'il nomme « Speculative Design » : « societal problems could be addressed by looking toward the future and finding solutions by speculating new perspectives. » (Al-Khufash 2021, 24). L'être ensemble et la véritable universalité devra passer par le partage du « queer ». Il imagine un futur ou la communauté Queer serait passée de la marginalité au centre d'une nouvelle société, « authentically inclusive and anti-racist » [. . .], faisant du mouvement queer une « norme » mondiale qui mènera à la « destruction of all the patriotical, colonial and capitalist systems ».

4 Conclusion

Pour conclure, comment penser les liens entre l'exil, la marginalité social et intellectuelle souvent afférente et les pensées sur l'universalité ? La position des intellectuels exilés est assimilable à celle de transfuges de classe (Bourdieu), déclassés par le bas mais qui souffrent pourtant des mêmes symptômes sociaux que les déclassés par le haut : « Engendrant un « habitus clivé », le décalage entre les dispositions héritées et les dispositions acquises « est souvent à la source du sentiment de « malaise » social, de « honte », de ceux qu'on désigne péjorativement comme les « déracinés » [. . .] » (Bourdieu et Wacquant 1992, 262). Les intellectuels exilés vivent en effet un changement de paradigme brutal dans le contraste qui existe entre la position d'exil et le refuge. Cette violence symbolique œuvre à deux niveaux : celui de l'expérience de l'étranger qui change de pays et de culture et celui du déclassement social parfois afférent. Si quelques instances valorisent ces parcours, les étapes pour arriver à cumuler du capital symbolique pour que le handicap devienne ressource constitue un chemin long et incertain. En outre, les gouvernements des pays d'accueil jouent un rôle dans la hiérarchisation politique et la légitimation différenciée des groupes d'exilés selon les pays d'origine, dont l'accès inégal à la reconnaissance dépend de leur capital politique et social (Dufoix 1999). Bien souvent, la position de refuge, de demandeur, est une position de dépolitisation par le statut de réfugié associé à la « racialisation » et stigmatisation de celles et ceux qui en bénéficient[28].

Nombreux sont celles et ceux qui convertissent, pour reprendre l'expression de Thomas Brisson, « la perte d'une communauté politique d'origine à la possibilité d'en imaginer la reconstruction sur des bases transnationales nouvelles » (Brisson 2018, 273). Le sentiment d'appartenance en exil est ancré dans l'expérience de sociabilité de l'exil dans les villes « globales » (Sassen 1991) comme Paris ou Berlin qui se dessinent comme des zones d'attraction pour les personnes déplacées[29]. On peut faire l'hypothèse que se créent aujourd'hui des sous-champs transnationaux d'intellectuels en exil.

Cet article constitue notamment une réflexion sur la possibilité de décrire différents discours vis-à-vis de l'universalité en fonction de différentes positions sociales, et subjectivités. Nous avons vu que la tension qui se joue dans la position des intellectuels exilés peut amener les intellectuels à prendre des positions plus ou moins universalisantes et critiques. Il faut étudier sociologiquement un certain nombre de paramètres pour comprendre la complexité du continuum des prises de positions dans l'épreuve de l'exil[30], entre défense et contraction identitaire ou ouverture sur le monde et les cultures étrangères ; ainsi que les différents types de positionnements vis-à-vis de l'universalisme occidental qui peuvent être adoptés. Avec l'exemple de ces deux penseurs, Omar Youssef Souleimane, et Mudar Al-Khufash, se dessinent deux façons de concevoir l'universalité, qui ont en partage la critique d'une universalité surplombante, ainsi que la défense de la liberté et de l'agentivité des identités. Cependant, Mudar Al-Khufash, et d'autres acteurs du projet collectif d'*Awhām*, dénoncent par une critique forte l'universalisme européen, identifié comme un système d'oppression, tandis qu'Omar Youssef Souleimane s'appuie sur certains de ses fondements pour nourrir son travail et ses luttes. Les modes d'intervention et de production des deux intellectuels sont également différenciés : d'un côté, Mudar Al-Khufash s'appuie sur le collectif et l'exploration de nouveaux modes d'expression esthétiques et narratives, pour porter un discours

---

28 Les actions mises en place par les Etats de départ (menace de représailles sur les familles restées sur place, confiscation du passeport etc.) ou d'accueil (reconnaissance du statut administratif et du droit de résidence) peuvent constituer un facteur de dépolitisation.
29 Comme le montre le rapport UNESCO (2016) *Cities Welcoming Refugees and Migrants*.
30 Il faut préciser que l'exil occupe une place différenciée dans les récits de vie et la construction du sens biographique et de son identité et sa place peut changer à différents moments biographiques (Breckner 2007).

critique intersectionnel, rappelant les modes d'intervention des avants-gardes. De l'autre, Souleimane a choisi les formes traditionnelles du roman et de la poésie pour trouver sa place dans la langue française, s'emparer de ses mots depuis l'exil, et interroger les enjeux identitaires de l'appropriation d'une nouvelle langue et culture.

En outre, le pays de l'exil nous semble être un élément de compréhension contextuel des façons dont les discours se présentent de façon différenciée : comme nous l'avons vu à travers les pensées d'Omar Youssef Souleimane et les voix d'*Awhām*, la critique déconstructiviste, décoloniale, queer, est bien plus présente dans les discours des intellectuels en Allemagne qu'en France, où l'attachement à un certain modèle, à un héritage intellectuel, perdure et où ces théories, perçues comme communautaristes, sont vivement débattues[31]. Ces phénomènes soulèvent la question de la circulation des savoirs et de la place symbolique, intellectuelle et affective qu'occupe la culture du pays d'installation dans la biographie des auteurs. Il faut cependant préciser que ces deux exemples ne sont pas voués à donner une représentation archétypale de deux positions qui seraient uniques, en France et en Allemagne, mais ils mettent en lumière une tendance qui nous semble pertinente pour l'analyse. La différence des engagements et des situations politiques qui ont amené les deux auteurs à l'exil est aussi un élément de compréhension de leur rapport à l'universalité. En effet, l'enjeu de l'universalisation des causes politiques et les moyens pour y parvenir est central dans l'élaboration d'un discours sur l'universel. Omar Youssef Souleimane (2021) s'est inscrit dans la lutte syrienne et s'est appuyé sur les pensées d'une gauche laïque et révolutionnaire pour revendiquer la démocratie, l'émancipation vis-à-vis des carcans religieux, et les droits humains fondamentaux en Syrie ; notamment une liberté citoyenne, politique et sexuelle telle qu'il la met en scène dans son roman *Le Dernier Syrien* (2020) qui retrace l'expérience et les aspirations d'un groupe de jeunes révolutionnaires. Dans ce contexte, revendiquer certains fondements de l'universalisme européen a pu nourrir cette lutte. De l'autre, Mudar Al-Khufash s'est battu et se bat pour la défense des droits humains des Palestiniens à l'échelle internationale, ainsi que ceux des personnes queers. Il s'appuie pour ce faire sur la valorisation des identités en marge et la critique d'un universalisme qui participe à leur invisibilisation.

La production d'une pensée sur l'universel, depuis la position de l'exil, ne saurait être réduite à une pensée unique. Étudier cette diversité permet tout

---

[31] Voir par exemple « Le décolonialisme, une stratégie hégémonique ». L'appel de 80 intellectuels en France. *Le Point*, 28 novembre 2018.

d'abord d'éclairer des pensées « non-occidentales »[32] qui ont été historiquement marginalisées, ainsi que d'interroger les effets concrets des trajectoires migratoires des intellectuels sur la circulation et hybridation des savoirs et des modèles d'engagements politiques contemporains.

Références bibliographiques

Academics for Peace. « Nous, enseignants-chercheurs de Turquie, nous ne serons pas complices de ce crime ! » Pétition du 10 Janvier 2016. https://barisicinakademisyenler.net/node/63 (consulté le 27 mars 2022).

Al-Khufash, Mudar. « Queeronomics : Neoliberal Co-Optation of Queer Masculinities. » *Awhām* 4 (2021) : 10–24.

Arendt, Hannah. « We refugees. » *The Menorah Journal* 31.1 (1943) : 69–77.

Ash, Mitchell G., et Alfons Söllner. Eds. *Forced Migration and Scientific Change. Émigré German-Speaking Scientists and Scholars after 1933*. Cambridge : Cambridge University Press, 1996.

Azuelos, Daniel. « L'exil dans l'exil. Les stratégies linguistiques contradictoires des exilés aux États-Unis (Thomas Mann, Klaus Mann, Hans Sahl, Oskar Maria Graf) ». *Études Germaniques* 252.4 (2008) : 723–735.

Baczko, Adam, Gilles Dorronsorro et Arthur Quesnay. « Le capital social révolutionnaire. L'exemple de la Syrie entre 2011 et 2014 ». *ARSS* 211–212.1 (2016) : 24–35.

Balibar, Étienne. *Des Universels. Essais et Conférences*. Paris : Galilée, 2016.

Ben-David, Joseph, et Randall Collins. « Les facteurs sociaux dans la genèse d'une nouvelle science. Le cas de la psychologie ». (1966). *Eléments d'une sociologie historique des sciences*. Joseph Ben-David. Ed. Gad Freundenthal. Trad. Michelle de Launay et Jean-Pierre Rotschild. Paris : Presses universitaires de France, 1997. 65–92.

Boucher, Manuel, Geoffrey Pleyers et Paola Rebughini. « Introduction générale ». *Subjectivation et désubjectivation : Penser le sujet dans la globalisation*. Ed. Manuel Boucher, Geoffrey Pleyers et Paola Rebughini. Paris : Éditions de la Maison des sciences de l'homme, 2017. 13–23.

Bourdieu, Pierre. *Les Règles de l'art. Genèse et structure du champ littéraire*. Paris : Seuil, 1992.

———. *Raisons Pratiques. Sur la théorie de l'action*. Paris : Seuil, 1994.

Bourdieu, Pierre, et Loïc Wacquant. *Invitation à la Sociologie Réflexive*. Paris : Seuil, 2014.

Breckner, Roswitha. « Case-Oriented Comparative Approaches. The Biographical Perspective as Potential and Challenge in Migration Research. » *Concepts and Methods in Migration Research*. Ed. Karin Schittenhelm. Conference Reader, 2007. 113–152.

Bridet, Guillaume. « Universalité de l'exil ? ». *Critique* 793–794.6-7 (2013) : 499–508.

Brisson, Thomas. *Décentrer l'Occident. Les Intellectuels Postcoloniaux, Chinois, Indiens et Arabes, et la Critique de la Modernité*. Paris : La Découverte, 2018.

Burnautzki, Sarah. *Les Frontières Racialisées de la Littérature Française. Contrôle au Facies et Stratégies de Passage*. Paris : Honoré Champion, 2017.

---

[32] Pour la dichotomie « occidentaux » / « non-occidentaux », voir le chapitre de Gisèle Sapiro dans le présent volume qui montre la naissance du récit d'un monopole occidental sur la science, construit par l'occultation des savoirs non-occidentaux.

Charle, Christophe. *Naissance des « intellectuels » 1880–1900*. Paris : Minuit, 1990.

——— . *Les Intellectuels en Europe au XIXe siècle. Essai d'histoire comparée*. Paris : Seuil, 1996.

Cohen, Elsie. *Le travail intellectuel et créateur dans les conditions de l'exil : Enquête sur les trajectoires et expériences d'intellectuel.es, étudiant.es et artistes en exil, aujourd'hui à Paris*. Mémoire de Master. Paris : EHESS, 2019.

Cohen, Elsie, et Anne Schultz. « Intellectual Migration(s). » *The Routledge Handbook of Intellectual History and the Sociology of Ideas*. New York : Routledge (à paraître).

Coser, Lewis. *Refugee Scholars in America. Their Impact and their Experiences*. New Haven, London : Yale University Press, 1984.

Crawford, Sally, Katharina Ulmschneider, et Jàs Elsner. *Ark of Civilisation : Refugee Scholars and Oxford University, 1930–45*. Oxford : Oxford University Press, 2017.

Dakhli, Leyla, Pascale Laborier, et Francis Wolff. Eds. *Scholars at Risk, Rescue Politics and Institutional Opportunities in Comparative and Long-term Perspective*. Wiesbaden : Springer, 2021.

De Swann, Abram. « Langue et culture dans la société transnationale ». Leçon inaugurale au Collège de France no. 143 (24 octobre 1997). Collège de France, Chaire Européenne, Paris.

——— . « A political sociology of the world language system (1) : The dynamics of language spread. » *Language Problems and Language Planning* 22.1 (1998a) : 63–75.

——— . « A political sociology of the world language system (2) : The unequal exchange of texts. » *Language Problems and Language Planning* 22.2 (1998b) : 109–128.

Detue, Frédérik, et Charlotte Lacoste. « Ce que le témoignage fait à la littérature ». *Europe* 1041–1042 (2016) : 3–15.

Dubar, Claude. « Formes identitaires et socialisation professionnelle ». *Revue française de sociologie* 33.4 (1992) : 505–529.

Dufoix, Stéphane. « Les légitimations politiques de l'exil ». *Genèse* 34 (1999) : 53–79.

Dunne, Michele, et Amr Hamzawy. *Egypt's political Exiles : Going Anywhere but home*. Carnegie Endowment for International Peace, mars 2019. https://carnegieendowment.org/2019/03/29/egypt-s-political-exiles-going-anywhere-but-home-pub-78728 (consulté le 27 mars 2022).

Fermi, Laura. *Illustrious Immigrants : The Intellectual Migration from Europe 1930–1941*. Chicago : University of Chicago Press, 1968.

Fleck, Christian. « The role of refugee help organizations in the placement of German and Austrian scholars abroad. » *Intellectual Migration and Cultural Transformation : Refugee from National Socialism in the English-Speaking World*. Ed. Edward Timms et Jon Hughes. Vienna : Springer, 2003. 21–36.

Fleury, Antoine, et Jilek Lubor. Eds. *Une Europe malgré tout, 1945–1990. Contacts et Réseaux Culturels, Intellectuels et Scientifiques entre Européens dans la Guerre froide*. Bruxelles, Berlin, Bern : P.I.E. Peter Lang, 2009.

Fourn, Léo. « Loin de la Syrie, loin de la Révolution ». *Revue des mondes musulmans et de la Méditerranée* 144 (2018) : 211–228.

Glasson Deschaumes, Ghislaine. « Penser une politique euroméditerranéenne de traduction ». *Diversité des langues et plurilinguisme. Culture et recherche* 124. Ministère de la culture et de la communication, 2011. 20–22.

Groppo, Bruno. « Exilés et réfugiés : l'évolution de la notion de réfugié au XXe siècle ». *Historia actual Online* 2 (2003) : 69–79.

Hagemann, Harald, et Milberg, William. Eds. « Refugees scholarship : the cross-fertilization of culture. » *Social Research and International Quarterly* 84.4 (2017). Special Issue.

Harchi, Kaoutar. « Pour en finir avec la croyance en l'universalisme littéraire français ». *AOC*, mai 2018.

Héran, François. « Et si la France prenait vraiment "sa part" dans l'accueil des réfugiés ». *De facto* 33 (2022) : 40–45. https://www.icmigrations.cnrs.fr/wp-content/uploads/2022/07/DF33.pdf (consulté le 18 avril 2023).

Hofmann, Franck, et Markus Messling. Eds. *The Epoch of Universalism 1769–1989/ L'époque de l'universalisme 1789–1989*. Berlin, Boston : De Gruyter, 2021.

INSEE. « Étrangers – immigrés ». *Insee Références*, Tef éditions, 2018. https://www.insee.fr/fr/statistiques/3303358?sommaire=3353488 (consulté le 27 mars 2022).

Jeanpierre, Laurent. *Des hommes entre plusieurs mondes. Etude sur une situation d'exil : Intellectuels français et réfugiés aux Etats-Unis pendant la Deuxième Guerre mondiale*. Paris : EHESS, 2004a.

———. « Une opposition structurante pour l'anthropologie structurale : Lévi-Strauss contre Gurvitch, la guerre de deux exilés français aux États-Unis ». *Revue d'Histoire des Sciences Humaines* 11.2 (2004b) : 13–44.

Jégo, Marie. « La Turquie condamne des universitaires à la prison ». *Le Monde*, 13 mai 2019.

Kleppinger, Kathryn. *Branding the « Beur » Autor, Minority writing and the Media in France 1983–2013*. Liverpool : Liverpool University Press, 2016.

Kouvouama, Abel, Gueye, Abdoulaye, Piriou, Anne, et Anne-Catherine Wagner. Eds. *Figures croisées d'intellectuels. Trajectoires, modes d'actions, productions*. Paris : Karthala, 2007.

Lalande, André. *Vocabulaire technique et critique de la philosophie*. Paris : Presses universitaires de France, 1993[1902–1923].

« Le décolonialisme, une stratégie hégémonique ». L'appel de 80 intellectuels en France. *Le Point*, 28 novembre 2018. https://www.lepoint.fr/politique/le-decolonialisme-une-strategie-hegemonique-l-appel-de-80-intellectuels-28-11-2018-2275104_20.php (consulté le 27 mars 2022).

Leperlier, Tristan. « Témoins algériens de la décennie noire en France ». *Europe* 1041–1042 (2016) : 178–192.

Loewenberg, Gerhard. « The Influence of European Emigré Scholars on Comparative Politics, 1925–1965. » *American Political Science Review* 100.4 (2006) : 597–604.

Loyer, Emanuelle. *Paris à New York. Intellectuels et artistes français en exil, 1940–47*. Paris : Hachette-Littératures, 2007.

Matonti, Frédérique, et Franck Poupeau. « Le capital militant. Essai de définition ». *Actes de la recherche en sciences sociales* 155.5 (2004) : 4–11.

Matonti, Frédérique, et Gisèle Sapiro. « L'engagement des intellectuels : nouvelles perspectives ». *Actes de la recherche en sciences sociales* 176–177.1 (2009) : 4–7.

Meerzon, Yana. « Theatre in Exile : Defining the Field as Performing Odyssey. » *Critical Stages/Scènes Critiques* 5 (2011). Online.

Mestci, Alihan. « En Turquie, les universitaires face au pouvoir ». *AOC*, 23 mars 2021.

Minor Universality. « Universalisme & savoir(s). Entretien avec Gisèle Sapiro ». *Les entretiens du groupe de recherche Minor Universality*, 2021. https://www.youtube.com/watch?v=AF-hEDCOGmI&t=15s&ab_channel=ERCMinorUniversality (consulté le 27 mars 2022).

Ngozi Adichie, Chimamanda. « The danger of a single story. » *TED Conference*, juillet 2009. https://www.ted.com/talks/chimamanda_ngozi_adichie_the_danger_of_a_single_story (consulté le 27 mars 2022).

Pasquet, Sophie. « La Maison des journalistes de Paris ». *Hommes & migrations* 1308 (2014) : 170–173.

Popa, Ioana. « Dépasser l'exil. Degrés de médiation et stratégies de transfert littéraire chez des exilés de l'Europe de l'Est en France ». *Genèses* 38 (2000) : 5–32.

———. *Traduire sous contraintes. Littérature et communisme (1947–1989)*. Paris : CNRS Éditions, 2010.

Poupeau, Franck « Universel/universalisation/construction de l'universel ». *Dictionnaire International Bourdieu*. Ed. Gisèle Sapiro. Paris : CNRS Editions, 2020. 869–870.

Reporters sans Frontières. *Guide Pratique pour les Journalistes en Exil.* 2012. https://rsf.org/sites/default/files/rsf_-_guide_pour_les_journalistes_en_exil_2012.pdf (consulté le 27 mars 2022).
Rösch, Félix. Ed. *Émigré Scholars and the Genesis of International Relations : A European Discipline in America ?* Basingstoke : Palgrave Macmillan, 2014.
Saïd, Edward. *Orientalism.* New York : Pantheon Book, 1978.
——— . *Out Of Place : A Memoire.* New York : A.A. Knopf, 1999.
——— . *Reflections on Exile and Other Essays.* Cambridge/MA : Harvard University Press, 2000.
Sapiro, Gisèle. Ed. *L'espace intellectuel en Europe.* Paris : La Découverte, 2009a.
——— . « Modèles d'intervention politique des intellectuels. Le cas français ». *Actes de la recherche en sciences sociales* 176–177 (2009b) : 8–31.
——— . « Exil et intellectuels transnationaux ». *Cahiers d'études germaniques* 83.2 (2022), à paraître.
Sapiro, Gisèle. « Le décentrement épistémologique conduit-il au relativisme ? » *Minor Universality / Universalité mineure. Rethinking Humanity After Western Universalism / Penser l'humanité après l'universalisme occidental.* Ed. Markus Messling et Jonas Tinius. Berlin, Boston : De Gruyter, 2023. 57–61.
Sapiro, Gisèle, Tristan Leperlier, et Mohamed Amine Brahimi. « Qu'est-ce qu'un champ intellectuel transnational ? » *Actes de la recherche en sciences sociales* 224.4 (2018) : 4–11.
Sassen, Saskia. *The Global City : New York, London, Tokyo.* Princeton : Princeton University Press, 1991.
Sayad, Abdelmalek. *La Double Absence. Des illusions de l'émigré aux souffrances de l'immigré.* Paris : Seuil, 1999.
Scholars at Risk. *Free to Think.* Rapports annuels 2015–2021. https://www.scholarsatrisk.org/free-to-think-reports/ (consulté le 27 mars 2022).
Seidel, Michael. *Exile and the Narrative Imagination.* New Haven/CT : Yale UP, 1986.
Souleimane, Omar Youssef. *Le Petit Terroriste.* Paris : Flammarion, 2018.
——— . « L'exil ne finira pas ». *Vivre l'Exil. Explorer des pratiques desexil de l'exil.* Ed. Marie-Claire Caloz-Tschopp, Valeria Wagner, Marion Brepohl, Graziela De Coulon, Ilaria Possenti, et Teresa Veloso Bermedo. Paris : L'Harmattan, 2019. 129–134.
——— . *Le Dernier Syrien.* Paris : Flammarion, 2020.
——— . « Peut-on rester de gauche et critiquer l'islam ? » *L'Express*, 15 mai 2021.
——— . *Une Chambre en exil.* Paris : Flammarion, 2022.
Steinmetz, George. « Ideas in Exile : Refugees from Nazi Germany and the Failure to Transplant Historical Sociology into the United States. » *International Journal of Politics, Culture, and Society* 23.1 (2010) : 1–27.
Tannous, Manon-Nour. *Chirac, Assad et les Autres. Les Relations Franco-Syriennes depuis 1946.* Paris : Presses universitaires de France, 2017.
UNESCO. *Cities Welcoming Refugees and Migrants.* Inclusive and Sustainable Cities Series. Paris : UNESCO, 2016. https://unesdoc.unesco.org/ark:/48223/pf0000246558 (consulté le 27 mars 2022).
Traverso, Enzo. *La pensée dispersée. Figures de l'exil judéo-allemand.* Paris : Léo Scheer, 2004.
Wagner, Anne Catherine. *Les nouvelles élites de la mondialisation : Une immigration dorée en France.* Paris : Presses universitaires de France, 1998.
——— . *La mondialisation des classes sociales.* Paris : La Découverte, 2020.
Walzer, Michael. « Les deux universalismes ». *Esprit* 187.12 (1992) : 114–133.
Wang, Simeng. *Illusions et souffrances. Les migrants chinois à Paris.* Paris : Éditions Rue d'Ulm, 2017.
Wierviorka, Michel. *La violence.* Paris : Balland, 2004.

Ananya Jahanara Kabir
Creolising Universality

Abstract: This essay returns to a founding figure of the discipline of creolistics, or Creole linguistics: the German scholar Hugo Schuchardt. I offer a close reading of the tract on the language he called "Malaioportugiesisch", or Malay-Portuguese, published in 1890 as *Kreolische Studien IX*. The critical apparatus that Schuchardt provides here deviated from the philological methods of the neogrammarians and their quest for universalism based on a hierarchy of languages bound together filially in a 'family tree'. Instead, Schuchardt privileges affiliation, proximity, and serendipitous encounter of unlike languages that result in unpredictable, improvised, and sensorially rich Creoles. In Schuchardt's imagination, Germanic, Romance, and Malay languages all come together to create new Creole possibilities for the world through revelling in porosity and impurity. These qualities enable us re-creolise creole as a concept, and creolisation as process and praxis. Creolising universality then emerges as a viable alternative to universalism's epistemic hegemonies.

Keywords: Hugo Schuchardt, creolistics, Malay-Portuguese, Dutch creoles, Portuguese creoles, creolisation, philology

> If minor formations become method and theory, then new analytics will be brought to the foreground to creolize the universalisms we live with today, doing so from the bottom up and from the inside out. It is this process of becoming theory of the minor that we are also calling creolization. (Shih and Lionnet 2011, 4)

> Some Portuguese expressions were also found on Dutch lips at that time... so Batavia's main canal road, the "Jonkersgragt" is better known by the name of "Roewa Malakka"; in addition to Dutch fish names, there are also "cabos", "pees leti" (milk-fish) and "pees porco" (swine-fish). (Schuchardt 1890, 17)[1]

> If we are to conceive of a meaningful sense of universality after European universalism, we need to interrogate the latter: what were the sources and emancipating "weapons of criticism" of a European universalism? (Messling and Hofmann 2021, 2)

---

[1] The original reads: "Mancher portugiesische Ausdruck fand sich damals auch auf holländischen Lippen... so ist die hauptsächlichste Kanalstrasse Batavias, die "Jonkersgragt" besser unter dem Namen "Roewa Malakka" bekannt; so werden neben holländischen Fischnamen auch "cabos", pees leti ("melk-visch"), "pees porco" ("verkens-visch"), verzeichnet."

What lies after the end(s) of universalism? The semantic ambition of that very word presents the first hurdle to moving beyond its remit. As Manuela Boatcă observes,

> scholarship on Orientalism, racism and critical whiteness have long taught us that prevailing norms function as unmarked [universalist] categories that may remain unqualified, unstressed, and at times altogether unnamed. Their negative or deviant counterpart, however, requires explicit naming (Boatcă 2021, 390).

Universalism, from this perspective, is the most flamboyantly universalist of all "unmarked [universalist] categories" (to use Boatcă's words). Like all unmarked "-isms", moreover, it is shackled to the geography, history, and values of an unmarked Europe–so much so that one may justifiably speak of a European universalism–as Markus Messling and Franck Hoffman do in my third epigraph above (Messling and Hofmann 2021, 2). "European" then emerges as a mark of the particular masquerading as universal; as they also point out, "for some time now, it has become evident that the proclaimed European universalism has indeed not been universal but followed rather the European temptation to universalise its own beliefs, norms, and interests" (Messling and Hofmann 2021, 3).

On scrutiny, the "Europe" on which this paradoxically particular universalism rests, reveals itself as a conglomerate of nation-states with disarmingly stable relationships between ethnolinguistic identity and cartographic boundaries, whose shadow lines persist beneath the supra-national European Union. The gleaming facades of the EU's buildings, in the heart of multi-denominational, multilingual, post-imperial Belgium are, however, a polished carapace.[2] They highlight, even while glossing over, the one-language-one-nation construct as rising out of the rubble of internecine wars over religion and territory, stretching back at least to the awkward suture of the medieval and modern periods of European history. The traumas of iconoclasm, counter-Reformation, and cultural and economic competition from the Islamicate worlds on Europe's eastern flanks and the Mediterranean's southern shores, all provide the deeper contexts for the confident universalising that, subsequently, Enlightenment Europe generated on the back of its colonising adventures. "Today", asseverate Messling and Hofmann, "European universalism, as an ideology, has come to an end", thanks to the seismic political shifts of the past century; the re-emergence of populist nationalism and fascist-racist tendencies; and "anti-colonial thought and critical studies (in a wider sense), all of which have confirmed universalism's thorough 'entanglement with capitalism and Western imperialism". Becoming-minor would seem to be a mode of rescuing this defunct and compromised

---

[2] On the carapace as fetish that conceals and reveals, see Mulvey 1991. See also Boatcă's argument for "coherent Europe" (2021, 303).

universalism from itself: but, since universalism purports to be everything and everywhere, where, and with what, do we start? (Deleuze and Guattari 1986 [1975], 27).

Creolising universality is my proposal, with the present participle form functioning both as an adjective describing universality and a verb, with universality as its object. I mobilise this dual force by returning to the emergence, within historical linguistics, of the concept 'creole'. What, precisely, does it name? This move is not a retrogression to the arguably narrow domain of linguistics from which creolisation must be freed before it can become an epistemological reset button. Rather, it constitutes a necessary part of the latter endeavour. As Shu-mei Shih and Françoise Lionnet argue in the quote that forms my first epigraph, to recognise creole phenomena as minor formations is the first step towards the creolising of theory (Shih and Lionnet 2020, 4). Likewise, Manuela Boatcă and Anca Parvulescu analyse Transylvania as "a minor formation in European history" to "contribute to the larger project of the creolization of Europe", and of the sociological analysis of Europe (2020, 23; see also Parvulescu and Boatcă 2023). For these thinkers, the concept of "minor formation" functions as a switch activating the process of *creolising theory*. Supplementing their efforts, I pause at a foundational moment in the *theorising of creole* as a "minor formation": the German philologist Hugo Schuchardt's pioneering work in creolistics, of which my second epigraph offers a taste. If, following Messling and Hofmann's injunction as set out in my third epigraph, we "are to conceive of a meaningful sense of universality after European universalism", we need, as they also urge, to return to that universalism's 'weapons of criticism'. My reading of Schuchardt posits that the most powerful of those weapons, textual criticism, and the principles of philology, contained *ab initio* the radical potential to dismantle universalism. As with the Haitian revolution, Schuchardt's creolistics exemplifies how "the universalistic claim of the centre has very early on been reversed on itself" (Messling and Hofmann 2021, 17).

Ensconced in Graz, Austria, Schuchardt contemplated, translated, analysed, and defined a linguistic situation as spatially remote to his own in the heart of Europe as it was taxonomically alien to his early training at Leipzig University in comparative Indo-European philology.[3] In 1891 he published as the ninth issue of his series *Kreolische Studien* (Creole Studies) a tract whose title, in English translation, is "the Malayo-Portuguese of Batavia and Tugu". This work presents several varieties of the non-Indo-European language comprehended under the term 'Malay' in maritime South-East Asia, to demonstrate their permeation by two

---

3 On Schuchardt's life and career, see Matauschek, 'Malay' (2014, 247–251); Cardoso's *Creole of Diu* (2018), gives an excellent account of Schuchardt's "remote" working methods. For a cutting-edge account of the philological, intellectual, and material historical dimensions of Schuchardt's networks, see now Castro, Cardoso et al. (2022).

European languages from different "branches" of the Indo-European family – the Germanic Dutch, and the Romance Portuguese. This process, and its linguistic consequences, is encapsulated in the second epigraph above (Schuchardt 1890, 17).[4] Why is Schuchardt drawn to this messy material, and how does he treat it, affectively and intellectually? In answering this question, I respond to the need, in Gary Wilder's words, to tell another story of Europe – one that is concerned less with "unmasking universalisms as covert European particularisms" than "with challenging the assumption that the universal is European property" (Wilder 2015, 9–10). Schuchardt's linguistic journeys creolise the universalism inherent in European philological methods to reveal, instead, the creolising universality catalysed by the transoceanic pathways of cultural encounter those journeys trace.

1 *Europäische Sprache in kreolischer Gestaltung*: Being creole

Despite obvious advances in the state-of-the-art since the discipline of creolistics was inaugurated by Schuchardt and his contemporaries, the question of what constitutes a creole language is far from settled.[5] There is nevertheless some consensus that, historically, linguistic creoles and para-linguistic processes we may call creolisation were compositely "the result of transformation of European cultural forms as they are transposed in another space beyond their established frames of reference" (Cheah 2011, 83). It is this sense of transposition that Schuchardt seeks to capture as he opens his tract on "Malaioportugiesisch" ("Malayo-Portuguese"), by calling it "Europäische Sprache in kreolischer Gestaltung" ("European language in creolised design").[6] What, however, is this creolised design, that even as it is announced on the page, has already incorporated within itself a European language, thereby undermining its ontological autonomy? How does *kreolische Gestaltung* come into being? Is it already equivalent to, or a discrete stage in a process leading to, "creole"? Several possibilities jostle in Schuchardt's tract. The title, *das Malaioportugiesische*, brings together the languages Malay and Portuguese in violent, momentary conjuncture, that recalls the deathly grappling of Hegel's master-slave

---

[4] Note that I have abbreviated the work differently in the epigraph so that the reader may start the essay with an immediate grasp of this work's geographical remit.
[5] For a useful overview of creologenesis and its taxonomies in a linguistic frame, see Bakker and Daval-Markussen (2013).
[6] Quotations from Schuchardt's 'Kreolische Studien IX' will henceforth be cited by page number parenthetically in the body of the text.

dialectic (Buck-Morss 2000). The title is, however, misleading. Over the work's two hundred and fifty-four pages, a far more complex, dilated and sedimented interlinguistic interaction in Batavia and Tugu unfolds than suggested by its portmanteau terminology comprised of two lexical elements.

Since Batavia originally named the area between the Rijn and the Maas rivers in the Netherlands, an important frontier zone between the Roman Empire and a tribe named the Batavi in late Antiquity (see Paluszek 2013; Kehoe 2015), it appears fitting that Schuchardt began his story with the arrival of the Dutch in this part of the world and the setting up of their reformed church. Yet this founding moment of a new Batavia is complicated by the fact that, before the Dutch, the Portuguese had already arrived here.[7] The need to communicate with the locals had led to the creation of what Schuchardt reports from his reading as a "sehr schlechtes und gemischtes Malaiisch" ("a very bad and mixed Malay", 2); indeed, Schuchardt has learnt from his studies to abandon "a very preconceived notion about the purity or corruption of Malay" (Matauschek 2014, 251). But the Portuguese too had left their linguistic mark in the form of "a broken dialect" (19), in the words of one of Schuchardt's informants, Arthur Coke Burnell, which he cites in the original English.[8] As my second epigraph illustrates, these remnants of Batavian Portuguese undergo further transformation in being rendered through Dutch orthography (e.g. "roewa" for "rua", or Portuguese "street"). At the same time, Portuguese terms cling to the naming and organisation of daily life–co-existing alongside, for example, Dutch names for tropical fish. "Kreolische Gestaltung" thus enters the archive as an assemblage of pre-existing fragments, "bad, mixed, and broken."[9]

Schuchardt uses these terms empirically rather than evaluatively. He is interested in, even excited by, the proliferation of fragments, of "Malabarisch" ("Tamil"), "Bengalisch" ("Bangla"), and a "verdorbene Portugiesisch" ("corrupted Portuguese"), all languages spoken by enslaved South Asians brought to Java by the VOC (4).[10] Dutch words contributed to this plasticity to generate unexpected linguistic newness.

---

[7] For specific linguistic consequences of the Portuguese being earlier than others, see Halikowski-Smith (2016) and Hoogervorst (2018).
[8] Henry Yule and Arthur Coke Burnell were also co-authors of the iconic glossary of Anglo-Indian terms, *Hobson-Jobson* (1886), which, as we shall see below, Schuchardt used in his own lexicographic work.
[9] This interpretation of Creoles and creolised languages as "bad" or "corrupted" versions of existing languages was widespread during the 19th century. For instance, the then Anglican Bishop of the Diocese of Central Travancore, John Martindale Speechly, remarked in 1869 that "in the seaport towns generally the worst Malayalam is spoken", because he noted the high admixture of Portuguese, Tamil, and Arabic lexis in the language of Calicut (Fernandes 2016, 800–801).
[10] For this transoceanic movement of the enslaved by the Dutch, see Wickramasinghe (2016) and Van der Velde (2020).

Schuchardt reports "eine mischblütige Dame" ("a mixed-race woman") improvising with "*eeu non kere comer*" ("I don't like eating") gatte" (8), whereas the italicisation (duplicated here from the original) emphasises how the entire sentence echoes Portuguese lexis until the surprise entry of Dutch "gate", glossed by Schuchardt as "Hühnersteiss" (German, "chicken chops", 8). Lest the adjective "mischblütig" push us toward privileging biological métissage as the catalyst for this mixed language, Schuchardt reminds us that the most fecund generators of the "kreolische Gestaltung" were Batavian-born Dutch children who absorbed the diverse languages spoken by the transoceanic enslaved in their parents employ, to end up speaking hardly a word of "gut Holländisch" ("good Dutch", 8). Their Dutch is studded with "lipe-tyole" words: an opaque descriptor which Schuchardt glosses as "schlechtes Portugiesisch" (bad Portuguese, 8) and aligns with "Liplap", citing the latter's definition in the Hobson Jobson Dictionary of Anglo-Indian English as 'a vulgar and disparaging term given in the Dutch Indies to Eurasian (Yule and Burnell 1886, 395). In Java, Schuchardt notes, "Liplap" is a synonym for "Kreole" (9); both terms encompass Dutch children born overseas; children born of a European father and "Indianische" ("of the Indies", 9) mother; and children of far more mixed parentage ("vielmehr vermischte Abkunft", 9).

2 *Geschlagene Wurzeln, ausgestreute Reiskörner*: Analysing creole

For Schuchardt, being creole is less about genetic propagation and more about cultural innovations from dispersed fragments. He analyses creoleness as the product not of opposed binaries, but of unpredictable admixtures of unspecified proportions. The languages that creolise each other can be closely related, somewhat related, or completely unrelated to each other; creolised languages born out of specific contact situations can spur on further processes of creolisation in parallel situations elsewhere. Schuchardt invokes the "vermischte Ehe" ("mixed couple", 9) as progenitor of racially métis children, but more interesting to him are those cultural métis who eschew the dictates of social hierarchy and blood in preferring the company of the domestics and the enslaved *vernacular* component– in their households, over that of their European-born parents. While, within theories of linguistic creolisation, such children will eventually be seen as "ground zero" for the emergence of creoles from pidgins (see Bakker and Daval-Markussen 2015, 142), they enter Schuchardt's schema with a different valence. These Batavian-born Dutch children are not a point of origin for "Malayo-Portuguese". They illustrate merely a watershed moment in ever-proliferating processes of cultural encounter, whereby transoceanic worlds, cultures, and languages come together within new social structures. Not simply through *filiation*, then, but through *affiliation and affinity*, does this "liplap" creole habitus emerge.

Schuchardt mobilises etymological knowledge to unpack a transoceanic sweep compressed within "Liplap", a creolised word for creole identity. Drawing on philological methods of the neogrammarians he trained alongside at Leipzig University, he includes East Frisian "labben" and German "labbern", as its cognates (9). It is important to note the wider context. These Indo-European connections were feeding into the racialisation of language families via the visual metaphor of the tree, first popularised by philological development of the *stemma codicum* to present relationships between variant manuscripts of a text, on which linguistic family trees were subsequently modelled.[11] Schuchardt initially calls up that metaphor in his own understanding of Malayo-Portuguese; the very first line of *Kreolische Studien IX* contains an observation on the wide and deep roots ("weite und tiefe Wurzeln") struck ("geschlagen") by the Portuguese language in maritime South East Asia (1). However, this opening soon yields to affiliative vectors for creologenesis. Escaping the tree metaphor signalling genetic descent, Schuchardt's analysis begins recalling, instead, his collaborator Johannes Schmidt's wave model for linguistic innovation (Schmidt and Schuchardt 1873; see also Matauschek 2014, 252). "Liplap", for instance, becomes unmoored from the Indian Ocean by the echoes of Germanic cognates, washing up on the shores of the North Sea, even as Batavia was transplanted from the latter to become a place-name in the former. Simultaneously, transoceanic currents tug "liplap" back to Java, as Schuchardt explicates its oscillating vowels through Malayan reduplication in forms such as "tjola-tjala". Through mimicry of this structure, he suggests, the Dutch words 'lip' and 'lap' combine in an altogether new formation (1890, 9–10).

As Isabella Matauschek convincingly demonstrates, Schuchardt's interest in Malayo-Portuguese arose from his distaste for philological methods that were becoming paradigmatic through the influential epistemic model of the Indo-European genealogical tree (Matauschek 2014, 252; see also Ploog 2015). The consequent racialisation of linguistic interconnections led to the intellectual devaluing of Indo-European languages and their relegation to lower or less-evolved cultural status. Notions of superiority and corruption were transformed into heuristic tools, and critical editions of manuscripts of all kinds increasingly devoted to weeding out

---

11 The *stemma codicum* originated in humanist scholarship on the New Testament and was popularised by classical philologist Karl Lachman; see, in this context, Most 2005. The first person to use it graphically to explain relationships between languages and build linguistic family trees thereby was August Schleicher. For a fuller account of these developments, and their implications for philology in the service of colonialism and empire, see Kabir (2011, 85–88).

"interpolations" and instating "corrections" in efforts to extricate putatively "clean" originals. Turning to Malayo-Portuguese illustrates Schuchardt's overall effort to generate linguistic taxonomies alternative to the universalist position being granted to the tree model by the Neogrammarians. He broke ranks in seeking out languages formed through the human necessity to communicate in and through adversity and risk. The resistance of these contact languages to arboreal taxonomies in turn demanded non-arboreal heuristic structures for their analysis. Hence the violence of "geschlagen" ("struck") that Schuchardt ascribed to the rooting of Portuguese in the Malay-speaking world, is replaced a year later by a gentler image drawn from rice cultivation methods of monsoon Asia (Schuchardt 1891, 199). Now, Schuchardt compares his encounter with language fragments from this world to the rice grains scattered ("ausgestreut") during the first phase of those methods. The second phase, of transplanting rice saplings into neat rows or *sawah*, is how he understands his own assembling of those fragments.

3 *Kong alegriea / voll Lust*: Becoming creole

This image of the *sawah* appears in a review dated 1891 that Schuchardt offered on his own work on Malayo-Portuguese – an unusual academic decision to which I shall return below. As a metaphor, it fits quite well his adaptation of handwritten manuscripts he had assembled from contacts in South-East Asia, for printed material fit for philological purpose (Twenty-four pages of discussion on the historical and social context which the Dutch found in the East Indies are followed by over a hundred pages of texts of verse, prose, and word lists from Tugu and Batavia). Variant versions of the verse fragments, each marked by a Greek letter, occupy vertical columns spread out over facing pages. For the prose, Malayo-Portuguese and Malay versions of the same tracts occupy symmetrical vertical columns on the page. The vocabulary lists (Malayo-Portuguese with Malay translations) are presented in slimmer columns, two sets to a page. The verticality of these differently sized columns is the philological equivalent of the *sawah*. It is offset by the horizontal sweep of explicatory notes which contain the critical apparatus. This presentation is visually reminiscent of standard philological transformation of the vagaries of manuscript to cleaned-up pages of print. Simultaneously, from between the rectilinear march of lines and columns, something seemingly contrary to philological work seeps out – an affect that, following the declaration of the very first verse Schuchardt prints under "Lieder" ("songs"), I want to call 'alegria'.[12]

---

[12] For an explication of his methods and apparatus, see Schuchardt (1890, 19–23).

"Alegria", Portuguese for "joy", appears in two versions of this verse, quatrain 1, within the construction "kong alegriea" (24), which Schuchardt translates as "voll Lust" (32). The German word, *Lust*, like *alegria*, encompasses joy, pleasure, and desire. The verse's account of social dancing on Friday evening moves "alegreia" from individual to collective joy. Allusions to quadrille formation are elaborated by Schuchardt in his notes: the dance is "wechselreich" ("full of turns and variations", 32); a "leader" ("Führer") "joyfully guides" ("guidoor kong alegreia", 24) the dancers through these variations. These details vivify the verse, releasing its graphic inscription of *alegria* into an embodied affect transmitted through the dancers. A community of and in dance is brought into being. Schuchardt continues on this theme in his notes on the word "kaverinjoe/kaferinjo" in quatrain 3 (24). Usually rendered "kafrinho" in Portuguese-influenced orthography, the term (which occurs in both feminine and masculine endings) is lexically a diminutive of "kaffir", an Indian Ocean term for "African"; it also names an Indian Ocean creole quadrille, memorialising the creolisation process in its referencing of Africancity.[13] Drawing on all these dimensions, Schuchardt reconstructs a "young Kaffer girl" ("Kafferlein", 32, 33), references "an old Portuguese dance" ("einen alten portugiesischen Tanz", 32) attested in Ambon as *Kafarinju* and in Timor as *kafarinja*, and mentions his personal collection of erotic songs in Ceylon-Portuguese titled "Cafrinha" (32). In spinning out these embodied, affective connotations, particularly of words he finds difficult to explain philologically, Schuchardt's critical apparatus becomes a *creolising* apparatus.

"Sehr räthselhaft" ("very puzzling", 37): one can see Schuchardt shaking his head as he pores over his materials. "Ist mir dunkel" ("I find it obscure", 39–40, *et passim*), he frequently exclaims in the notes. Freely admitting the limits of exegesis with regard to creole languages, Schuchardt attempts neither to reconstruct a pure version from available variants, nor reconcile their divergences through lexical or syntactic 'corrections'. Instead, through these words he conjures up copious details of a lived world-- of fruit, flowers, vegetables, and edibles mentioned in the verses. The discussion of what kind of fish might "pees porkoe" denote takes up almost a full page (34), going through multiple translations in Malay, French, German, and Portuguese, scientific taxonomies, as well as taste and size, before settling on the central European variety, "Kaulbarsch", which came to him in an epiphany: "So übersetze ich im letzten Augenblick" ("that's how I translated it at the last minute", 34, n. 1). Matters of taste fascinate him, whether it be the

---

[13] For a detailed discussion of the relationship between *kaffer* and *kafrinho/a*, including all spelling variations, see Kabir (2021, 20–22); for Indian Ocean creole quadrilles, see Kabir (2020), and for the Kafrinho/a as Indian Ocean dance and music genre, see Radhakrishnan (2021).

sour fruits of tropical trees, unfamiliar food combinations such as manioc from Bengal "enjoyed" ("genossen", 34) with Chinese crabs; or rice with sambal, "eine Reiszuspeise, deren Hauptbestandtheile fein geriebener spanischer Pfeffer und Salz sind" ("a condiment for rice whose main ingredients are finely grated Spanish pepper and salt", 40). Unfamiliar words are compared across the board to cognates and direct translations, only to lead us away from standardisation towards profusion and variegation. Schuchardt, who never left Europe, revels vicariously in the creole sensorium; but it is his method that allows him to extract its *alegria* from between the lines.

4 *Tischtuch von Pisangblättern*: Performing creole

This method deals with variation as polysemy, and difference as variety; its hermeneutic intention is to expand rather than reduce meaningful possibilities. We can observe this method at work through certain figures evoked in the *Lieder* that he explicates in apparently racialised terms. His "Kafferlein" is joined by a "Djondivrouwe" (25), a term he explains as Dutch "jongejufvrouw", and translates as "reinblütige Europäerin" ("pure-blooded European woman", 33). The mention of a "tolbaan" ("turban", 26) in one verse evokes "Mohren" ("Moors", or "Muslims", 33), even while the replacement of "tolbaan" by "topi" (glossed by Schuchardt as "europäischer Hut", or "European hat", 34) in the corresponding verse of the Malay variant,[14] evokes another European, male and hat-wearing this time. However, these categories are never reorganised into binaries that will yield a master-category of Creole. Rather, like the broadcasted rice grains, they are "ausgestreut" ("scattered") fragments of a sensuous world that break out of their philological rearrangement in the sawah-like rows and columns on the page. Dancing, singing, flirting, making merry, they spread newness and innovation through the streets of Batavia and Tugu: "roewa per roewa laba noba" (26; In Schuchardt's translation, "Strasse für Strasse trägt er die Neuigkeit", 36). Schuchardt's apparatus offers enchanted entry-points into these contact zones of improvisation and encounter, whether those be the imagined streets or indeed the "Tischtuch von Pisangblättern" ("tablecloth of Pisang leaves", 41): his translation of the phrase "taflak fola figèra" (30), where a Dutch-derived name ("taflak") for a European household item, is recreated through dried tropical leaves described in Portuguese-derived lexis ("fola" from "folha", 'leaf"; "figéra" from "figuera", "figtree").

---

14 See the four versions of quatrain 8 across Schuchardt (1890, 26–27) where "tolbaan" in the three Creole versions is replaced by "topi" in the Malay counterpart.

Alongside this linguistically and materially creolised tablecloth, the verse assembles "oenga rabana oenga gitèra / Oenga alfada oenga istèra" (30), which, Schuchardt translates as "ein Tamburin, eine Guitarre | Ein Kissen, eine Matte" (a tambourine, a guitar, a pillow, a mat, 41). These fragments of a creole habitus connect the transculturating worlds of the Mediterranean Sea with the Atlantic and Indian Oceans. "Rabanna" recalls the Mascarene percussion instrument *ravane*, and the guitar belongs to a long history of stringed instruments evolving between Iberia, Andalusia, and Asia. Although Schuchardt does not gloss the musical instruments, similar pathways of cultural encounter are opened up by his explications of the soft furnishings that also crowd this verse: "alfada wie auf (as in) Ceylon (alfàde: Moraes Silva) > almohada", he reminds us (41), although "almohada" itself is left uncommented upon, probably because its Arabic derivation would have been only too obvious to his readers. Philological method is mobilised to trace not the roots that anchor words to old worlds, but the routes through which they travel to, and make, new ones. Schuchardt compares different attestations to calibrate semantic shifts that occur in the process, often within the same lexical fields–as with the possibilities for "pees porkoe" that he offers, which include the near-identical German "Seeschwein" and "Meerschwein", French "marsouin", and Dutch "zeevarken" (all of which mean, more or less, "sea-swine", 34). His intention is always to proliferate with nuance the lexical field in question, rather than collapse difference by amalgamating nuance into pre-existing taxonomies.

"Diese halbkreolische Art" ("this half-Creole type") is how Schuchardt refers to the creole verses he transcribes and translates in *Kreolische Studien IX* (1891, 199). This phrase implies neither binaries nor essences that creolise together into stable cultural products. Instead, it indicates a range of creolised and creolising possibilities that emerge out of the unpredictable shimmer of contact. It is apposite to recall here that Schuchardt's interest in creolisation as a linguistic process arose out of his investigations of Lingua Franca as a historical contact language of the Mediterranean world. The possibility of drawing from it lingua franca as a universalist "paradigm for understanding the dynamics of trafficking and translation" lay in the future (Allan and Benigni 2017, 3) yet Schuchardt certainly pioneered the use of the historical Lingua Franca as a tool "to destabilize the presumptions of coherent national literary, linguistic or cultural traditions" (Allan and Begnini 2017, 5).[15] In so doing, he was not, to return to Wilder's words with which I closed the introduction to this essay, merely "unmasking universalisms as covert European particularisms"; neither was he propagating, I would argue, a minor form of universalism as

---

[15] On the distinction between the historical Lingua Franca and the theoretical concept of lingua franca, see Brosch (2015).

a substitute for a universalism unmarked, but silently assuming "major" status. Rather, his investigations performed creolisation as deconstructive method, with a built-in capacity to undo the deleterious consequences of scholarship driven by a hunger for universalism: "Our task consists solely in understanding a new structure: as for example the one underlying the Lingua Franca– as a function of an idiosyncratic process" (Schuchardt 1980, 68–69).

5 *Sind nicht durch eine feste Grenze zu trennen*: Re-creolising creole

In favouring idiosyncrasy over standardisation, Schuchardt took intellectual risks that did not pay off in his lifetime. As mentioned above, he had to take the solipsistic step of reviewing his own study of Malayo-Portuguese, because specialists neither of Romance languages nor of Malay were willing to engage with it. We note the classic creole conundrum: too much in-between-ness can leave 'creole' forever between two stools. The dissemination of his ideas has suffered a similar fate. Although Schuchardt has been given his rightful place in historical linguistics by much later generations of scholars (Matauschek 2014, 246–7; 261–62; Castro, Cardoso et al. 2023), his work has never been considered within wider discussions of creolisation as a theory of cultural encounter. It is time to re-engage with it, however. Schuchardt's investigations into contact languages have the potential to intervene within several debates in intellectual history and cultural theory. On the one hand, they constitute the perfect lever to prise open the nationalist and territorialist foreclosing of philology as a discipline in order to let in an alternative "philology of the sea" (Allan and Benigni, 2017). Close-reading him, as I do here, therefore, is one response to Shih and Lionnet's search for new analytics that mobilise creolisation to make minor formations into method and theory. On the other, Schuchardt's emphasis on an epistemic continuum of go-between vehicular languages, including Creoles, pidgins, and Lingua Franca, enables us re-evaluate debates over moving creolisation from the domain of linguistic taxonomy to the understanding of culture more broadly understood.

Ulf Hannerz's proclamation that "we are all being creolised", and Stephan Palmié's scepticism regarding such "proliferation of concepts of creolisation" (Hannerz 1987, 557; Palmié 2006, 434), articulate the opposing positions in this debate. Both come with problems: Hannerz's universalising embrace of "becoming-creole" is susceptible to Palmié's critique of the theoretical extrapolation of localised and historically situated social usages of creole. But if Hannerz embraces uncritically the fuzzy boundaries between "creole/creolised/in creolization" and "noncreole, uncreolized or–creolizing", as Palmié decries, the latter, in turn, draws too rigid a boundary between language and culture when he separates creolistics from the examination of cultural processes (Palmié 2006, 434). Yet their respective positions converge in a shared inability to recognise that the transformative potential of creole phenomena arises precisely from their escape of both universalism and particularism, and a corresponding neglect or, in the case of Palmié, even misreading, of Schuchardt. While Palmié agrees that "that the work of Schuchardt and his contemporaries in creating creolistics had the potential to disrupt the race=culture=language equation and reigning arboreal, proto-Darwininan metaphorics of an emergent historical linguistics," he erroneously reduces Schuchardt's methods to "isolating linguistic defects and reifying what a proper language should look like, how it ought to be acquired, and who should be speaking it" (Palmié 2006, 444). Hannerz, on his part, wants to press the "creolist point of view" in service of "a macro-anthropology of culture which takes into account the world system and its centre-periphery relation", but he cannot surmount the binaries this view rests on (Hannerz 1987, 556).

To return to Schuchardt, then, is to appreciate an intellectual honesty and avoidance of "ideologically charged terminology that Hugo Cardoso observes in his treatment of the Creole of Diu (2018, 24) along with a cluster of hermeneutic approaches that Schuchardt shared with fellow-enthusiasts for the variegated world of Luso-Asian creoles. Like the governor of Diu Perry da Câmara, whose inputs were essential for his work on Diu creoles, Schuchardt's search was for the "solução" (solution) to lexical puzzles, not their correction (Cardoso 2018, 24). Most importantly, like the Goan-born philologist Sebastião Rodolfo Delgado, Schuchardt interpreted available evidence in terms of a linguistic continuum rather than discrete, segmented, and compartmentalised language-forms of which Creole was one version (Cardoso 2018, 20).[16] Indeed, as he clarifies in his auto-review of 1891, Schuchardt had found it impossible to draw a firm boundary ("nicht durch eine feste Grenze zu trennen") between Malay, 'Portuguese, and indeed any other linguistic elements from the welter of materials contained in the manuscripts he put into print as *Kreolische Studien IX*.[17] Hannerz's recognition of a creolising spectrum of culture is closer to the ontology of Schuchardt's being-creole than is Palmié's dismissal of mere congeries of historically contingent local "individualities" (Hannerz 1987, 552, 555; Palmié 2006, 443), yet Schuchardt's achievement was to enjoy and

---

16 In fact, when later, Dalgado published his article on the "Indo-Portuguese dialect" of the Bombay region, he, too, according to Cardoso (2018), described the socio-linguistic landscape there in terms of a "linguistic continuum".

17 Schuchardt (1891, 200): "wie sich die speciell malaioportugiesischen Wörter von den allgemein nicht durch eine feste Grenze zu trennen sind, so auch nicht die letzteren von den allen Portugiesen ganz geläufigen Wörtern asiatischen Ursprungs."

work from the very "congeries" Palmié berates. On his creolising spectrum, linguistic variegation does not disaggregate into formative constituents from which the mechanisms of creole can be reconstructed, but possesses ontological validity within, and as, "the inner form of creole".[18]

In this recognition of inner form, we can also sense Schuchardt's desire to compensate for that which he never experienced: the sounds of the creole habitus he was so passionate about recreating. Schuchardt may have dismissed the gulf between the oral and the learned-on grounds of pragmatism: the situation was not so dire, he declared, that he needed to rush off on a voyage halfway across the world to listen to creole languages being spoken (Schuchardt 1891, 199). Yet, lurking here is also a romantic streak, whereby the philologist, like the poet John Keats in "Ode on a Grecian Urn", accepts that "heard melodies are sweet, but those unheard / are far sweeter. . . ." Schuchardt mobilises all his senses to enter the creole languages he was drawn to by the need to surpass universalist philological principles. Indeed, he demonstrates that going beyond universalism is to creolise it. A *creolising universality* is the result. Reading Schuchardt is to obtain from him the resources to *re-creolise creole* as a concept, and creolisation as process and praxis. Schuchardt was attracted to this word and its worlds, because of the potential they bear as antidotes to reification through binaries. Creolising universality is to use creole to navigate a route through the Scylla and Charybdis of "major" and "minor". "Time to overcome the obsessions and to get to an end with the *European tristezza*", as Messling and Hofmann declare, in their allied quest for a "common negative universal that can serve as a moral fundament of a world-society" (2021, 35). In the words of the French Caribbean band Kassav', singing in Antillean Creole, Schuchardt finds for us "the key that opens the door"–the door to creolised worlds and *mentalités*, the door beyond tristezza.[19] Using that key, we pass through that door, to dance in the streets *kong alegriea* and spread the good news of becoming-creole: "roewa per roewa laba noba."

---

18 Schuchardt (1891, 200): "Als meine Hauptaufgabe habe ich es betrachtet die Einwirkung des Malaiischen in der innern Form des Kreolischen nachzuweisen."
19 Kassav', "Kavalyé o Dam": "Maman ma trouvé klé-la / klé-la pou ouvé pot-la / pot-la si lakarayib" ('*Maman* found for me the key, the key that opens the door–the door of the Caribbean').

References

Allan, Michael and Elisabetta Benigni. "Lingua Franca: Towards a Philology of the Sea: Introduction." *Philological Encounters* 2.1–2 (2017): 1–5.
Bakker, Peter and Aymeric Daval-Markussen. "Creole Studies in the 21st Century: A Brief Presentation of the Special Issue on Creole Languages." *Acta Linguistica Hafniensia* 45:2 (2013): 141–150.
Boatcă, Manuela. "Thinking Europe Otherwise: Lessons from the Caribbean." *Current Sociology* 69. 3 (2021): 389–414.
Boatcă, Manuela and Anca Parvulescu. "Creolizing Transylvania: Notes on Coloniality and Inter-Imperiality." *History of the Present* 10.1 (2020): 9–27.
Brosch, Cyril. "On the Conceptual History of the Term Lingua Franca." *Apples: Journal of Applied Language Studies* (2015): 71–85.
Buck-Morss, Susan. "Hegel and Haiti." *Critical Inquiry* 26.4 (2000): 821–65.
Cardoso, Hugo C. "The Creole of Diu in Hugo Schuchardt's archive." *South Asian Studies* 34.1 (2018): 17–32.
Castro, Ivo, Hugo C. Cardoso, Alan Baxter, Alexander Adelaar, and Gijs Koster. Eds. *Livro de Pantuns, Um Manuscrito Asiático do Museo Nacional de Arqueologia, Lisboa/ Book of Pantuns, An Asian Manuscript of the National Museum of Archeology, Lisbon.* Lisboa: Imprensa Nacional, 2022.
Cheah, Pheng. "Crisis of Money." *The Creolization of Theory*. Eds. Françoise Lionnet and Shu-mei Shih. Durham/NC: Duke University Press, 2011. 83–111.
Deleuze, Gilles and Félix Guattari. *Kafka: Towards a Minor Literature*. Transl. Dana Polan. minneapolis: University of Minnesota, 1986 [1975].
Fernandes, Gonçalo. "The First List of Malayalam Words at the End of 15th Century by a Portuguese Seaman." *Boletim do Museu Paraense Emílio Goeldi. Ciências Humanas* 11 (2016): 793–809.
Halikowski-Smith, Stefan. "Languages of Subalternity and Collaboration: Portuguese in English Settlements across the Bay of Bengal, 1620–1800." *International Journal of Maritime History* 28.2 (2016): 237–267.
Hannerz, Ulf. "The World in Creolisation." *Africa* 57.4 (1987): 546–559.
Hoogervorst, Tom. "Sailors, Tailors, Cooks, and Crooks: On Loanwords and Neglected Lives in Indian Ocean Ports." *Itinerario* 42.3 (2018): 516–548.
Kabir, Ananya Jahanara. "Whitley Stokes, Scribbles and the Scholarly Apparatus." *Ireland, India, England: The Tripartite Life of Whitley Stokes*. Eds. Elizabeth Boyle and Paul Russell. Dublin: Four Courts Press, 2011. 78–97.
——— . "Creolization as Balancing Act in the Transoceanic Quadrille: Choreogenesis, Incorporation, Memory, Market." *Atlantic Studies: Global Currents* 17.1 (2020): 135–157.
——— . "Rapsodia Ibero-Indiana: Transoceanic Creolization and the Mando of Goa." *Modern Asian Studies* 55.5 (2021): 1581–1636.
Kehoe, Marsely L. "Dutch Batavia: Exposing the Hierarchy of the Dutch Colonial City." *Journal of Historians of Netherlandish Art* 7.1 (2015): 1–35.
Matauschek, Isabella. "Malay-Latin of the Pacific: Hugo Schuchardt's Pursuit of Language Mixing and Creole Languages in the Malay World." *Indonesia and the Malay World* 42 (2014): 246–267.
Messling, Markus, and Franck Hofmann. "On the ends of universalism." *The Epoch of Universalism / L'époque de l'universalisme, 1769–1989*. Eds. Markus Messling and Franck Hofmann. Berlin / Boston: De Gruyter, 2021. 1–39.
Most, Glenn W. "Editor's Introduction." *The Genesis of Lachmann's Method*. Ed. Sebastian Timpanaro. Transl. Glenn. W. Most. Chicago: Chicago University Press, 2005. 1–32.

Mulvey, Laura. "Xala, Ousmane Sembene 1976: the Carapace that Failed." *Third Text* 5.16–17 (1991): 19–37.

Palmié, Stephan. "Creolization and its Discontents." *Ann. Rev. Anthropol.* 35 (2006): 433–456.

Paluszek, Przemysław. "De Mythische 'Batavia' in de Gouden Eeuw– Een Poging tot Reconstructie: Het Scheppen van de Nationale Ruimte." *Neerlandica Wratislaviensia* 23 (2013): 53–73.

Parvulescu, Anca and Manuela Boatcă. *Creolizing the Modern: Transylvania across Empires*. Ithaca/NY: Cornell University Press, 2022.

Ploog, Katja, "Le 'Negerportugiesisch' de H. Schuchardt et la dynamique des langues." *Etudes créoles* 33.2 (2015): 1–27.

Pratt, Mary Louise. *Imperial Eyes: Travel Writing and Transculturation*. New York, London: Routledge, 2007.

Radhakrishnan, Mahesh. "'Shake it and Dance'. Portuguese Burgher Identity and the Performance of Káfriinha." *The Asia Pacific Journal of Anthropology* 22.2–3 (2021): 140–161.

Schmidt, Johannes, and Hugo Schuchardt. *Die Verwantschaftsverhältnisse Der Indogermanischen Sprachen: And Über Die Lautgesetze: Gegen Die Junggrammatiker*. Cambridge: Cambridge University Press, 2013 [1872].

Schuchardt, Hugo. "Kreolische Studien IX. Über das Malaioportugiesische von Batavia und Tugu." *Sitzungsberichte der Philosophisch-Historischen Classe der Kaiserlichen Academy der Wissenschaften* 122.9 (1890): 1–256.

———. "Review of 'Kreolische Studien IX'." *Literaturblatt für germanische und romanische Philologie* 12 (1891): 199–206.

———. "The Lingua Franca." *Pidgin and Creole Languages: Selected Essays*. Ed. and transl. Glenn G. Gilbert. Cambridge: Cambridge University Press, 1980. 65–89.

Shih, Shu-mei, and Françoise Lionnet. "Introduction." *The Creolization of Theory*. Eds. Françoise Lionnet and Shu-Mei Shih. Durham/NC: Duke University Press, 2011. 1–34.

Van der Velde, Paul. *Life under the Palms: The Sublime Life of Anti-Colonialist Jacob Haafner*. Trans. Liesbeth Bennink. Singapore: NUS Press, 2020.

Wickramasinghe, Nira. *Slave in a Palanquin*. New York: Columbia University Press, 2020.

Wilder, Gary. *Freedom Time*. Durham/NC: Duke University Press, 2015.

Yule, Henry and Arthur Coke Burnell. *Hobson-Jobson: being a Glossary of Anglo-Indian Colloquial Words and Phrases and of Kindred Terms Etymological, Historical, Geographical and Discursive*. London: J. Murray, 1886.

Part IV: **Restitutions and Reparations**

Quatrième partie : **Restitutions et réparations**

Bénédicte Savoy
Statues Also Trample

Abstract: This contribution gives back to the objects exhibited in the great European museums a part of their history, a history of the violence of their dispossession. It renders visible some of the internal contradictions and flagrant tensions that constituted the very idea of the museum itself, taking as a starting point the statue of Jean-François Champollion in the courtyard of the Collège de France in Paris. Champollion's statue is both an unbearable and precious document, and it says more about the history of heritage in Europe than most books on the subject. It always reminds us that in the Western world, the shiny, golden medal of culture and knowledge has a reverse side of symbolic and real violence. We must strive to think them together, as a single contradictory unit. At the museum, this means seeing the objects where they are, and where they no longer are. This introspection is an effort consisting of collectively tying these objects in our museums back to the history that brought them to our countries, and back to the people who now live where they used to be.

Keywords: Jean-François Champollion, Collège de France, Louvre, restitution, museums, Egypt

Upon entering the Collège de France – not in the institutional sense but physically, with one's feet, body, eyes, all senses and preoccupations of the moment – one is greeted, at the middle of the main courtyard, by a statue of Frédéric-Auguste Bartholdi, the famous designer of the Statue of Liberty. It represents Jean-François Champollion. Everybody knows Champollion. Born during the French Revolution, he was too young to participate in Bonaparte's expedition in Egypt, but he was an auditor at the Collège de France from his teenage years, was appointed curator of Egyptian collections at the Charles X Museum (the Louvre) at the age of thirty-six, and became the first person to hold a Chair of Egyptology at the Collège de France a few years later. He perfectly represents a generation of Europeans who were actors and witnesses of the great boom in universal museums in nineteenth-century Europe.

Note: This article is an excerpt from my inaugural lecture at the Collège de France on 30 March 2017, originally published in French with a preface by Antoine Compagnon (Savoy 2017).

Translated by Liz Carey Libbrecht

It is hard for me to describe the stupor, or rather the incredulous dismay that I experienced when, in the Collège de France's courtyard, I looked at Champollion's statue for the first time. I mean, *really* looked at it. I was early for an appointment. I had seen it a thousand times before, of course, but one tends not to look much or well at these monuments to national glories that the Third Republic has scattered across our cities. They were commissioned by public institutions and are outstanding examples of the alliance between ideology and aesthetics, especially when, in the late nineteenth century, the State used them to reach the ordinary man and woman on the street. Nowadays, we see them without seeing them. They are part of the "urban landscape" so aptly described in the late 1970s by Maurice Agulhon who, then already, noticed that public statuary was looked at "neither by drivers who go by fast, nor by pedestrians who, for many reasons, are no longer inclined to stroll" (Agulhon 1978, 165).

I had a bit of time and I looked at Champollion. The statue represents a monumental 2.40-meter-tall young man, who seems to be about thirty years old. He is wearing the tight-fitting frock coat, skin-tight breeches, and short riding boots that were worn in Europe around 1800. He has sideburns. He is resting on his elbow, his chin on his hand, and gazing at the floor in an indefinable manner, so altered by weather and pollution is the surface of his face. The white marble of which he is made is abraded and dirty. His left leg is very high, like that of a traveller who set his foot on a stone during a break. But his foot is not set on a stone (Figure 1). It is a decapitated statue of Ancient Egypt, the majestic and broken head of a pharaoh who could be Ramses II. The statue's pedestal bears Champollion's name in large letters. On the right-hand side, the work is dated and signed: Auguste Bartholdi, 1875 (Vidal and Kempf 1994).

The scholar's boot on the pharaoh's sacred head... Upon seeing this, I was seized by a dread that Walter Benjamin (and my German friend, scholar Karine Winkelvoss) call the "memory of the unseen" (see Winkelvoss and Beyer 16–17 May 2014; see Winkelvoss 2018, 185–197).[1] The return of repressed colonialism in a fortuitous crossing of divergent timelines: mine, that of a Berlin-Parisian mortal of the year 2017 who has never really paid attention to the political iconography of great men on the street and is waiting for an appointment at the Collège de France; and his, that of a century-and-a-half-old marble statue which, for decades, freely and openly, has been telling anyone who would hear it the same story that it was already telling in 1875, when France and Europe dominated the world. In Western art, the iconography of the foot on the severed head is kept for representations of

---

[1] Benjamin talks of "images which we have never seen before we remember them" (*Bilder, die wir nie sahen, ehe wir uns ihrer erinnerten*) (Benjamin 2005).

David vanquishing Goliath; or, when the head belongs to a ferocious beast, to images of archangels or saints slaying the demon. What was Bartholdi trying to say? I do not know.

Figure 1: Champollion, marble statue of Bartholdi, drawing by Sellier. *Le Magasin pittoresque* (vol. XLIV, July 1876, 233).

What I do know, however, is that Champollion's statue says more about the history of heritage in Europe than any book, any class or any inaugural lecture on the subject. It is like an allegory of that history, in the oldest sense of the term, which meant 'to speak loudly in public, in a different mode'. To me, what it lays out for all to see, with its made-to-last statuary insolence, is the alliance between the three libidos: the one that is sensually directed towards the beauty of the pharaoh's face; the one that is intellectually committed, together with the young scholar, to deciphering the remains of a lost civilisation; and the one that is manifested, with a foot on a head, in an act of domination.

Looking at it today, Champollion's statue is both an unbearable and precious document. It publicly invites us, in one of the institutions most able to do so, to think the un-thought aspects of Europe's heritage and museums.[2] It reminds us at all times, under open skies, that in the Western world, the shiny, golden medal of culture and knowledge almost always has a reverse side of symbolic and real violence; that there is a diurnal side to heritage in Europe as well as a nocturnal

---

[2] Cf. the contradictions of European universalism that Markus Messling develops through Bartoldi's statue as already inherent in Champollion's scientific thought; see above all Messling (2022, also 2015).

side; that these two aspects are inseparable from each other; that we must strive to think them together, as a single contradictory unit. At the museum, this means seeing the objects where they are, and simultaneously seeing them where they no longer are, that is to say, in the regions from which they were taken. It means enjoying the beauty and the knowledge that have been accumulated in our cities over centuries, but enjoying them with full awareness of the conditions in which these objects were collected, in asymmetrical economic, military, and epistemological contexts. It means rendering visible, in order to master them better, the internal contradictions and the glaring tensions that have been at work in the very idea of museums since its origin. It means paying close attention, in this context, to the gazes and voices of the dispossessed, and keeping in mind what Barbara Cassin and her research team have so convincingly shown: that the words *museum* and *heritage* and the associated concepts, are among the most eminently untranslatable terms in European languages (Cassin and Wozny 2014).

Champollion was four years old when France implemented its doctrine of liberated heritage, according to which the arts – as a product of liberty – should be gathered in the country of liberty, that is to say, in France. He was six when the Directory ordered that hugely famous ancient statues discovered in Rome during the Renaissance and permanently kept in the Pope's collections ever since, the *Apollo Belvedere* and *Laocoön and His Sons*, be confiscated from the Vatican and transported to Paris to be exhibited in the Louvre. He was seven when *The Wedding at Cana*, painted by Veronese for the Venetian monastery of San Giorgio Maggiore, was removed from its refectory wall and taken to France. He was eleven when the British army confiscated part of the discoveries made in Egypt from Bonaparte's scholars, among which was the famous Rosetta Stone, which was sent to London as a military trophy and exhibited ever since in the British Museum. He was twenty-six when the British government decided to buy the Parthenon frieze's hundred and twenty tons of marble, of which the diplomat Lord Elgin organised and funded the transfer from Greece to England, and which Athens is still claiming back to this day.

In the nineteenth century, the French triad of museums, nation, and heritage, so masterfully studied by Dominique Poulot (1995), extended its grip to the whole of Europe. Berlin, London, Paris, Vienna, and Saint Petersburg, most notably, invested dizzying sums in developing their museums, which are now *our* museums. They would spy on one another. The very young disciplines of art history, archaeology, and ethnology each cast their nets on Europe and the world. In unified Italy, the museums of London, Paris, and Berlin scoured the art market and vied with one another in ingenuity to obtain authorisations to export major artworks. The Spanish Golden Age fascinated northern capitals. In only a few years, Berlin gathered the largest collection of Rembrandt paintings ever formed outside of the

Netherlands. During the same period, the last quarter of the nineteenth century, an elite of private collectors from the cosmopolitan upper class of the business bourgeoisie acquired ancient artworks of extraordinary worth on the art market, and gathered world-class collections in all of Europe's large cities – including Constantinople/Istanbul, Moscow, and Athens. Decorative arts, medieval sculpture and silver and goldsmiths' works, the arts of Islam and of the Far East, paintings from the Italian Renaissance and seventeenth-century Dutch prints and drawings, would compete on the art market for the attention of these well-informed and wealthy collectors, who were often motivated by philanthropic and patriotic sentiments. Whether one was French, British, or German, investing in a collection of ancient art was then not only a sign of culture and taste, but also an act of patriotism, with governments encouraging collectors to bequeath or donate pieces from their collections to national museums, and collectors largely adhering to this system (Long 2001, 45–5, 2009, 84–104).

With, amongst others, Adolphe Schloss, David and Pierre David-Weill, Alphonse Kahn in Paris, Calouste Gulbenkian and the Rothschilds in Paris and London, James Simon in Berlin, the Camondos in Istanbul and later in Paris, the most prominent collectors of these days were often from Jewish families that regularly gratified public museums with spectacular donations. This part of history is overlooked all too often: these collections, built between the 1860s and the beginning of World War I, were precisely those that were systematically despoiled for racial reasons in Nazi Germany and the countries that it occupied in the late 1930s and early 1940s.

This explains that what in France is called the Musées nationaux récuperation (MNR – "National Recovery Museums"), about 2,000 artworks despoiled from French Jewish families during the Occupation, returned to the French state after the war, but which the latter has not yet given back to the legal successors of the families in question, are largely composed of decorative art objects, drawings, prints, precious tapestries, and paintings by former masters: Rubens, Boucher, Chardin, Fragonard, and so on. To read the MNR's catalogue – and to remember that, on top of these 2,000 works, the French state recovered another 15,000 from Germany after 1945, which it sold for the benefit of the administration of state-owned real estate, the *Domaines* ("POP: la plateforme ouverte du patrimoine") – is to make an impressive dive into the wealth and quality of nineteenth-century French private collections.

So, in the nineteenth century, when the European art market was expanding at unprecedented rates, the improvements to railways and steamboats, along with an acceleration of trade and competition between European powers in the colonies, made the heritage of mankind a major political stake for national assertion policies in Europe. The history of art has never been a neutral science. Similarly, as Alain

Schnapp (1997) and Ève Gran-Aymerich (2007) have shown, ethnology and archaeology have been part (as they are now) of precise political, diplomatic, and military contexts, in which tourism and religion have played an increasingly important part. Starting in the 1850s, biblical archaeology spread to all the territories mentioned in the Bible: Egypt, Mesopotamia and current Lebanon, Syria, Jordan, and Israel.

Those were golden times for European museums, when their collections would fill up with papyrus fragments and thousands of cuneiform tabs and rolls, which constituted such a wealth of text that archaeologists are still far from having deciphered them all to this day. In the same period, the Ottoman Empire sold spectacular remains of Greek civilisation in Asia Minor to archaeologists from European capitals, starting with Berlin. The ruins of the Pergamon Altar and the market gates of Miletus, for instance, were sent in hundreds of wooden crates from modern-day Turkey to be added to the antique collections of Berlin's Museum Island, where they were reconstructed in bold and innovative ways. Colonies in Africa, Asia, and Oceania also paid a heavy tribute to Europe in terms of heritage.

In the nineteenth century, artworks were collected not only during scientific campaigns, but also during wars for territory and trade. During the Second Opium War in China, the French and British army jointly pillaged treasures in the Summer Palace in Beijing. The most spectacular pieces taken then were deposited at Empress Eugénie's "Chinese museum" in Fontainebleau. Part of them can still be seen there to this day.

In 1897, the British army led an infamous punitive expedition in the Kingdom of Benin, in the south of current Nigeria, which marked the arrival in Europe of a body of works commonly known as the "Benin Bronzes". Over the past few years these artworks have been the subject of claims, which European museums and governments have systematically turned down. These bronzes are a set of several hundred metal fragments produced between the sixteenth and eighteenth centuries, richly decorated with animal and human figures in the round (Figure 2). They were taken from their original sites, transported to London in around 1900, deposited in part at the British Museum and, for the rest of them, sold on the art market, where the museums of Berlin and Hamburg acquired many. Nowadays, these bronzes are mainly owned by the museums of London, Oxford, Hamburg, Berlin, Dresden, Leipzig, and New York.

When the bronzes entered European capitals, around 1900, the Kingdom of Benin was presented – and this is a quote – as a "cultural exception" on the African continent; with a 1932 German article going as far as to call it "close to a civilization".³ Astounded art historians saluted the virtuosity of these works, which reminded them of European Renaissance or Baroque art. They had difficulty accepting them as the production of an African people.

Figure 2: Benin Bronze. Image: Photograph published in Eckart von Sydow (1932, 379).

But they were not alone. Around 1900, the whole of Europe struggled to believe that other cultures, other existences, other desires existed independently from it. In his famous letters on "The crisis of the mind" (1919), a text that was initially published in English, in London, for a British audience, Paul Valéry asserted of Europe that:

---

3 "In diesem Umkreis bildet Benin die Enklave einer relativen Hochkultur, deren Geschichte noch ein Rätsel ist, das nach einer Lösung verlangt" (von Sydow 1932, 380). On the history of "Benin Bronzes", see Greenfield (2007, 124–128).

> Other parts of the world have had admirable civilizations, [. . .]. But no part of the world has possessed this singular physical property: the most intense power of radiation combined with an equally intense power of assimilation.
>
> Everything came to Europe, and everything came from it. Or almost everything (Valéry 1956 [1911 and 1919], 23–26; see Achille Mbembe's reading of this excerpt, 2016, 98).

Yet in terms of heritage accumulation, this "everything" did not come without resistance. Since ancient times, dispossessed people have had their word. For a European historian, they are undoubtedly harder to grasp than the victors' discourse. But these words exist and are the soil in which contemporary claims regarding displaced cultural goods have their roots. In the late 1880s, a young Egyptian intellectual Ḥasan Tawfīq al-ʿAdl, who had left Alexandria to live in Berlin for a few years, noted in his travel diary these few words exchanged with an employee of Berlin's Egyptian museum:

- "So", he asked jokingly, "how do you find your treasures in our country?"
- Very well presented, Sir, and you have made a fine effort to preserve such beauty. I am glad that they are in your country, where they can remind you of Egypt. However, it is obvious that the most legitimate right to keep them is ours (al-ʿAdl 2008).[4]

Given some effort to look for these missing words, one will find early traces of them outside of Europe. But they can also be found, in great numbers, inside of Europe itself, in this Europe whence "everything came", and where the accumulation of precious objects from foreign lands has never been a subject of collective approval nor of general consensus.

Starting in the late eighteenth century, from Paris to London and from Rome to Weimar, massive transfers of cultural goods and the violence that underpinned them triggered troubled reactions in enlightened circles. In England, Lord Byron revolted against the transfer of Athens' Parthenon frieze to what he called England's "Northern climes abhorred".[5] In France, Antoine Chrysostome Quatremère de Quincy vigorously protested against the Directory's policy of artistic conquests in Italy, and dedicated some admirable pages to a description of the sacred unity which, according to him, binds an art object to its original context:

> Neither in the fog and fumes of London, nor in the rain and mud of Paris or the ice and snow of Saint Petersburg; neither in the midst of Europe's large cities' commotion nor in this chaos of distractions of a people necessitously occupied with merchant tasks can one develop this profound sensitivity for fine things (Quatremère de Quincy 1989, 116).

---

4 On the museums of Berlin in particular, see al-ʿAdl (2008, 279–288).
5 *"And snatched thy shrinking Gods to Northern climes abhorred!"* (Byron 1980 [1812], 3–186).

Half a century later, Victor Hugo wrote a now famous letter to express his disgust at the sack of the Summer Palace in Beijing and denounce a crime of European barbarity on Chinese civilisation (Hugo 1894 [1861], 253–256).[6]

In 1920, the journal *L'Esprit nouveau* published a memorable inquiry titled "Faut-il brûler le Louvre?" ("Should we burn down the Louvre?") (1920, 1–8, 1921, 960–962). In 1923, Paul Valéry wrote of his disgust upon visiting the Louvre, and described an "accumulation of excessive and therefore unusable capital" in what he called a "house of incoherence". To which he added: "our heritage is crushing us" (Valéry 1960 [1923], 1290–1293). Two years later, in Berlin, art critic Carl Einstein compared the museum of ethnology to a gigantic "cold room where the trophies accumulated by the white man's greedy curiosity lie bloodless" (1926, 590; see also Einstein 1921). The crisis of museums that we think we're diagnosing today is at least a century old.

And yet. There is also a diurnal face to this primitive accumulation of cultural capital in eighteenth- to twentieth-century Europe: individual and collective emotions, aesthetic fertilisations and unexpected crystallisations, which are at the very heart of the ideas of culture and humanity. *Culture*, not in the fixed sense of a "sum of knowledge", but rather in the dynamic sense of an elaboration, a construction; a sense that the German language captures with the term *Bildung*. For, in museums, immortal objects (that is, them) cross, from generation to generation, the timelines and the preoccupations of mortals (that is, us), and have on them a germinating power; the power, through their interactions, to make things, ideas or forms, which had not yet happened, happen. To paraphrase the Collège de France's motto, one could say that, in a museum, we "observe culture in the making". Here are three brief examples.

In 1901, Guillaume Apollinaire, then aged twenty, wrote one of his first literary essays in Berlin. He was touring Germany with a family that had hired him for a year to teach French to their daughter. He did not know what his future would look like. In Berlin, the Pergamon Museum had just opened (Figure 3). It presented a life-size reconstruction of the altar of Zeus that Prussian archaeologists had discovered twenty years earlier in the province of Izmir, in modern-day Turkey. The altar is adorned by a monumental frieze: "the Gigantomachy", which represents the victory of the gods over the giants, of order over disorder. The frieze is made of one hundred and twenty 2.3-meter-high slabs. Apollinaire,

---

[6] There does not seem to be any published translation of this letter, though several sources offer the same version online, see for instance: https://www.napoleon.org/en/history-of-the-two-empires/articles/the-chinese-expedition-victor-hugo-on-the-sack-of-the-summer-palace/.

planted before them, wrote in a mixture of enthusiasm for the work's savage beauty and caustic ferocity towards the German people:

> How beautiful it is! What a magnificent poem in stone! The earthly, marine and infernal Olympian gods, the animals, the giants, the monsters furiously entangle their sometimes-mutilated limbs, the torsos of goddesses rear upon the arms of heroes, faces contort and mouths bite. This work, that craftsmen carved in very large grain stone, is so imbued with the divine that the traveller forgets the crowd of handlebar-moustached visitors and ugly females, and wishes for the hour when the slaughterer's bulls will bellow (Apollinaire 1902, 146–147).

The text, which was published in *La Revue Blanche*, marked the beginning of Apollinaire's literary career. Thus, in Berlin, the savage creativity of the second century BCE Greeks met that of a slightly lost young man, born in Rome of a Polish mother and an Italian father (Apollinaire was granted French citizenship only in 1916). From this encounter in the museum – as well as from others, of course – emerged one of the most prominent voices on the early twentieth century's French literary scene.

Figure 3: Berlin's Pergamon Museum as it was presented from 1901 to 1907. Image: Anonymous photograph, 49.4 × 52.3 cm, Berlin, Architekturmuseum des Technischen Universität, inv. No. F 2059 © Architekturmuseum, Technische Universität Berlin.

In the same period – this was March 1900 – the Munich composer Richard Strauss was in Paris to conduct the Orchestre Lamoureux for two concerts. Romain Rolland took him to the Louvre. They were both thirty-five at the time. Romain Rolland was a lecturer in art history at the École normale supérieure. Strauss had also studied art history, but had become the conductor of the Berlin Opera's orchestra. Rolland wrote in his diary that "[Strauss] has true taste in terms of painting, and his taste is fashionable. He admires Chardin very much [. . .]. He is amused by Fragonard [. . .]; he is disappointed by Boucher. He is not severe enough with Greuze; he has a bit too much sympathy for Vernet's landscapes, and he recognizes the great Watteau's superiority; he says that this *Embarkation* [Figure 4] is a kind of *Märchen-malerei.* The happiness and ease that radiate from this eighteenth century move him pleasantly" (Strauss and Rolland 1950, 136, quoted from Schuh 1960, 59–98, 84–85).[7] As for Strauss, after visiting the Louvre, he wrote in his diary "Ideas for a ballet called *The Island of Cythera*, inspired by Antoine Watteau" (Strauss 17 May 1900, quoted from Schuh 1960, 85).

In the following weeks and months, long before Watteau's works reached Debussy and touched his heart, the young Strauss started composing the music for a vast ballet called *Kythere* (opus AV 230, Trenner 201), which remained fragmental but which provided some of the themes of *Der Rosenkavalier, Ariadne auf Naxos*, and *Josephslegende* (Schuh 1960). Pierre Rosenberg called the *Pilgrimage to the Isle of Cythera* "at once a pause and an action, an instant, but beyond all time" (2007, 901). This fine wording could be used to describe museums in general. They are all at once, the stopping of artworks, which are immobilised and forever imprisoned in displays and on walls, and the powerful, gripping action of these works on the generations that pass before them.

Figure 4: Antoine Watteau: *Pilgrimage to the Island of Cythera*, also called *The Embarkation for Cythera*, 1717. Oil painting on canvas, 129 × 194 cm, Louvre Museum, Department of paintings, inv. 8525. Public Domain.

---

7 I am very grateful to Wolf Lepenies for drawing my attention to this event.

One last example: the Egyptian art of the Amarna period in the crazy Berlin of the pre-World War I years. The Amarna period is this short break in ancient Egyptian history, when Pharaoh Akhenaton decided to desert the gods, the political capital and the aesthetics of his predecessors and impose a new capital, a new worship and a new art. During excavations conducted in 1912, an archaeologist from Berlin discovered the workshop of an Amarna sculptor. It contained tools, models, about twenty portraits among which some were of Queen Nefertiti, and some plaster casts. With the approval of the French authorities, which were then the administrators of Egypt's antiques, the set was shipped to Berlin and almost all of it was exhibited in the Museum Island during the winter of 1913–1914. Artistic avant-gardes and popular newspapers were dumbfounded. These faces came from the dawn of time (Figure 5) and yet were so similar – as writers of the time put it – to the people of 1913 that their radical realism made a political object out of Amarna art. Newspapers insisted on the democratic aspect of this "art for all", which would strongly move even the least cultivated visitors of the museum. Marxist journals would congratulate themselves on finding in these sculptures the categories that preoccupied them elsewhere. In December 1913, the *Sozialistische Monatshefte* ("monthly Socialist review") even explained that the Amarna faces resembled those of "anyone on the street"; that some were like "an ultimate aristocratic filtering" of mankind, whereas others (the plasters) seemed to have been cast "on proletarians" (Stern 1913, 1720–1721).

Egyptian heads from the fourteenth century BCE enrolled in the International Workers' class struggle. An eighteenth-century French painting which, two hundred years later, spawned music. Two-thousand-year-old Hellenistic marbles gave birth to an avant-garde poem in Berlin. There are numerous combinations and examples of unexpected cultural fertilisation through European museums. Special mention can be made of the painter André Derain for the turmoil he experienced at the British Museum in London in 1906. He was then twenty-six and it was the first time, according to Philippe Dagen, that a western painter paid attention to non-European sculpture. Once he had regained his hotel room, Derain spent the night writing an exalted letter to his friend Henri Matisse:

> I have blackened four sheets of paper that I have given up on sending you. It is such a mess of ideas, such a chaos of sensations, of reasoning, that you would really think I have gone mad. [. . .] I have been at the British Museum for the fifth time. There lay all jumbled up, so to speak – pay attention: the Chinese, the Africans, the Egyptians, the Etruscans, Phidias, the Romans, the Indies. My ideas were so confused before all this that I had to leave. I have insinuated myself in environments, in lives other than mine. I have therefore broadened my conscience by something else than words. Sensations alone, defined with, by shapes, colours. [. . .] It is no longer an idea, but the absolute idea, the conscience of being (quoted from Labrusse 1999, 52; see also Dagen 1994, 173–174, and Dagen 2010).

Figure 5: Sculptures and live plaster casts discovered in Tell el-Amarna. Photographic montage published as "Portraits of 1370 BC from an Egyptian studio" in *Illustrated London News* (19 March 1927, 3).

The awareness of being and the taste for Otherness; an incorporation of the Other into the substance of Self; de-centring and re-centring. There is no doubt that museums are among the places where the "singular physical property of Europe", to use Paul Valéry's words again, its extraordinary absorption and assimilation power, is visible at it strongest. Museums are, or have long been, the sites of formal encounters with vast worlds, the archives of human creativity, some of the places where History fertilises the future. And, if I were not afraid of pomposity and if so many European museums had not been excessively commodified and "touristified" over the last few years, I could almost say that they are the house of the mind.

But what then, of the places where objects no longer are? What is there to say to those who are outside the house and have been deprived from their goods by History's violence and asymmetry? How could one justify a situation in which the ones have access to the heritage of a mankind from which the others are physically and economically excluded? How could we tolerate the symbolic and real capital generated by these museums not being shared? And how could we not want – by museums, through museums, because they have given us so much and because we have taken so much – to engage in a fairer policy for the dispossessed?

In 1940, while he was fleeing from Nazi persecution, Walter Benjamin diagnosed traditional historians' inability to empathise with defeated people. It is meaningful that he did it in one of the rare passages of his oeuvre in which he mentions artistic conquests and spoils of war. With whom do historians identify when they write History, wonders Benjamin. With the victor.

> Whoever has emerged victorious participates to this day in the triumphal procession in which the present rulers step over those who are lying prostrate. According to traditional practice, the spoils are carried along in the procession. They are called cultural treasures [. . .]. There is no document of civilization which is not at the same time a document of barbarism, barbarism taints also the manner in which it was transmitted from one owner to another (Benjamin 1968 [1955], 256).[8]

We, Europeans, who have received and passed on, and are still passing on these objects, are on the side of the victors. And in a way, this too is a "heritage that is crushing us". But it is not our fate. The good news is that, today, the history of Europe having been what it has been for centuries – a history of enmity between our nations, of bloody wars and of discriminations that were overcome with great difficulty after World War Two –, we have sources and resources within ourselves to understand the sadness, or the anger, or the hatred of those who are in other parts of the world, further, poorer, weaker, and have been subjected in the past to the "intense absorbing power" of our continent. Or, to say things more plainly, all we have to do now to empathise with the dispossessed is to make a tiny effort of introspection and step sideways a little.

I will take a French example, but which was then relevant to the whole of Europe. In the 1920s, a powerful America had just taken the leadership of the international community. In Toulouse, a young lawyer gave a speech for the start of intern lawyers' new year, which was immediately awarded a prize, published, and broadcast. It was titled *L'Elginisme*, in reference to the Count of Elgin, the Athenian Parthenon frieze one. But in this young lawyer's *Elginism*, neither Greece nor England were mentioned. Instead, America and its dollars were

---

[8] For the French version, see Olivier Mannoni's excellent translation with Patrick Boucheron's foreword (2013, 64–65).

making the young man fret – as they did jurists and public opinions of the time in other parts of Europe.

> Mister President of the Bar, Gentlemen [. . .],
>
> Armed with a notebook and a Kodak, a second-rate second-hand goods dealer has travelled up and down the city and the land, with worn out soles and threadbare trousers. He has written down everything that seemed antique to him and transmitted his discoveries to his correspondent [in New York]. [. . .] Every day, universally known, visited and described marvels of our architecture are uprooted from French soil to be exported to other continents. [. . .]. [Of course,] it is necessary that some of our finest works go to foreign lands to serve as ambassadors of our taste and our civilization. What is, however, becoming intolerable, is that foreigners methodically come here to disfigure what the great Ruskin called "the beloved face of the Fatherland". Alas! We, Gentlemen, stand before this sorry sight.
>
> In times past, destruction came from ignorance. [. . .] Nowadays, it comes from appreciation for the venal value of what has above all a "soul value". [. . .] Go no more to Sens to see the great flamboyant windows of the refectory before which Jacques Clément, the half-mad monk, pondered the assassination of King Henry III; they were sold for 20,000 francs to an American lady who will use them to light a music room. The door of Abbeville [. . .] recently left its Francois I courtyard and is headed for an unknown destination. The Gothic staircase which stood so picturesquely with its three floors of woodwork in a courtyard of Morlaix is now entirely in a museum in London, sitting between an electric spotlight and a central heating unit. You would not find Villeneuve-lès-Avignon's beautiful cross anymore [. . .]; it has been in New York for five years, and it is a miracle that the old abbey of Moissac still keeps its remarkable thirteenth-century frescoes. [. . .] Thus, were we to cross out of guides all that can no longer be seen here, we would write all of the history of our French art, and the list of irreparable losses to our country would be long (de Gorsse 1927, 8–12).

As I read these lines, I think of Benin.

Of course, we should not mix everything up. We should not put on the same plane the dismantling of collections formed in the late nineteenth and early twentieth centuries by patriotic Jewish European families, led by Nazi fanatics in a general context of racial persecution, and the transfers from Italian and German public museums to Revolutionary and Napoleonic France in the name of ideals such as freedom, public education, and the progress of arts and knowledge. We should not confuse post-1915 despoiling of the Armenian people and the "second-hand goods dealer armed with a notebook, a Kodak" and dollars, who scoured French provinces in search of good deals at around the same time. Neither, of course, should we mix up the bloody plunders of colonial wars and the nineteenth-century archaeological campaigns. In studying massive heritage displacements – and thus in raising the issue of restitution –, one must always pay meticulous attention to the historical, cultural, ideological, and symbolic context in which these displacements took place, and to the specific nature of each case. The very credibility of our research is at stake.

So we must not mix everything up. Neither, however, should we fear to tackle contentious issues. Tackling the history – be it of gold or of lead – of art heritage in Europe from the eighteenth to the twentieth century, and doing it today, from Paris, from Berlin, from London, or from the Collège de France, which is the finest, the freest, the most dignified place to do it, is first and foremost undertaking a process of introspection. It seems to me that this introspection on heritage, in Europe, is the first mark of friendship and respect that we could show to those who have enriched us. True introspection is neither a matter of flogging oneself, nor of deleting anything, nor of rushing to return things of which some people, including outside of Europe, may think that they are better kept here for now.

Introspection is the effort consisting in collectively tying these objects in our museums back to the history that brought them to our countries, and back to the people who now live where they used to be. It is consciously embracing the burdening part of our history as Europeans "to whom all came" and making it visible and thinkable. It is to pay extreme, constant, and critical attention to the voices of all those who, inside and outside of Europe, make heritage a political issue. In sum, it is to try to do what Achille Mbembe invites us to do, "to cross [multiple places] as responsibly as we can, as the heirs that we all are, but in a totally free and, where needed, detached relationship. In this process, which involves translation as well as conflict and misunderstandings, some questions will dissolve by themselves. Then, in relative clarity, will emerge requirements, if not of a possible universality, at least of an idea of the Earth as that which is common to all of us, as our common condition" (Mbembe 2016, 178).

The dividing line does not run between others and ourselves; it lies between the immortals – that is, the objects in museums – and the mortals – that is, us.

References

Agulhon, Maurice. "La statuomanie et l'histoire". *Ethnologie française* 8.2–3 (1978): 142–172.
Al-'Adl, Hasan Tawfīq. *Riḥlat Ḥasan Afandī Tawfīq al-'Adl, 1887–1892*. Cairo, 2008.
Apollinaire, Guillaume. "Le Pergamon à Berlin". *La Revue blanche* (15 May 1902): 146–147.
Benjamin, Walter. "Theses on the Philosophy of History." *Illuminations*. Ed. Hannah Arendt. Transl. Harry Zohn. New York: Schocken Books, 1968 [1955]. 253–264.
Benjamin, Walter. "A Short Speech on Proust." *Walter Benjamin: Critical Evaluations in Cultural History*, vol. II: *Modernity*. Ed. Peter Osborne. London: Routledge, 2005.
———. *Sur le concept d'histoire*. Transl. Olivier Mannoni. Paris: Payot & Rivages, 2013.
Byron, George Gordon. "Childe Harold's pilgrimage", chant II, xv. *The Complete Poetical Works*. Ed. Jerome J. McGann. 7 vols. (1980–1993), vol. 2. Oxford: Clarendon Press, 1980 [1812]. 3–186.

Cassin, Barbara and Dominique Wozny. Eds. *Les intraduisibles du patrimoine en Afrique subsaharienne*. Paris: Demopolis, 2014.

Dagen, Philippe. *André Derain. Lettres à Vlaminck*. Paris: Flammarion, 1994.

———. *Le Peintre, le poète, le sauvage. Les voies du primitivisme dans l'art français*. Paris: Flammarion, 2010.

De Gorsse, Pierre. *L'Elginisme*. Toulouse: Vidaillon, 1927.

Einstein, Carl. "Das Berliner Völkerkunde-Museum, Anläßlich der Neuordnung." *Der Querschnitt* 6.8 (1926): 588–592.

———. "Faut-il brûler le Louvre?" *L'Esprit nouveau* 8 (1921): 960–962.

Gran-Aymerich, Ève. *Les Chercheurs de passé. 1798–1945. Aux sources de l'archéologie*. Paris: CNRS Éditions, 2007.

Greenfield, Janette. *The Return of Cultural Treasures*. Cambridge: Cambridge University Press, 2007.

Hugo, Victor. "L'expédition de Chine – au capitaine Butler". Hauteville House: 25 November 1861. *Victor Hugo, Actes et Paroles II: Pendant l'exil (1852–1870)*. Ed. Émile Testard. *Édition nationale. Victor Hugo*, t. 40. Paris: Librairie de l'Édition nationale, 1894. 253–256.

Labrusse, Rémi. *Matisse. La condition de l'image*. Paris: Gallimard, 1999.

Long, Véronique. "Les collectionneurs d'œuvres d'art et la donation au musée à la fin du XIXe siècle: l'exemple du musée du Louvre". *Romantisme* 31.112 (2001): 45–54.

———. "Les collectionneurs juifs parisiens sous la IIIe République (1870–1940)". *Archives juives* 42.1 (2009): 84–104.

Messling, Markus. *Les Hiéroglyphes de Champollion. Philologie et conquête du monde*. Revised and augmented edition. Transl. Kaja Antonowicz. Grenoble: UGA Éditions, 2015.

———. "Champollion devant l'universalisme républicain". *La Vie des idées* (Collège de France), 27 septembre 2022. https://laviedesidees.fr/Champollion-devant-l-universalisme-republicain.html (last accessed, 22 November 2022).

Ministère de la Culture. "POP: la plateforme ouverte du patrimoine". http://www.culture.gouv.fr/documentation/mnr/MnR-pres.htm (last accessed, 26 October 2021).

Mbembe, Achille. *Politiques de l'inimitié*. Paris: La Découverte, 2016.

Poulot, Dominique. *Musée, nation, patrimoine*. Paris: Gallimard, 1995.

Quatremère de Quincy, Antoine Chrysostome. *Lettres sur le préjudice qu'occasionnerait aux arts et à la science le déplacement des monuments de l'art de l'Italie* also called *Lettres à Miranda*. Ed. Édouard Pommier. Paris: Macula, 1989.

Rosenberg, Pierre. *Dictionnaire amoureux du Louvre*. Paris: Plon, 2007.

Savoy, Bénédicte. *Objets du désir. Désir d'objets*. Paris: Fayard, 2017.

Schuh, Willi. "*Das Szenarium* und die musikalischen Skizzen zum Ballett *Kythere*." *Richard Strauss Jahrbuch 1959/60*. Bonn: Boosey and Hawkes, 1960. 59–98.

Schnapp, Alain. *The Discovery of the Past*. New York: Abrams, 1997.

Stern, Lisbeth. "Ägyptische Funde." *Sozialistische Monatshefte* 26 (1913): 1720–1721.

Strauss, Richard and Romain Rolland. *Correspondance / fragments de journal*. Paris: Albin Michel, 1950.

Sydow, Eckart von. "Bronzen aus Benin." *Die Kunst für Alle* 12 (1932): 378–380.

Winkelvoss, Karin. "Erinnerung an das nie Gesehene – Vergegenwärtigung und Geistesgegenwart der Bilder. Einleitung." *Zeitschrift für Kunstgeschichte* 81 (2018): 185–197.

Winkelvoss, Karin and Andreas Beyer. "Le souvenir du jamais vu". Conference paper presentation. *Centre allemand d'histoire de l'art*. Paris, 16–17 May 2014.

Valéry, Paul. "The Crisis of the Mind." *The Athenaeum* (London), 11 April 1911 and 2 May 1919, 2nd Letter, reproduced in "The crisis of the mind". *The Collected Works of Paul Valéry*. Ed. J. Matthews. Transl. Denise Folliot and Jackson Mathews Vol. 10. Princeton: Princeton University Press, 1956. 23–26.

———. "Le problème des musées". *Le Gaulois* (4 avril 1923). *Œuvres*, t. II: *Pièces sur l'art*. Paris: Gallimard, 1960. 1290–1293.

Vidal, Pierre et Christian Kempf. *Frédéric-Auguste Bartholdi (1834–1904): par l'esprit et par la main*. Lyon: Les Créations du Pélican, 1994.

Albert Gouaffo
Décentrer la question des restitutions : l'exemple des biens culturels issus de contextes coloniaux en Afrique face aux micro-histoires régionales

Abstract: Although the question of returning African heritage taken away by Europeans in the colonial context has been raised in the public arena since the political independence of African nations in the 1960s, each time it has been suppressed and forgotten. In his 2017 declaration in Ouagadougou, French President Emmanuel Macron underlined France's willingness to return temporarily or permanently African cultural property located in French museums when it is established that it was looted or forcibly removed in a colonial context. As a result of Macron's stance and the report he commissioned by Felwine Sarr and Bénédicte Savoy on the issue of restitution, other European countries such as Germany have been forced to clarify the provenance of their collections and to determine their origin and the contexts of their acquisition in order to establish a dialogue with the concerned communities. The present contribution builds on an inter-university cooperation project on transcultural memorial topography to show that reflections on the restitution of cultural goods from colonial contexts should take two aspects into account: on the one hand, communities of African origin that were autonomous nations at the time and, on the other hand, today's nation-states that emerged from political independence. I therefore draw on the trans-regional paradigm of global history as a methodological approach to address issues of restitution, reparation and compensation in an appropriate and equitable manner.

Keywords: African cultural heritage, provenance research, restitution, reparation, compensation, historical justice

1 Introduction

Le travail sur la mémoire du nazisme en Allemagne a longtemps occulté celui sur le colonialisme. Quelques raisons peuvent être avancées pour expliquer cet état de choses. D'une part l'Allemagne, par rapport à ses voisins Français, Anglais, et Hollandais, pour ne citer que quelques-uns, a minimisé son passé colonial en Afrique qui n'a duré qu'une trentaine d'années. Le traumatisme lié à la perte brutale de ses possessions coloniales à la fin de la Première Guerre mondiale (Schnee 1923–1924) a poussé les Allemands à considérer cette période de leur histoire avec l'Afrique comme un accident qui méritait d'être classé. Après quelques tentatives, dans les années 1970, de redécouvrir ce passé dans le sillage du conflit Est-Ouest par les historiens marxistes de l'ex-RDA[1], mais aussi dans le contexte de la révolte estudiantine de mai 1968 en ex-RFA, cette période de l'histoire germano-africaine est vite retombée aux oubliettes. Seule la critique postcoloniale, la diaspora africaine, la société civile allemande, mais particulièrement le gigantesque projet « Humboldt-Forum »[2] qui a transformé l'ancienne résidence de l'empereur Guillaume II en un musée ethnographique mondial, ont remis à l'ordre du jour la question des répercussions de la colonisation sur la société allemande. La méconnaissance de la période coloniale et la persistance des idées héritées de la colonisation ne facilitent non plus la collaboration entre les peuples. D'autre part, au Cameroun, ancienne colonie allemande, la situation n'est non plus reluisante. La méconnaissance de ce passé allemand a cédé place à une nostalgie qui ne traduit qu'une maîtrise approximative de cette partie de notre histoire. Les barrières linguistiques et surtout la non-maîtrise de l'écriture gothique et de la *Kurrentschrift* (ancienne écriture manuelle de l'allemand) rendent le décryptage des archives quasi impossible pour l'historien camerounais. Il se contente dans la plupart des cas des sources orales qu'il peut retrouver ici et là ou des traductions françaises et anglaises qu'il peut rassembler. Les Camerounais se souviennent de l'Allemagne, et c'est le cas avec la crise anglophone actuelle (Guimatsia 2016), pour se guérir de la violence coloniale française ou anglaise (cf. Gouaffo 2005, 2011).

Fort de ce contexte, repenser les relations entre l'Allemagne et le Cameroun devient un impératif. Comme je l'ai auparavant soutenu, la création d'une germanistique postcoloniale pourrait-être une façon de décentrer les perspectives civilisatrices et hégémoniques de l'Allemagne coloniale. Il s'agit non seulement de décoloniser les savoirs universitaires, notamment en recontextualisant la germanistique encore considérée comme une exclusivité allemande (Gouaffo 2021), mais aussi de regarder dans notre passé douloureux pour penser un futur commun. L'appropriation de la langue incorporée d'abord de manière répressive et dans la violence peut permettre aux chercheurs camerounais de revisiter cette histoire partagée selon leurs propres modalités. La question de la restitution des biens culturels africains issus du contexte colonial offre une opportunité idoine pour relire, dans une perspective postcoloniale, les relations entre la métropole (l'Allemagne) et la colonie (le Cameroun). Pour que cette négociation ait lieu, il faut que les deux par-

---

[1] Je fais allusion ici aux travaux de Helmuth Stöcker (1968) et aux autres historiens de l'ex-RDA.
[2] Le Humboldt-Forum va coûter 595 millions d'euros au contribuable allemand. Cf. Bowley (2018).

ties fassent le bilan de ce qui les lie et qu'une recherche fondamentale transdisciplinaire soit menée de commun accord avant toutes négociations sur les questions de restitution, de circulation ou de conservation des biens culturels des anciennes colonies stockés en grande partie dans les musées européens[3]. Il nous faut mener ensemble une recherche exploratoire car nous connaissons à suffisance les réticences et toute la rhétorique que l'Europe a développé et continue de développer pour conserver jalousement ce patrimoine postcolonial[4]. En effet, on ne peut pas revendiquer ou partager que ce que l'on ne connaît pas quantitativement et qualitativement. Une exposition que nous avons organisée dans la cadre du projet « Liaisons coloniales » du 26 juillet au 16 août 2018 au musée des Civilisations de la ville de Dschang au Cameroun a permis de mesurer l'étendue de l'ignorance des populations, lorsque les photos de certains objets de leurs communautés stockés au musée ethnographique de Mannheim, le Reiss-Engelhorn-Museum, ont été exposées[5].

La réaction immédiate du public a été d'en savoir plus pour réclamer leurs restitutions. Bénédicte Savoy et son collègue sénégalais Felwine Sarr ont jeté un pavé dans la marre en prescrivant, dans leur rapport commandé par le président français Emanuel Macron, que les objets d'art effectivement pillés ou acquis par la violence par la France dans le contexte colonial en Afrique subsaharienne (au moins 88000 dont 70000 au musée du Quai Branly) soient restitués aux communautés d'origine (Sarr et Savoy 2018, 75 ; Horton 2018). Vu l'importance et la richesse en savoirs pour les communautés d'origine, l'université doit prendre ses responsabilités.

Je pense, comme l'artiste franco-algérien Kader Attia, que la restitution reste quand même une façon de panser les blessures de la colonisation à travers leur transformation en cicatrice douloureuse (Attia 2021). Mais autant faut-il que les débats et actions faites à la faveur des restitutions se décentrent. En ce sens, les problématiques de restitution sont une opportunité pour les chercheurs de l'histoire coloniale de décentrer plus généralement la question des réparations, afin que les acteurs des périphéries prennent la place centrale qui leur a été longtemps confisquée (Wallerstein 1980–1984).

---

3 Un inventaire que nous avons réalisé dans le cadre d'une recherche de provenance des objets culturels issus du contexte colonial et présents dans les musées publics allemand indique que 60000 pièces ont été pillées entre 1884 et 1920. Voir le lien sur le site de la TU Berlin : https://www.kuk.tu-berlin.de/menue/forschung/einzelne_forschungsprojekte/umgekehrte_sammlungsgeschichte_ein_kommentierter_atlas_zum_materiellen_erbe_kameruns_in_deutschen_museen/.
4 J'en veux pour preuve le refus du gouvernement français de restituer les objets royaux du Benin, après sa fracassante déclaration sur la restitution des biens symboliques africains qui seraient acquis illicitement par la France. Cf. Lecaplain (2017).
5 Plus d'informations sur cette exposition sur le site www.deutschland-postkolonial.de.

Cela a été l'objectif du projet *Liaisons coloniales* dont nous présentons les résultats ici et qui interroge, à l'échelle locale et régionale, la transmission de la mémoire coloniale et les productions de micro-récits historiques en Allemagne et au Cameroun. Notre étude de cas est une proposition de contribution aux réflexions du projet Minor Universality qui cherche à mettre en lumière les narrations qui émergent en dehors des grands récits hégémoniques de l'Occident afin d'ouvrir « des contextes locaux de manière à faire émerger une nouvelle conscience sensible, incarnée ou intellectuelle d'une humanité partagée[6] ». Le projet que nous avons mis en place a spécifiquement cherché à dépasser le « nationalisme méthodologique » afin de favoriser le localisme en mettant l'accent sur les régions comme échelle d'observation. En a résulté la mise en lumière des micro-récits des régions, souvent menacées par les métarécits nationaux, mais qui, pourtant, jouent un rôle fondamental dans la perspective d'une réparation par la restitution des biens culturels spoliés, et, ce faisant, la construction d'un avenir partagé.

2 Relations culturelles entre métropole et colonie. Une relecture mémorielle à partir du paradigme transrégional

Chez les théoriciens de la mémoire en Europe, que ce soit le sociologue Maurice Halbwachs, l'historien Pierre Nora, l'égyptologue et angliciste Jan et Aleida Assman ou le philosophe Paul Ricœur, la mémoire a été envisagée et forgée sous un prisme national. Cette conception ne prend pas en compte le contexte colonial où la notion de nation au sens de l'État centralisé n'existait pas encore. En plus, ces théoriciens ne tiennent pas compte de la diversité culturelle et historique, du caractère interconnecté, polyphonique et même superposé de la mémoire dans un même espace national. Nous avons essayé dans le cadre du projet « Liaisons coloniales » Grasland – Rheinland[7] un nouveau paradigme qui est la mise en relation symétrique des espaces et des régions afin de leur permettre d'échanger et de dialoguer d'égal à égal. Les questions de recherche ont été les suivantes : Comment

---

[6] ERC Consolidator Grant *Minor Universality. Narrative World Productions After Western Universalism.* https://www.uni-saarland.de/fr/chercheurs/minor-universality/le-projet.html

[7] Il s'agissait d'un partenariat entre le département d'Histoire de l'Université de Düsseldorf et le département de Langues Étrangères Appliquées de l'Université de Dschang, mais d'autres disciplines connexes comme la germanistique et les études médiatiques faisaient partie de ce projet de recherche pédagogique (*Lehrforschungsprojekt*) financé par la Fondation Alexander von Humboldt. Plus d'informations sur www.deutschland-postkolonial.de.

est-il possible d'échanger sur l'histoire coloniale entre les descendants des ex-colonisés et des ex-colonisateurs ? Qui détermine quelle histoire doit être racontée et de laquelle l'on doit se souvenir ? Avec le paradigme transrégional, et en relation avec l'histoire globale, le « nationalisme méthodologique » a été dépassé et les études littéraires, historiques et médiatiques ont été mises à contribution pour écrire les micro-histoires des régions. Nous avons essayé de dépasser le cadre d'interprétation de l'État-nation en allant au niveau de la région et en interrogeant les liens entre les régions dans le passé et dans le présent. L'approche classique existant jusqu'alors qui étudie le lien colonial entre l'Allemagne et le Cameroun comme entités nationales et homogènes, est remise en question. Nous avons plutôt opté de parler des régions aux frontières fluides comme le grasland du Cameroun d'un côté et de la Rhénanie de l'autre afin d'interroger l'ancrage local des mémoires coloniales et les éventuelles particularités régionales. Deux régions sur deux continents différents, la Rhénanie en Allemagne avec ses prairies d'une part et les hautes terres de l'Ouest-Cameroun avec ses savanes d'autre part, ont été mises en relation pour examiner leurs liens historiques et contemporains. Dans ce cadre, un atelier scientifique a eu lieu à Düsseldorf. Les méthodes transdisciplinaires de recherche sur la mémoire et la recherche historique ont été présentées dans divers panels.

3 Un projet de recherche transdisciplinaire révélateur d'une histoire interconnectée

Le projet nous a permis d'organiser des séminaires conjoints avec des collègues et étudiants des deux universités, à Düsseldorf d'abord, et à Dschang ensuite. Dans l'ensemble, il a été question de sensibiliser nos étudiants des deux espaces nationaux à revisiter, à travers la recherche dans les archives, les traces physiques de cette partie de leur histoire entrelacée, et ceci non pas à partir d'un prisme national, mais régional, c'est-à-dire décentré, pour mieux cerner les dynamiques qui s'y dégagent ; puis de commettre un ouvrage scientifique (Gouaffo et Michels 2019) sur cette démarche qui permet de lire en contrepoint les métarécits circulant sur les deux espaces nationaux et qui ombragent les micro-récits des régions tous aussi importants pour la gestion du vivre-ensemble.

Et, enfin, de sensibiliser le public des deux espaces géographiques sur les lieux de mémoires coloniaux allemands des *grassfields* tels que la prison de Dschang, l'Université de Dschang qui fut créée par les Allemands comme école d'agriculture (Ackerbauschule) en 1910, la ferme pastorale de Djutitsa, la mission pallotine Saint-Joseph, devenue Sacré-Cœur, les villages Fontem, Foto, Bana et

Bali comme point d'ancrage dans la conquête allemande du *grassfield* camerounais. Cinq mémoires de Bachelor/Licence en histoire ont été consacrés à certains de ces lieux par des étudiants allemands (Engler 2017 ; Karakis 2017). Les étudiants de médias et cultures de l'Université de Düsseldorf ont réalisé avec nos étudiants dans le cadre du projet de recherche pédagogique un film documentaire (Laumeyer et al. 2017).

Comme résultats de ce projet, je me réjouis du fait que des enseignements conjoints ont été réalisés en 2016 dans les deux sens avec des étudiants et chercheurs des deux Universités et dans leurs campus respectifs. Les résultats intermédiaires de ce projet de coopération ont été présentés à Düsseldorf en 2017 sous forme d'exposition dans le musée de cette ville (*Stadtmuseum*) et au musée des civilisations de Dschang en juillet 2018. Une table ronde a été organisée sur le thème du projet à l'intention du public allemand, un atelier d'histoire s'est tenu à l'intention des enseignants d'histoire des lycées à Düsseldorf et, enfin, une visite guidée sur les traces coloniales de cette ville a été réalisée.

Les étudiants de Licence, de Master et de Doctorat en Études Germaniques de l'Université de Dschang ont densifié leurs connaissances en recherches historiques et médiatiques et sont désormais bien outillés pour être des médiateurs de musée ou des chercheurs sur la provenance. Un cours d'été de deux semaines a été organisé à leur intention, par les collègues de Düsseldorf, au cours duquel ils ont été initiés à la lecture des documents d'archives.

Un site internet interactif et éducatif a été construit pour renseigner davantage sur le patrimoine commun des *grassfields* et de la Rhénanie. Douze lieux de mémoire interculturelle ont été identifiés, dont six dans le grassfield et six en Rhénanie, et mis en relation. Il est prévu que le site doit élargir la recherche sur d'autres lieux. Ce site est plurilingue (allemand, français anglais)[8].

Quelles sont les perspectives de ce projet pour la question de restitutions des biens culturels africains emportés en Europe et les possibilités pour la négociation de nouveaux rapports dé-coloniaux ? Dès l'entame de mon propos, j'ai précisé que pour la partie africaine en général et camerounaise en particulier, on ne peut parler de la restitution que lorsque cette partie dispose d'assez d'informations tant quantitativement que qualitativement sur l'inventaire de ses biens culturels emportés en Allemagne pendant la colonisation qui se chiffre autour de deux millions d'objets (Habermas 2018). Il s'agit de répondre plus précisément aux questions suivantes : Comment les différents objets ont-ils été acquis et à quelles fins politiques et scientifiques ont-ils servi ? Que faire de cet héritage dans le futur ?

---

8 Adresse du site web : www.deutschland-postkolonial.de (consulté le 20.10.2021).

Selon Jonathan Fine et Hilke Thode-Arora (2018, 57–58) la recherche de provenance s'intéresse à l'étude de la propriété et des conditions de propriété d'un objet depuis sa création jusqu'à nos jours. Il s'agit là de l'une des tâches fondamentales d'un musée – indépendamment de l'existence ou non d'une demande de restitution pour les objets de collection. Il est nécessaire non seulement de comprendre la chaîne de changement de propriétaires, mais aussi de reconstituer les circonstances dans lesquelles les biens ont été acquis. Les sources non européennes, écrites et orales sont importantes, l'examen stylistique de l'objet aussi (cf. Rein 2017, 26–31).

La recherche sur l'origine des objets issus de contextes coloniaux fait appel à une grande variété de sources. Il ne fait aucun doute que les sources écrites primaires utilisées dans le cadre du changement de propriétaires sont primordiales. Elles donnent des informations sur le contexte d'acquisition. Comme pour toute recherche historique, d'autres sources primaires sont nécessaires à l'instar des legs, des articles de journaux contemporains, des photographies, lettres, journaux intimes, livres (par exemple mémoires) et autres publications. Les sources secondaires, telles que les ouvrages scientifiques, les livres et les publications sont aussi nécessaires.

Notre projet de recherche nous a conduit aux constats suivants : En scrutant les espaces étudiés et en traçant quelques protagonistes au cours du projet, nous avons découvert quelques acteurs de transfert des biens culturels des *grassfields* vers l'Allemagne dont il conviendrait d'étudier sérieusement les actions. Il s'agit du natif de Düsseldorf, Eugen Zintgraff, qui fut le tout premier Allemand à fouler le sol du *grassfield* camerounais en 1891. Il a ramené des objets culturels en Allemagne (essentiellement des objets de représentation de pouvoir tels que les lances et les pipes dont une partie se trouve au Musée ethnographique de la ville de Braunschweig (*Das Städtische Museum*). Un autre acteur de transfert et non des moindres est le couple Franz et Marie Pauline Thorbecke, respectivement géographe et peintre qui furent envoyés dans les *grassfields* en 1911 par la Société Coloniale Allemande (*Deutsche Kolonialgesellschaft*) pour une exploration scientifique. Il reçut non seulement le financement de cette société, mais aussi du *Reiss-Engelhorn Museum* de Mannheim, de l'Université de Heidelberg et du Musée ethnographique de Berlin Dahlem. Il ramena des objets dont 1300 ont été donnés au musée de Mannheim, six corps préparés auraient été transmis à l'Université de Heidelberg et une partie des objets et archives sonores envoyés à Berlin. Marie Pauline Thorbecke a fait des photographies lors de leur exploration qui se trouvent au Musée de Cologne (*Rautenstrauch-Joest-Museum*). Un autre protagoniste actif dans le grasland dont nous n'avons pas suivi la trajectoire est Adolf Diehl, représentant de l'une des plus grandes plantations du Cameroun allemand, la *Deutsche Gesellschaft Nordwest-Kamerun*. Parmi les grands donateurs des 16 500 objets en provenance du Cameroun qui se trouvent au Musée ethnographique de Stuttgart (*Lindenmuseum*), figure Adolf Diehl avec 2268 objets[9].

Les échanges avec la partie allemande au sujet de la restitution montrent que l'Allemagne est juge et partie. Elle ne considère pas la restitution comme une nécessité, mais comme une question éthique, car selon le droit allemand ces objets font partie du patrimoine de l'État fédéral, des Länder ou des communes et sont de ce fait inaliénables. Nous devons éviter de nous cloisonner dans ce juridisme, car la recherche montre que – je m'appuie sur les résultats de recherche du *Lindenmuseum* de Stuttgart, des 25 300 objets répertoriés dans ce musée venant d'Afrique, 2200 proviennent du Sud-ouest africain et 16 500 ont été collectionnés au Cameroun. Les collections africaines de ce musée se situent entre 1884 et 1920. Les grands collectionneurs sont des militaires (plus de 41,5 % des objets), ce qui est révélateur de ce que ces objets furent emportés par la violence. Ils collectionnèrent ces objets en guise de trophées de guerre pendant les conquêtes de l'intérieur. Ils sont pour la plupart des officiers de la Schutztruppe, l'armée coloniale allemande, et des chefs de stations militaires. En ce qui concerne le musée ethnographique de Berlin, jusqu'en 1914, une grande partie des 55 000 objets d'origine africaine dont dispose ce musée provient du Cameroun (Krieger 1973, 104). Une recherche systématique sur ces collections n'a jusqu'à présent pas eu lieu. Un autre aspect concerne les objets détruits pendant la guerre. Il est utile que la recherche de provenance fasse la lumière sur ces collections.

Nous devons pour cela ne pas réduire la question du la restitution à la seule opération de retour des objets, mais la considérer dans un sens large comme une négociation paritaire sur un patrimoine commun. Il s'agit non seulement de négocier les modalités de circulation de ces biens dans les deux sens, mais également de clarifier les modalités de la copropriété. Les uns ne doivent pas posséder les objets véritables alors que les autres se contentent juste de leurs images en ligne dans les musées virtuels. Encore faut-il disposer de la technologie nécessaire pour pouvoir les découvrir en ligne.

Nous devons nous entendre sur la nature et la fonction de musée. Le musée est une institution qui a pour fonction de collecter, de conserver et de diffuser les informations sur des biens culturels. Ce modèle de musée comme espace de conservation ne correspond pas à l'esprit de conservation de biens culturels en Afrique qui fait de biens culturels des objets vivants. Les objets peuvent être exposés au public, mais en même temps les communautés les utilisent pour leurs

---

9 Il s'agit ici d'un premier inventaire dressé par Gesa Grimme, après une recherche sur la provenance des objets originaires de la Namibie, du Cameroun et de l'archipel Bismarck au Lindenmuseum de Stuttgart. Cf. Grimme (2018, 95–129).

rituels respectifs. Certains de ces espaces de conservation sont en plein air. L'Afrique doit envisager la restitution de ces objets comme une opportunité d'investissement et de création d'emploi dans le secteur du tourisme. Economiquement, ça devrait être très rentable dans le long terme. Les Allemands doivent assister les ex-colonies dans ce processus de reconstruction de leurs mémoires comme une sorte de réparation symbolique. Une autre question qui fait problème entre l'Afrique et l'Europe est la fonction de l'art dans la société. En Europe, traditionnellement, l'art était lié au beau, au noble au vrai au sens aristotélicien du terme. L'objet d'art y est défini par sa beauté. Il est objet de contemplation et n'a pas de fonction prédéfinie. C'est le résultat d'un travail créatif et original d'un créateur dont il porte la signature comme propriétaire unique. En Afrique subsaharienne de l'époque précoloniale et coloniale, l'art – ou disons mieux l'objet culturel – est d'abord conçu pour répondre à un besoin précis. Il a un usage prédéterminé. Les objets sont surtout fonctionnels et doivent remplir leur mission primaire en tant qu'objet sacré ou de représentation d'un pouvoir ou d'une personnalité royale dès lors qu'ils sont patrimonialisés, c'est-à-dire considérés comme bien culturel. Ils sont placés dans leur milieu naturel et ne sont accessibles à la communauté qu'à des occasions précises : fêtes annuelles, cérémonies d'épuration, sentence de tribunal coutumier, etc. Les objets spirituels deviennent des sujets vivants et participent à la célébration des aïeux. Enfermés dans les réserves des musées en Europe, ils sont en captivité. Il faut les délivrer et les ramener dans leur patrie d'origine.

La notion de propriété en occident et en Afrique pour ce qui concerne les objets d'art est à revoir. En occident, l'objet d'art appartient à un individu et il est unique. C'est d'ailleurs cela qui a facilité la recherche de provenance et la restitution des objets spoliés par le régime nazi. La production d'objets d'art en Afrique est essentiellement communautaire. On a des familles d'artisans, de forgerons et de sculpteurs sur bois par exemple. L'art en Afrique est essentiellement fonctionnel. Une fois sacralisé, il appartient à la communauté qui est représentée par un chef. L'objet d'art n'est pas nécessairement fait pour être exposé au public. Quand il est une représentation de la lignée, il est conservé en privé et ce n'est qu'à des occasions exceptionnelles qu'il est mis à la disposition du public. Les objets relevant du patrimoine sont à dissociés des objets usuels ou d'ornement. Par le processus de patrimonialisation ou de consécration, un objet courant peut changer de statut et devenir un élément d'identification de toute une communauté. À ce niveau, le créateur original de l'objet se retire et la communauté devient son propriétaire. C'est le cas par exemple d'un trône, symbole du pouvoir.

4 Les biens culturels issus de contextes coloniaux en Afrique comme possibilité d'imaginer un futur décolonial

Les biens culturels africains ne sont pas uniquement des objets d'art. Ils sont pour beaucoup d'entre eux des sujets (ancêtres, dieux, représentants de dynasties). C'est pourquoi l'Afrique n'avait pas à l'origine de musée en tant que lieu de collecte, de conservation et d'exposition au sens européen du terme. Les musées en Afrique ont émergé dans le contexte colonial en tant qu'activités de loisirs pour la population européenne dans les colonies, principalement dans les colonies de peuplement où la population européenne était relativement nombreuse, comme la Namibie et l'Afrique du Sud ou le Kenya. Vu sous cet angle, les objets de culte camerounais dans les musées européens sont en déportation, car ils ne sont pas dans leur environnement naturel pour communiquer et communier avec leurs populations d'origine. De la danse de la société secrète, il n'en reste dans les musées européens que des tambours et des costumes de danse. La communication qui est censée prévaloir entre ce monde et l'au-delà via les objets de culte est rompue. Lorsqu'on veut humilier un peuple entier, on commence par ridiculiser ses dirigeants en collectant et en confisquant les symboles de pouvoir comme le trône, les instruments de défense comme les arcs et les flèches. La fierté du peuple disparaît. On porte ensuite atteinte à la spiritualité en taxant les symboles de cette spiritualité de fétiches et en mettant ces objets en captivité ou en les détruisant quand on ne peut pas les emporter. Comme conséquence directe, les traditions ancestrales se meurent.

J'insiste ici sur la politique de restitution plutôt que sur la restitution en tant que terme juridique, car il ne s'agit pas d'un simple acte matériel de restitution. Nos chefs et résistants assassinés ne reviennent pas à la vie par le retour des objets spoliés. Le droit de propriété justifié par des factures du marché de l'art devient aussi problématique dès lors qu'il est établi par les descendants légitimes que l'objet acheté provient d'un vol.

La politique de restitution devrait être un processus de négociation entre les descendants des sociétés colonisées et colonisatrices. Pour cela, un pacte minimum consensuel de mesures de décolonisation devrait être négocié par les deux parties sur un pied d'égalité. Les décideurs politiques des deux côtés sont appelés à agir. Le pacte minimal de la politique de restitution dont il est question ici ne peut se formuler pour l'instant qu'en termes d'interrogations : Comment décentrer l'interprétation des musées ethnographiques comme instruments de construction de l'État-nation et d'exercice de violence symbolique sur l'altérité extraeuropéenne ? Comment donner la parole aux autres, et faire parler l'objet autrement en contexte de mondialisation dans lequel les espaces sont ouverts et interconnectés ? Comment partager plus équitablement le patrimoine et les richesses issues de la colonisation au sens le plus large ?

Il faut que la métropole et la colonie sortent des représentations et des impensés liés au passé et travaillent l'histoire et les imaginaires d'une relation qui restent à décoloniser (Sarr et Savoy 2018, 67). Les musées ethnographiques européens sont des archives publiques de ce système d'appropriation et d'aliénation que fut la colonisation. Penser la restitution des biens culturels issus de la colonisation implique davantage une exploration du passé. Il s'agit de bâtir les ponts vers des relations futures plus équitables guidées par le dialogue, la polyphonie et la réciprocité. Le geste de la restitution ne saurait être considéré comme un acte d'assignation identitaire ou de cloisonnement territorial de biens culturels. Ce geste invite au contraire à ouvrir la signification de ces objets et à offrir la possibilité d'être appropriés ailleurs. Sur un continent africain où 60 % de la population a moins de 20 ans, il en va d'abord et avant tout de l'accès de la jeunesse à sa propre culture, à la créativité et à la spiritualité d'époques certes révolues, mais dont la connaissance et la reconnaissance ne sauraient être réservées aux seules sociétés occidentales (Sarr et Savoy 2018, 15). L'Afrique ne peut être privée de son patrimoine. Les ressources héritées de la jeunesse africaine doivent être conservées en Afrique et servir au développement spirituel, culturel et économique des Africains, au même titre que celles héritées de la jeunesse européenne sont conservées en Europe et servent au développement culturel des Européens.

Il est du devoir moral de l'Europe d'aider les peuples africains à retrouver leur confiance en se reconnectant avec leur passé pour envisager l'avenir avec sérénité (cf. Sarr 2016).

5 Conclusion

De ce projet transdisciplinaire sur la topographie mémorielle transculturelle axé sur les *graslands* du Cameroun et la région de la Rhénanie, il ressort que l'Europe et l'Afrique se côtoient intensément depuis le 19ᵉ siècle, mais malgré leurs échanges intenses, les deux parties, pourtant liées par une histoire commune, se connaissent très peu. Les résultats de notre recherche montrent que les relations sont entrelacées mais restent superposées, fermées, car peu connues, sujettes aux idées coloniales. C'est un appel à aller au-delà des cloisonnements, notamment en procédant à une restitution claire, transparente, dépourvue des idées malicieuses d'intérêts propres pour refonder les relations culturelles qui restent encore une relation controversée. On assiste de part et d'autre à des monologues déguisés en dialogues. Notre projet de recherche pédagogique (*Lehrforschungsprojekt*) a montré que les deux parties, à savoir la métropole et la colonie, ont besoin d'une décolonisation mentale. Cela suppose la volonté de se regarder dans les yeux avec tout ce que cela comporte comme charge émotionnelle de part et d'autre. La présence des biens culturels africains en Europe offre une opportunité de repenser notre monde, de lutter contre l'injustice épistémique en œuvrant pour un savoir partagé. Ce patrimoine partagé nous renseigne sur l'interdépendance des relations entre les anciennes métropoles et leurs anciennes colonies. Les conditions nécessaires à l'émergence d'une nouvelle relation sont : la transparence, l'esprit d'équité et surtout l'acceptation du tort colonial pour un pardon et un oubli qui restent possibles.

Le paradigme transrégional comme approche méthodologique sur la recherche en mémoire culturelle a permis de lire la complexité des relations entre métropoles et colonies en contexte colonial. Cette approche nous a permis de comprendre que tant au niveau national qu'au niveau régional, il existe des micro-récits de la mémoire dignes d'être prise en compte au même titre que les métarécits nationaux. Ces micro-récits témoignent eux aussi des universalités possibles, latérales qui sont étouffés par l'universalisme vertical de la nation. Notre analyse montre qu'en matière de restitution ou rapatriement des biens culturels spoliés par l'Allemagne impériale, une prise en compte des acteurs nationaux (l'État postcolonial qui n'existait pas au moment de la translocation des biens) et les acteurs régionaux (chef de village, gardiens des traditions ancestrales) est indispensable. À l'époque coloniale à laquelle les objets ont été pillés, l'État postcolonial dans sa forme juridique actuelle n'existait pas. C'étaient des communautés plus ou moins indépendantes qui vivaient en interaction économique, culturelle et politique. Les négociations difficiles sur la mémoire de la guerre coloniale allemande en Namibie pour lesquels l'État allemand privilégie l'État namibien sans consulter les Hereros et les Namas en tant que communautés les plus victimes de la violence coloniale allemande prouvent à suffisance que le paradigme transrégional est probant pour vider le malentendu colonial.

Références bibliographiques

Attia, Kader. « C'est la reconnaissance de l'histoire des blessures qui est fondamentale ». *Affaire en cours. Podcast avec Marie Sorbier*. Radio France, 2021. https://www.radiofrance.fr/franceculture/podcasts/affaire-en-cours/c-est-la-reconnaissance-de-l-histoire-des-blessures-qui-est-fondamentale-2714513 (16 juin 2022).

Bowley, Graham. « In Deutschland reißt ein neues Museum alte Wunden auf. » *The New York Times*, 10 décembre 2018. https://www.nytimes.com/2018/10/12/arts/design/humboldt-forum-berlin-deutschland.html (16 juin 2022).

Engler, Saliha. *Die Gründung der Universität Dschang*. Bachelorarbeit. Institut der Geschichtswissenschaften. Heinrich-Heine-Universität Düsseldorf, 2017.

Fine, Jonathan, et Hilke Thode-Arora. « Provenienzforschung – Forschungsquellen, Methodik, Möglichkeiten. » *Leitfaden zum Umgang mit Sammlungsgut aus kolonialen Kontexten*. Ed. Deutscher Museumsbund e.V. Berlin, 2018. 57–64.

Gouaffo, Albert. « Se guérir de la violence coloniale ? Jean Ikelle-Matiba et René Philombe font face aux colonialismes français et allemand ». *Violences postcoloniales. Perceptions médiatiques, représentations littéraires. Actes du colloque du 17 au 18 juin 2005 à Sarrebruck*. Ed. Isaac Bazié et Hans-Jürgen Lüsebrink. Münster : LIT, 2005. 49–63.

———. « Écrire par devoir de mémoire. L'histoire coloniale allemande dans la littérature camerounaise francophone ». *Mont Cameroun. Zeitschrift für interkulturelle Studien zum deutschsprachigen Raum* 2 (2011) : 79–91.

———. « Eine Sprache gehört nicht. » *Rhinozeros. Europa im Übergang 1*. Ed. Markus Messling, Franck Hofmann, Teresa Koloma Beck et Priya Basil. Berlin : Matthes & Seitz, 2021. 32–41.

Gouaffo, Albert, et Stefanie Michels. Eds. *Koloniale Verbindungen – transkulturelle Erinnerungstopografien. Das Rheinland in Deutschland und das Grasland Kameruns*. Bielefeld : Transcript, 2019.

Grimme, Gesa. « Provenienzforschung im Projekt 'Schwieriges Erbe : Zum Umgang mit kolonialzeitlichen Objekten in ethnologischen Museen'. » Abschlussbericht. Ed. Linden Museum Stuttgart. Staatliches Museum für Völkerkunde, 2018. https://www.lindenmuseum.de/fileadmin/user_upload/images/fotogalerie/Presse__Veranstaltungskalender/SchwierigesErbe_Provenienzforschung_Abschlussbericht.pdf (28.10.2022).

Guimatsia, Sa'ah François. « Le problème anglophone au Cameroun : Comment éteindre le volcan en éruption ? » L'Harmattan (blog), 10.12.2016. https://www.editions-harmattan.fr/auteurs/article_pop.asp?no=31905&no_artiste=18165 (17 juin 2022).

Habermas, Rebekka. « Kolonialgeschichte lässt sich durch Restitutionen nicht entsorgen. » *Deutschlandfunk*, 25 novembre 2018. https://www.deutschlandfunk.de/rueckgabe-von-raub-kunst-kolonialgeschichte-laesst-sich-100.html (17 juin 2022).

Horton, Mark. « Returning looted artifacts will finally restore heritage to the brilliant cultures that made them. » *The Conversation*, 23 novembre 2018, http://theconversation.com/returning-looted-artefacts-will-finally-restore-heritage-to-the-brilliant-cultures-that-made-them-107479 (25 juin 2022).

Karakis, Yagmur. *Vom Kameruner Grassland nach Mannheim – Die Sammlung Thorbecke 1911/12 in den Reiss-Engelhorn-Museen Mannheim/From Cameroonian Grassfield to Mannheim – The collection Thorbecke 1911/12 in Reiss-Engelhorn-Museen Mannheim*. Institut für Geschichtswissenschaften. Heinrich-Heine-Universität Düsseldorf, 2017.

Krieger, Kurt. « Hundert Jahre Museum für Völkerkunde Berlin. Abteilung Afrika. » *Baessler Archiv. Beiträge zur Völkerkunde (Neue Folge, XXI)*. Ed.Kurt Krieger et Gerd Koch. Berlin : Dietrich Reimer, 1973. 101–140.

Laumeyer, Robin, Nina Jean Norin, et Vanessa Viola Neuhaus. « Koloniale Verbindungen. » Film documentaire réalisé sous la direction de Martin Doll. Heinrich-Heine-Universität Düsseldorf et Université de Dschang, 2017. http://deutschland-postkolonial.de/#kurzdokumentarfilme-koloniale-verbindungen-204729 (20.10.2021)

Lecaplain, Guillaume. « La France refuse de rendre les objets royaux du Benin ». *Libération*, 23 mars 2017. https://next.liberation.fr/culture/2017/03/23/la-france-refuse-de-rendre-les-objets-royaux-du-benin_1555888 (18 juin 2022).

Rein, Annette. « Wie muss heutige koloniale Provenienzforschung aussehen? » Tagungsbericht. *Museum Aktuell* 241 (2017) : 26–30.
Sarr, Felwine. *Afrotopia*. Paris : Philippe Rey, 2016.
Sarr, Felwine et Bénédicte Savoy. *Rapport sur la restitution du patrimoine culturel africain. Vers une nouvelle éthique relationnelle*. Paris : Phillipe Rey / Seuil, 2018.
Schnee, Heinrich. « Die koloniale Schuldlüge. » *Süddeutsche Monatshefte* 1 (1923–1924): 93–138.
Stöcker, Helmuth. Ed. *Kamerun unter deutscher Kolonialherrschaft*. Berlin : Deutscher Verlag der Wissenschaften, 1968.
Wallerstein, Immanuel. *Le Système du monde du XVe siècle à nos jours*. T. I : *Capitalisme et économie-monde : 1450–1640* ; t. II : *Le mercantilisme et la consolidation de l'économie monde européenne*. Trad. Claude Markovits. Paris : Flammarion, 1980–1984.

Khadija von Zinnenburg Carroll

Repatriation From the Universal Museum: *Iyagbon's Mirror* as a Performance of Minor-Universals

Abstract: In 2020 Mwazulu Diyabanza of the Yanka Nku Panafrican movement demonstratively entered a series of museums in France and Belgium and stole back African art works declairing they had been looted in the first place. This act of counter appropriation sent a wave of responses from legal to artistic around Europe. One of these was orchestrated by Samson Ogiamien and the Onyrikon theatre, which the author joined in the capacity of a collaborating artist and theorist reflecting upon the various modes of counter appropriation (and minor universality) occurring in restitutions around Europe. This chapter describes *Iyagbon's Mirror*, the performance work that resulted.

Keywords: Benin Bronzes, Nigeria, repatriation, appropriation, casts, copies

> I ask for Oluyenyetuye bronze of Ife – The moon says it is in Bonn
> I ask for Ogidigbonyingboyin mask of Benin – The moon says it is in London
> I ask for Dinkowawa stool of Ashanti – The moon says it is in Paris
> I ask for Togongorewa bust of Zimbabwe – The moon says it is in New York
> I ask I ask I ask for the memory of Africa – The seasons say it is blowing in the wind – The hunchback cannot hide his burden — Niyi Osundare
>
> ... I ask for Uhun Ila bronze head of Benin – The moon says it is in Vienna ... — Samson Ogiamien

What kind of platform is repatriation for a discussion of minor universality in the terms set out by this volume (Messling 2019; see also Hofmann and Messling 2021)? Following work I have done on theatre and 'productive universals', this chapter will investigate this question of repatriation from the perspective of a performance titled *Iyagbon's Mirror* (2017–ongoing).[1] This work is part, for me, of the five-year European Research Council project *REPATRIATES and New Originals* that compares different repatriations around the world from the perspective of the stakeholder communities and artist's responses, in this case to the return being made from Europe to Nigeria. In this project, I am

---

[1] Full credits of *Iyagbon's Mirror* can be read on the festival website: https://www.lastrada.at/en/cie-onyrikon-samson-ogiamien-fr-ch-at-ng/, see also Carroll (2019).

exploring the potential of replicas to mediate the spaces left in museums when looted artifacts are repatriated.[2]

Figure 1: *Iyagbon's Mask in Graz*, 2021. Photo credits: Khadija von Zinnenburg Carroll.

Iyagbon is a female deity who mothers the earth, for which the artist Samson Ogiamien created a mask which is the central character of *Iyagbon's Mirror*. The mask is taken on a journey by the theatre company Onyrikon, which reverses the usual provenance of the looted Benin Bronzes. Accompanied by actors and musicians in a two-hour play that moves through space along different stations, the audience is led in a procession of the mask to a ritual. In the middle, Samson Ogiamien addresses the Iyabgon mask and tells us that it and other things in his collections "were never meant to be in the museum" (Carroll 2021b, see Figure 1).

Ogiamien is a royal lineage from Benin City, an heir to the techniques of bronze casting that are still practised by the Royal Guild of Casters. In the Edo language the word for memory, *sa-e-y-ama*, means literally to cast in bronze. Edo is not a written language and the bronze sculptures that accompany ceremonies

---

[2] This research has received funding from the European Research Council (ERC) under the European Union's Horizon 2020 research and innovation programme (grant agreement No. 101001407 – REPATRIATES). www.repatriates.org.

in the palaces are the vessels of cultural memory (Plankensteiner 2016, 22–27; see also Carroll 2022b). In the final scene *of Iyagbon's Mirror* an auctioneer sells the mask and thereby brutally extracts it from the sacred context that is built up by the ritual that has just been performed (Carroll 2021b, see Figure 2).

Figure 2: *Iyagbon's Mask – auction scene in Rosengarten, Graz.* Samson Ogiamien and Onyrikon, performance still, 2021. Photo credit: Alberto Marchesis.

The assumption that is often made that restitution works towards returning original treasures to a place that is salvaging these after the erasure of modernisation and colonisation, is surprisingly countered by the example of Samson Ogiamien, a bronze sculptor and founder of the Edo Cultural Forum in Graz, Austria. On a studio visit he takes me to a glade near a river on rural farmland in lower Styria in central Europe, where there is an inconspicuous metal drum in the ground. This could be mistaken for a rusty home-made coffee table in the garden. Ogiamien peels aside the lid and reveals a coal pit and the remains of his last copper casting session.

In Benin casting is not done with a mould that can reproduce many of the same sculpture. While the one other Styrian bronze caster (near Ogiamien's studio) uses moulds to mass produce sculptures, Ogiamien is always making originals. What is interesting about Ogiamien is that he is both a contemporary artist, trained as such in Graz (which is why he moved to Austria) and also a bronze sculptor steeped in the manufacture of and activism for the restitution of bronze sculptures from Benin City. His sculpture, Iyagbon mask, is an assemblage of Benin Bronzes in a single piece, an over life size, baroque meta-melt. The technique of recycling metal that the bronze (and copper) casters use is an interesting material and also conceptual process in which existing artefacts are literally melted down into a new piece.

1 Repatriation as minor-universal

The general narrative theory underlying minor universality analyses narratives like *Iyagbon's Mirror* that construct the world to understand the in-common and the way universality is generated and generative of our communities and societies. The world of the museum and the narrative of breaking out of the deathly display within it to return to life in the world is one central narrative in *Iyagbon's Mirror*. There is a twist to the story in that the Iyagbon's Mask, which is broken free, is a sculpture that then becomes part of a ritual; whereas in the world of repatriation it is ritual masks and other objects that became art works in the museum. Contemporary art that is made to constitute a ritual is something the maker of Iyagbon's Mask, Samson Ogiamien, has in-common with many artists who are using similar strategies to shift their work out of hegemonic institutions into performative social engagements. These seek to create emotive responses so that people can identify on an emotional level with the stakes of return for those vested in repatriation claims. The format of ritual performance is an immersive one that involves people, even if only as the audience.

While Savoy's *Statues also Trample* (this volume) speaks of the sudden, eye-opening shift in experiencing the Jean-François Champollion sculpture (see also Messling 2022) – the kind of equestrian military monument that the Austrian writer Robert Musil (in 1927) said evades our attention (already in the early twentieth century cityscape) – the sculptures I am looking at in this chapter are of a very different regard (Musil 1986, 320). The Benin Bronze and copper, wood and fabric effigies are made for the shrines of the palaces. Worshipped, sung, prayed to, and moved about, they are central to moments of great attention, rather than being perched up on a high plinth and ignored.[3]

The architectures of display that museums use, like the parergon of plinths and vitrines, alarm censored barriers and frames, universally shift the lived

---

[3] This is what Akšamija and I argued also in *Living Monuments*, at the Venice Biennale, Rumanian Pavilion in 2007 (Akšamija and Carroll 2007, 4–6).

artefact into a space of stasis (Carroll 2017, 25–45; Carroll 2022b). Whatever specificity it came from is flattened to some extent by this force of the museum, which artists have set out to counter in many interventions and institutional critiques, from Fred Wilson and Daniel Buren to contemporary artists such as Piju Lawiyola, Kader Attia, Memory Biwa, and Victor Ehikhamenor.

The urge to smash the glass of the vitrine is also ubiquitous. Michael Taussig wrote it into his *Cocaine Museum* (1993) and the *Black Panther* movie popularised the idea. Most recently the first scene of *Iyagbon's Mirror* freed the mask of Iyagbon from the glass case in a ritual smashing of the vitrine. The experience of sharing a space with the breaking of glass, the sound especially, first of the smashing glass, then of the alarm that is set off, and finally of the fragments of security glass, are quite different to reading or watching such a scene on a screen or in a book.

The first scene of *Iyagbon's Mirror* intended to create an atmosphere of tension and unease. The actress Estelle Ntsende moves among the audience and begins to quietly and then in ever increasing tones speak to individuals as if she were just *en passant*:

(She speaks to someone randomly as they look at the exhibition.)
Do you think it's normal that this piece is in this museum?
(To another person, still in private.)
Excuse me, do you know how this work got here?
. . .
(To another person, still in private.)
Excuse me, are you aware that a large part of the collections in our museums comes from colonial looting?
. . .
(She speaks louder, to everyone.)
Can we accept that today the majority of African cultural heritage is in European museums? Stolen Massively imprisoned
In London, Vienna, Belgium, Berlin, the Vatican, Paris, Switzerland and also in Austria

THE GUARD *(sitting on his chair).*
Madam, I beg you to lower your voice, please.
Would you like to sit down, some water?
ESTELLE. *(She sings)*
THE GUARD. I ask you to lower your voice, please.
ESTELLE. For too long this voice has been silenced.
So no, I will not lower my voice.
What if we could give these masks a voice again, could we understand their words?
The past is present! The past is present! The past is present! The past is present!
THE GUARD. Madam, an artistic performance is about to begin, if you don't stop, I will be obliged to accompany you to the exit.

The first guard leaves and comes back with reinforcements. They are at a distance, communicating with each other and watching her.
ESTELLE. In this museum that is supposed to pay tribute to the past, I look for the names of the people who made these objects and what I see,
on the walls, on the labels, are the names of the plunderers, the missionaries, the colonisers.
I don't ask for anything, I don't claim anything. As Mwavulu Dyiabanza says: "You don't ask a thief if you can have your property back. You don't ask a thief if you can take back your property"
And I am not asking for reparation
No
Repair, repair, repair what, repair, who
Who repairs, who?
THE GUARD. Madam, I'm going to ask you to move towards the exit please
ESTELLE. Me? You? We?
Who repairs? Who repairs imaginaries? Who repairs memories? Who repairs souls? Repair yourself.
. . .
(She approaches Iyagbon.)
Help me, help us, help me to free these works. This work wants to get out. Let's free it together. Free it.
(The guards approach to stop her. One guard tries to grab her and another one signals her to calm down.)
A GUARD. Calm down, Madam. It's not worth it.
THE OTHER GUARD *(to the audience)*. It's all right, let's keep calm.
(The other talks in a low voice to the walki talki asking for outside help.)[4]

(Cainero, unpublished, first staged 2017)

As one sees in the film "Iyagbon's Mirror" (Carroll 2021b), people in the audience begin to intervene and try to help her, thinking this is a spontaneous outburst and not scripted action. Making a film of *Iyagbon's Mirror,* I am taken by the Tarkovskian moment that a white dog with an owner dressed also entirely in white, walks through the performers who are all masked in black (see Figure 3). Walker and dog remain oblivious to the dancers, the mask on a carrier, and the hundred odd audience, and walk through the middle of the shot as if scripted. I film this and think of *Stalker*'s dog that appears on the set for Tarkovsky, unplanned but, in his words, the apotheosis of his direction. In the dripping green soil of both these sets, the light instinct of the dog is oblivious to the existential drama of the human world. That in *Iyagbon's Mirror* this is accompanied by a human, white-skinned, dressed in white and with white dog makes their obliviousness reflect the lack of response or reference to African culture locally in Graz (Carroll 2021b; 2022a). Like in most of

---

4 Thank-you to Juri Cainero, director of Onyrikon and of *Iyagbon's Mirror*, for sharing his script with me.

Europe, the African diaspora lives their culture in relative separateness to the mainstream.

Figure 3: *Iyagbon's Mirror – first ritual scene in Rosengarten Graz*, 2021. Video still from a film by Khadija von Zinnenburg Carroll.

Naomi Vogt has argued in her work on rituals in contemporary art, and her participation in a performance I made in 2018 called *Processions for Tupaia*, in particular, that cues she knows from Jewish rituals shape the way she is able to respond to performances. She writes for example about how she instinctively doesn't turn her back to the main ritual object (Vogt 2022). However, the white dog and walker did not show any sign of seeing that there was a performance and ritual taking place in a space, which for this purpose becomes focussed by witnesses. My own experience would tell me that to cross uninvited into a space of ritual is taboo, because it disrupts the energy focussed on the performances on the ground prepared for them. There are minor-universalities but there are also parallel universes, and the white dog and walker were in one of them.

They were also not the only ones, on the second day, in the same space, two locals practising Qi Gong placed themselves within the world created by *Iyagbon's Mirror* and the Onyrikon performers. While the audience watched *Iyagbon's Mirror* being performed, in the near background there were quiet martial artists carrying on their evening brocades. Eventually, perhaps because I began to film them, one of the La Strada festival organisers went up and told them to stop because the audience might mistake them as part of the performance. This amused me because the limits of a ritual, the sum of this world of *Iyagbon's Mirror*, could not be in our control. The oblivious, white walkers or martial artists, would enter and become part of our world, the limits of which we cannot script and thereby hermetically seal.

Something Samson Ogiamien often emphasises is that "we are in the same boat" (Carroll "Samson Ogiamien introduction" 2021a, Figure 4). That is both the victims and perpetrators, the Europeans and Africans, for want of more nuanced dichotomies or categories, are both afflicted by the legacies of colonialism. It is through our collaboration that we begin to heal these wounds. I will argue in what follows that the process of reparation or repatriation might be read as a minor-universal.

The reason the repatriation debate recurs, as Savoy and Sarr have historicised in their report for French President Macron *Relational Ethics* (2018), is, because it is a symbolic transfer, potent with the potential to signal awareness and willingness to repair this colonial wound (Sarr and Savoy 2018; see also Savoy 2021). By performing together in public space, collective action becomes foregrounded rather than an individual monetary interest, which often derails repatriation claims. Since the theatre allows us to create a micro universe in which to experiment with ideas, *Iyagbon's Mirror* built precisely the boat in which we are all sailing in the wake of the third passage (Sharpe 2016).

Figure 4: *Iyagbon's Mirror – Samson Ogiamien*. Performance still, 2021. Photo credit: Nicola Milatovic.

2 Object to subject

The premise of our artistic research on repatriation is that we will expand our knowledge of human/object relations.[5] Advancing beyond the European conception of an object in a universal museum to what Mbembe has called "not mere objects but active subjects" (Mbembe 2020). The agency imbued in works through performance and ritual in the ways reenacted in Iyagbon's Mask are also addressed by Felwine Sarr:

> The notion of originality here is fluid. It was thought that once the artist made two copies of an object, both were authentic; doubling had no bearing on the power of either. When many African communities experienced the theft of their masks, for instance, they made identical copies of them, and their spiritual charge was transferred from the old to the new, rendering those examples we find today exhibited in the West spiritually empty: their immaterial content was channelled into a new physical body. We are less concerned here with an original object's multiplication, but rather a spiritual essence's appropriation of a physical form. An object is made real through its ritualisation. (Sarr 2019, 162)

The legal personhood finally given to non-humans has shown that material artifacts, in an intimate relational sphere, are the locus of moral rights (Morris and Ruru 2010; Miller et al. 2010, 294; Ruru 2018, 215–224). As Achille Mbembe notes, from an African perspective, artifacts have a subjectivity (2020), and their agency adds a further dimension, I argue, to claims for repatriation. The notion that objects are not merely things that illustrate ideas but subjects that have their own influence and agency in the relationships they constitute is adopted in the Bill of Rights for Works of Art that Artwatch released in 1992 (Artwatch 1992). This bill eschews restoration (which often radically alters the original object) and argues in favor of a notion of the agency and integrity of the artwork. The idea of the Bill of Rights for Works of Art as equivalent to bills of human rights needs to be interrogated in regard to the law used to justify restoration, which is often an instrument of political power. The Bill of Rights for Works of Art seeks to criminalise restorations that undermine a work of art's inalienable right to remain where and as it is. By treating the artwork as an entity with inalienable rights, it implicitly makes a comparison with the Bill of Human Rights from which the Artwatch bill derives its title.

Yet for most of us it is difficult to perceive reciprocal affects—such as love—from "inanimate" things. Because the object cannot speak to us in our language,

---

5 *Iyagbon's Mirror* is part, for me, of the ERC Consolidator REPATRIATES project of which I am the PI. The research team includes Jessyca Hutchens working in Australia, Memory Biwa working in Namibia, Tamara Newton in the UK, and Martha Fleming as project manager.

we think we cannot gauge the agency it possesses. We do not seem to know whether it has a life and whether it can be seen to reciprocate. Animists have no qualms in attributing agency to an object that might help or harm a person. In exchange, humans ventriloquise for objects, the performers of *Iyagbon's Mask* carried and danced and made music until the bronze mask indeed appeared to come to life. In the real world process of repatriation the activists and artists, the lawyers and museums also speak for what they claim the object wants. The voices of their human clients, the market, and the politics of the state enter the conversation with another range of unheard voices. To the polemicised opposition between the perspectives of archaeologists and museum curators toward looted art can be added the oft-occluded perspectives on repatriation of Indigenous non-European stakeholders.

The term "inalienable" describes the inseparableness of an object from a person or a group's identity. This has been studied by anthropologists such as Lévy-Bruhl, who found in 1914 that Melanesian languages have two types of nouns distinguished by a prefix to indicate the difference between alienable and inalienable things (Lévy-Bruhl 1914 cited in Chappell and McGregor 1996, 3). The inalienable relates to parts of the body, kin, and spatial relationships and objects closely related to a person (and all other nouns were presented by a free possessive morpheme). These certain things, such as the body, family, and the home and its contents, are the inalienable right of their owners to possess and control. It is the objects, in this intimate relational sphere, that are in possession of moral rights and are thus justified in claims for repatriation. The inalienable is interpreted in two ways, that which cannot be transferred and cannot be waived.

Making things and land alienable through capital, through the transformation of these once inalienable beings into equivalents in money, is what Karl Marx theorised in *Das Kapital* (1990–1992 [1867]). Vladimir Lenin would later modify Marx's economic theories by describing the function of financial capital in profiting from colonialism in his 1917 book *Imperialism, the Highest Stage of Capitalism* (Lenin 2005 [1917]). Marx spoke about alienation and predicted the kinds of alienation people would experience when their labor and everything associated with them became a currency rather than something they had intrinsic possession of. Dispossession of land and things became a dispossession of time, place, and sense of self. A process of disalienation is the attempt to regain some of these relationships to land, things, and people, likewise alienated through capitalism and colonialism.

Figure 5: Earliest known photograph of Oba's compound, Benin City, May 1891. Photo credit: Cyril Punch. Public Domain.

3 Repatriation as "negative universalism"

At the center of the ontological divide that exists in the process of decolonisation is the assumption that the museum in possession of a collection can assimilate it into a universal understanding. Yet it is clear from research conducted on colonial collections that holders' knowledge about them is scant and lacks the cultural context that could place them within the ontologies in which they were created. Being put on display, without the power to determine that display, has a perverse history from colonial exhibitions to zoos and anthropology museums that persistently attract audiences with their spectacles of othering.

The universal museum privileges the art historical value of the collector but does not offer narratives beyond a European biography and a moment of reception history. Former director of the British Museum David M. Wilson described the institution as a universal museum that stands as a "museum for *all* nations" (Wilson 1989). This is the ideal rather than the defined neutrality that the encyclopedic museum propagates—because this "universal model institution" is actually, and revealingly, called the "British" Museum and sits in the center of London.

The debate over repatriation has drawn the heads of museums and archaeologists into polemical opposition. Museum directors such as Neil McGregor, Philip de Montebello, and James Cuno eloquently defend the universal museum against claims that might jeopardise their institutions' ownership of treasures and have based their careers on their opposition to repatriation. Their reactionary turn to universalism undermines the affective and healing potential of repatriation (Cuno 2010). Ariella Aïsha Azoulay has written about the "Declaration on the Importance and Values of Universal Museums" signed by eighteen directors of major museums in the United States and Europe in 2004:

> Not surprisingly, the category used by museum directors, boards, and staff to counter restitution claims is "retention." The choice of a rival word that shares the prefix "re" is not innocent. It seeks to impose a kind of symmetry between two sides in a dispute, and rather than substantively engage with restitution claims, responds to them superficially in order to bury them as soon as possible and be able to pursue business as usual, as if the reasons for restitution should have no impact on the museum profession. In both cases, the prefix "re" serves to refer to a prior situation and to anchor a claim in it: museums seek to retain, to keep holding, what is already in their hands, while those who push for restitution seek recognition of their initial ownership of the object (Azoulay 2004, 145–146).

Setting the universal against the national is a powerful argument. It allows James Cuno to say that all claims upon objects from universal museums are driven by nationalism (Cuno 2010). Since nations are relatively recent constructs, the authenticity of original objects is seen as clear defense against co-optation into these "imagined communities." Cuno begins his book *Who Owns Antiquity?* (2010) with an image of the Parthenon Marbles and quotes from the key theorists of nationalism: Benedict Anderson, Anthony D. Smith, and Nayan Chanda (Anderson 2006 [1984]; Smith 2009; Appiah 2006; Cotter 2006). Especially useful to Cuno is the skeptical position of the British-Ghanaian philosopher Anthony Kwame Appiah, who cleverly outlines the unknowns of provenance and purpose and the certainty that the modern nation-states did not exist at the time of the objects' creation.

With the shift in museology to include Indigenous curatorial voices, national museums have become more representative of "the people" who Appiah (2006, 38) says are conflated with the nation. The Pitt Rivers Museum in Oxford, the Museum of Archaeology and Anthropology Cambridge, the British Museum, the Maritime Museum London, and the National Museum of Australia are among other museums that have taken initiative to invite Indigenous artists and researchers to work critically on their collections. Nevertheless, as Dan Hicks has written in *The Brutish Museums*, "Where discipline does come into things is where the academic fields of anthropology and archaeology repress the knowledge of the brutality of 'acquisition' in the form of loot, knowledge that, when we see it, shatters our image of the museum, forces us to question ourselves, to question what the curation of 'world culture collections' today actually means" (Hicks 2020, 51).

There are museum curators who are not staunchly opposed to repatriation but excitedly tell stories of its failure. Maybe it is my own insistence on addressing the topic that gets these conversations so heated that the museum directors take cover behind its walls and laws; they do not want to be responsible for any damage during their tenure.

"We gave back a Māori head," one director of a European museum told me, "and they keep writing each year with a standard request; they don't even bother to change the letter." This director is particularly irritated by the lack of differentiation and lack of respect shown to him. He wants something back, something in return for the repatriation that was made before his arrival in the museum. In his return letters he asks where the Māori head is now, and he says he receives no reply. He wrote to the embassy in New Zealand, and they were the only ones to respond with a letter of thanks for the repatriation. He concludes that the Māori do not actually care about the head. He is not going to repatriate anything further because they have failed to reply to his demands to know where the head now resides. "What about the possibility that they don't want to tell you where the head is?" I respond. It is a hot day. We are sitting in the sun and he is drinking wine, but the emotional temperature goes up far beyond the effects of wine in the heat––the loss of control over possessions and gift-giving processes can certainly drive people wild.

One might say the museum director and I, having a conversation in the sunshine, are "working" with the collection. We have a break to discuss the individual fields in which we are toiling. We think of ourselves as making things "work" in the process of our discussion, like making fallow land productive through labor. Rather than leaving objects from the collection lying unseen in underground suspension, our working with them justifies them being kept, in much the same way that settler agriculture was used to justify the dispossession of Indigenous people from their land during colonisation.

The museum director tells me a second story to try and convince me of the validity of his stance on repatriation. A collection of Peruvian mummies was offered for sale to the European museum. The museum declined but was then offered them for free. The museum declined again but offered to mediate the return of the collection to Peru. Two archaeologists from Peru came in a delegation to assess the mummies. Such mummies are among the most terrifying objects I have ever encountered in a storeroom. The ones in the Ethnological Museum in Berlin-Dahlem are simply bodies: crunched up but very recognisable as human beings, cowering on the shelves as if just recently deceased, with all the necessary rituals omitted.

The archaeologists from Peru visited, wrote their report, and the government selected some of the mummies to be returned. Others remained and were buried in a named grave in a Swiss cemetery. Time passed and the image of one of the Peruvian mummies went viral on the internet, with reports that started in Peru then spread further afield and picked up on the "indecent" burial of the remaining mummies in the Swiss cemetery. The director is getting heated again, this story of the undead is not terribly clear, but the problems are familiar. The archaeologists recommended the return of all the mummies, but the government concealed this, perhaps for reasons as banal as transportation costs. Once again, the museum is made to look responsible, despite its limited role as mediator, and is left feeling politically manipulated.

The issues around repatriation highlight the legal or clinical detachment of the institution toward the material life, the lived history of an object and its previous owner. In the confusion of ethics and economics, in the debate about ownership and repatriation, a disentanglement of what is possible from what is desirable might reveal what is meant by wanting something "back." The question of repatriation is therefore one of historical loss and contemporary gain.

Dacia Viejo-Rose writes of the dislocation of material culture, in which it becomes "like a divining instrument tracing for the lifelines of the territory from which it came, yet its stillness seems to indicate the broken connection between the object and the territory, a distance of time, space and meaning, too vast now for the dialogue to start up again. This silence has an effecting presence, for without the conversation, the references linking objects and places remain dislocated. What does reunion look like when both object and place have changed?" (Viejo-Rose 2016, 103–133).

In the case of *el Penacho*, the Aztec feather crown in the Weltmuseum Vienna, the "reunion" Viejo-Rose speaks of sometimes takes the form of collective protest outside the museum. At other times, Mexican visitors put their hands on the glass of the vitrine and speak to *el Penacho*. Through these gestures, the holy and resplendent green feathers, once part of sixteenth-century collections of early colonial featherwork, are now part of the history of the encyclopedic display and part of the modern museum. A set of deeper continuities exists between the sixteenth and twenty-first century collections. This is not only a post-Holocaust moment in which repatriation has come into the light; there are older exchanges, styles of collection and relationships to be considered, which realign possible futures.

The universalism that the museum claims is in fact itself partial to a particular philosophy that is in no way universal. Humanism, which has existed in a parallel space and time, cannot explain to us the humanitarian thinking of other cultures. This is another reason why place is of critical importance when assessing the rights of objects. For while the universal museum idea lives on in the extraction of objects from their locations, there is a strong counterargument that every excavation puts those objects in danger, particularly within a dominant power of scientific collection that will in turn degrade the meanings of objects both in the present and in the future.

The critics of repatriation cling to universalism and cite the likes of Terence's famous statement "I am human and I think nothing human is alien to me" alongside other pompous voices from Greco-Roman antiquity (Jenkins 2016, 219). Art historian Tiffany Jenkins does just this in her book *Keeping Their Marbles* (2016). Notably, the Wikipedia entry cut-and-paste job that Jenkins does in this book shows in every regurgitation of standard (and often dated) history that so much is incommensurable without a deeper engagement. The first chapter of *Keeping Their Marbles* (2016) tells the history of the British Museum's earliest collections through popular misconceptions of the history of Captain Cook. It appears that all the work of scholars on the Pacific in recent years, who have nuanced and complicated this heroic narrative of British imperialism, is alien or at least unknown to a polemic like the one adopted by Jenkins.[6]

A process of de-universalising positions on the European Enlightenment ideals of universality differentiates them as belonging to a particular historical moment, along with other historical ontologies around the world that would have very different understandings of the same collection. What is missing from the more familiar tropes of the repatriation debate in Europe is a deeper knowledge of those traditions of thought and ways of being, or 'indigenous ontologies' that are given space through relationships between the ancestors and the living, kindled by repatriations.

Appiah, Messling, and others would argue it is idealistic to imagine that alienated objects can be disalienated through repatriation and ritual such as *Iyagbon's Mirror*. Indeed testing the efficacy of performance as ritual is part of what interested me in joining Onyrikon and Samson Ogiamien to make a film of *Iyagbon's Mirror*. It strikes me that the ceremonies artists create often function as rituals in the sense that the audience undergoes an embodied transformation. Understanding what or why the ceremony is taking place is also not a prerequisite for being involved, as Naomi Vogt's work on invented rituals in contemporary art shows. Especially performative re-enactments, of the kind that *Iyagbon's Mirror* stages, or artists like Jeremy Deller, Yael Bartana, Mike Kelley, and Pierre Huyghe have made, raise challenges to the ideas of inventing traditions that have circulated in

---

6 For more on this subject see the chapters by Pauline Reynolds and Julie Adams, Huw Rowlands, Katerina Tiewa and Harriet Parsons and my introduction with Simon Layton to Carroll (2022c).

more traditional academic discourse. The participative dimension of re-staging requires more than a critical regard from the viewer and can produce and reinvent social realities.[7] I have experienced this first hand and turned my camera to documenting the process, for example in my film *Te Moana* (2020), which follows a repatriation from the UK to Maori in Aotearoa New Zealand.[8] The repatriated in that case created a funeral for ancestors, a dimension that merely calling repatriation Eurocentric cannot encompass. There is much that remains incommensurable, wounded, and unresolved in repatriations, which is all part of the complexity of processes at work within them. As artists, performers, and collaborators on artistic research with stakeholder communities we are in a unique position to reflect on the movement of the originals within the same medium that they are – bronzes recast, spoken words resung, ceremonies reenacted.

Figure 6: *Iyagbon's Mirror – Edo Cultural Forum Graz performing the last scene*, 2021. Photo credit: Khadija von Zinnenburg Carroll.

---

7 This is also the direction of argument in Naomi Vogt's forthcoming book *Inventing Ritual: Moving images of Social Reality in Contemporary Art*.
8 This is explored in greater depth also in Carroll (2021a).

References

Akšamija, Azra, and Khadija von Zinnenburg Carroll. "Living Monument." *Memosphere. Rethinking Monuments*. Eds. Mihnea Mircan and Meta Haven: Design Research. Frankfurt: Revolver, 2007.

Anderson, Benedict. *Imagined Communities: Reflections on the Origin and Spread of Nationalism*. New York: Verso, 2006 [1984].

Appiah, Anthony Kwame. "Whose Culture is it?" *New York Review of Books* (9 February 2006): 38.

Artwatch. "Bill of Rights for Works of Arts." *Artwatch*, 1992. http://artwatch.org.uk/archive/ (last accessed, 5 January 2022).

Azoulay, Ariella Aïsha. "Declaration on the Importance and Values of Universal Museums." *Potential History*. Paris: ICOM (2004): 145–146.

Caneiro, Juri. Iyagbon's Mirror. Unpublished theatre script. First staged: Arzo, Switzerland, 2021.

Carroll, Khadija von Zinnenburg. "The Inbetweenness of the Vitrine: Three Paraerga of a Feather Headdress." *The In-Betweenness of Things: Materialising Mediation and Movement between Worlds – A Cabinet of Curiosities*. Ed. P. Basu. London: Bloomsbury, 2017: 25–45.

———. "The Aesthetics of Classification and the Politics of Taxonomy: Wilhelm Blandowski's Encyclopaedia as Theatre, 1849–1859." *Productive Universals – Specific Situations. Analysis and Intervention in Art, Architecture and Urbanism*. Ed. N. Zschocke. Berlin: Sternberg, 2019.

———. "El Penacho, the lack of provenance and the gains of decolonization: Ethical, technical or political reasons for restoration." *Das Museum im kolonialen Kontext*. Vienna: Bundeskanzleramt, 2021a.

———. *Iyagbon's Mirror*. Dir. Khadija von Zinnenburg Carroll. Digital video (2021b), 7:25mins. https://vimeo.com/640260056 (10 November 2022).

———. "On Properties of Relation, in the Process of Repatriation." *21: Inquiries into Art, History, and the Visual — Beiträge zur Kunstgeschichte und visuellen Kultur* 1 (2022a): 259–267.

———. *The Contested Crown: Repatriation Politics between Europe and Mexico*. Chicago: Chicago University Press, 2022b.

———. *Tupaia, Captain Cook and the Voyage of the Endeavour: A Material History*. Ed. Khadija von Zinnenburg Carroll. London: Bloomsbury, 2022c

Chappell, Hilary, and William McGregor. "Prolegomena to a Theory of Inalienability." *The Grammar of Inalienability: A Typological Perspective on Body Part Terms and the Part-Whole Relation*. Eds. Hilary Chappell and William McGregor. Berlin, New York: De Gruyter Mouton, 1996: 3.

Cotter, Holland. "Who Owns Art?" *The New York Times* (29 March 2006). https://www.nytimes.com/2006/03/29/arts/artsspecial/who-owns-art.html (last accessed, 1 December 2022).

Cuno, James. *Who Owns Antiquity? Museums and the Battle over Our Ancient Heritage*. Princeton: Princeton University Press, 2010.

Hicks, Dan. *The Brutish Museums: The Benin Bronzes, Colonial Violence and Cultural Restitution*. London: Pluto, 2020.

Hofmann, Franck, and Markus Messling. "On the ends of universalism." *The Epoch of Universalism 1769–1989. L'époque de l'universalisme 1769–1989*. Eds. Franck Hofmann and Markus Messling. Berlin, Boston: De Gruyter, 2021. 1–39.

Jenkins, Tiffany. *Keeping Their Marbles: How the Treasures of the Past Ended Up in Museums . . . and Why They Should Stay There*. Oxford: Oxford University Press, 2016.

Lenin, Vladimir. *Imperialism, the Highest Stage of Capitalism*. "Marxists Internet Archive", 2005. First published 1917 in pamphlet form: https://www.marxists.org/archive/lenin/works/1916/imp-hsc/ (last accessed, 25 February 2022).

Lévy-Bruhl, Lucien. "L'expression de la possession dans les langues mélanésiennes". *Mémoires de la Société de Linguistique de Paris* 19.2 (1914): 96–104.

Marx, Karl. *Das Kapital: A Critique of Political Economy*. London: Penguin Classics, 1990– 1992 [1867].

Mbembe, Achille. "Wilde Objekte." *Anton Wilhelm Amo Lectures Vol.6*. Eds. Matthias Kaufmann, Richard Rottenburg and Reinhold Sackmann. Transl. Matthias Kaufmann. Halle: Martin-Luther-Universität-Halle-Wittenberg, 2020. 13–50.

Messling, Markus. *Universalität nach dem Universalismus. Über Frankophone Literaturen der Gegenwart*. Berlin: Matthes & Seitz, 2019.

———. "Champollion devant l'universalisme républicain." *La Vie des idées* (Collège de France), 27 September 2022. https://laviedesidees.fr/Champollion-devant-l-universalisme-republicain.html (last accessed, 22 November 2022).

Miller, Robert J., Jacinta Ruru, Larissa Behrendt, and Tracey Lindberg. *Discovering indigenous lands: The doctrine of discovery in the English colonies*. Oxford: Oxford University Press, 2010. 294.

Morris, James D.K., and Jacinta Ruru, "Giving voice to rivers: Legal personality as a vehicle for recognising Indigenous peoples' relationships to water." *Australian Indigenous Law Review* 14.2 (2010): 49–62.

Musil, Robert. "Monuments." *Selected Writings*. Ed. Burton Pike. Transl. Burton Pike. London: Bloomsbury, 1986. 320.

Plankensteiner, Barbara. "Samson Ogiamien and the Art Traditions of the Kingdom of Benin." *Yaruya. The sculptor Samson Ogiamien between African tradition and European reality*. Graz: Kunsthaus Graz, 2016.

Ruru, Jacinta. "Listening to Papatūānuku: A call to reform water law." *Journal of the Royal Society of New Zealand* 48.2–3 (2018): 215–224.

Sarr, Felwine. "The Museum as a Device of Recolonization?" *Look for Me All around You, Sharjah Biennale 14*. Ed. Claire Tancons. Sharjah: Sharjah Art Foundation, 2019: 162.

Sarr, Felwine, and Bénédicte Savoy. "The Restitution of African Cultural Heritage: Toward a New Relational Ethics." Transl. Drey S. Burk. French Government Report. 2018. http://restitutionreport2018.com/sarr_savoy_en.pdf (last accessed, 5 January 2022).

Savoy, Bénédicte. *Afrikas Kampf um seine Kunst. Geschichte einer postkolonialen Niederlage*. München: C.H. Beck, 2021.

Sharpe, Christina. *In the Wake: On Blackness and Being*. Durham/NC: Duke University Press, 2016.

Smith, Antony D. *Ethno-symbolism and Nationalism: A Cultural Approach*. New York: Routledge, 2009.

Taussig, Michael. *Mimesis and Alterity*. Chicago: University of Chicago Press, 1993.

Viejo-Rose, Dacia. "Eternal, Impossible, Returns: Variations on the Theme of Dislocation." *The Importance of Being Anachronistic: Contemporary Aboriginal Art and Museum Reparations*. Ed. Khadija Von Zinnenburg Carroll. Melbourne: Discipline, 2016. 103–133.

Vogt, Naomi. "I Didn't Know What I Was Doing: Tupaia's Postcolonial Funeral and Ritual Art in Britain." *Tupaia, Captain Cook and the Voyage of the Endeavour: A Material History*. Ed. Khadija von Zinnenburg Carroll. London: Bloomsbury, 2022.

———. *Inventing Ritual: Moving images of Social Reality in Contemporary Art*. Forthcoming.

Wilson, David M. *The British Museum: Purpose and Politics*. London: British Museum Publications, 1989.

Part V: **Human Rights and Universal Rights**

Cinquième partie : **Droits humains et droits universels**

Jean-Luc Chappey et Laurens Schlicht
Utopies égalitaires. De l'égalité aux techniques d'égalités : retour sur le « sauvage de l'Aveyron », 1799–1830

Abstract: The article raises the question of how different conceptions of equality were discussed during the phase immediately after the authoritarian take-over of state power in France by Napoléon Bonaparte. We use the case study of the so called "Wild Boy" Victor de l'Aveyron, who became a scientific and administrative subject of concern at around 1800, the period in which he has been found in the forests of the Department of Aveyron. By analysing political, scientific, and administrative discourses on human "equality," the article demonstrates how a universal concept of equality, as it is expressed, for example, in the Declaration of the Rights of Man and of the Citizen has been implemented in governmental strategies that categorised, mediated, and graduated kinds of equality of different types of human beings. The article thus shows how, in the decades after 1800, a stable system of administrative and scientific classificatory criteria for people was formed, transforming a universal system of equality into a system of governing and moderating inequalities.

Keywords: French revolution, history of the human sciences, Victor of Aveyron, equality, administration and science

> « Tous les hommes sont égaux par nature et devant la loi ».
> Déclaration des droits de l'homme et du citoyen de 1793, article 3

> « L'égalité consiste en ce que la loi est la même pour tous, soit qu'elle protège, soit qu'elle punisse. L'égalité n'admet aucune distinction de naissance, aucune hérédité de pouvoirs. »
> Déclaration des droits de l'homme et du citoyen de 1795, article 3

Plaçons-nous d'emblée en 1799. À la suite du coup d'État des 18–19 brumaire an VIII (9–10 novembre 1799), la Révolution française connaît une inflexion majeure marquée par un tournant autoritaire. Le pouvoir exécutif est renforcé, les libertés individuelles réduites, la presse muselée. Se revendiquant toujours républicain, Napoléon-Bonaparte tourne néanmoins le dos aux principes de liberté et d'égalité encore défendus sous le Directoire. Cette rupture avec les idéaux portés depuis 1789 est certes progressive mais bien réelle. En cette même année 1799, un jeune garçon, « Victor », est capturé dans les forêts d'un village proche de Saint-Affrique. Le « Sauvage de l'Aveyron » fait ainsi une entrée tonitruante dans l'Histoire. Dès 1797, les habitants des villages alentours ont alerté les autorités de la présence d'un enfant errant, d'une dizaine d'années, incapable de communiquer et dont le comportement est qualifié d'anormal (cf. Chappey 2017 ; Benzaquén 2006). Quelle est la source de son anormalité qui le fait apparaître aux yeux de ses contemporains comme un « phénomène extraordinaire »[1] ? Est-il vraiment incapable d'être socialisé et d'intégrer la communauté civique ? Ces questions sur le statut et les formes de marginalité ou de déviation de l'enfant sont au cœur du projet anthropologique porté par les membres de la Société des observateurs de l'homme (1799–1804) fondée au moment de sa découverte (cf. Chappey 2002). Dans cet article, nous voudrions considérer l'étude du cas de « Victor » comme un point de départ pour retracer la transition entre l'idéal d'égalité porté par les révolutionnaires et les républicains du Directoire et de nouvelles pratiques scientifiques et administratives qui, à partir du Consulat, tendent à légitimer et à organiser de nouvelles formes d'inégalités entre les individus et les populations.

Plus largement, il apparaît que le « moment 1800 » est particulièrement important pour comprendre comment des idéaux universels (« droits » universels ou « égalité » universelle), se rapportant à l'héritage des Lumières, encore revendiqué par les contemporains, vont être progressivement intégrés aux modalités de gouvernement pour devenir des objets de pratiques administratives. Le cas « Victor » ouvre des perspectives pour interroger les progressives adaptations des principes des Lumières, particulièrement ceux touchant aux projets de régénération et d'utopies pédagogiques, à la mise en place de nouvelles formes de pouvoirs et de dominations qui caractérisent les périodes consulaires et impériales. Il s'agit donc d'interroger les points de bascule à partir desquels se construit la sortie de la Révolution : des nouvelles formes de domination sociale, sexuelle ou raciale aux nouvelles pratiques de gouvernement des hommes et de la nature, le « cas » Victor doit permettre de mieux comprendre comment l'idéal d'égalité, encore défendu par les républicains du Directoire, disparaît progressivement derrière les combats contre les inégalités.

Comme l'ont montré de nombreuses recherches, la notion d'égalité s'impose comme centrale dans les discours politiques des XVIIe et XVIIIe siècles. Avant même 1789, les Frondes de 1648–1653, puis les conflits entre les nobles, les Parlements (jansénistes) et le roi au XVIIIe siècle, ont placé l'égalité comme un des enjeux centraux des dynamiques conflictuelles qui traversent le champ politique. L'historiographie récente est riche de nombreuses études portant sur l'analyse de différentes formes d'égalité étudiée, sous l'angle de la théorie politique et de l'histoire des idées

---

[1] Cf. Gineste (2004, 284), qui reproduit ici un article sur le « sauvage de l'Aveyron » dans la *Décade philosophique* de l'année 1800.

(Rosanvallon 2011 ; Stuurman 2017 ; Israel 2006), comme pratique épistémique dans les sciences (Elwick 2021 ; Alder 1998) ou encore, comme enjeu économique (Piketty 2013). Markus Messling a, par exemple, souligné l'importance de l'égalité dans la construction de la modernité : il soutient que, depuis la suppression des inégalités naturelles et des « privilèges » pendant la Révolution, les discours légitimant les inégalités (sociales ou raciales) ont dû recourir à de nouvelles stratégies d'argumentation (Messling 2019, 47). Immanuel Wallerstein souligne encore que « [t]he great political question of the modern world, the great cultural question, has been how to reconcile the theoretical embrace of equality with the continuing and increasingly acute polarization of real-life opportunities and satisfactions that has been its outcome » (Wallerstein 2003, 650). De son côté, Jean-Fabien Spitz invite à mieux comprendre les articulations et contradictions entre le combat en faveur de l'égalité et les pensées républicaines en France entre les XVIIe et XIXe siècles (Spitz 2005).

Nous souhaiterions montrer comment la question des pratiques d'égalité s'est fractionné après 1800 à partir de la formalisation de nouvelles sciences humaines et sociales et l'émergence de nouvelles pratiques administratives. D'une part, l'État développe, à travers des diverses pratiques comme les enquêtes préfectorales ou les topographies médicales, un besoin de savoir sur les formes et les mesures et les niveaux des inégalités au sein des populations : qui sont les pauvres et à quel point les pauvres sont-ils pauvres ? En quoi consiste la pauvreté ? À quel point encore, les sourds et muets sont sourds et muets et qu'est-ce que c'est, la surdi-mutité ? À quel point les aliénés sont-ils aliénés et ne pourraient-ils pas encore remplir une fonction « utile » dans l'État ? D'autre part, sur le plan discursif, les constellations sociales développent de nouveaux récits pour interpréter la déviation et construire un partage légitime entre les inégalités (dites « naturelles ») et les revendications d'égalité. L'appel à l'égalité ne détruit-il pas toute forme d'ordre social, politique, comme le pense Antoine Rivarol[2] ? Quelles étaient les inégalités naturelles, quelles étaient les inégalités artificielles (« factices »), et dans quelle mesure différaient-elles (Cabanis 1823 [1791–1793], 205–206) ? On constate que ces questions se posent à tous les niveaux de la société dès lors que la demande d'égalité est devenue possible pour tous les hommes.

Pendant la période révolutionnaire, le combat pour l'égalité a changé de forme et de nature : il ne concerne plus les droits (politiques, culturelles ou religieux) des élites, mais s'étend aux catégories populaires et aux revendications économiques et

---

2 « [. . .] elle [la nature] a voulu des hommes égaux avec des conditions et des fortunes inégales, comme nous vouons des anneaux inégaux pour les doigts inégaux : d'où résulte l'harmonie générale » ; « L'inégalité est [. . .] l'âme des corps politiques, la cause efficiente des mouvements réguliers et de l'ordre » (Rivarol [1797], 16–17).

sociales. L'émergence d'un mouvement populaire particulièrement dynamique (à travers le mouvement des sans-culottes) montre comme ces sollicitations constituent le moteur de la mobilisation des catégories populaires dans les villes comme dans les campagnes, obligeant les élites révolutionnaires à reprendre à leur compte une partie de ces revendications. Tout en limitant les droits politiques d'une partie du peuple, la république « bourgeoise » du Directoire aspire à instaurer une égalité pour tous en promouvant la propriété, le travail et l'instruction. Le Consulat et l'Empire, en promouvant de nouveaux dispositifs de gestion de la société et des populations, constituent des périodes de rupture : tournant le dos à l'idéal égalitaire, ces régimes cherchent à légitimer de nouvelles formes d'inégalités et de hiérarchies entre les individus et les populations.

1 Le « sauvage de l'Aveyron » et l'idéal de régénération

L'histoire du jeune « sauvage de l'Aveyron », est désormais bien connue (Cf. Chappey 2017 ; Benzaquén 2006)[3]. À la fin de l'année 1799, au moment même où la France change de régime politique, un garçon d'une dizaine d'années est finalement capturé par des chasseurs dans des bois situés près de Lacaune, un petit village du département de l'Aveyron. Suscitant la curiosité des populations locales, il alimente également l'intérêt des élites du département qui, dans le contexte d'incertitude politique ouvert par le coup d'État du 18-19 novembre an VIII (1799), cherchent à attirer l'attention des nouvelles autorités parisiennes. Dès le début du mois de janvier 1800, le maire de la commune de Saint-Sernin annonce, dans les journaux parisiens, qu'il vient de découvrir un « véritable » enfant sauvage, réveillant autant l'intérêt des philosophes et des savants que la curiosité du plus grand nombre (cf. Gineste 2004, 158–159). Aussitôt, la machine médiatique s'emballe et le nouveau ministre de l'Intérieur, Lucien Bonaparte, décide de transférer au plus vite l'enfant à Paris. Il n'arrive finalement dans la capitale française qu'en août 1800, confié alors aux bons soins du directeur de l'Institut national des sourds et muets, l'abbé Ambroise Sicard, et aux membres de la Société des observateurs de l'homme, une société savante créée quelques mois plus tôt autour d'un projet scientifique : la construction d'une « science générale de l'homme » définie sous la notion d'anthropologie (cf. Chappey 2002). Pour ces derniers, l'enfant

---

[3] Sur les usages de l'enfant sauvage dans l'histoire des sciences humaines, voir *Revue d'histoire des sciences humaines* 38 (2021).

considéré comme sauvage constitue une réelle opportunité pour mieux étudier les origines du langage et comprendre les modalités du développement de l'entendement et des facultés humaines. En un mot, le jeune sauvage doit permettre d'interroger les différentes étapes du processus de civilisation et de répondre à la question centrale : comment devient-on un homme civilisé ? En même temps, la question centrale des techniques d'observation est posée (cf. Schlicht 2020) : comment observer et mesurer les différentes étapes des progrès de la civilisation sur un être humain réel ? À partir de la mobilisation des connaissances existantes, le garçon est donc pris en charge par des personnes qui ont déjà développé des techniques d'observation et de classification dans des contextes éducatifs et psychiatriques.

Le premier à se pencher sur le cas n'est autre que le médecin Philippe Pinel (1745–1826), célébré pour avoir radicalement transformé les soins accordés aux aliénés : aux hôpitaux pour ces « aliénés », à la Salpêtrière et à Bicêtre, Pinel a mis progressivement au point un « traitement moral » lui permettant de construire un dialogue avec un insensé qui est désormais perçu comme un malade susceptible d'être soigné et de retrouver la raison (cf. Goldstein 1987, 65–71). Le fou cesse d'être un être irrémédiablement malade, condamné à l'isolement voire à l'exclusion, et la notion de guérison de la folie prend le devant de la scène. Néanmoins, après avoir travaillé avec de nombreux enfants, Pinel, au contact de l'enfant venu de l'Aveyron, se montre particulièrement pessimiste quant aux possibilités de l'éduquer ou de l'instruire. Selon lui, s'il convient de s'en occuper pour des raisons philanthropiques, cet enfant, qui ne parle pas et semble indifférent aux tentatives faites pour entrer en contact avec lui, est un idiot, incapable de faire le moindre progrès[4]. Ce jugement d'une des personnalités scientifiques les plus importantes du pays est pourtant remis en cause par un jeune médecin encore inconnu, Jean-Marc-Gaspard Itard, qui, juste nommé à l'Institut des sourds et muets de Paris, affirme au contraire pouvoir soigner et éduquer l'enfant. Ses deux rapports de 1801 et 1806 adressés au ministre de l'Intérieur sur ses méthodes et ses succès dans l'éducation de Victor sont très différents. Alors que le premier rapport exprime l'espoir d'une socialisation complète de Victor, le deuxième rapport contient des tonalités plus sceptiques, voire réellement pessimistes, ce qui a souvent conduit à la supposition que l'expérience d'Itard aurait mené à un « échec » (Bruland 2008, 38 ; McDonagh 2008, 73 ; Mannoni 1965). En effet, le fait que Victor ne puisse pas participer aux échanges sociaux comme tout le monde contredit les objectifs initiaux d'Itard. D'autre part, l'« échec » supposé d'Itard contribue à relancer une discussion et une pratique qui conduiront à la création d'institutions dédiées à une « éducation spéciale » des individus dé-

---

4 Pinel présente son *Rapport* devant les membres de la Société des observateurs de l'homme en 1800 (cf. Gineste 2004, 324–338).

viants au cours du XIXe siècle (Schlicht 2021). Ils répondent à la reformulation de l'idée d'égalité : égal, oui, mais seulement dans une certaine mesure, d'une certaine manière. Le fait que le niveau d'optimisme diffère dans les deux rapports de 1801 et 1806 peut donc être considéré, selon nous, comme une adaptation à l'évolution des pratiques de gouvernement des hommes. On peut retracer ce glissement dans les sphères politiques et scientifiques.

2 Les débats politiques après la Terreur

Si ce débat suscite l'intérêt des autorités et du public, c'est qu'il dépasse largement les frontières de la controverse scientifique pour s'ouvrir à des enjeux politiques. La question du « sauvage » et de la « civilisation » fait en effet référence à des débats qui renvoient à la nature même du projet politique de la République du Directoire et du nouveau régime Consulaire. Pour comprendre ces enjeux, il convient de remonter quelques années antérieures et revenir aux origines politiques et intellectuelles de la République du Directoire. Nous pouvons voir ici comment, en réaction à la Terreur, diverses revendications plutôt radicales des premiers jours de la Révolution sont remises en question. Entre autres, et en rapport avec le sujet qui nous occupe, l'idée limpide de l'égalité de tous les citoyens a été invalidée de manière pratique et discursive.

Au lendemain de la chute de Robespierre, les montagnards, encore en place au sein de la Convention nationale, se divisent : une partie d'entre eux, rejoints par des modérés, forment bientôt une nouvelle majorité politique, les Thermidoriens, qui entendent rompre avec l'idéal démocratique de l'an II et réduire le poids politique des sans-culottes. À partir de novembre 1794, les Thermidoriens mettent ainsi en cause le dirigisme économique et s'attaquent aux démocrates accusés d'avoir provoqué la « Terreur », une notion inventée pour stigmatiser la période du gouvernement révolutionnaire assimilée désormais aux violences et à la barbarie[5]. En floréal an III/mai 1795, un des rédacteurs de la nouvelle Constitu-

---

5 Il existe une réflexion sur le concept de la « terreur » et ses enchaînements avec les stratégies politiques. Ronen Steinberg (2015) montre comment le concept de la « terreur » a été pris d'un discours médical et, en effet, a été utilisé par Robespierre pour une certaine idée de la politique. Après la terreur, ces traditions médicales et politiques, se sont combinés pour construire une critique de la Terreur, particulièrement lisible dans le discours contre la Terreur de Jean-Lambert Tallien, qui s'appuie sur une ébauche de Pierre-Louis Roederer (cf. Jainchill 2008, 204–206). Après le règne de la terreur, Lezay-Marnésia réfléchit au lien entre la terreur et l'histoire de la révolution. Cet auteur suppose fortement que les terroristes ont formé leur règle sur la base d'une idée trompeuse de l'égalité (Lezay-Marnésia 1797, 31).

tion, Pierre-Charles-Louis Baudin des Ardennes, peut ainsi affirmer que « l'expérience démontre . . . qu'il est des hommes nés avec une supériorité incontestable de génie comme il en est de taille plus haute [. . .]. Les citoyens les plus jaloux de l'égalité ne peuvent prendre ombrage de l'homme aisé ni du savant » (Baudin des Ardennes 1795, 6). Sophie Wahnich a fait valoir que cette nouvelle vision du « peuple » sert à installer une nouvelle interprétation de la politique (Wahnich 2009, 72–73 ; cf. Baczko 1994 [1989]). Si certaines demandes d'égalité restent politiquement exprimables, émerge un espace de décision réservé à une élite politique. Les inégalités culturelles et intellectuelles servent désormais à légitimer un nouvel ordre politique, une République « sans révolution » ni démocratie, et une nouvelle distinction entre une élite civilisatrice, appelée à gouverner, un peuple à civiliser et à gouverner. La participation politique semble ainsi reposer sur une aptitude, des compétences particulières, qui doivent s'ajouter au capital financier[6]. Autre membre de la Commission des Onze chargée de rédiger la nouvelle constitution, Jean-Denis Lanjuinais construit l'équivalence entre ignorance et incapacité politique et affirme en juillet 1795 la nécessité des citoyens « ignorants » à s'en remettre à des guides : « qui de nous pourrait encore soutenir le spectacle hideux d'assemblées politiques en proie à l'ignorance crasse, à la basse avidité, à la crapuleuse ivresse ? [. . .] Il faut que celui à qui l'intelligence n'a pas été donnée, consente à prendre celle des autres comme guide [. . .]. Le temps des flagorneries populaires est passé » (*Réimpression de l'ancien Moniteur*, t. 25, 196).

Cette conception dirigiste et gradualiste de l'égalité des Lumières et de la participation politique était également ancrée dans des conceptions préexistantes. On la retrouve, par exemple, dans les conceptions anticolonialistes et égalitaires de Condorcet. Cofondateur de la Société des amis des noirs, ce dernier défend l'idée de l'égalité des « races », des sexes, mais dans la perspective même qui semble être reprise, et acceptable, par les Thermidoriens[7]. C'est là une ambiguïté des Lumières dont les représentants envisagent la « libération » des peuples selon

---

6 Les discours de Destutt de Tracy sont étudiés par Head (1985) ; pour une histoire de la construction des « aptitudes » basée sur plusieurs stratégies scientifiques cf. Carson (2017). La critique de la conception libérale émergente du sujet politique est trop détaillée et trop ancienne pour être présentée ici. Il est toutefois intéressant de constater que les acteurs libéraux eux-mêmes ont très tôt identifié et exprimé le lien entre le progrès économique et les libertés politiques des classes moyennes. Pierre Louis Roederer, en 1831, pense que la Révolution a été le produit d'une « passion de l'égalité » (Roederer 1831, 9), mais, en même temps, constate que cette passion était pour la plupart le résultat du désir de dépasser les ancêtres. Cette « passion de l'égalité » n'est, pour Roederer, pas une « égalité de fait », mais plutôt le fondement pour l'« amour des distinctions » (Roederer 1831, 8).
7 Cf. Condorcet (1966 [1795]), qui souligne qu'on doit éduquer les peuples avant que tous les droits de liberté et d'égalité peuvent être exercés. Cf. également son texte sur l'esclavage des « nè-

une perspective graduée et indirecte. Le peuple reste considéré comme un « enfant » auquel il convient d'enseigner les moyens d'accéder à la liberté et à l'égalité. Les hommes des Lumières ne sont pas forcément des démocrates : dès 1789, de nombreux philosophes et « héritiers des Lumières » prennent ainsi leurs distances face à ce qu'ils considèrent comme des débordements populaires. Les peuples ne peuvent donc pas être libérés immédiatement, mais seulement lorsqu'ils sont prêts. Cette forme d'égalité est donc toujours liée au contrôle par un pouvoir central ou des élites qui savent et peuvent faire en sorte que, sous la conduite de la raison, la vérité s'impose sous la bonne forme et au bon rythme. Gouverner au nom de la raison revient souvent à restreindre l'expression de revendications visant à instaurer immédiatement un régime de liberté et d'égalité. On voit donc que deux axes de contrôle et deux besoins de catégorisation s'ouvrent dans cet art de gouvernement : une connaissance des différences dans le progrès de la civilisation, ainsi qu'une connaissance des limites naturelles de l'égalité. Dans cette perspective, les savants du nouvel Institut national des sciences, arts et lettres sont appelés à remplir une nouvelle mission : construire une nouvelle science susceptible de mieux connaître les hommes et de donner aux législateurs les outils nécessaires à les gouverner. La République du Directoire se construit ainsi sur un idéal pédagogique et une utopie régénératrice : le peuple français, puis progressivement tous les peuples européens vivants sur les territoires conquis par les armées françaises, sont ainsi considérés comme des « enfants » qu'il convient de civiliser et d'éduquer afin de les maintenir dans de « justes bornes » et d'en garantir les « bonnes mœurs ». On comprend l'importance assignée par les autorités politiques du Directoire au « traitement moral » mis en œuvre par Philippe Pinel : comme le médecin auprès des fous, les législateurs républicains doivent empêcher le peuple de (re) devenir fou, barbare et violent (Steinberg 2015). Afin de mener à bien cette entreprise de civilisation, il convient de lutter contre tous les facteurs et causes d'une sauvagerie définie comme le résultat de l'isolement. L'apprentissage du langage, la valorisation de toutes les formes de communication deviennent ainsi des moyens de civiliser les populations, de perfectionner les mœurs et de régénérer la nation[8]. Pour permettre cette entreprise ambitieuse, il convient encore de transformer les environnements dans lesquels vivent les populations, en promouvant encore la circulation des hommes, des idées et des choses (Chappey et Vincent 2019). Peu à peu, l'image se dessine d'un nouvel art du gouvernement qui contrôle différents milieux, différents espaces d'action dans lesquels les différences peuvent

---

grès ». Dans ce dernier texte, Condorcet souligne qu'on doit réparer les maux qu'on a commis pendant la colonisation, mais qu'on doit choisir prudemment le moment (Condorcet 1781, 14).
[8] Ceci s'applique également dans la perspective des territoires colonisés ou à coloniser et devient clair, par exemple, dans l'*Esquisse* de Condorcet ; voir Condorcet (1966 [1795], 269–272).

être tolérées tant qu'elles n'entrent pas en conflit avec les intérêts du gouvernement central. De l'hygiène publique à l'apprentissage des langues en passant par l'histoire naturelle, tous les savoirs sont ainsi mobilisés pour constituer une « encyclopédie vivante » (Pierre-Jean-Georges Cabanis, cf. Chappey 2002, 67 suiv.) à laquelle les membres de la Classe des sciences morales et politiques de l'Institut national doivent particulièrement donner corps. On constate ainsi combien sont intrinsèquement lié l'idéal républicain et le projet de civilisation : le projet politique des républicains du Directoire renvoie en effet à un processus par lesquels toutes les populations et les individus doivent devenir « meilleurs ». En 1800, alors que se met en place le Consulat dont le projet politique reste à construire, la question posée par l'enfant sauvage de l'Aveyron est donc essentielle : est-il vraiment possible de civiliser un individu, de le rendre « meilleur », et dans quel sens cela est-il possible, avec quelles techniques ? Derrière cette question, c'est finalement l'avenir du projet républicain qui est en jeu d'où l'intérêt immédiat que suscite cette découverte dans le monde politique et scientifique. Derrière le destin de Victor et le « pari d'Itard » se jouent celui de l'idéal républicain tel qu'il fut défini par les élites du Directoire. En 1800, Bonaparte est encore soutenu par la grande majorité des membres de la nébuleuse des philosophes et administrateurs (pour la plupart membres d'une groupe appelée « Idéologues »[9]) qui espèrent encore qu'il parviendra à « régénérer » la population[10]. Après cinq années de fonctionnement de la République directoriale, nombreux parmi les partisans de la République espèrent faire émerger un peuple « raisonnable ». Ils participent à la construction d'un espace politique de « l'extrême centre » qui amalgame comme extrêmes royalistes et démocrates pour mieux les délégitimer (Serna 2019).

La publication en 1807 par les presses impériales du mémoire d'Itard adressé au ministère de l'Intérieur est un aveu d'échec. Ce mémoire marque finalement l'émergence d'une nouvelle grille de lecture (fondée sur des principes scientifiques) pour interpréter la « civilisation » et les différences individuelles. D'une part, pour Itard, en dépit des efforts menés depuis 1800, il est impossible d'éduquer le jeune enfant, ravalé dès lors au statut d'idiot. S'il ne se résout pas à reprendre les arguments de Pinel, Itard reconnaît que les progrès réalisés par l'enfant sont très limités et qu'il est désormais impossible d'atteindre le plein suc-

---

9 Terme désignant un groupe d'acteurs, actifs dans les cercles des « sciences de l'homme » à l'Institut des sciences et dans la politique au moment du Directoire. Participant à « l'invention de la Terreur », ce groupe exprime l'espoir de construire une forme de gouvernement contrôlée par les sciences de l'homme et la science sociale. Cf. (Wokler 2000 ; Head 1985).

10 Sean Quinlan retrace l'histoire du concept de la « régénération » après la Terreur et l'implication idéologique et pratique des acteurs des sciences de l'homme dans le coup d'État de Napoléon (Quinlan 2004).

cès que l'on espérait. Quelques semaines plus tard, les autorités publiques décident de cesser de payer les dépenses nécessaires à l'entretien de l'enfant au sein de l'Institut national des sourds-muets. Privilégiant désormais l'approche anatomopathologique, Itard se détache, sans pourtant la renier totalement, l'approche éducative et l'idéal de régénération[11]. Ce revirement peut être considéré à la lumière des transformations plus générales qui caractérisent alors les formes de gouvernement et l'ordre politique. D'autre part, Itard s'inscrit dans un contexte plus large de redéfinition de l'idée de « thérapie » à la fois en psychiatrie et dans d'autres institutions qui s'occupaient de ce qui était perçu comme une déviance. La nouvelle approche consiste à diviser l'idée d'égalité humaine : comme le dit l'article 3 de la Constitution de l'an III (1795), il y a égalité de tous devant la loi. Il n'y a plus d'égalité « par nature » comme le dit le même article 3 de la Constitution de 1789. L'égalité humaine peut ainsi devenir un objet de diverses pratiques qui sont développés pour la mesurer, catégoriser, et interpréter. Cette dernière égalité peut donc devenir un point de départ pour les techniques d'égalité.

3 Techniques de savoir et techniques d'administrer

Vers 1800 se forme un nouveau comportement des constellations étatiques et sociales pour maîtriser des populations et des individus. En dépit du maintien du titre de « République » dans les actes officiels, l'idéal républicain est rapidement mis en cause par le régime consulaire à partir de 1799. Dès le mois de janvier 1800, la liberté de la presse est fortement réduite et la répression politique s'abat sur de nombreux opposants. Contrairement à la légende, l'arrivée au pouvoir de Bonaparte n'est pas acceptée par tous les Français et il existe des programmes politiques concurrents crédibles dont il s'évertue à supprimer les représentants. C'est dans cette perspective qu'est orchestrée l'élimination par la force des membres du courant néo-jacobin. Cette répression politique particulièrement violente sert à mettre en place une nouvelle forme de pouvoir où les décisions centrales doivent désormais descendre « du haut » : dès 1800, la nouvelle Constitution marque un renforcement de l'Exécutif aux dépens des conseils. Si ces derniers perdurent (Corps Législatif, Sénat...), le pouvoir

---

[11] Dans son *Traité des maladies de l'oreille et de l'audition* (1821) Itard affirme que l'éducation connaît des limites naturelles. Par exemple, dans la perspective du *Traité* chaque oreille avait son « sensibilité particulière » (Itard 1821, t. II, 427).

législatif voit ses prérogatives diminuer au profit d'institutions qui servent de relais à la volonté du Premier Consul.

Les frontières entre les discours politiques et les théories scientifiques, en particulier les théories médicales, restent particulièrement poreuses, la Révolution française poursuivant une tradition déjà ancrée sous l'Ancien Régime. Les questions et interprétations portant sur la nature de l'homme étaient déjà présentent dans les années 1790, offrant des justifications possibles pour une version dirigiste d'organisation de l'État. L'une de ces interprétations de la formation d'un homme raisonnable était axée sur le lien entre le cerveau et les capacités intellectuelles. Cette réinterprétation du rôle du cerveau montre comment les convictions politiques et les interprétations scientifiques de l'homme ont évolué en parallèle après 1800. L'utilisation par la politique de raisonnements issus des sciences et de métaphores politiques dans les sciences humaines a déjà été examinée[12]. Dans le cas des sciences de l'homme, ce lien est particulièrement étroit, d'autant plus que ses acteurs ont accédé à des postes de décision dans l'État après 1795. Un débat central, mené ici par les médecins et les politiciens, portait sur le lien entre le « physique » et le « moral », particulièrement marqué par les textes de Pierre-Jean-Georges Cabanis et l'interprétation du cerveau. Les premières années du Consulat sont donc marquées par une transformation progressive de l'interprétation donnée au rôle du cerveau dans l'organisation physique et morale de l'homme. En 1795, une controverse oppose Cabanis et le médecin Samuel Thomas Sömmering sur le rôle joué par le cerveau dans le processus de la vie (cf. Gessinger 2013) : contre l'idée d'un principe vital contenu dans le cerveau, le premier défend le principe d'un principal vital réparti dans le corps tout entier et produit de la circulation entre les organes. Pour Cabanis, le cerveau ne saurait ainsi constituer un organe autonome et détaché du reste du corps. Or, au moment où la Constitution tend à légitimer le renforcement et l'autonomie de l'Exécutif, la question d'une autonomie du cerveau refait surface avec force. En 1801 en effet, un médecin réputé, Jacques-André Millot présente aux membres du Tribunat un nouvel ouvrage dans lequel il interroge la possibilité d'améliorer les hommes et en souligne les limites. En effet, selon lui, l'entreprise de régénération fondée sur l'éducation se heurte à des limites naturelles liées aux plus ou moins grandes aptitudes du cerveau. Millot pense qu'il existe donc des inégalités naturelles entre les différents individus qui ne sauraient être corrigées :

> Il faut donc qu'il y ait dans ces différents cerveaux une disposition particulière qui donne aux uns et refuse aux autres l'aptitude et le degré d'attention nécessaire à l'acquisition de la

---

12 Georges Gusdorf, notamment, a avancé la thèse selon laquelle l'impact des Idéologues était principalement dû au fait qu'ils ont donné aux techniques politiques un vocabulaire efficace (Gusdorf 1978, 389–390).

> science, de l'esprit et du génie [..]. Nous devons croire que c'est dans le cerveau, dans le fluide nerveux qu'il filtre, que consiste la différence qui se trouve non seulement entre les hommes et les brutes, mais encore entre un homme d'esprit et un sot. Willis ayant disséqué le cadavre d'un imbécile, lui trouva le cerveau plus petit qu'il ne l'est ordinairement [. . .] (Millot 1803 [1801], 27–28).

Selon Millot, « l'éducation ne crée rien en nous [. . .] elle ne fait que développer nos dispositions » (Millot 1803 [1801], 31). Ici aussi, nous voyons comment les scientifiques après 1800 divisent de plus en plus l'idée d'égalité naturelle. D'une part, de nouveaux objets scientifiques sont créés qui sont considérés comme les causes de l'inégalité. Le cerveau est un exemple particulièrement frappant car, du point de vue de l'histoire des sciences, une chose est au moins claire : aux alentours de 1800 il n'existait aucune connaissance certaine de quelque nature que ce soit sur le lien entre le cerveau et les aptitudes. Le cerveau est créé comme une « black box », pour ainsi dire, comme un espace vide dans l'espace des connaissances. On estime que, même s'il n'est pas encore possible de connaître avec certitude les raisons de la diversité des aptitudes dues au cerveau, les techniques de recherche seraient utiles et possibles pour découvrir progressivement les racines profondes de l'inégalité entre les hommes. Les pratiques de la phrénologie chez Joseph Gall et Johann Caspar Spurzheim en sont la première conséquence, d'autres étapes suivront (cf. Gessinger 2013). C'est l'un des exemples clés de la création de systèmes de connaissance pour mesurer et pour gouverner l'inégalité. De son côté, après plusieurs années consacrées au jeune enfant découvert dans les forêts de l'Aveyron, Itard ne peut que constater l'impossibilité d'éduquer l'enfant complètement. En récapitulant les résultats de ses efforts dans son dernier rapport, Itard, certes, peut souligner quelques progrès, surtout il remarque que Victor, à cause du « traitement physique et moral » aurait commencé à entendre la « voix de l'humanité » (reproduit dans Gineste 2004, 566). Néanmoins, dans ce second rapport Itard présente une « étonnante variété dans les résultats » et que, par exemple, les facultés intellectuelles « se développent d'une manière lente et pénible » (ibid., 564). Par rapport aux cinq « maximes » du premier rapport, les résultats effectivement obtenus ont été, en effet, maigres. Par exemple, la première maxime du rapport de 1801 promet qu'on pourrait « attacher » Victor « à la vie sociale », ce qui de toute évidence a mené à un échec (Itard 1894 [1801], 12). En dépit des espoirs qu'il a fait naître, Victor est irrémédiablement rangé du côté des « idiots » par les nouveaux experts de la science de l'homme, Gall et Spurzheim, dont la science craniométrique permettrait de statuer sans faille sur la nature des individus (cf. Carson 2017). Même s'elle n'acquiert pas le statut de science officielle, l'introduction et les débats autour des théories physiognomoniques de Gall et de Spurzheim instaure une nouvelle perspective de lire l'humanité : si elle reprend le paradigme des rapports du physique et du moral, la science des crânes postule, même si ses promoteurs s'en défendent, une forme de déterminisme naturaliste aux comportements individuels (Reneville 2020). Le médecin, partisan de Cabanis, Louis-Jacques Moreau de la Sarthe ne s'y trompe pas. Dans la *Décade philosophique*, ce dernier met en garde les effets de cette théorie sur le fonctionnement des pratiques judiciaires, dénonçant la part de déterminisme qu'elle fait désormais peser sur les justiciables (Moreau de la Sarthe 1804).

En 1807, les publications par les presses de l'imprimerie impériale du récit de voyage de François Péron et du rapport sur l'enfant sauvage d'Itard, marque encore une rupture majeure quant à l'idée de perfectibilité. Pour Péron, le recours aux mesures de la force musculaire grâce au dynamomètre permet d'établir une coupure franche entre les populations européennes et les populations dites « sauvages ». S'il constate la possibilité de certains progrès dans les populations européennes envoyées dans les colonies (en observant par exemple les colonies pénitentiaires anglaises), il semble exclure tout progrès de la part des populations indigènes dont le destin semble immanquablement se réduire au statut de dominés (Chappey 2002, 466). Les sociétés sauvages ou extra-européennes ont bien une histoire, mais une histoire naturellement différente de celle des sociétés européennes.

Symbole de cet ordre nouveau, le Code civil de 1804 fixe durablement les inégalités entre les hommes et les femmes. Si ces dernières ont pu être considérées comme « inférieures » du fait de leur organisation physique et physiologique (Roussel et Moreau de la Sarthe), c'est désormais la loi qui fixe leur état de leur dépendance au pouvoir masculin. La femme, réduite au rang d'épouse et de mère, se voit rabaisser dans un statut de dépendance face au mari et au père, l'égalité constituée par le noyau familial volant en éclat (cf. Verjus 2010).

4 Égalités politiques *vs* inégalités naturelles

À partir des années 1802–1804, le climat politique connaît des transformations progressives, mais profondes. Au sein des institutions scientifiques et administratives, on assiste à une offensive particulièrement agressive contre les différents projets intellectuels, portés par la classe des « sciences morales et politiques » de l'Institut national ou par les membres de la Société des observateurs de l'homme. Cette société vise à constituer une science générale de l'homme (ou anthropologie), science qui devait encadrer le projet plus général de régénération et de civilisation auquel se rattachait l'idéal républicain défendu sous le Directoire. Sans forcément se confondre avec, cette offensive portée contre le rôle civilisateur des savants se juxtapose à la campagne orchestrée par les partisans du rétablissement de l'esclavage et de l'inégalité entre les « races humaines » (Chappey 2019 ; Doron 2016). Dès 1800–1801, des ouvrages, de nature plus ou moins scientifique, font de nouveau écho aux théories polygénistes (largement mises en sommeil sous le Directoire) et aux idées concernant les différences « naturelles » entre les différentes « races ». Ces théories, qui servent à légitimer l'expression de véritables aberrations racistes (pensons au pamphlet de Louis-Narcisse Baudry de Lozières, *Les égarements du négrophilisme* publié en 1802), mettent en cause l'idée d'une histoire commune de l'humanité et établissent une véritable coupure entre, d'un côté, les peuples susceptibles de participer au processus de civilisation (les peuples européens et catholiques) et, de l'autre, ceux qui, par nature, seraient exclus de l'histoire et, de ce fait, voués à être asservis (Benot 1992). Sans forcément considérer qu'il existerait un lien entre ces différents phénomènes, il reste évident que cette campagne d'imprimés où se cristallisent la mise en cause de l'idée de progrès par la raison et de la conception monogéniste de l'espèce humaine participe à la justification et à la légitimation prise par les autorités de rétablir la traite des esclavages en 1802[13]. Il s'avère désormais que les possibilités données à la perfectibilité des individus et à la civilisation des populations ne sont pas identiques chez tous les hommes de la Terre : selon leurs « races » et leur couleur de peau, les populations ne peuvent prétendre à atteindre le même degré de perfectionnement, une thèse qui permet de revendiquer une supériorité naturelle aux populations blanches. Parmi ces dernières, des inégalités apparaissent selon leurs modes de vie, leurs coutumes et leurs professions. Contre l'idée de perfectibilité et la possibilité de penser un processus de civilisation intégrant chaque individu et chaque société humaine, l'idée se fait jour que la « civilisation » constitue désormais une qualité distinctive quasi naturelle à partir de laquelle il devient possible de hiérarchiser les différents individus, communautés et peuples. Tous les domaines de la société sont touchés par ce processus qui tend désormais à établir, selon des critères présentés comme « naturelles » de nouvelles hiérarchies et de nouvelles frontières au sein des populations, frontières et hiérarchies considérées désormais comme fixes et infranchissables. Ainsi, la nouvelle loi sur l'instruction publique du 1er mai 1802 (11 floréal an X), qui crée les lycées, est la première étape d'une transformation générale des institutions pédagogiques (qui aboutit à la création de l'Université en 1808) qui les transformations en lieu de sélection sociale dont l'accès est progressivement réservé aux seuls fils d'héritiers voués à devenir des serviteurs de l'État. Amorcée sous le Consulat, cette inflexion antirépublicaine, qui s'appuie sur la mobilisation de savoirs sur l'homme se poursuit sous l'Empire, caractérisant le « tournant autoritaire » du régime qui voit se ren-

---

[13] À la suite du Traité d'Amiens qui permet à la France de récupérer quelques territoires coloniaux, la loi du 20 mai 1802 (30 floréal an X) rétablit officiellement l'esclavage dans toutes les colonies françaises. Dans les territoires où il avait été supprimé (Guadeloupe, Martinique, Saint-Domingue), l'esclavage est rétabli par la force.

forcer le pouvoir d'un seul sur tous les domaines de la société. Ce tournant peut être illustré par les théories complexes défendues par le jeune médecin Jean-Joseph Virey dont l'originalité est sans doute de juxtaposer une conception polygéniste de l'espèce humaine avec une conception historiciste qui fait désormais prévaloir la coupure entre sociétés européennes et extra-européennes. Dans son ouvrage publié en 1808, il affirme ainsi que

> la force du corps distingue les bêtes brutes entr'elles : la force de l'ame est le premier titre de l'homme et sa noblesse originelle. Et de même que nous surpassons les animaux par la raison, plus nous augmenterons cette faculté, plus nous serons capables de surpasser aussi les autres hommes ; c'est par là que le blanc domine le nègre ; l'homme civilisé, le sauvage ; l'Européen, les autres peuples, et que l'habilité, le génie emportent toujours l'avantage, à la longue, sur les obstacles contre lesquels la force elle-même est impuissante (Virey 1808, viii).

Il crée ainsi une histoire spécifique du « nègre » et des peuples africains qu'il fonde particulièrement sur les usages des nombreuses représentations iconographiques issus des travaux de l'anatomiste hollandais Petrus Camper sur l'angle facial : il y a là un usage scientifique de l'approche esthétique, le « beau » étant toujours rangé du côté du blanc[14]. Cette perspective entre la stigmatisation esthétique et le la théorie de la civilisation est particulièrement présente dans son *Histoire naturelle du genre humain* (1800–1801) :

> Nous décrirons ici les caractères généraux de chaque race humaine qu'on peut diviser principalement en belles et blanches, en laides ou brunes et noires. La perfection physique de notre espèce ne peut s'opérer que dans les liens de la civilisation, et surtout dans le calme du bonheur domestique, dans une douce sécurité politique. Plus un peuple est avancé dans ses institutions sociales et dans sa morale, plus il y a de beauté, de noblesse, d'élégance et de grâces dans les formes des individus qui le composent (Virey 1800–1801, t. 1, 145, 293–294).

Si Camper affirmait que le « beau » est toujours relatif et dépend de la culture et de l'organisation des sociétés, Virey tend, au contraire, à « fixer » la beauté et la laideur dans des formes naturelles (Doron 2016). On connaît encore les fameuses illustrations de Camper reprises par Virey dans son *Histoire naturelle du genre humain* comparant le « Profil de l'Apollon ; celui du nègre et celui de l'orang-outang » (Virey 1800–1801, t. 2, planche III). Alors que la civilisation européenne se construit par un « retour » à l'esthétique antique justifiant le rejet « hors de la civilisation » du « nègre », l'assimilation systématique du noir avec les représentations du corps du « Hottentot », participe de la naturalisation d'une dualité entre

---

[14] L'histoire de cette esthétisation des hierarchies entre les supposées « races » est bien analysée par Bindman (2002).

la beauté et la laideur qui renforce encore la naturalisation des différences[15]. Comme le souligne Claude Blanckaert : avec Virey, « le monde africain s'autonomise de façon radicalement négative » (Blanckaert 1988, 122). Cette utilisation de critères esthétiques comme supports de (dis-)qualification raciale participe plus largement au processus de mise en ordre sociale et politique de l'Empire (comme le montre encore la mutation des représentations des « pauvres »). Ainsi de la physiognomonie à la phrénologie de Gall, on peut constater la mise en place d'un nouveau régime de visibilité qui, renvoyant à un nouveau régime des savoirs (marquée encore par la disparition en 1807 de la fameuse *Décade philosophique*), participe à la construction d'un nouvel ordre politique et social qui se caractérise par un mouvement de naturalisation des inégalités sexuelles, raciales ou sociales : alors que l'idéal républicain permettait de penser un possible progrès au sein des races, des sexes et des milieux sociaux, le Consulat et l'Empire reconstituent progressivement des frontières infranchissables entre les « races » noires et blanches (esclavage, 1802), entre les femmes et les hommes (Code civil de 1804), entre « sauvages » et « civilisés ». Sur le plan des relations diplomatiques, la mise en place de l'Empire instaure une hiérarchie « naturelle » entre la France et les autres nations et états européens. C'est donc l'ensemble des dispositifs et des supports de lecture du monde social qui connaît des transformations majeures entre le Consulat et l'Empire.

5 Conclusion

C'est précisément ce « système général des inégalités », dont Pierre Rosanvallon décrit les modes de fonctionnement statistiques, qu'on peut reconstruire à partir de Victor, l'enfant « sauvage » (Rosanvallon 2011). Comme nous l'avons montré, de diverses pratiques administratives et scientifiques se sont groupées tout autour de Victor et Itard, qui accompagne Victor pour un certain temps. La mort de Victor en 1828 n'est plus aussi importante pour le monde scientifique et administratif qu'auparavant. L'espoir d'une égalité intégrale a perdu sa force, les pratiques administratives sont plutôt occupées par les questions en quelque sorte plus concrètes : comment organiser les hommes d'une manière qui garantit la stabilité de l'État, qui fait progresser les hommes inutiles pour l'industrie nationale, et qui conserve les sphères d'inégalité existantes telles que la famille patriarcale. Les individus comparables à Victor sont désormais rangés dans les institutions spéciali-

---

[15] Dans *Under Representation. The Racial Regime of Aesthetics*, David Lloyd (2019) parle du choc causé par le spectacle de corps noirs considérés comme un danger porté à la civilisation.

sées pour « idiots ». Ces institutions ont, des plus en plus, des compétences à classifier différentes sortes d'« idiots » et de choisir des procédés de soins ou d'éducation (Schlicht 2021). Ces individus ne font pas partie des hommes « normaux », mais en même temps, on ne peut pas dire, qu'ils sont conçus comme totalement hors de la sphère de la civilisation. Ils sont civilisables d'une certaine manière, pour un certain degré. C'est une première manière de limiter les espaces d'égalité, mais de définir les frontières d'une perspective perméable. Bien qu'on doive contrôler les conditions de cette perméabilité, on ne veut pas exclure la possibilité que certains individus peuvent s'intégrer dans le groupe productif qui est la base de l'utilité économique et politique des hommes. Ainsi, on peut décrire d'une manière générale l'inégalité dynamique et adaptative qui établit à la fois les frontières entre les groupes de personnes et les procédures qui répondent aux erreurs de répartition des individus à ces groupes ou aux constructions de groupe dans leur ensemble.

Une autre stratégie consiste à délimiter des frontières entre les divers groupes d'hommes : un groupe civilisé (et surtout blanc), d'un côté, et un groupe exclu de la civilisation, sauvage, (et très souvent noir), de l'autre. Ces formes racistes et colonialistes d'attribution identitaire d'une inégalité de principe ont une fonction différente de l'inégalité locale, dynamique et adaptative attribuée à Victor. L'étude du destin de Victor montre comment les formes de contrôle de l'inégalité à l'intérieur d'une nation et les fonctions d'exclusion de l'inégalité fondamentale vers l'extérieur ont pris des fonctions complémentaires. La thèse d'Étienne Balibar selon laquelle le racisme et le nationalisme sont mutuellement dépendants est ici vérifiée (Balibar et Wallerstein 1997, 54–55). Ce qui est nouveau dans le cas de Victor, c'est qu'il permet de mettre au jour les processus à partir desquels les sciences, les administrations et les gouvernements ont co-produit les systèmes d'organisation des inégalités humaines. Contrairement aux idées reçues, les pratiques scientifiques (la médecine, la psychiatrie) ne se sont pas vu confier uniquement le rôle de justifier et légitimer la détention d'individus inutiles. Comme on peut le constater dans les récits ultérieurs d'Itard, les sciences humaines avaient trouvé leur voix dans le concert de ceux qui jugeaient les différences humaines. Pendant ce temps, un système complexe de différenciation et de hiérarchie voit le jour. Ce système crée des partages entre les citoyens à part entière, les citoyens qui travaillent sans appartenir à la communauté politique mais bénéficient d'une certaine protection de l'État, les citoyens qui travaillent mais qui sont exclus de l'espace politique et ne peuvent prétendre qu'à une protection minimale de l'État, voire en sont complètement dénués. Pour les membres des institutions scientifiques et administratifs qui participent à la mise en place de ces nouvelles normes de gouvernement, les gains en termes de carrières sont réels.

L'universalisme « universel » qui n'accepte pas les exceptions et les variations locales est intégré ou traduit dans un système universel et dynamique d'évaluation des citoyens. Ces derniers sont considérés comme égaux précisément parce qu'ils sont tous évalués selon les mêmes normes et les mêmes techniques. S'impose ainsi un régime différencié qui séparent les égalités locales, négociables, qui définissent les limites entre les espaces des citoyens, les espaces des presque-citoyens, et les espaces des non-citoyens. La frontière entre citoyens et non-citoyens était déjà l'objet des sciences et de l'État dans les débats sur la « race » et « limpieza de sangre » pendant la Reconquista. La frontière entre citoyens et presque-citoyens et la recherche sur l'ampleur des aptitudes intellectuelles commence avec Victor dans le « moment 1800 » et ne cesse de se renforcer au cours des années suivantes. Pour comprendre le contact entre les sciences de l'homme, les constellations administratives et les structures de l'État, le cas de Victor reste bien exemplaire, un cas à partir duquel les professionnels des sciences de l'homme et les élites politiques et administratives se mettent à définir et à légitimer des barèmes d'aptitudes et des degrés de compétences.

Références bibliographiques

Alder, Ken. « Making Things the Same : Representation, Tolerance and the End of the Ancien Régime in France. » *Social Studies of Science* 28.4 (1998) : 499–545.
Baczko, Bronisław. *Ending the Terror. The French Revolution after Robespierre*. Cambridge : Cambridge University Press, 1994 [1989].
Balibar, Étienne et Immanuel Wallerstein. *Race, nation, classe*. Paris : La Découverte, 1997.
Baudin des Ardennes, Pierre-Charles-Louis. *Anecdotes et réflexions générales sur la Constitution*. Paris : Imprimerie nationale, floréal an III/1795.
Baudry de Lozières, Louis-Narcisse. *Les égarements du nigrophilisme*. Paris : Migneret, 1802.
Benot, Yves. *La démence coloniale sous Napoléon*. Paris : La Découverte, 1992.
Benzaquén, Adriana. *Encounters with Wild Children. Temptation and Disappointment in the Study of Human Nature*. Montreal / London : McGill-Queen's University Press, 2006.
Bindman, David. *Ape to Apollo. Asthetics and the Idea of Race in the 18th Century*. London : Reaktion Books, 2002.
Blanckaert, Claude. « J.J. Virey, Observateur de l'homme (1800–1825) ». *Julien-Joseph Virey. Naturaliste et anthropologue*. Éd. Claude Bénichou et Claude Blanckaert. Paris : Vrin, 1988 : 97–182.
Bruland, Hansjörg. *Wilde Kinder in der Frühen Neuzeit. Geschichten von der Natur des Menschen*. Stuttgart : Franz Steiner, 2008.
Cabanis, Pierre-Jean-Georges. « Quelques principes et quelques vues sur les secours publics. » *Œuvres complètes*. T. 2. Paris : Bossange Frères, Didot, 1823 [1791–1793].
Carson, John. *The Measure of Merit. Talents, Intelligence, and Inequality in the French and American Republics, 1750–1940*. Princeton : Princeton University Press, 2017.

Chappey, Jean-Luc. *La société des observateurs de l'homme : (1799–1804) ; des anthropologues au temps de Bonaparte*. Paris : Société des Études Robespierristes, 2002.
——. *Sauvagerie et civilisation. Une histoire politique de Victor de l'Aveyron*. Paris : Fayard, 2017.
——. « À la recherche du premier écrivain noir. . . Sur la possibilité d'une 'littérature des nègres' autour de 1800. » *Poétique et politique de l'altérité. Colonialisme, esclavagisme, exotisme. XVIIIe–XXIe siècles*. Ed. Karine Bénac. Paris : Garnier, 2019. 217–234.
Chappey, Jean-Luc and Julien Vincent. « A Republican Ecology ? Citizenship, Nature and the French Revolution (1795–1799). » *Past and Present* 243.1 (2019) : 109–140.
Condorcet, Marie Jean Antoine Nicolas Caritat, Marquis de. *Réflexions sur l'Esclavage des Nègres*. Neuchâtel : Société Typographique, 1781.
——. *Esquisse d'un tableau historique des progrès de l'esprit humain. Fragment sur l'Atlantide*. Paris : Ed. Sociales, 1966 [1795].
Doron, Claude-Olivier. *L'homme altéré : races et dégénérescence (XVIIe–XIXe siècles)*. Ceyzérieu : Champ Vallon, 2016.
Elwick, James. *Making a Grade. Victorian Examinations and the Rise of Standardized Testing*. Toronto : University of Toronto Press, 2021.
Gessinger, Joachim. « 'Talking Heads' or the Naturalisation of Language at the End of the 18th Century », 2013. https://wg.geschichte.uni-frankfurt.de/epi-m/Konferenz-Papers.html (30 novembre 2022).
Gineste, Thierry. *Victor de l'Aveyron. Dernier enfant sauvage, premier enfant fou*. Paris : Hachette Littératures, 2004.
Goldstein, Jan. *Console and Classify. The French Psychiatric Profession in the Nineteenth Century*. New York, Cambridge : Cambridge University Press, 1987.
Gusdorf, Georges. *La conscience révolutionnaire. Les Idéologues*. Paris : Payot, 1978.
Head, Brian William. *Ideology and Social Science. Destutt de Tracy and French Liberalism*. Dordrecht : Martinus Nijhoff Publishers, 1985.
Israel, Jonathan. *Enlightenment Contested. Philosophy, Modernity, and the Emancipation of Man*. Oxford : Oxford University Press, 2006.
Itard, Jean Marc Gaspard. *Rapports et mémoires sur le sauvage de l'Aveyron, l'idiotie et la surdi-mutité*. Paris : Progrès Médical, 1894 [1801].
——. *Traité des maladies de l'oreille et de l'audition*. Paris : Chez Méquignon-Marvis, 1821.
Jainchill, Andrew. *Reimagining Politics after the Terror*. Ithaca/NY : Cornell University Press, 2008.
Lezay-Marnésia, Adrien. *Des causes de la Révolution et de ses résultats*. Paris : Imprimerie du Journal d'économie publique, 1797.
Lloyd, David. *Under Representation. The Racial Regime of Aesthetics*. New York : Fordham University Press, 2019.
Mannoni, Octave. « Itard et son sauvage ». *Les temps modernes* 233 (1965) : 647–663.
McDonagh, Patrick. *Idiocy. A Cultural History*. Liverpool : Liverpool University Press, 2008.
Messling, Markus. *Universalität nach dem Universalismus. Über frankophone Literaturen der Gegenwart*. Berlin : Matthes & Seitz, 2019.
Millot, Jacques-André. *L'Art d'améliorer et perfectionner les générations humaines*. Paris : Migneret, 1803 [1801].
Moreau de la Sarthe, Louis-Jacques. « Exposition et critique du système du docteur Gall sur la cause et l'expression des principales différences de l'esprit et des passions lues à l'Athénée de Paris ». *Décade philosophique* (2e trimestre an XII/1804) : 257–265.
Piketty, Thomas. *Le capital au XXIe siècle*. Paris : Éditions du Seuil, 2013.

Quinlan, Sean M. « Physical and Moral Regeneration after the Terror : Medical Culture, Sensibility and Family Politics in France, 1794–1804. » *Social History* 29.2 (2004) : 139–164.

Réimpression de l'ancien Moniteur. Paris : Plon frères, 1847.

Reneville, Marc. *Le langage des crânes. Une histoire de la phrénologie*. Paris : La Découverte, 2020.

Rivarol, Antoine. *De la philosophie moderne*. s.l., s.d. [1797].

Roederer, Pierre-Louis. *L'Esprit de la Révolution de 1789*. Paris : Chez les principaux libraires, 1831.

Rosanvallon, Pierre. *La société des égaux*. Paris : Éditions du Seuil, 2011.

Schlicht, Laurens. *tabula rasa. Die Erforschung des menschlichen Geistes im Kontext der Société des observateurs de l'homme, ca. 1780–1830*. Tübingen : Mohr Siebeck, 2020.

———. « Connaître et éduquer l'"idiot" – de Jean Itard, à l'enquête prussienne de 1883, au *Anschauungsunterricht* dans le Kalmenhof aux alentours de 1900 ». *Revue d'histoire des sciences humaines* 38 (2021) : 119–138.

Serna, Pierre. *L'extrême centre ou le poison français : 1794–2019*. Ceyzérieu : Champ Vallon, 2019.

Spitz, Jean-Fabien. *Le moment républicain en France*. Paris : Gallimard, 2005.

Steinberg, Ronen. « Trauma and the Effects of Mass Violence in Revolutionary France. » *Historical Reflections* 41.3 (2015) : 28–46.

Stuurman, Siep. *The Invention of Humanity. Equality and Cultural Difference in World History*. Cambridge/MA : Harvard University Press, 2017.

Verjus, Anne. *Le bon mari. Une histoire politique des hommes et des femmes à l'époque révolutionnaire*. Paris : Fayard, 2010.

Virey, Julien-Joseph. *Histoire naturelle du genre humain*. Tome 1 et 2. Paris : Dufart, 1800–1801.

———. *L'Art de perfectionner l'homme ou la médecine spirituelle et morale*. Paris : Déterville, 1808, t. 1.

Wahnich, Sophie. *Les émotions, la Révolution française et le présent. Exercices pratiques de conscience historique*. Paris : Éditions du CNRS, 2009.

Wallerstein, Immanuel. « Citizens All ? Citizens Some ! The Making of the Citizen. » *Comparative Studies in Society and History* 45.4 (2003) : 650–679.

Wokler, Robert. « From the Moral and Political Sciences to the Sciences of Society by Way of the French Revolution. » *Annual Review of Law and Ethics* 8 (2000) : 33–45.

Sergio Ugalde Quintana
La violence et la construction du « commun » : la littérature internationaliste écrite au Mexique dans les années 1940

Abstract: This paper analyses three moments in the representation of political violence in the literature written and published in Mexico in the early 1940s: the violence previous to the Mexican Revolution, that of the Spanish Civil War and that of the Second World War. Each of those periods is studied through the analysis of a literary work: the case of the violence in Mexico is analysed through the novel *La Rosa Blanca* by the German B. Traven; that of the Spanish Civil War, through the novel *Aquí el alba comienza* by the French journalist Simone Téry; that of the Second World War, through the book *Poemas de guerra y esperanza* by the Mexican writer Efraín Huerta. These three examples show that the political violence during the first half of the twentieth century incited, in the literature published in Mexico City during those years, a reflection on the "common" based on an active cosmopolitan conscience.

Keywords: Mexico, literature, violence, cosmopolitanism, common

1 La construction du « commun »

Entre les années 1930 et 1940, la ville de Mexico devint un laboratoire d'expérimentation esthétique doté d'un fort sens social. La Seconde Guerre mondiale en Europe, la guerre civile espagnole et les nombreux problèmes politiques sur le continent américain poussèrent un nombre considérable d'artistes et d'écrivains à émigrer vers la capitale mexicaine. D'importantes personnalités du monde intellectuel espagnol, français, allemand, italien, chilien, brésilien et guatémaltèque furent accueillies par le régime de Lázaro Cárdenas à la fin des années 1930 et par celui de Manuel Ávila Camacho dans les années 1940. Beaucoup d'entre elles entreprirent des projets communs dans lesquels elles échangèrent des perspectives et des expériences afin de développer différentes approches esthétiques ; toutes ces personnes avaient une conscience claire du moment critique qu'elles vivaient, mais aussi une ferme conviction de l'existence de principes partagés et communs. Des figures telles que le Français André Breton, l'Autrichien Wolfgang

Paalen, l'Allemande Anna Seghers, l'Espagnol Luis Buñuel, ont coexisté dans l'espace culturel mexicain avec le Chilien Pablo Neruda, le Péruvien César Moro, le Brésilien Jorge Amado et les Mexicains Diego Rivera, Frida Kahlo, José Revueltas, Efraín Huerta, entre autres.

L'ambiance de guerre qui marqua les quatre premières décennies du vingtième siècle, ainsi que tous les changements dans l'imaginaire social qu'elle entraîna, furent le point de départ d'une remise en question de l'idée d'« universalisme » occidental et d'une recherche des éléments « communs » entre les différentes cultures du monde. Dans le cas mexicain, comme j'essayai de le montrer dans ma contribution au livre *L'époque de l'universalisme (1769–1989)*, la création de prix littéraires et la fondation d'institutions favorisèrent une politique culturelle en accord avec la nouvelle situation de l'époque (Ugalde 2021a, 125–140). Afin d'identifier dans la littérature les mécanismes de représentation d'un sentiment de communauté internationale et, par conséquent, de cosmopolitisme, je prendrai comme point de départ deux romans et un recueil de poèmes publiés dans la capitale mexicaine entre 1940 et 1944 : *La Rosa Blanca* de l'Allemand B. Traven, *Aquí el alba comienza* de la Française Simone Téry et *Poemas de guerra y esperanza* du Mexicain Efraín Huerta. Dans ces trois livres, le sens de la communauté internationale se concrétise. L'extrême tension entre la crise de l'universel et la proposition d'un projet de résolution communautaire peut peut-être constituer un point de départ pour repenser, au XXIe siècle, ce que nous avons en « commun » après la montée des discours du particularisme.

2 B. Traven ou les citoyens du monde

L'énigmatique écrivain de langue allemande qui publia plusieurs romans et nouvelles sous le nom de B. Traven arriva au Mexique au milieu des années 1920. Sa carrière antérieure est pleine d'énigmes. Ses biographes affirment qu'il aurait participé à la révolte pour l'établissement de la République soviétique de Bavière en 1919 sous le nom de Ret Marut. En raison de son activisme anarchiste, il fut condamné à mort en 1919 et sauvé par un simple hasard. Il s'enfuit aux États-Unis, puis au Mexique, et adopta plusieurs pseudonymes tout au long de sa vie : Hal Croves, Traven Torsvan (Guthke 1987, 107–166). En 1924, installé dans la ville de Tampico, dans le nord-ouest du Mexique, il voyagea dans le pays et s'intéressa particulièrement à la vie des communautés indigènes du Chiapas. Dans cette région, il écrivit plusieurs œuvres de fiction qu'il publia dans une maison d'édition berlinoise. Ses romans furent rapidement traduits en anglais et dans d'autres langues. Ses best-sellers firent de lui un phénomène de l'édition. B. Traven devint un auteur très lu, mais à la personnalité impénétrable. L'écrivain garda sa biographie mystérieuse jusqu'à sa mort dans la ville de Mexico en 1969.

L'un des premiers romans que B. Traven publia après son arrivée au Mexique, et avec lequel il initia sa relation étroite de solidarité avec la vision du monde indigène mésoaméricaine, est *La Rosa Blanca* (*Die weiße Rose*), un récit sur l'extrême violence utilisée par les compagnies pétrolières américaines pour s'approprier des territoires exploitables au Mexique au début du XXe siècle. Le roman fut publié pour la première fois en allemand en 1929 par la maison d'édition berlinoise Büchergilde Gutenberg. Il fallut un peu plus d'une décennie pour que le livre paraisse en espagnol. La traduction espagnole fut publiée en août 1940 par Cima, une petite maison d'édition active au début de cette décennie et dont le catalogue comprenait des auteurs tels qu'André Maurois.

À cette époque, B. Traven était déjà un auteur connu et commenté par le public mexicain. Des éditeurs espagnols, argentins et mexicains l'avaient fait connaître dans le monde hispanophone. En 1931, *El barco de los muertos* (*Das Totenschiff. Die Geschichte eines amerikanischen Seemanns*, 1926) parut à Madrid aux éditions Zeus ; en 1936, les Ediciones Imán de Buenos Aires publièrent le roman *Puente en la Selva* (*Die Brücke im Dschungel*, 1929) ; en 1938, la maison d'édition Cima de Mexico publia *La rebelión de los colgados* (*Die Rebellion der Gehenkten*, 1936). Des fragments de ses romans furent publiés dans des journaux de Mexico tels que *El Nacional* et *El Popular* et dans des magazines tels que *Ruta* (Traven 1938, cf. Meyer-Minnemann 2012, 95–97). Bientôt, la solidarité avec le monde indigène mexicain que B. Traven représentait dans son œuvre commença à être commentée par les intellectuels mexicains. Le jeune écrivain José Revueltas, militant du Parti Communiste, publia une critique enthousiaste du *Puente en la Selva* en août 1938. Le titre de cet article en dit beaucoup sur la ferveur avec laquelle le livre a été lu : « Un livre exceptionnellement mexicain » (Revueltas 1938, 5). L'œuvre de l'énigmatique B. Traven fut également commentée dans les journaux militants de la gauche mexicaine. Le magazine *Frente a Frente* le qualifia de meilleur propagandiste du Mexique à l'étranger (Anonyme 1936). Dans *El Popular*, le journal du mouvement ouvrier du Mexique, et dans *Ruta*, magazine communiste, quelques articles sur son œuvre furent publiés à la fin des années 1930 (Geoffroy 1938). Efraín Huerta, un jeune poète et journaliste, fit également allusion à lui et le commenta dans ses contributions à la revue *Así* (Huerta 1941, 26).

C'est ainsi qu'en août 1940, la parution de la version espagnole de *La Rosa Blanca* représentait une continuation du dialogue avec le champ intellectuel et littéraire mexicain. Le roman fut traduit, apparemment sans l'autorisation de B. Traven, par le poète salvadorien Pedro Geoffroy Rivas, qui vivait alors en exil au Mexique, et par l'écrivaine Lya Kostakowsky, de parents russes mais née à Leipzig et réfugiée au Mexique depuis 1925. Dans les premières pages de l'édition mexicaine, les éditeurs soulignaient l'importance de l'ouvrage : « Nous sommes convaincus que M. Bruno Traven [. . .] comprendra que notre seul souhait était de mettre à la disposition des lecteurs mexicains une œuvre qui immortalise la marche douloureuse de l'Indien mexicain au moment de l'expansion sanglante du capitalisme mondial » (Ijac 1940, 1).

En effet, le roman de B. Traven montre la voracité et la violence d'une compagnie pétrolière américaine qui s'empare des terres d'une population indigène dans le nord de l'État de Veracruz ; avec cette dépossession, Condor Oil Co. détruit non seulement un lieu idyllique, mais aussi un sens de la communauté. Il est très clair que la traduction, la publication et la diffusion de ce roman s'inscrivaient dans le contexte de la nationalisation du pétrole par le régime de Cárdenas en 1938 (Zogbaum 1992, 26–36). Le conflit de *La Rosa Blanca* s'articule autour d'une dichotomie fondamentale : la logique du capital transnational versus la logique d'une communauté indigène. Les valeurs et les principes sont complètement différents, voire antagonistes. La première poursuit le profit à tout prix ; la seconde veut vivre et travailler en harmonie avec la nature. Pour la compagnie pétrolière, la principale valeur est l'argent ; pour la communauté indigène, les pièces de monnaie n'ont aucune signification et leurs terres n'ont aucun prix.

« Rosa Blanca » est le nom de l'hacienda où vit une communauté indigène de soixante-dix familles sous la direction de Don Jacinto Yáñez. L'endroit est représenté comme un lieu paradisiaque au milieu d'un environnement tropical. La nature, les animaux, les habitants, les règles de coexistence et les traditions forment un univers bienveillant qui fonctionne comme un organisme vivant. Don Jacinto est la figure tutélaire de cette communauté et en même temps le médiateur entre la nature et les personnes qui l'habitent : « La Rosa Blanca [. . .]. Elle lui a parlé. Elle lui a souri. Elle s'est personnifiée. Il l'a entendue chanter » (Traven 1940, 30)[1]. Don Jacinto connaît toutes les manifestations de son hacienda et est capable de les interpréter ; il connaît la signification de chaque son, de chaque mouvement et de chaque détail de ce monde. Cet espace enchanteur et vivant est désigné, à plusieurs reprises dans le roman, comme une patrie : « Il savait tout. Les cris et les hurlements de la perruche furieuse lui parvenaient, non pas comme des sons isolés,

---

[1] Une histoire textuelle de ce roman fournirait des données très intéressantes. La traduction mexicaine non autorisée de 1940 était basée sur l'édition allemande de 1929. Cependant, en 1951, B. Traven publia une autre édition en espagnol de cette œuvre, traduite par Rosa Elena Luján, qui est complètement différente de l'édition de 1940 et, par conséquent, de l'édition allemande de 1929. Les détails des différences textuelles fourniraient des indices sur l'adéquation et l'adaptation du projet littéraire de B. Traven au contexte de la Guerre froide vécu ces années-là au Mexique. A propos de l'histoire textuelle des autres œuvres de B. Traven, voir Dammann (2012), Guthke (2012), Potapova (2012), Meyer-Minnemann (2012), et Rall (2012).

mais comme une note, comme une de plus parmi les cent mille tonalités du chant éternellement égal, accueillant et familier de la Rosa Blanca » (Traven 1940, 41)[2].

L'image du sinistre et du violent émerge face à la logique de cet espace communautaire et idyllique, extrêmement attirant pour une personne ayant un passé anarchiste comme B. Traven. La compagnie pétrolière Condor Oil Co. est caractérisée dès les premières lignes comme vorace et dévastatrice. Cette société ne se soucie pas de la nature ni des personnes qui l'habitent ; tout ce qui l'intéresse c'est le pétrole et l'argent qu'elle peut en tirer. Les premières et dernières lignes du roman témoignent de cette logique : « Parmi les grandes compagnies pétrolières américaines qui avaient étendu leurs activités au Mexique, la Condor Oil Co. n'était certainement pas la plus importante ni la plus puissante. Mais c'était celle qui avait le plus gros appétit » (Traven 1940, 3). Le directeur qui dirige cette entreprise, M. Collins, est un homme sans scrupules et prêt à tout pour obtenir plus de bénéfices : « Nous ne nous soucions pas de l'homme. Seul le pétrole est important » (Traven 1940, 374). Tout comme Don Jacinto et Rosa Blanca forment une unité organique, M. Collins et la Condor Oil Co. se métamorphosent en un seul être, dans ce cas, monstrueux et terrifiant. Avant de devenir directeur de la compagnie pétrolière, Collins avait provoqué une crise financière majeure à Wall Street. Son but était de profiter largement de cette débâcle. Il en résultera des grèves ouvrières partout, des licenciements massifs et, bien sûr, une répression violente :

> M. Collins [. . .] n'a pas dressé la liste des pertes, [. . .] de celles qui s'étaient suicidées, de celles qui étaient allées à l'asile d'aliénés, de celles qui gisaient dans les hôpitaux. Ce sont les mauvais généraux qui s'inquiètent de ceux qui sont tombés. [. . .] Et pendant que le prolétariat enterre ses morts, pleure et parle de ses déchus, son adversaire a le temps de planifier la nouvelle boucherie (Traven 1940, 178–179).

Le drame entre ces deux logiques apparaît rapidement. Sous les terrains de la « Rosa Blanca » se trouve un énorme et riche gisement de pétrole. La Condor Oil Co. veut acheter l'hacienda. Don Jacinto est réticent à la vendre. Face aux refus constants du chef indigène, M. Collins charge l'un de ses employés de résoudre le problème. Abner, un avocat corrompu, dupe Don Jacinto et l'emmène en Californie. Une fois aux États-Unis, il le fait assassiner. Avec la mort de Don Jacinto, l'entreprise n'a plus d'obstacle pour prendre possession des terres. Ils ont falsifié des documents et signé un contrat aux États-Unis qui leur permettait de s'emparer de l'endroit dans le pays voisin, d'expulser ses habitants et de commencer à extraire

---

[2] Tous les textes littéraires cités ont été traduits de l'espagnol vers le français par moi-même (S.U.Q.). Je tiens à remercier Elsie Cohen pour sa relecture.

du pétrole. Tout comme le corps de Don Jacinto a été massacré en Californie, la « Rosa Blanca » est outragée au Mexique : le bâtiment principal du XVIe siècle est démoli ; l'église du XVIIe siècle est abattue ; les arbres et les cabanes sont rasés. À la fin du roman, l'hacienda communale, la « Rosa Blanca », gît saignée et torturée. L'espace paradisiaque a été transformé en un lieu répugnant et sale.

Dans l'histoire du roman, le début du massacre de la « Rosa blanca » coïncide avec le début de la Révolution mexicaine. La violence transnationale se confond avec la violence locale. La population mexicaine, trop préoccupée par les affrontements et les batailles internes, est inconsciente du pillage que les compagnies pétrolières infligent au Mexique. La Condor Oil Co. profite de la confusion et du chaos révolutionnaire pour tirer un bénéfice financier de son vol jusqu'au dernier moment. Au milieu de ce scénario désolant, le narrateur du roman souligne un développement positif qui a émergé de cette tragédie. Les habitants de la « Rosa Blanca », violemment expulsés de leur petite patrie, ont dû développer une conscience globale. Avant d'être dépossédés de leurs terres, ils ne s'intéressaient qu'aux détails de ce qui se passait chez eux. Ils voient maintenant qu'ils ont été victimes d'une logique internationale et que des personnes dans d'autres parties du monde subissent les mêmes conséquences. Les habitants de la « Rosa Blanca » sont passés du rôle d'habitants d'un petit paradis à celui de citoyens de la terre. Le sens du cosmopolitisme est accentué ; la solidarité internationale aussi.

> Ils avaient perdu une belle patrie, une patrie aimée [. . .]. Mais quand ils ont appris à voir, [. . .] ils ont reconnu qu'à la place de leur petite patrie, ils en avaient acquis une plus grande qui avait aussi sa beauté. [. . .] [Cette nouvelle patrie] n'était pas limitée à l'horizon [. . .], elle semblait n'avoir aucune limite et englobait toute l'humanité, tous les pays [. . .]. Et il arriva un jour [. . .] où ils purent dire à juste titre : « Nous sommes devenus plus riches que nous l'étions [. . .], parce que nous sommes maintenant des citoyens du monde [. . .], parce que nous comprenons le monde et les autres hommes [. . .]. Et parce que nous comprenons un plus grand nombre d'hommes, notre amour est devenu plus grand. Y a-t-il un bien plus précieux pour l'homme que de voir son amour grandir ? » (Traven 1940, 347).

Ce sentiment de solidarité mondiale représenté par l'œuvre de B. Traven fut très bien accueilli par certains intellectuels mexicains de l'époque. Dans un récit de voyage sur le sud-est mexicain, la journaliste Elvira Vargas utilisa par exemple 16 épigraphes de ce roman pour introduire chacun de ses chapitres. Au début du volume, elle écrit : « Je dédie ce livre à B. Traven, un homme qui a compris mon pays avec son cœur » (Vargas 1941, 1). De cette façon, la tragédie d'une collectivité indigène servit de catalysant pour représenter un sens de la communauté globale et transnationale. L'habitant dépossédé de la petite hacienda du nord-ouest du Mexique est devenu un citoyen du monde. Leur perte était aussi un gain ; la violence a provoqué un sentiment d'appartenance planétaire :

Ils n'étaient plus seulement les habitants d'un petit morceau de terre [. . .]. Ils ont reconnu que le monde était vaste et que la collaboration humaine s'étendait à l'ensemble de la planète. [. . .] Ils ont senti se développer en eux le premier germe de la pensée que tous les hommes de la terre sont solidaires et forment une grande famille (Traven 1940, 30).

3 Simone Téry ou la solidarité

À peu près au moment où le roman de B. Traven était discuté dans les cercles culturels de la ville de Mexico, la journaliste et romancière française Simone Téry arrivait au port de Veracruz, fuyant la violence de la Seconde Guerre mondiale. Dans un texte publié quelque temps plus tard, l'écrivaine raconta avec émotion ses premières impressions à son arrivée dans le pays qui l'avait accueillie. Elle se souvient, non sans ironie, qu'en débarquant au port de Veracruz le 5 mai 1941, elle fut surprise par la chaleur enivrante des tropiques et les festivités qui entouraient la ville. Alors que la journaliste demandait à un passant quelles étaient les raisons de la fête qui se déroulait à ce moment-là, il lui répondit : « Vous ne savez pas ce qu'est le 5 mai ? Eh bien, c'est le jour où nous avons donné une énorme raclée aux Français à Puebla. » Téry se retourna et s'enfuit pour éviter d'être identifiée comme une citoyenne française. De retour à l'hôtel, elle consulta un journal et constata que les manchettes annonçaient, également de manière festive, la grande amitié franco-mexicaine promue par le président de la République Manuel Ávila Camacho. Après avoir raconté cet accueil particulier, la journaliste relate ses expériences au Mexique en tant que réfugiée politique :

> Avant la guerre, j'avais parcouru la plupart des pays du monde, à l'exception de l'Amérique latine ; mais aujourd'hui, après avoir vécu trois ans au Mexique, je dis à mes amis : « Si un jour vous vous voyez, comme nous nous sommes vus, exilés, pauvres, malheureux, allez vivre au Mexique ». C'est le pays qui a ouvert ses portes le plus libéralement aux réfugiés [. . .], à ceux qui avaient toujours combattu le fascisme, à ceux qui mouraient dans les camps de concentration, en attendant d'être [. . .] livrés à Franco, Hitler ou Mussolini (Téry 1944a, 5).

Ce récit, caractéristique des exilés européens des années 30 et 40 au Mexique, était typique d'une figure comme Simone Téry : une intellectuelle liée à l'exil républicain espagnol et associée à divers espaces créés par l'institution mexicaine post-révolutionnaire durant ces années. L'article cité ci-dessus est la dernière des 54 contributions que l'écrivaine française publia, entre janvier 1943 et juillet 1944, dans le journal du mouvement ouvrier *El Popular*. Il était logique que Téry participe au journal. Son expérience et sa réputation de journaliste la précédait. L'écrivaine était issue d'une famille associée au monde des grands quotidiens (Stewart 2018, 71–96). Sa mère, Andrée Viollis, était une célèbre reporter et voyageuse ; son père, Gustave Téry, avait fondé et dirigé le quotidien de tendance socialiste *L'Œuvre*. Téry était née et avait grandi dans un environnement journalistique. Ses premières œuvres devinrent connues au milieu des années 1920. Les livres *En Irlande. De la guerre d'indépendance à la guerre civile (1914–1923)* (1923) et *L'Île des bardes. Notes sur la littérature irlandaise contemporaine* (1925) combinent ses passions politiques et littéraires. Parallèlement à son intense activité journalistique, Téry écrivit et publia un roman dans le Paris de l'entre-deux-guerres : *Passagère* (1930). En 1935, elle voyagea en Union soviétique, une expérience qui définit sa vision politique et sa future carrière intellectuelle et professionnelle. À son retour en France, elle adhéra au Parti Communiste. Peu après, avec les premières nouvelles du soulèvement de Franco contre le gouvernement de la République espagnole, Téry s'installa dans la péninsule ibérique et devint correspondante de guerre. Entre 1937 et 1938, elle rédigea de nombreux rapports, qu'elle compila peu après dans un volume intitulé *Front de la liberté. Espagne 1937–1938* (1938). Pendant son séjour en Espagne, elle rencontra Juan Chabás, un intellectuel, homme politique et écrivain bien connu de la génération de 1927, qu'elle épousa ensuite. Avec Chabás, elle se réfugia en France après la défaite de la République espagnole. Quelque temps plus tard, Téry et Chabás quittèrent l'Europe et commencèrent leur exil américain, avant d'aboutir leur périple au Mexique en mai 1941.

Comme c'était le cas pour de nombreux intellectuels européens réfugiés au Mexique, Téry trouva dans les institutions journalistiques et éducatives fondées par le leader du mouvement ouvrier Vicente Lombardo Toledano un espace d'engagement public. Dans ses articles de *El Popular*, un journal fondé par Lombardo Toledano, elle écrivait sur la Seconde Guerre mondiale et la politique extérieure française, y abordait des questions littéraires. C'est le cas de l'un de ses premiers textes publiés dans ce journal. Il s'agit d'une contribution intitulée « Por Hemingway doblan las campanas » (« Pour Hemingway sonne le glas »). Dans cet article, Téry (1943a) fait une critique frontale du roman *Pour qui sonne le glas*. Elle y discrédite la manière dont le romancier américain avait représenté la guerre civile espagnole et affirme qu'avec ce texte, Hemingway avait voulu faire « une œuvre au succès commercial certain », mais pas « un grand livre ». « Tout le faux romantisme espagnol des voyageurs étrangers, de Mérimée à Barrés, se trouve chez le 'réaliste' Hemingway » (Téry 1943a, 5). Téry disqualifia le prétendu « réalisme » d'Hemingway en raison du manque de cohérence dans la construction des personnages, de la vision stéréotypée de l'Espagne et de l'exotisme de ses pages. La conclusion tirée de cette analyse était claire. Il n'y avait pas encore de roman qui représentait la fraternité, l'héroïsme, la douleur, la joie et l'« explosion de la vie créative » que la guerre civile espagnole avait apportés avec elle. Il fallait nécessairement que quelqu'un effectue ce travail. Ce qui est curieux, c'est qu'au même moment, Téry écrivait son roman sur cet événement. Les arguments qu'elle avance contre Hemingway semblent justifier son propre projet.

Ce fait peut être confirmé lorsqu'en mars 1944, peu avant son retour en France et la fin de son exil mexicain, Simone Téry (1944b) publia son roman *Aquí el alba comienza*[3]. Le livre était dédié « au Major Général Manuel Ávila Camacho, et à l'ancien président, le Major Général Lázaro Cárdenas ». L'ouvrage fut publié par la maison d'édition Astro, une petite maison d'édition qui avait dans son catalogue des œuvres d'écrivains communistes. Une particularité du volume de Téry est qu'il ne fait pas référence à un traducteur. Ce fait suggère que l'écrivaine a elle-même écrit cette version de l'œuvre en espagnol. Comme certains spécialistes l'ont souligné, le roman s'inscrit dans le cadre des discussions esthétiques sur le réalisme socialiste qui ont émergé du Congrès des écrivains soviétiques de 1934 (Verdès-Leroux 1983, 284–285). Cependant, malgré l'évidence de ce fait, plusieurs éléments indiquent une autre voie possible d'interprétation esthétique du roman.

L'œuvre est à la fois une histoire d'amour et un roman de formation. Il raconte l'histoire de Jeannette, une jeune Française naïve qui, rejetée par son petit ami, décide de quitter Paris et de se rendre en Espagne pour chercher la mort. Elle s'engage comme correspondante pour un magazine et part pour Barcelone. Elle arrive dans une Espagne en pleine guerre civile. Là, paradoxalement, elle trouve l'intensité de la vie. Elle s'implique rapidement en réaction à ce qu'elle a vu et entendu, et rédige ses chroniques de guerre. La jeune fille naïve se transforme et s'engage pour une cause. Au fur et à mesure que le récit avance, l'héroïsme de l'armée républicaine, la solidarité des brigades internationales, le drame de la bataille de Teruel et le siège de Madrid sont présentés. En même temps qu'elle dénonce ce qu'elle voit, elle rencontre son grand amour : Ramón, un soldat de l'armée de la République aux convictions communistes. Avec lui, elle trouve la paix au milieu de l'agitation de la guerre. L'œuvre conclut avec l'image du couple à bord d'un bateau quittant Barcelone pour la France. Ils regardent tous les deux le coucher du soleil. Jeannette s'exclame à mi-voix : « Tout est perdu . . . Tout est fini ». Le narrateur déclare : « Un sourire est alors apparu sur le visage triste de Ramón. Il souleva la tête de Jeannette et la regarda dans les yeux, toujours souriant, comme si ce soleil couchant avait été pour lui une aurore : – Non, – répondit-il. Maintenant, ça commence » (Téry 1944b, 922). Ces derniers mots du narrateur et de Ramón font référence au titre du roman en espagnol : ce qui commence est l'aube, le lever du soleil, l'aurore.

---

[3] En 1945, Téry publia le roman en français, chez l'éditeur new-yorkais Bretano's, sous le titre *Où l'aube se lève*. Des années plus tard, elle réécrivit le roman et en publia une deuxième édition : *La porte du soleil*. Récemment, Anne Mathieu a préparé une nouvelle édition de l'œuvre pour L'Harmattan.

Deux éléments se distinguent dans ce roman. La première est l'imbrication de l'histoire et de la fiction. Certains critiques ont souligné les relations intertextuelles entre le travail journalistique de Téry sur la guerre civile espagnole, rassemblé dans *Front de la liberté. Espagne 1937–1938*, et le roman *Aquí el alba comienza*. Deuxièmement, la représentation d'un sentiment d'irréalité dans la guerre est remarquable. À plusieurs reprises, la protagoniste expérimente, dans des situations extrêmes, une altération de la perception. Ce qui est réel, en raison de l'intensité de l'expérience, acquiert un manteau d'irréalité. Ainsi, malgré l'impératif d'élaborer une esthétique conforme au réalisme socialiste, il existe des moments d'intimité subjective qui perturbent ce paradigme. Il s'agit sans doute d'un héritage des techniques d'exploration de la subjectivité, apprises dans les expérimentations des récits d'avant-garde, que Téry représenta dans son roman *Passagère* (1930). On peut le constater, par exemple, dans le passage suivant : « Un silence surnaturel régnait dans la ville [de Madrid] [. . .]. Mais le silence d'une ville en guerre est un silence pétrifié. Jeannette a traversé une ville fantôme. [. . .] Mais tout était si irréel [. . .] que Jeannette sentait que peu à peu, elle aussi devenait un fantôme » (Téry 1944b, 157).

Les allusions à l'irréalité et au sens fantasmagorique de Madrid sont complétées par d'autres appréciations de la perception altérée de la protagoniste : « Ici tout était intense, tragique, stimulant ; [. . .] et Jeannette avait conscience que la vie pouvait exploser à tout moment [. . .]. A partir de maintenant, tout lui semblait irréel » (Téry 1944b, 201). Il faut également ajouter que, dans la représentation de la guerre, Téry met l'emphase sur des éléments importants pour évaluer le sens du « commun » fondé sur la violence de la guerre. En effet, on pourrait dire que l'élément qui articule le récit est le sentiment de la solidarité. Tout d'abord, la protagoniste se rend dans un pays voisin pour soutenir la lutte de la République. Deuxièmement, il y a de nombreux moments dans le roman où tous les groupes politiques se rassemblent pour réussir l'unité d'un front populaire. Le narrateur montre un groupe uni réunissant des anarchistes, des communistes et des socialistes. Troisièmement, la pièce souligne la participation des brigades internationales. Tout cela crée un sentiment de solidarité qui permet l'union, malgré les différences, dans un projet commun. La solidarité devient alors un élément de cohésion. Le point commun est le sentiment de solidarité. Il est important de noter que l'œuvre fut écrite à une période pendant laquelle Téry collaborait avec *El Popular*. Le roman était dans l'orbite de ce que le journal promouvait : la création d'un univers commun, partagé, internationaliste.

4 Efraín Huerta ou l'espérance

Dès le début de sa carrière littéraire, Efraín Huerta fréquenta la poésie et le journalisme. Ses premières publications sont une série de plaquettes de belle facture : en août 1935, il publia *Absoluto amor* (*Amour absolu*) et, en novembre 1936, *Línea del alba* (*Ligne de l'aube*). Il trouva rapidement un moyen de subsistance dans l'écriture journalistique. En novembre 1936, il commença à collaborer au *Diario del sureste*, une publication de gauche distribuée dans la péninsule du Yucatán ; un an plus tard, il commença à contribuer à *El Nacional*, l'organe officiel du gouvernement mexicain et défenseur des politiques sociales du Cardenismo[4]. Dans les deux journaux, le jeune Huerta travaillait comme éditorialiste. Cependant, c'est en août 1939, lorsqu'il eut rejoint le journal *El Popular*, qu'Efraín Huerta assuma un rôle important dans le monde de la presse périodique mexicaine. Dans ce journal, organe officiel du mouvement ouvrier au Mexique, il remplissait diverses fonctions : il faisait partie du comité de rédaction ; il dirigeait la section littéraire, « Crítica, Poesía y Polémica » ; il était responsable de l'espace éditorial anonyme « El hombre de la esquina » (« L'homme au coin ») il signait l'espace « Las paredes oyen... » (« Les murs ont des oreilles ») sous le pseudonyme de Juan Ruiz, et écrivait de nombreux articles de fond. D'après toutes ces informations, on peut affirmer que Huerta a joué un rôle central dans le développement de la page éditoriale et dans le type de littérature que le journal promouvait au cours de ces années[5]. Malgré ses nombreuses obligations journalistiques, le jeune écrivain n'abandonna pas la poésie. Dès son entrée dans l'univers des grands quotidiens, son projet lyrique s'inscrivit dans une tradition qui alliait préoccupations esthétiques et politiques. Il fut clairement influencé par le Chilien Pablo Neruda, les Espagnols Arturo Serrano Plaja et Rafael Alberti et l'Argentin Raúl González Tuñón. Dans la même dynamique, Huerta écrivit une série de poèmes dans lesquels il dépeignit la violence de l'époque. Il traita d'abord de la guerre civile espagnole, puis des événements de la Seconde Guerre mondiale. Toutes ces compositions peuvent être lues dans le contexte de son intense activité journalistique au cours de ces années. *El Popular* était le forum idéal pour la présentation et la diffusion de certains de ces poèmes. Il existe un lien étroit entre l'écriture de ses articles, les notes journalistiques dans le journal et l'écriture de sa poésie. Dans chacun d'eux, on retrouve la profonde angoisse de la violence historique et la ferme conviction d'un avenir plein d'espoir.

---

4 Une sélection des textes qu'il publia dans les deux journaux a été compilée dans Huerta (2006).
5 Entre le 18 août 1939, date de la première publication de « El hombre de la esquina », et mars 1944, période où apparaissent ses derniers écrits signés, Efraín Huerta publia près de 1100 textes dans le journal du mouvement ouvrier ; cf. Ugalde (2021b, 9–56).

Dès le début de la guerre européenne, *El Popular* promut une vision très critique du nazisme. Ceci devint clair par ses pages d'actualités et éditoriales. En mars 1943, la manchette d'*El Popular* montrait son inquiétude face à la guerre. Les armées nazies dévastaient les lieux qu'elles traversaient. Dans sa collaboration anonyme, par exemple, Efraín Huerta rend compte du massacre de la communauté juive en Pologne par les nazis : « Il faut imaginer un ghetto entier rendu fou de terreur [. . .]. La Gestapo, à cette occasion comme à d'autres, a utilisé les services d'une meute spécialisée dans la persécution des Juifs. Des dizaines d'entre eux ont été horriblement déchiquetés par les crocs des chiens de garde » (Huerta 1943a, 5).

Dans le contexte de la diffusion de ces nouvelles, quelques jours plus tard, le dimanche 28 mars 1943, fut publié le poème « La Oración por Tania (Joven guerrillera soviética ahorcada por los nazis) » [« La prière pour Tania (jeune guérillero soviétique pendu par les nazis) »]. Huerta y recrée un double sentiment de deuil et de haine. La première partie du poème montre un profond chagrin. Un matin d'hiver froid dans la ville de Petrishevo, le corps sans vie d'une jeune combattante soviétique est suspendu à un arbre. Les nazis l'avaient pendue :

> Sous le ciel d'hiver, un matin
> tu étais un arbre,
> un arbre de torture et de martyre,
> [. . .]
> Les loups venaient pour toi. Ils t'ont trouvé,
> ils t'ont mutilé et arraché ta voix,
> ils t'ont fouetté, les nazis.
> (Huerta 1943b, 5)

Après cette représentation de la violence historique, le poète élabore une oraison funèbre à la mémoire de la combattante assassinée. La structure anaphorique du poème, fondée sur la répétition constante du mot « haine », donne un sens rituel et funéraire à la composition :

> Haine, haine fidèle !
> Une haine parfaite ! Respiration, tremblements.
> Haine au terrible mensonge et au pillage,
> haine au dévastateur et au pyromane,
> la haine pétrifiée, la haine purifiée,
> haine pour des centaines de raisons et de sang.
> Merveilleuse haine
> (Huerta 1943b, 5).

Le poème, écrit au moment où le monde apprenait la nouvelle de l'avancée nazie sur l'Union soviétique, fut conçu par Huerta à son bureau dans la rédaction du journal. L'expression de la « haine » n'est pas nouvelle dans sa poésie. L'un de ses poèmes les plus emblématiques porte le titre de « Declaración de odio » (« Déclaration de haine »). Ce poème, écrit en 1938 et publié dans divers magazines et journaux de l'époque, est l'un des textes que publia *El Popular*. Dans le même contexte, où l'incertitude régnait quant aux affrontements de la guerre en Europe, Huerta écrivit d'autres poèmes qui dépeignaient la violence de la guerre, mais aussi un principe d'espérance.

À la fin du mois de mai 1942, Reinhard Heydrich, le plus haut responsable de la Gestapo en charge du protectorat de Bohême et de Moravie, est assassiné par la résistance tchèque. La nouvelle fut commentée au Mexique par la presse antifasciste et antinazie. José Revueltas, par exemple, exprima son enthousiasme, mais aussi son inquiétude, dans un article d'*El Popular*. Hitler, confronté au meurtre du second d'Himmler, avait déclenché un terrible massacre. Un village entier avait été rasé. Revueltas écrivit sa note alors que les premières nouvelles de l'extermination de la population de la petite ville minière de Lydice arrivaient : « En représailles de la mort de Herr Henker – 'Monsieur le Bourreau' – les nazis ont exécuté 187 otages en Bohême et en Moravie, dont trente-deux femmes ; cinq mille autres personnes sont emprisonnées dans les camps de concentration, attendant anxieusement de subir sur leurs dos la vengeance furieuse d'Hitler » (Revueltas 1942, 5). L'événement commençait à peine à révéler ses conséquences. Peu à peu, l'histoire de cette dévastation devint publique. Huerta, attisé par les nouvelles du massacre, écrivit « Elegía de Lídice » (« Elégie de Lydice ») à la fin du mois d'août 1942. Le poème, écrit avec une rigueur métrique stricte (28 alexandrins, 11 heptasyllabes et 1 hendécasyllabe), déplore avec douleur et angoisse la destruction du village :

> Petite martyre, toi, Lydice déchirée,
> pleurs de fièvre et de poudre, de terreur sanglante,
> fleur de deuil décimée,
> Lydice des sanglots et des angoisses perçantes,
> le froid glacial du paysage de cendres et de croix
> 						(Huerta 1943c, 33).

Après avoir montré la scène de dévastation, le poème, dans ses trois dernières strophes, révèle l'espoir d'une renaissance de Lydice sur le sol américain. Deux villages, l'un aux États-Unis, au bord des Grands Lacs, et l'autre au Mexique, à la périphérie de la capitale, ont reçu le même nom que la ville dévastée.

> Regarde ta substance, ton essence vaincue,
> s'élever dans les Grands Lacs,
> à côté du Mississippi,
> où un village frère a pris ton nom,
> ton profil de jeune fille, ton corps percé.

> Et regarde comment, dans une autre vallée d'une beauté inhumaine,
> au pied des montagnes aussi, Lydice martyr,
> ton sang trouve un chemin pour rêver ses fruits.
> Tu es dans notre sein, Lydice américain,
> Lydice mexicain
>
> (Huerta 1943c, 34).

Le poème est daté du 22 août 1942. Quelques jours plus tard, une localité de Mexico a été baptisée du nom de San Jerónimo Lídice. A la une d'*El Popular*, la note suivante est apparue :

> Un acte simple et profond d'affirmation antinazie aura lieu dimanche prochain 30 [. . .] dans la petite localité de San Jerónimo, dans le District Fédéral. La cérémonie – qui consiste à changer le nom de la localité – trouve son origine dans une cérémonie similaire qui s'est déroulée dans une jolie petite ville de l'Illinois. Les habitants, apprenant que Lydice, la ville minière de Tchécoslovaquie, avait été effacée de la carte par les nazis en représailles à la mort du bourreau Heydrich, ont décidé de changer le nom de leur localité natale et de la baptiser du nom désormais disparu de Lydice. Lydice est ainsi devenu un symbole noble [. . .] : le symbole de la volonté de tous les peuples de ne pas disparaître (Anonyme 1942, 1).

La guerre nazie a suscité des actes de solidarité internationale, et la poésie d'Efraín Huerta a laissé un témoignage à la fois de l'horreur de la violence et du sentiment d'espoir d'une communauté internationale. Le même chagrin est évident dans le poème « Elegía y esperanza » (« Elégie et espérance »). La composition, écrite en 33 vers alexandrins et un heptasyllabe, modèle un double sentiment. D'une part, on se lamente sur les pertes de vies humaines dues à l'horreur de la guerre ; d'autre part, on construit une aura de résistance à la barbarie de la guerre. Le poème oscille entre la douleur et le chant, entre les ombres et la lumière, entre le meurtre et l'aube, entre les larmes et la musique. Ce double sentiment est constamment souligné dans une série de distiques disséminés dans le poème :

> Mais là où les nazis font pousser la fumée
> la douce musique du ventre de Rachel est née.
> [. . .]
> Mais là où les nazis tuent un sourire
> on entend le murmure clair d'un troupeau de moutons.
> [. . .]
> Mais là où les nazis pendent une vierge
> le blé fleurit et le pain est partagé.
> [. . .]
> Là-bas, sur cette terre de torture et de cendres,
> la chanson est revenue à la lumière et l'espoir était
> comme une prophétie lumineuse et étoilée
>
> (Huerta 1943c, 43).

Cette dualité réaffirme clairement le sentiment commun que le poète veut faire prévaloir : face à la violence historique de la Seconde Guerre mondiale, le poème chante l'espoir. Il convient de noter que tous les poèmes susmentionnés (« La prière pour Tania », « Élégie de Lydice », « Élégie et espérance ») furent rassemblés et publiés en juillet 1943 dans le livre *Poemas de guerra y esperanza* (*Poèmes de guerre et d'espérance*). Le volume fut publié par la maison d'édition Tenochtitlán, une très petite entreprise dirigée par un exilé républicain espagnol, Álvaro Arauz, qui était un collègue d'Efraín à *El Popular*. Une partie du champ littéraire mexicain rejetait ce type de poésie[6]. Peu de personnes manifestèrent publiquement leur sympathie pour le projet d'Huerta. Parmi la minorité qui célébra la publication du volume, on trouve Simone Téry. L'écrivaine se félicitait de la publication du livre et regrettait que les lecteurs de poésie n'aient pas célébré l'existence du volume. « Cela fait plusieurs semaines que *Poemas de guerra y esperanza* est sorti, et j'ai à peine vu une note dans la presse mexicaine. [. . .] C'est comme si le livre avait été publié sur la lune » (Téry 1943b, 5). Pour elle, la tradition à laquelle s'associe la poésie de Huerta est très claire : Vladimir Mayakovski, Louis Aragon, Pedro Garfias et Pablo Neruda :

> Les poèmes de guerre et d'espérance sont des chants [. . .] ; ce sont des cris de lutte, d'amour et de foi du Mexique en guerre. Ce sont des images visionnaires de la douleur et de l'espoir de l'humanité, ce sont des images prophétiques du nouveau monde qui est en train de naître. [. . .] Efraín Huerta est un témoin et un accusateur [. . .]. Ses poèmes sont, avec ceux de Pablo Neruda, parmi les plus grands que cette guerre de la vie contre la mort ait jamais suscités (Téry 1943b, 5).

Dès le titre de son recueil de poèmes, Huerta annonce les deux axes de la littérature de l'époque : d'une part, la description de la violence guerrière nazie ; d'autre part, la construction d'un sentiment du « commun » sur la base d'un horizon futur en espérance et en humanité.

5 Cosmopolitisme, solidarité et espérance dans la construction du « commun »

A partir des trois œuvres examinées ici, on peut dégager quelques idées sur le sens du commun élaboré à partir de la littérature écrite au Mexique dans une période de profondes crises. Pour commencer, il est très clair que les trois écri-

---

[6] Un exemple de cette réaction négative se trouve dans la critique que María Ramona Rey a écrite sur le livre. Dans ce texte, elle déplore l'existence de la poésie combative de Huerta et exprime son souhait que le poète revienne à la poésie amoureuse (Rey 1943, 55).

vains se trouvent dans une position très particulière : B. Traven élabore une allégorie de la perte du paradis et une projection des citoyens du monde basée sur l'empathie avec les communautés indigènes mexicaines dépossédées par les transnationales du pétrole ; Simone Téry montre un sens de la solidarité internationale basé sur la tragédie de la guerre civile espagnole ; Efraín Huerta élabore sa poésie basée sur un principe d'espérance face à l'horreur de la barbarie nazie. Dans le récit de B. Traven, la violence de la dépossession conduit à une conscience cosmopolite. Les indigènes violentés développent un sentiment d'appartenance mondiale ; ils passent du statut d'habitants d'une petite patrie à celui de citoyens du monde. Dans le roman de Téry, l'intensité d'une guerre hallucinatoire trouve son contrepoint dans les différentes formes de solidarité humaine. Les combattants, au-delà des convictions idéologiques, sont organisés autour d'un idéal commun : défendre la République. Dans les poèmes d'Efraín Huerta, un double processus est en jeu : l'indignation et la haine face aux excès guerriers du nazisme, et la revendication de l'espoir comme principe de résistance face à la brutalité historique.

Peut-être que les représentations littéraires des différents personnages qui convergeaient dans un espace internationaliste tel que la ville de Mexico entre les années 1930 et 1940 peuvent nous amener aujourd'hui à considérer ce que nous avons en « commun » après les crises constantes de violence. La construction du « commun », vue de ces représentations littéraires de la violence, implique l'assomption consciente d'au moins trois principes discursifs : le cosmopolitisme, la solidarité et l'espoir.

Références bibliographiques

Anonyme. « Simbólico acto de fervorosa afirmación antinazi, en el pueblo de S. Jerónimo, D.F. ». *El Popular* [Mexico] (27 août 1942) : 1.

———. « Bruno Traven ». *Frente a Frente : Órgano Central de la Liga de Escritores y Artistas Revolucionarios* (25 mars 1936) : s.p.

Dammann, Günter. « Die Rückübersetzung von Traven-Romanen ins Deutsche während des Exils der Büchergilde Gutenberg in Zürich. » *B. Traven. Autor – Werk – Werkgeschichte*. Ed. Günter Dammann. Würzburg : Königshausen & Neumann, 2012. 13–28.

Geoffroy Rivas, Pedro. « La Rebelión de los colgados de Bruno Traven ». *Ruta* 3 (août 1938) : 56–57.

Guthke, Karl S. *B. Traven. The Life Behind the Legends*. Trad. Robert C. Sprung. Chicago : Lawrence Hill Books, 1987.

———. « Vergangenheitsgestaltung. Die Baumwollpflücker : deutsch, englisch, amerikanisch. » *B. Traven. Autor – Werk – Werkgeschichte*. Ed. Günter Dammann. Würzburg : Königshausen & Neumann, 2012. 29–56.

Huerta, Efraín. « El infierno del chicle III ». *Así* (4 janvier 1941) : 24, 26 et 65.

———. « El hombre de la esquina. Asesinatos en masa ». *El Popular* [Mexico] (2 mars 1943a) : 5.
———. « La Oración por Tania (Joven guerrillera soviética ahorcada por los nazis) ». *El Popular* [Mexico] (28 mars 1943b) : 3.
———. *Poemas de guerra y esperanza*. Mexico : Tenochtitlán, 1943c.
———. *Aurora roja. Crónicas juveniles (1936-1939)*. Ed. Guillermo Sheridan. Mexico : UNAM / Pecata minuta, 2006.
Ijac, Carlos. « Nota de los editores ». *La Rosa Blanca*. Bruno Traven. Trad. Pedro Geoffroy Rivas et Lia Kostakowsky. Mexico : Cima, 1940. 1-2.
Meyer-Minnemann, Klaus. « Traven spanisch : *Die Brücke im Dschungel* – (Un / El) *Puente en la selva*. » *B. Traven. Autor – Werk – Werkgeschichte*. Ed. Günter Dammann. Würzburg : Königshausen & Neumann, 2012. 95-114.
Potapova, Galina. « B. Travens Roman *Das Totenschiff*. Fassungsgeschichte eines Werks zwischen der Erstausgabe und dem Edierten Text der Gesamtausgabe. » *B. Traven. Autor – Werk – Werkgeschichte*. Ed. Günter Dammann. Würzburg : Königshausen & Neumann, 2012. 57-94.
Rall, Dieter. « Travens Erzählung *Der Großindustrielle*. Fassung, Übertragungen, Bearbeitungen. » *B. Traven. Autor – Werk – Werkgeschichte*. Ed. Günter Dammann. Würzburg : Königshausen & Neumann, 2012. 115-128.
Revueltas, José. « Un libro excepcionalmente mexicano ». *Diario del sureste* (7 juillet 1938) : 5.
———. « Herr Henker ha muerto ». *El Popular* [Mexico] (6 juin 1942) : 5.
Rey, María Ramona. « Efraín Huerta, Poemas de guerra y eperanza ». *Rueca* 8 (1943) : 55.
Stewart, Mary Lynn. *Gender, Generation, and Journalism in France, 1910-1940*. Montreal : McGill-Queen's University Press, 2018.
Téry, Simone. « Por Hemingway doblan las campanas I ». *El Popular* [Mexico] (6 mars 1943a) : 5.
———. « Efraîn Huerta, un poeta de México ». *El Popular* [Mexico] (5 août 1943b) : 5.
———. « Nosotros no olvidaremos a México ». *El Popular* [Mexico] (31 juillet 1944a) : 5.
———. *Aquí el alba comienza*. Mexico : Editorial Astro, 1944b.
Traven, Bruno. « La Rosa Blanca ». Trad. Pedro Geoffroy Rivas et Erwin Friedeberg. *Ruta* 1 (juin 1938) : 30-35.
———. *La Rosa Blanca*. Trad. Pedro Geoffroy Rivas et Lia Kostakowsky. Mexico : Cima, 1940.
Ugalde Quintana, Sergio. « Littérature, culture nationale et guerre ». *The Epoch of Universalism / L'époque de l'universalisme (1769-1989)*. Ed. Franck Hofmann et Markus Messling. Berlin, Boston : De Gruyter, 2021a. 125-140.
———. Ed. *Prosas de guerra y esperanza, Efraín Huerta en El Popular (1939-1944)*. Mexico : UNAM / Almadía, 2021b.
Vargas, Elvira. *Por las rutas del sureste*. Mexico : Cima, 1941.
Verdès-Leroux, Jeannine. *Au service du parti : le Parti Communiste, les intellectuels et la culture 1944-1956*. Paris : Fayard, Minuit, 1983.
Zogbaum, Heidi. *B. Traven : A Vision of Mexico*. Wilmington : Scholarly Resources Inc., 1992.

Stefan Helgesson
Universality From Within: The Challenge of Black Consciousness in 1970s South Africa

Abstract: The aim of this essay is to address the problem of universality by way of Black Consciousness in apartheid South Africa in the 1960s and 70s. In contrast to Souleymane Bachir Diagne's notion of lateral universality, which is premised on encounters across differences, the argument here is that Black Consciousness begins with an inward turn. This "separatism", with its pronounced philosophical tenor in work by Steve Biko and others, needs however to be read dialectically, as a movement towards future modes of connection. Perhaps surprisingly, such a dialectical approach will also demonstrate how apartheid – the ultimate state-backed denial of universality – can be seen historically as the enabling condition of Black Consciousness. The optimistic conclusion to draw from such a reading is that oppression and racism tend to carry the seeds of their own undoing, allowing renewed modes of universality to emerge from within.

Keywords: Black consciousness, apartheid, South Africa, Steve Biko, Barney Pityana, Black theology

"Black man, you are on your own!" (Biko 2004, 108) This early rallying call for Black Consciousness can be read both as defiant and desperate. In its gendered locution, it posits a state of insurmountable existential separation. The "Black man" is cast out into the world – *thrown*, if we resort to Heideggerian vocabulary. This was a statement of fact under the extreme political conditions of apartheid South Africa, but also a challenge to think existence anew *from* that fact. In analogy with Descartes's *cogito ergo sum*, "Black man, you are on your own" sets a baseline for reflection and action. Of this, at least, the black man could be certain: of his isolation and loneliness in a hostile society.

In order to craft an argument around universality and Black Consciousness in early 1970s South Africa, it is essential to begin with this philosophical ground zero – for all its flaws. There is broad agreement that the outlook of leading Black Consciousness thinkers at the time was fatefully male-centred. The writings of the young Steve Biko speak exclusively of black *men* and failed, as Mark Sanders puts it, to produce "a critique of existing gender relations" (2002, 177), even as they in so many other respects revolutionised the perception (and even conception) of South African society. But this imperfect horizon of solidarity need not undermine the project of Black Consciousness as such. If "man" draws our attention today, negatively, one should observe that "black" also indicates a limitation. Black Consciousness *begins* with the recognition – both painful and proud – of particularity. We may in other words read the implication of "Black man, you are on your own" as follows: embodied beings can stake a claim in the world only by first acknowledging their particular mode of immanence. The potential contribution of Black Consciousness to our current attempts at conceptualising universality lies here: not by claiming the high ground of what Souleymane Bachir Diagne criticises as vertical universalism, imposed from above, nor by establishing the universal laterally, as Diagne suggests, but by descending to the specific, finite situation where any thought of universality must begin and end (Diagne and Amselle 2020, 42–44). In relation to Diagne's important formulations on universality, Black Consciousness presents an intriguing alternative: rather than attaining the universal through encounters across differences, it begins in withdrawal and proceeds from there.

The commentary on Black Consciousness is extensive and diverse, and this brief essay makes no claims to cover the field or present an entirely new interpretation of the movement. Its limited aim, in the context of the present volume, is to identify some of Black Consciousness's enabling conditions and notable features in the early 1970s, particularly its contingent conception of "race." The emphasis on the universal potential of Black Consciousness separatism might seem counterintuitive, but as Toth and Nicholls (2020) convincingly argue, its assumed "separatism" needs to be read dialectically, as a movement towards other modes of connection. This is where I locate its key relevance (and challenge) to our contemporary debates.

To consider Black Consciousness as a philosophy, as do among others Mabogo P. More (2008) and Mark Sanders (2002), offsets the more widely circulated political account of the movement. In the dismal decades of apartheid in South Africa – so the political narrative begins – state repression reached its apex after the Sharpeville massacre in 1960. Liberation movements such as the ANC (African National Congress) and the PAC (Pan-African Congress) were banned, as was the South African Communist Party. Many anti-apartheid leaders went into exile; those who couldn't or chose not to were arrested and prosecuted, most famously in the Rivonia trial which saw the conviction of Nelson Mandela in 1964. This clampdown was accompanied by the introduction of draconian censorship laws and the extension of the authority of the secret police, all of which led the South African 1960s to become the "silent decade".

It was in the absence of the ANC and PAC, the narrative then continues, that Black Consciousness emerged, with Steve Biko and Barney Pityana among its prominent early leaders. This started as an intellectual movement among students, but once we get to the Soweto uprising of 1976, it had, after the formation of the Black People's Convention (BPC) in 1973, become a political force to be reckoned with. From that point on, a synthesis of Black Consciousness and the non-racial tendency of the ANC would emerge in the 1980s, culminating in the stand-off with state power that ultimately led to the transition to democracy beginning in 1990.

This account is not factually incorrect, but the problem is precisely its predefined *political* slant. To outside observers, this may sound confusing. How could Black Consciousness ever *not* be political? Already its foundational moment in 1969, when Biko and Pityana led the break-off of the black student group SASO from the "non-racial" (but white-dominated) student organisation NUSAS, was after all politically charged. And to repeat the point I introduced above: How can a movement known for its separatism be claimed to articulate a mode of universality? However, as Sanders observes and Daniel Magaziner (2010) confirms in his in-depth study of the movement, the tendency to place Black Consciousness "in a history of political resistance to apartheid understood as a clash of clearly defined political forces" (Sanders 2002, 176) is a misleading simplification. Black Consciousness needs instead to be understood from within its own conditions of possibility. In this way, it also becomes apparent how a movement towards the universal can (and indeed *must*) begin from an acknowledgement of the particular.

Ironically and inevitably, the main enabling condition of Black Consciousness was nothing less than apartheid itself, as this system of governance had evolved since 1948. Poorly understood in its concrete manifestations outside of specialised academic circles today, the word "apartheid" itself has become an abstract signifier, almost synonymous with "evil." It is perhaps no longer racism's "last word," as Jacques Derrida (1986) once suggested, but it tends to be understood as the epitome of racism itself. The risk with such usage is twofold: it dehistoricises apartheid in South Africa (as Anne McClintock and Rob Nixon (1986) already claimed in their early critique of Derrida), and it skirts over the inescapably context-bound workings of racism and racialisation in any given society. This also means that any lessons we may draw today from Black Consciousness need always to be recalibrated in view of historical change, a view that diverges from the alternative understanding of "philosophy" as concerned with the a priori and hence generalisable aspects of being, knowing, and acting. As More argues, philosophy in black South Africa needs instead to be understood as a diverse undertaking, both in terms of genre and foci – an "open but diverse discursive field in which ontological, epistemological, ethical, moral, social, political, and especially existentialist traditions emerge" (More 2008, 46). For our purposes, it is not least the existentialist dimension of Black Consciousness, in view of apartheid's crushing impact on existence, that is of relevance.

When the Afrikaner-dominated National Party won the whites-only election in South Africa in 1948, "apartheid" was a slogan and a catchword, not a detailed plan of action. It was only in the coming years that an intricate system of laws and policies would eventually shape the totalitarian system of "grand apartheid," resulting in the nadir of the 1960s sketched out above. Imagined most insistently by Hendrik Verwoerd, its infamous "architect", apartheid had from the beginning been sold to the white electorate as a means to secure jobs for whites and control the expansion of the black urban population. The contradictions of its attempt to reconcile backward-looking Afrikaner nationalism and the demands of a rapidly industrialising capitalist economy (with its need for a growing labour force of skilled workers) bore however the seeds of its own undoing.

This becomes particularly clear in the domain of education, which is also where Black Consciousness would ferment and have its main impact. Legislated in 1953 and implemented from 1955 onwards, so-called "Bantu Education" was a cornerstone of apartheid policy. Up until the 1950s, only a tiny minority of African children had been granted access to formal education, mainly in schools run by missions. Being predominantly rural, these schools had almost no uptake among the growing numbers of urbanised Africans in the 1940s and 1950s. According to Jonathan Hyslop (1999), Bantu Education was therefore in the first instance an attempt to control black urban youth by making them acquiescent with the system and employable at the lower rungs of the economy. To do so required, moreover, that the state take charge of education – which is why Bantu Education spelled the end of the mission school system.

It was an explicitly racist set-up. There is no need here for a hermeneutics of suspicion – it is all in the open. In Verwoerd's motivation for introducing the Bantu Education Act, he bluntly stated that there "is no place for [the Bantu] in the European community above the level of certain forms of labour" and for that reason Africans must not receive training aiming at "absorption in the European community" (quoted in Dubow 2014, 55). It is for this reason that Bantu Education was identified by the ANC and its allies as one of the main evils of apartheid. Their high-profile protest campaign against Bantu Education in 1955 and 1956 was however largely ineffectual, partly because many parents in the urban areas saw Bantu Education as better than nothing. This is the paradox: even as it was underfunded and condescendingly racist in its constitution, Bantu Education also entailed an expansion of primary education. The small numbers of African children receiving any primary education at all in the 1950s had doubled to two million by the mid-60s. In other words, while one intention with the Act was to curtail an incipient African elite that had received a better and more egalitarian education at mission schools and posed a potential political threat to the government, Bantu Education also provided, in Dubow's estimation, "limited opportunities that had not previously existed for the majority" (2014, 57). Both Dubow and Hyslop see this is a crucial factor in understanding why there was a relatively high level of compliance with the system, at least in the 1960s.

To the extent that group identities are shaped by prevailing material circumstances, it is therefore the case that by 1970, an entire young generation of black South Africans had the experience of Bantu Education in common. This was a sub-standard system of schooling, organised according to the apartheid ideologues' fantasy of "tribal" identities among Africans (the first few years were to be taught exclusively in local African languages). Yet, a kind of schooling it was. Straddling as it did the contradictions underwriting apartheid in general, it also had contradictory results, ushering the majority of school-goers to their underclass station in life while creating a common, resistant identity that – nurtured by Black Consciousness – would explode on the scene in 1976. Just as importantly for making sense of Black Consciousness, the education system also opened the door (reluctantly) for a select few to segregated institutions of higher education that began to be established out of economic necessity the late 1950s. The most famous of these "apartheid universities" is the University of Western Cape (immortalised in Zoë Wicomb's short story "A Clearing in the Bush", 2000 [1987], 63–81; see also Sanders 2019), which catered for "Coloureds". It was however the "Bantu" University of the North, also known as Turfloop, that would initially be the hotbed of Black Consciousness.

When Steve Biko, in one of his opinion pieces published under the pseudonym "Frank Talk" between 1969 and 1973, stated that "I have lived all my conscious life in the framework of separate development" (2004, 29), this needs in other words to be understood as more than a neutral statement of fact. "My friendships," he wrote, "my love, my education, my thinking and every other facet of my life have been carved and shaped within the context of separate development" (2004, 29). The "my" here refers of course to himself, but should also be read metonymically, as standing in for everyone and anyone who credibly can use the first-person pronoun in relation to this period and political order. It should also be taken literally: if his education and thinking has been shaped by apartheid, so has his "consciousness" – his Black Consciousness. The idea may seem provocative, but draws on Sanders's understanding of the resistant potential of Black Consciousness being conditional on complicity. Black Consciousness was, perversely and profoundly, *produced* by apartheid. It is its dialectical inversion, taking the phantasm of separate development to one of its logical extremes: Black man, you are on your own. From that position, it eventually became possible to think existence anew, unconstrained by white supremacism.

But it is of course a simplification to privilege a system of governance, and apartheid specifically, as the source of a radical philosophical renewal. Biko himself had in fact skirted the margins of Bantu Education, managing to access education in the remaining fragments of what had originally been mission-initiated institutions such as Lovedale (today Fort Hare) in the Eastern Cape and the Catholic college St Francis in Durban. In those contexts, Biko was exposed to liberal, mostly English-speaking circles among white South African society. This social fraction – always a minority among whites – saw itself as staunchly opposed to the supposedly atavistic, backward outlook of apartheid. "Non-racialism" was its guiding principle, as it long had been also for the ANC. The political and moral rationale for non-racialism was that it negated apartheid's group thinking. In the 1955 Freedom Charter, the central visionary document of the ANC and its allies, a society of full and equal rights for all was imagined: "The rights of the people shall be the same, regardless of race, colour or sex"; "There shall be equal status in the bodies of state, in the courts and in the schools for all national groups and races" ("The Freedom Charter" 1955).

Between the abstract universalism of the Charter – and, by extension, of the default white liberal position – and the Black Consciousness intellectuals lay however the unbearable facticity of race in South Africa. Hence, the main target of Black Consciousness around 1970 was not primarily the apartheid state but the non-racial stance of white liberalism – on the understanding that it perpetuated white patronage of blacks. By setting up relationships between "token blacks and guilty white consciences in search of succor" (Magaziner 2010, 29), it was seen as the ostensibly benign but particularly insidious side of a racist system, not its negation. In the essay "Black Consciousness and the Quest for a True Humanity," Biko presents his own take on the dialectic:

> For the *liberals*, the *thesis* is apartheid, the *antithesis* is non-racialism, but the *synthesis* is very feebly defined. [. . .] Black Consciousness defines the situation differently. The thesis is in fact a strong white racism and therefore, the antithesis to this must, *ipso facto*, be a strong solidarity among the black on whom this white racism seeks to prey (2004, 99).

Here the picture begins to clear. If apartheid sectarianism and liberal inclusiveness are considered as jointly formative of Black Consciousness, which thereby functioned as a dialectical rejoinder to both, one can begin to understand the full extent of its philosophical and political potential. When Biko and Pityana split off from NUSAS in 1969, they made use of apartheid's segregationist logic only to invert it by establishing a new ground for subjectivity *as blacks*: a negation of the negation. From this followed the tremendously significant "inclusive" definition of blackness. Instead of reproducing the apartheid state's ethnic fictions, an ethos emerged in Black Consciousness that understood "black" to include all those groups who were legally subordinate in South Africa. In this way, once again, segregationism was inverted and a space for connection among Africans, Coloureds and Indians emerged. Although there also were tendencies to consider blackness as a thing of its own, the prevailing Black Consciousness approach was to see it as a contingent fact and not an essence. At one point, Biko could even say that "[w]e have set out on a quest for *true humanity*" (2004, 108; emphasis added), explicitly invoking a "distant horizon" (2004, 108) of non-racialism. This is a further indication of how Biko and Black Consciousness *claimed* subjectivity, and in so doing, assumed the right to define – dynamically – humanity on their own terms.

A question that remains to be asked, however, is just *how* the Black Consciousness thinkers arrived at their philosophically innovative position. The conventional explanation would be that they were inspired by the négritude movement, Frantz Fanon, existentialism, and Black Power in the United States (More 2008, 48). All of this is correct, yet it bypasses a dimension of early Black Consciousness that is harder to assimilate in contemporary mainstream decolonial discourse: its theological grounding. The landscape of Christianity in late 1960s South Africa, both black and white, was diverse and increasingly divided between the white Dutch Reformed Church's affirmation of apartheid and a wide range of churches that could be anything from politically quiescent to vocally resistant. This diversity notwithstanding, Christianity as such served indisputably as a common ground and shared vocabulary for a majority of South Africans – both white and black – at the time. Because of the National Party government's self-identification as "Christian," and due to the Calvinist dogma that the church should be formally separate from the state, this meant that there was a certain scope for debate and dissent *within* church contexts that was lacking elsewhere in a heavily repressive society. It is therefore less surprising than it might seem that the first seeds of Black Consciousness were sown in the ecumenical University Christian Movement (UCM), founded in 1967 (Dubow 2014, 157).

In dialogue with theological developments at the time – as I discuss more in detail below – early Black Consciousness thinkers crafted far-reaching critiques of South Africa that struck at the soft centre of collective identities and political convictions in the country. Indeed, few things disturbed the regime as profoundly as challenges to its theological doxa. Besides the UCM, two other organisations were at the vanguard of this development, namely, the Christian Institute (banned in 1977) and the South African Council of Churches (SACC). The Study Project on Christianity in Apartheid Society (Spro-Cas) initiated by SACC and the Christian Institute in 1969 dovetailed with early developments in Black Consciousness. Albeit a white-administered undertaking, Spro-Cas not only fostered multiracial study groups in churches (creating unprecedented spaces for dialogue) but published a series of reports such as *Anatomy of Apartheid* and *Apartheid and the Church* – both of them edited by Peter Randall (1970 and 1972) – that would soon lead to the formation of the highly influential radical publishing house Ravan Press. (The publisher, incidentally, of J. M. Coetzee's early novels.)

Spro-Cas did not always meet with the approval of Black Consciousness advocates, yet both parties shared a common trajectory towards theological radicalisation. From the point of view of Black Consciousness, what mattered was the insistence on situational theology that recognised the validity of black experience in South Africa as directly connected to the universalist claims of Christianity. When put on trial in 1974, Kaborane Gilbert Sedibe, president of the Student Representative Council at the University of the North, claimed that the charges against him were "an evil indictment . . . against God for having created me black [and] an indictment against Christ for having said that I am a free man" (quoted in Magaziner 2010, 2). God as creator did not make mistakes, the reasoning went – hence blackness was fully divine in its own right. By failing to acknowledge this, apartheid was a form of heresy. Just as importantly, however, situational theology was put to use to address the distortions produced by the legacy of mission churches in South Africa and their devaluation of African traditions.

Biko was particularly vocal in his critique of the hypocrisy and complicity of mission churches (Biko 2004, 58–65), yet more broadly in the Black Consciousness movement there were tensions between different theological impulses at the time. What the debates had in common was the need to arrive at a *relevant* articulation of Christian faith that spoke directly to the concerns of the oppressed in South Africa yet remained true to deeply entrenched religious vocabularies and convictions. Magaziner identifies three strands of theology that were of importance in this revisionist labour. One was secular theology, championed by among others Harvey Cox (1965) in an attempt to accommodate the realities of rationalist modernity. Another was Black Theology in the USA – as elaborated in particular by James Cone (1969) – and a third was African Theology, linked especially to the work of John Mbiti (1969) from Kenya. These were all to varying degrees pitched as resistant theologies, yet none was immediately applicable to the South African situation. Secular theology lacked an analysis of race, and Cone was seen by several influential black voices in the South African churches as being *too* context-bound (that is, American) and one-sided in his conflictual approach – precluding even the possibility of a non-racial future.

The indigenising impetus of African Theology, interestingly, created another type of problem because of its essentialising emphasis on African traditions. In analogy with the uneasy South African reception of négritude (Mphahlele 1962, 40), blacks from the industrialised and urbanised context of South Africa occasionally found it hard to identify with experiences elsewhere on the continent, where local "tradition" was often less fragmented and more integrated in the lifeworld. Importantly, as Magaziner observes, African Theology's "celebration of

Africanness was politically untenable in the quest for wider black unity, and it came perilously close to supporting the absolute difference between whites and Africans" (2010, 91).

What ensued was therefore a local inflection of these internationally circulating theologies, geared towards relevance in the South African context and increasingly messianic. The notion of the messiah evolved into an image of a black liberator, transforming each instance of pain and suffering into a sign of ultimate and inevitable victory. Having reached that point, one can see that the apartheid regime had been astute in identifying Black Consciousness as a threat to *them*: no matter what increasingly horrendous form state repression took – including the heinous torturing and killing of Steve Biko in 1977 – each new moment of pain was absorbed by this faith in eventual deliverance.

Looking back on these developments today is to peer into a different world from ours. Even at the time, there were Black Consciousness advocates who by the mid-1970s nostalgically recalled the early, earnest beginnings of the movement (Magaziner 2010, 11–14). Soon enough, the political dynamic overwhelmed the nuances of philosophical and theological reflection. In 1976, South Africa entered a protracted state of crisis that would abate only with the new democratic dispensation in 1994. Other crises have followed in ANC-ruled South Africa, but the conditions motivating Steve Biko's original challenge to the apartheid system have transformed dramatically. In a counterfactual world where Biko had lived on, one can only imagine that the coordinates of his mode of Black Consciousness would have had to be reorganised in view of majority rule, the growth of the black middle class and the emergence of new forms of inequality. In brief, his thinking, as we know it, was very much of its moment and cannot be transposed wholesale to our own.

That said, one motivation for this essay has been the revival – at least rhetorically – of Black Consciousness through the #RhodesMustFall and #FeesMustFall movements that rocked the South African universities in 2015 and 2016 under the banner of "decolonisation" (Ntloedibe 2019; Shabangu 2020). These were student revolts, fuelled by the evident failures of the so-called "rainbow nation" in South Africa and the sluggishness of universities to adapt the syllabus to a changed society. Indeed, the students have asked just how changed it really is. Capital and land remain disproportionately (but not exclusively) in white hands and the economic disparities are even worse than in 1994. Exploitation is undeniably a consistent feature of South African society. Yet, an analysis of contemporary power relations will just as evidently yield an adjusted understanding of "race." In other words, racial solidarity, under the general rubric of "decolonisation," cannot carry the *same* meaning in South Africa today as it did in 1970. If Black Consciousness achieved a much-needed sense of clarity as it withdrew from white society, the lines today seem blurred, and the political mood is marked by disappointment and bewilderment (Van der Vlies 2017).

We are, also in the Europe where I reside, living in an age of race-thinking, expressed both as anti-racism (Black Lives Matter being the most successful example) and – troublingly – anti-anti-racism (France's ultra right-wing demagogue Éric Zemmour is a topical example). The stakes here concern both the incapacity (or refusal) in many parts of Europe to confront its own history of colonialism and the continued marginalisation and ostracisation of visible minorities. Actual claims on behalf of racial belonging are however always thoroughly context-dependent, often strategic, and cannot therefore be embraced *or* dismissed a priori. It is a mode of thinking that can be destructive, or even serve to camouflage other power relations, but the acknowledgement of racist hierarchies and political deployment of socially entrenched differences may likewise assist in moving subjects into a new and more enabling social space. My own instincts in these matters, formed through my generational belonging, my personal background in southern Africa (both South Africa and Mozambique) and, no doubt, my racial positioning as white, are thoroughly non-racial. To express this as clearly as possible, I find that placing a premium on visual and/or cultural differences among people always comes with a cost that needs to be weighed against the costs of *not* doing so. I tend therefore to understand the contradictions of racial thinking dialectically. In other words, at least until a utopian state of universal justice is realised, I fail to see how one single position in this relational matrix can be fixed once and for all. Instead, we are confronted with a temporal process through which social relations evolve and unfold, both conflictually and dialogically. The litmus test for this process is normative: does it point in the direction of an always emergent universality or not? In this regard, Black Consciousness in South Africa, with its inclusive and de facto open-ended definition of blackness, provides us with one of the most profound lessons in challenging the status quo and (re-)opening the horizon of universality.

References

Biko, Steve. *I Write What I Like*. Johannesburg: Picador Africa, 2004 [1978].
Cone, James H. *Black Theology and Black Power*. New York: Seabury Press, 1969.
Cox, Harvey. *The Secular City: Secularization and Urbanization from a Theological Perspective*. New York: Macmillan, 1965.
Derrida, Jacques. "Racism's Last Word." *"Race," Writing, and Difference*. Transl. Peggy Kamuf. Ed. Henry Louis Gates, Jr. Chicago: Chicago University Press, 1986. 329–338.
Diagne, Souleymane Bachir, and Jean-Loup Amselle. *In Search of Africa(s): Universalism and Decolonial Thought*. Transl. Andrew Brown. Cambridge: Polity, 2020.

Dubow, Saul. *Apartheid 1948–1994*. Oxford: Oxford University Press, 2014.
"The Freedom Charter." 1955. Historical Papers, Witwatersrand University.
Hyslop, Jonathan. *The Classroom Struggle: Policy and Resistance in South Africa 1940–1990*. Pietermaritzburg: University of Natal Press, 1999.
Magaziner, Daniel R. *The Law and the Prophets: Black Consciousness in South Africa, 1968–1977*. Athens, OH: Ohio University Press, 2010.
Mbiti, John. *African Religions and Philosophy*. London: Heinemann, 1969.
McClintock, Anne, and Rob Nixon. "No Names Apart: The Separation of Word and History in Jacques Derrida's 'Le dernier mot du racisme'." *"Race," Writing, and Difference*. Ed. Henry Louis Gates, Jr. Chicago: Chicago University Press, 1986. 339–353.
Mphahlele, Ezekiel. *The African Image*. New York: Praeger, 1962.
More, Mabogo P. "Biko: Africana Existentialist Philosopher." *Biko Lives! Contesting the Legacies of Steve Biko*. Ed. Andile Mngxitama, Amanda Alexander, and Nigel C. Gibson. New York: Palgrave Macmillan, 2008. 45–68.
Ntloedibe, France Nkokomane. "Where Are Our Heroes and Ancestors? The Spectre of Steve Biko's Ideas in Rhodes Must Fall and the Transformation of South African Universities." *African Identities* 17.1 (2019): 64–79.
Randall, Peter, editor. *Anatomy of Apartheid*. Johannesburg: Spro-Cas, 1970.
———. *Apartheid and the Church*. Johannesburg: Spro-Cas, 1972.
Sanders, Mark. *Complicities: The Intellectual and Apartheid*. Durham/NC: Duke University Press, 2002.
———. "The Space of the University: Time, and Time Again." *Cambridge Journal of Postcolonial Literary Inquiry* 6.2 (2019): 257–271.
Shabangu, Mohammad. "Education and the Practice of Freedom: Towards a Decolonisation of Desire." *Social Dynamics* 46.1 (2020): 132–149.
Toth, Hayley G., and Brendon Nicholls. "A Dialectical Literary Canon?" *African Identities* 18.1–2 (2020): 41–63.
Van der Vlies, Andrew. *Present Imperfect: Contemporary South African Writing*. Oxford: Oxford University Press, 2017.
Wicomb, Zoë. *You Can't Get Lost in Cape Town*. New York: Feminist Press, 2000 [1987].

Nicole Fischer et Fatma Hotait
Penser l'universel à travers le féminisme islamique

Abstract: This article seeks to understand the building of theoretical archive as one of the main challenges in transnational feminist solidarity. As identified in the works of Lugones, Spivak, and Mohanty, we consider Western hegemonic knowledge production as inadequate for representing the interests of white feminists and feminists of color alike and therefore examine the practices of knowledge production from a minority point of view, that of Islamic feminism. By doing so, we engage in breaking up dominant binary approaches in favor of a decolonial point of view. The key point of our examination of Islamic feminism, however, will rely less on the praxis of knowledge production, but on its transmission and the way it offers an alternative way of bridging theory and action. Since Islamic feminism can be conceptualised as a transnational feminism, it seeks to consolidate the categories of global and local, which will be our key point about how to think universality in feminism.

Keywords: transnational feminism, Islamic feminism, intersectionality, decolonial feminism, universality

1 Introduction

Le féminisme est souvent conceptualisé comme se situant à l'intersection entre l'activisme dans toutes ses dimensions et la théorie, et se présente comme une référence pour une pratique activiste capable d'initier des changements concrets à partir d'une compréhension structurelle de l'organisation du vivre ensemble d'une société[1]. En tant que mouvement collectif, il vise à représenter une partie de la société ayant subi une marginalisation, cherchant à dénoncer les multiples formes de discriminations dans lesquelles ce positionnement subordonné en faveur des groupes dominants se décline. Le féminisme dépend du langage politique de représentation qui exige un

---

1 « Feminist practice as I understand it operates at a number of levels : at the level of daily life through the everyday acts that constitute our identities and relational communities; at the level of collective action and groups, networks, and movement constituted around feminist vision of social transformation; and at the levels of theory pedagogy, and textual creativity in the scholarly and writing practices of feminists engaged in the production of knowledge » (Mohanty 2003, 5).

sujet afin d'articuler ses intérêts à partir d'une identité établie sur le terrain politique. Alors que parler au nom de l'identité « femme(s) »[2] est indispensable comme stratégie politique pour thématiser l'inégalité sociale collective, c'est aussi mobiliser et renforcer une catégorie identitaire dont l'insuffisance supposée a été utilisée pour légitimer les inégalités, les inscrivant profondément dans la structure sociétale. Parler au nom de l'identité, c'est utiliser la grammaire d'une nature juridique du sujet, tout en étant soumis.e.s aux modes de pouvoir que la fabrication de cette catégorie et son inscription dans le système politique et linguistique ont créées. Parler au nom des « femmes », c'est manœuvrer sur un terrain qui essentialise et altérise tout ce qui n'est pas « homme » pour le passer au second plan (Butler 2006, 2–3). Si la politique identitaire reste problématique et sans alternative afin d'assurer son partage politique, l'activisme féministe cherche à intégrer un contre-pôle qui réussit à sortir de la terminologie – dans laquelle il s'articule pourtant – ainsi que les limitations de pair avec la position depuis laquelle il doit agir. Le fondement théorique, deuxième composante du féminisme, cherche à rendre visibles les mécanismes qui assurent ce positionnement sociétal et à développer une définition du soi qui va au-delà du discours hétéronormatif, qui rompe avec les logiques de fabrication d'identité qui, selon Butler, crée les effets du pouvoir que l'on appelle sexisme, tout en restant opérationnel dans le présent (Butler 2006, 7).

Cet article vise à problématiser le rôle de la théorie comme étant le lieu « où les relations de pouvoir sont, d'un côté, remises en question, et de l'autre fortifiées et constituées à nouveau[3] » (Schultz 2007, 2). Ainsi, nous chercherons à démontrer que c'est précisément la recherche du commun, voire de l'universel, qui peut diviser les luttes féministes et rendre impossible la solidarité à l'échelle globale et qu'il est primordial que les réalités de vie des femmes se déclinent au niveau local. Comme Dhawan le souligne, même si : « Chaque crise a une dimension du genre et des conséquences au niveau du genre, il n'y a pourtant pas de solution pour des problèmes que l'on pourrait identifier comme globaux »[4] (Ruppert 2020, 29). Les

---

2 Cet article traite des structures de pouvoir entre différents groupes sociaux. Nous utiliserons des termes tels que « non-blanc.he.s » et « femme » pour décrire des personnes catégorisées dans des groupes non dominants. Lorsque nous employons les termes tels que « homme » ou « whiteness », nous nous référons à des groupes dominants. Nous utilisons ces termes avec une distance analytique : ces catégorisations et les effets de pouvoir qui en découlent, émanent de la manière dont les personnes sont perçues et non de la manière dont elles s'identifient. La coïncidence de l'identité personnelle et l'identité assignée est possible, mais non significative pour l'analyse des structures et des effets de pouvoir qu'envisage cet article.
3 « In dem Herrschaftsbeziehungen einerseits in Frage gestellt, andererseits gestärkt und neu konstituiert werden. »
4 « Jede Krise hat eine Genderdimension und genderspezifische Konsequenzen; trotzdem gibt es keine universellen Lösungen für Probleme, die als global angesehen werden. »

crises diffèrent selon les régions du monde dans lesquelles elles apparaissent, et requièrent des stratégies et des outils de luttes adaptés aux foyers d'action.

Si nous soulignons l'importance de la composante locale afin d'assurer une compréhension complexe de ce que signifie « habiter le monde » en tant que femme, nous tenons à relever le mérite de la perspective transnationale pour les luttes féministes. Ina Kerner nie la possibilité de prendre du recul par rapport à la globalité des défis et estime que l'absence d'une communication transnationale féministe sur le terrain peut créer des angles morts au niveau de la théorie, créant ainsi le risque de tomber dans ce qu'elle appelle un « provincialisme » (Kerner 2020, 82)[5].

Notre article propose un outil de résistance issu du féminisme islamique qui vise à mobiliser des féministes au niveau mondial tout en mettant en avant le local. Cette approche vise à faire dialoguer les positions en pensant une culture de transfert du savoir, où l'autorité de traduction de ce savoir en action se décline par la proximité au terrain de la féministe. Ainsi, l'engagement féministe ne s'engage pas à établir des certitudes monologiques : des certitudes, qui peuvent, nous le verrons, être un point de branchement de domination pour celles qui en profitent ou qui réclament une autorité en matière de théorisation. De cette manière, le global et le local en seront consolidés, ce qui à nos yeux est la base démocratique du partage et de la résistance.

Premièrement, nous démontrerons pourquoi la lutte féministe nécessite une *archive du savoir* : une véritable contre-position aux mécanismes de pouvoir qui opèrent dans nos sociétés et pourquoi les différences sont, selon nous, l'outil le plus puissant pour lutter contre un système qui conçoit les différences comme une entrave à tout résistance potentielle. L'approche historique de cette première partie nous aidera à développer une compréhension desdites problématiques et à formuler les exigences et les contours que devraient prendre l'universel dans les luttes féministes transnationales. Dans une deuxième partie, nous présenterons le féminisme islamique comme formation de résistance. Ce féminisme met en valeur les différences entre femmes afin de révéler leur potentiel créateur. Cet exemple, que nous analyserons de manière approfondie autant historiquement, académiquement et globalement, nous permettra de poser les jalons pour une mouvance féministe globale et transnationale.

---

5 Le terme « international » impliquerait une coopération féministe qui s'intègre dans les manières dont la période coloniale a façonné le monde. Le terme « transnational » transporte l'accent décolonial, anticapitaliste et activiste de l'approche, voir le concept de « feminist democracy » (Alexander et Mohanty 1997, xxvii).

2 Hétérosexualisme, domination et colonialisme

Dans *Heterosexualism and the colonial/modern gender system*, la philosophe féministe argentine Maria Lugones introduit l'hypothèse que notre savoir sur les genres peut être retracé jusqu'à l'époque coloniale, époque durant laquelle ce savoir fut développé comme outil de pouvoir des colonisateurs sur les colonies dont l'organisation sociale reposait sur le principe de bénéfice économique. Elle caractérise le concept de genre comme, entre autres, un mode relationnel, de subjectivité, et de répartition de travail : un concept qui pénétrerait dans tous les domaines de la vie. Cet aspect était en effet indispensable afin d'instaurer le degré de contrôle nécessaire à l'expansion du capitalisme mondial. Tout en soulignant le potentiel analytique de ces savoirs sur le genre, elle critique l'eurocentrisme inhérent à ce savoir, et complexifie le concept de *colonialité* du pouvoir d'Aníbal Quijano. Ce dernier argumente que l'émergence du concept de *race* et de racisme à l'époque coloniale était un présupposé pour l'instauration d'un nouvel ordre mondial, tel que le nécessitait le capitalisme mondial, sur la base de modes de pouvoir-savoir qu'il désigne comme « the deepest and most enduring expression of colonial domination » (d'après Lugones 2007, 191). À l'échelle mondiale, le système européen des classes sociales (Lugones 2007, 191), qui organisaient la répartition du travail jusqu'à présent, sont transposées dans de nouvelles catégories d'identités : des identités géoculturelles qui seraient ensuite hiérarchisées en fonction d'une certaine forme de savoir pour mettre en place des logiques de distribution en faveur des colonisateurs. Quijano retrace cette hiérarchisation et montre qu'elle dépend d'une certaine production de savoir qui obscurcit le caractère violent des rapports d'exploitation en les naturalisant, phénomène au cœur de la pensée eurocentriste. Il se consacre alors à l'analyse du racisme sous une perspective marxiste, pour conclure qu'une nouvelle organisation du monde est nécessaire à la réalisation des intérêts économiques des colonisateurs. Il souligne en ce sens l'importance d'une épistémologie qui présenterait l'expérience du monde comme conséquence de sa compréhension eurocentriste. Ce sont des paramètres idéologiques qui construisent une causalité immédiate entre l'expérience du monde et sa conception, qui la rendent plausible et intersubjectivement valide, à un degré tel qu'une distinction nette entre savoir et vécu n'est plus possible. Afin de répondre de manière conceptuelle à cette particularité, Quijano propose de penser la modernité et la *colonialité* comme des axes autour desquels des relations de pouvoir s'articulent. Quijano démontre que les logiques biologisantes des *races* humaines sont idéologiquement surdéterminées en faveur des intérêts d'expansion et de pouvoir des colonisateurs, et précèdent le discours pseudo-scientifique et pseudo-rationnel propre à la modernité. Ce discours stipule l'infériorité d'une partie de l'humanité et légitimise sa domination par autrui, mettant ainsi en évidence son caractère fictif. Parallèlement, les similarités conceptuelles du genre lui échappent.

Lugones critique la compréhension de sexe et de genre de Quijano, qui les pense comme un domaine de réparation du pouvoir régulé par les axes dudit système qui maintient le contrôle sur le « sexual access, its resources and products » (Lugones 2007, 190). Selon elle, la théorie de Quijano oublie de contourner « the heterosexual and patriarchal character of the arrangements [. . .] themselves [. . .] as oppressive » (Lugones 2007, 191), que sa théorie assume comme des faits donnés, et reproduit alors les processus biologisants qui sont nécessaires afin de penser « resources [. . .] to be female » (Lugones 2007, 195).

3 Femmes blanches et femmes de couleur : dynamiques d'une oppression

L'auteure cherche à mettre en évidence comment le système global, eurocentriste et capitaliste s'articule autour du complexe sexe/genre, dépendant de la catégorie de la *race,* et comment il configure ainsi des catégories d'identité et les mécanismes d'oppression/de pouvoir découlant de cette catégorisation. Elle comble cette lacune dans la pensée de Quijano et enrichit son analyse avec le paradigme de l'intersectionnalité afin de comprendre « race as gendered and gender as raced » (Lugones 2007, 203). Elle distingue alors une face claire et une face obscure de la colonialité, qui a créé différents mécanismes de contrôle à l'intérieur des colonies et au sein des pays colonisateurs autour des domaines du travail, de la subjectivité et de l'intersubjectivité, de l'autorité collective et du sexe, et démontre ainsi que « this gender system was as constitutive of the coloniality of power as the coloniality of power was constitutive of it » (Lugones 2007, 203). En effet, les deux outils théoriques qu'elle emploie se complémentarisent : la logique des axes du modèle de Quijano élargit le paradigme de l'intersectionnalité, à savoir que l'intersection entre les catégories genre et *race n*e constitue pas uniquement une optique d'analyse en vue des victimes du racisme, mais que le fait de faire partie du groupe dominant, la *whiteness,* résulte lui-aussi en un phénomène complexe que l'auteur synthétise en deux catégories. Les deux faces décrites par Lugones peuvent être résumées ainsi :
1. La face claire : la vie commune de l'homme blanc et la femme blanche est définie en présentant la production comme tâche masculine et la reproduction comme tâche féminine. Elle y enchaîne des mécanismes d'exclusion et d'inclusion du domaine public. Le pouvoir de décision public est par conséquent centré sur l'homme blanc. Elle définit le paradigme de pouvoir sous-jacent comme hétérosexiste et patriarcal, qui se manifeste chez la femme blanche comme étant

compulsory and perverse [. . .] since the arrangement does significant violence to the powers and rights of white bourgeois women and serves to reproduce control over production and white bourgeois women are inducted into this reduction through *bounded sexual access* (Lugones 2007, 207)[6].

2. La face obscure : celle-ci surpasse largement la face claire, notamment en termes d'oppression et de violence, puisque l'identité de la femme blanche est construite en fonction de l'homme blanc, qui constituait la norme masculine, et qu'elle aussi est centrée comme norme de façon analogue. C'est précisément son altérité supposée par rapport à la femme blanche – caractérisée comme pure et passive, assurant la domination ethnique et coloniale de l'homme blanc – qui a construit la fiction de la femme de couleur comme sexuellement déviante, lubrique et débridé. Elle sera sexuellement exploitée ensuite, exploitation appuyée par un récit de la docilité dont elle fait l'objet.

Il est d'une importance décisive de souligner que les femmes de couleur étaient perçues « as animals in the deep sense of 'without gender' sexually marked as female, but without the characteristics of femininity » (Lugones 2007, 202–203). Cette vision cimente ultérieurement la domination des femmes blanches dans le système hétérosexualiste et patriarcal, et démontre le caractère relativement privilégiant du *sexisme blanc*. En même temps, l'instauration du système de relations entre les sexes coloniaux résultait du fait que la femme de couleur avait, de l'intérieur, accès à la catégorie « femme ». Cette catégorie étant pensée à travers la face claire, les femmes de couleur et leur réalité de vie se voient évincées non seulement de l'analyse historique de Quijano mais également de l'historiographie (Lugones 2007, 203). Ainsi, une optique théorique complexe, sensible à l'enjeu entre genre et race, est nécessaire afin de mettre en évidence les modes d'oppressions auxquelles les femmes de couleurs furent soumises. La même attention analytique est requise pour les rendre visibles d'un point de vue historique. De plus, et cela constitue une essence particulièrement pertinente du travail de Lugones, les femmes blanches sont soumises à une forme de sexisme – qui est pourtant la façon dominante de le penser – intrinsèquement lié à leur *whiteness,* un facteur également peu pris en compte dans le féminisme, comme critique Spivak : « the First World feminist must learn to stop feeling privileged as a woman » (Spivak 1981, 158). Dans son essai *French Feminism in an International Frame,* elle implique que la théorisation du féminisme français échoue à former une contre-position par rapport à la position dans laquelle le système patriarcal les place. Si Luce Irigaray et Julia Kristeva, féministes psychanalytiques, cherchent à

---

6 Nous soulignons.

conceptualiser la femme comme celle qui n'est pas identique à elle-même, voire celle qui ne peut pas être représentée, elles ne considèrent pas les effets divergents qui résultent de la position de la femme selon la catégorie de *race* et conceptualisent les femmes non-blanches de couleur comme une extension du soi. À l'exemple de Luce Irigaray, qui actualise la théorie de Lacan sur la constitution du sujet par un complexe féminin et conceptualise la subjectivité féminine, Spivak montre les effets de pouvoir que cet achèvement de subjectivité peut avoir sur la femme subalterne. Le statut hiérarchique de l'objet ne peut être vidé de son potentiel d'oppression, au contraire : la projection du statut de l'objet reste constitutive pour la fabrication du sujet, et ainsi répercutée sur autrui. Pour rester dans le vocabulaire psychanalytique, la femme non-blanche ne peut être autre que le miroir dans lequel la femme blanche se reconnaît.

Mohanty relève qu'une suprématie d'interprétation de la part d'une partie des féministes réduit les autres femmes au statut d'objet d'étude, les essentialisant sous l'étiquette de « femme tiers-monde » et les réduisant à des cas de figure (*tokenism*) d'un principe universel par rapport auquel la propre oppression peut être étudiée dans des contextes non familiers, et par conséquent abstraits. À travers la compréhension linéaire de la modernité, les femmes non-blanches sont l'espace de projection qui permet de mettre en scène les propres succès émancipateurs, en contraste avec l'immobilité temporelle présupposée de cette première, rendant les femmes blanches aptes à ouvrir le chemin et guider le reste des femmes « au-delà du patriarcat ». En d'autres mots : le féminisme blanc répète le même geste impérial qui a mis auparavant les femmes de couleurs dans la position d'opprimées. L'exclusion de la femme de couleur de la catégorie « femme », tel que le démontre Lugones dans son analyse, est (inconsciemment) réitérée à cause d'une lacune théorique. Le discours normatif qui met au centre le *whiteness*, lui conférant l'air d'être non-marqué, ainsi que le marquage du genre féminin, résulte dans une non-considération du statut privilégié de la femme blanche par rapport à la femme de couleur, universalisant de manière problématique l'identité féminine.

L'intention même de se solidariser avec les femmes de couleur peut prendre une dimension désubjectivante en supposant une expérience féminine homogène comme base commune. Le féminisme ne peut, tel est le but de notre argumentation, être pensé d'aucune position sociétale sans considérer les formations historiques issues du colonialisme, l'émergence du capitalisme global et les processus de normalisation autour des identités de genre qui structurent nos sociétés.

On a vu que ces processus sont intimement liés à des modèles épistémiques dominants, et même que la violence épistémique précède la violence manifeste, légitimant l'oppression de certains groupes. C'est sous cette perspective que se formulent les exigences envers la théorisation féministe et son transfert au niveau transnational. Il est primordial de décentraliser certains savoirs européens afin d'éviter ses logiques binaires qui soit négligent, soit décomplexifient les multiples formes d'oppressions auxquelles les femmes sont soumises à l'échelle mondiale et qui ne vise que le côté clair du système sexe/genre. Une approche décoloniale nous semble ainsi adaptée afin de problématiser les processus de normalisation issus de l'impérialisme, ainsi que pour théoriser les positions divergentes d'un point de vue historique pour rendre possible un dialogue d'égale-à-égale.

À notre sens, il est indispensable de laisser coexister différentes manières de comprendre le monde sous lesquelles les femmes issues de différents milieux puissent maintenir l'autorité sur les récits qu'elles produisent et les modes de narrations dans lesquelles elles visent à formuler leurs positions. La focalisation sur une compréhension universaliste pourrait résulter dans le masquage des positions hétérogènes des femmes selon leurs contextes de vie actuelle et créer des effets hégémoniques (Waller et Marcos 2005, xxv). Par ailleurs, comme le souligne Vergès, cette multiplication des positions théoriques ainsi que leur circulation est un bénéfice pour toute féministe, lui permettant d'envisager des idées allant outre ce qu'un seul bagage théorique lui aurait permis de prendre en considération. D'autres expériences de discrimination, et de sources de savoir peuvent ainsi être légitimées et constituer une forme d'apprentissage : « Une féministe ne peut prétendre posséder 'la' théorie et 'la' méthode [. . .] Elle se pose la question de ce qu'elle ne voit pas [. . .]. Elle doit réapprendre à entendre, voir, sentir pour pouvoir penser » (Vergès 2019, 33).

Ces conclusions aident à éviter une culture du savoir qui prétend l'universalité du patriarcat. Un féminisme transnational devrait laisser des marges de manœuvre à chaque activiste. La proposition d'un agenda fixe risque de libérer une femme dans une partie du monde pour en opprimer une autre dans un contexte différent (Spivak 1981, 179). L'enrichissement de la théorie féministe par du savoir local et contextuel semble une stratégie prometteuse afin d'assurer l'efficacité des luttes féministes sur le terrain. Pour ces raisons, nous ne proposons pas un outil de résistance issu du féminisme islamique pour remplacer l'ordre du savoir eurocentriste par un qui soit islamo-centriste. Au lieu de cela, nous voudrions attirer l'attention sur le fait que le féminisme islamique, dans sa pratique, réussit à réfuter des modes de pouvoir impérial ainsi que patriarcal, en délaissant le concept des frontières (que ces modes ont eux-mêmes mises en place) nationales par exemple, et ne cherche non plus pas à les déplacer – ce qui pourrait mener à les reproduire à travers d'autres moyens de différenciation – mais plutôt à les *transcender*.

Par ailleurs, le féminisme islamique refuse de traduire des concepts théoriques en une directive activiste formulée. Ainsi, la conception théorique peut être comprise comme une pratique collective universelle, et non universalisante. L'imbrication de l'archive du savoir dans des contextes locaux de manière concrète est bénéfique à chaque féministe, puisqu'elle peut ainsi calibrer son utilité en l'enrichissant par son propre savoir. Un pont entre l'activisme local et global peut ainsi être réalisé à partir d'une culture de transfert sensible. Appréhender la solidarité féministe comme un « achievement » au lieu d'un présupposé est « the result of active struggle to construct the universal on the basis of particular/differences » (Mohanty 2003, 7). Ainsi, nous allons nous pencher sur les outils qui nous permettrons d'arriver à cette solidarité globale.

4 L'exemple du féminisme islamique en tant que courant féministe global et unificateur

> Le féminisme islamique est au cœur d'une transformation qui cherche à se faire jour à l'intérieur de l'islam. Transformation et non réforme, car il ne s'agit pas d'amender les idées et coutumes patriarcales qui s'y sont infiltrées, mais d'aller chercher dans les profondeurs du Coran son message d'égalité des genres et de justice sociale, de ramener ce message à la lumière de la conscience et de l'expression et d'y conformer, par un bouleversement radical, ce qu'on nous a si longtemps fait prendre pour de l'islam (Badran 2010, 25).

4.1 Un mouvement fédérateur à l'échelle globale

À présent, nous analyserons les clés du féminisme islamique et pourquoi il peut servir de modèle pour repenser un courant féministe global et retracerons l'histoire du féminisme islamique[7] ainsi que ses différents courants et leurs procédés. Nous précisons qu'il est fondamental de comprendre qu'il n'y a pas un modèle statique de femme musulmane : nous distinguons ici (1) les femmes musulmanes dans les pays à majorité musulmane – de l'Indonésie à l'Iran, le Golfe, le Kosovo, etc. : chaque pays a ses particularités, sa langue ou dialecte, sa culture, son histoire islamique et ses différentes écoles. (2) Les femmes musulmanes dans les pays à minorité musulmane : on distinguera la diaspora musulmane aux États-Unis notamment, qui sera plus sensible à des questions de *race*, ainsi qu'au clivage *black/white*. Ces clivages sont beaucoup moins présents en Europe, où par

---

[7] Nous utiliserons tout au long de cette partie le terme féminisme islamique et non féminisme musulman. Nous faisons ce choix pour distinguer le féminisme qui puise ses sources du Coran et des textes islamiques, du féminisme initié par des femmes musulmanes mais qui ont une vocation laïque. Le féminisme islamique ne représente pas l'ensemble des féministes de foi musulmane : il englobe des féministes qui se regroupent sous le paradigme des textes et croyances islamiques pour faire leurs revendications féministes. La religion, la transmission de celle-ci, ainsi que les écritures sacrées et religieuses sont donc ici au cœur des recherches.

contre la religion est plus taboue selon les pays. Ainsi, les féministes musulmanes aux États-Unis ou en Europe n'auront pas les mêmes sensibilités. Les unes seront plus affectées par les freins dus à des discriminations « raciales » et d'autres par les freins dus à des discriminations religieuses (par exemple interdiction du port du voile)[8]. Enfin, nous voulons souligner le fait que nous nous inspirons des clés du féminisme islamique comme modèle pour atteindre un féminisme universel et l'utiliserons donc comme grille de lecture. Cela ne signifie pas que ces féministes revendiquent un féminisme universel.

4.2 Approches féministes et diversité

Nous distinguons trois positionnements principaux au sein du féminisme islamique (Sirri 2017, 28–29) : (1) la position strictement basée sur la (re)lecture et l'interprétation des textes et traditions qui vont venir composer le *Weltanschauung*, l'idéologie et philosophie islamique, notamment le Coran, la Sunna mais également la *turath* – l'ensemble des traditions accumulées au fil des centenaires (Duderija 2015, 46). (2) Une approche, moins centrée sur les textes coraniques et les textes rapportés (*hadiths*), se positionnant sur une forte opposition non seulement face au patriarcat régnant plus ou moins dans les communautés musulmanes, mais aussi face à la position paternaliste de l'Occident. On peut parler ici d'une approche décoloniale[9]. (3) Ce positionnement pourra être défini comme déconstructiviste, voulant abolir les modes de pensée binaires, tout en remettant en cause l'essentialisation de la catégorie « femme » dans la société. Ces approches montrent la diversité des besoins des femmes musulmanes. Toutefois, en dépit de ces différents positionnements, l'*Islamic Feminism* reste soudé, du moins en apparence. La mouvance féministe islamique a l'atout de pouvoir jouir d'une « auto-compréhension » de ses membres puisqu'elles évoluent toutes avec les mêmes principes religieux et le même canon de

---

[8] À l'heure actuelle, seul le port de la burqa est interdit par certains pays européens, dont la France, dans l'espace public, légalement justifié par une interdiction de se couvrir le visage. Si le port du voile n'est pas interdit en soi en France, il y a une interdiction des signes religieux « ostentatoires » à l'école entre autres, dont le voile fait partie, mais le port des signes religieux « discrets » restent possibles. Une loi européenne en vigueur depuis 2017 stipule de plus que certaines entreprises peuvent imposer à leurs employé.e.s une interdiction de signes religieux et/ou politiques ostentatoires. Enfin, un principe de « neutralité » doit être respecté pour les fonctionnaires du service public en France, interdisant de ce fait le port du voile.

[9] Francoise Vergès (2019) définit le féminisme décolonial comme étant un féminisme luttant contre ce qu'elle définit comme étant la « colonialité du pouvoir », c'est-à-dire l'ensemble des inégalités structurelles qui perdurent dans la société depuis la fin de la colonisation. Elle oppose le féminisme décolonial au féminisme qu'elle définit de « civilisationnel ».

valeurs, et ce, malgré les différences d'interprétations, de questionnements et même d'écoles religieuses. Ainsi, un des facteurs principaux de cette unité est le double rejet auquel font face les féministes musulmanes : pour beaucoup de féministes *blanches*, religion et féminisme sont incompatibles, encore plus dans le cas de l'islam. De l'autre côté, les conservateurs estiment qu'elles modifient la parole divine : « Quand il n'est pas dénoncé comme le cheval de Troie de l'islamisme, le féminisme islamique est perçu comme un non-objet scientifique, voire comme un oxymore » (Latte Abdallah 2010, 11). S'attaquant à plusieurs combats, l'optique critique du féminisme islamique est intersectionnelle : la contestation de la prévalence du *White Feminism* et par cela une approche antiraciste, post- et décoloniale, la contestation d'une lecture des textes coraniques et des *hadiths* à travers une loupe presque exclusivement masculine et la revalorisation voire repensée totale de la place de la femme. Cela rappelle le *Black Feminism*, qui a bouleversé la vision binaire et manichéenne du féminisme blanc, en visant « [s]a tendance – et ses théorisations – à se replier implicitement sur une compréhension de la domination qui prend la situation de certaines femmes pour la situation de toutes les femmes, pour la modalité universelle de leur assujettissement, le 'solipsisme blanc' du féminisme » (Dorlin 2010, 274).

C'est sur ce principe universel que se base le féminisme islamique puisqu'il représente « le premier discours féministe à base théologique à rencontrer un tel écho et à attirer des femmes de milieux sociaux aussi divers » (Badran 2010, 26). Ce mouvement, comme le *Black Feminism*, dépasse toute frontière géographique et nationale et va unifier ses membres sous le toit du paradigme islamique, qui ne connaît pas d'ancrage national. Selon Frantz Fanon, les nations sont fondées par des hommes pour servir leurs intérêts politiques puisque le concept de nation, tout comme celui de race, n'a « qu'une assise théorique des plus ténues ». Il apparente les nations à une « coquille vide », donnant l'occasion à une bourgeoisie nationale d'utiliser le nationalisme pour maintenir son pouvoir, notamment dans un contexte de contrôle hégémonique (Ashcroft et al. 2006, 151–152). Si l'on ajoute à cela la condition de double oppression subie historiquement par les femmes (oppression du colon et oppression des hommes), nous remarquons une troisième forme d'oppression parmi les femmes non-blanches : le manque de crédibilité et l'attitude paternaliste des femmes blanches à vouloir les libérer. Pour Badran, le pouvoir unificateur du féminisme islamique est dû à plusieurs facteurs :

> L'association de l'exégèse à la pratique, la notion centrale islamique d'égalité absolue aux yeux de Dieu et de la loi[10], mais également le moment historique de l'apparition du mouve-

---

10 Le principe d'égalité (al musawa) devrait assurer l'absence de discrimination dans l'application de la loi islamique : il n'y a pas de position supérieure ou inférieure.

ment islamique féministe, qui voit le jour et excelle dans la maîtrise des moyens de communications globaux et instantanés. Il s'agit du seul mouvement féministe religieux à avoir su fédérer autant de membres [. . .] (Badran, 2010, 26).

Cela nous amène à analyser les débuts de ce mouvement, les raisons de sa naissance ainsi que l'environnement politique et sociétal des premières féministes islamiques.

5 Les prémices du mouvement

Les premières réflexions féministes au sein de pays majoritairement musulmans ne sont pas nées à la suite de l'apparition du féminisme occidental mais de manière parallèle. Leur posture était anticoloniale, mais également nationaliste, contrairement au courant actuel qui a une tendance transnationale. Les raisons de cette tendance nationaliste des débuts est logique, puisque les mouvements nationalistes des pays du « tiers-monde » se sont construits simultanément aux formes de nationalisme américaine et européenne au cours du XXe siècle. (Ashcroft et al. 2006, 151), notamment en réaction à la construction-même de ces nations par l'Occident. Margot Badran et Miriam Cooke vont dégager trois périodes clés du féminisme islamique (cf. Alak 2015, 32) :

1. Le féminisme invisible (1860–1920), basé sur la critique des rôles sociaux des genres. Cette première vague prend place notamment en Égypte dans les milieux bourgeois et à travers la littérature et la poésie : un courant non accessible à toutes.
2. L'activisme social (1920–1960) : ce mouvement n'est plus élitiste, s'organise et se vulgarise. Il restera toutefois « léger » dans ses revendications, « se contentent de réclamer certaines formes juridiques et d'exhorter les hommes à améliorer leur comportement », notamment dans le cadre familial (répudiation, polygamie, implication dans la vie de famille . . .). Toutefois, le cadre conceptuel de la famille reste intact (Badran 2010, 29).
3. Le renouveau (1970– actuel) : le religieux est au premier plan, avec des figures féministes mettant l'islam au cœur de leur engagement social et politique. On s'éloigne des discours dociles des décennies précédentes : les féministes brandissent un discours d'égalité des sexes en islam et « s'attelèrent à dénouer le lien apparemment inextricable entre islam et patriarcat » (Badran 2010, 29).

Aujourd'hui, les féministes musulmanes sont très actives sur internet, avec des pôles d'intérêt différents en fonction des régions géographiques. En plus des figures majeures du féminisme islamique contemporain[11], qui ont une vocation plus académique, nous assistons à l'essor du féminisme islamique *mainstream*. Ces femmes revendiquent leurs droits par rapport à plusieurs thèmes : la domination masculine, le patriarcat, l'exclusion des mouvements féministes *blancs*, la discrimination raciale ou professionnelle. Nous pensons à *Muslim Girl* aux États-Unis, *Muslim Feminist* au Royaume-Uni, *Lallab* en France ou *Sisters in Islam* en Malaisie.

6 Outils stratégiques de mise en pratique

Si nous utilisons le féminisme islamique comme inspiration pour penser l'universel dans le féminisme, il présente également ses limites, notamment dans des pays plus conservateurs, où les féministes doivent contourner la censure. Toutefois, nous choisissons de nous concentrer ici sur les outils qui nous permettrons de donner des *inputs* pour arriver à un *agencing* féministe universel.

Dans la tradition classique, le moyen de connaître une règle juridique était *l'ijtihad* : l'effort individuel du juriste pour arriver à une conclusion quant à une norme juridique (Gleave 2012, 26). Un autre outil est le *tafsir*, l'exégèse et commentaire coranique, qui permet à chacun.e d'interpréter les textes. Nous définirons l'exégèse comme l'interprétation pratique et l'herméneutique comme la théorie de l'interprétation, « comprenant à la fois la compréhension des règles de l'exégèse et l'épistémologie de la compréhension – l'étude de la construction du sens dans le passé et leur relation avec la construction du sens dans le présent » (Adis 2015, 47).

Le *tafsir* va concéder à chacun.e le pouvoir de remettre en cause l'interprétation et la lecture masculine des textes. Amina Wadud porte cette pratique à son apogée, dénonçant la lecture souvent apologétique des féministes – y compris la sienne – du Coran et de certains passages. La raison de l'évolution du *tafsir* tel qu'envisagé par Wadud est développé dans *Inside the Gender Jihad* (2005) :

> Ce qu'il faut dire et redire [. . .] c'est que l'on peut discuter le texte, le contester et même lui dire non [. . .] Personnellement, je suis tombée sur des passages où la façon dont le texte dit ce qu'il dit est tout simplement inadéquate ou inacceptable, quels que soient les efforts interprétatifs qu'on lui consacre [. . .] Avec le développement de nos disciplines postmodernistes et déconstructivistes, nous jugeons possible d'être guidés par un texte sans pour autant nous laisser borner par son expression littérale (Wadud 2005, 190–197).

---

[11] Nous pouvons citer entre autres Amina Wadud, Riffat Hassan, Ziba Mir Hosseini, Zahra Ali, Stéphanie Latte-Abdallah, Noura Erakat, Fatima Mernissi, Asma Lamrabet.

Ainsi, si certaines pratiques prévalant à l'époque ont été « tolérées et encadrées » plutôt que d'être totalement bannies, elles devraient pourtant l'être à notre époque. Certains passages concernant par exemple le fait de battre les femmes « sont des usages dont le rejet est conforme à l'esprit et aux principes élevés du Coran ainsi qu'aux conceptions actuelles de justice et d'égalité ». Ce point de vue féministe va préférer réfuter un passage plutôt que de se « lancer dans des exégèses qui restent prisonnières de la scolastique patriarcale » (Badran 2010, 37).

La féministe Aysha Hidayatullah dégage six stratégies d'interprétation principales parmi les féminismes islamique, chrétien et juif, que Duderija définit de « quasi-scriptural hermeneutics » (Duderija 2015, 48) puisqu'elle emploie une terminologie alternative à celle de l'herméneutique traditionnelle. Les « stratégies de la théologie féministe » dénombrées dans *Feminist Edges* sont : (1) la critique de l'hypothèse selon laquelle les hommes seraient les destinataires normatifs de la Révélation ; (2) la critique de la représentation de Dieu en tant qu'homme et des prophètes en tant que patriarches ; (3) la contextualisation historique des textes divins et prophétiques ; (4) l'étude du langage de la révélation ; (5) l'interprétation des textes à la lumière des expériences de vie des femmes ; et (6) la redécouverte des récits des figures féminines significatives de l'histoire religieuse ancienne[12]. Parmi ces six stratégies, les cinq premières comportent de forts éléments d'herméneutique scripturale (Duderija 2015, 48).

Ainsi, depuis sa naissance, le féminisme islamique s'est concentré sur la production de savoir, ce qui constitue un « objectif plus positif que de se contenter de répéter les faits déjà bien connus et admis de l'histoire de la domination patriarcale sur les interprétations religieuses et l'autorité en général » (Abou-Bakr 2020, 174). Si les femmes ont jusqu'à présent été exclues du *tafsir*, il est primordial de produire une propre « contre-bibliothèque » des textes et interprétations existants.

7 Lecture et positionnement

Une lecture intéressante est celle de la féministe et académicienne Omaima Abou-Bakr, qui défend une lecture intertextuelle des écrits (Abou-Bakr 2013, 2014, voir aussi 2020). Elle dénombre quatre grands domaines du féminisme islamique : (1) le *tafsir*, (2) la spiritualité et le soufisme : validation à travers l'exploration du principe de féminité, distinguant la place de la femme dans le discours soufi de la

---

[12] Nous pensons à Asma Sayeed, qui a fait un travail de mise en avant des femmes dans l'histoire islamique, notamment dans la diffusion des *hadiths*.

place dans le discours juridique, (3) la revendication d'une révision du *fiqh* (jurisprudence) à travers un travail activiste transnational, (4) le pan historique, en deux axes : a) la mise en avant de l'histoire des femmes qui ont forgé la vie publique et religieuse islamique prémoderne et b) la consolidation des productions académiques et intellectuelles des femmes musulmanes.

Cette grille de lecture prend en compte des textes non religieux pour analyser et relire l'histoire. Elle utilise la théorie critique de l'intertextualité introduite par Julia Kristeva, qui consiste dans l'idée qu'on ne peut comprendre un texte sans prendre en compte les textes écrits auparavant. Le texte est ainsi une production vivante qui contient des éléments souvent inconscients de l'auteur.e. Un exemple évoqué par Abou-Bakr est celui des textes de Nazirah Zein el Din au XXe siècle, connue pour avoir vivement critiqué et remis en cause les traditions misogynes. Zein el Din les a subis elle-même, ayant été refusée à l'Université St-Joseph de Beyrouth, qui réservait l'accès à l'enseignement aux hommes (voir Badran and Cooke 2004 [1990]). Dans *Al Sufur wa al Hijab* (1928), « elle adresse un texte virulent aux hommes, qu'elle dénonce pour leur « trahison » envers les principes du Coran et de la Sunna, empêchant les femmes de s'instruire et donc d'être à leur même niveau intellectuel, les évinçant ainsi de la société » (Abou-Bakr 2020, 180). Ce qui est intéressant est qu'elle dénonce la formule « naqisat aql wa din » sans pour autant en citer le hadith[13]. Le fait que le texte ne comporte pas le *hadith* en lui-même mais la formule est un élément crucial :

> Dans tous ces appels et ces plaidoyers hautement passionnés, réagissait-elle [. . .] au seul hadith absent qui semble planer au-dessus de tous ses arguments ? La présence implicite du texte primaire ne détermine-t-elle pas la production du texte aussi bien que sa réception par un lecteur également informé ? [. . .] Selon elle, cette stratégie de lecture qui suscite « des connaissances tacites et implicites dans les textes [. . .] pointe l'agencement dans la production de connaissance spécialisée avec de nouveaux outils analytiques. » Ainsi, il « s'agit de créer l'opportunité d'explorer et découvrir la tension inconsciente ou la résistance à cette hégémonie patriarcale » (Abou-Bakr 2020, 181–183).

---

[13] « Naqisat Aql wa Din », extrait d'un hadith sunnite rapporté par Abu Said al Khudri, est un exemple de pourquoi le projet féministe islamique de réinterprétation est si important. *Naqisat* a été traduit comme « déficientes ». Toutefois, dans le Coran, ce terme est employé différemment, en termes de « réduction ». Ainsi, les femmes ne sont pas « naqisat » dans le sens de moins intelligentes, mais ont une charge réduite dans le « aql wal din » (raison et religion) : d'un côté, elles ne sont par exemple pas appelées à témoigner pendant un procès et de l'autre, elles sont exemptées de prière et de jeûne pendant les menstruations.

8 Un *agencing* féministe global : la clé pour un féminisme universel

Fortes de ces éléments d'analyse sur le succès du féminisme islamique, nous plaidons pour un *agencing* du féminisme global, avec pour objectif de le rendre universel. Nos clés sont (1) les droits et intérêts de toutes les femmes et féministes doivent être respectés et considérés sans ordre de priorité. Il est primordial qu'aucune féministe ne traite une autre avec condescendance, avec l'envie – même si de bonne foi – de vouloir la libérer ou en ayant une attitude justement « paternaliste » à ses égards. (2) chaque féministe doit pouvoir interpréter comme elle l'entend : nous sortons ici d'un cadre religieux et ne parlons donc plus de *tafsir* bien évidemment. Que ce soit au niveau des lois, des usages, du langage et vocabulaire utilisé au quotidien, jusqu'à aller sur une publicité qui peut paraître sexiste pour une et non pour l'autre : chacune doit pouvoir se faire une idée de ce qu'est le féminisme pour elle et ce qu'il doit lui apporter. (3) Une relecture de l'histoire de sorte à la rendre moins masculine et une mise en avant des figures féminines du passé, leur rôle et leur importance dans la société, dont l'histoire est souvent enterrée au profit des hommes comme uniques preneurs des décisions. Le féminisme est le principe selon lequel chaque femme doit pouvoir faire et choisir ce qu'elle souhaite. En créant cet espace d'expression et de respect, chaque féministe pourra se sentir part d'un mouvement global et universel, qui ne pourra n'en être que fortifié.

9 Conclusion

Le but de notre recherche était ainsi de mettre en évidence les disparités et défaillances au sein du féminisme global et de permettre, à travers l'exemple du féminisme islamique, de mettre en évidence des points d'amélioration. La cause de l'exclusion des femmes de couleurs, et ainsi de leurs besoins et leurs revendications, des priorités féministes *mainstream*. L'effet hégémonique, notamment sous l'époque coloniale, a en effet placé la femme de couleur en dessous de la femme blanche, la rendant supérieure à elle, tout en restant inférieure à l'homme. L'exemple du féminisme islamique que nous avons utilisé permet de décrypter comment une mouvance féministe doublement – voire triplement discriminée, par les féministes *mainstream* car elles considèrent que le féminisme islamique est tout bonnement un oxymore, mais aussi par les musulmans conservateurs car les voyant comme des réformistes de la parole divine. Une troisième discrimination, même si non généralisée, peut se voir auprès de certains hommes qui considèrent le féminisme comme un « caprice » des femmes. Malgré ces préjugés de tous bords, le féminisme islamique a su s'organiser, s'imposer autant académiquement qu'auprès du grand public, notamment avec l'avènement des réseaux sociaux, et ce malgré la diversité considérable de ses membres, que ce soit au niveau géographique, religieux, éducatif etc.

Il nous est ainsi primordial d'assister à la construction d'un féminisme transnational, dépassant les frontières des pays et des groupes d'identité et remettant le statut de la femme à la place centrale de la lutte féministe, englobant ainsi les besoins de toutes les femmes. À la vue de notre étude, nous plaidons ainsi pour un *empowerment* premièrement au niveau local, qui va permettre aux activistes d'affirmer et exprimer leurs besoins et leur légitimité à être qualifiées de féministes. Pour parvenir à un *agencing* global, il est primordial que les féministes soient « formées » et sensibilisées à pouvoir (1) exprimer leurs points de vue sans craindre d'être jugées ou moquées, (2) apprendre à accepter la manière de chacune d'appréhender le féminisme, même si celle-ci est incompatible avec la leur. La mise en avant des figures féminines importantes et non seulement blanches ou occidentales au niveau sociétal, historique et féministe sera crucial pour cette mise en réseau transnationale. Tous ces efforts devraient conduire à une archive de connaissances, une « contre-bibliothèque » féministe et allant contre toute notion de frontière. Cette base de données doit être non seulement transnationale, mais accessible à tou.te.s et intersectionnelle. Nous tenons toutefois à mettre en avant les limites de l'universalité, car dans le cas du féminisme islamique, ce dernier présuppose l'appartenance à une certaine religiosité de ses membres. Même si les féministes islamiques n'ont évidemment pas le même prisme idéologique, elles travaillent toutes sous le paradigme islamique qui les réunit sous un même canon de valeurs.

Références bibliographiques

Abou-Bakr, Omaima. Ed. *Feminist and Islamic Perspectives : New Horizons of Knowledge and Reform*. Giza : Women and Memory Forum, 2013.

———. « Trends and Directions in Contemporary Islamic Feminist Research. » *Arab Feminisms. Gender and Equality in the Middle East*. Ed. Jean Said Makdisi, Noha Bayoumi, et Rafif Rida Sidawi. London / New York : I. B. Tauris, 2014. 333–343.

———. « Le féminisme islamique et la production de la connaissance : perspectives dans l'Égypte post-révolutionnaire ». *Féminismes islamiques*. Ed. Zahra Ali. Paris : La Fabrique, 2020. 173–191.

Alak, Alina Isac. « Islamic Feminism(s): A Very Short Introduction. » *Analize – Journal of Gender and Feminist Studies* 4.18 (2015) : 31–38.

Alexander, M. Jacqui, et Chandra T. Mohanty. *Feminist Genealogies, Colonial Legacies, Democratic Futures. Thinking Gender*. New York : Routledge, 1997.

Ali, Zahra. Ed. *Féminismes islamiques*. Paris : La Fabrique, 2020.

Ashcroft, Bill, Gareth Griffiths, et Helen Tiffin. Eds. *The post-colonial studies reader*. 2nd edition. London, New York : Routledge, 2006.

Badran, Margot. « Où en est le féminisme islamique ? » *Critique internationale* 46.1 (2010) : 25-44.

Badran, Margot, et Miriam Cooke. Eds. *Opening the Gates. An Anthology of Arab Women's Writing*. Bloomington : Indiana University Press, 2004 [1990].

Butler, Judith. *Gender trouble : feminism and the subversion of identity*. London : Routledge, 2006.

Dorlin, Elsa. « Black Feminism Revolution ! La Révolution du féminisme noir aux États-Unis ». *Genre, postcolonialisme et diversité de mouvements de femmes*. Ed. Christine Verschuur. Genève : Graduate Institute Publications, 2010. 263-275.

Duderija, Adis. « Toward a Scriptural Hermeneutics of Islamic Feminism. » *Journal of Feminist Studies in Religion* 31.2 (2015) : 45-64.

Gleave, Robert. « 1. La charia dans l'histoire : ijtihad, épistémologie et 'tradition classique' ». *La charia aujourd'hui. Usages de la référence au droit islamique*. Ed. Baudouin Dupret. Paris : La Découverte, 2012. 23-34.

Kerner, Ina. « Provinzialismus und Semi-Intersektionalität : Fallstricke des Feminismus in postkolonialen Zeiten. » *Feministische Studien* 38.1 (2020) : 76-93.

Latte Abdallah, Stéphanie. « Le féminisme islamique, vingt ans après : économie d'un débat et nouveaux chantiers de recherche ». *Critique internationale* 46.1 (2010) : 9-23.

Lugones, María. « Heterosexualism and the Colonial / Modern Gender System. » *Hypatia* 22.1 (2007) : 186-209.

Mohanty, Chandra Talpade. *Feminism without borders : decolonizing theory, practicing solidarity*. Durham/NC : Duke University Press, 2003.

Ruppert, Uta. « Einleitung. Zukunftsbilanz. Annäherungen an Transnationale Feminismen 25 Jahre nach Peking. » *Feministische Studien* 38.1 (2020) : 4-20.

Schultz, Ulrike. « Feminismus zwischen Identitätspolitiken und Geschlechterkonstruktionen. Gibt es einen Raum für internationale feministische Solidarität ? » *gender . . . politik . . . online*, 2007. https://www.fu-berlin.de/sites/gpo/tagungen/tagungfeministperspectives/ulrike_schultz.pdf (consulté le 30 septembre 2021).

Sirri, Lana. *Einführung in islamische Feminismen*. Berlin : W_orten und Meer, 2017.

Spivak, Gayatri Chakravorty. « French Feminism in an International Frame. » *Yale French Studies* 62 (1981) : 154-184.

Vergès, Françoise. *Un féminisme décolonial*. Paris : La Fabrique, 2019.

Wadud, Amina. *Inside the gender jihad. Women's reform in Islam*. Reprinted. Oxford : Oneworld, 2005.

Waller, Marguerite, et Sylvia Marcos. « Introduction. » *Dialogue and difference : feminisms challenge globalization*. Ed. Marguerite Waller et Sylvia Marcos. New York : Palgrave Macmillan, 2005. xix-xxxi.

Olivier Remaud
Raconter le vivant

Abstract: When narrating takes the living as its subject, we never tell a single story. To believe that we are narrating just one story is to be mistaken about what telling the living means. Storytelling means here describing ecosystems, symbiotic relationships between heterogeneous non-human beings including the elements. So much so that each time there is a story, there are simultaneously many others. In our context of climate crisis and biodiversity extinction, the argument that materialities are not there without reason interacting with biotic beings, and increasingly destroyed by the human hand, reminds us how much part of the future lies under our feet, above our heads, in soils, clouds and ocean depths.

Keywords: ecologies, storytelling, non-humans, Gaia hypothesis, Aldo Leopold, Val Plumwood

Il en est qui se taisent et qui découvrent des univers insoupçonnés derrière le lourd rideau des phrases toutes faites. Ils préfèrent le silence au tumulte des mots. D'autres parlent comme s'ils étaient portés par un torrent de montagne dont le débit augmente à mesure qu'il dévale les pentes. Ils goûtent l'ivresse des flux de matière. Entre le vide et le plein, peu d'entre nous racontent. Tout récit exige des efforts de description. La tâche n'est pas simple. Elle implique de la patience, de l'exactitude, de l'ingéniosité. Mais l'enjeu en vaut la peine. Plus on décrit et plus se manifestent des êtres jusqu'ici invisibles, des figures effacées, des peuples négligés. Le monde s'enrichit de personnages nouveaux. Qui raconte fait émerger des associations hétérogènes et imprévues. Nous sommes invités à abandonner nos préjugés et à formuler autrement les relations entre les vivants.

On dira ici qu'est vivant tout être qui abrite des processus lui permettant de transformer les flux d'énergie et de matière qui l'animent. Cette définition légitime a priori l'activité de description. Elle rompt avec l'imaginaire hiérarchique qui ne s'intéresse qu'aux deux règnes humain et faunique et augmente le nombre

---

Note : Ce texte reprend en partie les arguments et les références de plusieurs séances de mon séminaire de recherche à l'École des Hautes Études en Sciences Sociales (EHESS) sur « Ce que dialoguer avec la Terre veut dire ». Pour toutes leurs questions et observations, je remercie les étudiant.e.s qui y ont assisté (dont Marc Decitre, Lucia Della Fontana, Aurore Franco, Capucine Garnier-Muller, Jade Nijman, Marion Picard, Emma Wolton).

des vivants à considérer puisqu'elle redonne leur pleine dignité tant aux êtres minuscules et imperceptibles qu'aux milieux dans lesquels ils évoluent. Dans quelle mesure le fait-elle vraiment ?

Avec leur « hypothèse Gaia », James Lovelock et Lynn Margulis ont montré dès les années 1970 que les bactéries et les végétaux avaient modifié, par leur activité photosynthétique, l'atmosphère de la Terre au point de la rendre vivable. Cette hypothèse a été vivement critiquée. Il n'y a là rien de surprenant : nombre d'intuitions ayant révolutionné les paradigmes de la science ont d'abord été reçues comme des romans, des fabulations peut-être agréables mais dénuées de rigueur. Le fait de réunir des protagonistes variés dans une même intrigue, celle de la Terre en l'occurrence, devait trahir une erreur de méthode autant qu'un défaut épistémique. Les esprits réductionnistes de l'époque se sentaient contredits par l'ajout d'une complexité dans l'analyse des rapports entre la biosphère et ses composants. La théorie de la tectonique des plaques n'avait-elle pas subi le même sort ?

Les arguments principaux de l'hypothèse Gaia ont fini par s'imposer dans les faits et les esprits. Au-delà des juridictions de la géochimie et de la microbiologie, ils ont été vérifiés depuis dans d'autres champs de recherche, dont la climatologie. Aujourd'hui, les scientifiques la valident lorsqu'ils s'intéressent aux échanges entre l'eau, les gaz et les minéraux qui produisent les sols comme les êtres vivants, ou analysent les courbes d'évolution et leurs rétroactions sur le climat des cycles biogéochimiques de la « zone critique » qui s'étend des cieux aux roches. La conclusion est claire : tout interagit dans le système terrestre, des pierres aux humains en passant par les sols, les nuages et les océans, les molécules, les microbes et les mycéliums, les plantes et les animaux. La planète n'est pas un organisme mais elle a une sorte de « physiologie » instable. Elle peut être dite « vivante » car elle contient des dynamiques de transformation de la matière qui incorpore des flux d'énergie[1].

Je voudrais illustrer ce dernier argument avec un passage de l'*Almanach d'un comté des sables*. Dans un chapitre intitulé « Odyssée », Aldo Leopold (2000, 138–143) raconte la grande aventure de l'évolution en confiant les rôles principaux aux constituants fondamentaux de la matière. Il prête un pouvoir spécial aux plus petites parties des corps simples : « X » et « Y » sont deux « atomes itiné-

---

[1] Voir l'article de Lovelock et Margulis (1974) dans la revue *Tellus*. Au fil des années, les positions ont un peu divergé (Hache 2011, 83–93). Tantôt entité « thermostatique » dotée de propriétés régulatrices (Lovelock), tantôt réseau d'organismes « symbiotiques » (Margulis), « Gaia » repose néanmoins chaque fois sur la capacité des vivants à convertir l'énergie radiante du soleil en une énergie chimique qui se recycle. Sur ce dernier point et pour une approche scientifique de la « physiologie » de Gaia, on lira avec profit le livre de Tyler Volk (1998).

rants ». Bien que différentes, leurs trajectoires manifestent des modes spécifiques de coexistence entre des êtres vivants.

Le premier atome se libère d'une roche calcaire à la faveur d'une racine d'arbre insistante. D'emblée, il contribue à former des chaînes trophiques. Il agit vite puisque « en l'éclair d'un siècle » – l'équivalent d'un bref instant du point de vue géologique – il circule déjà à travers l'écosystème des grandes prairies des États-Unis. Il se diffuse dans tous les vivants : il saute de la fleur au gland, du cerf qui mange le gland à un Indien qui tue le cerf pour le dévorer à son tour. L'atome court de péripéties en péripéties. On le retrouve dans d'autres plantes, puis un bison, une crotte de bison, un lapin, une chouette, d'autres Indiens, un renard, un aigle, un castor, et toujours, à répétition, les sols dont il est familier, jusqu'à un bayou. Il sort de cette étendue d'eau marécageuse et finit par revenir à la mer, son « ancienne prison », qui l'avait piégé dans la roche plusieurs centaines de millions d'années auparavant à la suite du retrait des eaux paléozoïques. L'atome X parcourt le « système sanguin de la Terre ». Il multiplie les excursions rocambolesques dans les processus vitaux, se niche dans les corps d'autres êtres et aide la biomasse de la prairie à se stabiliser. Leopold résume la propre odyssée de X en écrivant que « pour chaque atome perdu dans la mer, la Prairie en extrait un autre des roches en décomposition ». Un tel écosystème est homéostatique. Il s'autorégule puisqu'il compense ses dépenses d'énergie et de matière par de nouveaux apports. Ses strates organiques sont variées. Sa « caisse d'épargne » est bénéficiaire.

Tout change avec l'autre atome. L'histoire de Y débute pourtant de la même manière : il s'échappe lui aussi de la roche-mère et entame son errance grâce à une racine qui s'insinue dans des crevasses. Mais cette fois-ci, la prairie semble dépeuplée. Des fleurs et des prédateurs ont disparu du paysage. On n'entend ni ne voit plus le pigeon migrateur. Il y a une raison à cette situation : les attelages de bœufs ont pris le dessus, les étendues sont trop cultivées. Le fermier cultivateur a nettoyé les champs de leur précédente faune, il a fait le choix de l'exploitation intensive et s'est retrouvé à privilégier la luzerne, puis le maïs. Les sols se sont rapidement appauvris et l'érosion a augmenté au point de n'offrir à l'atome nomade qu'une prison nouvelle, moins accueillante que la mer tourmentée des premiers âges : Y échoue dans la « vase huileuse » des égouts de barrages, trace gluante de l'ancienne ardeur des rivières qui profitaient des glissements de terrain pour fuir hors de leur lit.

Dans l'histoire de X, la prairie regagne toujours ce qu'elle perd. Avec Y, les atomes nutritifs se dissolvent plus vite qu'ils ne réapparaissent en s'extirpant de la roche pour s'engager dans le circuit aventureux de la vie. Le voyage de l'atome Y est bien plus court que celui de X, ses étapes sont moins fréquentes et ses métamorphoses plus réduites. Autrement dit, les hôtes sont moins nombreux. La prairie a perdu sa fertilité.

Elle n'est plus en mesure de se renouveler car son « système circulatoire » s'est simplifié à l'excès. La caisse d'épargne de son écosystème est devenue déficitaire. La prairie porte aujourd'hui les marques d'un paysage d'abord façonné par la culture de blé, puis déstructuré par l'industrie de l'élevage laitier. De X à Y, la Terre vivante a été altérée.

Les cycles de la planète sont longs quand les rythmes bio-géologiques gouvernent. Ils deviennent brefs sous la pression de l'industrie agricole. La Terre résiste aux perturbations si son « système circulatoire » est préservé. Dans le cas contraire, les écosystèmes ne s'autorégulent plus. Les interconnexions entre les organismes doivent donc rester complexes et conserver leur lenteur si l'on veut que les milieux se renouvellent. Toute communauté biotique dépend par ailleurs de ses éléments abiotiques. Les plantes, les animaux, les bactéries, les champignons et les détritivores (qui transforment la matière organique en nourriture pour les plantes) sont liés aux sols, à la topographie, aux variations du rayonnement solaire, aux pluies, aux vents, à la température, aux nutriments, aux éléments et autres composants chimiques (nitrogène, phosphore, carbone de dioxyde, eaux, mercure, pesticides, etc.)[2]. Un écosystème ne dépérit pas si ses chaînes trophiques demeurent longues et s'il peut répéter ses cycles en maintenant une grande variété de plantes et d'animaux. Sinon, il perd sa capacité régénérative. Au moment où il formule avec un peu d'avance l'équivalent d'une hypothèse Gaia, Leopold suggère que la Terre ne retrouvera pas indéfiniment son équilibre.

Dans ce court chapitre, il est question de processus naturels aujourd'hui bien connus : la photosynthèse, l'assimilation de nutriments, la hiérarchie entre prédateurs et herbivores, la migration d'un écosystème à l'autre ou encore, la reproduction. Leopold raconte le cycle entier de la matière à travers la séquestration du carbone, la minéralisation de l'organique, la décomposition, la fixation du nitrogène atmosphérique par les plantes, l'érosion ou la météorisation (ce processus par lequel les roches se cassent, se réduisent et produisent les minéraux utilisables par les plantes, cf. LEAF 2021 [2004], 16–41). Nous ne sommes pas devant une grande fresque désincarnée. Les innombrables chemins de l'évolution et les nœuds de dépendance entre les vivants sont décrits à partir des biographies sensibles de deux composants infinitésimaux, un peu comme dans les contes classiques où le moindre détail porte une signification universelle. Les éléments s'entremêlent, des atomes ancestraux deviennent les contemporains d'êtres à la vie brève, les échelles de durée se télescopent. Le récit de X montre en quoi l'histoire de la Terre est une

---

2 Je renvoie ici au programme LEAF de l'Université du Wisconsin Stevens Point qui promeut l'éducation à la forêt. La première leçon pour la classe du guide LEAF (2021[2004]), intitulée « The Forest Odyssey », est construite à partir du livre d'Aldo Leopold, LEAF (2021 [2004], 16–41).

histoire interspécifique commune. Celui de Y nous rappelle combien les lieux de la planète sont modifiés et les équilibres vitaux détruits par une intervention humaine mal conduite.

Ce double récit est à la fois inspiré et exact. Il démontre le caractère vivant de la Terre. Avec le terme d'« odyssée », Leopold fait peut-être un clin d'œil évolutionniste à Homère. Les voyages des deux atomes ne ressemblent pourtant pas à ceux d'Ulysse. D'une narration à l'autre, on change radicalement de scène. Les atomes n'éprouvent aucune nostalgie. Même si ce terme n'apparaît pas dans le texte d'Homère, l'*Odyssée* est un récit d'errance qui exprime la souffrance de l'exil et l'inépuisable désir du retour chez soi. Le dieu Poséidon ne cesse de dresser des obstacles, au point que la confrontation d'Ulysse avec la mer semble éternelle. François Hartog montre que l'onde prend tous les aspects : elle est libre et haute, sa houle est forte, ses rivages sont inquiétants, ses rouleaux impitoyables, ses gouffres dénués de fond. Mais Ulysse est rusé. Il possède la « métis », cette forme d'ingéniosité qui permet de réagir aux circonstances imprévues. Dans ses errances, il trouve des chemins. Il passe d'un lieu à un autre, se glisse dans les interstices du monde au gré de rencontres tantôt risquées tantôt agréables. Il est à la fois empêché et aidé par les dieux. Il s'arrête devant les « portes d'Hadès », aux « bords extrêmes de l'Océan », refuse l'immortalité, il a peur, il pleure et manque de se noyer, de mourir « sans gloire », emporté par la mer qui abolit les traces et les mémoires. Il en réchappe pourtant et revient à Ithaque, parmi les siens, après avoir planté sa « bonne rame dans la Terre ». L'odyssée d'Ulysse est l'histoire d'un retour à la terre toujours retardé par les puissances de la « mer grise » (Hartog 1989 ; Homère 1989, 95, 181). Le voyage de l'atome X, lui, se conclut dans l'océan. Il n'y a pas de dieux et les autres êtres non-humains sont bien plus nombreux dans l'*Almanach d'un comté des sables*. Leopold sait que toutes les odyssées chantent des rencontres inopinées entre des personnages singuliers. Avec ce terme, il donne une puissance de description inédite à son récit scientifique.

Afin de mettre en perspective les périples de X et Y, je souhaiterais évoquer un autre écrivain qui a été fasciné par les atomes. Dans *Le Système périodique*, Primo Levi nous livre un ensemble d'histoires autobiographiques placées sous le signe des mêmes composants fondamentaux. Il met notamment en scène un atome de carbone qui passe, lui aussi, par tous les états et tous les corps (Levi 2005, 264–267). À la suite d'un coup de pic, l'atome en question devient vent, il est rabattu sur le sol, respiré par un faucon, puis expulsé dans un torrent. Il s'unit ensuite à des chaînes organiques « stables », se fixe dans une feuille de vigne, s'assemble à d'autres atomes, devient hexagonal, se dissout dans l'eau et se transforme. Il se mélange à une molécule de glucose, se diffuse dans le vin, est bu par un être humain dont il occupe le foie durant un moment. De là, il est à nouveau renvoyé, connaît une fois encore le vent, voyage beaucoup, s'ancre finalement dans le tronc d'un arbre, se mue en nymphe et devient papillon en se lovant dans l'un de ses mille yeux. Mais le papillon meurt et l'atome se niche alors dans l'humus. Il reprend son envol au bout de longues années et ne cesse ainsi de sortir et de rentrer dans le cycle de la vie (« tous les 200 ans environ »). Tant et si bien, écrit Levi, « que l'on peut affirmer que la photosynthèse n'est pas l'unique voie par laquelle le carbone devienne vivant mais aussi la seule qui rende l'énergie solaire chimiquement utilisable ».

Après s'être exprimé en chimiste, l'écrivain précise qu'un tel itinéraire, si « compliqué » et si « obligé », ne donne qu'une image faible de ce qui ressemble par ailleurs à un authentique « happening à l'échelle du millionième de seconde et dont les acteurs, par leur essence même, sont invisibles ». Le « premier rêve littéraire » de Levi était de décrire ces personnages que l'on ne voit pas à l'œil nu. Dès le début, celui-ci avait noué son désir de narration à la tâche délicate de raconter ce qui n'apparaît pas, sauf à travers les lamelles d'un microscope. La « description verbale » demeure l'objectif à atteindre. Mais une telle entreprise est toujours « défaillante ». Le langage est un outil trop humain pour s'ajuster aux mystères des rythmes terrestres dont les atomes témoignent. Il s'épuise vite.

Dans cette brève histoire de carbone, Levi ne se définit pas moins comme un « conteur » invétéré. Il assume autant la fragilité que l'inventivité de son approche littéraire. Il sait combien il avance sur un chemin de crête, entre l'exigence d'une écriture de vérité et l'utopie d'une science de l'invisible, là où s'enchevêtrent les histoires réelles de personnages infinitésimaux, là où aucune intrigue ne connaît plus de fin :

> On peut démontrer que cette histoire, entièrement arbitraire, est cependant vraie. Je pourrais raconter d'innombrables histoires différentes, qui toutes seraient vraies, toutes littéralement vraies, dans la nature des métamorphoses, dans leur ordre et dans leur date. Le nombre des atomes est si grand qu'il s'en trouverait toujours un dont l'histoire coïncide avec n'importe quelle histoire, fruit d'une invention capricieuse. Je pourrais raconter des histoires à n'en plus finir (Levi 2005, 467).

Exposer l'infinité contingente du vivant, débrouiller les mailles du tissu évolutif, emprunter les mêmes labyrinthes que les vivants microscopiques dont les trajectoires coïncident, autant d'arguments qui évoquent l'« odyssée » de l'*Almanach*[3]. Levi confirme que nous dépendons intimement des interactions physiques surprenantes entre les membres d'espèces très différentes et que nous sommes ce que l'on nomme, depuis les travaux de Lynn Margulis, des « symbiotes » qui se

---

[3] Julianna Lutz Newton (2016 [2006], 406, note 162) évoque également le parallèle entre Leopold et Levi. Pour une autre description du cycle accompli par un atome de carbone (peut-être inspirée de Leopold), voir Volk (1998, 14–15).

déploient au gré de circonstances particulières. Dans son ouvrage intitulé *The Symbiotic Planet*, la microbiologiste écrit que « we animals, all thirty millions species of us, emanate from the microcosm » (Margulis 1998). Elle rappelle de cette manière que l'évolution est toujours une co-évolution. Avec leurs récits d'atomes, Leopold et Levi s'efforcent de décrire ces microcosmes qui portent une forme d'universalité non évidente mais partout présente. Ils racontent les assemblages horizontaux entre les êtres qui transitent d'un lieu à un autre, d'un organisme à un autre. Ils collectent les indices et traquent les métamorphoses de ces relations « transcorporelles[4] ». Chaque fois, ils constatent la « résistance[5] » des symbiotes (Margulis 1998, 14).

Leur choix de la voie narrative est un choix antiréductionniste. Ils font le pari que l'activité de description parvient à expliquer le monde parce qu'elle est capable de rendre toutes ses connexions internes sensibles. Ils ne simplifient rien puisqu'ils dramatisent les mille et une aventures physiques des atomes. Mieux : ils les maximisent. Dans ces textes, le récit est en quelque sorte son propre anabolisant tellement il adhère aux vivants, suit chaque trajectoire, accumule les histoires et se déploie dans un horizon toujours ouvert. On n'y découvre pas seulement des relations, on comprend également que la narration contribue à « produire plus de relations » encore (Ingold 2013, 128). La narration sert la science plutôt qu'elle ne la contredit. Une fois les atomes réinjectés dans le processus biotique, les innombrables associations chimiques qu'ils produisent sont revalorisées. Il en va de même pour les agencements lithiques, les minéraux et, par dérivation, les autres matérialités. Leopold et Levi formulent bien un message à caractère universel : raconter le vivant, c'est témoigner de toute l'étendue de nos compagnonnages ontologiques[6].

En lisant ces textes, j'ai repensé à l'essai sur *Le Narrateur* (Benjamin 1991). Qu'est-ce que raconter pour Walter Benjamin ? Je retiendrais ici deux arguments principaux. D'abord, le narrateur revient toujours métaphoriquement d'un pays lointain, d'un lieu où il a vécu des expériences qu'il s'efforce ensuite de restituer auprès d'un public. Ce qu'il dit à celles et ceux qui l'écoutent a de l'autorité. Une

---

4 Pour le terme de « transcorporel », voir l'entretien de Stacy Alaimo avec Julia Kuznetski (2020).
5 J'emprunte le lexique de la « résistance » à Serenella Iovino et renvoie ici à son article « Il chewing gum di Primo Levi » (Iovino 2020, 240).
6 Donna Haraway, Vinciane Despret, Jane Bennett et Anna Lowenhaupt Tsing, pour ne mentionner que ces quatre autrices, nous invitent depuis des années à trouver de nouvelles forces dans les récits. Il s'agit de faire monter sur la scène de nouveaux personnages afin de libérer des schémas d'interactions inaperçus. Le but est reconnaître non seulement l'« agentivité » des entités matérielles mais aussi la richesse des cohabitations possibles entre les humains et les non-humains.

aura se dégage de ses récits. Elle vient de leur dimension d'expérience. Le narrateur procède comme un artisan. Il raconte ses histoires à la manière d'un potier qui monte un bloc d'argile avec ses mains et un tour mécanique. Il manie et remanie, en véritable obsédé du détail, pour transmettre un savoir vécu. Ses histoires ne sont pas linéaires mais denses, fissurées, stratifiées. Aucune vie ne se vit comme un trait continu tiré d'un seul geste. Ensuite, le narrateur chez Benjamin raconte afin qu'on se souvienne. Qui l'écoute devient lui-même, automatiquement, un potentiel narrateur. Un jour, il racontera « à son tour » ce qu'il a vécu. Il le fera car ce qu'il a entendu lui aura semblé utile. Le narrateur est de « bon conseil ». Ce qu'il raconte s'inscrit dans la mémoire. Ses récits expriment la sagesse d'une vie réfléchie. Ils véhiculent des enseignements que personne n'oublie. Aussi Benjamin écrit-il qu'« un bon conseil, en effet, est peut-être moins réponse à une question que suggestion à propos de la continuation d'une histoire (qui est en train d'être développée). Pour qu'on nous le donne, ce conseil, il faut donc que nous commencions par nous raconter » (Benjamin 1991, 208–209).

Dans la narration, il ne s'agit pas de se livrer en tant qu'individu. Le narrateur n'est pas un romancier. Le diagnostic de Benjamin sur le genre du roman est sévère : cette forme littéraire brise la compagnie, selon lui, elle isole l'auteur autant que le lecteur. Chacun songe dès lors au « sens de la vie » qu'il y trouvera. Bien calé dans son existence personnelle, il néglige la vie telle qu'elle se déroule avec ses leçons pratiques. Le roman est individualiste. Il apparaît avec le livre qui enferme le lecteur dans une bulle. Il se caractérise par une surcharge d'informations et d'explications. Il a perdu le style épuré de la chronique qui, elle, épouse au contraire les allures de l'expérience. Dans le roman, on ne raconte pas.

Benjamin oublie sans doute d'apercevoir le narrateur dans le romancier, la Schéhérazade capable de bâtir des récits sans s'arrêter, et tous les spécialistes des odyssées d'atomes. À l'image de la narratrice des *Mille et une nuits*, nous racontons aujourd'hui le vivant afin d'éviter la mort, pour faire en sorte que la Terre soit sauvée. C'est là notre épopée contemporaine. De plus en plus, les genres mélangent leurs styles et la frontière entre la fiction et la non-fiction se dissipe : chaque texte porte un peu de roman, de récit et d'essai. La narration est de toute façon une question de salut, c'est-à-dire d'avenir. Elle vise à créer une « mémoire universelle », pour reprendre cette expression du *Narrateur*, afin de mieux envisager le futur. Quand on raconte, on lutte contre tout nihilisme, on décrit des excès de réalité pour ranimer un monde qui a été dés-animé. Au XXIe siècle, un tel objectif exige de prendre au sérieux des peuples entiers d'éléments invisibles et de faire la place aux êtres issus de ladite « zone critique ». Ce sont l'atmosphère, l'hydrosphère, la lithosphère et la pédosphère qui vont contribuer à l'opération de sauvetage. Les écosystèmes et les récits ont une cause commune, ils observent une même loi « terrestre[7] » : maintenir la pluralité des voix biotiques dans leurs entremêlements avec tous les composants abiotiques[8].

Ce programme ambitieux est pleinement assumé dans un texte fascinant et encore trop peu commenté. Il s'agit de l'article de Val Plumwood (2007) intitulé « Journey to the Heart of Stone ». L'autrice y développe d'abord une critique, depuis devenue récurrente dans le domaine des sciences sociales du vivant, à l'encontre du dualisme qui structure la rationalité scientifique. Puis elle exprime un choix philosophique majeur, comme une exigence de vie nouvelle. Elle propose en effet « a radically intentionalising anti-reductionist writing of the world (that) might make visible whole new interspecies dialogues, dramas and projects previously unimaginable, that can re-open the door to the world of wonder ». Ce projet a pour condition de réinvestir « with speech, agency and meaning the silenced ones, including the earth and its very stones, cast as the most lifeless and inconsiderable members of the earth community ». C'est là « a decentring program » qui vise à élargir notre sensibilité et à briser toutes les frontières entre les êtres animés et non-animés, autant qu'une véritable « task for writing » (Plumwood 2007, 18–19). L'enjeu est limpide : redonner voix et visibilité aux innombrables populations du « more-than-human world » dont nous dépendons tant. On n'y parviendra pas sans réaliser un « cultural change » complet.

La gageure de Plumwood consiste dès lors à nous assurer que cette tâche est à notre portée et que nous pouvons l'expérimenter dans nos corps propres. La Terre et ses roches sont vivantes. Le philosophe amérindien Vine Deloria ne décrit-il pas leur grande force aux yeux des Indiens du Dakota du Nord qui vivent chaque jour à leur contact ? Avec lui, Plumwood nous redit que les pierres sont des êtres parfaits, à la mobilité lente, et qu'elles ont créé leurs lieux à l'échelle d'une durée qui nous échappe. Elles savent comment les autres êtres doivent se conduire. Elles nous parlent à leur manière de la vie et de la mort, du temps et de la fugacité des choses.

Le style du texte change au bout de peu de pages. Après les considérations introductives, Plumwood se mue en narratrice. Elle raconte comment les pierres ont bouleversé son approche du monde et l'ont éloignée des artifices du langage et des déclarations d'intention. Un beau jour, elle décide de construire sa maison avec ce qu'elle trouvera autour d'elle. Plus elle travaille et plus elle s'interroge sur les ryth-

---

7 Je renvoie ici à Bruno Latour (2000, 2017) chez qui le terme de « terrestre » fait écho à celui d'« attachement ».

8 Aurions-nous là un exemple d'« horizon utopique des récits topiques » ? C'est la formulation que Camille de Toledo place en tête de l'initiative des « droits de la nature » dans *Le Fleuve qui voulait écrire* (Toledo 2021).

mes géologiques, leur lenteur, leurs soubresauts, leur beauté. Une relation charnelle, de plus en plus intime, se noue avec les pierres. Elle devient attentive aux singularités matérielles de son environnement proche et repense même à Henry Thoreau ou Gary Snyder qui se sont ré-attachés à leurs lieux de vie. Elle aperçoit enfin une pierre qui retient son regard plus que d'ordinaire. Elle veut connaître les raisons qui font qu'elle est posée là, aujourd'hui, sous ses yeux. Elle se met à creuser le sol et finit par dégager une masse dont les contours demeuraient cachés dans l'épaisseur de l'humus. Majesté, révélation, deux modes auxquels s'ajoute l'excitation d'un « new love » : c'est en ces termes qu'elle décrit l'excavation de sa « cordolith or Heartstone ». Il s'agit bien d'un coup de foudre : « Clearly, this stone had called me ». L'expérience est intense. Elle s'apparente à une fusion, une identification de corps à corps, aux antipodes de tout instrumentalisme :

> The psychological distance of instrumentalism means you can change the stone Other without risk of mutuality – being changed in turn by that other. But the real stone lover takes stones seriously as ends in themselves, attending to them in their own rights and key constituents of their place. Both pleasure and significance may be the more intense for climbers who can see themselves as primarily using stones but as being in conversation with them, physical intimacy being a way to bring over the stone's own remarkable features and formations. Such people can talk of stones in the dialogical terms of encounter (Plumwood 2007, 22–23).

Qui pratique l'escalade ou l'alpinisme a de la chance : il peut dialoguer avec les pierres. Dans sa relation haptique avec la roche, il fait l'expérience d'une mutualité originale. Progresser en adhérant aux parois, se faire presque lichen pour mieux lécher tel ou tel bloc, c'est reconnaître que les pierres sont là, avec leurs histoires propres. Impossible de rester indifférents. L'ici de l'élément lithique se justifie sans recours à aucune instance, il s'impose et nous affecte profondément. Le toucher fait exploser la sphère de l'individu fermé sur lui-même. Plus de monade isolée parmi d'autres monades isolées, uniquement des liens réciproques et intimes. Jeffrey Cohen le rappelle avec force : « To tell a story with stone is intensely to inhabit that preposition *with*, to move from solitary individuations to ecosystems, environments, shared agencies, and companionate properties » (Cohen 2015, 11–12)[9].

Plumwood décrit toutes les étapes de son « voyage au cœur de la pierre ». Elle traverse une grande variété de lieux et revient même dans des territoires déjà arpentés. Elle y découvre des régimes de présence qu'elle n'avait jamais vraiment remarqués. Elle se remémore le gros rocher suspendu qui se tenait au-dessus du lieu où un crocodile s'est jeté sur elle en 1985. Rétrospectivement, elle l'honore comme

---

9 Italiques de l'auteur.

le double symbole de sa vulnérabilité et de son endurance. Si elle a commis l'erreur de s'aventurer en connaissance de cause dans les méandres de l'East Alligator River de l'Arnhem Land, tout au nord de l'Australie, là où un prédateur l'a considérée comme une proie et non comme une personne humaine, elle a en effet miraculeusement survécu à cette atroce expérience (cf. Plumwood 2013). Elle évoque enfin des peintures rupestres émouvantes d'animaux disparus, dont le Thylacine, ce loup marsupial aussi appelé loup de Tasmanie.

L'odyssée propre de la philosophe dans les mondes matériels, parmi les cailloux et les rochers, illustre les conjonctions traditionnellement curieuses entre les pierres et les humains. Plumwood expérimente une altérité imprévue, immaîtrisable, et le charme de sa « géophilie » soudaine est même si puissant que ces rencontres deviennent des « aventures » au sens médiéval du terme, riches en surprises et en rebondissements[10]. Elle réaffirme la vie des pierres, par-delà tous les hasards vrais ou faux :

> The Question is this : can we write stone teaching, stone acting, stone speaking, stone guiding, without being trapped in the familiar 'New Age' or gothic romantic repertoire of the dualistic, the irrational and the romantic discourses that instrumental culture has set aside for us – the permitted realm of exceptionality and intentionality allocated for superstition, the haunted, or the supernatural, the eerily inexplicable ? Can we write stone as much from SCIENCE as from ART, from philosophy as from poetry, from reason as from emotion ? Can we write nature as action, responsive partner for everyday stone and daily experience not just for the occasional impression or exceptional place ? For it is the former we will need if we are to change our everyday lives, to have a sense of how the earth supports us and how we take it for granted [. . .] (Plumwood 2007, 33–34)[11].

Il s'agit là d'une véritable défense et illustration de la Terre vivante, celle qui nous soutient et dont nous n'interrogeons plus vraiment la réalité. Plumwood enveloppe son raisonnement général dans une expérience avec les pierres qui excède les pouvoirs du discours analytique autant que sa tendance à penser avec des contraires (la science, la philosophie, la raison vs. l'art, la poésie, l'émotion). Elle nous pousse à raconter nos propres apprentissages auprès des éléments, nos familiarités retrouvées avec les roches, en bref à développer nos connivences quotidiennes avec le monde matériel. Il est urgent, nous dit-elle, de débarrasser ces relations des fausses mythologies. Vivre pleinement avec des matières n'a rien d'irrationnel. Ce devrait même être notre lot commun.

Le texte se poursuit dans cet esprit jusqu'à sa fin. Plumwood y décrit le rôle que joue le grès dans la bonne santé de la flore mellifère des bruyères et des marais, des oiseaux qui en dépendent et des travailleurs saisonniers qui récoltent le

---

10 Je reprends ces deux termes à Jeffrey J. Cohen (2015).
11 Majuscules de l'autrice.

précieux nectar. Elle saisit combien les pierres sont à l'origine de tout ce qui vit, combien elles sont essentielles aux écosystèmes. Elle est captivée par le travail de l'érosion qui désagrège et ré-agrège les ensembles rocheux en formant des conglomérats et des sédiments. Les histoires nomades des pierres qui ne cessent de se déplacer, de la montagne à l'océan, l'absorbent entièrement. Dans ces expériences lithiques se cache une énigme qu'elle veut éclaircir.

Elle y tient car elle a identifié un dialogue possible avec la Terre. Les sonorités qui résonnent « comme des voix » et les mouvements qui se transmettent « comme des actes » l'ont convaincue que la matière possède son « agentivité créatrice ». Dans sa description des pierres, Plumwood présente « la nature à la voix active ». Comme dans d'autres textes, elle n'hésite pas à utiliser un « vocabulaire intentionnel » qui lui semble apporter, en général, la preuve d'une « bien meilleure rationalité ». Aussi nous demande-t-elle de « prendre très au sérieux la stratégie intentionnelle pour les non-humains ». Il s'agit de mieux vivre avec les êtres « auxquels nous sommes apparentés » (Plumwood 2020, 46).

Au moment de conclure, Plumwood s'interroge sur les raisons pour lesquelles elle s'est tenue à l'écart des pierres, sans jamais vraiment les regarder. Pourquoi est-elle demeurée si longtemps « incurious » ? Était-ce de l'arrogance ou de la naïveté ? C'est là une autre énigme. Aujourd'hui, l'essentiel est ailleurs. Pour s'éveiller au vivant, Plumwood nous recommande d'accomplir, nous aussi, « a different kind of journey, a conceptual journey that moved stone from the background of consciousness to the foreground, from silent to speaking, from mindless vacancy to intentional actor, from the ordinary to the extraordinary, the wonderful, even the sacred ». Elle a changé de cap après avoir dénoncé son ancienne cécité d'humaine. Dans le sillage de sa rencontre tragique avec le crocodile, revitalisée par ses amours lithiques, elle se définit comme une « animiste philosophique » (Plumwood 2007, 35 ; 2020, 46)[12].

Val Plumwood a critiqué à plusieurs reprises les arguments de l'écologie dite « profonde » – notamment sa survalorisation de l'« identification » entre les êtres ou son incapacité à reconnaître la différence comme telle et les logiques de domination insidieuses. Ses récits avec les pierres la rapprochent étonnamment de séquences qu'Arne Naess a lui-même vécues.

On sait que ce dernier avait l'habitude d'aller travailler dans son chalet montagnard de Tvergastein, à l'est de Bergen. Dans un entretien avec Christian Diehm (2004), il évoque son irrépressible besoin de demeurer longuement dans ce lieu pour vivre l'expérience patiente d'une familiarité avec tout ce qui vit là. Il dispose

---

[12] Sur les rapports entre l'animisme, les sciences du vivant et les matérialités, je me permets de renvoyer à mon livre *Penser comme un iceberg* (Remaud 2020).

de cette manière son corps à l'empathie avec les vivants. Des choses que la biologie considère comme inertes deviennent douées d'une présence forte. À propos des rochers qui entourent et surplombent son chalet, il confie à son interlocuteur :

> [. . .] I have known the rocks at Tvergastein since I was very young and they *look* at me. I *look* at them and they *look* at me. Therefore I stopped treating them as if they weren't alive. There are some big rocks near my hut at Tvergastein – they are part of Hallingskarvet – and I was very interested in why they were here. There are large fissures in the rock above Tvergastein, and they expand as water freezes in them. Every year, they grow a little, and after so many years the rocks fall down. Gradually they lose their very nice position at the top of the mountain with a tremendous view, and tumble down to a flat place. Learning about the history of these big stories near the hut and about what has happened to them – it's a way of experiencing even rocks as alive (Diehm 2004, 14–15).

Diehm objecte qu'il tombe dans le piège de l'anthropomorphisme. Mais à cette remarque, Naess répond d'une manière surprenante. D'abord, le sentiment que les roches vivent et qu'elles le regardent vient de la façon dont il se considère lui-même :

> I am something that contains in me those stones, and have for so many years, such that I couldn't move them. As I feel the sense of belonging to Tvergastein, my motivation is always, without any reflection, adapted to this feeling of being-there-together. Here the ecological self gets a meaning because ecology has to do with what you *do* with the surroundings (Diehm 2004, 15)[13].

Les pierres sont là, il n'est pas question de les bouger et les histoires qu'elles abritent témoignent de liens avec le milieu de la montagne auquel Naess appartient. Pas vraiment de romantisme ici mais surtout de l'écologie (pour reprendre une opposition d'Isabelle Stengers). Le romantisme se caractérise par la quête infinie d'une vérité perdue et la volonté d'ériger un passé légendaire en norme de l'avenir. L'écologie, elle, décrit des relations entre les êtres. Or tout comme Plumwood, Naess estime que la matière fait partie du vivant.

Ensuite, ce dernier affirme que s'il « humanise » les pierres, c'est au fond parce qu'il « pétrifie » les humains eux-mêmes – peut-être vaudrait-il mieux traduire par « lithifie ». Le jeu de langage (*humanizing the stones / stoning the humans*) exprime une expérience de réciprocité complète : « the movement is mutual; it goes the other way also » (Diehm 2004, 15). Plumwood emploie le même terme de « mutualité ». Tandis qu'ils s'opposent sur le plan des arguments, les deux philosophes partagent ainsi des séquences lithiques. Les pierres n'annulent pas les critiques formulées à l'encontre de l'écologie profonde. On dira qu'elles offrent simplement un plan d'immanence qui démontise un peu les oppositions entre le même et l'autre, le sujet et l'objet, la nature et la culture. Tout se passe comme si certaines rencontres matérielles obli-

---

13 Italiques de l'auteur.

geaient à « situer autrement la différence », à la « requalifier » totalement[14]. Sans doute est-ce nécessaire si l'on veut entendre les innombrables voix de la Terre auxquelles les scientifiques s'intéressent eux-mêmes depuis des décennies[15].

L'une des conséquences du changement climatique est que les choses inertes deviennent subitement vivantes. Un peu à la manière des « hyper-objets » qui se signalent, chez Timothy Norton, par leur caractère collant, qui adhèrent à nos vies et la pénètrent : chargée d'acides, la pluie devient dangereuse pour tout le monde sur la planète. Tels sont les mots d'Amitav Ghosh dans *The Great Derangement* (2016). Notre environnement se montre de plus en plus « uncanny ». Au point que nous sommes contraints d'inventer d'autres façons de représenter les événements dits « naturels ». Il ne nous est plus possible de raconter le monde comme nous le faisions auparavant. Nous devons remiser les manières classiques d'écrire la nature. Ce ne sont que des métaphores de nous-mêmes, les miroirs de nos procédés d'association qui nous ont maintenus exclusivement entre humains. De nos jours, nous n'avons pas d'autres choix que de reconnaître la présence « inhumaine » de la nature, la force des tremblements de terre, des tsunamis, des tornades, des méga-feux. Passer de l'indifférence tranquille à la conscience angoissée impose de changer d'outils. Nous sommes entrés dans une époque inédite, dénuée de tout « précédent » : celle de la crise climatique.

Amitav Ghosh affirme que le réalisme littéraire masque les moments où se manifeste la réalité et ignore les effets surprenants d'une nature non humaine autant que sa puissance destructrice. Il rapporte les débats qui ont agité la discipline naissante de la géologie, entre le gradualisme et le catastrophisme. La littérature a, selon lui, étouffé la « longue durée » et ses régimes d'exception. Elle a embourgeoisé l'environnement, domestiqué les mondes sauvages, brisant toutes les continuités à la manière des arpenteurs coloniaux qui ont découpé et fragilisé les territoires qu'ils traversaient. Les interférences terrestres de l'hypothèse Gaia, positives comme négatives, ont été rendues « unthinkable » (Ghosh 2016). Aujourd'hui qu'il nous faut appréhender tout autrement nos liens avec le vivant, le « temps épais[16] », dirait Donna Haraway, reprend tous ses droits. En détailler les métamorphoses, telle est la nouvelle mission de la littérature[17].

---

[14] Ces deux expressions sont respectivement de Donna Haraway (2016, 2019) et de Vinciane Despret (2009).
[15] S'agissant du débat que Plumwood mène avec Naess, on lira son ouvrage intitulé *Feminism and the Mastery of Nature* (Plumwood 1991) ainsi que l'article de Diehm (2003) « The Self of Stars and Stone ». Quant aux voix de la Terre, l'éco-acoustique examine de plus en plus les interactions entre la géophonie, la biophonie et l'anthropophonie (selon les termes de Bernie Krause).
[16] L'expression de « temps épais » se trouve par ailleurs dans Caeymaex et al. (2019).
[17] Je résume les arguments principaux de la première partie du livre d'Amitav Ghosh (2016). On notera que Ghosh applique sa critique générale à ses propres romans.

De Benjamin à Ghosh, le débat sur la narration reste ouvert. Qu'il me suffise pour conclure de rappeler que dès le moment où l'écriture prend pour objet le vivant, on ne raconte jamais une seule histoire. Croire qu'on raconte *une* histoire, c'est se tromper sur le sens de ce que raconter le vivant veut dire. Raconter signifie décrire des milieux et des manières d'établir des relations entre des êtres hétérogènes. Tant et si bien que chaque fois qu'il y a un récit, il y en a simultanément beaucoup d'autres. Le jugement de Ghosh sur le roman d'avant est sans doute excessif. Mais il vise juste sur un point. Les puissances de la narration sont infinies. Dans notre contexte d'urgence, le sentiment selon lequel les matérialités ne sont pas là sans raison, plus ou moins détruites par la main humaine, nous redit combien une partie de l'avenir se tient sous nos pieds, au-dessus de nos têtes, dans les sols, les nuages et les abysses des océans.

Décrire nos réciprocités avec les éléments, voilà une tâche qui exige d'« écouter et (de) raconter des histoires qui se bousculent ». Anna Lowenhaupt Tsing (2017, 77) propose avec raison cette attitude comme « méthode ». Avec Frédérique Aït-Touati (2019), je suggère de l'appliquer aux multiples interactions des êtres biotiques et abiotiques. Peut-être pourrons-nous alors déchiffrer la « polytemporalité » de la Terre, nous réconcilier avec ses rythmes lents et dissiper notre « chronophobie » structurelle, obsédés que nous sommes encore par le « présentisme » (Bjornerud 2018). Qui a dit que le « deep time » des géologues nous empêcherait de nouer des relations d'intimité avec les éléments ?

Références bibliographiques

Aït-Touati, Frédérique. « Récits de la Terre ». *Critique* 1.860–861 (2019) : 5–16.
Benjamin, Walter. « Le Narrateur. Réflexions à propos de l'œuvre de Nicolas Leskov ». *Ecrits français*. Trad. Jean-Maurice Monnoyer. Paris : Gallimard, 1991. 205–229.
Bjornerud, Marcia. *Timefulness. How Thinking Like A Geologist Can Help Save The World*. Princeton : Princeton University Press, 2018.
Caeymaex, Florence, Despret Vinciane, et Pieron Julien. Eds. *Habiter le trouble avec Donna Haraway*. Bellevaux : Editions Dehors, 2019.
Cohen, Jeffrey J. *Stone. An Ecology of the Inhuman*. Minneapolis : University of Minnesota Press, 2015.
Despret, Vinciane. « Comprendre l'homme à partir de l'animal ». *Pouvoirs* 4.131 (2009) : 5–17.
Diehm, Christian. « The Self of Stars and Stone : Ecofeminism, Deep Ecology and the Ecological Self. » *The Trumpeter* 19.3 (2003) : 31–45.
———. « 'Here I stand' : An Interview with Arne Naess. » *Environmental Philosophy* 1.2 (2004) : 6–19.
Ghosh, Amitav. *The Great Derangement. Climate Change and the Unthinkable*. Delhi : Penguin Books India, 2016.
Hache, Emilie. *Ce à quoi nous tenons. Propositions pour une écologie pragmatique*. Paris : La Découverte, 2011.

Haraway, Donna. *Staying with the Trouble*. Durham/NC : Duke University Press, 2016.

———. « Avec le terme chthulucène, je voulais que l'oreille entende le son des terrestres ». Entretien avec Catherine Vincent. *Le Monde* (31 janvier 2019).

Hartog, François. « Des lieux et des Hommes ». Postface à Homère. *L'Odyssée*. Trad. Philippe Jaccottet. Paris : La Découverte, 1989, 415–428.

Homère. *L'Odyssée*. Trad. Philippe Jaccottet. Paris : La Découverte, 1989.

Ingold, Tim. *Marcher avec les dragons*. Trad. Pierre Madelin. Bruxelles : Zones Sensibles, 2013.

Iovino, Serenella. « Il chewing gum di Primo Levi. Piccola semantica della resistenza al tempo dell'Anthropocene » *MLN* 135.1 (2020) : 231–254.

Kuznetski, Julia. « Transcorporeality : An Interview with Stacy Alaimo. » *Ecozon* 11.2 (2020) : 137–145.

Latour, Bruno. « Factures / fractures : de la notion de réseau à celle d'attachement ». *Ce qui nous relie*. Ed. André Micoud et Michel Peroni. La Tour d'Aigues : Editions de l'Aube, 2000. 189–208.

———. *Où atterrir ? Comment s'orienter en politique*. Paris : La découverte, 2017.

LEAF. Wisconsin's K-12 Forestry Education Program : *LEAF Guide (9–12 Unit)*. University of Wisconsin Stevens Point, 2021 [2004]. https://www3.uwsp.edu/cnr-ap/leaf/Pages/9-12-Wisconsin-Forestry-Lesson-Guide.aspx (13 avril 2022).

Leopold, Aldo. *Almanach d'un comté des sables*. Trad. Anna Gibson. Paris : GF-Flammarion, 2000.

Levi, Primo. « Le système périodique ». *Œuvres Complètes*. Trad. André Maugé. Paris : Robert Laffont-Bouquins, 2005. 462–468.

Lovelock, James et Lynn Margulis. « Atmospheric homeostasis by and for the biosphere : the gaia hypothesis. » *Tellus* 26.1–2 (1974): 2–10.

Lowenhaupt Tsing Anna. *Le Champignon de la fin du monde. Sur la possibilité de vivre dans les ruines du capitalisme*. Trad. Philippe Pignarre. Paris : La Découverte, 2017.

Lutz Newton, Juliana. *Aldo Leopold's Odyssey. Rediscovering the Author of A Sand County Almanach*. Washington : Island Press, 2016 [2006].

Margulis, Lynn. *The Symbiotic Planet. A New Look at Evolution*. London : Phoenix, 1998.

Plumwood, Val. *Feminism and the Mastery of Nature*. New York : Routledge, 1991.

———. « Journey to the the Heart of Stone. » *Culture, Creativity and Environment. New Environmentalist Criticism*. Ed. Fiona Becket et Terry Gifford. Amsterdam, New York : Rodopi, 2007. 17–36.

———. *The Eye of the Crocodile*. Canberra : Australian National University Press, 2013.

———. *Réanimer la nature*. Trad. Laurent Bury. Ed. Diane Linder. Paris : Presses universitaires de France, 2020.

Remaud, Olivier. *Penser comme un iceberg*. Arles : Actes Sud, 2020.

Toledo, Camille de. « Du langage des êtres de la nature ». *Le Fleuve qui voulait écrire. Les auditions du Parlement de Loire*. Paris : Les Liens qui libèrent / Manuella éditions, 2021. 7–19.

Volk, Tyler. *Gaia's Body. Toward a Physiology of Earth*. New York : Copernicus, 1998.

Contributors

Isaac Bazié is full professor at the Department of Literary Studies, regular member of the Centre de recherche des études littéraires et culturelles sur la planétarité (CELCP), and director of the Laboratoire des Afriques Innovantes (LAFI) at the Université du Québec à Montréal (UQAM). He is also president of the Canadian Association of African Studies (CAAS). (bazie.isaac@uqam.ca)

Anil Bhatti is professor emeritus at the Centre of German Studies, Jawaharlal Nehru University, New Delhi. He holds an honorary doctorate from the Universität Zürich, and was awarded the Jacob and Wilhelm Grimm Prize by the German Academic Exchange Service (DAAD) in 2001, as well as the Humboldt Research Award by the Alexander von Humboldt Foundation in 2011. (anilbhatti@hotmail.com)

Jean-Luc Chappey is professor of the History of Science at Université Paris 1 – Panthéon-Sorbonne, director of the Institut d'histoire moderne et contemporaine (Paris 1/ENS/CNRS), and principal investigator of the project *Harmonia Mundi. Du mouvement mesmérien à l'internationale magnétiste* funded by the LabEx Histoire et anthropologie des savoirs, des techniques et des croyances. (jean-luc.chappey@univ-paris1.fr)

Elsie Cohen is doctoral researcher in the ERC project *Minor Universality. Narrative World Productions After Western Universalism* at Saarland University, preparing a PhD in cultural sociology in co-tutelle with the EHESS (Paris). (elsie.cohen@uni-saarland.de)

Leyla Dakhli is tenured senior researcher in History at the Centre d'histoire sociale des mondes contemporains (CNRS, Université Paris 1 – Panthéon-Sorbonne), and principal investigator of the project *DREAM. Drafting and Enacting the Revolutions in the Arab Mediterranean* funded by the European Research Council. (dakhlileyla@cmb.hu-berlin.de)

Souleymane Bachir Diagne is full professor at Columbia University in New York in the departments of French and of Philosophy, and is currently Director of the Institute of African Studies. Awardee of the Prix Édouard Glissant (2011), he is a member of UNESCO's Council on the Future. (sd2456@columbia.edu)

Nicole Fischer is doctoral researcher preparing a PhD in French Literature at the chair for Romance Literatures and Comparative Literary and Cultural Studies at Saarland University in co-tutelle with Université Paris 3 – Sorbonne Nouvelle. (nicole.fischer@uni-saarland.de)

Albert Gouaffo is full professor of German Literature, Culture, and Intercultural Communication at the University of Dschang in Cameroon. He is principal investigator of the project *Collection History in Reverse. Art and Culture from Cameroon in German Museums* funded by the German Research Foundation (DFG) and of *Re-connecting 'Objects': Epistemic Plurality and Transformative Practices in and beyond Museums* funded by the Volkswagen Foundation. (albert_gouaffo@yahoo.fr)

Contributors

Stefan Helgesson is full professor of English at Stockholm University, and a senior research associate in English at Rhodes University. Ordinary member of the Academia Europaea, he leads the Swedish research initiative *Cosmopolitan and Vernacular Dynamics in World Literatures* funded by the Riksbankens Jubileumsfond (Swedish Foundation for Humanities and Social Sciences). (stefan.helgesson@english.su.se)

Fatma Pia Hotait is PhD student at the chair for Romance Literatures and Comparative Literary and Cultural Studies at Saarland University. (fatmapia.hotait@uni-saarland.de)

Christopher Hutton is chair professor in the School of English and Associate Dean in the Faculty of Arts at the University of Hong Kong. Life member of the Hong Kong Academy of the Humanities, he is partner of the project *Minor Universality. Narrative World Productions After Western Universalism* funded by the European Research Council. (chutton@hku.hk)

Ananya Jahanara Kabir is professor of English Literature at King's College London. Principal investigator of the project *Modern Moves: Kinetic Transnationalism and Afro-Diasporic Rhythm Cultures* funded by the European Research Council, she was awarded the Infosys Humanities Prize, as well as the Humboldt Research Award of the Alexander von Humboldt Foundation (both 2018). (ananya.kabir@kcl.ac.uk)

Mario Laarmann is PhD student and lecturer at the chair for Romance Literatures and Comparative Literary and Cultural Studies at Saarland University. He is member of the executive board of the Society for Caribbean Research (SoCaRe). (mario.laarmann@uni-saarland.de)

Markus Messling is chair professor of Romance Literatures and Comparative Literary and Cultural Studies at Saarland University and principal investigator of the project *Minor Universality. Narrative World Productions After Western Universalism* funded by the European Research Council. (markus.messling@uni-saarland.de)

Rukmini Bhaya Nair is honorary professor at the Department of Humanities and Social Sciences, Indian Institute of Technology Delhi (IITD) and global professorial fellow at the Department of Languages, Linguistics and Film at Queen Mary University of London (QMUL). (rukmini.bhaya.nair@hss.iitd.ac.in)

Olivier Remaud is professor of Philosophy at the École des hautes études en sciences sociales (EHESS) in Paris. In 2013, he was awarded the Friedrich Wilhelm Bessel Research Award by the Alexander von Humboldt Foundation. (remaud@ehess.fr)

Gisèle Sapiro is professor of Sociology at the École des hautes études en sciences sociales (EHESS) and research director at the National Center for Scientific Research (CNRS) at the Centre européen de sociologie et de science politique in Paris. Ordinary member of the Academia Europaea, she was awarded the CNRS silver medal in 2021. (sapiro@ehess.fr)

Bénédicte Savoy is professor of Modern Art History at the Institute of Art Studies and Historical Urban Studies at Technische Universität Berlin. Ordinary member of the Berlin-Brandenburg Academy of Sciences and Humanities, amongst her many prizes, she was awarded the Gottfried Wilhelm Leibniz Prize by the German Research Foundation (DFG) in 2016. (benedicte.savoy@tu-berlin.de)

Contributors — **371**

Maria-Anna Schiffers is doctoral researcher in the ERC project *Minor Universality. Narrative World Productions After Western Universalism* at Saarland University and a PhD candidate at the chair of Romance and Comparative Literary Studies at the University of Potsdam. (mariaanna.schiffers@uni-saarland.de)

Laurens Schlicht is senior lecturer at the chair of Romance Literatures and Comparative Literary and Cultural Studies at Saarland University. He was awarded the Kopper Prize by the Goethe-Universität Frankfurt am Main in 2016. (laurens.schlicht@uni-saarland.de)

Hélène Thiérard is postdoctoral researcher in German Studies and Comparative Literature in the ERC project *Minor Universality. Narrative World Productions After Western Universalism* at Saarland University. (helene.thierard@uni-saarland.de)

Jonas Tinius is scientific coordinator and postdoctoral researcher in Cultural Anthropology in the ERC project *Minor Universality. Narrative World Productions After Western Universalism* at Saarland University. He is also associate member of the Centre for Anthropological Research on Museums and Heritage (CARMAH) at Humboldt-Universität zu Berlin. (jonas.tinius@uni-saarland.de)

Sergio Ugalde Quintana is research professor at the Centre for Linguistics and Literary Studies (CELL) at El Colegio de México and partner of the project *Minor Universality. Narrative World Productions After Western Universalism* funded by the European Research Council. (sugalde@colmex.mx)

Khadija von Zinnenburg Carroll is associate professor of History at the Central European University, honorary chair of Global Art History at the University of Birmingham, and principal investigator of the project *REPATRIATES: Artistic Research in Museums and Communities in the process of Repatriation from Europe* funded by the European Research Council. (carrollk@ceu.edu)

Index

The following terms are of such significance to this book that they appear too frequently to be reasonably listed with page notes here. We ask of the readers to use their own judgement and the possibilities afforded by open-access to browse the pdf using the search function to find the most suitable cases of use. The terms are: Berlin, colonialism, culture, European, langue, minor, museum, translation/traduction, universalism/universal, world.

1769 138, 306
1789 18, 38, 285, 286, 292, 294
1799 285, 286, 288, 294
1948 325, 326
1955 14, 178, 326, 328
1973 325, 327
1989 27, 121, 122, 138, 306

'ach al-cha'b (song by L'Zaar, Weld Legriya and L'Gnawi) 163
Abderrezak, Mahmoud 163
Abellio, Raymond 81
Abu-Lughod, Lila 15
Académie arabe du Caire (l') 170
Adorno, Theodor Wiesengrund 2, 15, 21
al-'Adl, Ḥasan Tawfīq 240
aesthetics 21, 47, 49, 114, 119, 120, 122–127, 129, 132, 151, 234, 244
African; Africain(s) (l'/les), africain(e/s); Afrikaner 5, 6, 36, 49, 61, 62, 86, 91, 94, 98, 99, 101, 102, 151, 176, 178, 195, 223, 238, 251–253, 256, 258, 260–262, 265, 269, 270, 273, 299, 300, 323
Afrique 92–96, 98–100, 102, 200, 251–253, 258–261, 269
– Afrique du Sud 100, 260
– Afrique Sub-saharienne 192
– Afrique-monde 92–93, 95, 98
Afrofuturism 125
afromondial/e, afromondiaux 96–101
Agulhon, Maurice 234
Akhenaton (Pharaoh) 244
Algeria, Algerian; Algérie, Algérien(ne)s, algérien(ne) 1, 6, 8, 11, 14, 66, 160, 166, 167, 169, 196, 197, 253
Almanach 354, 357, 358
al-Shabbi, Abul Qassim 171

Althusser, Louis 129
Amérique latine 192, 311
ANC (African National Congress) 324–326, 328, 331
Animism 109, 364
Anthropocene (Age of) 105, 137, 138, 150–152
Anticolonialism, anticolonial 36, 119, 126, 160, 291, 346
Apartheid 100, 323–331
Apollinaire, Guillaume 78, 241, 242
Arendt, Hannah 194
Aristote; Aristotle 80, 140, 175, 176, 178, 179, 184
Arnhem Land 363
Asholt, Wolfgang 122
atome (l') 355, 357, 358
Attia, Kader 157, 253, 269
Augé, Marc 93, 94
authoritarianism 37
autosociobiographical 131
Aveyron 285, 286, 288, 289, 293, 296
Ávila Camacho, Manuel 305, 311, 313
Axial Age (Achsenzeit) 137–141, 143, 147

Badiou, Alain 1, 16, 17–19
Badran, Margot 345, 346
Bakhtin, Mikhail 80
Balibar, Étienne / Balibarian 35, 37–40, 204, 301
Bandung 121
Bangla 219
Bantu 179, 326, 327
baobab 91–93, 96, 102
Barthes, Roland 8, 20, 182, 185
Bartholdi, Frédéric-Auguste 233–235
Batavia 215, 217, 219–222, 224
Baudrillard, Jean 80
Baudry de Lozières, Louis-Narcisse 298
Bears 106, 108, 111, 112

Benin Bronze 238, 239, 265, 266, 268
Benjamin, Walter 139, 182, 234, 246, 359, 360, 367
Bergson, Henri 79, 83
Berkaoui, Farah 170
Berlin
– Congress Hall 27
– Wall 138
Bicêtre 289
Biko, Steve 323–325, 327–331
Bill
– of Human Rights 273
– of Rights for Works of Art 273
Black Consciousness 323–332
Black People's Convention 325
Blanckaert, Claude 300
Boatcă, Manuela 216, 217
Bolzano, Bernhard 43, 45
Bonaparte, Lucien 288, 293, 294
Bonaparte, Napoléon 19, 138, 233, 236, 285
Bongie, Chris 126
Boni, Tanella 93, 94, 96, 98, 101
Bourdieu, Pierre 21, 57, 63–68, 119, 125, 130, 131, 194, 208
bourouda (frigidity) 170
Breton, André 305
Buckminster Fuller, Richard 84
Bulawayo, Noviolet 100, 101
Buñuel, Luis 306
Burnell, Arthur Coke 219
Burroughs, William 81
Butler, Judith 336

Cabanis, Pierre-Jean-Georges 295, 297
Cage, John 84
Camper, Petrus 299
Cárdenas, Lázaro 305, 208, 313
Cardenismo 315
Cardoso, Hugo 217, 227
Carpenter, Edmund 82
Casanova, Pascale 164, 181
Cassin, Barbara 39, 173–181, 184, 186, 236
Certeau, Michel de 165
Césaire, Aimé 35–39
Chabás, Juan 312
Chakrabarty, Dipesh 123

Chamoiseau, Patrick 92–94, 96, 98, 101, 119, 120, 124, 131, 133
Champollion, Jean-François 233–236, 268
Chiapas 306
Chinese novel(s) 51
Christ, Christianity, Christian 16, 17, 18, 85, 140, 151, 329, 330
Cima 307
civilisation 61, 66, 81, 82, 102, 105, 235, 238, 241, 289, 290, 292, 293, 297–301
Clément, Jacques 247
Cohen, Jeffrey 362, 363
Collège de France 233, 234, 241, 248
Colonial Indifférence 142, 145
commun (le, un) 306, 314, 319, 320
communism, communist 25, 36–37, 121, 192, 205, 307, 313, 314
Communist Party, Parti communiste 36, 307, 312, 324
Condor Oil Co. 308–310
Condorcet, Marie Jean Antoine Nicolas Caritat (Marquis de) 291, 292
Cone, James 330
conjunction 129, 132, 133
– conjunctural reading 119, 130, 132, 133
– conjuncture 128, 129, 133, 218
Conrad, Joseph 45, 50, 52
Consulat, consulaire 286, 288, 290, 293–295, 298, 300
Cook, Kenneth 127
Cooke, Miriam 346, 349
Cosmos, cosmique 84, 92, 107
cosmopolitan; cosmopolitisme, cosmopolite(s) 28, 94, 95, 145, 192, 237, 305, 306, 310, 319, 320, 370
Count of Elgin 246
counter-culture 75
Counter-Reformation 216
Cox, Harvey 330
Cran, Rona 81
Creole, creole language, Creolising universality; créole, créolisation, créolité 120, 132, 133, 157, 160, 215, 217–228
Creole Studies, creolistics; *Kreolische Studien* 215, 217, 218, 221, 225, 227
critical whiteness 216

Cuba 50
cultural
– studies 119, 122, 127–130, 182, 369–371
– theory 46, 129, 133, 226
– practices 1, 16, 23, 43

Dagen, Philippe 244
Dakhlia, Jocelyne 160
Dakota du Nord (*North Dakota*) 361
Danticat, Edwidge 119, 120, 124
Darja (language) 161
Darwinian theory 151
décennie noire 196, 197
Decolonisation, decolonial; décolonisation, décolonial 1, 6, 37, 39, 61, 100, 119, 123, 126, 138, 147, 162, 164, 178, 206–208, 210, 252, 260–262, 275, 329, 331, 335, 337, 342, 344, 345
Deconstruction 21, 80, 107, 120–125, 127, 128, 178
deep time 367
Deleuze, Gilles 1–3, 6, 9–11, 15, 81, 123, 145
Deloria, Vine 361
Demanze, Laurent 128
democratic, de-democratization, démocratique 38, 127, 167, 244, 290, 331, 337
Derain, André 244
Derrida, Jacques 80, 107–108, 110–114, 123, 124, 144, 178, 182, 325
Dhawan, Nikita 336
dhoukoura (masculinity) 170
Diagne, Souleymane Bachir 159, 173–179, 181, 183, 185, 186, 323, 324, 369
Díaz, Junot 119, 120, 124
Diehm, Christian 364–366
difference(s), différence(s) 17, 35, 39, 40, 43, 44, 49, 50, 52–54, 58, 50, 64, 68, 86, 87, 95, 100, 105, 115, 129, 137, 142, 144, 145, 147, 176, 177, 197, 204, 205, 210, 224, 225, 274, 292, 293, 296, 298, 300, 301, 308, 314, 323, 324, 331, 332, 337, 343, 345, 364, 366
différance (Derrida) 44
Directoire 285, 286, 288, 290, 292, 293, 297, 298
Diu (Indo-Portuguese Creole) 217, 227

Diversity 28, 43, 45, 50, 85, 137, 146–149, 174, 176, 179, 180, 181, 184, 329
Du Bois, W.E.B. 46
Dubow, Saul 326, 327
Duderija, Adis 348
Dujardin, Édouard 78

East Alligator River 363
East India Company 142
Eckermann, Johann Peter 48–52
Eco, Umberto 39
écologie 75, 86, 353, 364, 365
écosystème 353, 355, 356, 360, 362, 364
Ecumenism, ecumenical 25, 37–39, 329
Ediciones Imán (publishing house) 307
Éditions Zeus (publishing house) 307
Einstein, Carl 241
Ellis, Nadia 128
Empire 137, 139, 141, 144, 151, 185, 219, 238, 288, 298, 300
– Age of 137, 138
– Austro-Hungarian / Habsburg 11, 44, 45
– British 49
Engels, Friedrich 36, 53
Enlightenment 2, 54, 76, 216, 279
Equaliberty; égaliberté 35, 38, 39
esclavage, esclavagiste 94, 95, 101, 291, 297, 298, 300
Ette, Ottmar 110, 184
Europe
– European modernity 109
– European Universalism 16, 37, 105, 107, 110, 114, 138, 173, 174, 178, 215–217, 235
– Eurocentric; eurocentriste 37, 175, 181, 208, 280, 338, 339, 344
Exotopie 100

F'Bladi Delmouni (Gruppo Aquile / Ultras Eagles) 168
Fanon, Frantz 1, 6, 11–14, 160, 329, 345
féminisme 335–337, 340–348, 350, 351
fiqh (Islamic law/jurisprudence) 349
First War of Indian Independence 142
Flaubert, Gustave 125, 127, 130, 131
floréal 290, 298

Forster, E.M. 45, 49
fou'oula (scheme for distinguishing between genders) 170
Foucault, Michel 11, 58, 60, 61, 123, 149
Fragonard, Jean-Honoré 237, 243
Fraternalism, fraternity; fraternité 25, 37, 310
French pavilion 1, 3–7, 13, 28
French Revolution 18, 233, 285
Frente a Frente (magazine) 307
Fukuyama, Francis 121

Gaia 353, 354, 356, 366
Gall, Joseph 296, 300
Garfias, Pedro 319
genre(s) 63, 81, 98, 109, 120, 125, 131, 150, 170, 194, 197, 223, 299, 325, 336, 338–343, 346, 360
Gestalt 84
Ghosh, Amitav 366, 367
Giedion, Sigfried 82
Ginzburg, Carlo 1, 18, 19
Glissant, Édouard 86, 110, 111, 114, 119, 126, 130
Globalisation (the/la), global; global(e) 2, 23, 25, 27, 43, 46, 75, 83, 85, 86, 91, 94, 96, 101, 105, 110, 115, 121, 123, 129, 147–149, 174, 177, 196, 207, 209, 251, 255, 310, 335–337, 339, 341, 343, 350, 351
Goethe, Johann Wolfgang (von) 21, 43, 44, 46–53, 198
Gramling, David 179, 180
Gran-Aymerich, Ève 238
Grant, George 82
Gruppo Aquile 168
Guadeloupe 298
Guattari, Félix 1–4, 9–11, 14
Gulbenkian, Calouste 237
Gusdorf, Georges 295
Havelock, Eric 82
Gnawi (L') 169
Gwichi'in (First Nations people of Canada and Alaska native people) 114

Habitus 20, 131, 132, 208, 221, 225, 228
Hadès 357
hadith(s) 344, 345, 348, 349
Hafiz 46–48, 52
Hall, Stuart 119, 128–133

Haraway, Donna 106, 107, 111, 113, 114, 359, 366
Haus der Kulturen der Welt 1, 27
Hegel, Georg Wilhelm Friedrich / Hegel-marxian / Hegelian 21, 35, 37, 44, 52, 53, 80, 121, 177, 218
Heidegger, Martin / Heideggerian 80, 177, 178, 323
Hemingway, Ernest 312, 313
Herder, Johann Gottfried / Herderian 45, 180
Heydrich, Reinhard 317, 318
Hidayatullah, Aysha 348
hogra (contempt, humiliation) 168, 169
Holloway, John 169
Homère 357
Hominisation 105
Hopi 83
Hottentot 299
Huerta, Efraín 305–307, 315–320
humain(e/s) 60, 61, 92, 95, 96, 98, 101, 159, 171, 194, 196, 198–202, 204, 208, 210, 283, 287–289, 294, 295, 297–299, 301, 311, 318, 320, 338, 353, 354, 357–359, 363–367
human-animal 106, 107, 111, 113, 114
Humanism 287
Humanité 92, 95–98, 101, 102, 194, 204, 254, 296, 298, 310, 319, 338
Humboldt, Alexander von 49, 50, 53, 254
Humboldt, Wilhelm von 175–177, 185
hybridity, hybrid 119, 120, 124, 127, 132, 133
Hyslop, Jonathan 326, 327

iconoclasm 216
idéal républicain 293, 294, 297, 300
identity/identities; identité(s) 11, 16, 17, 19, 20, 22, 24, 25, 43, 60, 92, 97, 109, 120, 125, 148, 157, 158, 162, 164, 174, 181, 184, 185, 191, 194, 199, 200, 202, 203, 207–210, 216, 221, 274, 327, 329, 335, 336, 338–341, 351
ijtihad (independent legal reasoning) 347
île-mémoire 93, 96
Ilyenkov, E.V. 43, 52
imagined communities 276
imperialism; impérialisme, impérialiste 36, 57, 120, 178, 192, 216, 274
India(n) 43, 44, 47, 49, 53, 127, 137–151, 219–223, 225, 329

individu(s) 93, 95, 193, 259, 286, 288, 289, 293–296, 298–301, 360, 362
interculturality, intercultural 40, 182, 185, 186
internationaliste 305, 314, 320
intersectionality ; intersectionnel(le) 210, 335, 339, 345, 351
intersubjectivité 339
intraduisible(s) 39, 68, 177, 179, 181, 182, 185
Irhal (protest slogan in Egypt and Syria: "Get out") 167
Irigaray, Luce 340, 341
islamo-centriste 342
Israel 207, 238
Itard, Jean-Marc Gaspard 289, 293, 294, 296, 297, 300, 301
Ittihad Riadi Tanger (club de foot) 168

néo-jacobin 294
janséniste(s) 286
Jaspers, Karl 138–140, 143, 147, 151
jins (gender/sex) 170
jinsâniyya (sexuality) 170
jounoussa (term to designate the "distinctive features between the male and female sexes") 170
Joyce, James 11, 79

kaffir (infidel) 223
Kahn, Alphonse 237
Kamchatka 108, 109, 114
karama (aspiration to dignity) 168
kayyâs (street) 161
Kerner, Ina 337
al-Khudri, Abu Said 349
kifaya ("Enough", Egyptian movement for change) 167
Kincaid, Jamaica 127
Klee, Paul 139
Kostakowsky, Lya 307
koiné 158
Kristeva, Julia 80, 340, 349
kullun yani kullun (protest slogan in Lebanon: "all, that means all") 167

La Voix de l'Algèrie libre et combattante (Voice of Fighting Algeria) 12

Labov, William 151
Lacan, Jacques 6, 178, 341
Lachman, Karl 221
Laferrière, Dany 119, 120
Laidlaw, James 16
Lanjuinais, Jean-Denis 291
Latin America 50
Latour, Bruno 361
Le ëppe Tuuru (protest slogan in Senegal: "too much is too much") 81
Leary, Timothy 81
Lebenswissen 110
Lee, Dorothy 82, 83, 86
Leroi-Gourhan, André 80
Lenin, Vladimir Ilyich 36, 274
Levi, Giovanni V, 1, 19
Levi, Primo 357–359
Levinas, Emmanuel 39
Lévi-Strauss, Claude 58, 59, 61, 63, 64, 66, 182, 202
Lévy-Bruhl, Lucien 64, 84, 274
Lezay-Marnésia, Adrien 290
Lieu-monde, lieux-monde(s) 92–96
Lingua Franca 177, 225, 226
Lionnet, Françoise 215, 217, 226
Lloyd, David 300
local; local(e) 14, 22, 53, 94, 96, 100, 101, 140, 193, 197, 207, 219, 227, 254, 255, 288, 301, 302, 310, 327, 330, 331, 335–337, 342, 343, 351
Lord Byron (George Gordon Noel, 6th Baron Byron) 240
Lorde, Audrey Geraldine 122
Louvre (Le) 233, 236, 241–243
Lovelace, Earl 119, 120
Lowenhaupt Tsing, Anna 359, 367
Lugones, Maria 335, 338–341
Luján, Rosa Elena 308
Lukács, Georg 43, 50
Lumières 81, 166, 204, 205, 286, 191, 292
Lydice/Lidice (Czech village) 317–319
Lyotard, Jean-François 40

Macaulay, Thomas Babington 143, 145, 151
madness 12, 109

Magaziner, Daniel 325, 330
Malayo-Portuguese 217, 218, 220–222, 226
Malinowski, Bronisław 45
Manto, Saadat Hasan 46
Margulis, Lynn 354, 358
marna (television) 163
Martin, Nastassja 105, 106, 108–115
Martinique 120, 132, 298
Marut, Ret (writer) 306
Marx, Karl / Marxism/ Marxist theory 25, 35, 53, 67, 151, 252, 274
mathuka ("she-bear") 112, 113
Matisse, Henri 244
Mawazine (international music festival in Rabat) 169
Mayakovski, Vladimir 319
Mbembe, Achille 25, 93, 98, 99, 162, 178, 240, 248, 273
Mbiti, John 330
McClintock, Anne 325
Mediterranean; Méditerranée 1, 14, 17, 98, 101, 157, 216, 225
medka (indigenous concept among the Evens, denoting people "marked by the bear") 112
Melville, Herman 46
Merleau-Ponty, Maurice 39, 40, 83, 174, 185, 186
Meschonnic, Henri 175, 176
Messling, Markus 19, 75, 86, 102, 106, 110, 122, 126, 138, 192, 193, 215, 216, 217, 228, 235, 279, 287
métissage; mestizaje 98, 132, 220
micro-history ; *microstoria* 1, 19
migrance 98–100
migrant(s); migrant(e/s) 49, 91–93, 96–101, 199, 201, 205–207, 209
Millot, Jacques-André 295, 296
minor, minor universalism, minor universality, minor universal(s), minor formation
Modernity 11, 16, 17, 22, 25, 76, 81, 105, 107, 109, 110, 119, 121, 123, 126, 127, 133, 174, 180, 330
Mohanty, Chandra 335, 341
Mohren 224
monde arabe 157–159, 162–164, 170
Monde(s)-ville(s), ville(s)-monde(s) 93–95

Mondialisation (the/la); mondialité 43, 92, 96, 99, 101, 162, 163, 261
More, Mabogo 324
Moreau de la Sarthe, Louis Jacques 297
Moyen-Orient 192, 205, 206
multiculturalism, multicultural 35, 40, 44, 144
multilingualism 22, 44, 47, 174, 175, 179–181
museum
– British 236, 238, 244, 275, 276, 279
– Island 238, 244
– Pergamon 238, 241, 242
Musil, Robert 45, 268

Naess, Arne 364–366
Nahda 158–160, 162–164
Nahw wa sarf (Arabic grammar) 163
naqisat (deficient/term of reduction in the Quran) 349
Nation, nationalism, nationalist; nationalisme, nationaliste(s) VI, 2, 3, 5, 14, 19, 24, 25, 36, 38, 43–46, 48, 53, 85, 110, 121, 132, 133, 158–162, 164, 166, 178–181, 183, 192, 195, 196, 198, 216, 225, 226, 234, 236, 237, 246, 251, 254, 255, 260, 262, 275, 276, 288, 290, 292–294, 297, 300, 301, 324, 326, 328, 329, 331, 342, 345, 346
Nefertiti 244
Négritude 35, 37, 39, 329, 330
Neruda, Pablo 306, 315, 319
Nesbitt, Nick 126
New Realism 122, 125, 133
Nicholls, Brendon 324
Nixon, Rob 325
nonhuman; non-human(s), non-humain(s) 2, 106, 107, 110, 273, 353, 357, 364
Norton, Timothy 366
NUSAS (National Union of South African Students) 325, 328

Occident (the/l'), occidental, occidentalism, disoccidentalised; occidental(e/s), occidentalisation, désoccidentalisé 39, 57, 59, 61–64, 66, 68, 92, 94–97, 102, 144, 167, 185, 192, 193, 209–211, 254, 259, 261, 306, 344, 346, 351
odyssey; odyssée 354–358, 360, 363

onde (l') 357
Onyrikon 265-267, 270, 271, 279
organique (l') 309, 356
Orient (the/l'), Orientalism, Orientalist, oriental; Orientalisme 3, 47-49, 62, 66, 144, 146, 151, 163, 167, 169, 185, 191, 192, 205, 206, 216
Otherness 106, 109, 144
ounoutha (feminity) 170

PAC (Pan-African Congress) 324
Palmié, Stephan 226-228
particularism; particularisme 26, 95, 191, 193, 196, 197, 205, 218, 225, 227, 306
Parvulescu, Anca 217
Paternalism 36
Péron, François 297
Petrishevo (Russian village) 316
Phaedrus 141
Photosynthèse 356, 358
Pinel, Philippe 289, 292, 293
Pityana, Nyameko Barney 323-325, 328
Plato 140
Plumwood, Val 353, 361-366
Pluriculturalism 44
poetry, poetic; poétique 15, 21, 23, 37, 43, 46-48, 51, 52, 80, 91-94, 96, 98-101, 110, 111, 115, 119, 126, 132, 171, 173-175, 180, 182-186, 197, 203, 205, 228, 307, 316, 319, 363
populist nationalism 216
postcolonialism, postcolonial, postcolonial present, post-postcolonialism; postcolonialisme, postcolonial(e/s), postcolonie, post-postcolonialisme 25, 35, 39, 44, 75, 97, 119, 121-124, 126, 128, 129, 132, 133, 137-139, 143-149, 157, 158, 161, 162, 174, 178, 185, 204, 252, 253, 262
postmodernism, postmodernist, post-postmodernism, post-postmodernist, postmodernity, postmodern; postmoderniste 61, 75, 81, 86, 119, 120, 122-124, 126, 129, 133, 144, 347
post-nationalism 132
poststructuralism, poststructuralist 75, 80, 120, 122, 123, 127

Poulot, Dominique 236
proletariat; prolétariat 36, 37, 309
provincialisme 337
Puri, Shalini 119, 132, 133

Quatremère de Quincy, Antoine Chrysostome 240
Que se vayan todos (protest slogan) 167
Queer 206, 208, 210
Quijano, Anibal 338-340
Quinlan, Sean 293

Rabanna (string instrument) 225
race (the/la), racism, racist; racisme, raciste 24, 25, 38, 46, 58, 61-63, 93, 132, 166, 197, 204, 205, 208, 216, 220, 227, 298, 299, 301, 302, 323-326, 328, 330-332, 338-341, 343, 345
Radio 1, 11-13, 26, 39, 83
Raja Casablanca (club de foot) 168
Ramses/Ramsès II 234
Rancière, Jacques 37, 119, 125-127, 129-131
Randall, Peter 329
Reconquista 302
relativisme 16, 22, 25, 26, 57-59, 63, 65, 67, 68, 79, 86, 105, 115, 123, 174, 177, 179
republicains 286, 293
resistance; résistance 1, 2, 11, 12, 14, 19, 38, 40, 86, 87, 177, 178, 182, 194, 222, 240, 317, 320, 325, 337, 342, 349, 359
révolution, Révolution française 6, 12-15, 18, 36, 38, 57, 60-63, 68, 80, 149, 157, 158, 165-167, 170, 199, 205, 210, 217, 233, 285-287, 290, 291, 295, 305, 310
Revueltas, José 306, 307, 317
Rif, Rifain(e/s) 167, 170
Rivarol, Antoine de 287
Rivas, Pedro Geoffroy 307
Rivera, Diego 306
Robespierre, Maximilien de 290
Roederer, Pierre-Louis 290, 291
Rolland, Romain 242, 243
Rosa Blanca 305-310
Rosanvallon, Pierre 300
Rosenberg, Pierre 243
Rosetta Stone 236

Roth, Joseph 45
Rothschild (family) 237
rythmes bio-géologiques 356

SACC (South African Council of Churches) 329
Saïd, Edward W. 62, 122, 191, 192, 194
Saint-Domingue 298
Saint-Éloi, Rodney 91–94, 96, 101
Saint-Sernin (municipality) 288
Salkey, Andrew 127
Salpêtrière 289
Sanders, Mark 323–325, 327
Sarr, Felwine 93–97, 101, 105–107, 109, 111, 113, 121, 123, 251, 253, 272, 273
Sartre, Jean Paul / Sartrian 6, 37, 66
SASO (South African Student Organisation) 325
Saussure, Ferdinand de 45, 75–77, 86, 144
Savoy, Bénédicte 251, 253, 268, 272
Sawah (song by Baligh Hamdi) 222
Schéhérazade 360
Schloss, Adolphe 237
Schmidt, Johannes 221
Schnapp, Alain 238
Schuchardt, Hugo 215, 217–228
Schwangere Auster (Pregnant Oyster) V, 1, 27, 27
Scott, David 25, 119, 121, 122, 126, 128, 129, 131–133
Second World War (WW II); Seconde Guerre mondiale 192, 201, 202, 305, 311, 312, 315, 319
Sedibe, Gilbert 330
Sedira, Zineb 1, 3–8, 13, 14, 16, 28
self-identity 109
Senghor, Léopold Sédar 35, 37
Sepoy Mutiny (Indian Rebellion) 142
sexist; sexisme, sexiste 38, 166, 336, 339, 340, 350
shaab (the word of the people) 166
Sharpeville 324
she-bear 112, 113
Shih, Shu-mei 217, 226
Sicard, Ambroise 288
similarity, similarities; similarité(s) 8, 22, 43, 45, 48–54, 111, 129, 175, 176, 338
Simon, James 237
Snyder, Gary 362
socialist revolution 36

Socrates 140, 141
Solbiac, Rodolphe 132
Sömmering, Samuel Thomas 295
Souleimane, Omar Youssef 195, 201, 203, 205, 206, 209, 210
South Africa 49, 323–332
Spinoza, Baruch 35, 68
Spitz, Jean-Fabien 287
Spivak, Gayatri Chakravorty 10, 123, 335, 340, 341
Spurzheim, Johann Caspar 296
Steinberg, Ronen 290
Strathern, Marilyn 111, 113
Strauss, Richard 242, 243
subjectivity; subjectivité 21, 22, 91, 180, 185, 199, 209, 273, 314, 328, 329, 338, 339, 341
Sunna 344, 349
symbiotes 358, 359

tafsir (exegesis, interpretation) 347, 348, 350
Tallien, Jean-Lambert 290
Tamil 146, 219
Tampico 306
Tawada, Yoko 173, 175, 180, 182–185
telfaz (television) 163
Terreur (la) 390, 293
Téry, Simone 305, 306, 311–314, 319, 320
thawra (revolution) 166, 167
Thermidorien(s) 290, 291
Thoreau, Henry 362
Thorez, Maurice 36
Tokenism 341
Toledano, Lombardo 312
Toledo, Camille de VI, 26, 361
Trabant, Jürgen 175, 176, 185
transcendence 130, 133
transculturalism 120
translation(s); traduction(s)
transnational(e) 68, 164, 181, 195, 204, 206, 209, 308, 310, 320, 335, 337, 341, 342, 346, 349, 351
transracialism 120
Traven, Bruno 305–311, 320
tristeza 228
truth-procedure 1

Tugu (city) 217, 219, 222, 224
turath (heritage) 344
Tvergastein (cabin) 364, 365

UCM (University Christian Movement) 329
Ulysse(s) 11, 79, 357
Universalism
– Creolising universality 215, 217, 218, 228
– European universalism 16, 37, 105, 107, 110, 114, 138, 173, 174, 178, 215–217, 235
– minor universalism 137, 144, 147, 149, 150
– negative universalism 275
– lateral universal; universalisme latéral 35, 39, 40, 178, 182, 185, 323
– universalité blanche 208
untranslatable(s) see intraduisible(s) 173, 175, 177, 178, 182, 183
urbanisation 94, 95

Valéry, Paul 239–241, 245
Vargas, Elvira 310
Venice Biennale 1, 3–7, 13, 268
Veracruz 308, 260
Verwoerd, Hendrik 326
violence symbolique 208, 260
Viollis, Andrée 311
Virey, Jean-Joseph 299, 300
Viśvasāhitya 53
vivant (le/s) 106, 107, 353–356, 358–361, 364–367
Viveiros Castro, Eduardo 217
Volk, Tyler 354

Wadud, Amina 347

Wahnich, Sophie 291
Wallerstein, Immanuel 15, 18, 37, 174, 253, 287
Watteau, Jean-Antoine 243
Weld Legriya 169
Weltanschauung 344
West 25, 26, 46–48, 53, 82, 119, 121, 123, 126, 191, 273
Western imperialism 216
whiteness 216, 336, 339–341
Whorf, Benjamin Lee 83
Wilder, Gary 218, 225
Williams, Raymond 149
Winkelvoss, Karine 234
Wisconsin 256
Wittgenstein, Ludwig 35, 45
World
– Exhibition(s) 2
– Literature 46, 53, 54, 122, 131
– Society 115, 128
worlding 113, 115

Yáñez, Don Jacinto 308
Yildiz, Yasemin 180
Ytnahaou ga (Algerian protest slogan: "they should go") 167
Yule, Henry 219
(*Ash-sha'b*) *yurid isqat al-nidâm* ("Down with the regime!", slogan emerged in the Tunisian Revolution) 167

Zaar (L') 169
Zein el Din, Nazirah 349
Zusammenhang 50–52

www.ingramcontent.com/pod-product-compliance
Lightning Source LLC
Chambersburg PA
CBHW061928220426
43662CB00012B/1835